The University of **Law**

This book must be returned to the library on or before the last date stamped below. Failure to do so will result in a fine.

Bloomsbury Library
T: 01483 216387
library-bloomsbury@law.ac.uk

Moorgate Library
T: 01483 216371
library-moorgate@law.ac.uk

Practical Derivatives

A Transactional Approach, Third Edition

Consulting Editors **Edmund Parker** and **Marcin Perzanowski**

Consulting editors
Edmund Parker and Marcin Perzanowski

Managing director
Sian O'Neill

Practical Derivatives: A Transactional Approach, Third Edition
is published by

Globe Law and Business Ltd
3 Mylor Close
Horsell
Woking
Surrey GU21 4DD
Tel: +44 20 3745 4770
www.globelawandbusiness.com

Printed and bound by Gomer Press

Practical Derivatives: A Transactional Approach, Third Edition

ISBN 9781911078173
EPUB ISBN 9781787421103
Adobe PDF ISBN 9781787421110
Mobi ISBN 9781787421127

DISCLAIMER
This publication is intended as a general guide only. The information and opinions which it contains are not intended to be a comprehensive study, nor to provide legal advice, and should not be treated as a substitute for legal advice concerning particular situations. Legal advice should always be sought before taking any action based on the information provided. The publishers bear no responsibility for any errors or omissions contained herein.

Table of contents

Preface

Edmund Parker
Marcin Perzanowski
Mayer Brown

Welcome to the third edition of *Practical Derivatives*.

Each edition has accompanied very different derivatives markets. The first edition was published when the derivatives markets were buoyant; the book was prefaced by a future general counsel of the 'International Swaps and Derivatives Association Inc' (ISDA), who wrote: "Now is an interesting time to be a derivatives lawyer. The situation has been this way for many years and does not look like changing." While we can repeat those words again with vigour in 2017, the second edition of *Practical Derivatives* was published in December 2010 as the derivatives markets were recovering slowly from the 2007/2008 financial crisis. In the aftermath of the crisis, the global leaders at the G20 summit in Pittsburgh in 2009 decided to introduce a plethora of regulatory initiatives to ensure that such a crisis would not happen again. Like a phoenix rising from the ashes, the derivatives markets have been making a steady come back ever since, as both market participants and regulators realised the benefits offered by different derivatives products: they help pensions funds manage their liabilities to pensioners, they offer protection to borrowers against rises in interest rates, they even help fight global warming and climate change through emissions trading.

While the years spanning the three editions of the book have been a genuine roller coaster, the derivatives markets have matured considerably over the period. This is reflected in each edition. Thus, a relatively short chapter on proposed regulatory changes in the first edition is now much longer, and is complemented by a different chapter on regulatory-driven, newly developed documentation for cleared over-the-counter derivatives. Numerous other new industry standard forms have also been published which we also cover in this new edition. Most notably, the credit derivatives markets have changed beyond recognition with the implementation of the new 2014 ISDA Credit Derivatives Definitions. The securities finance markets developed further as the new versions of the Global Master Repurchase Agreement and Global Master Securities Lending Agreement are gaining popularity.

This edition also covers standard documentation and market conventions for well-established derivatives classes such as equity derivatives, commodity derivatives (including designated chapters on emissions trading, weather derivatives and energy derivatives), as well as the ever-present interest rate and foreign exchange derivatives products. In addition to discussing the usual English law ISDA framework, this edition also covers market standard German derivatives documentation. In short, the purpose of this book is to provide a practical introduction and overview of all current trends in derivatives, including – in particular – their transactional, regulatory and documentation-related aspects.

The co-editors have enjoyed working with the book's authors immensely, as well as writing and co-writing their own contributory chapters. Edmund Parker would like again to thank his amazing wife Panthea and children Amir, Cameron, Sienna and Cordelia for all their support during the production of this book. Marcin Perzanowski would like to thank Alina, his wife, for her love, understanding and mental support to become more efficient; and Alicja, his daughter, for her patience when her dad used his paternity leave for reviewing the final edits to this book.

Corporate governance and derivatives end users

Paul Ali
University of Melbourne

1. Introduction

The basic function of a derivative is to transfer risk. Derivatives can be used to replicate the entire economic incidents of particular assets, as well as to break assets down into their component risks and transfer individual risks. There is, in principle, no reason why a derivative cannot be crafted for each of the risks to which particular assets are subject – a point that is well borne out by the rapid rate of innovation in the derivatives markets. Beyond the 'plain vanilla' derivatives linked to interest rate and currency risk that continue to dominate the over-the-counter (OTC) markets, it is now possible to transact derivatives linked to credit risk, currency convertibility risk, equity risk, macro-economic indicia (including inflation and unemployment rates), market access risk, volatility and weather risk, as well as derivatives replicating real estate investments and dynamic portfolios of securities and derivatives.

There are, however, certain factors common to all derivatives transactions, regardless of their complexity and innovative qualities. One such factor is corporate governance. This is a matter that has assumed considerably more importance in the wake of the global financial crisis. It is commonly the case that when an end user of derivatives suffers losses – particularly where the derivatives in question are complex and the user has significantly less expertise in transacting derivatives than the dealer that it booked the derivative with – the focus is on how the dealer has conducted itself towards the user. A critical issue is whether the dealer owes a duty of care to the end user to ensure that the derivative is suitable for the end user, in the context of the end user's personal circumstances and risk tolerance. This focus on the sell side of derivatives transactions tends, however, to obscure the fact that the buy side of the transaction – the end user – may itself be subject to a legal duty to ascertain for itself the suitability of the derivative, and that failure to do so may render the end user liable to its own shareholders or investors. Corporate governance encompasses inquiries of that nature. Thus, while the management of an end user may be mulling over whether they can recover derivatives-related losses from a swap dealer, their own investors could well be contemplating bringing a class action against them to recover those losses. That prospect confronts both end users that are corporations – which are transacting derivatives for their own account – and those end users that are institutional investors which are transacting derivatives using funds entrusted to them by their investors.

Corporate governance may be described as a system of principles governing the interaction between the management of a corporation, its owners and other parties with a financial stake in the corporation. The objective of these principles is to reduce the agency costs inherent in the separation of management from ownership and assure the owners and providers of finance of a return on their stake in the corporation.[1] A key concern of corporate governance is therefore the rules that govern the management of corporations.[2]

This chapter examines the corporate governance aspects of derivatives transactions from the perspective of corporations, as well as institutional investors. These two categories make up the principal end users of derivatives.[3] The former are business enterprises that use derivatives, typically, for the purposes of reducing the volatility of their earnings by hedging particular risks; the latter are professional investors that manage assets on behalf of others and use derivatives for the purpose of hedging, as well as for creating exposure by replicating all or a discrete portion of the economic incidents of physical investments. The institutional investor category includes:

- pension funds;
- insurance companies;
- mutual funds;
- hedge funds;
- not-for-profit organisations; and
- charitable endowments.[4]

The chapter outlines the duties to which the management of corporate end users are subject when entering into derivatives transactions and the analogous duties that apply to institutional investors. In both instances the relevant duty holders have been entrusted with the management of assets for the benefit of other parties: the officers of a corporation have vested in them the power to manage the corporation's business assets for the benefit of the corporation as a whole, while the institutional investor has been appointed to manage assets entrusted to it by its investors.[5]

---

1   See A Schleifer and RW Vishny, "A Survey of Corporate Governance" (1997) 52, *Journal of Finance* 737.

2   Another key concern is the relationship of the controlling shareholders with management and the non-controlling shareholders (eg, RJ Gilson, "Controlling Shareholders and Corporate Governance: Complicating the Comparative Taxonomy" (2006) 119, *Harvard Law Review* 1641).

3   The duties of the sellers of derivatives have been discussed extensively in the derivatives literature and are not considered in this chapter (eg, S K Henderson, *Henderson on Derivatives* (London: LexisNexis UK, 2003), Ch 14).

4   The institutional investor may invest the assets entrusted to it directly or indirectly via an intermediated vehicle, on a pooled or individual basis, and may or may not accept further assets for investment. This leads to a further subdivision of institutional investors into closed-end funds, commingled funds, funds of funds, master funds, master-feeder funds, open-end funds, separately managed funds and wrap funds. See further PU Ali, G Stapledon and M Gold, *Corporate Governance and Investment Fiduciaries* (Sydney: Lawbook Co, 2003) Ch 1.

5   The institutional investor (whether as it is the trustee of a pension fund, for example, or the general partner of a hedge fund) will typically be a corporation. The duties, however, owed by the institutional investor's management to the institutional investor itself are subordinate to those owed by the institutional investor to the investors on whose behalf it has undertaken to invest assets (as the fiduciary relationship that exists between the institutional investor and its investors means that, at a minimum, the former owes the latter a duty of loyalty and must not place itself in a position where its self-interest conflicts with the interests of the latter); see G McCormack, "Conflicts of Interest and the Investment Management Function" (1999) 20, *Company Lawyer* 2. In exceptional circumstances, a court may recognise a separate fiduciary duty owed by the institutional investor's management to the investors; see M Thomas and B Dowrick, "The Duty of Directors of a Corporate Trustee" (1998) 19, *Company Lawyer* 305.

2.   Corporate end users

Derivatives are typically used by corporate end users to reduce or extinguish their exposure to discrete risks and thus reduce the volatility of their earnings. A corporation can, for example, hedge the risk of an increase in interest rates by putting in place an interest rate swap under which it receives a floating-interest rate in exchange for paying a fixed-interest rate. Similarly, other derivatives can readily be transacted to protect the corporation against an adverse change in exchange rates or even the financial consequences of inclement weather.

2.1   Use of derivatives for non-hedging purposes

Corporations also use derivatives not to reduce or extinguish exposure to an existing risk, but to create or magnify exposure.[6] In this situation, derivatives are used to establish investment positions reflecting the corporation's view of, for instance, future interest rates or exchange rates. However, corporations are less likely to treat their treasury departments as profit centres in the current economic environment, given the sharply reduced tolerance for derivatives-related losses on the part of shareholders, especially where the losses are not attributable to hedging.

2.2   Legal capacity of corporate end users

Corporate end users are relatively unconstrained in their ability to enter into derivatives transactions. The doctrine of *ultra vires*, which makes void any acts by a corporation that are beyond the scope of its stated powers, has been rendered otiose as regards UK corporations.[7] Accordingly, UK corporations face no explicit constraints on their legal capacity to enter into derivatives transactions.[8] Similar steps to reduce the operation of that doctrine or to abolish it altogether have been taken in other markets whose laws are derived from English law.[9]

While the governing laws and constituent documents of corporate end users may be silent on the issue of derivatives (with the legal capacity to transact derivatives being found in the general powers of the corporation), corporations usually assume voluntary limitations on their use of derivatives. These limitations are expressed in their internal hedging polices and are an incident of the duty of care that applies to the directors and senior management of corporations.[10]

---

6   For a survey of the use of derivatives by corporate end users to create exposure, see CC Geczy, BA Minton and C Schrand, "Taking a View: Corporate Speculation, Governance and Compensation" (2007) 62, *Journal of Finance* 2405.
7   Companies Act 2006 (UK), Sections 31 and 39.
8   This is in marked contrast to the municipal end users that were responsible for much of the English case law concerning the legality of derivatives transactions – for example, PBH Birks and F Rose (eds), *Lessons of the Swaps Litigation* (London: LLP Press, 2000). The issue of authority in relation to derivatives is examined in detail in S Firth, *Derivatives Law and Practice* (London: Sweet & Maxwell, 2003), paras [2-083] to [2-102].
9   G Gunasekara and A Sims, "Statutory Trends and the 'Genetic Modification' of the Common Law: Company Law as a Paradigm" (2005) 26, *Statute Law Review* 82 at 90-91.
10   Limits on the use of derivatives may also be voluntarily assumed by the corporation for the purposes of adhering to 'best practices' corporate governance guidelines in the markets in which the corporation's securities are listed and to allay investor concerns about the potential for derivatives-related losses.

2.3 Duty of care

The only legal fetters on the use of derivatives by corporations are the duties owed by the corporation's officers (the directors and senior management) to the corporation itself – in particular, the duty of care.

The duty of care requires corporate officers to exercise the level of care and diligence that a reasonable person in the officer's position would display, having regard to the corporation's circumstances and the officer's responsibilities within the corporation. In terms of the use of derivatives, the officers of the corporate end user, in discharging their duty of care, must:

- clearly understand the general nature of the corporation's business and, in particular, the significant risks to which it is exposed (eg, currency risk in relation to inputs and sales, and interest rate risk in relation to borrowings and fundraising capacity);
- be able to formulate and monitor the implementation of a hedging programme (if required) to address those risks (which requires them to have a general understanding of hedging and the role of derivatives therein, and the risks associated with transacting derivatives; and
- be able to monitor the implementation of appropriate internal controls for transacting derivatives, in particular ensuring that the dealing role is separate from the settlement role.

The officers of a corporation will be personally liable for losses incurred on derivatives transactions if they fail properly to monitor the corporation's use of derivatives (whether this failure is due to the insufficiency of the corporation's internal controls or a lack of sufficient understanding of derivatives on the part of the officers). Moreover, these officers are unlikely, as regards these requirements, to be protected by the business judgement rule as a failure to ensure that one is familiar with the corporation's financial position or to monitor the corporation's policies and use of derivatives is not ordinarily considered to involve a decision by the officer to take or not take action.

The spectre of personal liability on the part of corporate officers for derivatives-related losses is well illustrated by one of the few cases from a major common law jurisdiction to deal specifically with the failure of a corporation's directors (and auditors) to monitor properly the corporation's use of derivatives: the Australian case of *AWA Ltd v Daniels*.[11] AWA imported the majority of its inputs (electronic components) from Japan. AWA's board decided to implement an in-house hedging programme to reduce AWA's currency exposure. However, an employee with no training or experience in foreign exchange trading was placed in charge of the programme. Moreover, the managers to whom this employee was required to report had no training or experience in foreign exchange trading either. The employee was basically left unsupervised and was thus the person solely responsible within AWA for foreign exchange trading. The employee also had responsibilities in relation to the settlement of such trades and was in a position to circumvent any internal

---

11   (1992) 7 ACSR 759; affirmed *Daniels v Anderson* (1995) 16 ACSR 607.

controls relating to the review of AWA's foreign exchange positions.[12] The employee began to trade speculatively in foreign exchange forward instruments and ultimately caused AWA to incur losses of A$50 million. AWA's directors and senior management (as well as its auditors) were held by the Supreme Court of New South Wales and on appeal, the New South Wales Court of Appeal, to have breached their duty of care to AWA and were personally liable for the foreign exchange losses incurred by AWA.

2.4   A positive duty to hedge?

It is doubtful whether the duty of corporate officers to employ due care when their corporation enters into derivatives transactions can be extrapolated into a positive duty to use derivatives.

The closest case on point (and one often cited to justify the existence of a positive duty to use derivatives) is the US case of *Brane v Roth*, a decision of the Indiana Court of Appeals.[13] The case involved a class action brought by the shareholders of La Fontaine Grain Cooperative against the cooperative's directors for losses suffered by the cooperative in its grain trading activities. The shareholders sought to recover those losses from the directors on the basis that the directors had failed to implement an adequate hedging programme to protect the cooperative's revenues.

Most of the cooperative's revenue (90%) was generated by its grain-trading activities. The board of the cooperative decided to implement a hedging programme to protect the cooperative from fluctuations in grain prices. To that end, the cooperative entered into a number of grain futures contracts. These futures contracts covered less than 1% of the cooperative's grain sales and the cooperative suffered losses due to a deterioration in grain prices.

The court decided that the directors were personally liable for the losses suffered by the cooperative. However, rather than articulating a positive duty to use derivatives (or to hedge), the court's decision turned upon the failure of the directors to acquire a sufficient level of understanding of hedging and the impact of hedging or not hedging upon the cooperative's revenues. The directors were thus in no position to implement or monitor a suitable hedging programme for the cooperative and the court considered that this breach of duty was a direct cause of the trading losses suffered by the cooperative. Accordingly, it was the failure of the directors to attain the requisite level of understanding of derivatives and hedging that constituted a breach of their duty of care (as they could not then make a properly informed decision about whether to implement a hedging programme), not their failure to transact derivatives.

Despite this, directors and other officers of corporations would be well advised to

---

12   Rogue traders such as the employee in the *AWA* case remain an exceptional phenomenon.; see further K D Krawiec, "Accounting for Greed: Unravelling the Rogue Trader Mystery" (2000) 79, *Oregon Law Review* 301. Of more concern to corporations (and their shareholders) is the failure of management to implement appropriate hedging policies; see further HTC Hu, "Hedging Expectations: 'Derivative Reality' and the Law and Finance of the Corporate Objective" (1995) 21, *Journal of Corporation Law* 3 at 25 ff.

13   590 NE 2d 587 (1992). See further ES Adams and DE Runkle, "The Easy Case for Derivatives Use: Advocating a Corporate Fiduciary Duty to use Derivatives" (2000) 41, *William and Mary Law Review* 595 at 644-646.

consider the use of derivatives to reduce the volatility of corporate revenues. Failure to do so may raise questions about whether the officers are sufficiently conversant with the corporation's business (and, more particularly, the material risks associated with that business) and are thus in a position to discharge their duty of care to the corporation. However, any such consideration of derivatives requires the officers to be sufficiently informed about (and understand) the nature of hedging, the role of derivatives in hedging and the risks attendant upon transacting derivatives.

In considering whether to use derivatives, the officers of a corporate end user should be cognisant of the risk that just as under-hedging may expose them to shareholder claims of dereliction of duty, so too may over-hedging. While it is obvious that hedging is not free, the officers of a corporation should be aware that hedging also necessarily involves the forgoing of returns. The stripping out of risk and the concomitant smoothing of corporate revenues may also reduce the prospects for outperformance by the corporation with a negative impact on shareholder wealth.[14] Moreover, the shareholders of the corporation may, through their investment in the corporation, seek exposure to the markets in which the corporation conducts its business and the elimination, for instance, of all currency risk may not be what these shareholders perceive to be in their best interests.[15] A balance must therefore be struck between the need to reduce or eliminate risks that are (or are perceived as likely to be) inimical to the financial health of the corporation and the desire to retain or create exposure to risks that are capable of contributing positively to the corporation's performance.

3. Institutional investors

Unlike the corporate end users of derivatives discussed above, institutional investors face two explicit legal constraints on their use of derivatives. The first relates to their actual legal capacity to enter into derivatives transactions – that is, whether an institutional investor is permitted to use derivatives (in the same way that the doctrine of *ultra vires* is used to limit the powers of corporations in the United Kingdom and other common law jurisdictions), while the second imposes prudential guidelines for any use of derivatives.

These two constraints are attributable to the more specialised or defined nature of the business enterprise of institutional investors compared to corporate end users of derivatives and the fact that, in contrast to the latter, institutional investors do not, by definition, invest for their own account. Neither of the two constraints is restricted in its application to derivatives. Instead, they are integral to defining the

---

14   The extensive use of derivatives (or other instruments, in particular finite reinsurance) to smooth out revenues may well attract regulatory scrutiny, including by the Financial Services Authority, as an attempt to mislead investors by presenting a distorted picture of the financial health of the corporation and the stability of its revenues – for example, CL Culp, *Structured Finance and Insurance* (Hoboken, NJ: John Wiley & Sons, 2006), pp563–568; S von Dahlen, "Finite Reinsurance: How does it concern Supervisors? Some Efficiency Considerations in the Light of Prevailing Regulatory Aims" (2007) 32, *The Geneva Papers* 283.

15   The rationale for hedging may also be undermined by the fact that many shareholders hold diversified portfolios and the corporation, through its use of derivatives to hedge unsystematic or issuer-specific risk, may be duplicating what their shareholders have already done; see further Hu, above at footnote 13, 30–31.

scope of the business enterprise of the institutional investor and the nature of the bargain between that institutional investor and the persons on whose behalf it makes investments (in particular, the two constraints establish the extent to which the persons for whom the institutional investor is acting have bargained for exposure to market-based or asset-specific risk).

In addition, the two constraints apply to institutional investors, regardless of the legal form selected to undertake their business enterprise. Thus, it is not relevant that pension funds are typically structured as trusts, while mutual funds may be structured as trusts or corporations, and hedge funds, private equity funds and venture capital funds may be structured as trusts, corporations or limited partnerships.[16] The constraints do not arise as a result of the particular form chosen by the institutional investor for the management of assets on behalf of its investors, but are inherent in the relationship between the institutional investor and the investors.

3.1   Legal capacity of institutional investors

It is highly unusual for institutional investors to be given the same freedom to transact derivatives as corporate end users. Instead, the legal capacity of institutional investors to transact derivatives is ordinarily limited expressly by their governing laws, including the Occupational Pension Schemes (Investment) Regulations 2005 in the United Kingdom and the Employee Retirement Income Security Act 1974 in the United States, and constituent documents.

(a)   Investment mandates

The most common source of such limits is the investment mandate, a discrete portfolio-level document which broadly describes the investment objectives and strategy of the institutional investor and limits not only the use of derivatives, but also the selection of securities and the assumption of debt by the institutional investor. This document sets out how the institutional investor will invest the assets entrusted to it by its investors. It often supplements the more principles-based limitations on the legal capacity of the institutional investor which may be found in the laws governing specific classes of institutional investor (especially pension funds and life insurance companies).[17]

The legal capacity to use derivatives will normally be expressed in negative terms – for example:

- the institutional investor may be permitted to transact certain types of derivative only (eg, exchange-traded derivatives or vanilla derivatives such as interest rate swaps, foreign exchange forward agreements, currency swaps and equity options);

---

16   See footnote 5.
17   In general, hedge funds face the fewest limitations in their investment mandates on the use of derivatives and routinely use derivatives to create leveraged exposure. By contrast, pension funds which are entrusted with the retirement savings of their investors usually face the greatest limitations on the use of derivatives. See further PU Ali, "Hedge Fund Investments and the Prudent Investor Rule" (2003) 17, *Trust Law International* 74.

- the institutional investor may be permitted to transact derivatives only for the purposes of hedging particular risks (eg, interest rate, currency and equity market risk) and prohibited from using derivatives to create exposure;
- the institutional investor may be prohibited from using derivatives to create short positions in general or to create naked (ie, uncovered or unhedged) short positions in particular;
- upper limits may be imposed on the allocation of assets by the institutional investor to derivatives positions and the level of leverage assumed through the use of derivatives; and
- the use of derivatives may be subject to the limits on the level of exposure to particular geographic regions, industries, markets, market sectors and asset classes.

It is therefore essential that the entry into the derivatives transaction by the institutional investor complies with the limits imposed in its investment mandate on the use of derivatives.[18] If, as is often the case with mutual funds that are open to investment by retail investors, the mandate limits the use of derivatives to hedging, the institutional investor will lack the legal capacity to transact derivatives for the purposes of creating exposure. The absence of the requisite legal capacity means that any derivatives entered into by the institutional investor for non-hedging purposes will be void, even where the derivatives in question have been fully performed, and the net payer (which may be the institutional investor or its counterparty) will be entitled to recover all payments made by it under the derivatives. Moreover, the institutional investor will be personally liable to its own investors for any losses incurred on the relevant portfolio in connection with the derivatives.

(b) Transformer transactions

Despite this, the limits imposed by investment mandates on the use of derivatives do not pose an absolute bar to the assumption of derivatives-related exposure. Those limits, regardless of whether they are expressed in terms of financial constraints (eg, limits on the level of leverage) or permissible uses (eg, limiting the use of derivatives for the purposes of hedging only), are, in common with other limits contained in the investment mandate, directed towards the legal form of the putative destination for the investment of the institutional investor's assets. Accordingly, an institutional investor that is precluded by the terms of its investment mandate from entering into a particular derivatives transaction can usually replicate the type and level of exposure obtainable via that transaction by entering into what may be generically described as a 'transformer' transaction.[19]

---

18   The investment mandate presupposes that what the institutional investor is doing actually constitutes 'investment'. There is the thorny issue of differentiating 'investment' from 'speculation', as the legal capacity to invest (whether via transacting derivatives or otherwise) does not embrace speculation. Both terms have evaded precise legal definition, but it is likely that a court, in assessing whether the institutional investor's entry into a particular derivatives transaction constitutes speculation as opposed to investment, would be guided by the case law on wagering and gaming contracts; see further MT Johnson, "Speculating on the Efficacy of 'Speculation': An Analysis of the Prudent Person's Slipperiest Term of Art in Light of Modern Portfolio Theory" (1996) 48, *Stanford Law Review* 419.

A transformer transaction involves, in essence, the interposition of a permissible investment between an institutional investor and the ultimate destination of the assets being invested by the institutional investor. This enables the institutional investor to overcome limitations in their investment mandates, governing laws or constituent documents on the entry into particular forms of transactions. It is possible for the institutional investor to achieve this result by allocating assets instead to other investment vehicles that in turn invest in derivatives. Two prime examples are hedge funds (which, unlike other institutional investors, face few, if any, limitations on their use of derivatives and routinely establish investment positions via derivatives) and commodity pools or managed futures funds (which invest in exchange-traded derivatives). In both cases, the institutional investor purchases units, shares or a partnership interest, and receives returns on its investment linked to the performance of an underlying portfolio largely comprising derivatives.

However, there are two key impediments to the use of hedge funds and managed futures funds to overcome limitations in an institutional investor's investment mandate. The first impediment stems from the fact that hedge funds and managed futures funds invest in a wide range of derivatives and that the institutional investor will have no control over the selection of derivatives by those funds. Accordingly, the indirect derivatives exposure achieved through this intermediated investment cannot be tailored to the institutional investor's requirements in the same way as an individual derivatives transaction. There is therefore likely to be a mismatch between the institutional investor's requirements and the derivatives-related exposure achieved through the use of hedge funds and managed futures funds.

The second impediment concerns the nature of the investment interests in hedge funds and managed futures funds. Those interests are typically structured as shares, units or other beneficial entitlements in a trust, or limited partnership 'shares'. A common feature of the investment mandates of many pension funds is the limitations imposed on the allocation of assets to shares and other equity instruments (eg, units and partnership interests). Moreover, money market funds are normally precluded from allocating assets to equity instruments, regardless of whether those equity instruments represent interests in a portfolio of derivatives that reference debt instruments.

One solution that has been developed is to structure a tranche of debt securities that incorporate a tailored risk. This risk may comprise the credit risk of a portfolio of corporate loans and bonds or the market risk of an entire market, market sector or customised portfolio of shares. This can be accomplished by establishing a special purpose vehicle to assume the particular risk and issue debt securities to the institutional investor. The cash proceeds obtained from the institutional investor in exchange for the debt securities are invested by the special purpose vehicle in a pool of relatively riskless assets (ie, highly rated, highly liquid assets such as UK gilts or US

---

19   Many transformer transactions have been crafted specifically to address the limits imposed by subordinate legislation and the increased regulatory capital requirements to which life and general insurance companies transacting derivatives are subject; see J Coiley, "Not so Toxic: Understanding and Negotiating Insurance Transformer Transactions" (2002) 17, *Journal of International Banking Law* 231.

treasury securities), and those assets are used to collateralise one or more derivatives transactions under which the requisite risk has been assumed by the special purpose vehicle. That risk is thus embedded in the debt securities acquired by the institutional investor, as the payment of principal and interest on the debt securities is contingent upon the risk failing to eventuate.

The institutional investor determines the type of risk to be assumed by deciding which of the very large number of such synthetic securitisations (where the risk being assumed is credit risk) and equity-linked or debt-linked transactions (where the risk being assumed is market risk) on offer to participate in. The level of risk is then determined by which of the differentially rated tranches of debt securities the institutional investor chooses to acquire and the quantum of the securities acquired.

Three developments in the market for the above transactions are worthy of further mention. First, institutional investors can readily acquire debt securities whose returns are linked to portfolios of actively managed credit derivatives and equity derivatives, as opposed to the static or lightly managed portfolios that are now commonplace.[20] Second, it is also becoming increasingly common for debt securities incorporating credit risk to be designed for individual institutional investors. The credit risk that is being transferred in these 'single tranche' transactions can be tailored to meet the exact requirements of individual institutional investors, in contrast to generic tranched structures that are designed to meet the requirements of a broad range of investors.[21] Lastly, the structures that have been used to create exposure to credit risk and market risk for institutional investors are now being deployed to create debt securities incorporating new types of derivative, such as fund-linked derivatives, equity default swaps and commodity trigger swaps. Although the global financial crisis represented a severe set-back for securitisation – leading to a sharp fall in transaction volumes, as well as much criticism of securitisation, particularly the securitisation of bank loans and home mortgages – there is little to suggest that there is anything structurally wrong with securitisation (as opposed to the conduct of some of those involved in putting together, marketing and advising on securitisation transactions) and, indeed, there has been a revival of deal-making in the major securitisation markets.[22]

The efficacy of securitisation or other transformer structures to bypass end user restrictions on transacting derivatives has been considerably undermined in Australia by a relatively recent decision of the Federal Court of Australia, *Wingecarribee Shire Council v Lehman Brothers Australia Ltd.*[23] This decision concerned the liability of a financial adviser for mis-selling synthetic collateralised debt obligations (CDO securities) to an Australian local council. In the course of finding the adviser liable for

---

20   For an overview of these dynamic structures see JJ de Vries Robbé and PU Ali, "Synthetic CDOs: The State of Play" (2006) 21, *Journal of International Banking Law and Regulation* 12.

21   Single tranche structures are discussed in JJ de Vries Robbé and PU Ali, "The Continuing Evolution of the Structured Credit Market" (2005) 20, Journal of *International Banking Law and Regulation* 628.

22   See E Fournier, "Securitisation is Back" (2009) 27(8), *International Financial Law Review* 18. For a powerful refutation of claims that structural flaws in securitisation contributed to the global financial crisis, see SL Schwarcz, "Protecting Financial Markets: Lessons from the Subprime Mortgage Meltdown" (2008) 93, *Minnesota Law Review* 373 at 387-394; SL Schwarcz, "The Future of Securitization" (2009) 41, *Connecticut Law Review* 1313 at 1318-1321.

23   (2012) 301 ALR 1.

misleading and deceptive conduct, negligence, breach of contract and breach of fiduciary duties, the Federal Court held that the securities acquired by the local council were 'derivatives' and, consequently, that the council's investment of its funds in those securities was in breach of the prohibition in the investment management agreement between the council and the adviser against investments in derivatives. The argument before the court on the legal status of the synthetic CDO securities proceeded on the basis that those securities were derivatives unless one of two exceptions to the statutory definition of 'derivatives' applied.[24] It is not necessary for the purposes of this chapter to explore those exceptions or the statutory definition: it suffices to state that the court was persuaded that securities linked to credit derivatives should be treated as derivatives because, like the underlying derivatives, the amount that the issuer of the securities was obligated to pay the investors in the securities was determined by reference to the value of 'something else' (this 'something else' is the reference to obligations in the case of a credit derivative and the credit derivative itself in the case of securities linked to such a derivative).[25] How persuasive this judicial treatment of derivatives-linked securities is for other common law jurisdictions remains to be seen, given that the adviser in the above case essentially conceded that such securities were presumptively derivatives.

3.2   Prudent investor rule

However, the mere fact that an institutional investor has the legal capacity to transact derivatives does not necessarily mean that such a course of action is a legally proper one for that investor. Institutional investors, because they invest assets on behalf of other persons, must also have regard to the suitability of the derivatives transaction and the need to ensure portfolio diversification. These requirements are embodied in the second legal constraint to which the use of derivatives (and, indeed, all other investments) by institutional investors is subject, known as the 'prudent investor' rule. That rule applies to all institutional investors in the United Kingdom and other markets whose laws are derived from English law.[26]

The prudent investor rule has, as its source, the duty of care that institutional investors owe to the persons on whose behalf they manage assets.[27] This duty is analogous to that owed by directors to the corporations on whose boards they sit. However, while directors and other corporate officers enjoy considerable flexibility

---

24   (2012) 301 ALR 1, 307.
25   Readers interested in the complexities of Australia's regulatory framework for derivatives and other financial products may wish to refer to, for instance, K Lewis, "When is a Financial Product not a Financial Product?" (2004) 22, *Company and Securities Law Journal* 103.
26   In the United Kingdom, refer to Sections 36(2)(a) and (b) of the Pensions Act 1995, Sections 4(1), (3)(a) and (b) of the Trustee Act 2000 and Regulation 4 of the Occupational Pension Schemes (Investment) Regulations 2005. By contrast, in the British Virgin Islands, for instance, the prudent investor rule has been ousted to facilitate the passive holding of shares by trustees in special purpose vehicles (eg, the issuers in securitisation transactions). However, that is not a role ordinarily undertaken by institutional investors. In the United States, the prudent investor rule – including an explicit requirement for diversification – applies to pension funds governed by the Employee Retirement Income Security Act 1974 (ERISA); refer to Sections 404(a)(1) and 1104(a)(1) of ERISA and ERISA Regulation 2550.404a-1.
27   The duty of care, whether owed by directors or institutional investors, is generally viewed as being recognised by both common law and equity. Refer, however, to RP Austin, "Moulding the Content of Fiduciary Duties", in AJ Oakley (ed), *Trends in Contemporary Trust Law* (Oxford: Oxford University Press, 1996), pp68–174, where the notion of an equitable duty of care is challenged.

in how they exercise the powers vested in them on behalf of a corporation, the freedom of institutional investors to act within the confines of their more limited legal capacity is further circumscribed by the prudent investor rule, which sets out guidelines as to how institutional investors are to manage the assets entrusted to them.

An institutional investor that fails to comply with the prudent investor rule will be personally liable to compensate its investors for the losses incurred on the relevant portfolio by the contravening derivatives transaction, as well as for any underperformance of the portfolio attributable to such a transaction.[28] Where, as will often be the case, two or more parties are responsible for the actual undertaking of investments by the institutional investor (eg, the institutional investor may be the trustee of a pension fund or mutual fund, and may have appointed one or more fund managers to select investments, as well as a custodian to administer those investments), the party from which the investors have obtained compensation for the portfolio losses or underperformance may reallocate its liability among those other parties via the equitable doctrine of contribution.[29]

The prudent investor rule requires institutional investors, when contemplating entry into a derivatives transaction, to have regard to the suitability of that transaction in the context of the investment objectives and risk parameters of the relevant portfolio (as expressed in the investment mandate) and the need for portfolio diversification.

(a) Investment suitability

The first stricture – that of investment suitability – can usefully be explained by reference to the US Uniform Prudent Investor Act 1994:[30]

- The institutional investor must, in investing and managing assets, consider the purposes, terms, distribution requirements and other material circumstances of the relevant portfolio;
- Investment decisions made by the institutional investor concerning

---

28   Where the contravening transaction has resulted in a gain for the portfolio, the investors may elect to affirm the breach and retain the gain. On the topic of investor remedies, see further L Ho, "Attributing Losses to a Breach of Fiduciary Duty" (1998) 12, *Trust Law International* 66; PU Ali and T Russell, "Investor Remedies against Fiduciaries in Rising and Falling Markets" (2000) 18, *Company and Securities Law Journal* 326.

29   In deciding how liability is to be shared, a court will have regard to whether one party has contributed more to the loss or underperformance than the others (while the fund manager is responsible for selecting investments, the trustee is responsible for monitoring the conduct of the fund manager and the custodian or other fund administrator may be responsible for ascertaining compliance with the investment mandate), is more morally blameworthy than the others, and has benefited personally at the expense of the investors; see C Mitchell, "Apportioning Liability for Trust Losses", in PBH Birks and F Rose (ed), *Restitution and Equity Volume One: Resulting Trusts and Equitable Compensation* (London: LLP, 2000).

30   Section 2. The act forms the basis of the prudent investor rule in the majority of the US states and under the US federal laws governing pension funds, and an equivalent version of the rule now applies in the United Kingdom and in other markets whose laws are derived from English law (refer also to footnote 26). As regards the United Kingdom, refer to Section 4 of the Trustee Act 2000 (UK) and *Nestle v National Westminster Bank plc* (1996) 10 TLI 112 at 115 (affirmed by the Court of Appeal [1993] 1 WLR 1260 at 1268 and 1276). See also HE Bines and S Thel, *Investment Management Law and Regulation* (New York: Aspen Publishers, 2nd ed, 2004), section 8.03; JH Langbein, "The Uniform Prudent Investor Act and the Future of Trust Investing, (1996) 81, *Iowa Law Review* 641.

individual portfolio constituents must be evaluated not in isolation, but in the context of the portfolio as a whole and as part of the overall investment strategy and risk and return objectives applicable to the portfolio (as expressed in the investment mandate); and

- The institutional investor must consider the role that each portfolio constituent plays within the overall portfolio, the expected return of that constituent and, within the context of the investment mandate, the need for liquidity, regularity of income and capital preservation or appreciation.

(b) *Suitability of derivatives*

Accordingly, in ascertaining whether a proposed derivatives transaction constitutes a suitable investment as required by the prudent investor rule, the institutional investor must consider the following issues:[31]

- What is the expected return from the derivatives transaction? This requires an assessment of matters such as:
  - the volatility of the expected return;
  - the method for valuing the derivatives transaction (mark-to-market or another method);
  - who is undertaking the valuation (and whether the institutional investor is in a position to assess the merits of the valuation); and
  - the taxation position in relation to payments to be made or received under the derivatives transaction.
- What are the costs of entering into the derivatives transaction?[32] Has the institutional investor obtained quotes from other derivatives counterparties? Will the institutional investor be required to lodge collateral to support its obligations under the derivatives transaction?
- What are the risks associated with the derivatives transaction? Is the institutional investor assuming a discrete risk under the transaction (eg, interest rate risk on a notional principal amount, credit risk on a single reference entity or on a portfolio of reference assets), or the full range of risks associated with the

---

31   It is possible that the courts may impose more onerous suitability standards in the case of pension funds compared to mutual funds, since the investment objectives of the former are often less transparent, and more amorphous and flexible, than those of the latter, and employees enjoy less freedom, and often none at all, in choosing what pension fund their contributions should be invested with than do investors in mutual funds who can not only select a mutual fund to invest in, but can also decide not to invest in any mutual fund. See Hines and Thel, endnote 27, section 4.03[A][2]. From a regulatory perspective, the specific question of the suitability of derivatives for pension funds or other institutional investors is usually subsumed entirely within the broader question of compliance with the regulatory adoptions of the prudent investor rule. That remains the case in relation to ERISA-regulated pension funds in the United States; see, for instance, ERISA Advisory Opinion 2013-01A concerning fund investments in cleared swaps which addressed the issue of whether the status of clearing members under ERISA would preclude funds from entering into cleared swaps, but did not otherwise specifically comment on the suitability of cleared swaps as fund investments. By contrast, in the United Kingdom Regulation 4(8) of the Occupational Pension Schemes (Investment) Regulations 2005 explicitly limits funds to investing in derivatives where the derivative contributes to a reduction of the fund's risks or facilitates efficient portfolio management, and where such an investment does not entail excessive risk for the fund. See further C Sims, "Legal Issues in Liability Driven Investment and Derivative Programmes" [2007], *Trust Law International* 165.

32   Insurance companies will also need to consider the costs of the derivatives transaction in terms of its impact on their regulatory capital requirements.

underlying assets (as in the case of an asset swap or total return swap)? Apart from these transaction-specific risks, what risks is the institutional investor assuming in relation to the derivatives counterparty (eg, operational risk, settlement risk and credit risk)? Does the expected return under the derivatives instrument fairly compensate the institutional investor for the risks that it is assuming? What steps has the institutional investor undertaken, or what steps are available to it, to mitigate those risks (eg, netting)?

- How liquid is the market for the particular derivative? Can the institutional investor readily unwind its position (by transferring the transaction to a third party) or enter into an offsetting transaction if it wishes to close out its position early?

- If its derivatives counterparty defaults, what remedies are available to the institutional investor? Can the institutional investor withhold payments due from it to the derivatives counterparty? How are the payments to be made on termination to be calculated? Is netting available?

(c)   *Portfolio diversification*

As regards the second stricture encompassed by the prudent investor rule (concerning portfolio diversification), the institutional investor must assess the impact of the derivatives transaction on the overall risk and return profile of the relevant portfolio. The prudence of entering into a derivatives transaction is thus to be considered not in isolation from the existing constituents of the relevant portfolio, but rather in the context of the entire portfolio. Consequently, a derivatives transaction which on its own might be considered too risky for the portfolio (eg, due to the novel nature of the risk being transferred under that transaction or the complexity of its structure) may nonetheless, due to its putative diversification benefits, constitute an acceptable investment once its risk and return profile has been aggregated with that of the other portfolio constituents.

(d)   *Modern portfolio theory*

This approach towards ascertaining the appropriateness of derivatives and other investments is predicated upon modern portfolio theory:[33]

> *The central principle of portfolio theory is that the risk of a portfolio is wholly distinct from the risk of any particular investment contained in the portfolio. The risk of a portfolio is a function of the interaction of its component investments. Thus, a trustee can use securities and instruments that are highly risky viewed in isolation to assemble a portfolio that is safe. Portfolio theory justifies the inclusion, in appropriate amounts, of stocks thought to be risky. It also justifies the use of financial instruments, highly volatile in themselves, that may be deployed so as to lower portfolio risk or to attain a portfolio of a given risk at a lower cost.*

---

33   JN Gordon, "The Puzzling Persistence of the Constrained Prudent Investor Rule" (1987) 62, *New York University Law Review* 52 at 67. See also Bines and Thel, endnote 27, sections 7.01 and 8.04; EC Halbach, "Trust Investment Law in the Third Restatement" (1992) 77, *Iowa Law Review* 1151,at 1159-1175, and Lord Nicholls of Birkenhead writing extra-judicially in "Trustees and their Broader Community: Where Duty, Morality and Ethics Converge" (1995) 9, *Trust Law International* 71 at 76.

This whole-of-portfolio approach towards the selection of investments for portfolios is concerned with the relationship between the risk and rates of return of particular instruments and how different combinations of instruments can be used to construct efficient portfolios (a portfolio is efficient if there are no other portfolios with the same level of return that can provide the investor with a lower level of risk).

The return on a portfolio and its overall riskiness are dependent on the correlation of returns between the various constituents of the portfolio.[34] In order to maximise returns for a given level of risk (or, in other words, to minimise the portfolio's overall risk exposure for a given rate of return), the institutional investor must diversify its portfolio. This involves devising a mix of instruments (including derivatives) for a portfolio that has a collective risk profile consistent with the institutional investor's investment objectives (as expressed in the investment mandate) and which is expected to generate the optimal aggregate returns for the portfolio for the particular level of risk assumed. This can be achieved by combining instruments that are negatively correlated, lowly correlated or uncorrelated to each other. The lower or weaker the positive correlation between different instruments in a portfolio, the greater their collective potential to reduce the overall risk profile of the portfolio or generate a greater aggregate return for the same overall level of risk. Hence, even where two instruments have the same risk and return profiles, modern portfolio theory favours the selection of the instrument that is negatively correlated to the instruments already held in the institutional investor's portfolio because the inclusion of that instrument would lower the overall risk of the portfolio.

3.3 Not-for-profit organisations and charities

The majority of institutional investors are commercial, collective investment vehicles, where an institutional investor (or a fund manager appointed by the institutional investor) pools the contributions of its investors for the purposes of generating a financial return for the benefit of those investors. However, that structure does not hold true for institutional investors that are not-for-profit organisations or charities (eg, university endowments, many of which, in the United States, routinely transact derivatives). In the case of not-for-profit organisations and charities, the assets held by the institutional investor are invested not for the benefit of investors who have contributed assets to the institutional investor in expectation of financial returns, but in fulfilment of the not-for-profit or charitable purposes of the institutional investor. Moreover, the assets held by these institutional investors come from donations where the donors have no expectation of (or entitlement to) the financial returns generated from the investment of the donations.

This difference in legal structure and rationale may necessitate a modification of the prudent investor rule when applied to not-for-profit organisations and charities, whether the institutional investor is intending to enter into a derivatives transaction or to invest in some other instrument.[35] Assessing the suitability of derivatives

---

34   See Bines and Thel, endnote 27, section 7.02[C], and also Ali, Stapledon and Gold, endnote 5, Ch 4.
35   See PU Ali, "Charitable Trusts and Hedge Funds" (2004) 11, *Journal of International Trust and Corporate Planning* 187.

transactions and their consequences for portfolio diversification, remains a valid concern even for not-for-profit organisations and charities. Nonetheless, unlike other institutional investors that invest for the overarching purpose of generating financial returns for their investors, not-for-profit organisations and charities, when entering into derivatives transactions, must also take account of the need to ensure that the capital value of the portfolio remains available for the continued pursuit of the not-for-profit organisation or charity's legal purposes.

This need for long-term capital stability suggests that, unless the portfolio diversification benefits are overwhelming and there are no suitable, more conventional substitutes, not-for-profit organisations and charities should avoid complex or exotic derivatives that are difficult to value and illiquid, and derivatives that incorporate a high level of leverage. This is likely to generate a bias in favour of vanilla derivatives to hedge, for instance, the interest rate and currency risk of portfolios or to fine-tune the asset mix of portfolios.

3.4   Concluding remarks on the use of derivatives by institutional investors
The prudent investor rule, in common with the duty of care that applies to the directors of corporate end users, does not create a positive duty to use derivatives.[36] Instead, the rule sets out only the parameters for the acceptable use of derivatives by institutional investors: when deciding whether to enter into a derivatives transaction, the institutional investor must consider the suitability of the derivatives transaction and the consequences for portfolio diversification of its entry into that transaction (assuming that the institutional investor is empowered to enter into the transaction, and that the transaction complies with any limits on the use of derivatives prescribed by the investment mandate).

As with corporate end users, there are two general uses to which institutional investors can put derivatives.[37] First, derivatives can be used to reduce or eliminate the exposure of a portfolio to particular risks, such as currency risk in the case of investments in foreign securities.

The use of derivatives for hedging purposes is, again, subject to a caveat against over-hedging. The investors for whose account the institutional investor undertakes the investment of assets have, even more explicitly than investors in a corporate end user, bargained for market exposure. This exposure to market-traded instruments, such as securities and derivatives, necessarily carries with it the risk of loss (due to market revaluation or the crystallisation of a loss on realising an investment position). Investing in market-traded instruments means that neither the preservation of the investors' capital contributions to the portfolio managed by the institutional investor nor the generation of positive financial returns on those pooled contributions is certain. Nonetheless, the investors have the opportunity to obtain a financial gain to compensate them for the risk being borne – which is what they have bargained for.

36   Cf G Crawford, "A Fiduciary Duty to Use Derivatives?", (1994-95) 1 *Stanford Journal of Law, Business and Finance* 307.
37   As in the case of corporate end users, institutional investors who use derivatives to increase, rather than reduce, portfolio risk are likely to find, particularly in the current economic environment, that their investors are far less likely to forgive any derivatives-related losses.

Thus, an institutional investor that lays off all material risks and delivers a return to the investors approximating that which could been derived from cash instruments or other relatively riskless assets is unlikely to be seen by either the investors or a court as having complied with the prudent investor rule and discharged its duty to the investors.

Second, derivatives offer an efficient means of creating exposure. Generally, a derivatives transaction (eg, an equity index swap, portfolio swap or total return swap) can be established to create exposure to an entire market, market sector, diversified basket of securities or the securities of a single issuer, for a fraction of the cost of establishing the same level of exposure through a physical investment in the assets referenced by the derivatives transaction. For portfolios that track or are benchmarked against a particular index, the use of derivatives may reduce basis risk and tracking error between the price performance of the portfolio and the benchmark index. In addition, no physical rebalancing need be undertaken to mirror changes in index constituents or their relative weightings.

Balanced against this is the fact that the inherent leverage in derivatives transactions carries the potential to magnify not only gains for the portfolio, but also losses. The use of derivatives may, in addition, increase the volatility of the portfolio's returns. Moreover, the derivatives in question may be illiquid, rendering it difficult for the institutional investor to rollover or unwind positions and for the value of the position to be readily ascertained. Accordingly, an institutional investor considering using derivatives to create exposure, needs to look beyond the efficiencies offered by derivatives and their potential for leveraged gains (and thus portfolio outperformance), and assess the individual suitability of the derivatives and the likely impact of transacting them on the portfolio's overall risk profile.

4.   Conclusion

Corporate end users are relatively unconstrained in their use of derivatives and enjoy considerable flexibility in determining whether derivatives should be used as part of a hedging programme or to establish investment positions. However, there is one qualification. As part of the duty of care owed to the corporate end user by its directors and other officers, those persons will, at the very least, need to ensure that they have sufficient understanding of derivatives in order to be able to make informed decisions about, and properly monitor, the corporation's use of derivatives.

By contrast, institutional investors are subject to explicit constraints on the use of derivatives, in terms of both their legal capacity to enter into derivatives transactions and their selection of derivatives for inclusion in the portfolios that they manage. When selecting derivatives, institutional investors must ensure that those instruments are suitable for inclusion in the relevant portfolio and consistent with the investment objectives and strategy (as well as the risk parameters) applicable to the portfolio. They must also ensure that the selected derivatives contribute positively to the diversification of the portfolio.

The courts, in evaluating the suitability and contribution to diversification of derivatives (and other instruments) selected by the institutional investor, will be guided by the precepts of modern portfolio theory. Modern portfolio theory, and in particular the positive models derived from it (eg, the capital asset pricing model), are not without their critics. However, until there is judicial or legislative recognition of the shortcomings of (or alternatives to) modern portfolio theory, institutional investors are advised to continue treating modern portfolio theory as the investment norm.

Regulation of OTC derivatives

Ruth Frederick
Senior legal counsel

1. Introduction

Derivatives, and in particular credit derivatives, have received a great deal of attention in the past few years due to their market size[1] and complexity, and the collapse or near collapse of certain financial institutions with substantial involvement in the 'credit default swap' (CDS) market. While 'over-the-counter' (OTC) derivatives were not in themselves the cause of the global financial crisis, the near-collapse of American International Group (AIG)[2] and Bear Stearns, and the bankruptcy of Lehman Brothers during 2008 – all three financial institutions heavily involved in the CDS market – have highlighted the extent to which the risks in the OTC derivatives market had gone undetected by both regulators and industry. This has revealed perceived shortcomings in the management and regulation of counterparty credit risk, as well as the lack of transparency[3] of the OTC derivatives market. These issues resulted in derivatives regulation coming to the forefront of debate in both the United States and Europe, and a global move to improve regulatory oversight and transparency in relation to the OTC derivatives markets.

This chapter examines the current framework governing the regulation of OTC derivatives in the European Union introduced in response to the events of 2008. As certain aspects of the regulations are yet to come into full effect, this chapter is not, however, intended to be a comprehensive guide to OTC derivatives regulation.

2. Counterparty risk and transparency risk

Broadly speaking, a derivatives contract is a financial instrument between two parties in which they agree to exchange cash or assets in amounts and on dates that are dependent upon certain future values or the occurrence of certain pre-defined future events and is intended to assist parties in, among other things, managing and sharing risk. One predominant risk associated with such an agreement is the risk of one of the parties not fulfilling its obligation to pay cash or deliver assets. This risk

---

1   According to statistics released by the Bank of International Settlements, as at December 2015 the notional amount of unsettled OTC derivatives contracts worldwide exceeded US$490 trillion. The total market value of outstanding derivatives contracts (which provide a more meaningful measure of risk than notional amounts) was at US$14.5 trillion as at December 2015 (www.bis.org/publ/ otc_hy1605.htm).
2   AIG issued over US$400 billion of unhedged CDSs. When the value of those swaps started to decline and AIG suffered two downgrades, its counterparties began calling for collateral to secure its payment obligations under those swaps, which resulted in AIG needing to be bailed out by the US Federal Reserve to avoid further systemic consequences.
3   In that it appeared more difficult to see behind the bilaterally negotiated OTC derivatives contracts.

is sometimes described as 'counterparty risk' or 'default risk'. Counterparty risk is sometimes difficult to evaluate because the exposure of the counterparty to various risks is generally not public information and such risk can worsen if a counterparty enters into similar contracts with one or more other market participants. It can be argued that if a large financial institution has accumulated large positions with other counterparties and then defaults, such counterparties may also suffer substantial losses, which in turn may create systemic risk in the markets generally.

The events relating to, among others, AIG and Lehman revealed an apparent lack of transparency in the OTC markets, as neither the regulators nor the market were aware of the extent of the CDS exposures that these institutions had accumulated. These concerns led to a call by regulators for more robust counterparty risk management, greater transparency and more stringent reporting requirements.

3.   Various perspectives on regulatory reform

The push for reform to the OTC derivatives market continues to progress at an international level.

3.1   Global perspective

During the 2009 G20[4] Summit, the G20 leaders agreed upon a commitment to "promote the standardisation and resilience of credit derivatives markets, in particular through the establishment of central clearing counterparties subject to effective regulation and supervision".[5] Subsequently, at their meeting in Pittsburgh on 25 September 2009, the G20 leaders made the following declaration:

> All standardized OTC derivative contracts should be traded on exchanges or electronic trading platforms, where appropriate, and cleared through central counterparties by end 2012 at the latest. OTC derivative contracts should be reported to trade repositories. Non-centrally cleared contracts should be subject to higher capital requirements. We ask the [Financial Stability Board][6] and its relevant members to assess regularly implementation and whether it is sufficient to improve transparency in the derivatives markets, mitigate systemic risk, and protect against market abuse.[7]

3.2   EU perspective

The European Commission's view is that legislation is required to allow the markets to price risk appropriately. Accordingly, the EU Regulation on OTC derivatives transactions, central counterparties and trade repositories (648/2012) (known as EMIR) came into effect on 12 September 2012. EMIR is the European Union's part of the global effort to increase the stability of the OTC derivatives markets, by seeking to reduce counterparty credit risk and boost transparency, as described further below.

---

4   The Group of Twenty Finance Ministers and Central Bank Governors (known as the G20 or Group of Twenty) is a group of finance ministers and central bank governors from 20 economies: 19 countries, plus the European Union.

5   G20 Declaration on Strengthening the Financial System, London, 2 April 2009.

6   The Financial Stability Board was established to develop and implement regulatory, supervisory and other policies in the interests of financial stability (www.financialstabilityboard.org).

7   Leaders' Statement, The Pittsburgh Summit, 24-25 September 2009 (http://ec.europa.eu/archives/commission_2010-2014/president/pdf/statement_20090826_en_2.pdf).

EMIR is essentially a framework regulation whose detailed rules regarding scope are determined by additional 'regulatory technical standards' (RTSs). EMIR contains three broad requirements:

- Reducing counterparty credit risk – the European Commission concluded that the global financial crisis demonstrated that market participants failed to price counterparty credit risk properly and that such risk could be managed using either bilateral or central clearing. Accordingly, OTC derivatives would need to be cleared through 'central clearing counterparties' (CCPs). The rules also impose numerous obligations on CCPs, including authorisation, prudential, organisational and conduct of business requirements, and contain requirements regarding interoperability between CCPs (each as summarised in section 7 below).
- Reducing credit and operational risk – OTC derivatives contracts that cannot be centrally cleared are subject to additional risk mitigation measures (eg, marking-to-market (readjusting the positions to current market value), higher levels of margin to protect against credit risk and higher regulatory capital charges).
- Increasing transparency – EMIR requires market participants to report all OTC and listed derivatives contracts to EU-approved or recognised trade repositories. Separately and in an attempt to improve market integrity and oversight, the market manipulation provisions of the Market Abuse Directive (2003/6/EC) have been extended to apply to derivatives.

Each of these requirements is described further below.

3.3 UK perspective and implementation of EMIR

As a regulation, EMIR has direct application in the United Kingdom without the need for significant UK legislation to implement it. However, some amendments were required to be made to UK law to facilitate compatibility between UK legislation and EMIR. For example, various amendments have been made to the Financial Services and Markets Act 2000 and the Financial Services and Markets Act 2000 (Over the Counter Derivatives, Central Counterparties and Trade Repositories) (Amendment) Regulations 2015[8] in relation to the authorisation and regulation of CCPs, and amendments have been made to the Companies Act 1989 to implement the EMIR rules regarding the segregation and transfer of assets in the United Kingdom.

The UK Financial Conduct Authority also amended its client asset rules[9] to implement EMIR's segregation and portability requirements.

3.4 US perspective

The Dodd-Frank Wall Street Reform and Consumer Protection Act, whose main purpose was to overhaul the US financial regulatory system, was signed into law on 21 July 2010. The act introduced changes that affect the oversight and supervision

---

8   www.legislation.gov.uk/uksi/2015/348/pdfs/uksi_20150348_en.pdf.
9   FCA Client Money Rules and Client Money Distribution (CASS 7 and 7A).

of financial institutions, creates a new resolution process for significant financial institutions, introduces more robust regulatory capital requirements, reforms the regulation of rating agencies and introduces changes within the securitisation market. The act required a number of studies to be conducted and significant additional rule-making to be introduced for the OTC derivatives markets. The rules relating to OTC derivatives are set out in Title VII of the Dodd-Frank Act. Broadly speaking, the Title VII reforms to the regulation of the OTC derivatives market include requiring:

- the mandatory clearing of all standardised OTC derivatives contracts through regulated CCPs;
- the movement of standardised OTC derivatives transactions onto regulated exchanges; and
- the promotion of transparency, which requires market participants to report trades to regulated trade repositories, increased margin requirements for derivatives contracts that are not centrally cleared, and the imposition of position limits to limit speculation in commodity derivatives underlying assets.

CCPs and trade depositories are also required to disclose information on open positions and trading volumes to the markets, and to disclose information on individual counterparty trades and positions to US federal regulators. OTC derivatives dealers that build up large exposures to counterparties are subject to a regime of prudential supervision and regulation, which includes conservative capital requirements, business conduct standards and certain additional reporting requirements.

4. EMIR requirements

The following paragraphs describe the scope and key requirements of EMIR in more detail.

4.1 Entities in scope

EMIR applies to counterparties to derivatives trades, CCPs and trade depositories. Certain central banks of EU member states and other public bodies are exempted.[10, 11]

The extent to which EMIR applies to counterparties to derivatives trades depends on whether the counterparty is a financial counterparty (described for the purposes

---

10   During July 2013 the European Commission adopted a delegated regulation exempting from EMIR the central banks and public bodies charged with or intervening in the management of the public debt in Japan and the United States. The Commission adopted a further regulation that would extend the list of non-EU central banks that are exempt entities under EMIR to include the central banks of Australia, Canada, Hong Kong, Mexico, Singapore and Switzerland. The proposed regulation needs to be approved by the European Parliament and European Council before it can come into effect.

11   EMIR excludes certain entities and transactions from the clearing requirement – namely:
- institutions such as the European System of Central Banks, other institutions responsible for managing public debt and the Bank for International Settlements (Article 1(4)); and
- multinational development banks, certain public sector entities (where they are owned by central governments and have explicit guarantee arrangements provided by central governments), the European Financial Stability Facility and the European Stability Mechanism (Article 1(5)).

Certain intragroup trades are excluded from the clearing obligation (Article 4(2)) and certain transitional provisions apply to pension funds, exempting them from the clearing obligation for a limited period of time (Article 89).

of this chapter as 'FC') or a non-financial counterparty (described for the purposes of this chapter as 'NFC'). If an entity is classified as a NFC, whether it is subject to certain aspects of EMIR depends on the volume of its derivatives trading activities.

4.2 Financial counterparties

An 'FC' is broadly defined in Article 2(8) of EMIR and includes investment firms,[12] credit institutions,[13] insurance undertakings,[14] assurance undertakings,[15] reinsurance undertakings,[16] undertakings for collective investment in transferable securities (ie, mutual funds based in the European Union) (known as UCITS funds)[17] – and, where relevant, their management companies – 'institutions for occupational retirement provision' (IORPs)[18] and 'alternative investment funds' (AIFs).[19]

The clearing obligation, the risk mitigation requirements for uncleared derivatives transactions and the reporting requirements all apply to FCs.

4.3 NFCs

An 'NFC' is defined in Article 2(9) of EMIR as "an undertaking which is established in the Union" other than FCs and CCPs. The European Commission recognises that NFCs use OTC derivatives to hedge against commercial risks directly linked to their business activities (eg, an airline or a shipping company hedging risk against a rise in oil prices). Accordingly, EMIR takes into consideration the purpose for which NFCs use OTC derivatives and the level of exposure to such contracts.[20] Consequently, NFCs are characterised under EMIR as either:

- NFCs whose OTC derivatives trading activities exceed the EMIR clearing threshold (described for the purposes of this chapter as 'NFCs+') (for a more detailed discussion on the clearing threshold, see the relevant paragraph in section 7.3(c) below); and
- NFCs whose OTC derivatives trading activities do not exceed the clearing threshold (described for the purposes of this chapter as 'NFCs-').

The EMIR reporting requirement applies to derivatives contracts entered into by all NFCs, irrespective of the level of OTC derivatives trading activities in which they engage. However, whether an entity is an NFC+ or an NFC- will affect whether and the extent to which that entity is subject to EMIR's clearing and risk mitigation requirements. With respect to risk mitigation, if an NFC exceeds the clearing threshold this also widens the scope of risk mitigation requirements that the NFC must comply with under Article 11 of EMIR. For example, the requirements to exchange collateral under Article 11(3) will apply to an NFC+, but not to an NFC-.[21]

12　Authorised under the Markets in Financial Instruments Directive (2004/39/EC) (MiFID).
13　Authorised under the Banking Consolidation Directive (2006/48/EC) (BCD).
14　As defined in the First Non-Life Directive (73/239/EEC).
15　Authorised under the Life Directive (2002/83/EC).
16　Authorised under the Reinsurance Directive (2005/68/EC).
17　Authorised in accordance with the UCITS IV Directive (2009/65/EC).
18　As defined in the Occupational Pension Funds Directive (2003/41/EC).
19　As defined in the Alternative Investment Fund Managers Directive (2011/61/EU).
20　Recital (29) of EMIR.
21　Article 11(2) of EMIR.

4.4   Exempted entities

Some entities are completely or partially exempt from EMIR – namely:

- members of the European System of Central Banks, other member state bodies performing similar functions and other member state public bodies charged with or intervening in the management of public debt; and
- the Bank for International Settlements.[22]

With the exception of the reporting obligation, the following entities are also exempt:

- multilateral development banks, as listed under Section 4.2 of Part 1 of Annex VI to the Banking Consolidation Directive (2006/48/EC);
- public sector entities within the meaning of point (18) of Article 4 of the Banking Consolidation Directive which are owned by central governments and have explicit guarantee arrangements provided by central governments; and
- the European Financial Stability Facility and the European Stability Mechanism.[23]

4.5   Which derivatives contracts are subject to EMIR

EMIR applies to derivatives contracts as defined in Annex 1 Sections C(4)–(10) of the Markets in Financial Instruments Directive (2004/39/EC) (MiFID). This includes certain options, futures, swaps, forwards rate agreements and any other derivatives contracts relating to securities, currencies, interest rates, yields, commodities, emissions allowances or other derivatives instruments, financial indices or financial measures.

MiFID provides no precise definitions of the terms used in Sections C(4)–(10) of Annex I and, in particular, of what amounts to a derivative. Consequently, there is still industry-wide confusion as to constitutes a derivative; the lack of a consistent and harmonised definition across the EU member states presents significant challenges in determining which products are subject to EMIR, particularly in the context of cross-border trading.

In the context of 'foreign exchange' (FX) trading, this uncertainly has meant that EU different member states have been left to interpret themselves how to differentiate between an FX forward and a spot FX transaction.

While MiFID (and thus EMIR) does not expressly exclude spot FX, it can be argued that spot FX transactions are not subject to EMIR as they do not fall within the relevant MiFID definition. As regards the EMIR clearing requirement, the European Commission recognises that FX transactions may not be required to be cleared as they present settlement risk rather than counterparty risk, which is what central clearing is intended to address.[24] However, in subsequent statements, the Commission appears to have implied that the central clearing requirement may

---

22   Article 1(4) of EMIR.
23   Article 1(5) of EMIR.
24   Recital (19) to EMIR.

30

apply to FX transactions. By way of comparison, the US Dodd-Frank Act exempts FX swaps and non-deliverable forwards from its clearing requirements (although there may be limited scope for non-deliverable forwards being subject to clearing in the United States in the future).[25]

To seek to address this issue, the European Securities and Markets Authority (ESMA)[26] and the Commission exchanged correspondence with the aim of finding a resolution.[27] Although the Commission intended to use the power conferred in Article 4(2) of MiFID to publish implementing regulations to clarify the definition of 'derivative', the Commission realised that it would be impossible to address the issue in this way. Consequently, the Commission stated that the uncertainty would be addressed through changes to be introduced through MiFID, which is to come into force on 3 January 2018. The Commission also welcomed further guidance to be issued by ESMA. However, as at the date of publication, ESMA had not yet issued any further guidance.

Accordingly, the proposed amendments to MiFID, known as MiFID II,[28] will seek to define 'spot FX'. In the latest draft MiFID II delegated regulation,[29] it is defined as a currency exchange contract in which delivery is scheduled to be made within the longer of the following periods:

- two trading days in respect of any pair of the major currencies[30] set out in Article 10(3);
- for any pair of currencies where at least one currency is not a major currency, the longer of two trading days or the period generally accepted in the market for that currency pair as the standard delivery period; or
- where the contract relates to a purchase or sale of a transferable security (ie, spot-for-settle transactions), the period generally accepted in the market for the settlement of that transferable security as the standard delivery period or five trading days, whichever is shorter.

What is an OTC derivatives contract? EMIR defines an 'OTC derivative' as a derivatives transaction that is not executed on a regulated market within the meaning of Article 4(1)(14) of MiFID or on a third-country market considered as equivalent to a regulated market in accordance with Article 19(6) of MiFID.[31]

---

25   www.treasury.gov/press-center/press-releases/Pages/tg1773.aspx.
26   ESMA is responsible for, among other things, regulating clearing houses. It began its operations on 1 January 2011 and replaced the Committee of European Securities Regulators, which was a network of EU authorities that promoted consistent supervision across the European Union.
27   ESMA wrote to the European Commission on 14 February 2014 requesting that the Commission clarify the definition of a 'derivative' or 'derivatives contract' under EMIR. The Commission replied on 26 February 2014 and wrote a further letter to ESMA on 23 July 2014.
28   Technically, MiFID II encapsulates a directive (Markets in Financial Instruments Directive (2014/65/EU)) and a regulation (Markets in Financial Instruments Regulation (600/2014) (MiFIR) – see section 9 below for more details.
29   Article 10 of Draft Delegated Regulation of 25 April 2016, supplementing the MiFID II Directive on the organisational requirements and operating conditions for investment firms and defined terms for the purposes of that directive.
30   US dollar, euro, Japanese yen, UK pound sterling, Australian dollar, Swiss franc, Canadian dollar, Hong Kong dollar, Swedish krona, New Zealand dollar, Singapore dollar, Norwegian krone, Mexican peso, Croatian kuna, Bulgarian lev, Czech koruna, Danish krone, Hungarian forint, Polish zloty and Romanian leu.
31   Article 2(7) of EMIR.

Regulated markets in the United Kingdom include ICE Futures Europe, the London Stock Exchange, NYSE Euronext London, the London International Financial Futures and Options Exchange and the London Metal Exchange.

Consequently, derivatives contracts that are traded bilaterally or on a multilateral trading facility[32] that is not presently a regulated market will be considered OTC derivatives contracts for the purposes of EMIR. Furthermore, derivatives contracts traded on organised trading facilities[33] will also be treated as OTC derivatives contracts for the purposes of EMIR. These derivatives contracts may, therefore, be subject to the clearing obligation.

Under EMIR, trades executed on regulated markets are not subject to the clearing obligation. However, these trades may be subject to a clearing requirement when MiFID II comes into force. This is because MiFID II requires the operator of a regulated market to ensure that all transactions in derivatives executed on its venue are cleared by a CCP.[34]

The risk mitigation requirement applies to all OTC derivatives contracts that are not subject to the clearing requirement. The reporting requirements apply to all listed (eg, traded on a trading venue) or OTC derivatives contracts. The clearing requirement applies only to those OTC contracts that have been declared by ESMA to be mandatorily cleared, via the publication of RTSs. At present, interest rate swaps and CDS indices will be the first types of derivatives product that will be subject to mandatory clearing (see below for more details).

5.   Risk mitigation

EMIR requires counterparties to OTC derivatives contracts that are not cleared by a CCP (either because the class of OTC derivative is not subject to clearing or the counterparties to the transaction are not subject to the clearing obligation) to mitigate their counterparty and operational risks by using a number of risk mitigation techniques prescribed by EMIR.[35, 36] The risk mitigation techniques are intended to reflect the protections that would have been awarded if the transaction had been centrally cleared and, broadly, comprise the following:

- procedures to monitor and mitigate operational and counterparty credit risk (including trade confirmations and robust reconciliation processes);
- daily marking-to-market of the value of outstanding transactions;

---

32   As defined in Article 4(1)(15) of the MiFID II Directive.
33   As defined in Article 4(1)(23) of the MiFID II Directive.
34   Article 29 of MiFIR.
35   Article 11 of EMIR.
36   Delegated Regulation 148/2013 supplementing EMIR on OTC derivatives, central counterparties and trade repositories with regard to regulatory technical standards on the minimum details of the data to be reported to trade repositories; Delegated Regulation 149/2013 supplementing EMIR regarding indirect clearing arrangements, the clearing obligation, the public register, access to a trading venue, non-financial counterparties and risk mitigation techniques for OTC derivatives contracts not cleared by a CCP; Delegated Regulation 150/2013 supplementing EMIR on OTC derivatives, central counterparties and trade repositories with regard to regulatory technical standards specifying the details of the application for registration as a trade repository; Delegated Regulation 151/2013 supplementing EMIR specifying the data to be published and made available by trade repositories and operational standards for aggregating, comparing and accessing the data; Delegated Regulation 152/2013 supplementing EMIR regarding capital requirements for central counterparties; and Delegated Regulation 153/2013 supplementing EMIR on requirements for central counterparties.

- exchange of collateral; and
- increased capital requirements for FCs to manage the risk not covered by collateral.

5.1 Which derivatives transactions do the risk mitigation requirements apply to?
As mentioned above, the risk mitigation requirements apply to OTC derivatives contracts that are not subject to the clearing requirement.[37]

5.2 When does the risk mitigation obligation apply?
If one or both of the conditions listed below are met, the OTC derivatives transaction will not be subject to the clearing requirement (in which case the risk mitigation requirements will apply):

- One or both of the counterparties is not subject to the EMIR clearing requirement (see the paragraph titled "To whom does the central clearing obligation apply" in section 7.3(c) below); and/or;
- The derivative is not among the classes of derivative that the Commission has determined to be subject to the clearing requirement (see section 7.3(b) below).

5.3 Who must comply with the EMIR risk mitigation requirements?
The risk mitigation requirements apply to some extent to all counterparties, although more requirements apply to FCs and NFC+s under EMIR[38] than to NFCs-.

5.4 Overview of risk mitigation requirements
EMIR requires that all FCs and NFCs that enter into uncleared OTC derivatives contracts must implement procedures and arrangements to measure, monitor and mitigate operational risk and counterparty credit risk,[39] as summarised below:

- the timely confirmation, where available, by electronic means, of the terms of the relevant OTC derivatives contract; and
- formalised processes which are robust, resilient and auditable in order to reconcile (which includes valuing) portfolios to manage the associated risk and to identify disputes between parties early and resolve them, and to monitor the value of outstanding contracts.

The scope of the rules is fairly wide. They apply to all financial institutions and funds subject to financial regulation under an EU directive, to all other (unregulated) entities established in the European Economic Area (EEA) and to certain third-country (ie, non-EU) entities.

(a) Confirmation of trades
All FCs and NFCs that enter into OTC derivatives contracts must have appropriate

---

37   Article 11(1) of EMIR.
38   Article 10 of EMIR.
39   Article 11(1) EMIR.

procedures and arrangements in place to ensure that trades are confirmed (where available by electronic means) as soon as possible and at the latest within specific deadlines ranging from one to seven days, depending on the classification of the counterparties involved, the derivative class and the date on which the trade was effected.

The European Commission adopted an RTS[40] which provides more granular detail on the risk mitigation procedures and arrangements required to be implemented by Article 11(1) of EMIR, as summarised below.

As mentioned above, the trade confirmation deadline depends on, among other things, whether the counterparty is an FC, NFC+ or NFC-. For example, transactions entered into by an NFC- have a longer confirmation timeline. The RTS also distinguishes between different types of derivatives contract (ie, CDS and interest rate swaps on the one hand, and equity, FX, commodities and other derivatives on the other hand). The table below sets out the various confirmation deadlines based on the above variables.

Derivative	Deadline[41]
Regime for FCs and NFCs+s	
CDSs and interest rate swaps entered into on or before 28 February 2014	T+2
CDSs and interest rate swaps entered into after 28 February 2014	T+1
All other derivatives entered into on or before 31 August 2013	T+3
All other derivatives entered into after 31 August 2013, but on or before 31 August 2014	T+2
All other derivatives entered into after 31 August 2014	T+1
Regime for NFCs-	
CDSs and interest rate swaps entered into on or before 31 August 2013	T+5
CDSs and interest rate swaps entered into after 31 August 2013, but on or before 31 August 2014	T+3

continued on next page

---

40   Article 12 of Delegated Regulation 149/2013.
41   These deadlines are extended by one business day where the contract is concluded after 4:00pm or with a counterparty in a time zone that does not allow confirmation by the set deadlines.

Derivative	Deadline[41]
Regime for NFCs-	
CDSs and interest rate swaps entered into after 31 August 2014	T+2
All other derivatives entered into on or before 31 August 2013	T+7
All other derivatives entered into after 31 August 2013, but on or before 31 August 2014	T+4
All other derivatives entered into after 31 August 2014	T+2

FCs are also required to be prepared to report (at the request of the relevant regulator) to the relevant regulator, on a monthly basis, the number of unconfirmed trades that have been outstanding for more than five business days.

(b)   *Portfolio reconciliation*
Prior to entering into a derivatives contract, FCs and NFCs must agree in writing the arrangements under which portfolios will be reconciled. Portfolio reconciliation must cover key trade terms that identify each derivatives contract and include at least the valuation attributed to each contract. The parties can appoint a third-party agent to carry out their portfolio reconciliation duties.[42] The times at which reconciliation must be performed vary from each business day to annually, depending on the classification of the counterparty and the number of contracts outstanding with any counterparty, as set out in the table below.

Classification of counterparty	Contracts outstanding	Frequency of reconciliation
FC or NFC+	500 or more	Daily
FC or NFC+	51–499	Weekly
FC or NFC+	50 or less	Quarterly
NFC-	More than 100	Quarterly
NFC-	100 or less	Annually

42   Article 13 of Delegated Regulation 149/2013.

(c) **Portfolio compression**

Portfolio compression comprises the termination of equal and offsetting trades with the same counterparty. The benefits of reducing the aggregate notional amount and number of trades with a counterparty include reduced cost and operational risk, as well as reduced counterparty credit risk. The RTS[43] requires that FCs and NFCs with 500 or more OTC derivatives contracts outstanding with a counterparty which are not centrally cleared have a process in place to analyse regularly (and, in any event, at least twice a year) the possibility to conduct a portfolio compression exercise in order to reduce counterparty credit risk. Note that the RTS does not specify that counterparties must carry out portfolio compression, but that market participants with significant portfolio sizes should consider whether compression is appropriate.

(d) **Dispute resolution**

The purpose of the dispute resolution requirements is to avoid unresolved disputes escalating and exposing counterparties to additional risks. Disputes should be identified, managed and, in certain cases, appropriately disclosed.

When concluding non-centrally cleared[44] OTC derivatives contracts with each other, FCs and NFCs must have agreed detailed procedures and processes relating to:

- the identification, recording and monitoring of disputes relating to the recognition or valuation of the contract and to the exchange of collateral between counterparties. Those procedures shall at least record the length of time for which the dispute remains outstanding, the counterparty and the amount which is disputed; and
- the resolution of disputes in a timely manner with a specific process for those disputes that are not resolved within five business days.

Financial counterparties must report to the relevant regulator any disputes between counterparties relating to an OTC derivatives contract, its valuation or the exchange of collateral for an amount or a value higher than €15 million and outstanding for at least 15 business days.[45]

Market participants (particularly NFCs) should be aware of the operational, cost and administrative impact that these requirements may have on them.

ISDA EMIR Portfolio Reconciliation, Dispute Resolution and Disclosure Protocol: In order to comply with certain EMIR risk mitigation requirements, market participants have had to amend their existing derivatives contracts to reflect such requirements. The ISDA EMIR Portfolio Reconciliation, Dispute Resolution and Disclosure Protocol[46] was published by the 'International Swaps and Derivatives Association Inc' (ISDA) to facilitate the amendment by market participants of their

---

43   Article 14 of Delegated Regulation 149/2013.
44   Recital 31 of Delegated Regulation 149/2013 states that the dispute resolution requirements apply to OTC contracts that are not centrally cleared.
45   Article 15 of Delegated Regulation 149/2013.
46   www2.isda.org/functional-areas/protocol-management/protocol/15.

contracts at a multilateral level, with the aim of complying with the portfolio reconciliation and dispute resolution obligations described above.

The ISDA EMIR Protocol works by amending the terms of, among other things, each ISDA Master Agreement entered into between two market participants that have adhered[47] (or agreed) to the ISDA EMIR Protocol. An investment manager may adhere to the ISDA EMIR Protocol on behalf of all or some of its clients or funds. Consequently, investment managers must ensure that they have such authority to adhere on behalf of their clients and funds.

The ISDA EMIR Protocol sets out provisions relating to portfolio reconciliation, dispute resolution and confidentiality waiver.

Portfolio reconciliation: Each adhering party needs to elect in the adherence letter whether it wishes to be a 'portfolio data receiving entity' or a 'portfolio data sending entity'.

A 'portfolio data receiving entity' is electing to receive only the portfolio data (comprising key trade terms) sent by its counterparty, following which it is under an obligation to compare such data against its own records. If the portfolio data receiving entity identifies a discrepancy in the data which it believes is material to the rights and obligations of the parties, then it must notify its counterparty, and the two parties must consult, in a timely manner, with the aim of resolving any such discrepancy. Failure by the portfolio data receiving entity to notify its counterparty of any discrepancy within five joint business days (ie, days that are both New York and London business days) is deemed to be an affirmation of the portfolio data.

If both parties elect to be 'portfolio data sending entities', both parties will send to the other party the relevant portfolio data and both parties are required to compare such data against their own records. Each party is required to notify the other party of any discrepancy in the portfolio data which it believes is material to the rights and obligations of the party, in which case both parties must consult in a timely manner to resolve the discrepancy.

The parties can agree amongst themselves the frequency of portfolio reconciliation subject to the minimum specified by EMIR (see section 5.4(b) above). An adhering party may also delegate the portfolio reconciliation requirement to a third party.

Dispute resolution: The ISDA EMIR Protocol sets out a dispute resolution mechanism which allows either party to identify a dispute by sending a dispute notice to its counterparty. The parties must then consult in good faith and in a timely manner to resolve the dispute. If any dispute is not resolved within five joint business days, then each party must escalate the dispute to internal senior members of staff. Adhering parties are still required to comply with existing dispute resolution provisions agreed elsewhere in their derivatives agreements (eg, those set out in the ISDA Credit Support Annex or any calculation agent dispute provisions). Adhering parties will, therefore, need to comply with any existing dispute resolution processes, as well as the ISDA EMIR Protocol.

47   Adherence is effected by completing an adherence letter via the protocol management section of the ISDA website and paying a fee.

Confidentiality waiver: The ISDA EMIR Protocol includes a confidentiality waiver provision which is unrelated to the EMIR risk mitigation requirements, but which is relevant for the obligation to report transactions to trade depositories.

The confidentiality waiver was proposed to address the concerns of certain market participants that wished to avoid the potential legal ramifications of disclosing information relating to their clients and counterparties. Under the confidentiality waiver provisions, adhering parties consent to the disclosure of transaction data (to trade depositories, or between the other party's head office, branches, affiliates or their respective service providers) to the extent required by, among other things, EMIR.

(e) *Mark-to-market valuation of outstanding contracts*

FCs and NFCs+ are required to mark-to-market on a daily basis the value of outstanding derivatives contracts. Alternatively, where market conditions prevent marking-to-market, reliable and prudent marking-to-model must be used.[48]

The RTS describes two market conditions that prevent marking-to-market of an OTC derivatives contract:

- the market is inactive; or
- the range of reasonable, fair value estimates is significant and the probabilities of the various estimates cannot reasonably be assessed.

The RTS acknowledges that a market would be deemed inactive for many reasons, including when quoted prices are not readily and regularly available, and when those prices do not represent actual and regularly occurring market transactions on an arm's length basis.[49]

(f) *Criteria for marking-to-model*

If adopting the marking-to-model approach, FCs and NFCs+ must have a model that:

- incorporates all factors that counterparties would consider in setting a price, including using as much marking-to-market information as possible;
- is consistent with accepted economic methodologies for pricing financial instruments;
- is calibrated and tested for validity, using prices from any observable current market transactions in the same financial instrument or based on any available observable market data;
- is validated and monitored independently, by a division other than the one taking the risk; and
- is duly documented and approved by the board of directors as frequently as necessary, following any material change and at least annually. This approval may be delegated to a committee.

---

48   Article 11(2) of EMIR.
49   Recital 32 of Delegated Regulation 149/2013 states that the dispute resolution requirements apply to OTC contracts that are not centrally cleared.

'Marking-to-market' comprises tracking the current market value of an asset so that losses or gains on a position (ie, each party's true exposure to its counterparty) can be calculated based on current market values. Marking-to-market is particularly relevant in the context of calculating how much collateral would be required to cover any loss in market value over a given time period. Alternatively, 'marking-to-model' is where a financial model is used to calculate a party's exposure. Where the marking-to-model approach is used, for the purposes of ensuring accountability, the board of directors are responsible for approving such model. These requirements will again impose additional operational, administrative and financial burdens on market participants.

(g)   ***Exchange of collateral***

FCs are required to have in place risk management procedures that require the timely, accurate and appropriately segregated exchange of collateral with respect to OTC derivatives contracts that are entered into on or after the date that EMIR came into force (ie, 16 August 2012). NFCs+ are required to have in place risk management procedures that demand the timely, accurate and appropriately segregated exchange of collateral with respect to OTC derivatives contracts that are entered into on or after the clearing threshold is exceeded.[50] Note that these requirements do not apply to NFCs.

The provision of collateral is intended to reduce credit risk by ensuring that there is sufficient collateral to offset losses caused by the default of a counterparty. Exchange of variation margin is also intended to reduce market risk. With respect to non-cleared OTC derivatives, higher collateral requirements coupled with greater capital charges are intended to incentivise market participants to centrally clear OTC derivatives transactions.

Further detail on collateral requirements: EMIR mandates[51] the European Supervisory Authorities[52] to develop standards that set out the levels and type of collateral and segregation arrangements required to ensure the timely, accurate and appropriately segregated exchange of collateral.

Consequently, Delegated Regulation 2016/2251 supplementing EMIR on risk mitigation techniques for non-centrally cleared derivatives contracts and dealing with the margin requirements for OTC derivatives transactions not cleared by a central counterparty was published in the *Official Journal of the European Union* on 15 December 2016 and came into force on 4 January 2017.

Broadly, the delegated regulation provides more detail on, among other things, permitted collateral and the minimum amounts of collateral to be posted under Article 11(3) of EMIR. In particular, it specifies the amount of initial and variation margin to be posted and collected, and the methodologies that can be used to calculate the minimum collateral requirements. With respect to initial margin,

---

50   Article 11(3) of EMIR.
51   Article 11(15) of EMIR.
52   The European Supervisory Authorities comprise ESMA, the European Banking Authority and the European Insurance and Occupational Pensions Authority.

market participants may adopt the RTS's pre-defined schedule based on the notional value of the contracts (which, arguably, might not more closely reflect risk) or a more complex internal modelling approach, where the initial margin is determined based on the modelling of the exposures. The RTS requires the transparency of any proprietary collateral model (so the counterparty can verify the margin calculation).

The RTS prescribes the methods for determining appropriate collateral haircuts, to address potential market and FX volatility of collateral. It also describes the operational and risk management procedures that would need to be adopted by counterparties. It grants the option to apply an operational minimum transfer amount of up €500,000 when exchanging collateral.[53] It also sets out a procedure for the granting of intragroup exemptions permitted under EMIR.[54]

Furthermore, it imposes segregation requirements to ensure that collateral is available if a counterparty defaults.[55] Market participants are also required to ensure the bankruptcy remoteness of collateral by putting in place the appropriate operational and legal arrangements. In addition, counterparties are required to perform an independent legal review of the segregation arrangements to verify that such arrangements meet the requirements of the RTS. Market participants must also be in a position to provide documentation supporting the legal basis for compliance of the arrangements in each relevant jurisdiction.

Initial margin and variation margin: Any collateral required to be delivered in connection with an OTC derivatives contract would constitute initial and/or variation margin. Initial margin is provided to cover any potential future exposures arising should the contract be unwound. Initial margin, to a great extent, therefore reflects the assessment of a counterparty's credit risk. If a counterparty has posted initial margin, but then subsequently defaults under the OTC derivatives contract, that collateral can be liquidated by the non-defaulting counterparty to offset any amounts that would have been due to the non-defaulting party on the close-out of the OTC derivatives transaction. Variation margin is exchanged between counterparties to cover daily (or other periodic) changes in the market value of the relevant OTC derivatives contract. Counterparties are required to calculate the variation margin at least on a daily basis.[56] However, the EMIR rules allow the exchange of variation margin to occur less frequently than on a daily basis in certain limited circumstances.

Permitted collateral: The RTS specifies the eligible collateral for the purposes of EMIR and lists a wide range of securities, including "sovereign securities, covered bonds, specific securitisations, corporate bonds, gold and equities". The RTS also sets out criteria intended to ensure that collateral is sufficiently diversified and is not subject to 'wrong way' risk.[57]

---

53   Article 25 of Delegated Regulation 2016/2251.
54   Articles 32–34 of Delegated Regulation 2016/2251.
55   Article 19 of Delegated Regulation 2016/2251.
56   Article 9 of Delegated Regulation 2016/2251.
57   Wrong way risk may arise where a counterparty has posted collateral whose value is positively correlated with the counterparty's own creditworthiness (ie, the collateral comprises securities issued by the counterparty).

Timing: Various aspects of the collateral requirements will be phased in, with market participants that trade greater volumes of OTC derivatives being required to comply with the rules earlier than smaller market participants (as described further below). The RTS adopts the revised timeframe and phase-in periods proposed by the Working Group on Margin Requirements of the Basel Committee on Banking Supervision and the International Organisation of Securities Commissions in a revised version of its Global Minimum Standards for Margin Requirements for non-centrally cleared derivatives (see below for more details).

The variation margin requirements applied from the date when the RTS came into effect (ie, 4 January 2017) for entities belonging to a group whose aggregate month-end notional amount of uncleared derivatives (for March, April and May 2016) exceeded €3 trillion. For all other market participants, the variation margin requirements came into effect on 1 March 2017.

The variation margin requirements will be phased in for deliverable FX forward transactions from the earlier of 31 December 2018 and the entry into force of the RTSs under MiFID II, which will apply a uniform definition of the term (which, as at the date of publication, is expected to occur on 3 January 2018). A three-year phase-in period applies to single-stock equity options and index options.

The initial margin requirements will also be phased in. Market participants belonging to a group whose aggregate month-end notional amount of uncleared derivatives exceeds (for March, April and May in the relevant year) €3 trillion will be required to post initial margin first. See the table below for each relevant threshold and the corresponding phase-in date.

Both parties have uncleared average annual notional amounts for March, April and May in the relevant year of:	Phase-in date
Over €3 trillion	4 February 2017
€2.25 trillion	1 September 2017
€1.5 trillion	1 September 2018
€0.75 trillion	1 September 2019
€8 billion	1 September 2020

At the time of publication, physically settled FX forwards and swaps and fixed, physically settled FX transactions associated with the exchange of principal of cross-currency swaps are exempt from the EU initial margin requirements (but not the variation margin requirements).

NFCs are exempt from the margin requirements.[58]

---

58   Article 11(3) of EMIR.

Many market participants have experienced difficulties and delays in amending existing collateral documentation and implementing operational changes to comply with the new margin rules. Consequently, a number of industry bodies wrote to ESMA and other EU-based regulatory bodies asking for "reasonable flexibility" to market participants in their aim to comply with the new rules. In response, the European Supervisory Authorities published a statement[59] on 23 February 2017 that they expect:

- domestic regulators "to generally apply their risk-based supervisory powers in their day-to-day enforcement of applicable legislation", taking into account the size of exposure to the counterparty plus its default risk; and
- that counterparties put in place alternative arrangements to ensure that the risk of non-compliance is contained.

The statement also set out the authorities' expectation that the current difficulties "will be solved in the coming few months". While the authorities also clarified that the statement does not amount to regulatory forbearance, the statement does contemplate some level of domestic regulatory flexibility in enforcing against non-compliance.

Basel Committee on Banking Supervision and International Organisation of Securities Commissions margin requirements for non-centrally cleared derivatives: In an attempt to ensure global consistency of margin rules for uncleared OTC derivatives, Delegated Regulation 2016/2251 is based on the Report on Margin Requirements for Non-centrally Cleared Derivatives published by the Basel Committee on Banking Supervision and the International Organisation of Securities Commissions in September 2013. A revised report was subsequently published in March 2015.[60] The report sets out a global policy framework that establishes minimum standards for margin requirements for non-centrally cleared derivatives. The framework is articulated through eight key principles, as summarised below:

- Appropriate margining practices must be put in place for non-centrally cleared derivatives.
- All financial entities and non-financial entities that are considered systemically important that trade non-centrally cleared derivatives must exchange initial and variation margin sufficient to counteract any counterparty risks.
- The methodologies for calculating initial and variation margin should:
  - be consistent across entities and reflect the potential future exposure (initial margin) and current exposure (variation margin) associated with the portfolio of non-centrally cleared derivatives in question; and
  - ensure that all counterparty risk exposures are fully covered with a high degree of confidence.

---

59   www.esma.europa.eu/sites/default/files/library/esas_communication_on_industry_request_on_
      forbearance_variation_margin_implementation.docx_0.pdf.
60   See Basel Committee on Banking Supervision and Board of the International Organization of Securities
      Commissions: Margin requirements for non-centrally cleared derivatives, March 2015 (www.bis.org/
      bcbs/publ/d317.pdf).

- To ensure that collaterals can be liquidated in a reasonable amount of time should a counterparty default, these assets should be highly liquid and should, after taking into account appropriate haircuts, be able to hold their value in a time of financial stress.
- Initial margin should be exchanged by both parties on a gross basis (ie, without netting of amounts collected by each party), and held in such a way as to ensure that:
  - the margin posted is immediately available to the collecting party in the event of the counterparty's default; and
  - the posted margin is protected against the bankruptcy of the collecting party.
- Intragroup transactions should be subject to appropriate regulation in a manner consistent with each jurisdiction's legal and regulatory framework.
- There should be global regulatory harmony to promote consistent and non-duplicative regulatory margin requirements for non-centrally cleared derivatives across jurisdictions. This is particularly beneficial for cross-border derivatives transactions.
- The report proposes that the margin requirements be phased in to assist with moderating transition and implementation costs.

Concerns regarding collateralisation requirements: Some market participants have raised concerns regarding the potential impact on cost and liquidity that would result from derivatives counterparties having to source and post liquid, high-quality collateral to satisfy these regulatory requirements.

Although Delegated Regulation 2016/2251 is broadly consistent with the equivalent US rules[61] on the collateralisation of uncleared OTC derivatives, there are a few significant divergences. For example, the US rules do not require individual segregation to be offered as an option by the collateral receiver to the collateral giver and for initial margin in the form of cash to be segregated. Furthermore, under the US rules initial margin must be held by an independent custodian (which is not required under the EU rules). The EU rules allow for various forms of variation margin, whereas the US rules stipulate that variation margin must be in the form of cash only. Contrary to the EU rules, there are no exemptions for intragroup transactions under the US rules. Both deliverable and non-deliverable FX forwards are subject to the EU rules, whereas under the US rules only non-deliverable forwards are required to be collateralised.

These differences between EU and US rules could be challenging in the context of cross-border transactions where counterparties are subject to both sets of rules (eg, transactions between EU and US entities). It is arguable that the differences could lead to market fragmentation or regulatory arbitrage (ie, market participants choosing to transact only in the jurisdiction with the more lenient regulatory regime).

---

61 Margin and Capital Requirements for Covered Swap Entities, 79 Fed Reg 57348 (24 September 2014) and Margin Requirements for Uncleared Swaps for Swap Dealers and Major Swap Participants, 79 Fed Reg 59898 (3 October 2014).

(h)   Increased capital requirements

EMIR requires that FCs "hold an appropriate and proportionate amount of capital to manage the risk not covered by appropriate exchange of collateral".[62] FCs will, therefore, be subject to increased capital requirements if collateral is not exchanged. Article 11(15)(b) of EMIR required the European Supervisory Authorities to develop draft RTSs specifying the level of capital required to comply with Article 11(4) of EMIR. Such draft RTSs are yet to be finalised. The European Supervisory Authorities published a joint consultation paper which provided their initial position on what proposals will be made in the draft RTSs.[63]

Rationale for the requirement: In the March 2012 Joint Discussion Paper, the European Supervisory Authorities explained that capital requirements engender two broad outcomes:

- to "contain the risks arising from OTC derivatives transactions" by being available to absorb unexpected losses with the aim of protecting a firm from becoming insolvent; and
- to incentive the move to standardised documentation and central clearing.

The RTSs will not seek to impose capital requirements on prudentially regulated firms (eg, investment firms, credit institutions, insurance undertakings, assurance undertakings, reinsurance undertakings and institutions for occupational retirement provision) as they are already subject to existing capital regimes which are deemed sufficient to address any risks not covered by the exchange of collateral.

However, on the basis that 'non-prudentially regulated financial counterparties' (NPRFC) (which includes UCITS and AIFs) are not subject to specific prudential capital requirements, the European Supervisory Authorities have taken the view that "it is not appropriate to establish specific risk-based capital requirements for NPRFCs through RTS without a corresponding regime ...".[64] The broad outcome is that AIFs and UCITS might not be subject to capital requirements, but will need to address risks arising from OTC derivatives through the exchange of collateral (as described above).

Third-country entities: Third-country entities are essentially non-European entities. Article 11(12) of EMIR provides that the risk mitigation requirements described above apply to OTC derivatives contracts entered into between third-country entities that would be subject to those obligations if established in the European Union, "provided that those contracts have a direct, substantial and foreseeable effect within the Union or where such obligation is necessary or appropriate to prevent the evasion of any provision of this Regulation". A strict reading of Article 11(2) means that non-EU counterparties may be subject to obligations to exchange collateral, but

---

62   Article 11(4) of EMIR.
63   Joint Discussion Paper on Draft Regulatory Technical Standards on risk mitigation techniques for OTC derivatives not cleared by a CCP under the Regulation on OTC derivatives, CCPs and Trade Repositories (JC/DP/2012/1), 6 March 2012.
64   *Ibid.*

only when they enter into transactions with each other. The risk mitigation requirements, therefore, appear to have broad extraterritorial scope.[65] Consequently, it is debatable whether and how EU regulators can detect or even enforce compliance with these requirements directly against third-party entities, particularly where the entities may not be regulated in their home jurisdiction.

(i) *Exceptions for intragroup transactions*
EMIR provides exemptions from the clearing and collateral requirements for certain intragroup transactions.[66]

Criteria for intragroup exclusions: The transaction must fall within the relevant definition of 'intragroup transaction' in Article 3 of EMIR. The counterparties must then meet a number of additional requirements under Articles 11(5)–(11) of EMIR, as broadly summarised below:

- The counterparties must be established in the same member state;
- The counterparties' risk management procedures must be adequately sound, robust and consistent with the level of complexity of the transaction; and
- There can be no current or foreseen practical or legal impediment to the prompt transfer of own funds or repayment of liabilities between the counterparties.

Broadly, a counterparty wishing to benefit from the exemption from the margin requirements for transactions with an affiliate must first apply to its competent authority or relevant regulator (eg, in the case of a UK entity, the Financial Conduct Authority) with evidence that it meets the relevant criteria. For an NFC transacting with an affiliate that is either an NFC or a third-country entity FC, such counterparty must notify its competent authority under Article 11 of EMIR that it intends to use the exemption, with evidence that it meets the relevant criteria.

Any counterparty that has benefited from an intragroup exemption must publically disclose that fact.[67] EMIR does not, however, exempt intragroup transactions from the reporting obligation or its other risk mitigation requirements.

6. **Transparency and reporting of transactions**
The global financial crisis also highlighted a lack of transparency on transactions and prices in the OTC derivatives markets, as well as the risks associated with CDS positions held by financial institutions and their exposures to other counterparties.[68] As a

---

65   Delegated Regulation 285/2014 supplementing EMIR with regard to RTSs on direct, substantial and foreseeable effect of contracts within the European Union and to prevent the evasion of rules and obligations defines contracts that may be considered to have a direct, substantial and foreseeable effect within the European Union or cases where it is necessary or appropriate to prevent the evasion of any provision of EMIR.
66   Articles 3, 4(2) and 11(5) to (11) of EMIR.
67   Article 11(11) of EMIR.
68   The Financial Services Authority (now the Financial Conduct Authority) notes in BP 2009/10 (see 2009 FRO, Section C, pp47, 65, 66, 71, 72 and box on p74; and 2009/10 BP, Section 2, pp19 and 22) that the global and economic financial crisis, among other things, has prompted regulators to review current arrangements for fixed income, credit derivatives, structured products and commodities, where a significant amount of OTC derivatives trading takes place.

consequence, regulators called for measures to improve the transparency of the OTC derivatives markets in relation to information (including information on pricing, positions and transactions) to be provided on a timely and comprehensive basis to the regulators.[69] The EMIR reporting requirement is intended to allow regulators to supervise the OTC derivatives markets efficiently for the purposes of identifying any systemic risk and market abuse, and also give market participants better access to reliable prices and the ability to assess risks and value positions more effectively.

6.1 Transaction reporting

Article 9 of EMIR requires counterparties and CCPs to report details of any derivatives contract that they have entered into to an EU-authorised or recognised trade depository. The term 'counterparty' is not defined in EMIR. However, ESMA has confirmed in its 'Questions and Answers' (Q&As)[70] that the term should be interpreted as meaning FCs and NFCs. The EMIR reporting obligation applies to OTC and listed or exchange-traded derivatives. The report must be made no later than the working day following the conclusion, amendment or termination of the contract. Market participants are permitted to delegate the reporting requirement to a third party. To assist with delegation, ISDA and the Futures and Options Association have published a template Reporting Delegation Agreement.[71]

Market participants are also required to keep a record of any derivatives contract that they have concluded and any amendment for at least five years following the termination of the contract. If there are no available trade depositories, market participants must report the transaction directly to ESMA. Both EU parties to the transaction must report, unless the parties agree that one party will report on behalf of the other party.

Timing and reporting deadlines: The reporting requirement came into effect on 12 February 2014 and applies to derivatives contracts entered into before 16 August 2012 which remain outstanding on that date or that were entered into on or after 16 August 2012.

With respect to derivatives transactions entered into before 12 February 2014, the reporting deadlines were as follows:

- Trades entered into on or before 16 August 2012 and still outstanding on 12 February 2014 had to be reported within 90 days of 12 February 2014 (ie, by 13 May 2014).
- Trades that were still outstanding on 16 August 2012, but which were terminated or expired before 12 February 2014, had to be reported within three years of 12 February 2014 (ie, by 12 February 2017).
- Trades entered into on or after 16 August 2012, but which were terminated

---

69 In its October 2009 communication, the European Commission stated that it should become mandatory to report all transactions to trade repositories, which would then report to regulators.

70 Questions and Answers, Implementation of EMIR, at www.esma.europa.eu/sites/default/files/library/2016-898_qa_xviii_emir.pdf.

71 See ISDA/FOA EMIR Reporting Delegation Agreement – 13 January 2014 and Reporting Guidance Note – 19 July 2013, at www2.isda.org/emir/.

or expired before 12 February 2014, had to be reported within three years of 12 February 2014 (ie, by 12 February 2017).[72]

Further legislation was published on 21 January 2017 granting a further two-year delay to the back-reporting requirement.[73]

Current trade repositories: As the reporting obligation is already in effect, market participants already have a framework in place to comply with the reporting requirement, either by using a third party or by reporting directly to a trade repository that is registered or recognised by ESMA. At the date of writing, the trade depositories registered with, and recognised by, ESMA were:[74]

- CME Trade Repository Limited (United Kingdom);
- DTCC Derivatives Repository Limited (United Kingdom);
- ICE Trade Vault Europe Limited (United Kingdom);
- Krajowy Depozyt Papierów Wartosciowych SA (Poland);
- Regis-TR SA (Luxembourg); and
- UnaVista Limited (United Kingdom).

UK approach: In addition to the EMIR reporting requirement, in the United Kingdom the Financial Conduct Authority, under the market abuse regime, currently requires that UK OTC derivatives contracts which reference assets traded on a regulated market be subject to the Financial Conduct Authority transaction reporting requirements. This is to enable the authority to monitor any market manipulation or exploitation activities.

Shortfalls of trade repositories: As mentioned above, the reporting obligation was introduced so that information on the risks inherent in derivatives markets will be centrally stored by trade depositories and be easily accessible by ESMA, other relevant regulators and central banks.

The dual reporting aspect of EMIR (ie, that both parties to the transaction are required to report data on the same transaction), coupled with problems associated with 'unique trade identifier' numbers (UTI) and the number of fields that need to be reported,[75] has meant that some trade depositories have struggled to reconcile or match trade data received in respect of the same trade from both counterparties, which, arguably, could result in increased costs and operational impact on market participants (particularly where they would have had to resolve and resubmit transaction reports). This issue could be compounded in circumstances where two counterparties on either side of the transaction report to different trade depositories.

Smaller market participants may find on-boarding with and reporting to trade depositories disproportionately costly. Furthermore, numerous repositories for various asset classes could result in defragmentation of trade information.

---

72 Implementing Regulation 1247/2012 laying down the implementing technical standards with regard to the format and frequency of trade reports to trade repositories according to EMIR.
73 Delegated Regulation 2017/104 and Delegated Regulation 2017/105.
74 www.esma.europa.eu/supervision/trade-repositories/list-registered-trade-repositories.
75 Some 85 data fields.

6.2 Regulation of trade repositories

EMIR legislates for the establishment and governance of trade depositories, as well as for new reporting obligations on market participants. It covers, among other things, trade depositories' authorisation and registration requirements, access and participation to a repository, disclosure of data, data quality and timelines, access to and safeguarding of data, legal certainty of registered contracts, governance and operational reliability.

Registration and recognition of trade repositories: A 'trade depository' is defined in Article 2(2) of EMIR as a legal person that centrally collects and maintains the records of derivatives.

Trade depositories must be registered with ESMA for the purposes of the trade reporting obligation under EMIR. The registration is effective for the whole of the European Union and not just the member state in which the repository is established.[76]

Articles 55–59 of EMIR set out, with the registration process (including the application for registration), the details[77] and the format[78] for the registration application, any required consultations with the applicant repository's local regulator, the time period for reviewing the application and notification of ESMA's decision. ESMA is also granted various broad powers relating to information requests, general investigations and on-site inspections of trade depositories.[79]

EMIR provides scope for non-EU trade depositories to seek recognition by ESMA to offer trade reporting services in Europe. In order to be recognised by ESMA, certain equivalence determinations need to be met, including that:

- the applicant is subject to an equivalent and enforceable regulatory and supervisory framework in another country which has been recognised by the European Commission;
- the relevant third country has entered into an international agreement with the European Union which provides for, among other things, the mutual exchange of information on derivatives contracts held in data repositories; and
- the relevant third country has entered into cooperation arrangements with the European Union regarding the sharing of information and the cooperation of supervisory activities.[80]

Supervisory requirements for trade repositories: Once registered, trade repositories are subject to robust requirements as set out in Articles 78–81 of EMIR. The requirements are split into four broad areas:[81]

- General requirements – trade depositories must have robust governance

---

76 Article 55(3) of EMIR.
77 Delegated Regulation 150/2013 supplementing EMIR with regard to regulatory technical standards specifying the details of the application for registration as a trade repository.
78 Implementing Regulation 1248/2012 with regard to the format of applications for the registration of trade repositories according to EMIR.
79 Articles 60–65 of EMIR.
80 Article 77 of EMIR.
81 Note that the list is not exhaustive.

arrangements, which include a clear organisational structure with clear lines of responsibility and adequate internal controls which prevent any disclosure of confidential information; effective arrangements must be in place to identify and manage any potential conflicts of interest; the repository must have objective, non-discriminatory and publicly disclosed requirements for market participants to access its services, and it must publicly disclose its fees for providing trade reporting services.

- Operational reliability – trade depositories must identify and minimise the sources of operational risk and implement adequate business continuity plans (eg, suitable back-up facilities).
- Safeguarding and recording – trade depositories must keep the information received by them secure, prevent any misuse and maintain such information for at least 10 years following termination of the relevant contracts. Trade repositories should also allow market participants to correct any information in a timely manner.
- Transparency and data availability – trade depositories must regularly publish aggregate positions by class of derivatives on the contracts reported to them; they must also make the information available to the regulators (including ESMA and any relevant non-EU regulator).

Sanctions: Articles 64–71 of EMIR set out the rules relating to fines and other sanctions that can be imposed on trade depositories if they fail to comply with any of the requirements under EMIR. ESMA has additional powers to impose fines and penalties on trade depositories under EMIR.[82]

7.   Central clearing

Following the global financial crisis, large financial institutions are no longer considered to be too big to fail – a view shared by industry and regulators alike. As a result, the European Commission sees the use of CCPs as key to mitigating the perceived systemic impact of a default of a major counterparty to an OTC derivatives contract and has, therefore, mandated that a greater proportion of the OTC derivatives industry adopt central clearing. Consequently, EMIR requires that all standardised contracts be cleared through a CCP.

A 'CCP' is defined in EMIR as a legal person that interposes itself between the counterparties to the contracts traded on one or more financial markets, becoming the buyer to every seller and the seller to every buyer.[83] Similar to the authorisation or recognition of trade depositories, to provide clearing services under EMIR CCPs must be either authorised (if they are EU CCPs) or recognised (if they are third-country (or non-EU established) CCPs) by ESMA. (See further below a summary of how CCPs are authorised and regulated.)

---

82   Delegated Regulation 667/2014 supplementing EMIR regarding the rules of procedure for penalties imposed on trade repositories by ESMA, including rules on the right of defence and temporal provisions. This regulation specifies the procedures to be followed by ESMA in the exercise of its power to impose fines or penalty payments, including rights of defence for trade repositories subject to sanctions.
83   Article 2(1) of EMIR.

7.1   What is clearing?

'Clearing' is defined in EMIR as "the process of establishing positions, including the calculation of net positions, and ensuring that financial instruments, cash or both are available to secure the exposures arising from those positions".[84] Broadly, clearing includes all activities from the time when two parties agree to enter into a transaction until that transaction is settled. The clearing process includes reconciliation of trades, risk margining and the management of credit exposures, to ensure that trades are settled smoothly in accordance with market rules. Reconciliation or trade matching will involve the matching of the terms of the transaction to ensure that they reflect each party's records. Risk margining and the management of credit exposures may involve the provision of collateral and margin to secure a party's performance under a transaction. Lastly, settlement, which is the last step in the post-trade process, involves the transfer of cash or assets between the parties to satisfy their respective payment or delivery obligations under the derivatives contract.

7.2   What is central clearing?

The following is a simplified explanation of central clearing. After two parties enter into a transaction, the transaction is either novated to a central counterparty which takes on the sole credit risk by becoming the buyer to every seller and the seller to every buyer under two new derivatives contracts,[85] or a back-to-back transaction is entered into with the central counterparty. If, for example, a bank that is counterparty to the transaction defaults, the CCP will honour the bank's payment or delivery obligations. A CCP would, therefore, remove bilateral credit risk as between its direct participants by assuming the position as the central counterparty to every trade. The diagrams below provide a simplified example of the contractual links between the parties to a centrally cleared transaction (although there are numerous and more complex clearing structures). The initial bilateral agreements (Diagram 1) are replaced by new agreements with the CCP (Diagram 2) with the result that the parties can net their exposures across the clearing house (Diagram 3).

The keys objectives of the EMIR clearing requirement are, first, to improve trade transparency and, second, to reduce counterparty or credit risk, which, in turn, will reduce systemic risk and lower the likelihood of systemic contagion (since counterparties are in effect 'insulated' from each other). 'Counterparty risk' is the risk that one of the counterparties defaults under the derivatives contract. As CCPs are subject to prudential and risk management requirements under EMIR (including capital requirements, margin requirements, liquidity risk controls and default fund

---

84   Article 2(3) of EMIR.
85   Pricing in relation to centrally cleared OTC derivatives contracts differs from that of an exchange-traded contract. In relation to the latter, the price of a trade is determined by the matching of anonymous buy and sell orders entered onto the exchange for which the parties are obligated to enter into the trade at the prices at which such orders meet. The difference between exchange trading and central clearing may have an impact on dealers, which, on an exchange, may not have the power to be price makers (as they would in bilaterally negotiated OTC derivatives contracts), thus making exchange trading more disadvantageous from a profit perspective. ("The regulatory drive towards central counterparty clearing of OTC credit derivatives and the necessary limits on this" by Adam Glass, *Capital Markets Law Journal*, Vol 4, No S1).

requirements),[86] the regulators argue that replacing bilateral counterparty exposure with a CCP will significantly reduce counterparty risk.

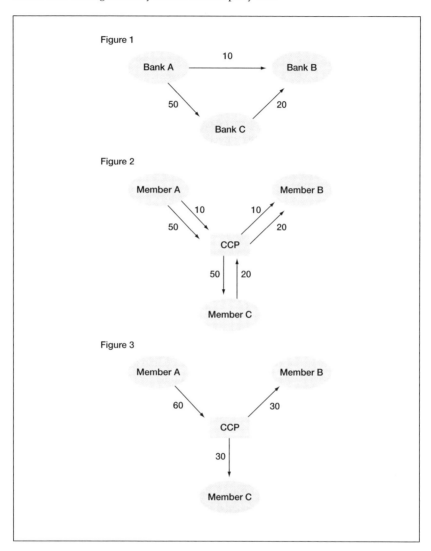

The above example also demonstrates a multilateral netting arrangement. Multilateral netting allows counterparties to set off amounts owed between them with the party owing the higher amount paying a single net sum. Multilateral netting does not eliminate counterparty risk, but instead reduces exposure between counterparties to the extent that it reduces the aggregate amounts owed between counterparties to a smaller net sum.

---

86   Articles 14–54 of EMIR.

In carrying out its functions as a CCP, the CCP will demand collateral from its participants based on daily mark-to-market valuations of their positions. This collateral will be put aside to create a buffer against any potential defaults. In addition to margin requirements, CCPs will require participants to contribute to a risk default fund to protect the CCP in the event of a default by a counterparty and the termination of a position not fully protected by collateral. The CCP's own capital and reserves may also be made available for this purpose. If the margining requirement and risk controls of the CCP are robust enough to cause the defaulting entity to cover its risk entirely, other participants will not share that risk, otherwise the risk will be borne by the members of the CCP and the CCP itself.[87]

Clearing can be effected directly or indirectly. 'Direct clearing' occurs when counterparties are members of the CCP through which the trade is cleared. 'Indirect clearing' occurs where a client of a clearing member clears trades for its own clients (see section 7.4(b) below).

7.3   Clearing requirement

EMIR requires that certain eligible OTC derivatives transactions be cleared through a CCP.[88] The CCP must be either established in the EEA and authorised by its local member state regulator,[89] or a non-EU CCP that is permitted to provide clearing services as recognised by ESMA.[90, 91]

For an OTC derivatives transaction to be eligible, it must satisfy certain criteria, in particular with regard to standardisation and liquidity. Furthermore, the European Commission must also formally determine that the class of derivatives is subject to the clearing obligation in accordance with the procedures set out in EMIR.[92] Information on the classes of derivatives contract that are subject to the clearing requirement and the CCPs authorised under EMIR to clear those contracts are available on ESMA's website.[93] See below for more details on the various ways in which products can be determined to be subject to the clearing requirement.

(a)   How does a CCP reduce counterparty risk?

Interposing a CCP between each counterparty does not eliminate counterparty risk because counterparty exposures merely shifts to the CCP. This potentially creates another systemic issue, as it concentrates risk in a relatively small number of entities (the CCPs themselves). The regulators are addressing this issue by considering how a CCP failure might be avoided or, at least, managed. For example, during August 2016 the Committee on Payment and Market Infrastructure and the International Organization of Securities Commissions published a consultative report "aimed at enhancing the resilience of [CCPs]".[94]

---

87   "Central Counterparties and Regulating CDS", *Derivatives Week*, 19 December 2008.
88   Article 4 of EMIR.
89   Article 14(1) of EMIR.
90   Article 25(1) of EMIR.
91   Article 4(3) of EMIR.
92   Article 5 of EMIR.
93   www.esma.europa.eu/regulation/post-trading/otc-derivatives-and-clearing-obligation.
94   www.bis.org/cpmi/publ/d149.pdf.

(b) **Which products are subject to mandatory clearing?**
EMIR provides a framework for the clearing obligation and ESMA is required under EMIR to draft a number of RTSs specifying, among other things, which particular class of derivatives is subject to clearing and the date or dates upon which the clearing obligation will arise for that class.

Accordingly, and in line with the bottom-up approach contemplated in Article 5(2) of EMIR (see below), ESMA submitted to the European Commission for endorsement various draft RTSs proposing to establish a clearing obligation on several classes of OTC interest rate derivatives.[95] Over time, the Commission has formally endorsed such RTSs. Following the Commission's endorsement, the next step in the EU legislative process is each time for the European Parliament and the European Council to review the RTSs; both institutions have a three-month period (extendable for a further three months) to object to the RTSs before they can be published in the *Official Journal of the European Union* and come into force.

The three types of derivatives product that are currently required to be cleared under EMIR are two types of interest rate derivatives and CDS indices.

(c) **Interest rate derivatives**
In accordance with EU legislation,[96] the interest rate products outlined below are subject to mandatory clearing.

G4 currency interest rate swaps: These consist of:
- basis swaps denominated in euro, pound sterling, Japanese yen and US dollar;
- fixed-to-float swaps denominated in euro, pound sterling, Japanese yen and US dollar;
- forward rate agreements denominated in euro, pound sterling and US dollar; and
- overnight index swaps denominated in euro, pound sterling and US dollar.

EEA currency interest rate swaps: These consist of:
- fixed-to-float interest rate swaps denominated in Czech koruna, Danish krone, Hungarian forint, Norwegian krone, Swedish krona and Polish zloty; and
- forward rate agreements denominated in Norwegian krone, Swedish krona and Polish zloty.

Clearing of CDS: RTSs mandating clearing for certain types of 'index credit derivatives' (CDS) were published in the *Official Journal of the European Union* on 19 April 2016, resulting in the following CDS becoming subject to mandatory clearing from 9 May 2016:

---

95 The RTSs also specify the date(s) from which the clearing obligation will take effect and the minimum remaining maturity of the OTC derivatives contracts that will be subject to frontloading (see the paragraph on frontloading below).
96 Delegated Regulation (EU) 2015/2205 supplementing EMIR; Delegated Regulation (EU) 2016/1178 supplementing EMIR; and Delegated Regulation (EU) 2016/592 supplementing EMIR.

- untranched iTraxx Europe Main Index, Series 17 onwards, 5-year tenor; and
- untranched iTraxx Europe Crossover Index, Series 17 onwards, 5-year tenor.

FX non-deliverable forwards: On 1 October 2014, and again under the bottom-up approach contemplated by Article 5(2) of EMIR, ESMA published a consultation paper and draft RTSs for the clearing of non-deliverable forward derivatives. Based on feedback that it received in response to the consultation paper, ESMA decided not to propose the central clearing of FX forwards at that stage.[97] ESMA may still, however, propose that the clearing obligation applies to these products in the future to address further market developments.

Furthermore, although some CCPs offer central clearing of equity and interest rate futures and options, ESMA has decided that the clearing obligation should not apply to these instruments at this stage.[98]

Timing: Central clearing will be phased in, with the largest market participants that are more active in the derivatives markets to commence clearing first.

To classify the extent of a market participant's trading activities and, hence, the deadline for central clearing, entities are categorised as Category 1, 2, 3 or 4, as follows:

- Category 1 entities are counterparties which, on the date that the relevant RTS comes into effect, are clearing members for at least one of the classes of OTC derivatives specified in the RTS;
- Category 2 entities are FCs and NFC+ AIFs which do not fall into Category 1 and which belong to a group whose aggregate month-end average notional amount of non-cleared derivatives for January, February and March 2016 exceeds €8 billion;
- Category 3 entities are FCs and NFC+ AIFs which are neither Category 1 nor Category 2 entities; and
- Category 4 entities are NFC+s that do not fall into the prior categories.

The implementation schedule for each category of counterparty to whom central clearing will become mandatory is set out on the next page.

ESMA proposed to postpone the phase-in date for central clearing by Category 3 firms until 21 June 2019.[99] ESMA's RTS published on 14 November 2016 acknowledged the difficulties that smaller derivatives market participants experienced in implementing clearing arrangements. As at the time of writing, the decision sat with the European Commission, which had three months to endorse the RTS. If the Commission endorses the RTS, there will be a period of non-objection by the European Parliament and European Council. Paradoxically, ESMA has not sought

97   Feedback Statement, Consultation on the Clearing Obligation for Non-Deliverable Forwards, 4 February 2015, 2015/ESMA/234.
98   Final Report, draft technical standards on the Clearing Obligation, Interest Rate OTC Derivatives, dated 1 October 2014, ESMA/2014/1184.
99   Final Report on the clearing obligation for financial counterparties with a limited volume of activity, dated 14 November 2016, ESMA/2016/1565, at www.esma.europa.eu/sites/default/files/ library/2016-1565_final_report_on_clearing_obligation.pdf33333.

Category of counterparty	Deadline for central clearing		
	G4 currency interest rate swaps	EEA interest rate swaps	CDS indices
Category 1	21 June 2016	9 February 2017	9 February 2017
Category 2	21 December 2016	9 August 2017	9 August 2017
Category 3	21 June 2017	9 February 2018	9 February 2018
Category 4	21 December 2018	9 August 2019	9 May 2019

to delay the clearing requirement for Category 4 firms (which are considered less active in the derivatives markets than Category 3 firms), which means that Category 4 firms may need to clear prior to Category 3 firms.

Frontloading: As mentioned above, details of the date from which mandatory central clearing will apply will be set out in the relevant RTS for each class of OTC derivatives. Some market participants will be required to centrally clear transactions that were entered into before the actual date on which clearing obligation commences. This is called 'frontloading'. To provide more background on how frontloading may arise, if a new CCP is authorised by its home regulator to clear a class of derivatives contracts, the local regulator is required to notify ESMA of such authorisation. ESMA will then recommend to the European Commission whether any new classes of derivative that will be cleared by the new CCP should be subject to the EMIR clearing requirement. The Commission will decide whether to adopt ESMA's recommendation. Frontloading has been particularly controversial due to uncertainty over which OTC derivatives contracts will become subject to the clearing obligation and the unknown duration of the frontloading period. To address this uncertainty, ESMA proposed in its consultation papers on this topic[100] that the frontloading period be split into two intervals:

- the interval between the notification by the local regulator to ESMA and the publication of the relevant RTS in the *Official Journal*; and
- the interval following the publication of the relevant RTS in the *Official Journal* and the formal date on which the clearing obligation takes effect.

ESMA stated that OTC derivatives contracts entered into during the first interval will not be subject to frontloading, whereas OTC derivatives contracts entered into during the second interval may be subject to frontloading. The determinant for whether an OTC derivatives contract entered into during the latter interval will be

---

100   Clearing Obligation under EMIR (no 1) 11 July 2014/ESMA/2014/799 and Clearing Obligation under EMIR (no 2) 11 July 2014/ESMA/2014/800.

subject to frontloading is whether, as at the date of the application of the clearing obligation for that class of OTC derivatives contract and for the counterparty in question, there is a certain minimum remaining maturity.

The European Commission has broadly accepted ESMA's recommendations in this regard, but decided to shorten the frontloading period further. In the final rules, the Commission has specified that the frontloading start date will not fall on the date on which the relevant RTS is published in the *Official Journal* (as originally proposed by ESMA) but, instead, it would fall on a future date as specified in each clearing RTS. This change was to give market participants some time to prepare for the new rules, while also addressing concerns expressed by the derivatives industry at the time.

The frontloading requirement applies to Category 1 and 2 firms and the timing is set out in the table below.

Category of counterparty	Start dates for frontloading		
	G4 currency interest rate swaps	EEA interest rate swaps	CDS indices
Category 1	21 February 2016	9 October 2016	9 October 2016
Category 2	21 May 2016	9 October 2016	9 October 2016

ISDA frontloading additional termination event: For market participants subject to frontloading, it may not be possible to clear such transactions by the time the frontloading obligation takes effect. In ISDA's view, the only way for counterparties to avoid breaching the frontloading requirement is to terminate the relevant OTC derivatives contract. Consequently, and to mitigate this risk, on 12 June 2015, ISDA published the EMIR Frontloading Additional Termination Event Amendment Agreement, which allows the parties to an ISDA Master Agreement (1992 or 2002) to amend the agreement to incorporate a new additional termination event relating to frontloading.

To whom does the central clearing obligation apply? The clearing requirement applies to derivatives transactions among and between FCs and NFCs+. It may also apply to certain third-country entities. If a counterparty is an FC, an NFC+ or a relevant third-country entity, this may not necessarily mean that its OTC derivatives transactions are subject to the clearing requirement as both counterparties to the trade need to be either an FC, NFC+ or relevant third-country entity.[101] Set out below are the various scenarios in which the clearing obligation can apply, as specified in Article 4(1)(a) of EMIR:

- between two FCs;

---

101   Recital 22 to EMIR states: "For an OTC derivatives contract to be cleared, both parties to that contract must be subject to a clearing obligation".

- between an FC and an NFC+;
- between two NFCs+; and
- between an FC or NFC+ and an entity established outside the EEA which would be subject to the clearing obligation if it were established within the EEA; or
- between two entities established outside the EEA, both of which would be subject to the clearing obligation if they were established within the EEA, provided that the contract has a "direct, substantial and foreseeable" effect within the EEA or where necessary to prevent the evasion of any provisions of EMIR (see further below for a discussion on the extraterritorial impact of EMIR).

Clearing threshold: The regulatory position in requiring NFCs to clear derivatives is that by exceeding the clearing threshold, NFCs would be trading significant levels of OTC derivatives on a speculative (ie, non-hedging) basis. Therefore, and to address the systemic risks summarised above, such trades are required to be subject to the clearing obligation.

In the context of the EMIR clearing requirement, NFCs will be required to clear OTC derivatives contracts where the notional value of OTC derivatives contracts over a given interval exceeds certain thresholds. ESMA has specified the tests used to determine whether or not an NFC has exceeded the clearing threshold.[102] The clearing threshold will be exceeded if the average of the gross notional value of the entity's OTC derivatives positions over a rolling 30-day period exceeds the relevant thresholds set out in the RTS (ie, an NFC+). The relevant thresholds are set out in the table below for five different asset classes:

Derivatives type	Clearing threshold (gross notional value)
OTC credit derivatives	€1 billion
OTC equity derivatives	€1 billion
OTC interest rate derivatives	€3 billion
OTC FX derivatives	€3 billion
OTC commodity derivatives and other OTC derivatives not defined above	€3 billion

Recital 29 to EMIR recognises that NFCs may use OTC derivatives to hedge commercial risks linked to their commercial or treasury financing activities, and that

102   RTS relating to the clearing threshold, Delegated Regulation 149/2013.

trades entered into for hedging purposes should not count towards the clearing threshold. Consequently, in making its determination the NFC must include all OTC derivatives contracts entered into by it and any other NFCs within its group (irrespective of whether the group members are inside or outside the EEA), but can exclude any contract entered into for hedging purposes. Broadly, 'hedging contracts' are contracts that are considered to be "objectively measurable as reducing risks directly relating to the commercial activity or treasury financing activity of the non-financial counterparty or its group". Delegated Regulation 149/2013 relating to clearing threshold provides more detailed criteria for establishing which contracts can be deemed to be entered into for hedging purposes.

ESMA confirmed in a Q&A[103] that OTC derivative contracts cleared on a voluntary basis should be included in the calculation of the clearing threshold.

The NFC is responsible for determining whether it has exceeded the clearing threshold and is required to notify ESMA and its relevant local regulator immediately if this is the case.[104] Again, in Regulation 149/2013, ESMA clarified that when a clearing threshold for one asset class is exceeded, the NFC will be deemed to have exceeded the clearing thresholds for all classes of OTC derivatives contracts. Therefore, if an NFC exceeds the threshold for credit derivatives, every other class of derivatives contracts would also be subject to clearing (including, eg, a derivatives contract entered into for the purposes of hedging only). If the clearing threshold is exceeded, the NFC+ must clear all relevant future contracts within four months of becoming subject to the clearing obligation. Furthermore, the NFC+ will cease to be subject to the clearing obligation if the rolling average gross notional as described above over 30 working days does not exceed the above thresholds. NFCs will need to have implemented processes to monitor and analyse their derivatives trading volumes constantly to determine whether the clearing threshold has been exceeded.

ESMA clarified in its 26 July 2016 Q&A[105] that derivatives contracts executed on non-EU exchanges that are equivalent to a regulated market in accordance with Article 19(6) of MiFID can be ignored for the purposes of determining the clearing threshold (since they do not constitute OTC derivatives contracts for the purposes of EMIR). However, derivatives traded on other non-EU exchanges will constitute OTC derivatives and will, therefore, be included in the calculation of the clearing threshold.

Furthermore, notwithstanding significant objections from the industry, OTC derivatives contracts that might be exempt intragroup transactions or that have been voluntarily cleared by an NFC may not be excluded from the clearing threshold calculation.

The requirement for NFCs to calculate whether or not they exceed the clearing threshold came into effect on 15 March 2013 (the date when Delegated Regulation 149/2013 came into effect).

---

103   Questions and Answers, Implementation of EMIR, 26 July 2016, ESMA/2016/1176 (www.esma.europa.eu/sites/default/files/library/2016-1176_qa_xix_emir.pdf), OTC Question/Answer 3, (b)2.
104   Article 10(1) of EMIR.
105   Questions and Answers, Implementation of EMIR, 26 July 2016, ESMA/2016/1176 (www.esma.europa.eu/sites/default/files/library/2016-1176_qa_xix_emir.pdf), OTC Question/Answer 1.

If an FC is trading with an NFC, the clearing obligation will apply only to the FC if the NFC is in fact an NFC+ (ie, the clearing threshold has been exceeded). The FC is not responsible for determining the status of the NFC. In its 26 July 2016 Q&A,[106] ESMA advised that FCs should obtain representations from NFCs as to the NFC's status on which they may rely. Consequently, FCs have sought warranties and/or representations from NFCs for NFCs to confirm their status for the purposes of the central clearing requirement of EMIR.

Third-country entities: A third-country entity that would be subject to the clearing obligation if it were established in the European Union (ie, it would be an FC or an NFC+) may be required to clear under EMIR if it enters into an OTC derivatives trade with:

- an FC or NFC+; or
- another third-country entity (that would be an FC or NFC+ if established in the European Union), if:
  - the contract has a direct, substantial and foreseeable effect within the EEA; or
  - the obligation is necessary or appropriate to prevent the evasion of any provisions of EMIR.

The clearing requirement may, therefore, apply directly to non-EEA entities.[107] ISDA and other industry representatives had raised concerns about the extraterritorial nature of EMIR, arguing that "legal uncertainty about extraterritorial application of such rules to contracts (and hence the potential for legal conflicts) will hamper markets that are the most global in nature".[108]

The application of the EMIR clearing requirement to third-country entities creates obvious challenges in the face of cross-border transactions for which one or more other parties are subject to their local regulatory requirements in addition to the EMIR requirements. For example, it is possible for a trade between an EEA entity and a US entity to be subject to clearing requirements both in the European Union (under EMIR) and in the United States (under the Dodd-Frank Act (see section 3.4 above)).

To avoid duplicative or conflicting rules, under EMIR[109] the European Commission may declare the regime in the relevant non-EEA state to be equivalent for the purposes of compliance with EMIR. Ultimately, this means that where one of the counterparties to a transaction which would otherwise be subject to the requirements of EMIR is established in a non-EEA state whose domestic regime is recognised by the European Commission as imposing equivalent requirements to EMIR, both counterparties will be deemed to have complied with EMIR.

106 Questions and Answers, Implementation of EMIR, 26 July 2016, ESMA/2016/1176 (www.esma.europa.eu/sites/default/files/library/2016-1176_qa_xix_emir.pdf), OTC Question/Answer 4.
107 Articles 4(1)(a)(iv) and (v) of EMIR.
108 ISDA, 'Association for Financial Markets in Europe' (AFME), British Bankers' Association (BBA) joint response to AFME BBA ISDA Response to First ESMA Discussion Paper, dated 16 February 2012, Draft Technical Standards for the Regulation on OTC Derivatives, CCPs and Trade Repositories, dated 20 March 2012.
109 Article 13 of EMIR.

The Commission has adopted 'equivalence' decisions to allow CCPs from (at the date of printing) 21 non-EU countries outside the European Union to clear EU derivatives transactions. However, further work is needed to address the ramifications of dual regulation.

RTS on transactions between two third-country entities: ESMA published RTSs relating to third-country entities[110] which shed light on how stakeholders interpret "contracts that have a direct, substantial and foreseeable effect within the EEA" and "prevention of evasion of EMIR". Below is a summary of the RTSs.

The following contracts between two third-country entities would be deemed to have a direct, substantial and foreseeable effect in the European Union:

- when at least one counterparty benefits from a guarantee provided by an EU FC, which:
  - covers a minimum aggregate notional amount of OTC derivatives exposures by the counterparty benefiting from the guarantee (where the guarantee covers all such liability, the minimum amount is €8 billion; where the guarantee covers a percentage of such liability the minimum amount is €8 billion divided by the percentage of liability covered by the guarantee); and
  - represents an amount which is at least 5% of the total OTC derivatives exposures of the FC providing the guarantee;
- contracts between two EU branches of non-equivalent third-country entities that would qualify as FCs if they were established in the EEA.

As regards preventing the evasion of EMIR, the RTSs provide that:

An OTC derivative contract shall be deemed to have been designed to circumvent the application of any provision of [EMIR] if the way in which that contract has been concluded is considered, when viewed as a whole and having regard to all the circumstances, to have as its primary purpose the avoidance of the application of any provision of [EMIR].

Consequently, a contract would be considered to be entered into for EMIR avoidance purposes if the:

primary purpose of an arrangement or series of arrangements related to the OTC derivative contract is to defeat the object, spirit and purpose of any provision of [EMIR] that would otherwise apply including when it is part of an artificial arrangement or artificial series of arrangements.

Exemption for intragroup transactions: Certain intragroup transactions are exempt from the central clearing requirement.[111] The definition of 'intragroup transactions' is very detailed and is set out in Article 3 of EMIR. Such exempt transaction will also be subject to the margin requirements (which form part of EMIR's risk mitigation requirements), unless it also benefits from the separate group

110 Delegated Regulation 285/2014 (which came into effect on 21 March 2014) supplementing EMIR.
111 Article 4(2) of EMIR.

exemption from those requirements. There are, however, no exemptions for OTC derivatives transactions between third-country entities.

The intragroup exemption does not automatically apply. To have the benefit of the intragroup exemption, counterparties must notify their relevant national regulator at least 30 days before the exemption is to be relied on.[112] Where two EEA counterparties are seeking the exemption, both must notify their national regulator(s) that they intend to rely on the exemption. The regulator(s) can object to the notification if the requirements under Article 3 of EMIR are not met (or cease to be met after the 30-day period).

Where one group entity is established in the EEA and the other is established in a third country, only the EEA counterparty must notify its regulator that the conditions in Article 3 are met. The exemption can be relied on only if such regulator expressly grants authorisation within 30 days of the notification (therefore, negative affirmation does not apply).

Pension scheme exemption: EMIR allows for a three-year exemption to the clearing obligation to be granted to certain pension scheme arrangements[113] with respect to OTC derivatives contracts that are "objectively measurable as reducing investment risks directly relating to the financial solvency" of arrangements (essentially, OTC derivatives that are used for hedging purposes).[114] The three-year exemption also applies to entities established for the purpose of providing compensation to members of pension scheme arrangements in case of default (eg, the UK Pension Protection Fund).

The exemption was granted because the European Commission recognised that stakeholders (particularly CCPs) needed time to develop technical solutions to allow for the transfer of non-cash collateral by pension scheme arrangements (CCPs generally accept only cash as variation margin, while pension scheme arrangements typically hold very little cash). The three-year exemption ran from the date on which EMIR came into force (ie, 16 August 2012), which means that the initial extension expired on 16 August 2015.

However, EMIR allows the Commission to extend the exemption period further by up to two years and again by an additional year[115] if the Commission considers that "the adverse effect of centrally clearing derivative contracts on the retirement benefits of future pensioners" remains unchanged. Consequently, and because the Commission opined that CCPs and the derivatives industry have not made sufficient progress in finding a solution to allow for the delivery of non-cash collateral,[116] on 5 June 2015 the Commission published a delegated regulation extending the transitional relief for another two years, to 16 August 2017.[117]

---

112   Article 4(2) of EMIR.
113   As defined in Article 2(10) of EMIR.
114   Article 89 of EMIR.
115   Article 85(2) of EMIR.
116   Report from the European Commission to the European Parliament and the Council under Article 85(2) of EMIR, dated 3 February 2015 (http://eur-lex.europa.eu/legal-content/EN/TXT/PDF/?uri=CELEX: 52015DC0039&from=EN).
117   Delegated Regulation C(2015) 3680 of 5 June 2015 (http://ec.europa.eu/finance/financial-markets/docs/derivatives/20150605-delegated-act_en.pdf).

7.4   Which OTC derivatives transactions must be centrally cleared

(a)   Procedure for determining the classes of derivative subject to the clearing requirement
Rather than apply to all OTC derivatives contracts, the EMIR clearing requirement will apply on an incremental, class-by-class basis. Two conditions need to be satisfied for a class of OTC derivatives to be subject to clearing – namely:

- a CCP must be authorised by its local EU member state regulator or (if the CCP is not established in the EEA) the CCP must be recognised by ESMA as being permitted to provide clearing services for the purposes of EMIR; and
- an RTS must have come into force specifying, among other things, that such class is subject to the clearing requirement and the date from which the relevant class must be cleared.

In determining which classes of OTC derivative should be cleared, ESMA will use one of two approaches contemplated by EMIR – namely, the bottom-up approach or the top-down approach,[118] each as summarised below.

Bottom-up approach: Broadly, under the bottom-up approach the clearing obligation may be triggered in relation to specific OTC derivatives contracts as a result of a CCP seeking authorisation from its local regulator to clear such OTC derivatives contracts.

When a CCP makes an application to its local regulator, the regulator must notify ESMA of that application. ESMA has six months after it receives such notification to submit a RTS to the European Commission. During this six-month period, ESMA must hold a public consultation (including with the relevant local regulator(s) of the CCP) and prepare and submit to the Commission draft RTS specifying, among other things, the class of OTC derivatives that should be subject to the clearing obligation, the date(s) on which the clearing obligation takes effect (including any phase-in), the categories of counterparty to whom the obligation applies and the minimum remaining maturity of OTC derivatives contracts to which the frontloading provisions apply.[119] The RTS (and hence the clearing obligation) will come into force some time after is it endorsed by the Commission.[120]

ESMA maintains a public register in which it publishes its notifications (see section 7.5 below).

Criteria adopted by ESMA: EMIR requires ESMA to take into account certain criteria when proposing certain classes of OTC derivative to be subject to clearing. The criteria to identify the class of OTC derivatives include the degree of standardisation of the contractual terms and operational processes, the volume and liquidity of the derivatives, and the availability of fair, reliable and generally accepted pricing information in the relevant class of derivatives.[121]

---

118   Article 5 of EMIR.
119   Article 5(2) of EMIR.
120   The RTS will be subject to a non-objection period by the European Parliament and the European Council after endorsement by the Commission.
121   Article 5(4) of EMIR.

In determining the date(s) from which the clearing obligation takes effect and the categories of counterparty to which the obligation applies, the relevant criteria includes the expected volume of the relevant class, whether more than one CCP already clears the same class (note that some market participants have raised concerns regarding the lack of CCPs to clear a certain class of OTC derivatives), the ability of the relevant CCPs to handle the expected volume and to manage associated risks, the type and number of counterparties active, and expected to be active, within the market for the relevant class, the period of time market participants need to prepare themselves for clearing and the risk management, legal and operational capacity of affected market participants.[122]

ESMA maintains and periodically publishes a list of CCPs that have been authorised by their local regulators as notified to ESMA by such local regulator.

With regard to non-EU CCPs seeking recognition under Article 25 of EMIR, a process similar to the bottom-up approach described above will apply. Furthermore, ESMA will have six months from the date when it completes the process for recognising the CCP to make a determination as to whether or not to recommend that a particular class of derivatives cleared by such CCP be subject to the EMIR clearing requirement.

If there are no longer any CCPs authorised or recognised to clear a class of OTC derivatives contracts under EMIR, the relevant class will no longer be subject to the clearing obligation and the top-down approach will apply.[123]

Top-down approach: Broadly, under the top-down approach the clearing obligation may be triggered in relation to specific OTC derivatives contracts as a result of ESMA, on its own initiative, determining that such OTC derivatives contracts – for which no CCP has at that time been authorised to clear – must be subject to the clearing requirement.[124]

Prior to making a determination, ESMA must conduct a public consultation and also consult with the European Systemic Risk Board and, where appropriate, relevant non-EU regulators.

(b) How can end users or clients access a CCP?

A CCP will deal directly only with a participant that it has accepted as a clearing member. However, clearing members represent a relatively limited number of market participants when compared to all firms that might need to clear under EMIR.

To allow smaller market participants to gain access to clearing, EMIR permits clearing to be made available to non-dealer (buy-side) market participants by allowing them to become clients of clearing members (unless they seek to become clearing members). This is achieved through a framework that permits clearing to be conducted in one of three ways:

- Become a clearing member only – a 'clearing member' is an entity which

---

122   Article 5(5) of EMIR.
123   Article 5(6) of EMIR.
124   Article 5(3) of EMIR.

participates in a CCP and which is responsible for discharging the financial obligations arising from that participation.[125] It is likely that most if not all buy-side firms will not be clearing members.

- Become a client of a clearing member – a 'client' is defined as an entity with a contractual relationship with a clearing member of a CCP which enables the entity to clear its transactions with that CCP.[126]
- Establish an indirect clearing arrangement with a clearing member – indirect clearing is permitted provided that such arrangement does not increase counterparty risk, and ensures that the assets and positions of the counterparty benefit from equivalent protection to that contained in Articles 39 (account segregation and portability) and Article 48 (procedures on default of a clearing member) of EMIR.[127]

An 'indirect client' is defined as "the client of a client of a clearing member".[128] For example, this arrangement exists where a client of a clearing member provides clearing services to its client (the indirect client). Hence, the client has an account with the clearing member, while the indirect client is a customer of that client.

EMIR[129] specifies, among other things, the types of indirect clearing arrangement that would meet the conditions in Article 4(3) of EMIR as summarised above – namely:

- Authorisation – a client of a clearing member may provide indirect clearing services only to its own client (ie, the indirect client) if the client of the clearing member is an authorised credit institution, investment firm or an equivalent third-country credit institution or investment firm.
- Contractual terms – the contractual terms of an indirect clearing arrangement are required to be agreed between the client of the clearing member and the indirect client, after consultation with the clearing member on the aspects that can impact the operations of the clearing member. The terms must include contractual requirements on the client to honour all obligations of the indirect client towards the clearing member.

7.5 ESMA's Public Register
ESMA is required to establish and maintain a public register on its website to specify the classes of OTC derivative subject to the clearing obligation. The register will also include details of the CCPs that are authorised or recognised to clear under EMIR, the dates from which the clearing obligation takes effect, including any phased-in implementation, any class of OTC derivatives subject to clearing as determined by the top-down approach, the minimum remaining maturity of contracts subject to frontloading and details of the CCPs whose local regulators have notified ESMA of their local authorisation for clearing and the date of notification (see the bottom-up approach section above).

---

125 Article 2(14) of EMIR.
126 Article 2(15) of EMIR.
127 Article 4(3) of EMIR.
128 Article 1(a) of Delegated Regulation 149/2013.
129 See Article 4(4) of EMIR and Article 2 of Delegated Regulation 149/2013.

7.6 Regulation of CCPs

As CCPs remain regulated at a national level by EU member state regulators, but provide services at an EU level, the European Commission has called for cooperative and collective oversight over CCPs to prevent market participants from cherry-picking the CCPs that may have the weakest form of supervision. Consequently, EMIR contains numerous requirements relating to the governance of the activities of CCPs including robust authorisation, prudential, organisational and conduct of business requirements for CCPs, as well as rules governing the interoperability[130] arrangements between CCPs (see section 7.6(d) below). EMIR also contains robust membership criteria, including capital and credit requirements, adequate capitalisation through the establishment of default funds and a margining and collateral management process. Certain aspects of these requirements are summarised below.

(a) Authorisation of CCPs

As mentioned above, EMIR specifies the process that must be followed to authorise CCPs for the purposes of providing clearing services in the European Union.[131] The process, which is relatively complex, is summarised below.

Where an EU entity wishes to provide clearing services as a CCP, it must apply for authorisation to its local member state regulator.[132] The applicant must provide its local regulator with all the relevant information necessary to demonstrate that it meets the requirements specified by EMIR. The domestic or local regulator must transmit the information to ESMA and to a college of other relevant regulators (see below). The local regulator has 30 working days following receipt of the application to determine whether the application is complete. If the application is incomplete, the local regulator must set a deadline for the applicant to provide additional information. Having finally determined that an application is complete, the local regulator must notify the applicant, the supervisory college and ESMA accordingly.[133]

Within 30 days of submission of a complete application, the applicant's local regulator must set, manage and chair a college of regulators to review the application. The college includes, among others:

- ESMA;
- the applicant's local regulator;
- regulators responsible for supervising the clearing members of the applicant that are established in the three member states with the largest contributions to the default fund of the CCP over a given period;
- regulators responsible for the supervision of trading venues served by the applicant;
- the regulators supervising CCPs with which interoperability arrangements have been established; and

---

130 However, some have argued that interoperability may have adverse systemic consequences if the weakest clearing house, which may be subject to default and be poorly capitalised and collateralised, causes the others to fail.
131 Articles 14 to 21 of EMIR.
132 Article 14 of EMIR.
133 Article 17 of EMIR.

- central banks that issue the most relevant EU currencies of the financial instruments to be cleared.[134]

Within four months of the submission of the completed application, the applicant's local regulator must conduct a risk assessment of the applicant and submit a report to the college. Within 30 days of receipt, the college must reach a joint opinion determining whether the applicant complies with the EMIR requirements. If no joint opinion is reached, the college should adopt a majority opinion (based on a simple majority of the members).[135]

Having taken the opinion of the college into consideration, the applicant's local regulator may grant authorisation only where, among other things, it is satisfied that the applicant complies with all of the requirements of EMIR.[136]

EMIR prescribes the process and outcome if there is no agreement between the local regulator and the college or no unanimous agreement is reached between different members of the college. For example, the applicant will not be authorised where all the members of the college except the local regulators in the applicant's jurisdiction unanimously opine that the applicant should not be authorised. EMIR also describes the circumstances where the matter may be referred to ESMA.[137]

In any event, the applicant's local regulator must inform the applicant, within six months of submitting a complete application, if authorisation has been granted or refused.

Once authorisation is granted, it is effective for the whole of the European Union.[138] Such authorisation will be granted only in respect of clearing activities and must specify, among other things, the services that the CCP is authorised to provide, as well as the classes of derivative covered by that authorisation.[139]

A CCP authorisation is not static. A CCP's obligations do not cease when it becomes authorised. CCPs are required to notify their local regulators of any material changes affecting the conditions of their authorisation.[140] Article 20 of EMIR describes the circumstances in which a CCP's authorisation may be removed, including not making use of the authorisation within 12 months of receiving it, or no longer being in compliance with the conditions of authorisation and not taking sufficient requested remedial action. Should any of the prescribed circumstances arise, and unless an urgent decision is needed, the CCP's local regulator must consult with the members of the college on the necessity to withdraw authorisation.

One of the key conditions to be satisfied for authorisation is that a CCP must have "permanent and available initial capital of at least €7.5 million".[141] The CCP must have sufficient capital (including retained earnings and reserves) that is proportionate to the risk stemming from its activities. Such capital must be sufficient

---

134   Article 18 of EMIR.
135   Article 19 of EMIR.
136   Article 17(4) of EMIR.
137   Article 17 of EMIR.
138   Article 14(2) of EMIR.
139   Article 14(3) of EMIR.
140   Article 14(4) of EMIR.
141   Article 16(1) of EMIR.

to ensure an orderly winding-down or restructuring of the CCP's activities over an appropriate time span and an adequate protection of the CCP against credit, counterparty, market, operational, legal and business risks which are not already covered by specific financial resources identified elsewhere in EMIR (eg, margin and default fund resources).[142]

(b)   *Recognition of non-EEA CCPs*

So far, this chapter has focused on EU CCPs seeking authorisation to offer clearing services under EMIR. However, EMIR provides a framework in which CCPs established in third countries (ie, non-EEA CCPs) may also apply to ESMA for recognition to provide clearing services in the European Union.[143] Certain conditions need to be satisfied before ESMA can recognise a non-EEA CCP including the following:

- ESMA must have consulted with the relevant college of regulators;
- The European Commission must determine that, among other things, the CCP is subject to a legal and supervisory regime in its country of establishment which is equivalent to the EMIR requirements for CCPs, and that such CCP is subject to "effective supervision and enforcement in that third country on an ongoing basis and that the legal framework of that third country provides for an effective equivalent system for the recognition of CCPs authorised under third-country legal regimes";
- Cross-border cooperation arrangements have been established between ESMA and the relevant third-country regulators; and
- The relevant third country has equivalent systems for anti-money laundering and combating the financing of terrorism to those of the European Union.

ESMA maintains a non-exhaustive list of third-country CCPs that have applied for recognition under EMIR.

(c)   *Supervision requirements for CCPs*

In order to qualify as CCPs and continue to be so authorised, CCPs must satisfy organisational, conduct of business and prudential requirements as set out in EMIR.[144]

(d)   *Organisational requirements*

EMIR's organisational requirements include those outlined below.[145]

General provisions: These include:

- having robust governance arrangements, such as a clear organisational structure with well-defined, transparent lines of responsibility, and effective processes to identify, manage and monitor risks;

---

142   Article 16(2) of EMIR.
143   Article 25 of EMIR.
144   Articles 26 to 50 of EMIR.
145   The RTS (Delegated Regulation 153/2013) relating to requirements for CCPs under EMIR specifies the minimum requirements under the above rules.

- maintaining a clear separation between the reporting lines for risk management and those for the other operations of the CCP;
- adopting, implementing and maintaining a remuneration policy that promotes sound and effective risk management, and does not create incentives to relax risk standards; and
- making its governance arrangements, the rules governing the CCP and its admission criteria for clearing membership available publicly free of charge.

Senior management and board: A CCP's senior management needs to be of good repute and experience, and at least one-third of its board members should be independent.

Risk committee: CCPs are required to establish a risk committee, which must be composed of representatives of its clearing members and independent board members.

Record keeping: CCPs are required to maintain, for at least 10 years, all records on the services and activities provided and following termination of a contract, all information on all contracts that it has processed.[146] CCPs are required to make such records and information and all information on the positions of cleared contracts available upon request by regulators.

Qualifying holdings: The local regulator of the CCP must be informed of the identities of the CCP's direct and indirect shareholders and can refuse authorisation if it is not satisfied as to the suitability of such shareholders.[147]

Conflicts of interest: A CCP must maintain and operate effective written organisational and administrative arrangements to identify and manage any potential conflicts of interest between itself (including its managers, employees or any person with direct or indirect control or close links) and its clearing members or their clients known to the CCP. CCPs are also required to implement adequate procedures aiming at resolving possible conflicts of interest.[148]

Business continuity: A CCP must establish, implement and maintain an adequate business continuity policy and disaster recovery plan aimed at ensuring the preservation of its functions, the timely recovery of operations and the fulfilment of the its obligations.[149]

---

146 The RTS (Delegated Regulation 153/2013) relating to requirements for CCPs under EMIR specifies the information to be retained and the format of the records.
147 A qualifying holding is any direct or indirect holding in a CCP that represents 10% or more of the capital or voting rights or a holding that makes it possible to exercise a significant influence over the management of the CCP.
148 Article 33 of EMIR.
149 Article 34 of EMIR and RTS (Delegated Regulation 153/2013) relating to requirements for CCPs under EMIR specifying the minimum content and requirements of the business continuity policy and disaster recovery plan.

Outsourcing: Where a CCP outsources functions, services or activities, it retains the regulatory responsibility of complying with its obligations and any outsourcing must comply with the specific conditions set out in EMIR.[150] CCPs are not permitted to outsource major activities linked to risk management without the approval of their local regulator.

(e)   ***Conduct of business rules***
EMIR's conduct of business rules include those outlined below.[151]

Best interests: CCPs must act fairly and professionally in accordance with the best interests of their clearing members and sound risk management. CCPs must have accessible, transparent and fair rules for prompt complaints handling.

Participation requirements: CCPs must establish, where relevant for each product type, the categories of admissible clearing member and the admission criteria. The criteria should be non-discriminatory, transparent and objective, so as to ensure fair and open access to the CCP. CCPs are also required to ensure that clearing members have sufficient financial resources and operational capacity to meet the obligations arising from participating in a CCP. CCPs must also review, on at least an annual basis, compliance by their members with these requirements.

Transparency: CCPs and their clearing members are to make various public disclosures such as the prices and fees associated with the services offered, including discounts and rebates. CCPs are also required to disclose to their clients and/or, where relevant, their local regulator the risks associated with the services offered and the price information used to calculate their end-of-day exposures to their clearing members. CCPs are also required to disclose publicly the volumes of cleared transactions for each class of instrument on an aggregate basis. CCPs are also subject to disclosure requirements relating to breaches by clearing members of the CCPs' admission criteria.

Segregation and portability: Under Article 39 of EMIR, CCPs must be able to identify and segregate the assets and positions of one clearing member from the assets and positions of any other clearing member and from their own assets. CCPs must offer two different types of account segregation to their clearing members:
- 'Omnibus client segregation' (OCS) – the minimum level of client protection permitted under EMIR – which consists of keeping separate records and accounts to enable the CCP's clearing members to distinguish in the accounts with the CCP the assets and positions of that clearing member from those held for the clearing members' clients; and
- 'Individual client segregation' (ICS), which is keeping separate records and accounts to enable each clearing member to distinguish in the accounts with

---

150   Article 35 of EMIR.
151   Articles 36 to 39 of EMIR.

the CCP the assets and positions held for the account of a client from those held for other clients.

Clearing members are also required to be able to distinguish their assets and positions from the assets and positions held for their clients (in their own accounts and in the account with the CCP). They must offer their clients, at least, the choice between OCS and ICS, and inform such clients of the costs and level of protection associated with each option. CCPs and clearing members must publicly disclose the levels of protection and costs associated with the different levels of segregation that they provide and must offer those services on reasonably commercial terms.[152]

While EMIR mandates that CCPs (and clearing members) offer OCS and ICS, CCPs generally offer a range of options of OCS accounts. Therefore, even where clients opt for an OCS account structure, clients will need to choose between different OCS account structures.

Under the OCS account structure, the clearing member's position and margin are separated from those of its clients, therefore protecting clients from the insolvency of the clearing member. However, the positions and margin of each of the clearing member's clients are commingled, which means that each client is exposed to the risk of a shortfall arising in the account as a result of the default or insolvency of another client. As mentioned above, CCPs are offering different types of OCS which include:

- net OCS account structure – the positions of all clients are offset against each other, resulting in a net margin amount being posted to the CCP. The net margin amount will be lower than the amount of collateral posted to the CCP under the gross OCS account structure (below). The clearing member will hold any excess margin. This account structure is the most popular structure adopted by EU clients in the exchange-traded derivatives markets;
- gross OCS account structure – each client's margin is calculated independently under the CCP's own methodology and the clearing member posts collateral representing the gross amount of each separate calculation to the CCP. Again, the clearing member will typically hold any excess margin;
- 'legally separated, operationally commingled' (LSOC) omnibus account structure – the LSOC account structure is similar to the account structure offering by US CCPs. It is similar to a gross OCS account, but excess margin demanded by the clearing member for the CCP is held by the CCP and not the clearing member; and
- ICS – that is, as explained above, an individual account at the CCP for one client of a particular clearing member. ICS offers greater protection than OCS as clients' positions and margin are not commingled. Excess margin is posted to the CCP and segregated from the margin of other clients. Given the greater levels of protection, the fees for the ICS account structure would typically be higher than those for the OCS account structures.

---

152   Article 39 of EMIR.

(f) ***Prudential requirements***

To provide a buffer against credit and market risk, CCPs are required to satisfy certain prudential requirements under EMIR,[153] include those outlined below.

Exposure management: CCPs must measure their liquidity and credit exposures to each clearing member (and other CCPs with whom such CCPs have interoperability arrangements) on a near to real-time basis.[154]

Margin requirements: CCPs must call for and collect margin to limit credit exposures from clearing members (and other CCPs with whom such CCPs have interoperability arrangements). Such margin shall be sufficient to cover potential exposures that the CCP estimates will occur until the liquidation of the relevant positions. Such margin should be sufficient to cover losses that result from at least 99% of the exposure's movements over an appropriate time horizon. CCPs are required to collateralise their exposures fully with all their clearing members, and, where relevant, with CCPs with which they have interoperability arrangements, at least on a daily basis. CCPs are also required to review regularly the level of margin to reflect current market conditions taking into account any potentially procyclical effects of such revisions. Margin must be called and collected on an intraday basis, at a minimum when pre-defined thresholds are exceeded. Margin needs to be segregated to ensure that the CCP is protected against the default of any other clearing members or the CCP itself.[155]

Default fund: To limit their credit exposures to their clearing members, CCPs must maintain a pre-funded default fund to cover losses arising from clearing member default and not already covered by margin. The default fund must not fall below a minimum amount set by each CCP. CCPs must establish a minimum size of contributions of each clearing member to the default fund and the criteria to calculate such contributions. The default fund must at least enable the CCP to withstand, under extreme but plausible market conditions,[156] the default of the clearing member to which it has the largest exposures, or of the second and third largest clearing members if the sum of their exposures is larger.[157]

Other financial resources: CCPs are required to maintain sufficient pre-funded available financial resources to cover potential losses that exceed the losses to be covered by margin and the default fund. Such pre-funded financial resources must include dedicated resources of the CCP and be freely available to the CCP. The default fund and such additional financial resources must be sufficient to buffer the CCP against the default of at least the two clearing members to which it has the

---

153   Articles 40–50 of EMIR set out detailed prudential requirements for CCPs.
154   Article 40 of EMIR.
155   Article 41 of EMIR.
156   The RTS (Delegated Regulation 153/2013) relating to requirements for CCPs under EMIR specifies the framework for defining the extreme but plausible market conditions that should be used when defining the size of the default fund.
157   Article 42 of EMIR.

largest exposures under extreme but plausible market conditions. CCPs may require non-defaulting clearing members to provide additional funds if another clearing member defaults.[158]

Liquidity risk controls: A CCP must have access to sufficient liquidity to provide its services. It must obtain the necessary credit lines to cover its liquidity needs in case its other financial resources are not immediately available.[159]

Default waterfall: EMIR specifies the order in which a CCP's financial resources should be applied on default of a clearing member – namely, first, margin posted by the defaulting clearing member should be used. Second, having exhausted the defaulting clearing member's margin, the CCP must use the default fund contribution of the defaulting member. Third, having exhausted the contributions of the defaulting clearing member and having used its own financial resources, the CCP may use the default fund contributions of non-defaulting clearing members. CCPs are not permitted to use margin posted by non-defaulting clearing members to cover losses resulting from the default of another clearing member.[160]

Collateral requirements: CCPs must accept highly liquid collateral with minimal credit and market risk to cover their initial and ongoing exposure to their clearing members. CCPs must apply adequate haircuts to asset values that reflect the potential for their value to decline over the interval between their last revaluation and the time by which they can reasonably be assumed to be liquidated. Liquidity and concentration risk must also be taken into account.[161] The types of collateral that can be considered as highly liquid include cash, gold, government and high-quality corporate bonds.[162]

Investment policy: EMIR prescribes how CCPs must invest their financial resources, which may be applied to cash or in highly liquid financial instruments with minimal market and credit risk.[163]

Default procedures: CCPs must establish procedures to deal with clearing members that fail to comply with the CCPs' participation requirements. CCPs are required to take prompt action to contain losses and liquidity pressures resulting from clearing member defaults, and must ensure that the closing-out of any clearing member's positions does not disrupt their operations or expose the non-defaulting clearing members to losses that they cannot anticipate or control. CCPs are required to agree

---

158   Article 43 of EMIR.
159   Article 44 of EMIR. The RTS (Delegated Regulation 153/2013) relating to requirements for CCPs under
       EMIR specifies the framework for managing liquidity risk.
160   Article 45 of EMIR. The RTS (Delegated Regulation 153/2013) relating to requirements for CCPs under
       EMIR specifies the methodology for calculating and maintaining the amount of CCPs' own resources to
       be used in accordance with the default waterfall rules.
161   Article 46 of EMIR.
162   Delegated Regulation 153/2013.
163   Article 47 of EMIR.

to trigger the procedures for the transfer of the assets and positions held by the defaulting clearing member for the account of its clients to another clearing member designated by all of those clients. That replacement clearing member is obliged to accept those assets and positions where it has previously agreed with the clients to act as a back-up clearing member. If the transfer to the replacement clearing member does not take place for any reason within a predefined transfer period specified in the CCP's operating rules, the CCP would seek to manage its risks actively in relation to those positions, including liquidating the assets and positions held by the defaulting clearing member for the account of its clients.[164]

Review of models, stress testing and back testing: The models and parameters adopted to calculate margin requirements, default fund contributions, collateral requirements and other risk control mechanisms must be regularly reviewed and subjected to rigorous and frequent stress tests.[165]

Settlement: EMIR requires CCPs to use central bank money to settle their transactions. Where this is not available, steps need to be taken to limit cash settlement risk.[166]

(g) *Interoperability*

Where two parties to a derivatives transaction choose a different CCP with which to clear their transaction, an arrangement would need to exist between the two CCPs to facilitate that trade. The two CCPs are, therefore, said to 'interoperate' in managing the risk and settlement obligations arising between them.

Article 2(12) of EMIR defines an 'interoperability arrangement' as an arrangement between two or more CCPs that involves a cross-system settlement of transactions. Thus, 'interoperability' is, broadly, where two or more CCPs interact with each other to permit a counterparty using one CCP to settle a transaction with a counterparty that has chosen an alternative CCP. Interoperability should ensure that a CCP is still able to meet its obligations to its clearing members even if the other CCP defaults. However, this could mean that each CCP is exposed to the potential default of the other CCP, as well as the potential default of the clearing member. This additional risk is addressed by fairly strict governance requirements under EMIR. For example, CCPs can enter into interoperability arrangements with other CCPs only where certain risk management, margin and approval requirements are met.[167] These include requirements relating to monitoring and managing credit and liquidity risk, monitoring and addressing interdependencies and correlations that arise from interoperability arrangements, and the provision of margin between interoperating CCPs.

Recital 73 to EMIR states that, in light of the additional complexities involved in an interoperability arrangement between CCPs, the scope of interoperability

---

164   Article 48 of EMIR.
165   Article 49 of EMIR and the RTS (Delegated Regulation 153/2013) relating to requirements for CCPs under EMIR which specifies the tests to be undertaken, the involvement of clearing members or other parties in the tests and the frequency and time horizons of the tests.
166   Article 50 of EMIR.
167   Articles 51–54 of EMIR.

arrangements is currently restricted to transferable securities and money market instruments. However, ESMA was required under Article 85(3)(d) of EMIR to submit by 30 September 2014 a report to the European Commission on whether an extension of the scope to other financial instruments would be appropriate. At the time of writing, ESMA had not yet issued this report.

In advance of the regulatory efforts on central clearing, investors have already requested that new structures be written into deals to mitigate counterparty default risk and market participants have already launched their own reforms. Consequently, many of Europe's largest clearing houses launched clearing operations ahead of the EU central clearing deadline. Furthermore, ISDA has been working alongside the industry to standardise swap documentation with the aim of facilitating central clearing. There are presently at least four recognised clearing houses in the United Kingdom (CME Clearing Europe Limited, ICE Clear Europe Limited, LCH.Clearnet Limited and LME Clear Limited)[168] and more may launch in due course. Furthermore, clearing houses are also expanding their clearing capabilities to clear a greater number of products.

7.7 Shortfalls of clearing

While clearing houses are seen as the solution for counterparty risk in the OTC derivatives market, some industry members argue that central clearing will not remove systemic risk from the market entirely, but will instead concentrate such risk on the CCPs,[169] and that unless CCPs are well capitalised and closely monitored, they can add systemic risk to the financial markets.

ESMA published the results of a stress test exercise for EEA CCPs.[170] The stress test was established to determine the resilience of EEA CCPs, as well as to identify possible weaknesses in CCP infrastructure. It focused on counterparty credit risk which CCPs would face as a result of multiple clearing members going into default along with market price shocks. The report also provides recommendations to address the perceived weaknesses in CCP internal methodologies.

ESMA tested the resilience of 17 EEA CCPs using combinations of clearing member default and market stress scenarios. The results indicated that, broadly, EEA CCPs are resilient to the stress scenarios used to model extreme but plausible market developments. However, under more severe stress scenarios, CCPs faced small amounts of total residual uncovered losses. Clearing houses are not, therefore, completely immune to failure.

8. Cross-border issues

Given that many derivatives transactions are conducted across multiple jurisdictions, stakeholders in the derivatives market have called for better coordination among global regulators on how these regulations will be applied to market participants that

---

168   www.bankofengland.co.uk/financialstability/Pages/fmis/supervised_sys/rch.aspx.
169   According to a panel of in-house bankers' counsel, speaking at the PLI conference on Securities Regulation in Europe during January 2010.
170   29 April 2016 (www.esma.europa.eu/press-news/esma-news/esma-publishes-results-eu-central-counterparties-stress-test).

engage in cross-border transactions. Global regulators have been urged to avoid duplicative or conflicting derivatives regulations, and to ensure that regulations are adopted consistently around the world.

For example, with respect to the EMIR clearing requirement, a US counterparty that is subject to and required to clear a transaction under the Dodd-Frank regime may be trading with a EEA counterparty that is subject to the EMIR clearing regime. It is accepted that it is practically, legally and operationally impossible to clear in two jurisdictions at the same time. Therefore, EMIR sets out a framework whereby the European Commission and ESMA may acknowledge and recognise the derivatives regulatory regimes of non-EU countries so that if an entity that is subject to EMIR is already complying with the equivalent rules of a non-EU country, that entity would be deemed to have complied with EMIR (sometimes described as the 'equivalent or substitutive compliance' principle).

ESMA advises the European Commission on the extent to which the derivatives regimes of non-EU countries are to be determined as equivalent for the purposes of EMIR. This advice is intended to assist the Commission in seeking to recognise the derivatives regulatory regimes of non-EU countries. Following ESMA's advice, the Commission has already determined that the derivatives regulatory regimes of a number of non-EU countries are equivalent for the purposes of EMIR.[171]

9. MiFID II and derivatives

In its 2009 communiqué, the G20 stated:

> All standardized OTC derivative contracts should be traded on exchanges or electronic trading platforms, where appropriate, and cleared through central counterparties by end 2012 at the latest.[172]

The European Commission agreed with this proposal with the view that adding exchange trading to central clearing will enhance liquidity and transparency as to trading levels and market conduct in the OTC derivatives markets.

The MiFID II Directive and MiFIR (ie, Regulation 600/2014) (together, MiFID II) is the legislation that replaces MiFiD and also forms the regulatory framework for the requirements applicable to investment firms, regulated markets and data reporting services. MiFID II will come into force on 3 January 2018. The MiFID II Directive is to be transposed into the domestic law of each EU member state. In the case of the United Kingdom, MiFID II will be transposed through the Financial Services and Markets Act 2000 (FSMA) framework (ie, the Financial Services and Markets Act 2000 (Markets in Financial Instruments) Regulations 2016) in the same way as MiFID was transposed. Although the MiFID II Directive and MiFIR should be read together, MiFIR deals more with derivatives regulation and interconnects with EMIR.

One of the key aims of MiFIR is to ensure that trading of certain OTC derivatives is conducted on regulated trading venues. It also addresses other market conduct issues, including access to CCPs and trading venues, regulated markets, multilateral

---

171   As at the date of publication, the relevant countries include Australia, Canada, Hong Kong, India, Japan, Singapore, South Korea, Switzerland and the United States.
172   G20 Declaration on Strengthening the Financial System, London, 2 April 2009.

trading facilities and organised trading facilities, and the recognition of equivalent non-EU trading venues.

In furtherance of the aim to improve transparency and oversight of OTC derivatives, one of the basic doctrines of MiFIR is that OTC derivatives contracts that are subject to the EMIR clearing requirement must (if admitted to trading or traded on at least one trading venue and also deemed sufficiently liquid)[173] be traded on an EU-authorised or non-EU recognised trading venue. Essentially, counterparties falling within the EMIR clearing requirement may also be required to trade certain types of liquid derivative that are eligible for EMIR clearing on a regulated trading venue (ie, a regulated market, a multilateral trading facility, an organised trading facility or non-EU equivalent venue).[174] Therefore, entities that are required to clear under EMIR will not be able to enter into derivatives contracts with each other away from a trading venue if the relevant derivative is required to be traded under MiFIR. ESMA will publish a list of derivatives that are subject to the trading obligation, the venues where they are admitted to trading or traded, and the dates from which the trading obligation takes effect.[175]

In line with the EMIR clearing requirement, the MiFIR trading requirement also applies to:

- FCs and NFC+s that trade derivatives with non-EU entities that would be subject to the clearing obligation if they were established in the EEA; and
- two non-EU entities if:
  - they would be subject to the clearing obligation if they were established in the European Union; and
  - where the contract has a direct, substantial and foreseeable effect within the European Union, or where such an obligation is necessary or appropriate to prevent the evasion of any provisions of MiFIR. Certain intragroup exemptions and a transitional period apply, broadly consistent with the exemption and transitional period under EMIR.

It is not yet known whether the classes of derivative subject to the MiFIR trading requirement will be a smaller subset of the classes subject to the EMIR clearing requirement, although this is likely.

10.   Position limits

10.1   What are position limits?

With the aim of promoting and maintaining stable and fair markets (eg, avoiding disproportionate price movements), preventing the control and manipulation of the market by a few market participants and limiting excessive speculation that may undermine the market, regulators and exchanges have in the past set limits on the total number of positions that a dealer or trader can hold in option contracts on the

---

173   Articles 28 and 32 of MiFIR.
174   Article 28 of MiFIR.
175   Article 34 of MiFIR.

same side (call or put) of the market. Depending on the exchange, position limits may be set as a number of contracts or as total units of the commodity. Some commodity exchanges allow exemptions from these limits in cases of good-faith hedges and certain risk management positions to qualified traders and arbitrageurs.

Position limits originated in the commodity markets and were historically applied to prevent large positions being amassed as the expiry of a physically settled contract approached, with the aim of:

- limiting concentrated and dominant positions; and
- promoting market confidence by preventing participants from incurring obligations to accept or deliver large quantities of physical commodities where they are not equipped to do so.

So far as the derivatives market is concerned, the European Commission has proposed a number of measures to combat manipulation (or creating disproportionate price movements) and concentration of speculative positions in the derivatives markets including to give regulators the scope to set position limits.

The MiFID II Directive provides a legislative framework in which EU-wide mandatory restrictions can be imposed on the size of commodity derivatives trading by specifying quantitative thresholds for the maximum size of a position in a commodity derivative that market participants can hold.[176]

MIFID II provides for the imposition of limits by each domestic member state regulator on the "maximum size of the net position which a person may hold at any time in a commodity derivative traded on a trading venue in an EEA state and economically equivalent over-the-counter contracts" and largely repeats the MiFID II requirements in relation to position limits.[177] The position limit regime will not apply to a position held by a non-financial entity hedging risks arising from its commercial activities. If an entity trades the same commodity derivative in sufficient volumes on trading venues in more than one jurisdiction, a single position limit may be set by the local regulatory body of the jurisdiction in which the largest volume of trading occurs.

One aspect of the position limit regime that has created challenges relates to its potential extraterritorial nature. In the case of position limits specified by the Financial Conduct Authority, such limits appear to apply to any person irrespective of their location if there is a link to a contract traded on a UK market. It is unclear how a link to the UK markets can be determined.

ESMA published two draft RTSs in relation to position limits. The RTSs address a number of areas including the methodology to be utilised by member state regulators to set position limits, the type of contracts in scope, and permissible aggregation and netting for the purposes of calculating a position. Position limits will apply to both cash-settled and physically settled commodity derivatives.

10.2   Position reporting

Under MiFID II, trading venues that trade commodity derivatives or emissions

---

176   Article 69(1) and (2)(p) of the MiFID II Directive.
177   Articles 57 and 58 of the MiFID II Directive.

allowances (or derivatives thereof) will be required to publish a weekly report with the aggregate positions held by different categories of persons (including investment firms or credit institutions, investment funds, other financial institutions and commercial undertakings) for each instrument traded on that trading venue. The report must articulate the number of long and short positions held by each category of person, changes since the previous report, the percentage of total open interest represented by each category of person and the number of persons holding a position in each category. UK regulated trading venues are also required to send the report to the Financial Conduct Authority and ESMA.[178]

UK investment firms trading in, among other things, commodity derivatives outside a trading venue must provide to the Financial Conduct Authority, on a daily basis, a complete breakdown of their positions in commodity derivatives or emissions allowances or derivatives thereof traded on a trading venue and economically equivalent OTC contracts, as well as those of their clients and the clients of those clients until the end client is reached.[179]

11. Conclusion

In summary, the EU regulatory framework includes standarding the terms of derivatives contracts, improving counterparty risk management through, among other things, increased use of clearing houses and by extending their use to a wider range of product types, and improving transparency by establishing trade depositories to which derivatives transactions are reported. Exchange trading will become mandatory for certain derivatives contracts. MiFID will also be amended to enable regulators to set position limits for commodity derivatives. As global regulators work to establish and implement rules for the regulation of OTC derivatives, a collective and cooperative approach is needed to prevent regulatory arbitrage and to ease cross-border derivatives trading. However, differences still remain between the European Union, the United States and other jurisdictions as to the scope of such regulatory reforms.

The industry has broadly welcomed the proposed regulatory reforms and agrees that while the regulation of OTC derivatives market is necessary (to address the perceived systemic problems discussed in this chapter), too much regulation might restrict the freedom of the markets to trade in derivatives and could limit the competitiveness[180] of the market.[181] Trade associations continue to work with policymakers to convey industry views on the regulatory proposals and their implications on stakeholders.

Further work is, however, needed to ensure a globally harmonised regulatory framework for the OTC derivatives market that does not inhibit the performance and evolution of the financial markets.

---

178   Article 58 of the MiFID II Directive.
179   Article 58 of the MiFID II Directive.
180   "Fresh regulations 'threaten' financial services", by Brian Groom, 19 January 2010.
181   ISDA has responded to regulatory proposals by asking that any new regulations should enhance the ability of market participants to manage their risk exposures and that regulators should carefully compare the positive and negative aspects of such proposals.

Close-out netting

Kunel Tanna
Mayer Brown

1. Background and introduction

Close-out netting serves an essential purpose in the 'global over-the-counter' (OTC) derivatives markets, allowing parties to evaluate counterparty exposures better, make more efficient use of credit lines and manage the burden of regulatory capital requirements. It brings systemic benefits by reducing risk across the whole network of market participants and promoting the liquidity and stability of the financial system. Effective close-out netting has proven to be a cornerstone of the modern financial markets over the years, with all other credit risk mitigation techniques arguably operating to deal with the residual credit risk left after close-out netting is applied.[1]

Indeed, various model insolvency law provisions published by multilateral organisations provide recommendations for the statutory enactment of safeguards for close-out netting (eg, by UNCITRAL[2] and UNIDROIT[3]), while supranational regulatory bodies (including the Financial Stability Board[4] and the Cross-border Bank Resolution Group of the Basel Committee on Banking Supervision[5]) strongly encourage market participants to use close-out netting owing to its beneficial effects on the stability of the financial system.

The most widely used standard form documentation in the international derivatives, repurchase and securities lending markets are designed as master netting agreements under which the parties can enter into a number of transactions and, in the event of an early termination, calculate the net exposure between the parties under those transactions.

This chapter considers the key legal issues that have informed the drafting of close-out netting provisions and examines the practical implications of these provisions in the context of English insolvency law. In particular, this chapter examines the derivatives master netting agreements published by the 'International Swaps and Derivatives Association Inc' (ISDA), possibly the most ubiquitous example of a master netting agreement used throughout the financial world.

---

1   Statistics prepared by the Bank of International Settlements have shown that net credit exposure among parties in the global derivatives market is between 75% and 90% lower than their gross credit exposure.
2   See the 2004 UNCITRAL Legislative Guide on Insolvency.
3   See the 2013 UNIDROIT Global Netting Principles.
4   See Key Attributes of Effective Resolution Regimes for Financial Institutions, 15 October 2014.
5   See the 2010 Report and Recommendations of the Cross-border Bank Resolution Group.

2. Close-out netting and the ISDA Master Agreement

2.1 Defining 'close-out netting'

Where counterparties have entered into multiple transactions under a master netting agreement, the occurrence of an event of default or a termination event would permit the non-defaulting party to terminate, or close-out, all of the affected transactions. Such early termination would typically follow the occurrence of any number of events that prejudice the continuation of the trades between the parties, which may or may not have a direct impact on the credit risk of continuing to trade with the counterparty. The most striking example of such an event is the insolvency of the counterparty, but may also include non-fault based events that render continuing to trade illegal or uneconomical due to changes in laws.

Upon an early termination, parties can determine an amount owing by one party to the other that represents the net values of all of those transactions instead of settling each separate transaction individually. To achieve this, counterparties include close-out netting provisions in their master netting agreements that provide a mutual, contractual process comprising three distinct stages:

- the early termination of all outstanding transactions under the master netting agreement;
- the valuation of the terminated transactions, typically on a mark-to-market basis; and
- the determination of a single, net sum payable by one party to the other with respect to those terminated transactions.

The obligation to pay this net sum represents the sole obligation to be settled under the master netting agreement and is typically due immediately following determination, notwithstanding that no debts may have been due and payable under the terms of the transactions prior to the early termination.

2.2 The ISDA Master Agreements

Looking at the standard form ISDA Master Agreements, a number of provisions set out the basis of close-out netting. Taken together, one finds the core of the close-out netting provisions in Sections 1(c), 5(a), 5(b), 6(a), 6(c), 6(d) and 6(e) of the ISDA Master Agreement. Set out below is a brief description of how each provision operates.

- By Section 1(c), the parties express their intention that all transactions entered into under the ISDA Master Agreement and the relevant confirmations form a single agreement between the parties, and that the parties would not otherwise enter into any transactions.
- Sections 5(a) and 5(b) specify the events of default and termination events, the occurrence of which will give rise to early termination rights; these are often modified by the parties in the ISDA Schedule.
- Section 6(a) governs the circumstances in which early termination may occur by notice given by the non-defaulting party to the defaulting party designating an early termination date (or automatically where the parties

have elected that automatic early termination will apply with respect to a party).

- Section 6(c) provides that the obligations of each of the parties under all transactions cease once the early termination date occurs (or is deemed to occur, where automatic early termination applies).
- Sections 6(d) and 6(e) together govern the method for determining the net balance and the obligation to pay such amount.

2.3 Treatment of scheduled obligations

At this point, it is useful to consider the treatment of the scheduled obligations under the terms of the transactions prior to their early termination. Reading Section 6(c) together with Section 2(a)(iii) of the ISDA Master Agreement (by which the performance of payment obligations is conditional on an early termination date having not occurred), the obligation to pay a scheduled amount in respect of any particular transaction is merely a conditional obligation and the right to receive that payment is merely a conditional right; likewise with the obligation to deliver in respect of any particular transaction and the parallel right to receive delivery.

As considered further in paragraph 7.1 of this chapter, prior to the scheduled payment date, the counterparties therefore accrue debt obligations under the terms of the transactions and, upon the occurrence of the scheduled payment date, they benefit from a conditional right to receive payment of that debt obligation, which right to receive payment (and the parallel obligation to make payment) arises only where the relevant conditions precedent have been satisfied. As such, the occurrence of the early termination date constitutes the irremediable failure of a condition to the effectiveness of the rights and obligations under a transaction. At that point, where there is no hope for the condition to be satisfied and the separate rights and obligations to be revived, the parties calculate the values of the outstanding positions and net those amounts to arrive at a single sum owed by one party to the other.

3. Distinguishing close-out netting

Practically and legally, it is important to distinguish close-out netting from the operation of set-off and from settlement netting, each of which applies to executory contracts, such as derivatives transactions, where the parties have obligations that remain to be performed over a period of time in accordance with the terms of the agreement.

3.1 Set-off

While conceptually and functionally distinct, there is some overlap between the operation of close-out netting and set-off from an economic perspective:

- 'Close-out netting' describes the process of calculating two parties' termination exposures to each other upon the early termination of transactions under a master netting agreement to determine a single, net balance.
- 'Set-off' is the application of payments owing by one party to its counterparty against the payments owing to it by the counterparty so as to extinguish any

payment obligations of the net creditor and leave the net debtor with a new, reduced payment obligation that reflects the difference between the original obligations.

The question of when the obligations are determined is key in establishing whether close-out netting or set-off is being used. Under close-out netting, transactions that are being terminated ahead of their scheduled maturity will be valued in accordance with the master netting agreement only once they have been terminated. Under set-off, however, the obligations will relate to amounts already determined and payable under separate agreements prior to being discharged against each other. It is helpful to note here that, unlike in the case of close-out netting, which applies to obligations under separate transactions under a single agreement, the right of set-off applies to legally distinct sums payable under different agreements.

Indeed, the third limb of the close-out netting process described in paragraph 2.1 of this chapter may (but need not) be achieved by way of contractual set-off. Some master netting agreements used in the financial markets adopt this approach – for example, the Global Master Repurchase Agreement jointly published by the Securities Industry and Financial Markets Association and the International Capital Market Association, which provides that monetary values are given to accelerated obligations and these values are then set off against each other. However, in the ISDA Master Agreements, as described above, the combination of the various provisions used achieves the same result without the use of contractual set-off. That said, the ISDA Master Agreement does not eschew contractual set-off entirely – see, for example, Section 6(f) of the 2002 ISDA Master Agreement, which gives the non-defaulting party certain set-off rights that come into play following the determination of the early termination amount.[6]

3.2   Settlement netting

Settlement netting applies where the two parties to an agreement each owes the other an amount payable on the same day and in the same currency with respect to a particular transaction (or multiple transactions, if the parties are able to accommodate this), as set out in Section 2(c) of the ISDA Master Agreement. Settlement netting results in the reduction of those payment obligations into a single, net payment obligation owed by one party only to the other, representing an amount that is the difference between the larger payment obligation and the smaller on that day. This applies likewise to delivery obligations with respect to the delivery of fungible assets (eg, gilts of the same type and description) on a particular day.

Practically, settlement netting serves many purposes, from reducing the 'daylight risk' of parties in different time zones (which opens the parties up to the risk that one party may become insolvent in its jurisdiction before it settles its payment

---

6   While the standard form 1992 ISDA Master Agreement does not allow a party to set off early termination amounts against sums due under other agreements, a set-off provision to this effect is often included in the bilaterally negotiated ISDA Schedule. There is a standard set-off clause in the User's Guide to the 1992 ISDA Master Agreement published by ISDA.

obligations, but after the other party has settled its payment obligations), minimising the operational burden of processing multiple payments, reducing the administrative risk of making an incorrect payment, and reducing the amount to which any withholding tax may be applied.

This presupposes that the payment obligations already exist and, accordingly, settlement netting is limited to comparable obligations being settled on the same day and in the same manner. Unlike close-out netting, settlement netting does not contemplate future or contingent obligations, and does not require the early termination of transactions or the determination of an early termination amount based on the mark-to-market value of all transactions under the relevant master netting agreement. It is simply the netting of scheduled payment obligations that arise in the course of a transaction and applies on a daily basis.

In the context of the ISDA Master Agreement, it is worth noting that the Court of Appeal has clarified that settlement netting under Section 2(c) of the ISDA Master Agreement operates before any payment obligation arises under Section 2(a)(i) of the ISDA Master Agreement.[7] That is, settlement netting will apply to all sums that accrue under a transaction on a particular day and the payment obligation that arises with respect to those sums will always be the net value of those sums. The corollary of this is that, where a condition precedent fails under Section 2(a)(iii) of the ISDA Master Agreement, it is the payment obligation in respect of the net sum that is suspended and not the separate gross sums (see further paragraph 7.3 of this chapter with respect to Section 2(a)(iii) of the ISDA Master Agreement and the Lehman Brothers litigation).[8]

4.   Early termination of master netting agreements

Unlike the acceleration of a simple loan after drawdown, for example, where the identities of the debtor and the creditor are clear (the borrower and the lender, respectively), and where the amounts payable at the point of breaking the loan are easily determinable (the outstanding amount of the loan plus any interest and fees), the early termination of a master netting agreement will require the parties to determine both the payer and the amount payable with respect to all of the transactions that are being terminated.

4.1   ISDA Master Agreements – an overview

The principal steps of the early termination procedure under the ISDA Master Agreements are illustrated in the diagram on the following page. Although the diagram is intended to set out the steps in chronological order, the documentation may require or permit that these steps be taken in a different order.

---

7   Four joint judgments: *Lomas v JFB Firth Rixson Inc*; *Lehman Brothers Special Financing Inc v Carlton Communications Ltd*; *Pioneer Freight Futures Co Ltd (in Liquidation) v Cosco Bulk Carrier Co Ltd*; *Britannia Bulk Plc (in Liquidation) v Bulk Trading SA* [2012] EWCA Civ 419 (together referred to here as *Lomas v Firth Rixson*).
8   See also *Pioneer Freight Futures v TNT Asia* [2011] EWHC 1888 (Comm).

Review of documentation	Determination of event of default/ termination event	Conditions to early termination
Designation of early termination date/ automatic early termination	Enforcement of security under credit support deed	Determination of market quotation/loss/ close-out amount and unpaid amounts
Application of posted collateral under credit support annex	Determination of interest on unpaid amounts	Conversion into termination currency
Adjustment for bankruptcy, illegality and *force majeure*	Application of set-off	Calculation of expenses
Preparation of calculation statement	Payment date	Expenses and accrual of interest after payment date

Parties should ensure that they have reviewed all of the relevant documents and circumstances that may affect the early termination mechanics, including the version of the ISDA Master Agreement being used, the amendments and elections made in the related ISDA Schedule, any collateral arrangements in place, any bilateral or multilateral amendments or protocols entered into, and any other overriding provisions in the transaction confirmations.

4.2 Designation of an early termination date

Where an event of default has occurred and is then continuing, or a termination event affecting all transactions has occurred (and automatic early termination has not been triggered), the non-defaulting party may (but is not obliged to) give notice to the defaulting party designating an early termination date with respect to all outstanding transactions. Any notice must be given in accordance with the notice provisions of Section 12 of the ISDA Master Agreement and any additional requirements set out in the ISDA Schedule, and any mandatory requirements for the service of notices should be strictly complied with.[9]

Once a notice designating an early termination date is effective, then:

---

9   The court in *Greenclose v National Westminster Bank* [2014] EWHC 1156 (Ch) found that Section 12(a) of the 1992 ISDA Master Agreement establishes an exclusive list of permitted methods of service; while the person sending the notice can choose between the prescribed methods set in the ISDA Schedule, it is limited to those specific methods of service.

- the early termination date will occur whether or not the relevant event of default or termination event is then continuing; and
- no further payments or deliveries are required to be made in respect of the terminated transactions (other than any early termination payments and interest thereon).

It should, however, be noted that, if it transpires that an event of default or termination event has not in fact occurred (or is not continuing) when the notice is given, then the notice will be invalid but will not of itself constitute a repudiation of the agreement.

Irrespective of the methodology being used to value the early termination amount, parties seeking to designate an early termination date should be aware that they will be required to determine the payments on early termination as soon as reasonably practicable or on a date commercially reasonable after the early termination date. To reduce the risk of challenge, it is prudent for parties, where possible, to be in a position to determine the early termination amounts on or soon after the designated early termination date.

4.3 Calculation of the early termination amount

Where derivatives transactions are terminated ahead of maturity, the early termination amount that becomes payable under the master netting agreement will necessarily be composed of the amounts that are already due and payable as well as the amounts that may have become due or payable had the transactions continued to maturity. Given that the nature of derivatives transactions is to shift the risk of fluctuations in the underlying variable from one party to another, the value of the individual transactions (and which party owes a net obligation to the other) will likewise fluctuate with the movements in the values of the underlying variable, and determining the value of these unascertained obligations will be among the most contentious parts of any close-out netting mechanism.

The ISDA Master Agreements provide for various methods for determining the early termination amount and it is important to establish which prescribed mechanism is to be used. The 1992 ISDA Master Agreement contains two methodologies – 'market quotation' and 'loss'[10] – and the parties elect which to apply in the related ISDA Schedule (typically in Part 1(f)). There is a further election in the 1992 ISDA Master Agreement as to whether the parties will use the 'first method' (where no early termination payment is required to be made to a defaulting party) or the 'second method' (where early termination payments are due irrespective of which party is in default). Lastly, where the market quotation methodology is specified, the 1992 ISDA Master Agreement provides a fall-back mechanism to the loss methodology where the determining party reasonably believes that the market quotation methodology would not produce a "commercially reasonable result". In

---

10   The terms defined in the ISDA Master Agreements are denoted by the use of single quotation marks when defined or used for the first time in this chapter. Thereafter, those terms are spelled without using any capital letters or punctuation marks, unless they appear in direct excerpts from the agreements.

the 2002 ISDA Master Agreement, there is only one prescribed method for determining the payments due on close-out – namely, the 'close-out amount' – and there is no provision for the election of the first method.

Market quotation: The market quotation methodology seeks to value the terminated transaction on the basis of what the determining party would have to pay (or would receive) for entering into a transaction with a market counterparty under the terms of which the determining party and the market counterparty would be required to make all payments and deliveries that would have been required to be made under the terminated transaction after the early termination date. Accordingly, the determining party is required to make the determination on the basis of quotations obtained in the market.

Notably, the quotations should be sought "on or as soon as reasonably practicable after the Early Termination Date" and should be provided "as of the same day and time (without regard to different time zones)", which should be selected in good faith to be a time which would permit a quotation to be given. The court in *Lehman Brothers Finance SA v Sal Oppenheim*[11] reaffirmed that it would be reasonable to delay getting quotations where illiquidity prevents the party from being able to receive live or actionable quotations on the early termination date. However, the court rejected an attempt by the determining party to rely on a retrospective valuation that preceded the early termination date.

Loss: The loss methodology requires the determining party to reasonably determine in good faith its total losses and costs (or gains) in connection with the terminated transactions. Generally speaking, it is the amount required to put the determining party in the position that it would have been in had the contract been performed.

Note that the loss should be determined as of the early termination date "or as soon as reasonably practicable thereafter". The court in *Fondazione Ensarco v Lehman Brothers Finance SA*[12] found that 'as soon as reasonably practicable' does not mean the same 'as soon as possible', and there are circumstances in which, notwithstanding that it is possible to get a quotation, it would not be reasonably practicable to do so (eg, in times of acute market illiquidity). It is possible that any contingency that occurs between the early termination date and the determination of the loss that would have affected the parties' rights and obligations under the terminated transactions can also be taken into account in determining the loss.

The courts have also considered that the market quotation and loss methodologies are intended to provide broadly the same result and that, if the market quotation methodology would produce a significantly different result, then it may be commercially unreasonable to use the market quotation methodology.[13] Parties should keep this in mind if they believe that the quotations provided would cause them to sustain a significant loss or to recover a significant windfall *vis-à-vis* the amount that would be determined under the loss methodology. Note also that

---

11   [2014] EWHC 2627 (Comm).
12   [2015] EWHC 1307 (Ch).
13   See *Peregrine Fixed Income Ltd v Robinson Department Store Public Company Limited* [2000] All ER (D) 1177.

the determining party is likely to be under a duty to act reasonably in mitigating its loss and should therefore not rely on the loss methodology to protect itself against unwinding hedge position at off-market prices.

Close-out amount: The close-out amount method is the sole methodology provided for in the 2002 ISDA Master Agreement. It is also imported into many 1992 ISDA Master Agreements through various multilateral protocols and bilateral agreements, so it is vital to establish whether any relevant 1992 ISDA Master Agreement is subject to such a protocol or agreement prior to initiating any valuation process.

The close-out amount method is intended to reflect the losses or costs (or gains) to the determining party under then-prevailing circumstances in replacing (or providing the economic equivalent of):

- the material terms of the terminated transactions (including the payments and deliveries that would have been required after the early termination date); and
- the option rights of the parties in respect of the terminated transactions.

The determining party is required to "act in good faith and use commercially reasonable procedures in order to produce a commercially reasonable result". Note that relevant information for determining any close-out amount may include:

- third-party quotations;
- relevant market data supplied by third parties; or
- quotations or market data generated from internal sources if such information is of the same type used by the determining party in regular course of its business for valuation of similar transactions.

The close-out amount should be determined as of the early termination date "or, if that would not be commercially reasonable, as of the date or dates following the Early Termination Date that would be commercially reasonable".

Where the market quotation methodology is specified under a 1992 ISDA Master Agreement (irrespective of whether there has been a fall-back to the loss methodology) or where a 2002 ISDA Master Agreement is used, the determining party must also determine the 'unpaid amounts'. Where the loss methodology is specified under a 1992 ISDA Master Agreement, account is already taken of these amounts in the determination of the loss.

4.4 Calculation statement

Section 6(d) of the ISDA Master Agreements requires that each party will provide the other party with a statement of its calculations. The statement is required to show the relevant calculations "in reasonable detail", including quotations obtained (and, in the case of the close-out amount method, any market data or information from internal sources used in making the calculations). The question of what qualifies as 'reasonable detail' was considered in *Goldman Sachs v Videocon*,[14] where the High

---

14   [2013] EWHC 2843 (Comm); [2014] EWHC 4267 (Comm).

Court held that simply stating that quotations have been obtained and illustrating the addition/subtraction of totals will not satisfy this requirement; instead, the determining party should show the quotations used, give details of the source(s), and either state what pricing model was used or demonstrate how it was used. The statement must also specify the amount that is due and (where applicable) give details of the account to which that amount is to be paid.

Other factors that a determining party may wish to consider when preparing the calculation statement (and, indeed, when carrying out its calculations) may include the following:

- including the termination currency in which the payment is to be made and details of any foreign exchange calculations made in respect of components of the termination payment denominated in currencies other than the termination currency;
- specifying the date on which the amount is due;
- including the calculations of the value of the credit support balance under any credit support annex and the resulting 'unpaid amount' or loss;
- including a statement of the realisation proceeds of posted collateral under any credit support deed and how these have been applied to the amounts owed (including accounting for any excess proceeds);
- specifying the interest accrued on unpaid amounts to the early termination date, the interest accrued on the early termination amount in the period from the early termination date to the date on which the amount is payable, and the relevant interest basis for the determination of interest after the due date for payment;
- including details of any amounts to be set off in respect of other obligations between the parties, including sufficient information to identify those obligations and any estimates used for amounts in respect of obligations that are not yet ascertainable; and
- including a statement of all expenses that are required to be indemnified pursuant to Section 11 of the ISDA Master Agreement.

5. An illustration of close-out netting

Having established the basis of close-out netting and the relevant provisions in the ISDA Master Agreement, it is worth briefly considering how close-out netting would operate in an insolvency scenario.

Party A and Party B enter into two physically settled commodity forwards under a market standard master netting agreement:

- Transaction 1 – on 1 January, Party A enters into a forward contract to buy 50,000 pounds of coffee beans from Party B with a settlement date of 15 March and a forward price of US$1.50 per pound.
- Transaction 2 – on 1 February, Party A enters into a forward contract to buy 500,000 pounds of sugar from Party B with a settlement date of 10 April and a forward price of US$0.25 per pound.

On 20 February, Party B enters into insolvency proceedings, triggering an event of default under the master netting agreement. Spot and forward prices for both coffee beans and sugar have moved since the transactions were entered into.

The early termination date occurs and both transactions are terminated at Party A's option (or automatically, if automatic early termination applies). Pursuant to the terms of the master netting agreement, the transactions are valued by Party A on a mark-to-market basis, where Transaction 1 yields an amount of £100,000 payable by Party A to Party B, and Transaction 2 yields an amount of £140,000 payable by Party B to Party A.

Close-out netting under the terms of the master netting agreement permits Party A to net the amounts such that it is left owing nothing to Party B, while it has a claim of £40,000 against Party B's estate (£100,000 minus £140,000). If the transactions were considered separate transactions and close-out netting did not apply under the master netting agreement, Party A would have had to pay the £100,000 owing under Transaction 1, while claiming for £140,000 against Party B's estate. Assuming that Party B's insolvency estate yields a dividend of 25%, the extent of Party A's losses in the close-out netting and the non-close-out netting scenarios would instead be as follows:

- where close-out netting applies, 75% of £40,000 = £30,000; and
- where close-out netting does not apply, 75% of £140,000 = £105,000, while also having had to settle its £100,000 liability.

In this simple scenario, applying close-out netting allows Party A to reduce its loss against Party B by an amount of £175,000 ((£100,000 + £105,000) minus £30,000).

Where this scenario is replicated thousands of times in distressed circumstances with exposures worth millions of dollars (eg, during the collapse of Lehman Brothers), it becomes clear how close-out netting can contribute to broader financial stability. Had Party A, and Party B's other counterparties, been subjected to losses on a gross basis, this would have an immediate knock-on effect, potentially pulling other counterparties into insolvency and throwing their respective counterparties into similar difficulties. (See further, paragraph 8 of this chapter relating to the special resolution regime for certain financial institutions.)

Of course, this is subject to the accommodation by the jurisdiction's laws of close-out netting provisions in insolvency scenarios and any other rights that may be granted to insolvency practitioners. For the purposes of the above illustration, it is important to note the following:

- Cherry-picking – notably, where close-out netting does not apply, the insolvency practitioner will be able to cherry-pick the profitable transaction (ie, Transaction 1 in this illustration), while disclaiming the unprofitable transaction (ie, Transaction 2 in this illustration). As considered further in paragraph 6.4 of this chapter, this may exacerbate the uncertainty of Party A's potential claim or liability at the time of Party B's insolvency, depending both on the actions of the insolvency practitioner and on any further movements in market prices.
- Insolvency set-off – were the close-out netting arrangements to fail in the case of these physically settled transactions, Party A would also not benefit

from insolvency set-off (which applies only to monetary obligations between two parties) and the transactions would likely be subject to termination on a gross basis. However, had the parties instead entered into two interest rate swaps, for example, then insolvency set-off would apply to Party A's benefit where close-out netting does not operate such that the transactions would be subject to termination on a net basis.

The section below considers further these and other rules that will apply to creditors and insolvency practitioners in an English law insolvency, and in particular how they may operate in the absence of effective close-out netting arrangements.

6. Enforceability of close-out netting under an English law insolvency

As demonstrated in the illustration above, it can be crucial from the relevant parties' perspective that the close-out netting process works in the event of the insolvency of the counterparty. In England, the general market view is that the common law supports the right of creditors to implement the close-out netting mechanism following the insolvency of an English counterparty. The enactment of the Banking Act 2009 (as extended by the Financial Services Act 2012)[15] and the Financial Collateral Arrangements (No 2) Regulations 2003[16] also puts netting with certain counterparties on a statutory footing.

When considering the insolvency analysis under English law, a number of items merit discussion in ensuring that close-out provisions will be enforceable as against an English company. The main ones among these are set out below with a consideration of how the close-out netting provisions in the ISDA Master Agreement operate.

6.1 The *pari passu* rule

As a cornerstone of English insolvency law, all unsecured creditors must share the available assets of the insolvent company equally in proportion to the debts due to those creditors, such that no one unsecured creditor is in a better position with respect to the assets of the insolvent company than any other unsecured creditor. Any provision of an agreement that has the effect of disposing of an insolvent party's property once the insolvency proceedings have commenced will be void. While there are certain exceptions – for example, creditors preferred by statute or dispositions that have been sanctioned by the court – public policy dictates that the *pari passu* rule must be the overarching principle.[17]

The courts have established that the *pari passu* rule invalidates arrangements that provide:

- for a creditor to receive more than its proper share of the insolvent party's available assets; or

---

15   The Banking Act 2009 provides for a special resolution regime for financial institutions in line with the European Bank Recovery and Resolution Directive (2014/59/EU). (See paragraph 8 of this chapter relating to the special resolution regime.)
16   The Financial Collateral Arrangements (No 2) Regulations 2003 implements the Financial Collateral Directive (2002/47/EC).
17   *Carreras Rothmans v Freeman* 1985 Ch 297.

- that debts due to the company on liquidation are to be dealt with other than in accordance with the statutory regime, notwithstanding that such arrangement may have been entered into in good faith for commercially justifiable reasons.[18]

Of course, and without detracting from the general principle, English courts recognise as enforceable a number of contractual mechanisms that are triggered upon the occurrence of the insolvency (distinct from what happens to the party's assets following the occurrence of the insolvency) – typical examples being the crystalisation of floating charges and the application of mandatory insolvency set-off (see paragraph 6.3 of this chapter relating to insolvency set-off).

In the context of the ISDA Master Agreement, the Court of Appeal in *Lomas v Firth Rixson* considered that the application of close-out netting would also not offend the *pari passu* principle. In coming to this conclusion, Lord Justice Longmore, handing down the judgment of the court, emphasised the distinction between, on the one hand, the underlying debt obligation that arises in accordance with the terms of the master netting agreement and, on the other hand, the related payment obligation to settle the debt obligation that arises pursuant to Section 2(a) of the ISDA Master Agreement. While the indebtedness occurs in the ordinary course of the transaction, the obligation to make a payment in respect of the indebtedness is subject to various conditions precedent including, importantly for the purposes of close-out netting, "the condition precedent that there is no Event of Default or potential Event of Default with respect to the other party has occurred and is continuing".

"Once one approaches the analysis on the basis that, under Section 2(a)(iii), one is only looking at the payment obligation, rather than the debt obligation, the whole machinery makes sense."[19] That is, notwithstanding that amounts continue to accrue giving rise to a debt obligation under the terms of the agreement, Section 2(a)(iii) prevents the debt obligation from becoming payable owing simply to the unfulfilled condition precedent, which payment obligation remains indefinitely suspended until the condition precedent is either waived or satisfied or if the early termination date occurs (at which point the early termination determinations will kick in pursuant to Section 6 of the ISDA Master Agreement; see paragraph 4 of this chapter). In effect, then, "Section 2(a)(iii) does not infringe the *pari passu* rule because it operates at most to prevent the relevant debt ever becoming payable. There is therefore no property which is capable of being distributed". (See further paragraph 6.2 of this chapter relating to the anti-deprivation principle.)

6.2 The anti-deprivation principle

Allied with the *pari passu* rule, the anti-deprivation principle intends to protect the value of the insolvent party's estate from attempts to evade the laws governing the

---

18   *Lomas v Firth Rixson.* See also *British Eagle International Air Lines Ltd v Cie Nationale Air France* [1975] 1 WLR 758.
19   Gloster J in *Pioneer Freight Co Ltd v TMT Asia Ltd* [2011] 2 Lloyds Rep 96, cited by Longmore LJ in *Lomas v Firth Rixson.*

insolvency by preventing the creditors of the insolvent counterparty from removing assets from the insolvent counterparty's estate to the detriment of the claims of the other creditors: "there cannot be a valid contract that a man's property shall remain his until his bankruptcy, and on the happening of that event shall go over to someone else, and be taken away from his creditors".[20] While the *pari passu* rule prohibits the distribution of assets after the occurrence of insolvency (irrespective of the trigger for the distribution, whether it was the counterparty's insolvency or any other termination event) – that is, it addresses "what happens in bankruptcy", the anti-deprivation principle applies only where the distribution is triggered by the counterparty's insolvency and that distribution deprives the insolvent counterparty's estate (and therefore its creditors) of property that would otherwise have formed part of it – that is, it addresses "what happens on bankruptcy".[21]

While this principle is deeply entrenched in English insolvency law, the litigation that followed the collapse of Lehman Brothers has revived interest in the anti-deprivation principle.[22] Recent case law has seen the courts nurturing the evolution of this principle by giving more weight to party autonomy to meet the demands of increasingly complex financial instruments,[23] while abstaining from finding that the anti-deprivation principle applies to "*bona fide* commercial transactions which do not have as their predominant purpose, or one of their main purposes, the deprivation of the property of one of the parties on bankruptcy".[24] The courts have declared that they will instead consider each transaction on its merits to see whether the contractual deprivation could be permissible as a "genuine and justifiable commercial response" to the consequences of the insolvency of a counterparty.

With respect to the ISDA Master Agreement, the courts have previously found that the function of the close-out netting provisions is to produce a net balance that is materially the same as the net balance that would be determined under the Insolvency Rules (as considered in paragraph 6.3 of this chapter), such that the estate of the insolvent company should receive fair value (determined under Section 6(e)) for the asset of which it is purportedly deprived (by the combined operation of Section 2(a)(iii) and Section 6(c)(ii)).[25] As such, and in so far as the relevant provisions cannot be said to have been drafted with the purpose of giving the non-defaulting party a disproportionate return as a creditor of the defaulting party, it is unlikely that the courts would consider the ISDA Master Agreement to offend against the anti-deprivation principle.[26] (See further paragraph 7 of this chapter relating to flawed asset arrangements and 'walk-away' provisions in the ISDA Master Agreements.)

6.3 Insolvency set-off

Set-off as a concept distinct from close-out netting was introduced in paragraph 3.1

---

20   *Ex p Jay, re Harrison* (1880) 14 Ch D 19.
21   *Belmont Park Investments Pty Ltd v BNY Corporate Trustee Services Ltd* [2012] 1 AC 383 (SC) (referred to here as the *Belmont* case).
22   See *Lomas v Firth Rixson*.
23   *Perpetual Trustee Company Limited v BNY Corporate Trustee Services Ltd* [2009] EWCA Civ 1160.
24   The *Belmont* case.
25   *Whitmore v Mason* (1861) 2 J&H 204; 70 ER 1031; *Borland's Trustee v Steel Bros & Co Ltd* [1901] 1 Ch 279.
26   *Lomas v Firth Rixson.*

of this chapter. Insolvency set-off involves applying amounts due between the insolvent debtor and a creditor where, before the debtor entered the relevant insolvency proceedings, there have been mutual dealings between them, so that the sums due from one party are set off against sums due from the other.[27] In England, the Insolvency Rules 1986 provide that insolvency set-off as it applies to eligible debts is mandatory, automatic and self-executing, such that no additional steps need to be performed by either of the parties and it is not possible to contract out of this. Importantly, insolvency set-off also applies where the claims have not been liquidated or are not contractually connected, and it is not necessary that the claims arise out of similar transactions or financial products.

However, there are two key limitations of insolvency set-off that affect derivatives transactions. First, the Insolvency Rules do not allow for delivery obligations to be taken into account – only sums due. This is of course of great importance where a transaction is to be physically settled in the absence of monetary obligations (commonly found with commodity derivatives transactions, such as in the illustration in paragraph 5 of this chapter).

Secondly, the Insolvency Rules provide that the insolvent company's insolvency practitioner, and not the non-defaulting party, will have the power to determine the value of any contingent obligations (which are central to many derivatives contracts, such as exchange-traded options). While this should not result in a materially different net balance, the valuation models and techniques and the timing of the determination by the insolvency practitioner may not match the valuation models and techniques and the timing of the determination in accordance with the ISDA Master Agreement. It is also notable that insolvency practitioners may lack the necessary resources and expertise to determine the value of contingent obligations properly – in particular in the case of highly structured derivatives transactions or in illiquid markets – and it may in practice be difficult to challenge the insolvency practitioner's determination.

Accordingly, a contractual approach that clearly governs how transactions are to be terminated and amounts netted on an insolvency is considered preferable to relying on the statutory rules, and it is important to ensure that this is not inconsistent with the application of insolvency set-off. In turn, after determining the early termination values and any unpaid amounts, those early termination values and unpaid amounts would be set off against any other sums due between the parties in accordance with the Insolvency Rules.

If, however, the contractual close-out netting provisions fail for any reason, then the Insolvency Rules would still apply to the individual transactions, albeit with the limitations outlined above.

6.4   Cherry-picking

English insolvency law permits the insolvency practitioner of an insolvent English company to require the performance by a counterparty of those transactions where

---

27   See Rule 2.85 (where a company enters into administration and administrator gives notice of intent to make distributions to creditors) and Rule 4.90 (where a company enters liquidation) of the Insolvency Rules.

the insolvent party is 'in the money', while disclaiming those transactions where the insolvent party is 'out of the money'.[28] In the absence of an effective close-out netting provision (or insolvency set-off), the counterparty would become an unsecured creditor of the insolvent party with respect to those individual transactions. The result would be that, while the insolvent company's estate recovers the full amount of its claim from the counterparty for the in-the-money transactions, the counterparty would likely receive just a fraction of its claim from the insolvent company for the disclaimed out-of-the-money transactions (see the illustration in paragraph 5 of this chapter).

However, under English law, an insolvency practitioner may disclaim only a whole (and not part only of a) contract[29] – that is, it cannot take the benefit of a contract without also taking the burden of it. To avoid the insolvency practitioner being able to cherry-pick individual transactions in these circumstances, master netting agreements such as the ISDA Master Agreement are purposely structured as a single agreement (see Section 1(c) of the ISDA Master Agreement), whereby all transactions entered into under it together form a single agreement comprising the master netting agreement, any schedule thereto and all confirmations evidencing transactions (if so evidenced, together with any other transactions – for example, collateral posted under a credit support annex), and which transactions, importantly, cannot be disclaimed individually.

A constituent part of the close-out netting provisions in the ISDA Master Agreement, Section 1(c) is key in allowing the parties to determine a single, net amount under Section 6(e) instead of the individual amounts that would otherwise have been payable (or receivable) under the separate transactions and thereby avoiding the insolvency practitioner's right to cherry-pick.

While some have raised concerns that the single agreement concept is a legal fiction and that each transaction should properly be considered as a distinct agreement, the courts have confirmed that "there is nothing artificial about the agreement of the parties... their agreement prescribes the substance of the legal relations into which they have freely chosen to enter".[30]

6.5 Multi-branch scenarios – special concerns

In the case of banks entering into transactions through branches located in countries outside their home country, close-out netting can be negatively impacted by ring-fencing. 'Ring-fencing' is when insolvency officials in another country treat a local branch's assets and liabilities as separate from those being adjudicated in the insolvent bank's home country. Even if cherry-picking among the local branch transactions is not permitted under local bank insolvency laws, the risk of ring-fencing is that a net profit on the branch transactions could be used to satisfy other creditors' claims against that branch. This would prevent the non-insolvent party from offsetting those profits against losses under other transactions with the

---

28   Section 178 of the Insolvency Act 1986.
29   *Re Bastable* [1901] 2 KB 518; *Re The Nottingham General Cemetery Co* [1955] Ch 683.
30   *BNP Paribas v Wockhardt EU Operations Swiss AG* [2009] EWHC 3116 (Comm).

insolvent bank and its other branches. If that happens, the non-insolvent party could be left seeking recovery from the insolvent bank of a loss that is actually greater than its contractual net claim under the multi-branch master netting agreement. By contrast, if the non-insolvent party's transactions with the local branch show a loss for the local branch, ring-fencing of that branch's transactions by its jurisdiction's insolvency authority should not cause a loss for the solvent party. Ring-fencing is primarily a concern when the branch transactions show either a profit or profits and losses that cannot be netted.

If a master netting agreement includes transactions with branches that do not qualify for close-out netting, then the netting of those transactions against qualifying transactions with branches located in jurisdictions where netting is effective may not be recognised. However, in these cases, close-out netting may be recognised for the qualifying transactions, provided that exposures under the non-qualifying transactions are managed on a gross basis. Nevertheless, as noted above, the non-insolvent counterparty could still be left seeking recovery from the insolvent bank of a loss that is actually greater than its contractual net claim under the multi-branch master netting agreement. This remains an inherent risk of doing business with a bank under a master netting agreement where its branch transactions can either be cherry-picked or ring-fenced, and counterparties should consider the issues carefully when doing so.

7. ISDA Master Agreement: flawed asset arrangements and walk-away provisions

7.1 Flawed asset arrangements

In order to mitigate the adverse consequences of insolvency laws, parties can attempt to introduce contractual 'flaws' in the assets granted to their counterparties to avoid being deprived of those assets on the counterparty's insolvency. For example, parties may seek to make certain contractual rights (eg, the right to receive payment of a debt obligation) conditional on the occurrence, or non-occurrence, of some event or circumstance, the failure of which condition would frustrate that right from becoming exercisable.

As considered above, Section 2(a)(iii) of the ISDA Master Agreement provides for the parties' payment obligations to be subject to "the condition precedent that no Event of Default or Potential Event of Default with respect to the other party has occurred and is continuing" and, where automatic early termination has not been activated, Section 6(a) gives the non-defaulting party the right (but not the obligation) to terminate the agreement following the occurrence of an event of default with respect to its counterparty.

Taken together, these provisions of the ISDA Master Agreement represent a typical flawed asset arrangement providing that, where an event of default has occurred with respect to a party, the non-defaulting party is within its rights both not to terminate the agreement and to refrain, potentially indefinitely, from making any further payments that would otherwise be owing to the defaulting party. Where the non-defaulting party is in the money, one would expect it to terminate the agreement and crystallise its claim against the defaulting party.

However, the indefinite option of inaction afforded by the combination of Section 2(a)(iii) and Section 6(a) is clearly very attractive where the non-defaulting party is out of the money and has a net liability to the defaulting party – and it is an option that many companies relied upon in the midst of the global financial crisis, giving rise to parallel litigation in New York and England to interpret Section 2(a)(iii) in accordance with local insolvency laws (each coming to markedly divergent conclusions, as discussed further in paragraph 7.3 of this chapter).

7.2   Walk-away provisions

Unlike a flawed assed arrangement that operates to prevent the asset ever properly vesting in the counterparty, a walk-away provision is one that allows a non-defaulting party to make lower payments than it would otherwise make, or no payment at all, to the defaulting party or its estate, even if the defaulting party would otherwise be a net creditor.

While there are no common law or statutory rules that specifically restrict the operation of walk-away provisions or otherwise prejudice those agreements that include walk-away provisions in an insolvency scenario, in the European Union, and in keeping with the Basel Accords,[31] the inclusion of a walk-away provision in a master netting agreement would disqualify the master netting agreement from being recognised as risk reducing for regulatory capital purposes,[32] and would also prohibit the relevant provision from being considered a 'close-out netting provision' under the Financial Collateral Arrangements (No 2) Regulations.[33] As such, the inclusion of walk-away provisions in agreements has fallen very much out of favour, especially with financial institutions that frequently rely on the beneficial treatment of close-out netting provisions in the context of regulatory capital requirements and financial collateral arrangements.

A typical walk-away provision appears in the 1992 ISDA Master Agreement where the parties select the first method for the purposes of Section 6, which provides that no early termination amount will be payable by the non-defaulting party to the defaulting party regardless of whether the defaulting party is in the money (also referred to as 'limited two-way payments'). This was also the default position under the 1987 ISDA Master Agreement, which provided for the defaulting party only (and not the non-defaulting party) to make payments on early termination. However, over time, the limited two-way payments option has become largely redundant owing to the evolving regulatory treatment of master netting agreements that contain a walk-away provision, and market participants now almost invariably opt for full two-way payments to apply, providing simply for amounts determined on early termination to be payable by the party that is out of the money to the party that is in the money, irrespective of which party is the defaulting party or the non-defaulting party. Observing the succession of the early termination provisions in

---

31   The Basel Accords comprise the recommendations on banking laws and regulations issued by the Basel Committee on Banking Supervision (acting under the auspices of the Bank for International Settlements) and have been broadly adopted globally by the G20 countries and regions.
32   Article 295(d) of the Capital Requirements Regulation (575/2013).
33   Article 12 of the Financial Collateral Arrangements (No 2) Regulations 2003.

various iterations of the ISDA Master Agreement, the shift in market opinion, in line with the global regulatory standards, is clear: while the 1987 ISDA Master Agreement allowed for limited two-way payments by default, the 1992 ISDA Master Agreement offered parties the opportunity to agree to use either the first method (limited two-way payments) or the second method (full two-way payments) and, in turn, the 2002 ISDA Master Agreement provides only for full two-way payments.

However, a walk-away provision may also appear in less recognisable forms and any provision reducing the payment by the non-defaulting party to the defaulting party should be considered carefully. While Section 2(a)(iii) of the ISDA Master Agreement (considered above) is not strictly speaking a walk-away provision in that it does not have a direct connection to the obligation to pay a net termination amount,[34] regulators around the globe have considered that the effect of this is sufficiently similar in nature to a walk-away provision that it merits closer review.[35] Notably, Section 2(a)(iii) represents a particular concern for regulators in insolvency scenarios where it may not be possible to cure the event of default (and, thereby, to satisfy the condition precedent to the payment obligations under the transactions), the result being that performance by the non-defaulting party of its obligations under the relevant transactions is permanently suspended allowing the non-defaulting party effectively to walk away from its liabilities. (See paragraph 7.3 of this chapter on Section 2(a)(iii) of the ISDA Master Agreement and the Lehman Brothers litigation.)

7.3 Section 2(a)(iii) of the ISDA Master Agreement and the Lehman Brothers litigation

As considered above, Section 2(a)(iii) of the ISDA Master Agreement has proven to be pivotal in determining whether the insolvent party's estate will be entitled to receive the early termination amounts that may otherwise be owing to it under the relevant master netting agreement, and it has recently been the subject of crucial litigation in New York and in England.

In a seminal case arising out of the Lehman Brothers bankruptcy, the US Bankruptcy Court for the Southern District of New York found that Section 2(a)(iii) constitutes an unenforceable *ipso facto* provision that operates to deprive the in-the-money insolvent party of its rights to receive payment under the agreement as a result of its insolvency, in contradiction with the bankruptcy safe harbour applicable to derivative transactions.[36] The judgment of the US Bankruptcy Court in effect forces the out-of-the-money non-defaulting party dealing with a counterparty subject to the Bankruptcy Code either:

---

34 Instead, it is simply a condition precedent to the payment of debts and, where the transactions are terminated ahead of maturity, the non-defaulting party will still have to make the full net payments to the defaulting party if the defaulting party is in-the-money (assuming that the parties have not agreed to use the first method in the 1992 ISDA Master Agreement).

35 See, for example, the United Kingdom HM Treasury consultation paper dated 16 December 2009 entitled *Establishing Resolution Arrangements for Investment Banks* (referred to here as the *UK Treasury Paper*, considered further below) and the Canadian Statutory Review of the Bankruptcy and Insolvency Act and the Companies' Creditors Arrangement Act 2014.

36 *In re Lehman Brothers Holdings Inc*, Case 08-13555 (JMP) (Bankr SDNY 15 Sept 2009) (*Metavante*).

- to keep the transactions and the master netting agreement in place and continue to make any scheduled net payments; or
- to elect to terminate the agreement and all relevant transactions within a reasonable period of time of the counterparty's insolvency (after the expiry of which reasonable period of time it will be deemed to have waived its right to terminate) and pay the net early termination amount to the insolvent counterparty.

The decision, effectively removing the indefinite option of inaction, turns very much on an interpretation of the Bankruptcy Code rather than purely on the impact of Section 2(a)(iii).

By contrast, as considered in paragraph 6.2 of this chapter, the courts in England in the parallel Lehman Brothers cases found that Section 2(a)(iii) is in fact a justifiable response to the commercial effects of the insolvency of a counterparty and the resultant indefinite option of inaction is a by-product of the balance struck between the parties.[37] The courts found that Section 2(a)(iii) protects the non-defaulting party from taking on additional credit risk where it performs its obligations, while the defaulting counterparty remains unable to meet its own. Given that the intention behind close-out netting provisions is to enable parties to manage and reduce their credit exposures arising from financial transactions, this interpretation stands to reason. Taking the example of an interest rate swap demonstrates the commercial justification behind this position, where (after the application of settlement netting) the non-defaulting party should not be obliged to continue to pay net amounts of the fixed leg of the swap where the insolvent counterparty is (and will likely continue to be) unable to satisfy any obligations that it may have over the course of the transaction to pay any net amounts of the floating leg of the swap.

That is, under English law, the fact that the defaulting party (which may be in the money) has no right to close out the agreement is considered to be the result of balancing the interests of a hypothetical non-defaulting party (which would otherwise have to pay net liabilities in full under a non-performing contract) and those of a hypothetical defaulting party (whose own net liabilities, in turn, would at best be met by a dividend from the insolvency estate): "The indefinite suspension of the payment obligation of the non-defaulting party (like any attempt to balance competing interests) may on one view be criticised as imperfect but it cannot be said to be uncommercial."[38] Accordingly, while the parties' respective rights would continue to accrue and net out, the defaulting party would not be able to enforce its right to be paid while the condition against it remained unsatisfied. That is, the debt obligation continues, while the related payment obligation is suspended (see also paragraph 6.1 of this chapter on the *pari passu* rule).

---

37   *Lomas v Firth Rixson*. In Australia, the courts had previously interpreted the ISDA Master Agreement in a manner consistent with the English courts (*Enron Australia Finance Pty Ltd (in liquidation) v TXU Electricity Ltd* (2003) 204 ALR 658).

38   *Lomas v Firth Rixson*.

7.4   Amendment to Section 2(a)(iii) of the ISDA Master Agreement

The judgments in the English courts and their disparity with the parallel case in the United States (including the apparent interpretation that Section 2(a)(iii) introduces a quasi walk-away provision into the ISDA Master Agreement) did not go unnoticed by national regulators, with the UK Treasury observing that Section 2(a)(iii) "was never intended to operate as a 'walk-away' clause and, until the recent financial crisis, it was normally assumed that the non-defaulting counterparty would, in virtually all cases, eventually terminate and close-out the outstanding positions". In particular, in light of the difficulties faced by the administrators of Lehman Brothers in England in recovering the net close-out value represented by those ISDA Master Agreements where counterparties relied upon Section 2(a)(iii) not to perform the outstanding transactions and also not to designate an early termination date with respect to them, the UK Treasury sought out the assistance of ISDA to encourage "the market to develop a solution that preserves any perceived benefit of Section 2(a)(iii) while providing sufficient certainty to the administrators as to the eventual timing of early termination and therefore realisation of the value of open transactions", emphasising that it would not rule out "further intervention (such as requiring bar dates) should the market fail to reach an adequate solution".[39]

In response, ISDA published a standard form of amendment in June 2014 to address the UK Treasury's concerns and to mitigate the effects of the indefinite option of inaction, which amendment may be adopted by parties on a bilateral basis. The amendment inserts a new provision (Section 2(f) in the 1992 ISDA Master Agreement and Section 2(e) in the 2002 ISDA Master Agreement), sub-section (iii) of which eliminates the condition precedent that no event of default has occurred and is continuing with respect to the counterparty on the 'condition end date', which occurs an agreed number of days negotiated by the parties (eg, 90 days) after a notice is given by the defaulting party to the non-defaulting party pursuant to the new sub-section (i) or (ii). If the event of default for which the notice was given is continuing on the condition end date, the out-of-the-money non-defaulting party can choose either to pay the deferred obligations to the defaulting party or to designate an early termination date under Section 6(a) of the ISDA Master Agreement and pay the net early termination amount to the defaulting party. The parallels between this amendment and the US Bankruptcy Court's judgment in *Metavante* are apparent.

While the amendment brings contractual certainty to market participants and appears to have appeased the UK Treasury, parties that wish to adopt the new provision need to agree actively either to include the new sub-section by amending their existing ISDA Master Agreements or to insert the relevant language into any future ISDA Master Agreements that they enter into. At present, there seems to have been a relatively limited uptake of the amendment by market participants and so parties will still have to fall back on the elaborate judicial interpretations where they have not incorporated it.

---

39   See the *UK Treasury Paper*.

8.   Special resolution regimes

8.1   The global financial crisis

Commentators have noted that the collapse of Lehman Brothers and the ensuing global financial crisis was exacerbated by counterparties closing out hundreds of thousands of derivatives transactions with the various Lehman Brothers entities, sending irreversible shockwaves through the financial markets and virtually assuring the failure of Lehman Brothers. As regulators across the globe sought to manage the fallout in the midst of the crisis, it became clear that their existing tools to prevent or tackle failures of systemically important financial institutions were insufficient. In particular, regulators lacked the power to suspend the rights of counterparties, which would allow the bank to be rescued before a run on its assets could take hold. As a result, and observing the impact of the collapse of Lehman Brothers, governments across the globe decided to use public funds to bail out a number of banks in order to stem contagion and effectively save the international financial markets from imploding.

National and international regulators and supervisory bodies have since committed huge levels of resource to addressing these issues, including the development of comprehensive bank recovery and resolution regimes (also known as 'special resolution regimes') applicable to systemically important financial institutions that are considered too big (or rather too important) to fail. According to the Financial Stability Board:

> *The objective of an effective resolution regime is to make feasible the resolution of financial institutions without severe systemic disruption and without exposing taxpayers to loss, while protecting vital economic functions through mechanisms which make it possible for shareholders and unsecured and uninsured creditors to absorb losses in a manner that respects the hierarchy of claims in liquidation.*[40]

In Europe, the 'Bank Recovery and Resolution Directive' (BRRD), published in June 2014, introduces a special resolution regime for the resolution of financial institutions within the European Union and aims to give national resolution authorities the necessary powers to manage failing financial institutions without prejudicing the broader financial market or economy. Notable among the tools brought in by the BRRD are statutory stays on parties' rights and obligations in a resolution scenario and 'bail in' rules to put creditors on the hook for losses incurred by the bank instead of national governments and taxpayers.

8.2   Statutory and contractual stays and the ISDA Protocols

The BRRD, transposed in the United Kingdom into the Banking Act 2009, introduces a statutory stay with respect to covered agreements entered into by certain financial institutions. In particular, it gives the Bank of England, as the national resolution authority, the power to suspend temporarily the termination rights of any counterparty to a covered derivatives master netting agreement with a covered bank, provided that the bank continues to perform its payment and other substantive

---

40   See 'Key Attributes of Effective Resolution Regimes for Financial Institutions', 15 October 2014.

obligations under the agreement. It further provides that a resolution action or a pre-resolution action by the Bank of England, the Prudential Regulation Authority, or the Financial Conduct Authority will not give rise to a counterparty's right to terminate a contract with the bank or to exercise its rights under any collateral arrangements.

While it is clear that these statutory stays, and parallel ones in other jurisdictions, would be enforceable within the jurisdiction as against the entities subject to the new regimes, there are concerns that the resolution authority's statutory powers under a special resolution regime would not be recognised in cross-border scenarios where one of the parties to an agreement (or indeed 'the agreement itself') is located outside the jurisdiction. The absence of the cross-border effectiveness of the statutory stay could severely undermine the effectiveness of the authority's resolution powers with respect to a failing institution.

In the absence of immediate legislative solutions that recognise the statutory regimes of other jurisdictions (which is a cumbersome and time-consuming process), regulatory authorities in various jurisdictions have, under a framework established by the Financial Stability Board, begun implementing rules requiring systemically important financial institutions established in their jurisdiction to obtain the consent of each of their counterparties (whether or not otherwise subject to that special resolution regime) for the prescribed statutory stays to apply to all relevant financial contracts between those parties. This has the effect of contractually recognising the resolution authority's statutory powers in the bilateral contracts, thereby avoiding any concerns that the statutory stays will not otherwise be enforceable.

In England, for example, the requirement to recognise contractually the statutory stays has been reflected in a change to the Prudential Regulation Authority rulebook,[41] the effect of which is that those financial institutions subject to the rules (as well as members of their global group) cannot enter into financial arrangements governed by the laws of a third country (ie, a country that is not a member state of the European Union) unless their counterparties enable them to meet the contractual stay recognition requirement. That is, notwithstanding that all of the compliance requirements under the new rules apply to the covered English entities only, the rules necessitate also the acknowledgment of compliance with the statutory stays by their counterparties.

With a view to minimising the administrative and operational burden of banks having to incorporate these contractual acknowledgments into all of their affected transactions on a bilateral basis, regulatory authorities from Germany, Japan, Switzerland, the United Kingdom, and the United States in November 2013 requested that ISDA revises the standard ISDA Master Agreements to incorporate these contractual stays for cross-border agreements to reflect the domestic statutory stays.

In response, ISDA (together with the Financial Stability Board and a working group of stakeholders) has since developed three multilateral protocols to which parties can adhere to incorporate the relevant contractual acknowledgments:

41   See Prudential Regulatory Authority Policy Statement PS25/15 'Contractual stays in financial contracts governed by third-country law', 13 November 2015.

- the ISDA 2014 Resolution Stay Protocol, now superseded in its entirety by the ISDA 2015 Universal Resolution Stay Protocol, is intended to be adhered to by the largest dealers in the market to recognise any statutory regimes that may apply to their counterparties (referred to here as the 'Original Protocols'); and
- the ISDA 2016 Resolution Stay Jurisdictional Modular Protocol is intended to be adhered to by all market participants on a case-by-case basis with respect to those specific statutory regimes that apply to them and their respective counterparties (referred to here as the 'JM Protocol').

While the Original Protocols, which were developed in advance of the final regulations in the relevant jurisdictions, contain relatively broad acknowledgements in their operative provisions to allow parties to recognise the special resolution regimes applicable to any of their counterparties that have also adhered to the Original Protocols, the operative provisions of the JM Protocol (as set out in the various 'jurisdictional modules') are intended to reflect the relevant regulatory requirements in the specified jurisdictions.

The JM Protocol is structured in two sections: the first containing the boiler-plate provisions that will apply to all adherants for the JM Protocol to operate, and the second constituted by the individual jurisdictional modules that will be tailored to the legal and regulatory requirements of a particular jurisdiction. This allows market participants to adhere separately to each jurisdictional module under the JM Protocol as it applies to that market participant (or its counterparty), rather than to adhere to the JM Protocol with respect to all jurisdictions. Note that the JM Protocol is designed to be a work in progress that is developed (by its jurisdictional modules) to allow market participants to comply with the relevant rules as they come into force in different jurisdictions. Notably, at the time of writing, the jurisdictional modules have been published with respect to the rules in the United Kingdom, Germany, and Japan only, with several others in the works.

By way of example, the UK Module, which was launched by ISDA at the same time as the JM Protocol, allows market participants to incorporate into their ISDA Master Agreements with other adhering market participants the relevant parts of the final rules published by the Prudential Regulation Authority without having to negotiate them bilaterally. That is, the institutions subject to the rules will be able to comply with them by adhering to the UK Module via the JM Protocol and then seeking parallel adherence by their counterparties (whether or not those counterparties would otherwise be subject to the rules). Those parties that are not be required to comply with the rules (either because they are not subject to the rules or because they do not trade with any counterparties that are subject to the rules) would not be obliged to adhere to the UK Module and subject themselves to the rules.

8.3   Bail-in and the ISDA Protocol

As considered above, the 2008 financial crisis required several failing financial institutions to be rescued by national governments (or 'bailed out'), with governments injecting funds into the institutions to bring them back to health and to ensure that the broader financial system remains intact. By contrast, 'bail-in' provides for the internal recapitalisation of a systemically important financial institution by writing-down its liabilities or by converting its liabilities into equity, thereby ensuring that shareholders and creditors shoulder the burden of re-capitalising the entity, as opposed to relying on external (typically, taxpayer) funds – or otherwise allowing the institution to fail, with the attendant consequences to the financial system – in a distressed scenario.

The BRRD provides that derivatives agreements should be subject to bail-in, but clarifies that it should not apply on a gross basis. That is, only the net early termination amount with respect to a master netting should be subject to bail-in – if the counterparty is a creditor with respect to a particular transaction but out of the money after the application of close-out netting under a master netting agreement, then that party will not be considered a creditor of the institution subject to the resolution regime for the purposes of bail-in.

Consequently, the BRRD (and the relevant transposing regulations) empowers the resolution authorities to terminate derivatives transactions and net them off against other transactions under a particular master netting agreement in order to apply the bail-in measures on a mandatory basis. While Article 49 of the BRRD (and the related regulatory technical standards) sets out the details of how derivatives liabilities are to be valued in the event of bail-in, it is unclear on the face of the BRRD whether the resolution authority has any discretion to move away from the valuation process specified in the relevant master netting agreement – instead, it is the UK implementation of Article 49 that clarifies that the valuation of derivatives transactions under a master netting agreement must be carried out in accordance with the terms of that agreement.

Note that, unlike the contractual recognition of the statutory stays considered above (which is not mandated by the BRRD, but is instead a policy pursued by the Financial Stability Board), Article 55 of the BRRD includes a contractual recognition requirement with respect to master netting agreements that are governed by a third-country law that may be subject to bail-in under the BRRD. Accordingly, ISDA has published the ISDA 2016 Bail-in Article 55 BRRD Protocol (referred to here as the Bail-in Protocol), which allows the relevant in-scope market participants to amend the terms of the affected master netting agreements efficiently on a multilateral basis to incorporate the requirements of Article 55 of the BRRD (and the related regulatory technical standards) as implemented in the relevant jurisdiction. In particular, where both parties to an affected agreement have adhered to the Bail-in Protocol, the parties:

- acknowledge and accept that certain liabilities arising under the master netting agreement may be subject to the relevant resolution authority's bail-in powers under the BRRD; and
- agree that they will be bound by the exercise of any bail-in power by the relevant resolution authority in respect of all transactions under the affected master netting agreement.

9.   Netting opinions

Lastly, it is worth noting that, with respect to the ISDA Master Agreements, ISDA commissions local law netting opinions with regard to the enforceability of the termination, bilateral close-out netting and multi-branch netting provisions of the 1992 and 2002 ISDA Master Agreements, and the opinions are updated annually. At the close of 2016, ISDA had received netting opinions from law firms in almost 60 jurisdictions, with a number of others commissioned.[42] Several other industry organisations commission similar opinions for other market standard master netting agreements for their members.[43]

Review of these opinions is crucial for market participants for several reasons:

- to ensure that financial counterparties can attain beneficial regulatory capital treatment for derivatives contracts pursuant to the Basel Accords;
- to ensure that parties can effect the close-out netting process in the relevant jurisdictions where their counterparties are based without offending local insolvency laws;[44] and
- to determine whether or not parties can calculate mandatory margin requirements on a net basis.[45]

Where an industry standard netting opinion does not exist with respect to a particular jurisdiction, market participants may be inclined (or required) to seek comfort themselves that close-out netting would be effective so as to ensure they can continue to trade with counterparties in those other jurisdictions.

---

42   See www2.isda.org/functional-areas/legal-and-documentation/opinions/.
43   For example, by the International Capital Market Association with respect to the Global Master Repurchase Agreements.
44   If not, parties should consider specifying that automatic early termination will apply with respect to the party incorporated in the non-netting-friendly jurisdiction.
45   While certain jurisdictions (including the European Union, Australia, Hong Kong and Japan) have proposed exemptions from the mandatory margin requirements for trades with counterparties established in non-netting-friendly jurisdictions, the final margin rules published by the Prudential Regulators in the United States do not allow for such exemptions.

Overview of industry standard documentation

Guy Usher
Fieldfisher

In this chapter, we identify a selection of structural and sometimes neglected issues which arise when industry standard documentation is used for over-the-counter (OTC) derivatives, as well as repurchase agreement (repo) and stock lending (or, collectively, 'securities financing'). We deliberately include no product-specific issues; nor do we go into depth on netting or collateral, which are the subject of separate chapters. However, we hope that there will be food for thought for the seasoned documentation negotiator, as well as plenty to digest for the uninitiated.

1. OTC derivatives documentation

1.1 Background

In the OTC derivatives market, the well-established international standard in documentation is that published by the International Swaps and Derivatives Association Inc (ISDA) (formerly, the International Swap Dealers Association).

ISDA embodies the efforts of a small group of swap dealers that, in 1983, identified the need to collaborate and coordinate on documentation for OTC derivatives. ISDA itself was formally established in 1985 with the primary aim of achieving standardisation in the inter-dealer market for transactions in interest rate and currency swaps. Until that time, swap dealers had each developed their own forms of contractual agreement which contained all the necessary contractual terms, and had to be individually checked and negotiated between each dealer in the market. As trading volumes increased, this became unworkable and a solution had to be found.

The first ISDA publication was the 1985 Code of Standard Wording, Assumptions and Provisions for Swaps (reissued in 1986 in a more enduring form). The Swaps Code effectively constituted a set of provisions and definitions for interest rate and currency swaps, as well as the non-transaction specific (relationship) terms which are now found in master agreements. While the Swaps Code was an impressive document at the time, and is the cornerstone of all subsequent publications, the embedding of transaction-specific terms together with provisions which documented the relationship between the parties was ultimately not an optimal solution. The Swaps Code was therefore followed in 1987 by the first forms of master agreement and definitions booklet. Things have come a long way since then, but this basic framework has persisted to this day. The timeline below picks out some key milestones in the development of ISDA documentation.

1985/6	The Swaps Code – interest rate and currency swap terms, as well as close-out provisions and other relationship terms
1987	The Interest Rate Swap Agreement and the Interest Rate and Currency Exchange Agreement – the first stand-alone master agreements The Interest Rate and Currency Exchange Definitions – the first set of stand-alone definitions and forms of confirmation (for interest rate and currency swaps)
1989/90	Cap and Option Addenda to the Interest Rate and Currency Exchange Definitions – extending the 1987 definitions to cover caps, collar and floors and options/swaptions. This also introduced suggested wording to change limited two-way payments to full two-way payments (more on this below)
1992	Local Currency Single Jurisdiction and the Multicurrency – Cross Border Master Agreement – the latter superseded the 1987 Interest Rate and Currency Exchange Agreement and is still in use today Confirmations for OTC Equity Index and Bond Option Transactions – the first long-form confirmations, created in response to market demand for these developing products Foreign Exchange and Currency Option Definitions – an established and mature product, but new to the ISDA documentation framework
1994	New York Law Credit Support Annex (CSA) – this enabled the market to expand in terms of trade volumes, and the types of counterparty that could participate in the derivatives market, and was a response to the greater focus on exposures and credit management. Like the period before the development of the master agreements, previously participants had produced their own forms which were unwieldy and required heavy checking/negotiation Equity Definitions – the equity derivatives market had matured sufficiently to warrant its own set of definitions Amendment to the 1987 Master Agreements to provide for full two-way payments
1995	English Law CSA and Credit Support Deed (CSD)

continued on next page

1996	British Bankers' Association Interest Rate Swaps and Forward Rate Agreement Bridges – a new method of extending coverage of the master agreements (and hence the scope of netting) to embrace more products from other, established markets and bring them within the ISDA framework Non-reliance Wording – standardised wording reflecting the diversification of players and increased risks of claims as a result
1998	European Monetary Union Protocol – a groundbreaking, multilateral contracting solution in an OTC (bilateral) environment to address the market issues/uncertainty thrown up by the introduction of the euro. The protocol approach has since been followed as a solution to fix large-scale documentation issues on many different occasions

The timeline is selective. Indeed, many of these publications have themselves since been superseded by updated versions. The purpose of the timeline is simply to illustrate the types of documentation solution which have developed and the evolution of the earliest products. Later products, of which there are many, have largely followed the same developmental path – long-form confirmation when the product first develops, followed by a set of transaction definitions once the market for the product is more mature.

1.2 ISDA documentation structure

The structure of the ISDA documentation at the relationship and transactional levels is illustrated in the diagram on the following page.

The rest of this chapter looks at selected structural issues arising from the documentation in the standard structure set out above. However, before doing that, let us consider some of the reasons for developing standardised documentation in the OTC derivatives market.

1.3 Why standardised documentation?

Other capital markets, including the loan and bond markets, have not expressed the same need to have such prescribed terms. There exists some standard documentation (eg, for syndicated loans and for commercial paper) and some standard or recommended provisions (eg, the International Capital Market Association recommended wording for bond issues), but generally the documentation tends to be more individually drafted and negotiated for each borrower/issuer and lender/dealer. So why are OTC derivatives different? There are a number of reasons for this.

Aside from the practical imperative of being able to document the legal terms of large numbers of transactions quickly (which should not be understated), certain significant fundamental differences between the loan and bond markets on the one hand, and the OTC derivatives markets on the other, warrant particular mention.

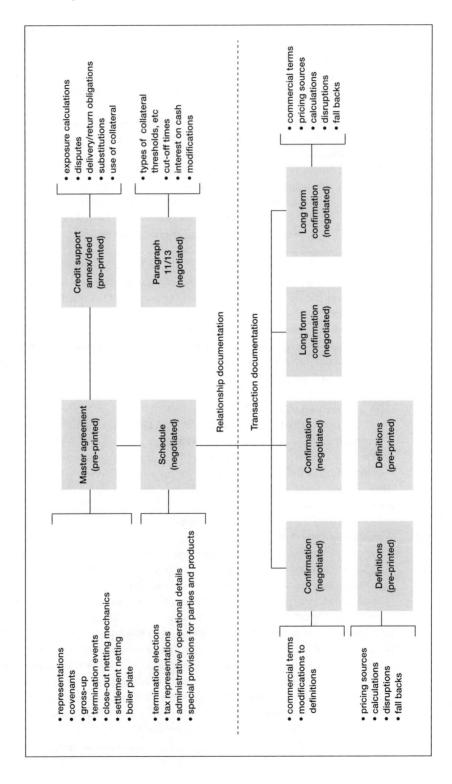

(a) Commonality of interests

The first is that loans and bonds are largely one-way obligations where the lender/dealer negotiates for one position and the borrower/issuer negotiates for the other. Lenders/dealers are infrequently borrowers/issuers at the same time. They instead have polarised positions. Derivatives are different. One transaction is capable of being an asset for one party at one time and a liability for that same party at another time as the transaction's value changes over time. Many transactions also involve several payments or deliveries being made by each party to the other at different times throughout the term of the transaction. Even with one-way transactions (eg, fully paid options), there might be multiple transactions of that type at any times where one party is a buyer and the other is a seller, and so between the same parties there may still be transactions which represent both assets and liabilities. In each case, there is therefore usually a commonality of interest between the parties involved: provisions which work for one party at one time would, or might, apply equally against it at another.

(b) Liquidity and pricing

An OTC derivative is priced based on the expectation, as at the trade date, of the future benefits that the transaction is expected to provide. This involves a projection as to future changes in rates and prices. This is one reason why, in an immature OTC derivatives market, transactions are typically traded on a matched-book basis, with the swap dealer simply placing itself between two parties which each require or desire the opposite in terms of protection/exposure to the underlying. As the market grows, swap dealers will take and hold unmatched positions and manage the risk on their books on macro basis through approximate or partial hedges from other unmatched (but economically reverse) positions. Swap dealers inevitably also have, or choose to keep, exposure to the relevant market which they can trade and make a profit (or a loss) for their own account.

One reason why this can happen more easily is that a market in a mature product will have an established, consistent pricing methodology. This means that a swap dealer knows that it can find someone to enter into transactions at a price within its expectations and is itself able to provide prices for transactions without reference to the pricing (or precise terms) of a specifically matched transaction. Standardisation of trade term documentation is essential in achieving pricing transparency (and hence liquidity), as it provides consistent terms against which prices can be calculated and quoted.

(c) Clearing, trade execution and information

Following the 2007/2008 financial crisis there has been a regulatory-driven push to move OTC derivatives transactions towards a centrally cleared model. We have seen this under the Dodd–Frank Wall Street Reform and Consumer Protection Act (Dodd-Frank) in the United States and Regulation 648/2012 on OTC derivatives, central counterparties and trade repositories (EMIR) in Europe.

Transactions can be cleared only if they are on identical terms and the central counterparty to the transaction is comfortable that these terms are sufficiently standardised that it can value and risk-manage its clearing members and its entire portfolio of transactions.

The same applies to the requirement to trade certain OTC derivatives on regulated markets or trading venues.

Another post-crisis regulatory initiative has been to require significant reductions in the time within which firms must confirm OTC derivatives transactions. Standardisation of trade terms enables this to happen without delays to trading, while documentation is negotiated.

(d)   ***Close-out netting and collateral***

The effect of default/insolvency of one party in derivatives transactions is very different from that in the bond and loan markets, where it is simply a question of accelerating the (one-way) obligation owed by the borrower/issuer to the lender/investor. By its (forward) nature, the value of a derivative is constantly changing with the value of the underlying and other variables. In the case of an interest rate swap, for example, the pricing of that derivative will change as interest rates change. In fact, it is not the actual change in interest rates which causes the derivative's value to change, but the change to the 'forward curve' for interest rates (ie, the market's prediction of when and how rates will change at relevant future times in the context of the remainder of the term of the interest rate swap).

This feature of derivatives is not be as significant if a derivatives transaction (once originally priced and entered into) takes its full course; but if the transaction does not run to its maturity because one party defaults, the position is very different. The non-defaulting party is suddenly open to the market risk that was previously covered by that derivative. The only way that the non-defaulting party can restore itself to the position that it was in before the default is to enter into a new derivative to replace the defaulted transaction. The price of entering into the replacement derivative on the same terms as the remainder of the original transaction will inevitably involve the non-defaulting party either:

- having to pay someone to enter into what is now an off-market transaction; or
- receiving an amount of money for so doing.

Whether it is a payment to or by the non-defaulting party will depend on whether the value of the derivative which has defaulted has moved against or in favour of the non-defaulting party.

The value of each derivative outstanding between the same two parties will also fluctuate. At any one time, some transactions may be positive and others negative in terms of value. The master agreement contains a mechanism to deal with this situation. Indeed, it is called a 'netting agreement' because it provides for offsetting these negative and positive values. Without the ability to net exposures on positions in this way, the potential loss to a party in the case of a default of the other could be as much as the sum of the transactions which have value to the non-defaulting party (which might ultimately yield zero recovery in the worst case), and it could conceivably have to pay out on those transactions, which have value to the defaulting party. This can arise due to the application of bankruptcy laws to the defaulting party, which are mandatory and can therefore override the contractual provisions. So dealers need to know with some certainty the size of the loss that they could suffer if their counterparty were to default at any time.

Derivative dealers typically are regulated entities and certain specific requirements apply to them in relation to capital that they need to cover for losses that they might suffer, including on their derivatives positions. The contingent liabilities (contingent as they arise only on a default) to which derivatives can give rise require capital cover as prescribed by the relevant regulatory rules. Since the introduction of the 1988 Basel Capital Accord (known as 'Basel I'), which sets down the agreement among the G10 central banks to apply common minimum capital standards to their banking industries (and as still embodied in Basel III), in order for a dealer in a G30 country to be able to recognise risk reduction through offsetting negative against positive positions in OTC derivatives transactions, there is a requirement to have a written netting agreement in place, and for firms to be confident that it will be enforceable upon a bankruptcy of its counterparties. This means that it needs to have legal opinions to that effect. Standardised documentation means that each bank or swap dealer does not individually have to obtain its own legal opinions on each and every netting agreement that it has with each counterparty in order to be able to calculate its capital requirement on a net basis. Instead, as long as its netting agreements are based upon the standard ISDA forms, it can rely on the standard industry netting opinions.

The same requirement applies in order for banks and swap dealers to recognise collateral as an effective risk mitigation technique for capital purposes against the net exposure that it has to any counterparty. Again, this leans heavily toward standardised collateral documentation (eg, the ISDA CSA), which is then backed by standard industry legal opinions published by ISDA.

1.4   ISDA Master Agreements
Three versions of ISDA Master Agreement are used in the global market:
- the 1987 Master Agreement (the Interest Rate and Currency Exchange Agreement);
- the 1992 Master Agreement (the Multicurrency Cross-Border version); and
- the 2002 Master Agreement.

While most newly originated agreements are based on the 2002 Master Agreement, legacy documents already in place mean that usage of the 1992 Master Agreement is probably still as common as the 2002 Master Agreement. There are very few 1987 Master Agreements in use today.

Each published master agreement has essentially the same structure and provisions. It consists of a pre-printed form (or 'front end') and a schedule, in which various elections and changes are made to the front end.

The schedule itself is divided into parts. The first four parts follow a standard layout. It is Part 5 that typically contains most of the departures from the standard front end; these will be a mixture of provisions that the entities themselves wish to see and those that are relevant to, or required by or for, counterparties of a particular type (eg, insurance companies or investment funds).

Provisions which apply generally to transactions of a particular type may, if appropriate, be added as further (non-standard) parts of the schedule. These might include:

- provisions for foreign exchange transactions (in order to facilitate shorter-form or electronic confirmations for those transactions);
- provisions for contracts for difference on equities, which are often formulated in a particular way to suit the trading systems developed by a particular broker-dealer; and
- provisions setting out standard disruption events and fall-backs for particular types of transaction, such as commodity derivatives (so that these are pre-prescribed).

Any guarantees or similar documents are separate, but are listed in the schedule so that the events of default in the master agreement also apply to these documents and the providers of them.

Common features of every ISDA Master Agreement are:

- coverage, inconsistency and single agreement provisions;
- a condition to payment provision (more of which below);
- provisions for settlement netting, with certain options available;
- basic representations and covenants, primarily as to the provision of documents and information specified in the schedule;
- tax representations, a and an agreement to provide any necessary tax forms;
- a tax gross-up provision, conditional on any tax representations given being correct;
- 'events of default' and 'termination events';
- 'close-out' calculation mechanics; and
- 'back end' – that is, provisions relating to matters such as:
  - notices;
  - default interest; and
  - law and jurisdiction.

It is important to remember that the ISDA Master Agreements do nothing on their own. If there are no transactions outstanding, then there is nothing for the master agreement to bite on or apply to.

So what is different between the different forms of master agreement? How have they evolved? All three share the features described above, so it is helpful to distinguish later master agreements from earlier ones.

(a)   *1992 Master Agreement v 1987 Master Agreement*
The big driver for replacing the 1987 Master Agreement related to the close-out mechanics and netting. A close second was the fact that the 1987 Master Agreement really only contemplated cash-settled transactions – there was no reference to physical deliveries being made. There are few other differences of note.

In terms of close-out netting, the main differences were the addition of the 'loss' method of determining the close-out amount and the change from limited two-way payments (a provision which allows a non-defaulting party not to have to pay a close-out amount to a defaulting party and which was embedded in the 1987 Master Agreement) to an ability to select two-way payments under the 1992 Master Agreement. This latter change was made in response to the fact that a limited two-way payments provision was, and still is, regarded as a 'walk-away' clause and the presence of such a provision means that net reporting of exposures is not permitted for capital adequacy purposes.

(b)   ***1992 Master Agreement v 2002 Master Agreement***
The main driver for the publication of the 2002 Master Agreement was a practical difficulty which had been experienced when implementing close-outs under the 1992 Master Agreement in certain situations. Many market participants preferred market quotation to loss as the termination calculation measure under the 1992 Master Agreement, as the latter was considered to be too subjective. Equally, however, significant practical problems had been experienced in actually obtaining the required quotations in the case of some of the well-known and major collapses that had occurred. While market quotation will ultimately fall back to loss, that does not negate the problem of having to go through the process of seeking the tradable quotes required by market quotation, which can take a considerable amount of time where many trades are outstanding. As it turned out, in the Lehman bankruptcy a number of parties also experienced some unexpected outcomes when using the loss methodology.

The solution adopted in the 2002 Master Agreement is a hybrid termination measure comprising a methodology which does not require actual quotations for replacement transactions, but enables the non-defaulting party to use indicative quotations and public or internal pricing sources in order to determine its loss (or gain) in respect of a terminated transaction, albeit by reference to external sources where available. In the 2002 Master Agreement, this is the 'close-out amount" methodology.

While there is no reason to think that the close-out amount methodology ought not to be enforceable, there is perhaps greater scope to challenge what is due on termination under a 2002 Master Agreement than in the case of market quotation or, indeed, loss, as there are both objective requirements (reference to prevailing market rates and a requirement to act reasonably) and subjective elements (because, at the end of the day, a close-out amount is still the actual loss/gain). Given that a bankruptcy official of a defaulting party is likely to be less conversant than the insolvent party itself with the intricacies of the derivatives transactions and markets, it is not unreasonable to expect it to require either objective evidence of market prices (back to market quotation, therefore) or evidence of actual losses (back to loss) before allowing claims in the bankruptcy.

Notwithstanding these potential issues, in the run-up to the Lehman Brothers default, a number of major banks and broker-dealers were concerned about the implications of having to use market quotation as the close-out methodology in the

1992 Master Agreements between them, in case one of them defaulted. So much so that, in August 2008, these banks entered into a multilateral agreement which adopted the 2002 Master Agreement close-out amount methodology in place of either selected methodology in any 1992 Master Agreements which existed between them.

Subsequently, ISDA published a protocol to enable adhering parties to elect for a similar 'upgrade' of their 1992 Master Agreements.

Three other changes from the 1992 to the 2002 Master Agreements are worthy of mention.

The first is the introduction of a multi-layered default interest regime. The intricacies of this are many, but the most substantive change relates to default interest. As a number of market participants facing a bankrupt Lehman discovered to their surprise, under the 1992 Master Agreement the obligation to pay interest on a termination payment due to a defaulting party is based on the defaulting party's cost of funds, which can be very high if that party is bankrupt at the time. These and other wrinkles were ironed out in the 2002 Master Agreement.

Another difference is the introduction of the concept of *'force majeure'*. The 2002 Master Agreement provides for a 'termination event' if a party is prevented from performing obligations due to *force majeure*. While in principle this may sound sensible, no definition or further clarification of the term *'force majeure'* is given.

'Force majeure' is not a term of art under English law, unlike in certain other jurisdictions. Instead, in the absence of a specifically agreed definition, it is a court that ultimately has to determine what it means in the context in which it is used. In the context of OTC derivatives transactions, it may be unclear what exactly might constitute *force majeure*, especially around the edges. As most sets of published ISDA definitions now deal with anticipated transaction-specific issues (eg, potential settlement disruptions), the *force majeure* concept at the master agreement level is presumably intended to apply more to 9/11-type situations or systemic problems, rather than to localised problems at the individual-transaction level. The potential issue with introducing a *force majeure* concept on an undefined basis is that the parties (at least to a 2002 Master Agreement) may simply not know whether a close-out has occurred in a given situation.

Let us consider one possible scenario. A party defaults. The other party claims that close-out has occurred and enters into replacement transactions to eliminate market risk on the transactions with the defaulted counterparty. The defaulted party then says that the default in question was beyond its control so that *force majeure* applies and the close-out did not occur – at least not at that time. What does the non-defaulting party do? Reverse the replacement transactions and enter into a series of options on the underlying derivatives until the matter is determined? Waiting for a court to determine whether force majeure had occurred is clearly not the answer.

Another change from the 1992 to the 2002 Master Agreement is the reduction of grace periods, particularly in the case of a failure to make a payment or delivery under a transaction or to transfer collateral under an English law CSA. The 2002 Master Agreement's shorter grace periods may have initially been regarded as less end-user friendly. However, end users these days are often equally concerned about broker-dealer defaults, given market events since 2007.

(c)   Structural points on master agreements

Two unrelated structural points are worth mentioning, neither of which is a standard ISDA election and both of which would apply regardless of which form of master agreement is used.

The first is the incorporation of ISDA definitions into the master agreement – not an uncommon practice. On the face of it, this seems sensible and is almost invariably the practice in some markets (eg, foreign exchange markets). You will almost certainly want the updated definitions to apply to any transactions entered into after the change takes effect (or rather after the new definitions are in use, which can be later than their publication), but do you want the replacement definitions to alter the terms of existing transactions (which may be long-dated and may have been specifically hedged or may have hedged a particular asset or liability)? Do the incorporation provisions deal with updates and supplements to definitions clearly? If they do intend to update automatically, both parties must be sensitive to the changes made. If they do not, then parties must be able to recognise which transactions are subject to which set of definitions. Not all changes are well known or well remembered. The change from non-automatic to automatic exercise for swaptions from the 1991 to the 2000 ISDA Definitions is a good example.

The second point to highlight concerns Section 2(a)(iii) of the ISDA Master Agreements. The simple point is that, under all of the ISDA Master Agreements, a non-defaulting party has the choice either to:

*   close-out where a default occurs; or
*   allow the transactions to subsist, but simply rely on Section 2(a)(iii) and stop making payments or deliveries (including the transfer or return of collateral under an English law CSA).

In many instances the existence of this right may not colour the non-defaulting party's decision as to whether to terminate its transactions. But what if the non-defaulting party has a significant liability at the time, thereby requiring it to make a payment to the defaulting party by virtue of the early termination? It could be better for the non-defaulting party not to terminate in this situation. Irrespective of the (net) termination values of the transactions, the non-defaulting party could also rely on this provision in order to refuse to make its contractual payments and deliveries, while insisting that the defaulting party makes its own. That is what each of the 1987, 1992 and 2002 Master Agreements provide for. There are polarised opinions on the wider implications of this particular provision and it has come under some scrutiny and criticism in the courts[1] and by regulators.[2] We now know that Section 2(a)(iii) is enforceable as a matter of English insolvency law.[3] However, it appears that Section 2(a)(iii) cannot be relied upon against a party subject to US bankruptcy proceedings.[4]

1   See *Enron Australia v TXU Electricity* [2003] NSWSC 1169, an Australian court decision; *Marine Trade SA v Pioneer Freight Futures Co Ltd* [2009] EWHC 2656 (Comm), an English court decision.
2   See UK HM Treasury consultation paper of December 2009, "Establishing Resolution Arrangements for Investment Banks".
3   *Lomas v JFB Firth Rixson Inc* [2012] EWCA 419.
4   *In re Lehman Brothers Holding Inc* No 08-13555 (SDNY 17 September 2009), known as the Metavante case.

1.5   CSAs/CSD

The ISDA credit support documents are central to most trading relationships in OTC derivatives and many participants simply could not, or would not, trade (at least to significant levels) without these risk management tools. So what types of credit support document are there and what are the differences between them?

Ignoring local law variants, there are:

- the New York Law CSA – this assumes collateral and exposures to be denominated in US dollars and, as is allowed under New York law, permits/provides for the outright transfer of collateral, as well as the creation of a security interest;
- the English Law CSA – this contemplates that the parties elect a base currency, but allows for collateral to be posted in other currencies as well. It provides for the outright transfer of collateral without any security interest being created (so that security perfection issues do not arise); and
- the English Law CSD – this differs from the English Law CSA in that it creates a security interest. As a consequence, the security perfection requirements need to be considered in applicable jurisdictions. However, unlike the English Law CSA, the CSD can be used to eliminate or reduce the risk of the collateral provider from a default of the collateral receiver. The CSD was rarely used before the financial crisis, but its use has increased since then with the risks associated with over-collateralisation (especially where there is initial margin posted) becoming as much of an issue as under-collateralisation. The recent rules on the margining of uncleared swaps under Dodd-Frank and EMIR have also meant increased use of CSDs for the same reason.

Unlike the New York Law CSA and the English Law CSD, the English Law CSA is not strictly speaking a credit support document under the ISDA Master Agreement; rather, it is structured as a transaction under the ISDA Master Agreement. Certain points are worth noting as a consequence of this structure.

The first is that, in terms of netting 'efficacy', the close-out netting provisions also need to be enforceable in context of the transaction which is the obligation to transfer (and retransfer) collateral. Accordingly, if the parties want to be sure that any collateral provided will not need to be returned by the collateral receiver to the collateral provider on a default (except as excess), the collateral receiver must be satisfied that close-out netting under the ISDA Master Agreement will not be adversely affected by the inclusion of the credit support annex as a transaction. By extension, if it is necessary to have legal opinion coverage of transactions under the ISDA Master Agreement for the efficacy of close-out netting for capital adequacy purposes, then that requirement applies equally to the transaction constituted by the English Law CSA.

A development of this is that the English Law CSA is really suitable for use only with an English law-governed ISDA Master Agreement, as otherwise there could be a transaction (ie, the credit support agreement) governed by laws different from those governing the master agreement. While it might not be fatal to do this, the ISDA legal opinions on netting and collateral do not contemplate mixing the governing laws in this way.

By virtue of the English Law CSA being a transaction, a failure to pay or deliver collateral under such credit support annex is, without modification, subject to the standard grace period for a failure to pay or deliver an event of default in the ISDA Master Agreement (ie, three local business days in the case of a 1992 Master Agreement, or one local business day in the case of a 2002 Master Agreement). As the New York Law CSA is a credit support document for the purposes of the ISDA Master Agreement, the grace period for failures to pay or deliver collateral under it is two local business days, whichever master agreement it relates to, as (like the CSD) this relies on the credit support default event of default (which has no grace period in itself).

1.6   Bridges and cross-product netting

In terms of the credit risk mitigation effect deriving from netting close-out, it is clearly beneficial in a default situation to be able to net down as many positive and negative trading positions against each other as possible. While this applies not only to derivatives, it is particularly relevant to them because of their peculiar characteristics mentioned earlier in this chapter.

We have also seen that the types of transaction which can be documented under an ISDA Master Agreement have expanded and continue to do so in terms of both new product markets and existing products being brought within the ISDA documentation framework.

This can be achieved in various ways using the ISDA documentation framework:

- through the creation of a set of definitions for transacting in established market products. The 1998 Foreign Exchange and Currency Option Definitions are one example. Both in London and in other markets, there were already market standard terms for foreign exchange transactions, but these were typically not documented under the ISDA Master Agreement umbrella before the definitions were published;
- through the publication of transaction-type bridges. The 1996 British Bankers' Association Interest Rate Swaps and Forward Rate Agreement Bridges are an example where interest rate transactions and forward rate transactions based on the British Bankers' Association standard terms were brought under the ISDA Master Agreement umbrella. In that case, the commercial terms of the transactions were still based on the association's terms, but the close-out netting terms in the ISDA Master Agreement applied instead of the equivalent British Bankers' Association terms; and
- through the publication of master agreement bridges. The 2001 Cross-agreement Bridge provides for net amounts calculated under other (non-ISDA) master agreements to be brought into the ISDA Master Agreement close-out netting regime, so that the ISDA Master Agreement effectively sits on top of those other master agreements and effectively offsets the net amounts under each underlying netting agreement against each other. Other master netting agreements have also been developed to achieve a similar result in a different way.

From a credit risk perspective, maximum transaction/position coverage under a single netting agreement is optimal, as long as it is legally effective and can be managed operationally. However, there are constraints to this, as not all regulators accept this as effective as risk reducing for regulatory capital purposes under a single set of rules. As a result, it may be necessary to compartmentalise exposures even when, legally, they could be netted down to a greater extent.

1.7   Confirmations

So far, we have looked mostly at the relationship documentation for OTC derivatives trading and some of the issues which stem from it. The nature of the transaction-level documentation must also be understood and gives rise to its own structural issues.

In a mature product market, OTC derivatives transactions are documented by a short-form confirmation. This incorporates (either specifically or generically through terms in the master agreement) the applicable product definitions, which prescribe how the scheduled payment/delivery obligations are established and any disruption or adjustment events and fall-backs which may apply. In an immature market, there may be a long-form confirmation which sets out all of the terms that apply to the relevant type of transaction. Once there is sufficient demand, the long-form confirmation provisions are typically embedded in a set of definitions (eg, setting out standard pricing sources, disrupts, etc) and the confirmations, which set out only the trade-specific details, then become short form. However, even where there are definitions for a particular product type, where transactions are more bespoke, hybrid or exotic, the confirmations will still need to contain provisions for calculating the payment and delivery obligations.

The other type of confirmation commonly used is the pre-master confirmation. This can be long or short form, depending on the transaction type. The distinction, as the name suggests, is that there is no agreed ISDA Master Agreement in place at the time that the transaction is entered into. Instead, the pre-printed (front-end) ISDA Master Agreement is incorporated into the confirmation (as regards both that transaction and other transactions entered into on the same basis).

It is important to note the differences between transacting pre-master on the one hand, and having a signed ISDA Master Agreement in place on the other. The following are features of a pre-master arrangement:

- Unless specified in a pre-master confirmation, it will not be clear which law (English or New York) applies or which termination currency applies.
- Unless specified in the pre-master confirmation, certain events of default (eg, cross-default) will not apply as they need to be 'switched on' in the schedule to the master agreement.
- Automatic early termination will not apply, so this may need to be switched on in the pre-master confirmation if necessary, depending on the jurisdiction of the contracting parties.
- Typically, no CSA/CSD will be made to apply at this point – this can be done in a pre-master confirmation, but it requires several elections to be made, so it rarely happens in practice. Once the new rules under Dodd-Frank and EMIR

for the margining of uncleared swaps take effect, this is no longer going to be a market option for participants that are subject to those rules.

- Typically, no guarantees or third-party credit support will be given until the master agreement is signed, even if it is referred to in the pre-master confirmation. Where it is given on a transaction-specific basis, it will normally need to be given again once the master agreement is signed to pick up the obligations under the signed master agreement.

Whether trading pre or post-master agreement, two structural aspects to be aware of are consistency and prevalence. The same issues must be addressed in any multi-layered documentation structure.

In ISDA documentation terms, the normal level of prevalence for a particular transaction is:

- confirmation (once signed/exchanged);
- trade call/communication (before confirmation signed/exchanged);
- definitions;
- schedule to master agreement – absent in the pre-master confirmation situation; and
- pre-printed master agreement.

Parties to an ISDA Master Agreement may agree to alter the standard order of prevalence. This must be done with some care and even then may not always be effective. As any agreement is capable of amending a previous agreement, even the standard or agreed modified order of prevalence is not without some uncertainty. Prevalence is, however, commonly changed where, in relation to particular types of transaction, the parties wish to incorporate or modify definitions – particularly in relation to foreign exchange derivatives, or to specify upfront terms (eg, fall-backs), most commonly seen in commodity derivatives.

Another approach to embedding such terms is through the use of master confirmation agreements, which can substantially simplify individual trade confirmations in markets such as equity and credit derivatives, where the elections or modifications to definitions to be made for individual transaction types are numerous and relatively complex. In recognition of the increasing use and advantages of this approach, ISDA and others have published standard forms of master confirmation agreement for use in particular products and markets, such as the US and Asian equity derivatives markets. There are also published forms of standard master confirmation agreement for various types of standardised credit derivatives transaction, particularly for indexed products. These and similar developments make it possible (through standardisation) to facilitate clearing and trading on platforms of what are highly complex transactions.

1.8   Protocols

As has already been seen, OTC derivatives documentation is multi-layered and multi-faceted. The size of the derivatives market also makes it difficult to negotiate and implement changes to documentation retrospectively where this is necessitated by changes or uncertainties in the markets in the underlying or changes to the legal or regulatory framework to which OTC derivatives are subject.

ISDA developed the protocol as a means of circumventing the impracticality of making such changes to contractual terms on a bilateral basis. The protocol is, in effect, like a contractual central counterparty. By adhering to a typical ISDA protocol, each adhering party agrees with each other adhering party that all relevant agreements between them are deemed amended as specified in the protocol.

The first example, unique in the financial markets at the time, was the 1998 Euro Protocol. This was designed to deal with the legal, commercial and operational issues and uncertainties surrounding the introduction of the euro.

It has since been followed by several other protocols, including protocols:

- to deal with physical settlement issues in the credit derivatives markets in the context of certain big-name defaults – the Big and Small Bang Protocols;
- to provide a framework for the novation process in certain derivatives products – the Novation Protocols;
- to 'marry up' contractually the CSAs/CSD – the 2002 Master Agreement Protocol; and
- to enable participants to change the close-out methodology in their 1992 Master Agreements for market quotation or loss to the close-out amount formulation – the Close-out Amount Protocol.

There have since been many more, particularly addressing regulatory compliance with Dodd-Frank, EMIR and Directive 2014/59/EU establishing a framework for the recovery and resolution of credit institutions and investment firms (known as 'BRRD'). Use of some ISDA protocols has been almost universal, but others have had patchy uptake.

The most ambitious ISDA Protocol yet is perhaps the 2016 CM[3] Protocol which does not provide a single outcome to adherence, but engages a process which provides a very large number of possible outcomes based upon some 28 data point elections which need to be made via a questionnaire in order to achieve an outcome at all. This protocol is a new style of arrangement as it is more akin to a bilateral negotiation through a series of elections which can be made. It is very complex and it will be interesting to see how much it is used.

1.9   Standardisation v commoditisation

ISDA documentation is a collection of standardised documentation solutions which have been developed and adapted to the markets and needs of the players involved in them. There is no doubt as to the value of standard documentation, and ISDA has been particularly progressive and responsive to this over many years.

However, people can confuse standardisation with commoditisation. ISDA documentation is aimed at OTC derivatives – privately negotiated, bilateral contracts. It is designed in a way to give the parties the flexibility to structure their trading relationship and the transactions which they wish to enter into. It is an essential and solid starting point, but is not necessarily suitable for all purposes without some or significant tailoring. It is primarily driven by the inter-dealer market, which comprises much of the overall market in terms of size. However, as the types of participant expand, the suitability of the standard documentation must be considered and questioned. Similarly, as OTC derivatives are increasingly used in more diverse and specific applications, the derivatives lawyer must be increasingly cognisant of the underlying, or the risks or positions which the derivative may be using to hedge or trying to replicate.

2. Repo and stock lending documentation

The trade association for the repo and stock lending markets – Securities Industry and Financial Markets Association (SIFMA) – and the industry association which promotes these agreements – the International Securities Lending Association – have published and developed their own standard master agreements for securities financing transactions.

The documentation in these markets is, in many ways, simpler than that used in the derivatives markets. This reflects the fact that repos and stock loans are relatively straightforward transactions, involving an outright transfer of securities in exchange for cash or other collateral (each transferred outright to the receiving party), and each master agreement covers only one product.

Although the repo and stock lending markets have traditionally been quite separate and have different market practices as a result, from a legal perspective the two are very similar in terms of structure and issues. In recent years, there has been greater cross-over and collaboration between the two markets, with equity repo becoming more common and stock lending being used for cash financing based upon fixed-income instruments (as opposed to simply for stock borrowing). The documentation for the two different products has also increasingly converged, to a point where the trade associations which promote them have been able to obtain joint opinions on the enforceability of close-out netting under both the standard documentation for repo and the standard documentation for stock lending. For these reasons, we look at the standard documentation in these two markets together.

2.1 Why have master documentation?

The main purpose of having master agreements in the context of repos and stock lending is to provide the transaction linkage that enables them to operate simply and efficiently by:

- facilitating the margining of transactions across the portfolio of transactions; and
- offering a pre-agreed exit strategy on a close-out in case one of the parties defaults.

The recognition of netting under the master agreement as risk reducing for regulatory capital purposes for repo and stock lending agreements is subject to the same requirements as for OTC derivatives (see section 1.3(c) above). Therefore, having standard forms of master agreement and industry-published legal opinions on the effectiveness of close-out netting under them greatly facilitates this.

2.2   **Master agreements**

The principal master agreements in use in the repo markets today are the 2000 and 2011 Global Master Repurchase Agreements (GMRAs) and in the United States, the 1996 Master Repurchase Agreement. Takeup of the 2011 GMRA has been slow to date and most newly originated master agreements outside the United States are still based on the 2000 GMRA. The 1992 and 1995 GMRAs are largely just legacy documents.

The principal master agreements in use in the stock lending market today are the 2000, 2009 and 2010 Global Master Stock Lending Agreements (GMSLA) and, to a lesser extent, the 1995 Overseas Securities Lending Agreement. Many newly originated stock lending agreements are still based on the 2000 GMSLA document at this time, but this is gradually changing to the 2010 version.

The documentation largely adopts the same format as the ISDA Master Agreement in terms of there being a pre-printed form and an annex (for the GMRA) or a schedule (for the GMSLA) which contains the party's bespoke elections and modifications to the printed form at the front.

There are also a number of supplemental standard annexes to the GMRA which are included when transactions on a particular type of underlying security (eg, gilts or Italian securities) are to be traded, or where the parties have agreed to trade in a particular way (eg, as an agent of a third-party principal or as an agent to multiple principals on a pooled basis). There are also agency provisions that used to be included in the body of the 2000 GMSLA which are also now contained in annexes to the 2009/10 versions and are very similar to the equivalent annexes to the GMRA.

All the standard master repo and stock lending agreements have a number of common features:

- coverage and single agreement provisions;
- basic representations;
- provisions relating to the margining of transactions;
- provisions dealing with the making of manufactured payments (ie, amounts which are equal to the dividends or coupons on the underlying securities or margin securities);
- provisions dealing with taxation of payments;
- events of default;
- close-out calculation methodologies; and
- back-end or boilerplate provisions.

The standard master agreement and standard annexes provide the basis for trading repos and for stock borrowing for most underlying securities on an uncommitted basis. As already mentioned, the master agreement is effectively a self-contained document relating to a single product. As a result, all the essential terms of each transaction type are included within it and not in a separate document. Again, this contrasts with the ISDA documentation structure.

2.3   **Events of default**

The events of default under a GMRA or a GMSLA are typically more limited in scope than those that apply under an ISDA Master Agreement. With the exception of bankruptcy and suspension or expulsion by securities exchanges or trading prohibitions imposed by a regulator affecting a party, the standard events of default are inward-looking events – in the sense that they are limited to defaults and similar issues under the master agreement and the transactions under it. They do not extend to extraneous events which might apply to the parties or other related entities. This is principally because repos and stock loans are almost invariably fully collateralised transactions so that, on a default, the risk of loss is generally considered to be small. This is also reflected in the favourable regulatory capital requirement for repo and stock lending. There is no concept of no-fault termination events in repo or stock lending master agreements.

Two aspects of the GMRA and GMSLA events of default are of particular interest.

The first is that, unlike under the ISDA Master Agreements, there are no grace periods for a failure to make a payment or delivery on the due date. This applies not only to payments and deliveries, but also to margin transfers. This makes the master agreement very credit-sensitive relative to the ISDA Master Agreements (which themselves often cross-default to repo and stock lending master agreements).

The second is the related, but separate, issue of delivery failures. It is not uncommon in the repo and stock lending markets for there to be delivery failures which are due to liquidity problems in the underlying securities. Market participants take differing views as to whether a party should be able to close out all transactions where this occurs. These differing views have led to different approaches being taken in the various versions of the master agreement which have been published for each product. In the 1992 GMRA it was an event of default if a party failed to make a delivery of securities. In the 1995 GMRA this event of default was omitted and in the 2000 version of the GMRA it was included as an elective event of default. Similarly, a failure to deliver securities was an event of default under the 2000 GMLSA, but this was omitted from the 2009 and 2010 versions of that document.

However, an expectant recipient of securities is not left without remedy if no event of default applies. Although it cannot close out all transactions for a delivery failure, it can effect a mini close-out in respect of the particular transaction affected by the liquidity problem.

2.4   Close-out methodologies

Although the precise mechanism for determining the amount payable on an early termination under the different versions of the standard repo and stock lending agreement has evolved over time, the basic principles are unchanged. The reason is that both repos and stock loans are simple products relative to a typical derivative. The close-out methodology therefore adopts a simplified methodology of advancing the maturity date and valuing the then-current cash/collateral leg and the then-current value of the delivery leg, before offsetting them against each other. This is much the same as with the acceleration by a lender of a cash loan. Unlike with a derivative, no valuation is made of the forward aspect of any transaction, although with a repo there is an ability to claim the costs of entering into a replacement transaction or hedge. In highly liquid, short-dated markets, this typically will get the parties to the right number. However, users of these master agreements should be aware of the lack of compensation that can be provided, particularly when using the master agreement for longer-term transactions or transactions in particular securities which are being used for a specific purpose.

2.5 Cross-product netting

Given the clear benefits of having as wide a transaction coverage under a single agreement as possible, you may ask, why not document repo or stock lending transactions under an ISDA Master Agreement, rather than under a separate master agreement? The answer is that while repos and stock loans can be documented under an ISDA Master Agreement (and, in the case of some bespoke transactions – for example, repos embedding equity or credit derivatives – they sometimes are, but more usually as a forward or a total return swap), the products and markets have developed and operate quite differently.

Two features that point against documenting repos and stock loans under an ISDA Master Agreement are as follows:

- Collateral – repos and stock lending transactions self-collateralise (there is no separate collateral annex or document). They collateralise based on current value of securities and accrued payments, and not the expected future values.
- Close-out – the methodologies which apply on a close-out are simpler and more specific in the case of repos and stock lending. Again, as noted above, there is no forward-looking element to a close-out of a repo or a stock loan.

Additionally it is not generally permitted for regulatory capital purposes to net off positions on off-balance sheet transactions (ie, OTC derivatives) with on-balance sheet transactions (which include repo and stock lending transactions). Although this is sometimes now permissible, subject to certain conditions, it is still not common in practice to do this.

Where parties do want to net off repo against stock lending positions or either against positions in OTC derivatives with the same entity, they are likely to use the Cross-product Master Agreement published by SIFMA. Like the ISDA Cross-product Agreement Bridge, this master netting agreement straddles the individual underlying master agreements and allows for the set-off of net exposures under each agreement to take place under a further netting arrangement. That arrangement sits above (and so does not interfere with) arrangements set out in the underlying master agreements. The Cross-product Agreement Bridge therefore has the attraction of not potentially contaminating the effectiveness of the close-out netting provisions of the underlying master agreements, but it is not itself supported by generic legal opinions on which market participants can rely. As noted previously, in contrast to the Cross-product Agreement Bridge, the ISDA bridge approach is to bring the net termination payments under non-ISDA master agreements into the close-out netting calculation under the ISDA Master Agreement.

Introduction to German derivatives documentation

Patrick Scholl
Mayer Brown

1. Introduction

It is possible to enter into almost any derivative transaction, securities-lending transaction and repurchase transaction under German law. In 1990 the first master agreement for swaps was introduced and in 1993 the first German Master Agreement for Financial Derivatives Transactions (known as 'DRV') was published on that basis. Since then, the standardisation of over-the-counter (OTC) derivatives and securities transactions developed in line with the international standardisation of these transaction types and resulted in a broad spectrum of standard forms for OTC derivatives and securities transactions under German law (together, the 'German standard forms').

The German standard forms may be obtained from the Bank-Verlag GmbH[1] and are drafted by working groups from the five associations which, together, make up the German Banking Industry Committee:[2] the National Association of German Cooperative Banks, the Association of German Banks, the Association of German Public Banks, the German Savings Banks Association and the Association of German Pfandbrief Banks. The Association of German Banks usually takes the lead in the preparation of the German standard forms, together with the participation of its members. The past and current German standard forms can therefore also be found on, and downloaded from, that association's website.[3]

This chapter describes the German law derivatives documentation in detail and gives insight into the practical aspects of using the German standard forms in an international context.

2. Systematic approach

Currently, there exist five German standard forms:

- the DRV;
- the German Clearing Framework Agreement;
- the German Master Agreement for Securities-Lending Transactions;
- the German Master Agreement for Repurchase Transactions (Repos); and
- the Framework Agreement for German Investment Funds or Luxembourg Investment Funds. This framework agreement enables fund managers to

---

1   www.bank-verlag.de/index.php?id=197.
2   https://die-dk.de/en/.
3   https://bankenverband.de/service/rahmenvertraege-fuer-finanzgeschaefte/deutscher-rahmenvertrag-fuer-finanztermingeschaefte/.

enter into each of the other master agreements for the account of the relevant fund and a segregation of fund assets.

Each of these German standard forms is a separate master agreement and creates the basis for a separate netting of all transactions executed under the relevant master agreement (which is often described as a 'netting set').

The German standard forms are drafted in German and are subject to German law, in particular the German Civil Code. They have been drafted in many respects on the basis of German statutory civil law principles and are consequently rather short compared with their international counterparts. When interpreting the German standard forms, international market participants should therefore bear in mind that, in addition to the contractual provisions set out in the forms, the Civil Code and, in particular, the basic principles of German contract law still apply.

The German standard forms are prepared on the basis of a bank-customer relationship and define one party (the bank) as the 'bank' and the other party (the customer) as the 'counterparty'. The forms are therefore, from the outset, bank-customer arrangements, which explains the balance that they strike. However, the German standard forms are also used between dealer counterparties. In most cases, the forms are used between such counterparties without material changes, even though only one of the dealers will be a bank for the purposes of the relevant German standard form. In limited cases it is, however, necessary to agree on supplemental (tailor-made) provisions to the German standard forms. Such supplemental provisions may, for example, be required for certain forms or annexes if both counterparties are regulated institutions or investment funds.

There exist (non-binding) English-language translations of some of the German standard forms. International counterparties sometimes agree on and sign the English-language versions rather than the German-language versions of the forms as a matter of convenience for negotiation purposes (see section 5.3 below on the aspect of using a German-language confirmation). It is important to note, however, that the legal opinions regarding the forms relate to the German-language forms, and that a final interpretation by a German court will also be based on a German version or retranslation of the relevant forms.

3. DRV

3.1 General[4]

The DRV can be subdivided into four thematically related parts:

- the scope and purpose of the DRV;
- the general transaction-related provisions;
- the default and close-out netting arrangements; and
- certain miscellaneous and elective clauses.

---

4   For ease of reference, the terms used in the following sections correspond to the terms used in the publically available translation of the DRV at https://bankenverband.de/media/contracts/RV-DRV-engl.pdf.

The DRV is in principal an agreement for risk mitigation purposes and therefore – like the ISDA (International Swaps and Derivatives Association Inc) Master Agreement – mainly focuses on the default provisions and close-out netting. Transaction-specific terms and conditions are set forth in certain annexes to the DRV which will be further outlined below (see section 3.3 below).

(a) **Purpose and scope**

The scope of the DRV is defined rather broadly. Clause 1(1) of the DRV refers to financial derivatives transactions that can be cash or physically settled and that may relate to interest rates, exchange rates, prices or any other calculation basis (including indices relating thereto), securities, precious metals or other financial instruments. Further, the DRV clarifies that financial derivatives transactions may also include options, transactions relating to interest rate protection or any other transaction with conditional (payment) obligations or that requires a party to render performance in advance. Due to its broad scope, the DRV can be used for many different types of derivative transaction. However, counterparties should be especially careful when contemplating using the DRV for a transaction type that is not covered by the relevant applicable netting opinion or that is outside of the scope of Section 104 (2) of the German Insolvency Code (see section 3.1(c) below).

Clause 1(2) of the DRV further provides for a so-called 'single agreement clause'. The single agreement clause stipulates that all transactions executed under the DRV constitute between themselves and together with the DRV a single agreement to achieve an aggregated risk assessment. The single agreement clause, which is similar to the corresponding provision used in the ISDA Master Agreement, serves to protect the DRV as a single netting set agreement. The DRV therefore enables regulated entities to benefit from regulator capital reliefs in relation to their OTC derivatives portfolios.

(b) **General transaction-related provisions**

Due to its primary function of creating the legal netting set between the counterparties to the DRV, the core provisions regarding the execution and content of transactions under the DRV are limited to some general and optional provisions. The DRV is very flexible and can be adjusted for particular transactions (ie, regarding specific terms) by way of standardised product-related annexes to it (prepared by the German Banking Industry Committee) or by way of individual agreements between the counterparties.

Individual transactions are executed by way of 'confirmations' in writing which should explicitly refer to the respective DRV between the counterparties. The terms of the confirmations prevail over the provisions of the DRV and are, as the DRV itself, governed by German law. Template confirmations for specific OTC derivatives can be found on the website of the Association of German Banks.[5]

In addition, the DRV provides for general clauses regarding due dates (Clause

---

5   https://bankenverband.de/service/rahmenvertraege-fuer-finanzgeschaefte/deutscher-rahmenvertrag-fuer-finanztermingeschaefte/.

3(1)) and a general payment netting for due amounts under the same transaction (Clause 3(3)), a general 'banking day' definition (Clause 4), as well as the three banking day conventions for 'following banking day', 'preceding banking day' and 'modified following banking day' in case a certain date is not a banking day (Clause 3(5)). The DRV further includes general provisions on the reference asset underlying the OTC derivatives and the calculation method for some interest rate-related transactions – in particular the method for calculating a fixed or floating amount leg of an OTC derivative – as well as a method to apply a discounting method in case of advance payments at the commencement of an interest period. In this context, the DRV further defines different types of day count fraction[6] and the calculation period.

(c)   ***Default provisions***

Against the background of Article 295 of EU Regulation 575/2013 on prudential requirements for credit institutions and investment firms (the Capital Requirements Regulation or CRR), the key elements of the DRV are – as it is the case for any other netting agreement – the default provisions which enable the recognition of contractual netting as a risk reducing feature. Contractual netting is considered as risk reducing by the CRR if the netting contract ensures that following a pre-defined default situation as set out in the netting contract, all bilateral obligations between the parties are netted and/or converted into a single net sum of the positive and negative mark-to-market values of all included individual transactions.

On the basis of the German statutory concepts for agreements with continuing obligations (*'Dauerschuldverhältnisse'*), the DRV may be terminated for material reason (*'wichtiger Grund'*). The DRV does not exclusively define the term 'material reason'. It does, however, clarify that a material reason shall be deemed to occur in case of non-payment or non-performance of an obligation by a party more than five banking days following a corresponding notice by the non-defaulting party. Besides this clarification, the term 'material reason' is open for interpretation. A court would use the statutory definition of 'material reason' set out in Section 314(2), sentence 2 of the Civil Code as a starting point. Pursuant to this provision, "there is a material reason if the terminating party, taking into account all the circumstances of the specific case and weighing the interests of both parties, cannot reasonably be expected to continue the contractual relationship until the agreed end or until the expiry of a notice period". A material reason usually encompasses situations which result in a material deterioration of the contractual relationship between the parties involved, and makes it unreasonable for one party to proceed with the contractual relationship. Thus, the hurdle for terminating the DRV is high and, even though case law could provide guidance, particular care should be taken when considering the termination of the DRV for reasons other than non-payment.

In addition, the DRV provides that the agreement terminates automatically in the event of insolvency (Clause 7(2)). This concept corresponds to the 'automatic early termination' in the ISDA Master Agreement, if automatic early termination has

---

6   In addition, the parties to the DRV may sign the additional agreement to Clause 6 of the 2002 DRV (*Zusatzvereinbarung zu Nr. 6 – Zinsberechnungsmethoden*), which provides for further day count fractions.

been elected in the schedule. An event of insolvency occurs with the filing of the relevant insolvency application and, thus, occurs prior to the opening of insolvency proceedings. To avoid a termination in case of an unjustified insolvency filing, the DRV stipulates the following additional conditions:

- a party to the DRV must have filed for the application itself;
- the respective party must be unable to pay its debts as they become due; and
- the commencement of the insolvency proceedings is otherwise justified.

Upon a termination of the DRV, all payment and other performance obligations under the DRV and all transactions hereunder cease to exist and close-out netting applies (Clause 7(3)). The close-out netting is based on a damage compensation principle (which also takes into account any financial benefit arising from the termination as a reduction of the damage claim) and results in a single compensation amount (also including unpaid amounts) (Clause 9(1)) denominated in euros payable by one party to the other. The valuation of damages or benefits due to a party following close-out netting is performed by the non-defaulting party and is based:

- on actual replacement costs (ie, the costs for the respective replacement transactions entered into by the non-defaulting party); or
- if no replacement occurs, on hypothetical replacement costs (ie, the amount that would be needed to enter into replacement transactions).

The debtor of the termination payment is the party that gains the overall benefit from the termination. The DRV, however, clarifies that a payment obligation by the non-defaulting party is limited in amount to the damages incurred by the defaulting party (the 'CAP clause').

If the calculation following the close-out netting results in a compensation claim against the non-defaulting party, the DRV provides that such a claim by the defaulting party becomes due only if there are no other claims by the non-defaulting party against the defaulting party arising from any other relationship between the two (Clause 9(2)). In case there are any such unsatisfied counterclaims by the non-defaulting party (including non-cash claims), the DRV applies set-off without the need for a set-off declaration or prior notice.

The German Federal Court of Justice recently ruled on the DRV close-out netting provisions in connection with the Lehman Brother insolvency. The court first stated that in an insolvency of a non-German counterparty to the DRV, Section 340(2) of the Insolvency Code applies and the validity of the close-out netting provisions is determined on the basis of the law governing the netting agreement itself – that is, German law. The DRV has therefore to comply with the statutory close-out netting provisions in Section 104 of the Insolvency Code, which are mandatory and may not be circumvented by contractual close-out netting. This in particular applies to the statutory requirements regarding the valuation of the close-out amount. The Federal Court of Justice further held that the close-out amount valuation provisions of the DRV are invalid insofar as the CAP clause provides for a limitation of the amount that can be claimed by the insolvent party. Thus, the estate of the insolvent party will be prejudiced by the contractual valuation provisions of the DRV when compared with the valuation provision in Section 104(3) of the Insolvency Code. In the specific case referred to above, the court therefore applied the calculation method of Section 104 of the Insolvency Code instead of the calculation method provided for in the DRV, but respected the close-out netting between the parties as such.

As a result of the Federal Court of Justice judgment, the Supervising Financial Authority issued a general decree stating that counterparties to the DRV shall continue to apply the DRV on the basis of its specific terms – that is, including the close-out netting provisions and its determination method. Moreover, the German Ministry of Finance and the Ministry of Justice and Consumer Protection initiated a legislative process for the purposes of amending Section 104 of the Insolvency Code to enable a more flexible approach to contractual close-out netting and certain deviations from the existing Section 104. A legislative amendment has been published[7] and at the time of writing, it was expected that it would come into force by the end of 2016.

(d) Elective clauses

Clause 12 of the DRV provides for a few elections that the parties can make, in particular with regard to applying an agreement-based payment netting instead of a transactional-based payment netting, as well as a gross-up obligation in case of a tax deduction together with a termination right for tax reasons with respect to the affected transactions. Lastly, the DRV allows for further individual negotiated terms. These can be set out in the placeholder in the form of the DRV or in a separate and supplemental document to the DRV (the 'other provisions').

3.2 Credit Support Annex

The 2001 Credit Support Annex enables the parties to the DRV to exchange margin collateral on a title-transfer basis. The basis of the calculation of the margin requirement between the parties is exposure driven. The 'exposure' is defined as the hypothetical single compensation claim that would arise upon termination of all transactions under the DRV pursuant to the close-out provisions of the DRV on the relevant valuation date. The applicable margin requirement can include additional amounts in favour of the collecting party, less any additional amounts agreed in favour of the posting party. The parties can also agree on a minimum threshold amount for each party. If the margin requirement on a certain date results in a margin shortfall, then the credit support provider has to post additional collateral assets. If the margin requirements result in a margin excess, then the credit support receiver (ie, the party entitled to receive collateral) is required to retransfer equivalent collateral assets to the credit support provider. The details of the margin requirements and the eligible collateral assets are agreed between the parties in the individual arrangements section of the Credit Support Annex. The annex also governs the payment of distributions and interest amounts on the securities posted

---

7   www.bmjv.de/SharedDocs/Gesetzgebungsverfahren/DE/Aenderungsvorschlag_Neufassung_104InsO.html.

as collateral and cash collateral. The annex contains no explicit provision with regard to a negative interest obligation on the collateral provider. It is, therefore, still subject to legal discussion whether the annex can be interpreted to mean that such an obligation exists. To overcome this legal uncertainty, the German Banking Industry Committee has published specific additional provisions which can be used by the parties to agree on a negative interest obligation of the collateral provider.[8]

The annex also supplements the default provisions of the DRV. The annex thus provides that a material reason is also deemed to occur if a due margin collateral transfer or a retransfer of equivalent collateral is not effected within one banking day of notification of the non-performance of such obligation. In case of a termination of the DRV, the value of the posted collateral will be included in the determination of the single compensation claim under the DRV as an unpaid amount. Securities collateral will be valued for the purposes of the close-out netting at the price of an actual or hypothetical sale of equivalent securities.

In view of the upcoming implementation of the margin rules under EU Regulation 648/2012 on OTC derivatives, central counterparties and trade repositories (EMIR), a new set of credit support documentation under the DRV is currently being prepared. It is expected that there will be a credit support annex for the variation margin and a credit support annex for the initial margin obligations of the parties subject to the relevant margin obligation.

3.3   Other annexes

There are several other annexes to the DRV, drafted by the associations making up the German Banking Industry Committee under the lead of the Association of German Banks, which can be obtained from the Bank-Verlag GmbH.[9] Most of the DRV's other annexes are product related, but there are also specific annexes which implement cross product-related aspects into the DRV, in particular in relation to the implementation of new legal requirements. Some of the annexes are accompanied by user guides published by the Association of German Banks on its website.[10]

The existing annexes to the DRV are summarised below:

- the 2014 EMIR Addendum – this enables the counterparty to implement the risk management requirements under EMIR (other than collateralisation);
- the 2015 Clearing Annex – this serves as an execution arrangement for transactions to be submitted for clearing under the DRV.[11] Under its terms, the initial non-cleared OTC transaction will be dissolved upon a successful clearing of such transaction;
- the 2016 FATCA Addendum – this implements certain requirements of the US Foreign Account Tax Compliance Act (FATCA) (Sections 1471–1474 of the 1986 US Internal Revenue Code);.

---

8   The suggested additional provisions for agreeing on a negative interest obligation under the annex are available here (in German only): https://bankenverband.de/media/contracts/BSA-Zinsregelung-Formulierungsvorschlag-20-02-2015.pdf.
9   www.bank-verlag.de/index.php?id=197.
10   https://bankenverband.de/service/rahmenvertraege-fuer-finanzgeschaefte/deutscher-rahmenvertrag-fuer-finanztermingeschaefte/.
11   See Section 2.1 of the chapter on client clearing documentation.

- the 2001 Annex for the Early Settlement through Cash Settlement – if the parties agree on call rights under transactions, the terms of this annex can be used to determine the cash settlement amount to be paid;
- the 2001 Annex for Foreign Exchange (FX) Transactions and Options – this annex implements product-specific provisions for FX, in particular the terms and conditions of an FX option. The currency-related definitions have to be set forth and agreed on in the relevant confirmations;
- the 2010 Annex for Equity Derivatives – the equity annex provides for several terms and conditions, definitions regarding equity and equity index transaction types, as well as market disruption events, adjustment events and settlement disruptions. Many terms and definitions were prepared in alignment with the 2002 ISDA Equity Derivatives Definitions;
- the 2013 Annex for Ccommodity Derivatives – this annex relates to cash-settled commodity transactions. It provides for terms of certain transactions types, in particular options, forwards, swaps and capped and floored commodity transactions, as well as market disruption provisions; and
- the 2001 Annex for Emission Allowances – this annex provides for specific terms regarding transactions for the physical settlement of emission allowances.

In addition, there are several annexes for counterparties which are German Pfandbrief issuers and intend to execute OTC derivatives for the cover register for German law-governed Pfandbriefe.[12] The use of OTC derivatives by German Pfandbrief banks is subject to the risk limitation provisions of the German Pfandbrief Act. In particular, a Pfandbrief bank has to ensure that its claims under OTC derivatives cannot be adversely affected in the event of the insolvency of the Pfandbrief bank or of the other cover pools.

Each of these DRV annexes is intended to be supplemental to the DRV. This means that the provisions of the DRV annexes prevail over the terms of the DRV.

3.4 Differences with the ISDA Master Agreement
The following are some key differences between the DRV and the ISDA Master Agreement:
- The DRV provides only for a limited number of options in its Clause 12. In particular, its core provisions are not set up in a modular or elective way and are thus, in principle, not subject to an individual composition as is the case for several clauses of the ISDA Master Agreement, which can be applied or disapplied in the ISDA Schedule. Therefore, the DRV provides no form of a schedule in which individual terms to certain core provisions can be agreed. If the contractual parties intend to make amendments to the DRV, the parties are free to agree on such individually negotiated terms as part of the 'other provisions' section.

---

12   A list of Pfandbrief issuers can be found on the website of the Association of German Pfandbrief Banks at www.hypverband.de/cms/_internet.nsf/tindex/en_925.htm.

- The DRV provides no early termination rights similar to the ISDA termination events (other than the optional tax termination right in Clause 12). Accordingly, if parties intend to have additional termination rights in place, they must agree such rights in the other provisions section. They should carefully consider whether such additional termination rights would constitute a material reason (resulting in a termination of the contract as a whole) or whether such termination rights would result only in a partial termination of certain affected transactions. In the latter case, additional amendments to the existing provisions of the DRV are required.

The German standard forms provide no particular terms for credit derivatives transactions. Credit default swaps are therefore currently being documented using the 2014 ISDA Credit Derivatives Definitions via a so-called 'bridge clause' (see section 5.2 below).

4. Clearing Framework Agreement

The Clearing Framework Agreement was published in 2013. This is a separate master agreement to the DRV. In contrast to the ISDA/FOA (Futures and Options Association, now FIA Europe) Client Cleared Derivatives Addendum, the DRV and the Clearing Framework Agreement provide for two separate netting sets that are not set off against each other, even during the insolvency of the clearing client. Accordingly, the close-out between the counterparties under the DRV and the Clearing Framework Agreement will result in two single compensation claims which – subject to the applicable insolvency laws – could be subject to an additional set-off, as provided under each of the DRV and the Clearing Framework Agreement.[13]

The scope of the Clearing Framework Agreement extends to client transactions resulting from the clearing of OTC derivatives, as well as the clearing of exchange-traded derivatives and spot transactions. Moreover, the Clearing Framework Agreement also includes OTC non-cleared futures on foreign currencies and precious metals which are not already subject to a master agreement and irrespective of whether reference has been made to the Clearing Framework Agreement. Hence, the Clearing Framework Agreement also partially covers these non-cleared OTC derivatives.

The structure of the Clearing Framework Agreement is based on the DRV. The Clearing Framework Agreement therefore contains similar default provisions to the DRV. For the purpose of valuing terminated transactions or the margin collateral provided, the Clearing Framework Agreement enables the parties to make use of the central counterparty's respective valuations. However, the Clearing Framework Agreement contains two additional default clauses which are not present in the DRV. In the event that the clearing member counterparty defaults, and where the client and the clearing member agreed on an omnibus or individual client segregation, the single compensation claim will be established per central counterparty if required by

---

13   For further details on client clearing agreement and the ISDA/FOA Client Cleared Derivatives Addendum, see section 4.1 of the chapter on client clearing documentation.

the rule book of the central counterparty. The Clearing Framework Agreement therefore respects the need for segregating the close-out claim in a clearing context.

The Clearing Framework Agreement also provides for a termination event in case of a default of a central counterparty. In this case, the transactions under the Clearing Framework Agreement which relate to the defaulted central counterparty will be terminated and result in a single compensation claim. The clearing member counterparty assumes no responsibility for the performance of the central counterparty, and its obligations following a central counterparty default are accordingly limited to the payment of the amounts actually received from the central counterparty.

The Clearing Framework Agreement also includes the margining provisions for cleared client transactions and introduces initial margin and variation margin requirements. These provisions, however, require an individual completion by the parties in line with any requirements of the central counterparty. As of today, these bilateral arrangements have to be done in supplemental arrangements prepared by the parties.

The German Banking Industry Committee also published annexes to the Clearing Framework Agreement specific to the central counterparty which parties should execute if a clearing takes place via the relevant central counterparty.[14] For further information on the Clearing Framework Agreement, the Association of German Banks issued a user guide in German.[15]

5.   Practical aspects

5.1   Use of individual agreements to the master agreements

As outlined above, the DRV and the Clearing Framework Agreement contain only a limited number of elective provisions or concepts as they are designed as agreements in bank-customer relationships. It is therefore not uncommon to agree on individual terms to the DRV or the Clearing Framework Agreement. Changes to the core concepts and provisions of the DRV or Clearing Framework Agreement should, however, be carefully analysed, in particular with respect to the scope of the available industry netting opinions.

If market participants want to use certain provisions or concepts in their ISDA-based derivatives documentation, they should take particular care when combining certain defined terms or principles with the DRV or Clearing Framework Agreement.

5.2   Use of ISDA standards via bridge clause

It is not uncommon to implement certain ISDA definitions into the DRV even if an annex is available for the same transaction type or reference asset. The main reason for the use of ISDA definitions with the DRV is the limitation of basis risk in case of a back-to-back hedging under ISDA documentation. Another reason is the desire to

---

14   https://bankenverband.de/service/rahmenvertraege-fuer-finanzgeschaefte/clearing-rahmenvereinbarung-vorlagen/.
15   https://bankenverband.de/service/rahmenvertraege-fuer-finanzgeschaefte/clearing-rahmenvereinbarung-vorlagen/.

make use of generally accepted market standards for certain transaction types, in particular with international swap counterparties. Lastly, the use of ISDA definitions is necessary if there is no existing standardisation under the DRV, which is particularly true for credit default swaps.

The ISDA definitions are incorporated into a DRV confirmation, which is and remains governed by German law, by using the so-called 'bridge clause'. The bridge clause was introduced to take into account the fact that the ISDA definitions are governed by English or New York law and are interpreted pursuant to market participants in accordance with such laws. The bridge clause therefore intends to prevent a situation where the ISDA definitions would be entirely governed by German law by stating that the interpretation of the ISDA definitions under English or New York law shall be taken into account. In addition to the bridge clause, certain individual clarifications to the relevant ISDA definitions might be required in the confirmation. This applies in particular to definitions or legal concepts used in the ISDA Master Agreement but not in the DRV (eg, default events and termination events). The relevant ISDA definitions should therefore be carefully reviewed to avoid inconsistencies with the DRV. Care should also be taken when a confirmation provides that the relevant ISDA definitions prevail over the corresponding provisions of the DRV. For example, the ISDA definitions should not take precedence over the core netting provisions of the DRV.

5.3 Use of English-language documentation

DRVs are often used between international counterparties. It is therefore not uncommon to use English-language confirmations under the DRV even if the DRV itself has been executed in German, which is true for most DRVs. The use of English-language confirmations nevertheless requires some caution. In particular, it is important to ensure that defined terms in the DRV are clearly recognisable in the English-language confirmation. It is therefore advisable to identify already existing defined terms of the DRV by using their German equivalent besides the English term, or to define the relevant term in the confirmation again. Furthermore, it is advisable to ensure that the confirmation is in itself comprehensive, as well as comprehensible. This will prevent the risk of language mismatches between the German-language DRV and the English confirmation. In case of a dispute, German courts will require a translation of the relevant English confirmation.

5.4 Amendments to the DRV

In contrast to ISDA conventions, there is currently no market-wide protocol solution to implement market-wide amendments to the DRV or any annex. In order to amend the DRV or any annex, it is therefore required to enter into bilateral amendment agreements with each individual counterparty. In case of new developments, the German Banking Industry Committee therefore prefers to prepare new annexes or certain standard wordings (eg, with respect to negative interest obligations) that can be executed in a separate document without the need to amend or re-execute the DRV itself.

6. Legal opinions

The German Banking Industry Committee obtains and regularly updates netting opinions for the purposes of Article 295 of the CRR for Germany, as well as several other jurisdictions like the United States, England, Switzerland or Austria. Market participants should therefore be able to conduct their netting analysis without the need for their own netting opinion. Accordingly, there are only limited cases where an additional or a drawdown netting opinion is required; however, counterparties should consider additional opinions if they (materially) modify the provisions of the DRV.

The author would like to thank Alexei Döhl and Matthias Wetzig for their critical review of this chapter.

Documentation for cleared OTC derivatives

Patrick Scholl
Mayer Brown

1.   Introduction

Following the publication of EU Regulation 648/2012 on over-the-counter (OTC) derivatives, central counterparties and trade repositories (EMIR), it became apparent that the documentation landscape for the trading of OTC derivatives would face significant change. EMIR introduced the general delegated power of the European Commission to adopt regulatory technical standards[1] (after receiving proposed draft rules from the European Securities and Markets Authority (ESMA)) which impose obligations on OTC derivatives counterparties to clear certain specifically named OTC derivatives contracts through an authorised or recognised central counterparty (CCP).

The first regulatory technical standards under EMIR in respect of the clearing obligation came into force in the European Union on 21 December 2015 and related to four categories[2] of interest rate OTC derivative denominated in the G4 currencies[3] (the G4 IRS). The G4 IRS clearing obligation will be phased in over a period of two years[4] and, for such purposes, the OTC derivatives market has been subdivided into four categories of market participant based on their experience and related trading volume.[5] The mandatory clearing in the European Union for the largest market participants, the clearing members for such interest rate OTC derivatives, commenced on 21 June 2016.

Since then, further rules relating to the clearing obligation have been introduced in the European Union covering certain untranched index credit derivatives[6] and two categories[7] of interest rate derivative denominated in Norwegian krone, Polish zloty or Swedish krona.[8] Those rules are also subject to a phase-in. The first category of large market counterparties, which are clearing members of the relevant index credit derivatives or the G4 IRS, clear from 9 February 2017 onwards.

---

1   See Article 5 of EMIR for further details regarding the clearing obligation procedure.
2   Basis swaps, fixed-to-floating interest rate swaps, forward rate agreements and overnight index swaps, each with specific maturity buckets.
3   Japanese yen, US dollar, euro and British pound sterling.
4   For further details, see Commission Delegated Regulation (EU) 2015/2205 of 6 August 2015 supplementing EMIR with regard to regulatory technical standards on the clearing obligation (the IRS G4 RTS). In July 2016, ESMA started a consultation on an extension of the start date for Category 3 counterparties, which are rather small and less systemically important market participants. See ESMA Consultation Paper, "On the clearing obligation for financial counterparties with a limited volume of activity", 13 July 2016, ESMA/2016/1125.
5   Article 2 of the IRS G4 RTS.
6   See Commission Delegated Regulation (EU) 2016/592 of 1 March 2016 supplementing EMIR with regard to regulatory technical standards on the clearing obligation.
7   Fixed-to-floating interest rate swaps and forward rate agreements, each with specific maturity buckets.
8   See Commission Delegated Regulation (EU) 2016/1178 of 10 June 2016 supplementing EMIR with regard to regulatory technical standards on the clearing obligation.

Once the relevant rules have come into force, OTC market participants covered by the clearing obligation will therefore not only have to have in place derivatives master agreements for their non-cleared OTC derivatives, but also clearing participation arrangements with CCPs under the CCP rule book and/or a client clearing arrangement with a clearing member of a CCP if a market participant is not a direct member of a CCP (ie, a client).[9] Hence, market participants subject to the clearing obligation are required to complement their derivatives master agreement with a set of new clearing documents, which have only recently been standardised and published, and get comfortable with CCP rule books, which have changed significantly due to the implementation of asset segregation and porting techniques required by Article 39 of EMIR for authorised CCPs.

This chapter gives an overview of the background and content of client clearing agreements and practical considerations related thereto.

2. What is client clearing?

Client clearing is a service run by clearing members for the benefit of their clients which allows the latter to participate in the clearing offering provided by a CCP for certain derivatives contracts. In this context, the term 'clearing' means (under EMIR) the process of:

- establishing positions, including the calculation of net obligations; and
- ensuring that financial instruments, cash, or both, are available to secure the exposure arising from these positions.[10]

In other words, this means that a the selected CCP which offers a clearing service for certain financial instruments or contracts ('CCP service') steps between trading counterparties and thereby assumes the capacity as buyer to any seller counterparty and the capacity as seller to every buyer counterparty under the cleared transactions. In order to limit the risks associated with its central position between the trading counterparties, the CCP will in particular require collateral and other default-based contributions – for example, by creating a default fund (which enables, and results in, a mutual loss sharing between members of the CCP).

The regulatory purpose of clearing is the reduction of counterparty credit risk by centralising the OTC derivatives trading relationship and the aggregate outstanding amount of derivative positions via CCPs in order to meet the overarching goal of reducing systemic risk in the OTC derivatives market. Consequently, CCPs have to implement effective risk management principles and establish robust margin collateral structures to protect themselves against the defaults of clearing members with respect to their own clearing positions or the clearing positions of their clients. The term 'position' therefore describes the positive or negative interest in payments or delivery under a certain cleared derivative contract.

There is no uniform client clearing structure in the global derivatives market.

---

9   Pursuant to Article 4 (3)(2) of EMIR, the clearing obligation can also be complied with through an indirect clearing arrangement. See section 2.2 below.
10 Article 2(3) of the IRS G4 RTS.

This chapter outlines the process of clearing and the submission of OTC derivatives contracts into clearing from an EMIR perspective.

2.1 Client clearing structure

The submission for clearing of a derivatives contract eligible for clearing between two market participants is in the first instance translated into different legal arrangements by the conclusion of two economically identical transactions between the CCP and two clearing members (each, a 'cleared CCP transaction'). The CCP thereby takes a commercially neutral position with respect to such cleared CCP transactions – for example, it assumes the seller's position *vis-à-vis* Clearing Member 1 and the purchaser's position *vis-à-vis* Clearing Member 2.

In the case of an OTC derivatives client clearing, the client first executes the OTC derivatives contract to be cleared (the 'initial OTC derivatives contract') with its market counterparty (the 'execution broker') under the terms of, for example, an ISDA (International Swaps and Derivatives Association Inc) Master Agreement and an execution agreement thereto (the 'execution agreement').[11] The execution broker can be either the client's clearing member or any other market participant (being either also a member of the relevant CCP or a client). The purpose of the execution agreement is to agree on the process for the submission to clearing, including the consequences of a failed clearing attempt. The client and execution broker will then apply the process required by the relevant CCP and involved services providers to submit and register the initial OTC derivatives contract with a CCP.

In the case of a successful submission to clearing, the initial OTC derivatives contract is then dissolved pursuant to the execution agreement and replaced by:

- two economically identical cleared CCP transactions between the CCP and the clearing members involved under the rule book (as described above); and
- an economically identical transaction between the clearing member and the client under the client clearing agreement (the 'client transaction').

The economic position of the client under the client transaction mirrors its economic position under the initial OTC derivatives contract. The clearing member assumes a neutral position between the CCP and the client and is therefore referred to as a 'riskless principal'. This process of concluding a cleared transaction is referred to as 'abstract novation'.

This basic clearing cascade structure involving an execution broker that is also the client's clearing member can be illustrated on the following page.

2.2 Indirect clearing

Market participants can also comply with the clearing obligation under EMIR by entering into an indirect clearing arrangement pursuant to Article 4(3)(2) of EMIR with a client of a clearing member (the client of a client is called the 'indirect client').

---

11   For example, the ISDA/FIA (Futures Industry Association) Europe Cleared Derivatives Execution Agreement, which can be downloaded from https://fia.org/articles/isdafia-europe-cleared-derivatives-execution-agreement-may-2014.

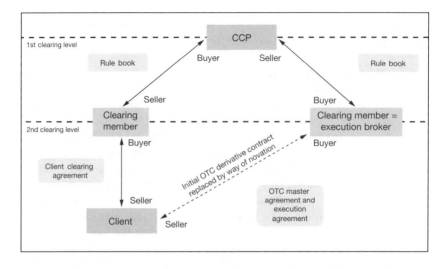

Indirect clearing arrangements are defined by Article 1 of Commission Delegated Regulation 149/2013 of 19 December 2012 as a set of contractual relationships between the CCP, the clearing member, the client of a clearing member and the indirect client that allows the client of a clearing member to provide clearing services to an indirect client. As a consequence, the basic clearing cascade structure will be extended by a third clearing level. Accordingly, in the case of a successful submission to clearing, the initial OTC derivatives contract between the execution broker and the indirect client is dissolved pursuant to the execution agreement and replaced by:

- two economically identical cleared CCP transactions between the CCP and the clearing members involved under the rule book;
- an economically identical client transaction relating to the indirect client between the clearing member and the client under the client clearing agreement; and
- an economically identical transaction between the client and the indirect client under an indirect clearing agreement ('indirect client transaction'). The economic position of the indirect client under the indirect client transaction mirrors its economic position under the initial OTC derivatives contract. The clearing member, as well as the client, each take a neutral position in the clearing cascade and are intended to be riskless principals.

The basic indirect clearing structure involving an execution broker that is also the indirect client's clearing member can be illustrated on the following page.

If a clearing member offers an indirect clearing service, the client clearing agreement will require specific amendments of its terms to capture the segregation requirements applicable to the clearing member and client under EMIR – in particular, the segregation of the assets and positions of the indirect client from the assets and positions of the client. Moreover, the indirect client and client will have to agree on an 'indirect clearing agreement'. Accordingly, the indirect clearing agreement serves the same purpose as a client clearing agreement and will therefore

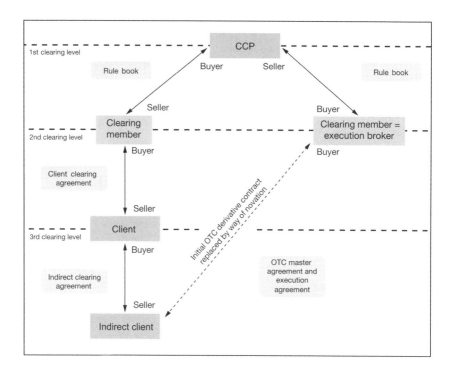

provide for similar provisions, but takes into account the fact that the indirect client faces three default scenarios – namely, the default of the CCP, the default of the clearing member and the default of the client. In particular with respect to the default of the client, the indirect clearing arrangement (which includes the client clearing agreement and the indirect clearing agreement) will have to implement legal techniques to comply with the segregation requirements under EMIR, especially Chapter II of Commission Delegated Regulation 149/2013.[12]

So far, there is no market standard documentation for indirect clearing and the legal frameworks for indirect clearing are still developing.

2.3　CCP clearing models

EMIR introduced the obligation for CCPs and clearing members to offer their clients two types of asset segregation model (each, a 'clearing model') to reduce or eliminate the risks faced by clients if their clearing member were to default.[13] Articles 39(2) and (3) of EMIR introduced two clearing models:

12　ESMA supports amendments to the current segregation requirements set out in Commission Delegated Regulation (EU) 149/2013. The proposal can be found in the ESMA final report, "Draft regulatory technical standards on indirect clearing arrangements under EMIR and MiFIR", of 26 May 2016, ESMA/2016/725.

13　The default risk of the clearing member is reduced and eliminated on the basis of the default management procedures of the CCP and the so-called 'lines of defence'. The main pillars are close-out netting, margin collateral, the default fund of the CCP and own dedicated amounts of the CCP. See for example the lines of defence of Eurex Clearing AG under www.eurexclearing.com/clearing-en/risk-management/lines-of-defense.

- the omnibus client segregation model (which is often referred to as an 'omnibus segregated account'); and
- the individual client segregation model (which is often referred to as an 'individual segregated account').

The 'omnibus client segregation model' is defined by EMIR as a record and account structure enabling each clearing member to distinguish in accounts with the CCP the assets and positions of that clearing member from the assets and positions of its clients. With respect to an individual client segregation model, EMIR requires separate records and accounts enabling each clearing member to distinguish in accounts with the CCP the assets and positions held for the account of a client and those held for the account of other clients or the clearing member itself. It is important to note that in case of an individual segregated account, Article 39(6) of EMIR requires that any margin collateral posted by the client for its cleared positions ('client margin') in excess of the client's margin requirement be also posted by the clearing member to the CCP ('forwarding obligation') and distinguished from the margin collateral of other clients or the clearing member. Client margin held in an individual segregated account should not be exposed to losses connected to positions recorded in another account (either of another client of the clearing member, or of the clearing member itself).

There are, however, no uniform legal structures for omnibus or individual segregated account offerings by European CCPs. In relation to omnibus segregated accounts, clients are often given the choice of alternative omnibus structures which either group all clients of a clearing member or only a limited group of clients of a clearing member within one specific account at the CCP. In addition, omnibus segregated accounts may provide for net or gross collateralisation requirements of the clearing member *vis-à-vis* the CCP. In the case of the net collateralisation requirement, the obligation of the clearing member to provide margin to the CCP is based on the net exposure of all its client positions credited to the relevant omnibus segregated account. Accordingly, the clearing member's margin obligation will benefit from netting effects between the individual client positions cleared and recorded in the relevant omnibus segregated account. By contrast, the gross omnibus segregated account is based on the idea of margining the net exposure per each omnibus segregated account client. Hence, there is no netting effect with other client portfolios in the relevant omnibus segregated account.

The clearing models are a decisive element for the portability requirement introduced by Article 39(10) of EMIR. 'Porting', in the context of client clearing, means the transfer of the clearing member's client positions to a replacement clearing client at the option of the relevant client (in the case of an individual segregated account) or the group of omnibus segregated account clients (in case of an omnibus segregated account). This, in the first instance, means the transfer of clearing member's cleared CCP transactions relating to the relevant client or clients to the replacement clearing member. However, as a consequence, the respective client transactions at the second clearing level should also be legally or economically transferred to the replacement clearing member. It is important to note that it will in each case depend on the relevant client clearing documentation and the insolvency laws applicable to the clearing member pertaining to how a porting of client transactions has to be legally structured.

As a result, an individual segregated account or a gross omnibus segregated account provides for a comparably higher likelihood that a porting of the cleared transactions to a replacement clearing member will take place and will be completed under the rule book than a net omnibus segregated account. This is an important consideration for clients whose clearing member defaults. In case of a net omnibus segregated account, it is very unlikely that the positions of an individual client will be ported in practice, on the basis that a net omnibus segregated account can usually be ported only as a whole to a single replacement clearing member, which requires the uniform selection of a replacement clearing member by all clients. Given that the transfer of a large clearing portfolio to a replacement clearing member might affect the own capital requirements of that clearing member and its regulatory leverage ratio, it would also be difficult to find a replacement clearing member. It is therefore very likely that net omnibus segregated accounts will be liquidated, as opposed to ported, resulting in the requirement for clients to re-establish their liquidated positions. Clients should take into account any such porting risks when selecting a certain clearing model.

2.4   Principal-to-principal relationship

Most of the clearing models offered by European CCPs are structured on a principal-to-principal basis. This means that the payment or delivery requirements under the cleared CCP transactions, as well as all margin requirements as against the CCP, are direct obligations of the clearing member under the rule book, and not obligations of the client. Consequently, the clearing member has then:

- a direct obligation to the client to make payments and deliveries under client transactions, or to return client margin; and
- a right to request payments and deliveries under client transactions.

This means that there is no direct contractual nexus between the CCP and individual clients, and that the clearing member is factually a conduit operating between the client and the CCP to effect any relevant obligations. Some CCPs, however, offer a direct legal transfer and return of client margin between the CCP and the client. Any such direct delivery reduces the risk of a clearing member default at the time when the client margin is held by the clearing member for onward delivery to the CCP or the client, respectively.

By contrast, under a so-called 'agency model', the client – in theory – directly legally faces the CCP on the basis of an agency arrangement with the clearing member. In order to protect the CCP for client defaults, the clearing member assumes a guarantee to the CCP regarding the client positions and, therefore, remains liable to the CCP. The agency model is predominant in the United States, but European CCPs also developed direct access models for clients to CCPs in order to mitigate the regulatory capital costs for clearing members offering client clearing.

3. **Client clearing agreement background and standardisation**

Client clearing agreements are not new sets of agreement; they were historically first created for exchange-traded derivatives. The documentation for exchange-traded derivatives is usually in the form of template modules for 'standard terms of business' provided by the Futures Industry Association (FIA). With the commencement of discussions about the future contractual structure of client clearing for OTC derivatives and the requirement to ensure compliance with EMIR, and in particular with the segregation requirements for cleared positions introduced by Article 39 of EMIR, it became apparent that new documentation standards would be required in addition to the existing OTC derivatives master agreements and the existing documentation for exchange-traded derivatives ('standard forms'). In 2013 ISDA published the ISDA/FOA (Futures and Options Association, now FIA Europe) Client Cleared Derivatives Addendum[14] and the FIA published the FOA Clearing Module[15] to give market participants the basis for a standardised set-up for client clearing. The German Clearing Master Agreement was published at the same time.[16] In France, ISDA and the French Banking Federation released the French Law Annex[17] to the ISDA/FOA Client Cleared Derivatives Addendum in August 2014 to be used as a supplement to a master agreement of the French Banking Federation for cleared transactions.

The focus of the standardisation was to create a standard form that works both for all European CCPs and their clearing models, and for all cleared financial instruments. The standard forms are therefore conceptually set up as CCP agnostic – that is, their terms make it possible to work with numerous CCPs services rather than just one specific CCP, in order to reduce the number of client clearing agreements between a clearing member and a client. This is obviously a challenging objective given the complexity of, and differences between, the clearing models and the governing laws involved, in particular the insolvency laws, as CCP, clearing member and client could each be located in different jurisdictions, including outside the European Union.

The importance of a client clearing agreement and its sophisticated drafting and elaborate negotiation strategies should therefore not be underestimated. A client clearing agreement is the principal contractual link to the first clearing level relationship between the CCP and the clearing member, and the basis for a well-functioning asset segregation and porting technique applied by the CCP.

The minimum contractual contents of a client clearing agreement can be summarised as follows:

- The client clearing agreement provides the contractual basis for the establishment of cleared transactions between the client and the clearing member which should economically match the cleared CCP transaction

---

14   The addendum can be found at www.isda.org/publications/isda-clearedswap.aspx.
15   The FOA Clearing Module is available for FIA members.
16   The English language version can be found at https://bankenverband.de/media/contracts/44537_0413a_ClearingRahmen_Engl_conven_CavVfSM.pdf. See also section 4 of the chapter on German derivatives documentation.
17   The French Law Annex can be found at www.isda.org/publications/isda-clearedswap.aspx.

(between the clearing member and the CCP) and be concluded around the same time. The cleared CCP transaction and the related client transaction are back-to-back transactions. Their existence and their content should be aligned and, in the case of amendments to the cleared CCP transaction, the related client transaction should be amended as well, or both should be terminated.

- The posting of client margin is agreed on the basis of the client clearing agreement. In line with the rule book, the clearing member and the client can agree on the posting of so-called 'initial margin' and 'variation margin'. Initial margin will be posted only by the client to the clearing member and intends to cover future uncertainties and the deterioration of positions and margin assets in case of a default until the time for the liquidation of the positions and margin assets. In addition, there is usually an exchange of variation margin between the client and clearing member to cover daily changes in the market value of the client portfolio and the posted margin collateral. It is possible that – subject to the rule book – the clearing member might be required to post variation margin to the client as well.
- Another important aspect of the client clearing agreement is the default handling if one of the parties in the clearing cascade defaults – that is, either the CCP, the clearing member or the client. The general contractual consequences provided for in the client clearing agreement is a close-out netting regarding the client transactions taking into account the value of the posted client margin (comprising both initial and variation margin). However, the client clearing agreement should also take into account potential porting solutions provided for by the CCPs. These porting solutions of CCPs can substantially deviate from CCP to CCP due to the laws, in particular the insolvency laws, governing the rule book. Accordingly, a close-out under a client clearing agreement might not be an adequate contractual reaction if a transfer of client transactions is envisaged by the porting offering of a CCP. Some CCPs, however, provide for both porting on the basis of a close-out netting of the cleared CCP transactions and client transactions, and an immediate re-establishment of the clearing cascade via a replacement clearing member.
- Lastly, client clearing agreements are important tools to protect the clearing member's riskless principal position and to implement regulatory capital requirements applicable to supervised institutions. Clearing members therefore will require a limitation of their obligations *vis-à-vis* the client if the CCP does not perform under cleared CCP transactions or even defaults.

In order to implement these minimum contractual contents in a CCP agnostic client clearing agreement, it is important that standard forms provide for sufficient flexibility to take into account differences in the clearing models and the porting mechanics of a CCP. A CCP agnostic client clearing agreement can therefore not be drafted without the possibility of agreeing on CCP specific provisions within the CCP agnostic structure.

4. Documentation standards

The two central standard forms for European principal-to-principal clearing models are the ISDA/FOA Client Cleared Derivatives Addendum and the FOA Clearing Model. The material contractual contents of these two client clearing documents are outlined below.[18]

4.1 ISDA/FOA Client Cleared Derivatives Addendum

(a) *Overview*

The addendum is not a standalone client clearing agreement. As its name suggests, the addendum supplements and forms part of a master agreement between the clearing member and the client, which can be the ISDA Master Agreement or a futures and options agreement drafted on the basis of the FIA standard forms (each, a 'master agreement'). Client transactions therefore form part of the whole portfolio of transactions executed under the master agreement, but are subject to the specific and prevailing provisions of the addendum.

An important aspect of the ISDA Addendum is the creation of the so-called 'cleared transaction sets'. This term groups client transactions by CCP clearing service and forms a basis for a separation and potential different treatment of any such cleared transaction sets. In particular, this is relevant for the purposes of the obligation to provide client margin, as well as for close-out netting and porting.

In order to achieve compliance with the rule book, the addendum creates a link to the rule book by way of the 'mandatory CCP provisions' and the 'core provisions'. 'Mandatory CCP provisions' are, for example, provisions of the rule book which the CCP determines as mandatory between the clearing member and the client and their client clearing agreement. In the event of any inconsistencies between the addendum and any mandatory CCP provisions, the mandatory CCP provisions will prevail in respect of the relevant cleared transaction set. 'Core provisions' are rule book terms and conditions which serve to protect the rules of the clearing model of the CCP – for example, in relation to the porting process established therein, and which have been published by the CCP for such purposes. The addendum respects this important linkage to the rule book by specifying that the application of a certain clause of the addendum is subject to the core provisions.

The main contents of the ISDA Addendum include the following:

- provisions for the establishment of transactions, their modification and termination (other than in case of a default);
- collateral terms regarding the requirement to post initial margin and variation margin and the determination of the margin requirement and the valuation of posted client margin;
- default provisions relating to the client, the clearing member or the CCP; and
- specific riskless principal-related clauses for the benefit of the clearing member, in particular the clearing member's protection of a payment

---

18   Terms in single quotation marks that are not defined in this chapter are however defined terms used in the relevant standard forms.

adjustment and a limited recourse in case of a shortfall in the amounts received by the clearing member from the CCP.

The addendum contains several optional clauses and, in particular in relation to the collateral terms, placeholders to be agreed and finalised by the clearing member and the client in the annex to the addendum. The annex therefore serves as an instrument to make the CCP agnostic addendum in certain aspects CCP specific.

(b) Conclusion of client transactions and modifications

Client transactions under the addendum arise automatically upon a clearing eligible trade being cleared through a CCP. In that context, 'cleared' means that an eligible trade has been submitted for clearing and the relevant CCP has become a party to a cleared CCP transaction with the CCP in respect of the eligible trade under the rule book.

In case of modifications relating to the cleared CCP transaction (or a termination of a cleared CCP transaction), the client transaction will usually be adjusted in the same way. However, if it is impossible or impracticable for the clearing member to adjust the client transaction, the clearing member may be entitled to terminate this client transaction and to request reimbursement for the loss suffered. The client, however, has the option to transfer the affected cleared CCP transaction and client transaction to a replacement clearing member.

(c) Collateral terms

The addendum provides for flexibility regarding the collateral arrangement between the parties. The clearing member and client may either apply the so-called 'collateral standard terms' of the addendum or agree on any other collateral terms. If the collateral standard terms are used together with an ISDA Master Agreement, the clearing member and the client automatically agree on the creation of a separate 1994 Credit Support Annex (New York law) or 1995 Credit Support Annex (English law) per cleared transaction set. Each such credit support annex will be deemed to form part of the client clearing agreement formed by the addendum with the Paragraph 11 provisions set forth in the relevant appendix to the addendum. Accordingly, the clearing member and the client can agree with respect to each CCP service on the specific terms for the client margin. This also enables the clearing member and client to take into account specific requirements or commercial aspects in relation to the applicable clearing models of the specified CCPs.

(d) Default provisions

The default provisions in the addendum are structured in an asymmetric way. In case of a default by the client, all client transactions, as well as all other transactions between the clearing member and the client, under the master agreement will be subject to the event of default provisions set out in the master agreement. With respect to the ISDA Master Agreement, this means that a close-out netting will occur at the same time in relation to all cleared and non-cleared transactions documented under the ISDA Master Agreement resulting in one single net amount taking into account all margin collateral provided for the cleared and uncleared transactions.

By contrast, in case of the default of a clearing member or a CCP, the addendum provides for a close-out netting only with respect of the affected cleared transaction set. Accordingly, if a clearing member defaults there will be a close-out netting and a single net amount per CCP service. This segregation of close-out claims enables a linkage to the asset segregation and porting techniques of the relevant clearing model. Only where such protections are not required, the addendum enables a set-off of these single close-out amounts. If a CCP defaults, then only the respective cleared transaction sets affected by such default will be closed out.

A clearing member default occurs under the addendum if the applicable CCP formally declares to the clearing member that an event constitutes a default in respect of the clearing member under the rule book, or if a certain event defined in the rule book – for example, an insolvency – results in the automatic termination of all relevant cleared CCP transactions. A 'CCP default' is a default, termination event or other similar event that entitles the clearing member to terminate cleared CCP transactions or results in an automatic termination. As a consequence of a clearing member default or a CCP default, the corresponding client transactions terminate at the same time as the cleared CCP transactions and without a declaration (or prior notification) by the client (in case of a client default) or the clearing member (in case of a CCP default).

The determination of the close-out amounts in case of a clearing member or CCP default is not based on the relevant master agreement. Instead, the addendum provides for a termination amount which will apply to each cleared transactions set, and will be determined for the client transactions of the relevant affected cleared transaction by reference to the values of the respective terminated cleared CCP transactions and the value of the client margin for such cleared transaction set. This ensures that client positions and client margin are considered per CCP services for the purposes of determining the close-out amount. The relevant client margin value is not specifically defined in the addendum. If parties select the collateral standard terms, the credit support annex provides several options for determining the value of client margin asset. The credit support annex in particular provides for a CCP valuation matching which enables the use of the valuation of the CCP for a specific client margin asset.

(e) ***Clearing member protections***
Subject to the terms of the relevant rule book, particularly in the case of a default by the clearing member, it is possible for the client to receive payment or delivery of securities directly from the CCP. This direct payment or delivery by the CCP is often referred to as a 'leapfrog' payment or delivery. The leapfrog payment or delivery, in particular if it relates to client margin, will not be reflected as such in the clause-out provisions applicable under the addendum following a clearing member default. Hence, in order to avoid double counting, the addendum provides for a payment adjustment which either:

- reduces the amount of any obligation of the clearing member towards the client by the amount of the leapfrog payment or delivery; or
- gives the clearing member a right to request the reimbursement of any

overpaid amount, as well as any losses incurred in connection with the leapfrog payment or delivery.

In light of the capital requirements listed under EU Regulation 575/2013 on prudential requirements for credit institutions and investment firms (CRR), clearing members are urged to incorporate a limited-recourse provision into the client clearing agreement to obtain an exposure rate of zero for client credit risk in respect of the client transactions. The addendum therefore provides that obligations of the clearing member are limited by, and contingent on, the actual performance by the relevant CCP. This limitation, however, does not apply if non-performance results from a netting or set-off pursuant to the rule book or a direct payment or delivery by the CCP to the client upon the occurrence of a clearing member default. These exemptions enable a successful liquidation or porting of the segregated cleared transaction sets.

In addition, the addendum provides for optional limitation of liability, indemnity and increased costs provisions. These provisions can be elected in the annex and negotiated in more detail between the parties.

(f)   *Further CCP-specific provisions*
Some European CCPs developed specific provisions for use with a client clearing agreement and a specific clearing model. These CCP-specific provisions are often intended to reinforce an insolvency analysis of the segregation and porting techniques of the relevant clearing model. Users of the addendum should therefore consider including such additional provisions as an appendix to the addendum.

4.2   FOA Clearing Module

The FOA Clearing Module is based on the addendum, but certain concepts and provisions of the addendum have been left out. The FOA Clearing Module has been drafted to enable clearing members and clients to use the FIA standard terms of business following the coming into force of EMIR. The FOA Clearing Module is primarily drafted for use with exchange-traded derivatives. The terms of the FOA Clearing Module, however, generally also enable the module to be used with cleared OTC derivatives, although the clearing member and client will have to make certain amendments to it, in particular if credit support annex-based collateral terms are to be used.

The main differences to the addendum are the following:

- The module does not provide for the concept of core provisions. It is therefore important to consider that a linkage to, and compliance with, the relevant clearing model has to be ensured by way of either mandatory CCP provisions or additional CCP specific provisions which should then prevail over the terms of the module.
- The module also provides for no specific clauses on modification events. Amendments to CCP transactions will be dealt with by the market action clauses in the FIA standard terms of business.
- There are no specific client margin provisions in the module. The module is

based on the assumption that client margin terms are already part of the FIA standard terms of business. However, it should be noted that those collateral arrangements might not be aligned to the concept of cleared transaction sets or a two-sided variation margining. An agreement on specific client margin provisions per CCP service between the clearing member and the client might therefore be required.

Similarly to the addendum, the terms of the module and the optional provisions therein will be completed and supplemented by the module annex.

5. Negotiating a client clearing agreement

When negotiating a client clearing agreement, the parties involved in the negotiation should be aware of the key commercial perspectives of the clearing member and the client. It is important to understand the background of the many negotiation topics that will come up when creating an access to a CCP.

5.1 Key perspectives for clearing members

As outlined above, clearing members are service providers that extend the clearing cascade to the end user and frequently analyse their client clearing offering with an emphasis on the effects of such offering on their own capital requirements and leverage ratios.[19] Against this background, clearing members will focus carefully during the negotiation process on their position as a riskless principal and the overall costs of their client clearing offerings. The riskless principal concept is, as mentioned above, already included in many parts of the existing standard forms – for example, provisions on limited recourse or payment adjustments. However, there are further aspects that clearing members will look at when finalising the elections provided for by the relevant standard form. Additional provisions on existing fees, additional fees and other rights to achieve a reimbursement of costs or losses in connection with client clearing are often proposed by clearing members in the 'other provisions' sections of the annex to the standard form.

5.2 Key perspectives for clients

Clients are primarily concerned with the protection of their client margin and their positions so that, in the event a clearing member's default, the margin does not become part of the clearing member's insolvency estate. In addition, clients that are financial counterparties and therefore subject to regulatory own-fund requirements will intend to structure their clearing arrangements in the most efficient way with regard to their own capital requirements. Under the CRR, this means that clients

---

19   See for example the ESMA Consultation Paper, "On the clearing obligation for financial counterparties with a limited volume of activity", of 13 July 2016 (ESMA/2016/1125) no. 13 on p8 (www.esma. europa.eu/sites/default/files/library/2016-1125_cp_on_clearing_obligation_for_financial_ counterparties.pdf). The leverage ratio concept does currently not appropriately take into account the risk-reducing effect of the margin collateral provided by the client, and clearing members might be required to hold extra capital against the margin collateral received. Clearing members should be enabled to offset initial margin received from clients against their future exposure from the client transactions.

might aim for a 2% risk weighting of their cleared positions (see section 6 below) and will therefore want to ensure that the respective requirements pertaining to bankruptcy remoteness, segregation and portability are complied with, in particular if the clearing member proposes changes to the standard forms.

Further, clients are concerned about the fees, additional costs and reimbursement risks passed on to them by the clearing members. The cost of client clearing is critical to the success of any mandatory clearing, and the market would benefit from further changes to the existing laws with a view to reducing any applicable clearing costs.

Lastly, clients should not be forced to put on hold or delay a clearing access via a second clearing member. An alternative clearing access is critical to reducing the impact of a clearing member's default on the client's ability to continue to be able to enter into cleared derivatives transactions.

5.3   Commonly negotiated provisions

There are several likely discussion points when negotiating a standard form between a clearing member and a client. However, the starting point of each negotiation should always be the client's choice of the relevant clearing model offered by the CCP. In particular, if a client opts for an individual segregated account, it is important to keep in mind the requirements of the rule book for the content of the client clearing agreement, as well as any available legal opinion on the insolvency remoteness of the clearing model. Caution must therefore be taken when agreeing to deviations from the standard form which CCPs might have analysed. Any deviation implies the risk of changing the legal analysis of a given clearing model.

(a)   Collateral elections

Under the existing standard forms, the clearing member and client will need to agree on the details relating to exchange of client margin. This in particular includes the details of any eligible currencies for cash collateral and the eligible securities for non-cash collateral, as well as any value deductions (known as 'haircuts') to take into account the risk of price movements regarding the non-cash collateral in a liquidation scenario. Clearing member and client will thereby take into account the list of assets that the relevant CCP service will accept as collateral. Otherwise, particularly in the case of the individual segregated account and the forwarding obligation, a collateral transformation arrangement between the clearing member and the client besides the client clearing agreement might be required.

The client margin requirement usually takes into account the margin requirement of the CCP *vis-à-vis* the clearing member for the client positions. Clearing members, however, often require excess collateral from the client to take into account their creditworthiness. Clients, by contrast, are interested in protecting liquidity and therefore want to limit any excess collateral. In the case of an omnibus segregated account, clients are taking an insolvency risk on the excess collateral if this will be held by the clearing member and not subject to any client asset segregation rules.

The clearing member and client will also have to agree on the transfer timings and the valuations of the client margin. The standard forms usually provide for a

CCP matching principle. In this case the clearing member and client agree to apply the valuations obtained by the CCP. However, it is often the case that clearing members prefer to make use of their own valuations.

Additional provisions are also negotiated if the rule book provides for a liquidation of client margin upon a clearing member default. In such a case, clearing members might require that the close-out netting calculation be adjusted to take into account the actual liquidation proceeds of the client margin instead of its market value as of the determination time specified in the standard form.

(b)   *Clearing access and transfer conditions*
Clearing members are unable to guarantee unconditional clearing access or a transfer of positions to another clearing member. However, clearing members often set out the conditions under which they will regularly accept the clearing of client transactions. Some of these conditions are often the basis for negotiations or clarifications, in particular if the client is subject to the mandatory clearing requirement.

(c)   *Costs, indemnities and limitation of liabilities*
Provisions regarding fees and general costs, increased costs rights of the clearing member (eg, in case of additional capital charges for the client clearing business), as well as indemnity provisions and limitation of liabilities for the clearing member, are common areas for negotiations. It is obvious that clearing members have a material interest in expanding their rights under the documentation in order to protect their riskless principal and own capital position. There is no uniform balance or compromise position in practice with respect to these provisions and, ultimately, it is a matter of negotiation and relationship that will conclude the agreement on such topics. However, it should be noted that clearing members often insist on their clauses and refer to their internal risk polices for the clearing service.

(d)   *CCP-specific negotiation points*
Clearing members have prepared and rolled out their additional standard terms to be included in the annex to the standard form. Any such clauses should be reviewed carefully when a specific clearing model is used, in particular in case of an individual segregated account, due to the complexity of the overlap between the rule book and the client clearing agreement. Regular negotiation points are, for example, additional provisions regarding the default of the clearing member, including any additional provisions regarding the liquidation of collateral, collateral substitutions or the consequences of a return of margin assets to the insolvent clearing member.

(e)   *Amendments*
Amendments to the standard forms might be time consuming, in particular if an amendment is required due to a change in law or a change in the rule book. Clearing members and clients therefore often negotiate unilateral amendment rights for the clearing members in certain scenarios. Clients usually prefer to have some controlling mechanism or at least a specific notice period to consider the changes and any consequences, such as moving positions to another clearing member.

6. Legal opinions

Clearing participants that are supervised institutions will require regulatory-driven legal opinions on the basis of Article 304, 305 and 306 of the CRR. ISDA and FIA therefore provide netting opinions regarding their standard forms for several jurisdictions. These opinions focus on clearing member insolvency on the one hand and client insolvency on the other.

In addition, under the requirements stipulated by Article 305(2) of the CRR, the client is entitled to calculate its own funds requirements in accordance with Article 306 of the CRR with a risk weight of 2% instead of 4%. These requirements are:

- bankruptcy remoteness;
- segregation;
- porting; and
- an independent, written and reasoned legal opinion that concludes that the client would bear no losses on account of the insolvency of its clearing member or of any of its clearing member's other clients.

Such segregation opinions have been obtained by certain CCPs or market associations and are therefore offered to clients. If there is no CRR segregation opinion available for a certain clearing model or jurisdictions, or the available opinions do not opine on all required legal aspects, clients might be required to obtain their own opinions to benefit from a capital relief.

The author would like to thank Alexei Döhl and Matthias Wetzig for their critical review of this chapter.

Designing derivatives structures

John D Finnerty
Rachael W Park
AlixPartners LLP

Derivative instruments play a fundamental and crucial role in finance and business. They are very useful in risk management, provided that they are structured and applied properly. They can improve economic efficiency when used appropriately to manage unwanted risk exposures. They can also assist portfolio managers in achieving more desirable portfolio risk-return profiles. However, numerous well-publicised problematic situations growing out of the misuse of derivatives serve as a stern reminder that harm can result when they are misapplied.

The global over-the-counter (OTC) derivatives market peaked at US$35 trillion of gross market value in December 2008, but had declined to approximately US$15 trillion as of December 2015.[1] The market for derivatives remains an important part of the worldwide capital market.

This chapter describes the basic types of derivative instrument and explains how financial engineers use them to design derivatives structures to meet derivatives users' financial objectives.

1. What are derivatives?

'Derivatives' are financial instruments whose value depends on the value of some specified underlying asset price, reference rate or index. They have been written on shares of stock, bonds, commodities, currencies, credit spreads and assorted indices. Derivatives are used either to take on selected risks, which may include (perfectly legal) speculation, or to hedge specific risks. Derivatives channel risks away from hedgers that wish to avoid them to speculators that are willing to bear them at lower cost. They enable market participants to manage interest rate and other risk exposures cost effectively.

Figure 1 shows the size of the key derivatives markets as of December 2015 and their growth since 2001.[2] Growth peaked in late 2007/early 2008, just before the

---

1   Bank for International Settlements, "OTC Derivatives Statistics at end-December 2015", dated May 2016, and "Derivative Statistics", dated 4 May 2016, available at www.bis.org/statistics/derstats.htm?m=6%7C32. A portion of the reduction was due to portfolio compression, which reduced the notional amount outstanding by eliminating offsetting trades. According to the International Swaps and Derivatives Association Inc (ISDA), portfolio compression reduced the notional amount of OTC derivatives by US$25.7 trillion and US$48.7 trillion during 2011 and 2012, respectively. During the period 2007–2012, a total of US$250.1 trillion notional amount was eliminated via portfolio compression. See ISDA, "OTC Derivatives Market Analysis, Year-End 2012," dated June 2013 (updated on 9 August 2013).

2   Bank for International Settlements, "Semiannual OTC Derivatives Statistics", dated 4 May 2016, available at www.bis.org/statistics/derstats.htm?m=6%7C32.

Figure 1. Notional amounts of outstanding derivatives, 2002-2015

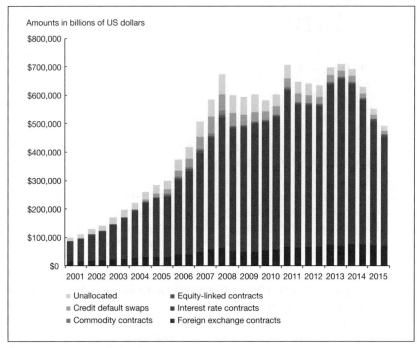

Source: Bank for International Settlements

international financial crisis of 2007–2009. Once the crisis passed, derivatives market growth has resumed, and the market has generally stabilised.[3]

2.   The basic building blocks

There are four basic classes of derivatives, called the 'basic building blocks': options, futures, forwards and swaps. These instruments play a fundamental role in structuring more complex derivatives.

2.1   Options

An 'option' is a contract that gives the holder the right, but not the obligation, to purchase (call option) or sell (put option) the underlying asset on or before a specified expiration date, for a price agreed at the transaction's outset (either a fixed price or one based on a formula). There are three principal styles of option:

- American style, which can be exercised any time before the expiration date;
- European style, which can be exercised only on the expiration date; and
- Bermuda style, which can be exercised on pre-specified fixed dates during the transaction's term.

---

3   The recent decline in the overall size of the OTC derivatives market was primarily driven by trade compression.

An option may be cash settled or physically settled. Physical settlement is the more commonly used form of settlement. It involves the actual delivery of the asset on which the option was written. Cash settlement does not require the actual delivery of the underlying asset and thus, is typically used for options written on assets that are not easily deliverable, such as foreign currencies or commodities. Under cash settlement, the settlement amount at the exercise date is equal to the intrinsic value of the option (the difference between the market value of the underlying asset and the option strike price) at that time.

Call options on stocks benefit the holder when stock prices rise because the payoff to the call option holder will be the amount by which the stock price exceeds the strike price on the exercise date. By contrast, put options on stocks benefit the holder in the opposite scenario because the payoff to the put option holder will be the amount by which the strike price exceeds the stock price on the exercise date.

Based on these 'plain vanilla' call and put options, financial engineers have developed options with more complex features, called 'exotic' options. The exotic options can be designed in various ways – for example:

- by combining plain vanilla call and put options, forward contracts, cash and the underlying asset (eg, bull/bear spreads, butterfly spreads, straddles, strangles);
- by allowing the option's payoff to be determined by a minimum/maximum/average price of the underlying asset during the option's life (eg, lookback options, Asian options);
- by terminating/initiating the option when the underlying asset's price reaches a certain level during a specified period of the option's life (eg, barrier options);
- by structuring another option on an option (compound options); and
- by allowing the option holder after a certain period of time to choose whether the option would be a call or a put (chooser option).

The exotic options are developed for various reasons, such as hedging, speculation, tax, regulatory, cost saving, or other purposes. A 'barrier option', as an example, is an option that is terminated or initiated when the price of the underlying asset reaches the predetermined barrier level during a specific period of the option's term. A barrier option can be either a 'knock-out' or a 'knock-in' option. A knock-out option expires worthless when the underlying asset's price reaches the knock-out barrier price, while a knock-in option starts worthless at inception and comes into existence when the underlying asset's price reaches the knock-in barrier price. Since barrier options limit the profit potential for option holders, barrier options are less expensive than equivalent plain vanilla options.

The asset underlying an option can be a stock, index, bond, commodity, currency, interest rate, or futures contract. When the underlying asset is an index, such as the S&P 500, Dow Jones Industrial Average or Nasdaq 100 stock index, the option is called an 'index option'.

When an option's payoff is dependent on an underlying interest rate, such as the yield on 10-year treasury notes, the option is called an 'interest rate option'. Interest rate call options are attractive to market participants that believe that interest rates will fall and bond prices will rise, while interest rate put options are attractive to those that want to hedge a fixed-income investment against the effect of a rise in interest rates (and resulting fall in price).

As of December 2015, the aggregate outstanding notional amounts of equity options, interest rate options and foreign exchange options were US$3.8 trillion, US$37.1 trillion and US$11.4 trillion, respectively, according to the Bank for International Settlements.

2.2   Forwards

A 'forward' is a contract between a purchaser and a seller to buy or sell an asset at a specified exercise price on or before a specified expiration date. The buyer, the holder of the long position, agrees to pay the contract price and receive delivery of the underlying asset at the expiration date, while the seller, the holder of the short position, agrees to receive the price and deliver the underlying asset.

At expiration, a forward contract can be either physically settled or cash settled. Under the physical settlement method, the buyer of a forward is obliged to pay the full price of the asset and the seller is required to deliver the underlying asset of the forward on the specified date. Cash settlement, by contrast, does not involve any physical delivery of the underlying asset; at expiration, the parties to the forward contract net out the difference in the value of their positions, and the one party with a net liability will pay the cash difference to the other. Cash settlement is preferred for the underlying assets that are inconvenient to deliver, such as the S&P 500 index, because, in this case, delivering the underlying 500 stocks would be inconvenient and extremely expensive.

For example, suppose that Party A enters into a forward contract to buy 1 million barrels of oil at $50 per barrel from Party B on a specific date. At expiration, suppose that the price of oil falls to $40. If the forward contract was physically settled, Party A is required to pay $50 million to Party B, and Party B is obliged to deliver 1 million barrels of oil to Party A. If the forward contract was cash settled, Party A is required to pay $10 million (= ($50 – $40) × 1 million) to Party B.

A forward contract carries default risk. The seller might fail to deliver the asset and the buyer might fail to pay for it. Credit risk is important in determining who can transact in the forward market. Access is usually limited to large corporations, governments and other creditworthy parties.

Forward contracts, and OTC derivatives in general, are typically cleared and settled either at a central counterparty clearing house (CCP) or on a bilateral basis. The degree of standardisation of contract terms determines whether the contract can be cleared at a CCP or not. If a contract is not sufficiently standardised that it can be cleared at a CCP, the counterparties are typically required to post collateral to mitigate the bilateral credit risk.

As of December 2015, the aggregate outstanding notional amounts of equity forwards and swaps, interest rate forwards, and foreign exchange forwards and swaps were US$3.3 trillion, US$58.3 trillion and US$36.3 trillion, respectively, according to the Bank for International Settlements.

2.3   Futures

A futures contract is similar to a forward contract, except that it is standardised and exchange traded, whereas a forward contract is non-standardised and traded OTC.[4] Futures therefore have greater liquidity than forward contracts. Unlike forward contracts, which realise gains or losses only on the settlement date, futures contracts are marked to market daily by an exchange clearing house. A futures contract carries very low default risk because of the daily marking to market, the exchange's margin requirements and the exchange clearing house guaranteeing each party's performance. In the United States, for example, futures markets evolved from forward markets when the Chicago Board of Trade (or CBOT) decided that it needed a mechanism to address the risk of contract default that had plagued the forward markets.[5]

2.4   Swaps

A swap agreement is a contract between two parties to exchange one stream of future cash flows for another on a stated notional amount. The most common types of swap are written on interest rates, foreign exchange rates, credit, commodities or equity. The most basic swap is a fixed-for-floating interest rate swap in which one party makes floating-rate payments and the other makes fixed-rate payments.

As of December 2015, the aggregate outstanding notional amounts of interest rate swaps and foreign exchange swaps were US$288.6 trillion and US$22.7 trillion, respectively, according to the Bank for International Settlements.

2.5   Distinguishing payoff profiles

Each of the basic building blocks has a distinctive payoff profile. These profiles are useful in crafting derivatives structures to satisfy users' risk-return preferences.

(a)   Options

As illustrated in Figure 2, options have an asymmetric payoff profile. A long position has an unlimited profit potential, but loss is limited to the option premium paid to buy it. By contrast, a short position has a limited profit potential, but unlimited potential for loss. The long call position earns a profit as the value of the underlying asset increases above the exercise price, whereas the short call position realises a loss. The long put position earns a profit as the value of the underlying asset decreases below the exercise price, whereas the short put position realises a loss.

For example, suppose that an investor believes that the stock price of a company is likely to decrease in coming months. Then the investor could purchase a put option on the company's stock. Assume that the company's stock is currently trading at $100, and the put option expiring in three months with a strike price of $100 is priced at $7. The investor would pay $700 (= $7 × 100 shares) for one put option, as one option is typically written on 100 shares of stock. After three months, assume that the price

4   www.legislation.gov.uk/uksi/2001/544/article/84/made.
5   Smithson, Charles W, Clifford W Smith, Jr and D Sykes Wilford, *Managing Financial Risk, A Guide to Derivative Products, Financial Engineering, and Value Maximization*, Richard D Irwin, Inc, 1995, p185.

falls to $80. Then the investor has the right to sell 100 shares of the company's stock at $100 while the stock is trading at $80, resulting in a profit of $2,000 (= ($100 – $80) × 100 shares) on the put option contract. As the investor paid a $700 option premium at inception, its net profit for the put option position will be $1,300. Let us assume now that the company's stock price rises to $120 after three months. In this case, the option would be worthless at expiration, so the investor would not exercise it, resulting in a net loss of $700 for the investor. Thus, the investor's put option has an asymmetric payoff profile as shown in Panel B of Figure 2.

Figure 2. Option pay-off profiles

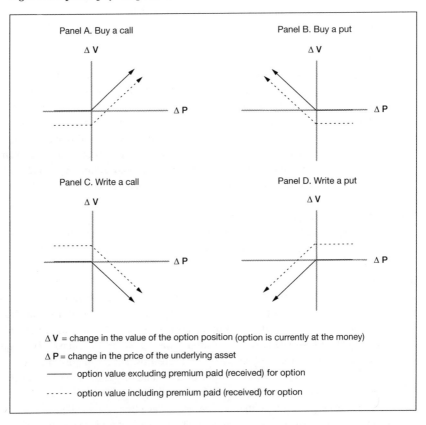

(b)   *Forwards and futures*
Unlike options, forwards and futures have symmetric payoff profiles, as illustrated in Figure 3. At the time when the forward or futures contract is initiated, the net present value of the contract is zero because the exercise price is equal to the expected future price. If the price of the underlying asset exceeds the exercise price at expiration, the holder of the long position makes a profit and the holder of the short position loses the same amount. Both long and short positions have an unlimited potential for profits or losses.

For example, consider an airline company that is concerned about future oil price appreciation and would like to lock in its future purchase price of oil. Suppose that the current oil price is $100 per barrel, and that the airline company enters into a forward contract to buy 1 million barrels of oil at $100 per barrel from a counterparty in one year. At expiration, suppose that the price of oil has fallen to $60 per barrel. Then, the airline company is required to pay $100 million to the counterparty in exchange for delivery of 1 million barrels of oil from the counterparty, which results in the net loss of $40 million (= ($60 – $100) × 1 million) on the contract for the airline company. If, however, the oil price had risen to $120 per barrel at expiration, the airline company would recognise a net profit of $20 million (= ($120 – $100) × 1 million). In both cases, the airline company buys oil for $100 per barrel. Thus, the airline company's forward contract has a symmetric payoff profile as shown in Figure 3.

Figure 3. A forward contract

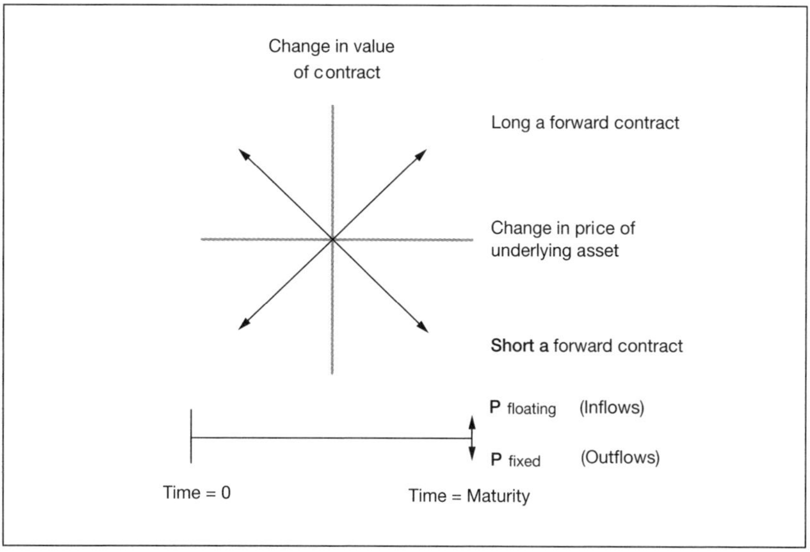

(c)   Swaps

Typically, at inception a swap has zero value and neither party makes a payment to the other. A plain vanilla interest rate swap involves the exchange of fixed-rate payments for floating-rate payments. On each settlement date, the parties exchange the net amount one owes the other, a practice called 'netting'. For example, if one party currently pays a floating rate on a loan but wants to pay a fixed rate, and another party pays a fixed rate but wants to pay a floating rate, the two parties can swap payment obligations to achieve their desired interest rate payment profiles by entering into a swap like the one illustrated in Figure 4. The floating-rate borrower agrees to pay fixed and receive floating in the swap to neutralise the effect of the floating rate on the loan. The fixed-rate borrower does the opposite, and both benefit.

Figure 4. An interest rate swap

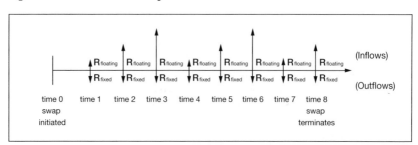

A plain vanilla currency swap is an exchange of interest payments on a loan denominated in one currency for interest payments on a loan denominated in another currency. At the start of the swap, the two parties exchange payments of principal. The swap specifies the notional principal amount that they need to pay at the start and at the end of the swap.

In an equity swap, the underlying asset is a share, basket of shares, a stock index or basket of stock indices. In a simple transaction, one party (Party A) makes (receives) a variable payment if the return on the stock or the index is positive (negative), while the other party (Party B) makes a variable payment based on an interest rate such as the London Interbank Offer Rate (LIBOR), when the payment is pegged to a floating rate. For example, if the price of the stock increases, Party A pays an amount based on the return on the stock to Party B and receives a LIBOR payment from Party B, based on a notional amount. However, if the price of the stock decreases, Party A receives the absolute value of the return amount from Party B in addition to the LIBOR payment. The equity swap allows Party B to gain exposure to the equity return without actually owning the shares of the stock.

A commodity swap is an agreement in which one party makes a payment based on the change in the trading price for a commodity, such as oil or natural gas, and the other makes a variable payment based on LIBOR. For example, an airline can enter into a commodity swap with a dealer to make floating payments based on LIBOR and receive floating payments determined by the change in the price of jet fuel to lock in the future purchase price of its fuel. If the price of jet fuel goes up, the airline makes a profit on the swap, which offsets its higher fuel cost.

2.6 Credit derivatives

A credit derivative is a contract whose value is derived from the credit risk of bonds, bank loans or other credit instruments of third-party reference entities (a corporate or sovereign). The underlying asset is the creditworthiness of the reference entity. Market participants can use credit derivatives to separate default risk from other forms of risk, such as currency risk or interest rate risk. The value of a credit derivative is linked to the change in credit quality of the obligations of the third-party reference entity. As credit quality changes, so do the values of the fixed-income security and the derivative.

The most common form of credit derivative is a credit default swap (CDS). A CDS

Figure 5. Credit default swap

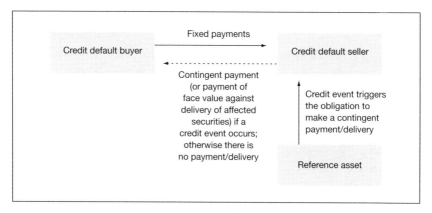

is a contract in which a credit protection seller agrees to make a payment equal to the difference between the face amount of a specified debt instrument, typically a loan or a bond, and its market value if a credit event, such as a default or a debt restructuring, occurs on the debt. Alternatively, the credit protection seller may accept delivery of a pre-agreed amount of affected bonds or loans of the reference entity, paying the credit protection buyer a pre-agreed, pre-default price for the securities, which are now trading at a post-default price.

In return, the protection buyer agrees to make a series of payments until default occurs or the CDS expires. The payoff structure is shown in Figure 5.

As of December 2015, the aggregate outstanding notional amount of credit default swaps was $12.3 trillion, according to the Bank for International Settlements.

Investors can also use credit derivatives to:

- take advantage of differences between their expected future default rates (eg, based on historical data) and the default rates implied by bond prices in a particular market sector; or
- profit from opportunities to arbitrage the differences in implied future default probabilities in two credit markets (eg, the bond market and the syndicated loan market).

3.   Using the basic building blocks to develop more complex structures

There are many ways to combine the basic derivatives building blocks to create different payoff structures. Creative financial engineers use the basic building blocks to create more complex derivatives structures for hedging, speculation, tax arbitrage or other purposes.

3.1   Basic design considerations

One of the objectives for designing derivatives is risk management through hedging. One can reduce the risk in the underlying asset by entering into a derivatives contract whose value moves in the opposite direction, provided that the derivatives instrument is properly structured.

Derivatives can also be used as investment vehicles. The instruments provide investors with the opportunity to make bets and make a profit (or loss) if the price of the underlying asset moves the same way as (or opposite to) what investors expect. Derivatives also provide leverage so that a smaller movement in the underlying asset price causes a much greater difference in the value of the derivatives. For example, a stock option provides a leveraged investment in the underlying common stock because the option premium represents a small percentage of the underlying share price.

Derivatives also provide an opportunity to circumvent regulatory restrictions or reduce taxes. For example, a prepaid forward contract enables a stockholder to achieve the same economic effect as selling the stock and receiving (most of) the cash proceeds while technically maintaining ownership of the stock. By doing so, one can defer the income taxes that would otherwise be due on the sale of the stock.

3.2 Alternative structures

Derivatives are usually structured to meet a particular financial objective, such as how to hedge a particular exposure to floating interest rates. There are often multiple combinations of the basic derivatives building blocks that will produce the same risk-return profile because the building blocks can be recharacterised in terms of each other. Probably the best-known such relationship is put-call parity, wherein every situation that can be described in terms of a call option has a parallel description in terms of a put option.

3.3 A futures contract as a series of forward contracts

As noted, futures contracts are marked to market daily. The value of the futures contract is paid or received at the end of each day. In effect, a futures contract is a series of daily forward contracts. A new forward contract is written each day and settled the next day throughout the life of the futures contract.

3.4 A swap as a series of forward contracts

An interest rate swap can be viewed as a series of interest rate forward contracts – one for each of the swap settlement dates. Paying a fixed rate on a swap and receiving LIBOR is the same as agreeing to pay the fixed rate (the forward price) in exchange for LIBOR (the underlying asset) on the settlement date.

3.5 A forward contract as a pair of options

Suppose that an investor buys a call option and sells a put option on a particular stock with the same strike price and expiration date. One option or the other will exercise, and the investor will receive the asset and pay the strike price for it. Accordingly, a long position in a call option coupled with a short position in a put option is equivalent to a long position in a forward contract (or a futures contract) because each structure will provide exactly the same returns to investors:

| long forward contract | = | long call option | + | short put option |

3.6   Swaptions

A 'swaption' (or 'swap option') is an option to enter into a swap. Although a swaption can be designed in various ways, it typically refers to an option on an interest rate swap. It gives the holder the right (without the obligation) to enter into a specified interest rate swap at a certain date in the future. For example, suppose that a firm knows that it will draw down a 10-year floating-rate bank term loan in six months and that it will want to enter into an interest rate swap to convert the loan into a fixed-rate loan. It can buy a six-month swaption giving it the right to enter into a fixed-for-floating interest rate swap to pay, say, 8% fixed and receive LIBOR on the agreed notional amount for 10 years. If the swap rate exceeds 8% in six months, the firm exercises the swaption. The swaption guarantees that the swap's fixed rate will not exceed 8%.

3.7   Interest rate caps, floors and collars

Three interest-rate derivatives instruments – interest rate caps, floors and collars – can be developed directly from the basic building blocks. They are used to structure floating-rate debt instruments to limit the holder's exposure to interest rate risk.

(a)   Caps

An interest rate cap is a series of call options on an interest rate, typically three-month or six-month LIBOR. An interest rate cap hedges the contract holder (eg, the issuer of a floating-rate note (FRN) whose interest rate is tied to three-month LIBOR) against a rise in interest rates. It is analogous to a put option on a debt security. For example, the buyer of a 5% cap on LIBOR will receive any excess of LIBOR over 5%.

(b)   Floors

An interest rate floor is a series of put options on an interest rate. An interest rate floor hedges the contract holder (eg, the owner of an FRN) against a drop in interest rates. It is analogous to a call option on a debt security. For example, an investor in FRNs that pay three-month LIBOR + 1% that purchases a 4% floor contract can never receive less than 5% interest in any period.

(c)   Collars

Buying an interest rate collar is like simultaneously buying a cap and selling a floor. A collar hedges against the interest rate falling outside a particular range. A collar always costs less than a cap at a given strike rate, because the premium received from the floor offsets part of the cost of the cap.

(d)   Caps, floors, collars and swaps

A collar with equal cap and floor rates is equivalent to an interest rate swap. For example, buying a 6% cap and writing a 6% floor both on three-month LIBOR is equivalent to going long a swap which pays 6% fixed and receives three-month LIBOR. The holder of the cap/floor combination will receive the excess of three-month LIBOR over 6% and pay the excess of 6% over three-month LIBOR, as with the 6% swap.

3.8   Usefulness of the relationships among the basic building blocks

Each building block can be transformed into any of the others through financial transactions. Because of these relationships, it is always possible to structure a complex derivatives instrument in multiple ways with the same payoff profile. One of the challenges facing a market participant that is considering entering into a derivatives transaction is to determine which equivalent structure will achieve the desired goal at the lowest cost.

3.9   Minimising counterparty default risk

One must also account for the default risk connected with any derivatives contract because the counterparty might default. If that happens, the holder of the derivatives instrument might lose the entire benefit of the contract unless the counterparty replaces the contract. Consider the fixed-rate payer in an interest rate swap. If the floating-rate payer defaults and interest rates have risen, it will cost the fixed-rate payer more for a replacement swap. Any cost saving must be measured net of contract default risk.

Structuring derivatives requires building in default risk protection to safeguard against the counterparty's default undermining the value of the derivative contract. In order to protect against a default, for example, one can insist that the counterparty be a AAA-rated bankruptcy-remote vehicle or require full collateralisation for any amounts that are owing to it under the contract. To mitigate the credit risk, the parties commonly use the legal frameworks provided by ISDA, which include standardised master agreements, credit support annexes and protocols for close-out, credit support, novation etc. A credit support annex, in particular, provides terms and rules regarding collateral arrangements to protect against the counterparty's default risk. It specifies the required collateral, such as the nature and types of collateral permitted under the contract, the minimum collateral transfer amount and the methodology for calculating the collateral amount. If there are multiple transactions between the parties under a particular ISDA master agreement, all the parties' positions are netted to a single aggregate net position.

4.   Designing structures to enhance risk exposures

Market participants can structure derivative instruments to increase their risk exposure, such as selling CDS to increase their credit risk exposure to a particular borrower with whose credit they are comfortable. Buying stock call options or selling stock put options increases the investor's equity risk exposure as compared to buying or selling the common stock because of the leverage inherent in an option. Selling stock call options increases the investor's equity risk exposure as compared to selling the common stock because of the unlimited potential for loss with the short call option position.

4.1   Enhancing credit risk with total return swaps

An investor can take on risk exposure to a company's debt (or its stock) by entering into a total return swap. The investor agrees to pay LIBOR (plus a spread) in return for the total return on the risky debt (stock). The receipt of total return payments mirrors the payments that the investor would receive if it owned the bond (stock). The investor has effectively leveraged its investment by borrowing the purchase price at LIBOR.

A total return swap can also be structured so as to magnify the investor's credit risk exposure, such as enabling investors to take on more credit risk than an equal position in an underlying instrument whose maturity matches the term of the swap. For example, a three-year total return swap based on a 10-year reference bond has the same credit risk price sensitivity as a 10-year note, and substantially greater credit risk price sensitivity than a three-year note. A longer maturity for the underlying reference bond increases the total return receiver's credit risk exposure.

4.2   Enhancing interest rate risk with inverse FRNs
Inverse floaters, also known as 'reverse floaters', 'bull floaters' or 'yield curve notes', increase interest rate risk exposure. A traditional FRN coupon adjusts each period in direct relation to changes in market interest rates. In fact, the market price should return to par value after each reset, unless the margin no longer sufficiently compensates for the default risk. Therefore, price changes are limited as compared to fixed-rate bonds of the same maturity. Inverse floaters are more volatile in price than fixed-rate bonds because the coupon moves in the opposite direction to interest rates.

4.3   Structured products
Interest rate swaps, fixed-rate notes and FRNs can be structured to conform to a specific view on future movements of interest rates, a currency or a commodity price. This is usually done by including one or more interest rate, currency or commodity options, respectively, in the structure of the swap or the note. These instruments are known as 'structured products'. Generally, those designed around an interest rate swap are called 'structured swaps' and those designed around a note are called 'structured notes'. Prior to a change in the accounting for derivatives, structured swaps were often preferred because it was easier to keep them off the balance sheet.

For example, a structured note with an Australian currency option might give the issuer a call option on the Australian dollar by paying reduced principal to the extent that the Australian dollar call option is in the money when the note matures. The note would pay an above-market coupon rate to compensate the note holder for the short position in the embedded foreign currency option. Such a note might be attractive to a financial institution that believes the Australian dollar is going to increase in value, but does not (or cannot) deal in foreign exchange options directly.

4.4   What structured products are designed to achieve
Market participants often have a view on interest rates. Even when there is no explicit forecast and no intended bet on the course of interest rates, there is an implicit view in each investment and new issue decision taken or postponed. For example, a simple decision to invest in back-to-back three-month treasury bills rather than buying six-month treasury bills has an implicit view – in this case, that the three-month treasury bill rate on the rollover date is likely to be above the rate

that the forward curve predicts at the time when the contract was entered into.

However, structured products are distinguished by the specificity of the view. The view can be structured in any number of ways, such as a specific interest rate staying within a particular interest rate band, or the difference between specified short-term and long-term interest rates changing in a particular way. One can bet on the direction of interest rates, changes in the shape of the yield curve, shifts in interest rate volatilities and so on.

4.5 Taking a view on the direction of interest rates

We have already discussed one structure that facilitates a bet on the direction of short-term interest rates – the inverse FRN. This first-generation product was subsequently modified to enhance its interest rate sensitivity.

An inverse FRN, barring default, is equivalent to purchasing a fixed-rate note, going short a swap (to pay floating and receive fixed) and buying an interest rate cap. Figure 6 shows how layering additional short swaps on top of a long position in an FRN creates different synthetic fixed-rate and floating-rate debt instruments. In Panel A, an investor purchases FRNs. In Panel B, the investor then sells a swap (to receive 7% fixed and pay LIBOR). The swap's notional amount equals the principal amount of the FRNs. Combining the long position in the FRNs and the short position in the swap produces a synthetic fixed-rate note paying 7.5%.

In Panel C, selling a second swap that is identical to the first (or doubling the notional amount of the first swap) transforms the synthetic fixed-rate note into a synthetic inverse FRN paying 14.5% – LIBOR. This synthetic instrument combines a long position in FRNs and two receive-7%-pay-LIBOR swaps. In panel D, selling a third identical swap converts the synthetic inverse FRN into a synthetic leveraged inverse FRN. The term 'leveraged' refers to the multiple applied to LIBOR – in this case, two. The coupon rate of the leveraged inverse FRN in Figure 6 declines twice as fast as the coupon of the inverse FRN as LIBOR rises. The leveraged inverse FRN pays interest at the rate of 21.5% – 2 × LIBOR.

Investors buy inverse FRNs rather than creating synthetics because the inverse FRN is simpler and carries less credit risk. Issuers of inverse FRNs usually have strong credit, often AAA-rated. The synthetic involves bearing credit risk on the underlying FRN, on the two swaps and on the cap. Also, some potential investors might be prohibited, by policy or regulation, from buying derivatives contracts. Embedding a derivative in a structured note, such as an inverse FRN, provides a way around such restrictions.

5. Designing structures to hedge risk exposures

Derivatives are used to reduce risk exposures through hedging. The need for such vehicles explains much of the rapid growth in the derivatives markets. A hedge guards against changes in an interest rate, the price of a commodity or a foreign exchange rate. Figure 7 illustrates the rationale for hedging interest-rate risk as an example. In Panel A, the firm's value decreases as interest rates increase. This may be due to interest rates increasing on the firm's floating-rate debt or to a rise in rates just as the firm is about to issue fixed-rate debt. If the firm can take a position in a

Figure 6. Creating synthetic inverse floaters

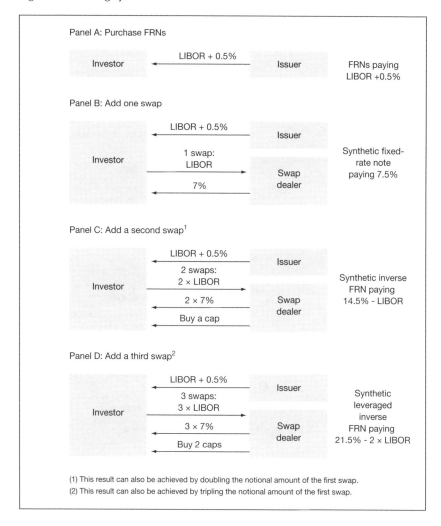

Panel A: Purchase FRNs

Investor ← LIBOR + 0.5% ← Issuer   FRNs paying LIBOR +0.5%

Panel B: Add one swap

Investor ← LIBOR + 0.5% ← Issuer
1 swap: LIBOR → Swap dealer
← 7%
Synthetic fixed-rate note paying 7.5%

Panel C: Add a second swap[1]

Investor ← LIBOR + 0.5% ← Issuer
2 swaps: 2 × LIBOR →
← 2 × 7%   Swap dealer
← Buy a cap
Synthetic inverse FRN paying 14.5% - LIBOR

Panel D: Add a third swap[2]

Investor ← LIBOR + 0.5% ← Issuer
3 swaps: 3 × LIBOR →
← 3 × 7%   Swap dealer
← Buy 2 caps
Synthetic leveraged inverse FRN paying 21.5% - 2 × LIBOR

(1) This result can also be achieved by doubling the notional amount of the first swap.
(2) This result can also be achieved by tripling the notional amount of the first swap.

derivative whose value will increase as interest rates increase, it can neutralise the impact of the interest-rate increase.

In Panel B, the value of the hedge position follows the dotted line. The position is carefully structured so that changes in its value offset changes in the value of the hedged asset. Panel B illustrates a perfect hedge. The value changes offset precisely so the value of the firm is unaffected. While perfect hedges are rare, proper hedging can substantially reduce a firm's exposure to interest rate or other risks.

5.1 Hedging with forwards and futures

Figure 7 illustrates how forward and futures contracts can be used to hedge interest rate risk. When interest rates rise, the values of both the firm and an interest rate

Figure 7. The rational for hedging

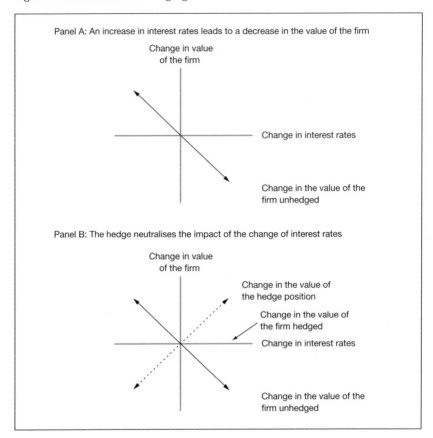

forward contract decrease. A short position in an interest rate forward contract moves in the exact opposite direction to firm value. Going short an interest rate forward or futures contract consequently provides a hedge against changes in firm value due to interest rate changes.

5.2 Hedging with options

Options provide a way to guard against a bad outcome and still have a chance at a good outcome. For example, life insurance companies sell products that promise a minimum rate of return. If interest rates fall sufficiently, it will fail to earn this minimum, and it will have a loss on the product. It can hedge its risk by buying call options on interest rate futures. Other firms would be hurt by rising interest rates. They can hedge their exposure by buying put options on interest rate futures.

One can view insurance as a put option. For example, auto insurance lets you put your car to the insurer if it is wrecked in an accident. Similarly, buying a put option lets the holder eliminate its exposure to bad outcomes, such as a large drop in share price or bond value.

Figure 8. Using an interest-rate swap to convert a floating-rate loan to a fixed-rate loan

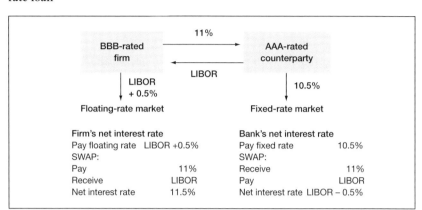

5.3   **Hedging foreign exchange risk with currency forwards or swaps**

The treasurer of a firm can use a currency swap, or a series of currency forwards, to transform cash receipts in a foreign currency into its currency of account. Suppose that a US firm sells products in the United Kingdom under a five-year contract that pays in sterling. It can structure a series of forward contracts to exchange the stream of sterling into US dollars at exchange rates that are agreed at the time when the forward contracts are entered into, which will fix its dollar receipts.

5.4   **Hedging interest rate risk with interest rate swaps**

A floating-rate borrower can hedge against a change in interest rates by entering into a swap to pay fixed and receive floating. Figure 8 illustrates how this hedge works. A BBB-rated firm borrows in the floating-rate market (eg, by entering into a bank loan). The LIBOR-denominated cash receipts under the swap offset the LIBOR-linked payments on the loan. Thus, the swap converts the floating-rate loan into a synthetic fixed-rate loan. The firm's interest cost changes from LIBOR + 0.5% floating to 11.5% fixed.

5.5   **Hedging credit risk with total return swaps**

A total return swap involves swapping an obligation to pay interest based on a specified fixed or floating interest rate in return for an obligation representing the total return on a specified reference asset or index. Such a swap transfers the total return (including interim cash flows and capital appreciation or depreciation) of a reference asset or index from one party to another. A lender can hedge its credit risk exposure on a debt instrument by entering into a total return swap in which it agrees to pay total return and receive LIBOR plus a spread. The total return payment stream depends on the credit standing of the borrower on the underlying loan. Such a transaction enables the lender to hedge the credit risk while leaving the loan on its books. Total return swaps are flexible – for example, allowing a lender to structure credit risk protection for, say, the last three years in the life of a five-year bond.

5.6 Hedging credit risk with credit derivatives

CDS buyers include lenders and fixed-income investors that have exhausted their credit limits to a client firm, but that want to lend additional funds or buy additional debt from that borrower. They can hedge their credit risk exposure by purchasing a CDS linked to the new loan. Similarly, a bank can free up additional lending capacity to a particular borrower by arranging a CDS to hedge part of its credit risk exposure on its existing bank lines to that borrower.

5.7 Hedging credit risk with credit spread options

Credit spread options enable investors to separate credit risk from market risk and other types of risk. Suppose that an investor wishes to protect against the risk that a particular bond's credit rating will be downgraded, in which case the credit spread would widen and the bond's price would fall. Buying a credit spread put option would provide the desired protection.

5.8 Hedging credit risk with a structured note

A structured note combines a conventional fixed-rate note or FRN with an embedded derivative instrument, such as an option or a swap, which links the payments on the note to the reference asset. A credit-linked note (CLN) is a particular form of a structured note in which the derivative instrument is a credit default swap or some other form of credit derivative. Typically, a CLN is a combination of a conventional note and a CDS.

A CLN allows the issuer to transfer a particular credit risk exposure to the purchaser of the CLN. In this structure, the issuer (seller) of the CLN is the protection buyer, and the investor (purchaser) of the CLN is the protection seller, which ultimately bears the credit risk.

CLNs are attractive to issuers that want to hedge against a credit default or a rating downgrade, which would adversely affect the value of one of their investments. They are able to customise the terms of the credit protection contract to satisfy their credit risk protection objectives. By contrast, investors purchase CLNs with the objective of enhancing the yield that they receive on their note investment. Many investors find CLNs attractive because they are able to gain access to the credit market, which might be unavailable to them otherwise.

5.9 Collared FRNs

A variety of innovative financial instruments has been introduced in the floating-rate securities market. Many contain embedded interest rate options. The coupon rate of a typical FRN resets each period at a reference rate, often LIBOR, plus a fixed margin. The coupon rate may be subject to a cap or a floor (or both) to limit the investor's interest rate risk.

6. Designing structures to alter cash payment profiles

A rich variety of derivatives structures has been developed to redirect the cash flows from a portfolio of assets so as to provide more appealing risk-return profiles.

6.1 Asset-backed structures

An asset-backed security passes through to security holders the cash flows from a portfolio of financial assets, such as mortgage loans. A representative list of securitised assets includes residential and commercial mortgage loans, automobile loans, credit card receivables, home equity loans and commercial bank loans. Complexity arises because principal and interest are not always passed through *pro rata*; there may be two or more classes (or tranches) of asset-backed securities, which are prioritised by their right to receive cash from the portfolio. The number of classes may be large – 60 or more – and the complexity of the priority rules can challenge even the most sophisticated investors.

6.2 Risk reallocation or reduction

The development of the asset-backed securities market has enabled financial institutions to structure derivatives to reduce or reallocate three principal types of risk associated with these assets.

(a) Prepayment risk

Most US residential mortgagors can prepay some or all the loan without prepayment penalty. Mortgage pass-through securities simply pass through mortgage prepayment risk to investors. Certain institutional investors, particularly life insurance companies and pension funds, limited their investments in mortgage pass-through securities because of their aversion to prepayment risk. Collateralised mortgage obligations were developed to prioritise the right to receive principal repayments, which reallocates prepayment risk exposure. Investors that have a preference for shorter-dated investments can purchase the highest-priority class, while investors that prefer longer-dated investments can buy the lowest-priority classes. Also, special securities classes can be structured to suit a particular investor's preferences for more or less prepayment risk exposure.

(b) Default risk

The Federal Home Loan Mortgage Corporation and the Federal National Mortgage Association provide payment guarantees for certain classes of residential mortgage loans. Mortgage-backed securities that are not guaranteed by these government-sponsored enterprises can be structured so as to prioritise the right to payments in the event that some of the underlying mortgages default.

(c) Interest rate risk

An unanticipated increase in interest rates will reduce the value of a fixed-rate loan. Mortgage-backed securities can be structured as interest-only and principal-only securities, which behave differently when interest rates change. For example, 'interest-onlys' increase and 'principal-onlys' decrease in value when interest rates increase. Consequently, these instruments can be used to manage interest rate risk exposure effectively.

6.3 Liability management structures

Derivatives are also used to tailor some of the standard provisions of conventional bonds, such as the redemption provisions.

(a) Call (optional redemption) provision

A call provision enables the issuer to call the bonds in whole (the entire issue) or in part (a portion) when interest rates drop, and to refund them at the lower interest rate then prevailing. Issuers must pay for this call option because it is disadvantageous to the bondholder. The cost depends on how the call option is structured. For example, a make-whole call provision, which is an indexed bond call option, generally costs the firm much less than a fixed-strike-price call option because the investor receives a higher redemption price.

(b) Put provision

A put provision gives bondholders the option to sell the bonds back to the issuer for par value on designated dates. This feature benefits investors and therefore increases the bond's value. If interest rates rise, thereby reducing a bond's value, investors can sell the bonds for par value and reinvest the proceeds at the higher prevailing interest rate.

6.4 Tax-oriented structures

Financial engineers can add value by designing derivatives that reduce the total amount of taxes paid. For example, derivatives can improve tax efficiency by deferring income tax liabilities or utilising tax losses more effectively. Suppose that a firm expects to earn $10 million per year for three years, but have losses the next several years as a result of large depreciation deductions. With an upward-sloping yield curve, the firm can enter into a fixed-for-floating swap to pay fixed and receive floating that will require net payments for three years and then net receipts thereafter. The net interest expense in the first three years and the net interest income in the later years will fit its tax situation.

Derivatives have also been misused in designing tax shelters. The BOSS (Bond Options Sales Strategy) and Son of BOSS abusive tax shelters are examples. One variant matched purchases and sales of nearly identical call options on a foreign currency. When exchange rates changed, one position had a gain and the other a loss. Tax promoters crafted a sequence of transactions that had the effect of recognising the capital loss while ignoring the gain due to a quirk in the partnership taxation rules. However, the taxpayers were not at risk because of the matching positions, and the US Internal Revenue Service has successfully challenged their tax deductions.

6.5 Regulatory arbitrage

Derivatives have been designed so as to achieve regulatory arbitrage, which is a practice through which investors capitalise on the differences in regulatory systems by shifting economic outcomes from one regulatory regime to another. For example, banks may prefer selling a series of interest rate swaps that settle every day for five years to selling a five-year swap that settles quarterly because the former requires banks to hold less capital.

The differences in regulatory regimes may also result in the flow of capital from markets that are more heavily regulated to other markets that are less heavily regulated. Recently, the implementation of the Dodd-Frank Wall Street Reform and Consumer Protection Act (commonly referred to as 'Dodd-Frank') in the United States in 2010,[6] which was initiated to overhaul the US financial regulatory regime, gave rise to regulatory arbitrage opportunities. In particular, Title VII of Dodd-Frank, among other objectives, seeks to mitigate counterparty credit risks and to increase transparency in the OTC derivatives market. The fact that the United States passed the OTC derivatives regulation ahead of other financial regulators around the world created important differences in derivatives regulation between the US derivatives market and international derivatives markets, which ultimately stimulated regulatory arbitrage. Derivatives dealers reacted to the tougher US derivatives regulatory regime by moving derivatives transactions offshore. US regulators in turn reacted to this shift by extending their regulatory reach to include offshore derivatives transactions conducted by financial institutions registered to operate a derivatives business in the United States.[7]

7. Conclusions

The financial markets have become more volatile. Firms have responded by seeking better ways to hedge their risk exposure, while hedge funds and other investors have sought ways to profit from this greater volatility. Financial engineers have responded by developing new derivatives structures that provide the desired risk-return profiles. The basic derivatives building blocks can be combined with traditional fixed-income instruments to design these more advantageous securities. There are usually multiple alternative structures available. The challenge is to determine which of the structures best meets the need most cost effectively.

---

6   Dodd-Frank Wall Street Reform and Consumer Protection Act, Pub L 111-203, H.R. 4173, signed into law on 21 July 2010.
7   US Commodity Futures Trading Commission (CFTC), Interpretive Guidance and Policy Statement Regarding Compliance with Certain Swap Regulations, 78 Fed Reg 45292, dated 26 July 2013.

Introduction to commodity derivatives

Edmund Parker
Marcin Perzanowski
Mayer Brown

1.   Introduction

The father of communist theory, Frederick Engels, wrote that "a commodity is a thing that has use-value; the latter exists in all forms of society, but in capitalist society, use-value is, in addition, the material depository of exchange-value".[1] This is a good definition. Things that have a use value as well as an exchange or tradable value include:

- bullion and metals, such as gold and aluminium;
- agricultural products, such as wheat, grain, livestock and cotton; and
- electricity and gas.

Twenty-first century commodities trading has broadened this definition to include freight pricing, permits for carbon dioxide emissions and other asset classes.

Many economists and political theorists have analysed commodities, including Adam Smith in *The Wealth of Nations* or Karl Marx in *Das Kapital*, but relatively little has been written to provide an understanding of commodity derivatives. Even less time has been spent analysing and discussing the documentation of commodity derivatives, even though commodity derivatives have existed for thousands of years and have been popular in Europe and the United States since the 19th century and before. This and the following chapter aim to fill the gap, at least partially.

For the purposes of this and the following chapter, we define a 'commodity derivative' as:

- a financial instrument;
- referencing an underlying commodity asset or other variable;
- from which the financial instrument's price or value is derived; and
- entered into by the parties for a purpose.

2.   The size and history of the commodity derivatives market

There are three categories of commodity derivatives financial instrument, each with different market sizes, characteristics and history:

- over-the-counter (OTC) derivatives;
- structured products; and
- exchange-traded derivatives.

---

1   Frederick Engels, *Synopsis of Capital* (1868).

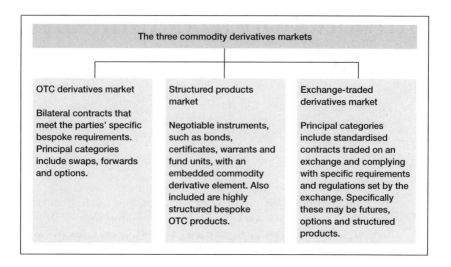

The three commodity derivatives markets

OTC derivatives market	Structured products market	Exchange-traded derivatives market
Bilateral contracts that meet the parties' specific bespoke requirements. Principal categories include swaps, forwards and options.	Negotiable instruments, such as bonds, certificates, warrants and fund units, with an embedded commodity derivative element. Also included are highly structured bespoke OTC products.	Principal categories include standardised contracts traded on an exchange and complying with specific requirements and regulations set by the exchange. Specifically these may be futures, options and structured products.

2.1   OTC derivatives

OTC commodity derivatives (ie, bilateral privately negotiated contracts) are nothing new. Bilateral forward contracts have been around for centuries and long precede the credit and interest rate derivatives markets. Forward contracts, where farmers agreed to sell their crops for an agreed price once harvested, were documented in ancient Egypt. Certainly, brokers have entered into forward and option contracts referencing freight rates (the cost of carrying goods by sea) since the 17th century.

The popularity of these products has increased significantly, as with all derivatives asset classes. The Bank of International Settlements' biannual reports provide the most reliable data on the overall size of the OTC market. Its end-of-year report disclosed that for the second half of 2015 there were more than US$1.3 trillion of outstanding OTC commodity swaps, forwards and options. This is a decline on previous years and this decline is likely to continue in numerical terms as regulatory requirements force standardised commodity derivatives instruments towards exchange clearing. More complex and bespoke transactions, though, will always be documented off-exchange.

2.2   Structured commodity products

The market for structured commodity products is growing. Each different negotiable financial instrument (eg, certificates or fund units) is called a 'wrapper'. Structured commodity products also include OTC derivatives contracts, which show a greater level of sophistication than so-called 'vanilla' products.

With many products privately traded and tailored to specific investor requirements, it is difficult to estimate the market's precise size.

Many major financial institutions have incorporated commodity derivative provisions into their medium-term note programmes. They can then issue debt where the return is linked to the performance of an underlying commodity asset, such as the gold price, a commodities index or the relative performance of a basket of commodities or indices. Major players in this area include Goldman Sachs,

Morgan Stanley and Deutsche Bank, among others. Some, including Goldman Sachs, also have commodities warrant programmes.

These programmes began in the 1980s and the more popular issue hundreds of series of notes, certificates and warrants to investors every year. These institutions will also structure bespoke OTC swaps for certain clients, providing a complex investment strategy in certain commodity assets.

2.3   Exchange-traded commodity derivatives

The financial markets of the 16th to 18th centuries introduced organised derivatives contracts trading with commodities and equities at the forefront. There are now several major players in the exchange-traded commodity derivatives market. These include ICE Futures Europe, a regulated futures exchange for global energy markets which lists the leading global crude-oil benchmarks and handles half the global trade in crude oil and refined-product futures. Present too is the London Metal Exchange (LME), which traces its origins to 1571 and the opening of the Royal Exchange. The LME offers futures and options contracts for base and non-precious metals such as aluminium, copper, nickel, tin, zinc and lead, plus two regional aluminium alloy contracts.

The London International Financial Futures and Options Exchange (LIFFE) – now called NYSE LIFFE and part of NYSE Euronext following its takeover by Euronext and Euronext's merger with the New York Stock Exchange – trades a number of commodity futures and option contracts, including a range of agricultural commodity contracts.

Eurex is a global derivatives exchange which is jointly operated by Deutsche Börse AG and SIX Swiss Exchange. Popular contracts traded on the exchange reference emissions allowances, bullion and agricultural derivatives.

CME Group Inc (formed through the merger of the Chicago Mercantile Exchange (CME) and the Chicago Board of Trade (CBOT)) also owns NYMEX. The CME is a financial and commodity derivative exchange based in Chicago. It was founded in 1898 and trades a variety of commodity derivative products. CBOT, which was established in 1848, is the world's oldest futures and options exchange and also trades a wide variety of contracts. NYMEX is a futures and options exchange comprising two divisions: the NYMEX division and the COMEX division. The NYMEX division trades coal, crude oil, electricity and uranium futures and options contracts. The COMEX division trades futures and options contracts referencing gold, silver, aluminium and copper.

3.   Understanding the four constituent parts of a commodity derivative

We define a 'commodity derivative' as a financial instrument referencing an underlying commodity asset or other variable, from which the financial instrument's price or value is derived, entered into by the parties for a purpose. By setting out the definition in this way, we show that a commodity derivative is made up of four constituent parts:

- a financial instrument;
- referencing an underlying commodity asset or other variable;

- from which the financial instrument's price or value is derived; and
- entered into by the parties for a purpose.

This allows us to analyse each constituent part in turn to form a fuller picture of the nature of commodity derivatives.

The financial instrument – the first constituent part – will fall into one of the three main categories of commodity derivative financial instrument:

- OTC derivatives;
- structured products; and
- exchange-traded products.

In the case of an OTC derivative, the financial instrument will be a swap, forward or option. In the case of a structured product it will be a note, certificate, warrant, fund unit or bespoke swap. In the case of an exchange-traded product, it will be a future, an option or one of the structured products.

The second constituent part – the underlying commodity asset or other commodity variable – will be a commodity such as bullion, other metals, agricultural products, freight prices, paper, gas, power, emissions allowances or a weather index. The commodity itself will be commoditised. For example, it might be a metric tonne of a certain grade of cocoa or a specific freight route in a vessel of a particular size for a specific weight of cargo.

The price or value of the underlying commodity asset from which the financial instrument derives its value – the third constituent part – may be the change in the price or an underlying commodity or future referencing it, or the level of an index over a period of time or between specific dates. Alternatively, it may be the relative price or level of different underlying assets over a period of time or specific dates. or the total return on single or multiple underlying assets (eg, indices or futures contracts) over a period of time. These prices or levels may be determined on specific or multiple dates and often in accordance with a formula.

The fourth constituent part – the purpose for which the parties enter into a commodity derivative transaction – can be many and varied. Reasons might include:

- commodity producers such as mining companies looking to hedge against sale proceeds being insufficient to cover production costs;
- manufacturers hedging against rises in raw material prices which would erode sale margins;
- speculators making leveraged investments in particular commodity asset classes, such as oil; or
- funds looking to diversify their investments away from traditional asset classes such as debt and equities.

We now look at each of the four constituent parts of commodity derivatives in further detail.

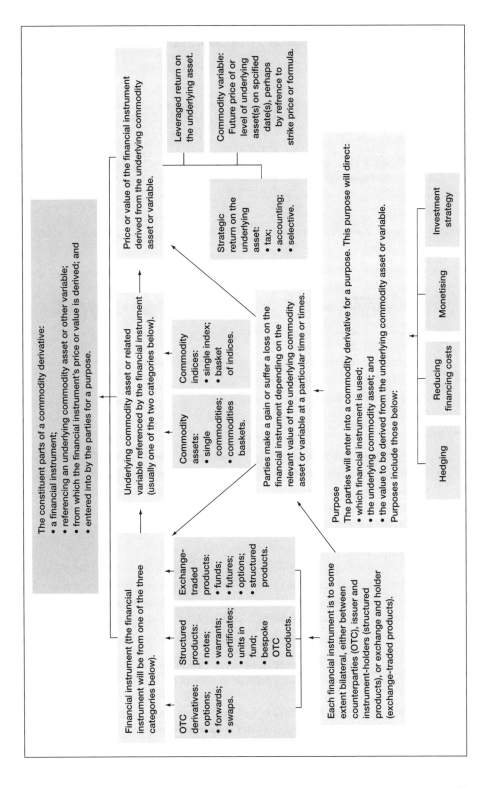

4. The first constituent part of a commodity derivative: the financial instrument

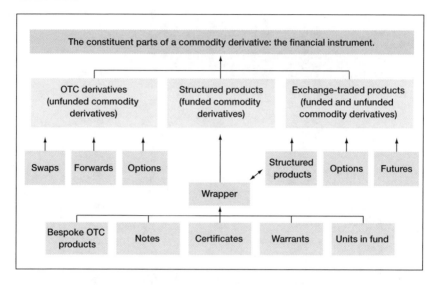

Any commodity derivative financial instrument will be a sub-type of at least one of the three commodity derivatives categories:

- OTC derivatives;
- structured products; and
- exchange-traded products.

An OTC derivative financial instrument will be a swap, a forward or an option. A structured product financial instrument will be a note, a certificate, a warrant, a unit in a fund or a bespoke OTC product. An exchange-traded product financial instrument will be a future or an option or, if it is listed on an exchange, one of the four types of structured product financial instrument.

4.1 OTC derivatives

There are three categories of commodity derivatives OTC financial instrument: options, forwards and swaps. Each type has various sub-types. Sub-types of option are European, American, Bermudan, Asian and barrier options. Among the sub-types of forward are contracts for difference, while sub-types of swap include index-linked and basket swaps.

(a) Options

An option is a bilateral contract. The buyer of the option acquires a right to buy (or sell to the seller of the option) a defined amount of an underlying commodity asset at a price agreed at the contract's outset (the strike price). This price will be either a specific price or one determined by reference to a formula or set of rules set out in the confirmation. The underlying asset is usually a single commodity or basket of commodities, or an index or basket of indices.

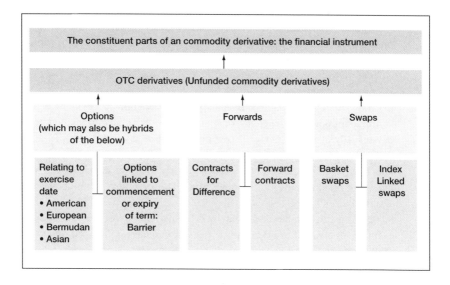

The option buyer pays an amount of money (a premium) to the option seller, as determined in the relevant transaction confirmation, to compensate it for providing the option.

Options are either call options or put options, and are also either cash settled or physically settled.

In a physically settled put option, the buyer has a right to sell a specified quantity of a commodity or basket of commodities (eg, one metric tonne of coal) to its counterparty at an agreed price (the strike price) on a future date. In a physically settled call option, the option buyer has a right to buy the same at the strike price.

Whether the option buyer chooses to exercise its option will depend on whether the underlying commodity asset is trading above or below the strike price. Naturally, the call option is worth exercising only if the underlying asset is trading above the strike price on the exercise date. Likewise, the put option is worth exercising only if the underlying asset is trading below the strike price on the exercise date.

In a cash-settled option, a put option buyer has the right to demand a payment from its counterparty if the settlement price (ie, the trading price of the underlying commodity or future, basket of commodities or futures or the level of a commodities index) is lower than the strike price (as provided in the confirmation) on the exercise date. Conversely, a call option buyer can demand a payment when the actual price (the settlement price) is higher than the strike price on the exercise date.

Options are also categorised by when they can be exercised. The three most common types are American, European, Bermudan and Asian.

An American option can be exercised on any trading day during the option's term; this means that it can be exercised at any time before its expiry. However, a European option can be exercised only on the day of its expiry (ie, its expiry date).

A Bermudan option is a half-way house between a European and American option. It can be exercised on specific days, as provided in the confirmation; these are called 'potential exercise dates'.

Options can be categorised using the method by which the strike price or exercise price is determined (if this is not specifically set out in the transaction confirmation). For example, an Asian option looks at the average price of the underlying asset over a period of time or on specific dates.

Another category of option is a barrier option (which has sub-sets called 'knock-in' and 'knock-out' options). In a knock-in transaction, a payment or delivery is contingent upon the occurrence of a knock-in event on any knock-in determination day (usually a trading day or predefined period or range of dates). In a knock-out transaction, the transaction will terminate without the option being exercised if a knock-out event occurs on any knock-out determination day. Knock-in and knock-out events will usually be the level of a share or index going above or below a specified level.

Options can also be categorised by being part of a particular trading strategy. For example, in a straddle, a derivatives user can purchase both a call option and a put option referencing the same underlying asset and with the same strike price. The strategy protects the derivatives user against volatility above or below a specific level in the trading price of the underlying asset.

(b)   *Forwards*

A forward transaction is a bilateral sale-and-purchase contract. In a physically settled transaction, one of the parties agrees to sell and the other agrees to buy a defined amount of the underlying commodity at a defined point in the future for a specified price (if the transaction is physically settled). In both cases, sale prices can instead be determined by reference to a formula or an average price over a number of dates.

In a cash-settled transaction, the parties exchange the difference between the actual trading price of the underlying commodity asset at the future date and the price set out in the confirmation.

A forward can also relate to an index (in which case it will be cash settled), and the parties will instead exchange payments based on a settlement price related to the level of the index at the future date as compared with the level set out in the confirmation.

(c)   *Swaps*

A commodity swap is a bilateral contract that allows a party to acquire economic exposure to an underlying commodity asset without the need to buy that asset. There are several variations.

Under these types of transaction, the swap references a commodity underlying asset, which can be a single commodity or basket of commodities, or an index or basket of indices. One or several measurement dates are set out in the transaction confirmation.

There are many bespoke variations depending on the underlying commodity asset. Generally speaking, though, each transaction has two parties: a fixed-amount payer and a floating-amount payer. On each payment date a fixed amount is paid. If the value of the underlying commodity asset has risen above a set level on a particular measurement date, the floating-amount payer will pay the fixed-amount payer an amount equal to the positive differential (multiplied by the transaction's notional amount and any mulitplier). If the value of the underlying commodity asset has fallen below the set level on the particular measurement date, the fixed-amount payer will pay the corresponding value of that differential to the floating-amount payer.

Different underlying commodity assets are treated differently from one another. Bullion swaps, EU emissions allowances, freight and other derivatives all have their own market norms. These are driven partly by market traditions and standards, and partly by the esoteric nature of the underlying asset itself.

(d) *Documentation platform for options, forwards and swaps*

Much of the OTC commodity derivatives market has standardised norms and documentation. The principal documentation platform for OTC derivatives is provided by the International Swaps and Derivatives Association Inc (ISDA). Documentation platforms for other underlying commodity asset classes have been provided by, among others:

- the European Federation of Energy Traders (EFET) for energy derivatives;
- the International Emissions Trading Association (IETA) for emissions allowances; and
- the Forward Freight Agreement Brokers Association (FFABA) for freight derivatives.

ISDA: ISDA, founded in 1985, is a latecomer to the commodity derivatives market. It accompanied the new players, the financial institutions and hedge funds – the traditional brokers were using commodity derivatives long before and already had their own market norms, traditions, documentation and trade bodies. The ISDA platform therefore was specifically designed to harmonise with existing market practices and trade organisations, while trying to add greater documentation sophistication developed in other derivatives areas, such as equity derivatives.

ISDA's suite of documentation for commodity derivatives consists of three inter-linking platforms: a primary platform, a secondary platform and a tertiary platform. The primary platform – a master agreement amended by a schedule and possibly a credit support document – is an umbrella agreement applicable to all derivatives areas covered by ISDA (eg, interest, foreign exchange, currency and credit). All transactions entered into under the master agreement form a single agreement, allowing amounts payable under the same currency to be netted in the same transaction and, if the parties elect, all transactions. On an early termination (eg, as a result of the bankruptcy of one of the parties), the amount due can be netted to a single amount.

The secondary platform consists of the 2005 ISDA Commodity Definitions. The 2005 Definitions are designed to be used with OTC confirmations relating primarily to option transactions, forward transactions and commodity swaps governed by an ISDA master agreement already entered into by the parties.

The 2005 Definitions provide a framework of agreed terminology, together with market standard fall-backs for when prices cannot be obtained or, for example, trading days for exchanges or the calculation of indices are disrupted.

The tertiary platform essentially consists of best-practice statements and guidance prepared by ISDA, to provide support for market participants in case there are any market disruptions.

EFET: EFET is a non-profit organisation whose membership is made up of more than 120 energy-trading companies from over 20 European countries. EFET's documentation platform operates in a similar manner to ISDA documentation.

It utilises a primary platform of general agreements. These operate similarly to the ISDA Master Agreement, except that they are product specific and relate to gas or electricity only. These general agreements are then amended, modified or supplemented through separate election sheets and/or appendices, just as one would amend the ISDA Master Agreement through the ISDA Schedule.

For gas, there is the EFET General Agreement Concerning the Delivery and Acceptance of Natural Gas. This governs all transactions for the purchase, sale, delivery and acceptance of natural gas. This general agreement also has an allowances appendix to facilitate emissions trading through the trading of EU emissions allowances. For electricity, there is the EFET General Agreement Concerning the Delivery and Acceptance of Electricity, which performs the same function.

EFET's secondary platform consists of a confirmation under which each individual transaction is documented. Each confirmation supplements and forms part of the relevant general agreement.

4.2   Structured products

For structured products, the financial instrument is called a 'wrapper'. The wrapper may be a certificate, note or warrant or, for more bespoke OTC commodity derivatives, the standard ISDA documentation framework. The specific format that a wrapper takes will depend on investor preference, efficiency, liquidity, and tax and regulatory issues.

Although notes or certificates can be issued as standalone instruments by an issuer (usually a financial institution or one of its specially created subsidiaries), for reasons of documentation efficiency they are more commonly issued under a programme. The programme will establish a master documentation platform, under which future issues of instruments will be documented.

The programme will have a prospectus which will be listed on a stock exchange. In Europe, this is most commonly the Luxembourg Stock Exchange or the Irish Stock Exchange. The prospectus will set out the conditions of any instruments issued under the programme. These conditions will usually adapt many of the provisions from the 2005 ISDA Commodity Definitions to make them suitable for inclusion in a certificate, note or warrant. The prospectus will also contain risk factors and disclosure on the issuer and any other relevant parties.

The programme will also have an agency agreement which will set out the roles and responsibilities of the various other parties to the transaction – such as the calculation agent and paying agents.

Each time the issuer issues instruments to investors, it will complete a final terms document. This will make various elections contained in the conditions (set out in the prospectus) and will set out the pricing information and specific terms (eg, the identity of the underlying asset) for the particular issue.

The final terms together with the conditions will be attached to a global instrument (which will represent all of the securities for a particular issue), and will be deposited into a clearing system. In Europe, this will usually be either one or both of Euroclear and Clearstream. The instruments can then be traded.

Sometimes, but not always, the individual issue of securities will be listed on the same stock exchange as the programme. This helps to make the securities more liquid and also meets the investment requirements of many institutional investors. This means that commodity derivatives structured products can also be exchange-traded products.

Another form of commodity derivatives structured product relates to investments in commodity funds. This is where an investor purchases units, or alternatively shares or preference shares, in a fund located in a low-tax or no-tax jurisdiction such as the Cayman Islands or Jersey. Alternatively, the fund may be located in a European Economic Area (EEA) jurisdiction as a scheme for undertakings for collective investment in transferable securities (or UCITS). The fund will invest in commodity underlying assets such as gold or copper; or it may track the performance or relative performance of various indices, or indeed follow various commodity investment or commodity derivative strategies, to generate an enhanced return for investors. The instruments issued by the fund will derive their value from the value of the fund. If the instruments issued to investors are listed on a stock exchange, the fund will be an exchange-traded fund. The listing allows increased liquidity for the fund's units.

An alternative structure can involve establishing a cell company, which then creates a separate segregated cell for each issue, whose assets are ring-fenced from the other cells. Other less common forms of wrapper include:

- structured deposits with financial institutions, the returns on which are usually linked to commodity indices;
- life insurance policies with returns usually linked to the performance of commodity indices; and
- trust certificates, which operate in a similar manner to protected cell companies (with a separate sub-trust be established for each issue and segregation between different sub-trusts).

4.3   Exchange-traded products

Exchange-traded commodity derivatives are commodity derivatives traded on an organised exchange. They provide, just as with trading in the underlying commodities, standardised contracts tradable through a central clearing house (also known as a 'central counterparty'). The principal exchange-traded commodity derivative products are futures, options and structured products.

Forwards and futures are similar, the main difference being the way in which they are traded. Forward contracts are OTC private bilateral contracts where each party takes a credit risk on the other. Futures contracts are standardised exchange-traded contracts with limited credit risk, as they will have the benefit of a central counterparty.

The futures markets developed promoting efficiency, market regulation and increasing investor confidence. The pricing, delivery provisions and other elements of each futures contract are standardised. Delivery of the underlying asset rarely occurs, with the initial contract being hedged.

While forwards have both credit risk and market risk (with the credit risk arising from exposure to the counterparty), futures aim to eliminate credit risk as far as possible, leaving only market risk. The central counterparty will transact only with brokers – these are institutions which are members of the exchange. Central counterparties are usually a part of an individual exchange or third-party entity, which acts as a buyer to every seller and a seller to every buyer. They minimise counterparty risk by taking margin payments in line with underlying exposure. The central counterparty therefore takes a limited credit risk on each broker and the brokers take a limited credit risk on their clients. No party takes any credit risk on an unknown party. Each broker will take an initial margin payment in the form of cash or securities from its client, which it holds in a margin account.

5. **The second constituent part of a commodity derivative: the underlying commodity asset**

In the case of commodity derivatives, the underlying asset being referenced by the financial instrument is almost always a single commodity or a basket of commodities, or a single commodity index or a basket of commodity indices.

In equity derivatives transactions, the underlying asset is fairly simple: shares or indices related to them. The complexity lies in the regulation, extreme volatility of the underlying asset and the sophisticated structures set up to manage these. In commodity derivatives, the most complex area is the variety of underlying assets and the adaptation of derivatives financial instruments to work with these – in particular, the different market norms which can exist in the mature markets that relate to them.

The most common assets underlying commodity derivatives transactions are agricultural products, energy, freight, metals, paper, emissions allowances and weather indices.

Commodity derivatives generally reference the price of an underlying commodity asset. To do that, the commodity must be standardised (ie, traded by reference to a specific price and quality (or grading). The quantity and quality will be specific to the particular underlying asset.

5.1 **Agricultural products**

Mature markets for trading agricultural derivatives have existed since the 19th century, and many of the older commodity derivatives exchanges were set up to trade futures and options referencing agricultural products. Some of the most popular underlying agricultural commodities include canola, cocoa, coffee, corn, cotton, livestock, milk, oats, orange juice, rubber, soya beans, sugar, sunflower seeds, wheat and wool.

Within these categories are various sub-categories of traded commodity:

- within coffee, there is washed arabica coffee and robusta coffee;
- within corn, there is yellow maize and white maize; and
- within livestock, there is dressed carcase, feeder steers, live steers and lean value hog carcasses.

Each commodity is traded in a standardised quantity. For example, cocoa is traded in tonnes; corn is traded in bushels; cotton and sugar are traded per pound; and cattle are traded on a per-kilogram basis.

Standardisation is vital in commodity derivatives and so financial instruments referencing individual agricultural commodities will almost always reference one of the prices published by a commodities futures exchange. These are then republished by information providers such as Reuters. Definitions for the most popular commodity prices are set out as commodity reference prices in Sub-Annex A to the 2005 Definitions.

The commodity reference price for cotton, for example, is set out as:

"COTTON NO.2-NYBOT" means the price for a Pricing Date will be that day's Specified Price per pound of deliverable grade cotton No.2 on the NYBOT of the Futures Contract, stated in U.S. cents, as made public by the NYBOT and displayed on Reuters Screen "0#CT:" on that Pricing Date.

Several things are apparent from this definition:

- the standardised quantity (pounds);
- the grading (deliverable grade cotton No 2 is a set of quality standards);
- the dollar pricing is the trading price of the related futures contract; and
- the commodity reference price is that republished on the specified Reuters screen.

5.2 Energy

Some of the most popular underlying energy derivatives include benzene, coal, diesel fuel, electricity, fuel oil, gas oil, gasoline, heating oil, jet fuel/kerosene, methanol, naphtha, natural gas and oil. Within these categories are many sub-categories of traded commodity.

Electricity, for instance, is divided into several groups of tradable commodity reference prices based on geography, with trading markets in particular for Australia, Europe (with sub-groups for the Benelux countries, France, Germany, the Nordic countries, Spain, Switzerland and the United Kingdom) and the United States.

The commodity reference prices for each group reference the price per megawatt for physical delivery of electricity. Each country or area will have several different commodity reference prices. For example, Sub-Annex A to the 2005 Definitions specifies four different traded prices for UK electricity commodity reference prices, relating to prices calculated by the London Energy Brokers' Association for the UK Power Indices:

- the Day Ahead Window Index;
- the Working Days Index;
- the Monday–Friday Peak Index; and
- the All Days Index.

There are many tradable electricity commodity reference prices and these represent just four. These prices are not necessarily published with derivatives in mind and are widely used in the spot markets.

Each of the other energy commodities also has several tradable commodity reference prices. Oil, for example, has:

- Brent crude oil;
- Dubai crude oil;
- baskets of crude oil imported into Japan, known as Japanese Crude Cocktail (Provisional); and
- West Texas intermediate light sweet crude oil.

5.3 Freight

Freight rates are the prices charged for carrying goods on a ship and are the underlying asset in freight derivatives; and freight derivatives involve a financial instrument which derives its value from the underlying asset of a freight rate. The complexity of the underlying assets and how these are traded makes freight derivatives a particularly complex area of commodity derivatives. The discussion below demonstrates both the difficulty and importance of understanding the intricacies of the underlying asset, both when dealing in the particular product and when documenting any particular transaction.

Freight rates are filled with nautical terminology. They are quoted on the basis of cost per metric tonne for transporting cargo on an agreed route, in a vessel of a particular size. These rates will differ according to the following, among other factors:

- whether the route is on a voyage basis or a time charter basis;
- the size of the particular vessel transporting the cargo; and
- the route taken.

Freight rates are volatile: prediction of future demand rests on sentiment about the future direction of world trade and the global economy, with unreliable and differing forecasts in this area correlating to volatility in the future direction of freight rates. Ships run on fuel, so movements in oil prices directly impact on freight rates. Particular freight rates are often directly referenced to the commodities being carried (eg, coal or iron ore). So movements in the pricing of the underlying commodity can also impact on freight rates.

Trading in freight derivatives is possible only if reliable market prices are available. These come from published indices, freight rates and trading prices. The principal provider of current freight market information is the Baltic Exchange (located in London and a centre of freight trading for hundreds of years). For tankers, Platts (an information provider) is important; and for wet route rates published by both the Baltic Exchange and Platt's, the prices published by Worldscale are used as a nominal base.

Worldscale is a joint venture between Worldscale Association (London) Limited and Worldscale Association (NYC) Inc. It operates as an online platform providing more than 320,000 flat rates for previously requested freight routes, on the basis of a standard-sized vessel carrying a standard cargo being charged at a daily hire rate. These rates are published annually and are supposed to represent the average market rates at the time of publication. Worldscale operates on a system of 'points of scale'. Parties then negotiate these dollar figures by adjusting them by Worldscale points. Each point away from 100 represents a percentage point of adjustment to the published rates. For example:

- 100 points means the published rate itself (or Worldscale Flat);
- 40 points means 40% of the published rate; and
- 180 points means 180% of the published rate.

These figures are expressed with the prefix 'WS', so in the preceding examples these would be expressed as WS100, WS40 and WS180.

5.4   Metals

Some of the most popular underlying metal commodities comprise aluminium, copper, gold, lead, palladium, platinum, silver, steel and tin.

Within these categories are various sub-categories of traded commodity, which are tradable commodity reference prices. For example, within aluminium there is high-grade primary aluminium traded on COMEX or the LME, and also aluminium alloy traded on those exchanges. For copper, there is grade-A copper and high-grade copper.

Bullion is one of the more complex categories of metals. Gold and silver are defined by reference to gold (or silver) bars or unallocated gold (or silver) complying with the rules of the London Bullion Market Association relating to fineness and good delivery.

Palladium and platinum are traded as palladium (or platinum) ingots or plate or unallocated palladium (or platinum) complying with the rules of the London Platinum and Palladium Market relating to good delivery and fineness.

The bullion market trades in ounces. However, 'ounce' has one meaning for gold and another for precious metals: for gold it means a fine troy ounce, while for silver, platinum or palladium it is just a troy ounce. This is a fine distinction, but one which reflects that there are many distinct trading environments for commodity assets and that commodity derivatives financial instruments must accommodate them.

5.5   Paper

The most popular type of underlying paper commodity assets includes containerboard, newsprint, pulp and recovered paper. Each category has several types of widely traded price in the commodity derivatives market.

5.6   Emissions allowances

Emissions trading derivatives consist of financial instruments such as swaps, options and forwards which derive their value from the underlying asset of permits giving the right to emit a defined quantity of a greenhouse gas.

Commodity derivatives trading involving emissions allowances is highly complex, as far as the underlying commodity asset is concerned. Currently the biggest area is based around the EU Emissions Trading Scheme (or ETS). This is the European Union's compulsory cap-and-trade project for trading carbon dioxide emission allowances. To date, it is the most ambitious and comprehensive emissions trading scheme ever created, although the United States is making strong efforts to develop its own scheme.

Each allowance represents the right to emit one tonne of carbon dioxide and each participating installation must surrender allowances equal to its actual carbon dioxide emissions. If its allocated allowances are not sufficient to cover its actual emissions, the affected installation must go into the market and purchase additional allowances to cover the shortfall. Failure to surrender sufficient allowances to cover emissions incurs a penalty per tonne of carbon dioxide emitted, as well as a requirement to make good the allowances in the following year. If the affected installation has an excess of allowances, perhaps through generating efficiencies, it can sell these into the market for a profit. The scheme aims to reduce carbon dioxide emissions by financially rewarding affected installations that reduce their emissions and penalising those that do not.

These permits have a tradable value, which varies based on their perceived scarcity. This makes them ideal underlying assets for commodity derivative transactions.

5.7 Weather indices and catastrophe swaps

Weather risk is hard to include as a commodity, but it is justified by the derivative market because of the impact that weather can have on the pricing of goods.

In the world of weather derivatives, the underlying commodity asset referenced is the variance in an index which measures the differences in temperature, precipitation, snow or wind as recorded at meteorological stations. The 2005 Definitions reference 28 of these – for example, those in Austria, Australia, Belgium, Canada, Switzerland, the Czech Republic, Germany, Denmark, Italy, Japan, South Korea, Mexico, New Zealand, Spain, Finland, Sweden, South Africa, the United Kingdom and the United States.

Two types of weather derivative are commonly traded. Under the first type, an aggregate weather variable for temperature, precipitation, snow or wind is measured over an agreed period of time at a meteorological station. The variables are compiled together by a calculation agent, with each increment of the variable above or below a threshold adjusting the number of weather index units in a notional index. If the number of weather index units is above or below a pre-agreed level at any measurement date, then one party will make a differential payment to the other, based on an amount per weather index unit.

Under the second type of weather derivative transaction, if a specified adverse weather event, such as a hurricane, occurs during the transaction's term, the party which is the seller will pay the other a fixed amount, based on the event's severity.

Weather indices, like emissions allowances and freight rates, are particularly complex assets.

5.8 Commodity indices generally

Investors in a commodity derivative often want the diversity of exposure to more than one commodity, perhaps to follow an investment strategy. This can be achieved by the financial instrument referencing movements in a commodity index or basket of commodity indices. Commodity indices are compiled by specialist index providers. These are usually financial institutions (eg, Goldman Sachs and Morgan Stanley).

The constituent items in a commodity index are not typically the trading price of the physical commodity, but instead the trading price of a commodity-linked futures contract. The constituent items are weighted as specified by the index's rules. The most commonly referenced commodity indices include the S&P GSCI (previously, the Goldman Sachs Commodity Index) and the Commodities Research Bureau Index.

6. The third constituent part of a commodity derivative: the value to be derived from the underlying asset

Under a commodity derivatives contract, one party will pay the other an amount linked to the value of the underlying commodity asset. This amount may be based on many types of election, which are agreed by the parties at the outset.

Examples of common values referenced to or extracted from the underlying asset	
Type	Description
Single commodity	• The total return on a single commodity futures contract. • The difference in trading price of a single commodity or commodity future on or between specific dates or against a specific price or formula.
Basket of commodities	• The total return on the basket of commodities or commodity futures. • The difference in trading price of the basket of commodities or commodity futures on or between specific dates or against a specific price or formula. • The difference in trading price between the constituent parts of the basket on or between specific dates, against a specific price or formula, or against each other.
Single index	• The total return on the single index (eg, the value of the return on the individual commodity futures comprising all or part of the index). • The difference in trading level of the single index on or between specific dates or against a specific level or formula.
Basket of indices	• The total return on the basket of indices (eg, the value of the return on the individual commodity futures comprising all or part of each index). • The difference in trading level of each of the indices on or between specific dates, against a specific level or formula, or against each other.

7. The fourth constituent part of a commodity derivative: purpose

7.1 Who are the market participants?

To understand why parties enter into a commodity derivatives contract, we must first look at who those parties are (ie, the key market participants in the commodity derivatives market).

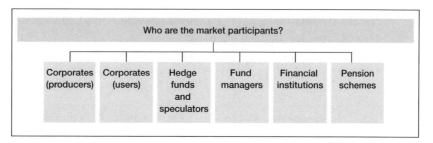

Almost all participants fall into one of the following categories:

- corporate entities (commodity producers);
- corporate entities (commodity users);
- hedge funds and speculators;
- fund managers;
- institutional clients; and
- pension schemes.

(a) Corporates (commodity producers)

Corporates that produce commodities are major users of commodity derivatives products. A commodity producer has many fixed costs in producing a commodity, and falling commodity prices can adversely affect profitability.

Owners and operators of coal mines may wish to forgo the potential upside of future increases in the coal price, to protect themselves against a potential market decline. An oil producer may wish to do the same by entering into an oil forward contract to hedge against a fall in oil prices. An electricity producer may wish to enter into a weather derivative to hedge against a mild winter reducing the demand for electricity. A shipowner may wish to enter into a forward freight agreement to hedge against a decline in freight rates eroding the profitability of its fleet.

(b) Corporates (commodity users)

Corporates that use commodities are major users of commodity derivatives products. A commodity user has many fixed costs in producing its product, and falling commodity prices can adversely affect profitability.

A steel producer will see increased costs if the price of coal increases and may wish to enter into a coal forward, agreeing to purchase coal at a fixed price on a future date. An airline might prefer to enter into a cash-settled jet fuel swap to lock in current jet fuel prices over an extended period, rather than pass fuel price increases onto its customers in the form of a surcharge. A coal importer may wish to enter into a forward freight agreement with the shipowner so as to hedge against an increase in freight rates eroding the profitability of its business.

Corporate commodity users are the natural end counterparties of corporate commodity producers. Here lies the great strength of derivatives: the ability of parties to trade risks and protect themselves against the unforeseen.

(c)   *Fund managers*
Fund managers are increasingly establishing funds that reference and trade different types of commodity. This represents an alternative asset for investors to invest in. This is something which was particularly attractive during the 2007–2009 credit crunch, with several commodities such as gold performing at record levels while equities and bonds have languished. Investment is generally in commodities futures. However, fund managers also make use of other derivative financial instruments for hedging and leverage purposes.

(d)   *Hedge funds and speculators*
The line between hedge funds and asset managers has become blurred in recent years, with hedge funds sometimes moving towards traditional long strategies and asset managers looking to participate in leveraged and shorting strategies.

Traditionally, hedge funds have looked to make returns from any type of market:
- in an upward market through leverage (perhaps through the use of options);
- in a downward market through shorting strategies; and
- in times of market volatility through leveraged trading strategies.

Hedge funds and other investors that look to make profits from movements in the value of an underlying asset alone are not popular with regulators and politicians. For example, in 2008 US Senator Byron Dorgan introduced the End Oil Speculation Bill, which would have cracked down on speculative commodity derivatives trading. It never made it into law. However, new US legislation now allows regulators to impose position limits on commodity derivatives. It still remains to be seen how this will affect hedge funds and speculative traders.

In their defence, these users argue that they bring liquidity to the market, which in the end benefits those participants that are hedging actual risk.

(e)   *Financial institutions*
Commodity derivatives can form a large part of a financial institution's business and relate to a significant source of its profits.

A financial institution may use commodity derivatives as a market maker, acting as a buyer to sellers and a seller to buyers. Here the financial institution makes its profits from being able to sell exposures to an underlying asset at a better rate than it purchases them.

An example of this would be a financial institution that enters into a forward freight agreement with a shipowner, where it agrees to pay the negative differential below a fixed freight rate at a future date, while the shipowner agrees to pay the financial institution the positive differential above the fixed freight rate at the future date (should that be the case). Simultaneously, the financial institution will enter into a back-to-back transaction with another of its clients, a coal importer, which is exposed to increases in the same freight rate. Here the financial institution agrees to pay the positive differential above the fixed freight rate at the future date, while the coal importer agrees to pay the financial institution the negative differential above the fixed freight rate at the future date (should that be the case).

The financial institution can charge favourable pricing differences in both transactions because it is making a market and is itself isolated from any movement in the freight rate. Alternatively, the end users – the shipowner and the coal importer – may be matched up by two financial institutions entering into a forward transaction with one another and then entering into corresponding transactions with the end users, creating a chain of transactions.

Financial institutions may also enter into commodity derivatives transactions on a proprietary basis, perhaps as part of an investment strategy.

(f) Pension schemes

Pension schemes invest the majority of their funds in bonds and equities. However, they are increasingly diversifying their assets to avoid overexposure to the equity markets. Investing in commodities as a separate asset class is likely to gain in popularity.

7.2 Reasons for using commodity derivatives

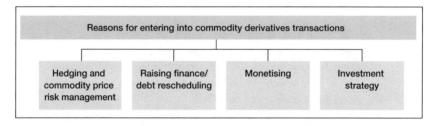

The principal reasons for entering into commodity derivatives contracts usually include one or several of the following:
- hedging, and commodity-price risk management;
- raising finance/debt rescheduling (or increasing debt capacity);
- monetising; and
- investment strategy.

Some of these overlap and, depending on the type of market participant, the importance of each motivation is likely to have different significance.

(a) Hedging and commodity price risk management

There are various reasons why a market participant may choose to hedge a commodity price. These include:
- reducing volatility in earnings;

- ensuring minimum cash flows;
- hedging a fixed proportion of production, guaranteeing prices to customers; and
- keeping the price of goods within a predetermined price range.

Hedging is principally done in relation either to end users' expenses or to earnings depending on a commodity price.

(b) Raising finance/debt rescheduling (or increasing debt capacity)

This area overlaps with hedging. Banks are usually more willing to lend to companies exposed to movements in commodity prices, which have effectively hedged themselves against those risks – or the banks are at least willing to lend at more favourable rates.

Where a borrower or debt issuer is particularly exposed – perhaps because it is a raw materials producer, such as a mining company – commodity-linked risk management instruments embedded in bond and loan structures can allow borrowers and lenders to decouple their exposure to commodity prices from the ability to pay.

These instruments embed a commodity derivative into the overall transaction structure.

For example, if a gold mining corporation enters into a facility agreement at a fixed or floating rate of interest, it faces gold price risk exposure. If the price of gold falls below the cost of production, then it will not generate enough revenue to repay the principal and interest on the loan.

For banks and borrowers to protect themselves against this risk, as part of the overall transaction structure, the borrower could enter into a cash-settled gold swap with a notional amount equal to the principal amount of the facility agreement. Under this swap, the mining corporation would pay the positive cash differential between the actual gold price on each measurement date above a set level (multiplied by the notional amount) and the hedging bank would pay the equivalent negative differential if the actual gold price happened to be below the set level on the relevant measurement date.

The hedging bank would in turn enter into equivalent opposite transactions with other market participants, making a return on the differentials between these two prices. The gold swap would remove some of the exposure to the underlying gold commodity price for both the mining corporation and the banks.

Other commodity-linked structures can involve the return of principal or return being linked to an underlying commodity price or basket of prices; or *in lieu* of interest, investors having the right to exercise a cash-settled call or put option.

Commodity bonds have also been used as part of debt-rescheduling programmes to reduce repayment obligations. Examples have included long-dated bonds issued by foreign-exchange-poor raw-material-rich countries, which link repayment of principal and payment of interest to the particular commodity export prices.

(c)   *Monetising*

Commodity prices can be very volatile. In recent years, we have seen extreme movements in the price of oil, for example. This volatility can make hedging essential for certain market participants. If the hedging proves useful, though, individual hedging contracts can themselves gain great value. For instance, if an oil producer entered into a series of options giving it the right to sell thousands of barrels of oil at $100 a barrel at three-month intervals, this contract would have little or no value if oil were trading at $120 a barrel. However, as has happened in recent times, if oil were trading at $50 a barrel, then if sold the contract would have significant value, entitling the new counterparty to sell oil at $50 a barrel more than the current price.

Market participants will from time to time seek to monetise these values. Indeed, in the structure described above, the mining companies and the banks involved might choose to sell on the embedded derivatives contracts if the price of gold collapsed, and use the resulting profits to pay down the principal of the loan. This practice was common in early 2009, as financial institutions sought innovative ways to rebuild their balance sheets.

(d)   *Investment strategy*

Commodity derivatives may form part of a fund's, corporate's or financial institution's investment strategy. Commodity derivatives can allow a user to achieve leverage, allowing for greatly enhanced returns (and, potentially, losses too).

Commodity derivatives can also allow users to pursue certain strategies taking a view as to the relative performance of one commodity or commodity future over the performance of other commodities or commodity futures within a basket.

Commodity derivatives can help investors to follow sophisticated strategies which decouple the risk of an individual commodity producer from the price risk of the underlying commodity it produces. An example of this is where an investor enters into a commodity futures which provides it with the upside return on a commodity (eg, coal) while selling short a particular gold producer's shares (ie, borrowing these shares, selling them into the market and hoping for a decline in price). This strategy would allow the investor to take a view that the commodity producers shares would decline in value relative to the value of the underlying commodity asset that it produces, while hedging itself against an increase in the share price due to an unrelated increase in the price of the underlying commodity.

8.   **Additional and inherent risks of commodity derivatives**

We have discussed the constituent parts of a commodity derivative in detail. Surrounding these constituent parts, though, are various additional and inherent risks and other relevant factors, which any user of commodity derivatives ignores at its peril. To some extent, these may even negate or temper the effectiveness of any applicable purpose for using commodity derivatives and must therefore be considered seriously.

The five relevant areas here can be divided into:

• structural and strategic factors;

- regulatory and tax risks;
- operational and documentation risks;
- counterparty risks; and
- liquidity risks.

Inevitably, there is some overlap.

8.1 Structural and strategic factors

The third limb of the definition of a 'commodity derivative' – "from which the financial instrument derives its value" – provides users with the opportunity to make gains as well as unexpected losses. And the ability of commodity derivatives to leverage losses as well as returns, mixed with the complexity of any strategy, means that there is an opportunity to get it badly wrong.

The complexity of strategies followed in commodity derivatives transactions can also make it more difficult for any user to gauge the risks involved accurately. This is particularly so where the institutional approvals given to enter into transactions may be sanctioned by personnel with a lesser degree of knowledge than those structuring these products.

For example, a commodity derivative which bases its return on the worst performing of three commodity derivative indices, by reference to a complex formula, may be particularly risky if bought by a pension fund that does not habitually engage in these types of finance transaction, but that is attracted to the potentially high return.

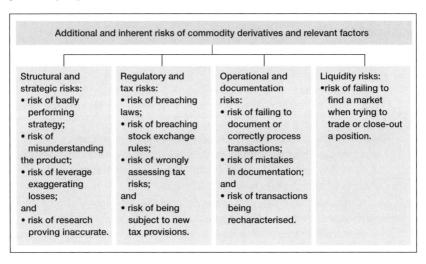

Many financial institutions which are leading market participants produce commodity derivatives research as one of their key client products. This research can cover ideas for new transactions and strategies, or may consist of analytical reports and briefings for new products. The risk that any research proves to be incorrect is significant in any commodity derivative.

8.2   Regulatory and tax risks

(a)   *Regulatory risks*

Since 2009 there has been an increasing regulatory focus on transparency, with regulators shining a light on the participants in the derivatives markets and the size of their exposures. This has translated into the Dodd-Frank Wall Street Reform and Consumer Protection Act in the United States, and the European Market Infrastructure Regulation (or EMIR) in the European Union. As a result, certain standardised trades are required to be traded through central counterparties and for certain transactions to be traded on an exchange. At this stage, however, commodity derivatives are not required to be mandatorily cleared, but this may change in the future.

The extent to which commodity derivatives transactions can be prohibited, preventing hedging of risk, or limited by forcing standardisation of trades (which prevents hedging of actual exposures by end users) will become an increased risk in commodity derivatives transactions. Further risks may arise where speculative trading is restricted and this results in reduced liquidity in the market, making it more costly and difficult for participants to close out transactions when they no longer have a need for them.

(b)   *Tax risks*

Where a commodity derivative allows a gain or loss to be deferred, failure to obtain proper tax advice can lead to a product user not obtaining the desired gains. Such arrangements can also run the risk of being recharacterised as tax avoidance techniques, leaving a product user perhaps subject to a large bill and/or proceedings against it.

8.3   Operational and documentation risks

(a)   *Operational risks*

What happens when a derivative product grows so quickly that the IT, back-office and middle-office support cannot keep pace with the product's growth? Trades can no longer be tracked and/or documented as quickly as parties enter into them. Inevitably, in these circumstances, operational risk increases. This is what has taken place in the credit derivatives market and equity derivatives market; it is also a concern in the commodity derivatives market.

Operational risk also arises where transactions are entered into without proper authorisation or due diligence being carried out, or where delays in the documenting of transactions mean that there is uncertainty as to the terms which were agreed. These can occur due to the sheer volume of transactions entered into by a market participant.

The first area is most apparent where two institutions enter into a relationship trading commodity derivatives (and perhaps other derivatives contracts as well), but the documentation process of agreeing and negotiating an ISDA master agreement (or other trade body standard documentation) and carrying out the requisite due diligence as to creditworthiness and legal risk does not proceed at the same pace.

The second area of confirmation backlogs has caused some concern. Without a confirmation in place, the process of ascertaining what was actually agreed between the parties can become open to dispute and extremely difficult to determine.

(b)   ***Documentation risks***

The first major question is whether the commodity derivatives documentation will work. Does it do what is intended and is it legal, valid, binding and enforceable? The OTC commodity derivatives market is now well established and the standardisation efforts of ISDA have reduced these risks as much as possible (eg, ISDA has obtained legal opinions in more than 40 jurisdictions around the world on various enforceability issues). However, there is still a risk – particularly with regard to more bespoke products and/or where UK or New York law is not used as the governing law – that documentation will not perform as intended and will not be legal, valid, binding and enforceable. Similar concerns exist for the documentation produced by other trade bodies.

8.4   Counterparty risks

In OTC commodity derivatives transactions, both counterparties are exposed to one another's credit risk. An option buyer, for example, is exposed to the risk that the seller will not be in a position to pay any cash settlement amount or physically deliver the commodity.

To a certain extent, counterparty risk is inherent in all derivatives transactions. The parties can deal with this risk using existing ISDA documentation architecture (ie, the credit support annex and/or other collateral and credit support-related documentation), or the margin provisions provided in other market-standard documentation. The new margin rules which are phased in all major jurisdictions from 2016 and 2017 will reduce these risks to some extent.

A further risk is that a counterparty does not have the correct legal authority to enter into a commodity derivatives transaction. The early landmark cases relating to derivatives and capacity occurred in the 1980s and apply to derivatives in general. Proper diligence on any counterparty is essential and will depend to a large extent on the type and jurisdiction of the relevant reference entity. Otherwise, the risk remains that any commodity derivatives contract could be unenforceable and/or that any payments due may not be recoverable.

Commodity derivatives structured products are often issued under the arranging financial institution's Euro medium-term note (or EMTN) programme. This exposes the noteholder to the credit risk of the issuing entity. Where a commodity derivatives structured product is issued by a special purpose vehicle (SPV), the financial institution arranging the transaction will usually also enter into an commodity swap with the SPV, pursuant to which the noteholder will be taking the credit risk on that swap counterparty.

8.5   Liquidity risks

Commodity derivatives and OTC structured products may not be as liquid as the underlying commodity futures that they reference. This may mean that the price of a commodity derivative against the relevant underlying obligations may become distorted and prone to wider fluctuations in price that the market price of the underlying asset.

9.   Restrictions on the development of the commodity derivatives market
The main restrictions that are preventing development of the commodity derivatives market can be summarised as follows:

- lack of knowledge;
- inadequacy of trading systems and trade infrastructure;
- lack of liquidity in the market in general;
- pricing issues;
- documentation inadequacies, particularly in relation to new products; and
- complexity of accounting and tax treatment of commodity derivatives.

9.1   Lack of knowledge
The perceived complexity of certain commodity derivative products actively prevents many potential market participants from purchasing or using products. Whereas these entities may be entirely comfortable with the mainstream commodity markets, the perceived dangers of leveraged losses may stop many entities from using commodity derivatives, even where products can hedge against losses of existing commodity exposures.

9.2   Inadequacy of trading systems and trade infrastructure
The costs of putting appropriate structures in place will deter many potential market participants from the market, as will the perceived risk if the infrastructure and systems do not prove sufficiently robust.

9.3   Lack of liquidity in the market
Concern regarding how easy it would be to close out or sell a particular commodity derivatives product can deter potential users of commodity derivative products. Whereas an exchange-traded option may be easy to trade, a structured commodity-linked note may not be.

9.4   Pricing issues
Return and losses on commodity derivatives products may be linked to bespoke and complex mathematical formulae. Difficulty in understanding these and the related risks involved will deter many users (in particular, retail users) from purchasing commodity derivatives products. Additionally, issues of opacity relating to how certain formulae are structured may also lead to concerns.

9.5   Documentation inadequacies, particularly in relation to new products
Derivatives documentation is structured for ease of use. This has the benefit of reducing the costs and related timeframes for documenting products. It also makes it easier for experts to understand quickly how a product works. However, the documentation is not constructed to be easily understood by the general user.

The effect of this can be to make the documentation extremely difficult to understand for non-derivatives specialists, even when they are finance lawyers. This can mean that necessary credit approvals for the usage of commodity derivative products can be difficult to obtain.

9.6 Complexity in the accounting and tax treatment of commodity derivatives

The multi-jurisdictional nature of many commodity derivatives can magnify the difficulties in applying the correct accounting and tax treatment to commodity derivatives products.

10. Conclusion

The commodities industry has suffered a rather difficult couple of years, with the prices going down significantly since the end of the so-called 'commodities supercycle'. At the same time, the lower prices mean that the world is not running out of resources. The volatility of this sector means that market participants will, when investing in commodities, have a chance both to make and lose a lot of money; and often both can happen in the same year! Commodity markets will continue to have their ups and downs and as history shows, a boom may be followed by a bust sooner than most would realise. This also means that there will always be a place for commodity derivatives, which offer market participants the ability to protect their exposure to the relevant commodity, or to speculate on the volatility of the prices.

Overview of the 2005 ISDA Commodity Definitions

Edmund Parker
Marcin Perzanowski
Mayer Brown

1. Introduction

If you are involved in over-the-counter (OTC) commodity derivatives, you need to understand the 2005 ISDA Commodity Definitions well enough to be able to review, advise on or maybe even structure or price commodity derivatives transactions.

The 2005 definitions are the flagship document in the International Swaps and Derivatives Association Inc's (ISDA) market-standard documentation platform for commodity derivatives. They provide the operative framework for OTC transactions. They also provide market-standard definitions and detailed fall-backs for when the unforeseen occurs – for example, when a market or trading is disrupted.

Doing the same job as the 2003 ISDA Credit Derivatives Definitions for credit derivatives and the 2002 ISDA Equity Derivatives Definitions for equity derivatives, the 2005 definitions are brought to life through incorporation by reference in an OTC confirmation. The 2005 definitions also contain many templates for those confirmations. A confirmation will also incorporate the parties' ISDA Master Agreement, as amended by its schedule, and possibly a credit support annex as well. In addition to setting out the pricing information for the transaction, the confirmation will select various elections to craft the transaction's terms, definitions and fall-backs, with the efficiency of the 2005 definitions providing market certainty and allowing complex OTC commodity derivatives products to be documented in just a few pages. As with all ISDA transactions, documentation efficiency trumps ease of understanding. To address this, ISDA has published an 18-page user's guide to accompany the 2005 definitions. This chapter goes into greater depth than the user's guide and makes extensive use of diagrams and worked examples to explain this asset class's complexities.

The terms defined in the 2005 ISDA Commodity Definitions are denoted by the use of single quotation marks when used for the first time in the body of this chapter. Thereafter, those terms are spelled without using any capital letters or punctuation marks (unless they are being defined, for instance).

2. History and structure of the 2005 definitions

ISDA was founded in 1985. Organised commodity derivatives markets have existed for hundreds of years. The result of this is that ISDA is the new kid on the block and the darling of the financial institutions and hedge funds – though not of traditional brokers, who were using commodity derivatives long before ISDA showed up. So, whereas ISDA definitional booklets such as those for equity and credit derivatives definitions have been driven from a financial institution and hedge fund perspective, the 2005 definitions take greater account of harmonising with existing market practice and organisations, while introducing the robust fall-back regime of other derivative asset classes. For example, the provisions relating to trading in the English physical electricity market interact with the Grid Trade Master Agreement published by the Futures and Options Association.

The 2005 definitions were developed to cover a range of commodity derivatives products and underlying commodity assets, as well as to reflect the developing market practices in the global derivatives industry. The 2005 definitions are ISDA's second version of a set of commodity definitions, succeeding the 1993 ISDA Commodity Derivatives Definitions. The 2005 definitions also combine the revised versions of the 2000 ISDA Supplement to the 1993 Commodity Derivatives Definitions and the earlier 1997 ISDA Bullion Definitions.[1]

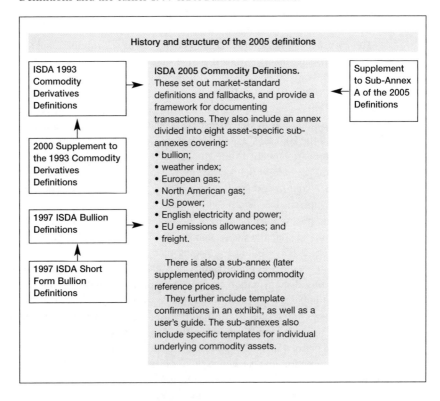

History and structure of the 2005 definitions

| ISDA 1993 Commodity Derivatives Definitions | → | ISDA 2005 Commodity Definitions. These set out market-standard definitions and fallbacks, and provide a framework for documenting transactions. They also include an annex divided into eight asset-specific sub-annexes covering: • bullion; • weather index; • European gas; • North American gas; • US power; • English electricity and power; • EU emissions allowances; and • freight.

There is also a sub-annex (later supplemented) providing commodity reference prices. They further include template confirmations in an exhibit, as well as a user's guide. The sub-annexes also include specific templates for individual underlying commodity assets. | ← | Supplement to Sub-Annex A of the 2005 Definitions |

2000 Supplement to the 1993 Commodity Derivatives Definitions

1997 ISDA Bullion Definitions

1997 ISDA Short Form Bullion Definitions

The structure of the 2005 definitions has changed considerably since the 1993 version. Whereas the 1993 definitions had only 42 pages, the new set of definitions (together with the exhibits, annexes and the user's guide) has been expanded to 526 pages. The 2005 definitions are also substantially greater in complexity and the range of products covered.

---

1   The Bullion Definitions were also available in a short version for use with physically settled transactions and were known as the 1997 ISDA Short Form Bullion Definitions.

One of the principal reasons for the drafting of the new 2005 definitions was to cover a wider variety of different types of underlying commodity asset.

In *Das Kapital*, Karl Marx viewed commodities as things that are bought and sold, with their value representing a quantity of human labour. The 2005 definitions have a broader approach to commodities than Marx; the traditional commodities (eg, gold, copper, gas, cocoa and oil) are covered, but more exotic commodities (eg, electricity, freight, the weather and EU emission allowances) are also included.

The main operative section of the 2005 definitions is quite short – it takes up only 26 of the 526 pages and contains 18 articles. It is quite similar in scope to the 1993 definitions. In addition to the operative section, there is an exhibit which sets out generic template confirmations that can be adapted for use with a wide range of underlying commodity assets. The new definitions also include eight lengthy annexes setting out special provisions for different types of underlying commodity asset.

Some of these sub-annexes provide suggested paragraphs which can be incorporated into an ISDA Master Agreement. For example, the sub-annex for Grid Trade Master Agreement transactions (physically settled electricity) includes provisions to be incorporated into an ISDA Master Agreement adding an electricity-specific additional termination event and event of default. The sub-annex for emissions allowances transactions includes elections relating to which party bears the burden of any penalties imposed when emissions allowances are not delivered on time. The sub-annexes also contain specific template forms of confirmation for the relevant type of underlying commodity asset.

The annexes cover in detail the following types of commodity derivatives transaction:

- bullion transactions (Sub-Annex B);
- weather index transactions (Sub-Annex C);
- European gas transactions (Sub-Annex D);
- North American gas transactions (Sub-Annex E);
- North American power transactions (Sub-Annex F);
- Grid Trade Master Agreement (electricity) transactions (Sub-Annex G);
- EU emissions allowances transactions (Sub-Annex H); and
- freight transactions (Sub-Annex I).

Articles X to XIII of the operative provisions of the 2005 definitions refer to each of the sub-annexes in turn. When parties incorporate the 2005 definitions into a confirmation, only the sub-annex relating to bullion transactions is deemed to be automatically incorporated. If the parties choose to, they can incorporate any of the other sub-annexes either into the schedule to the ISDA Master Agreement or specifically into the confirmation.

The 2005 definitions also include Sub-Annex A. This sets out market-standard definitions of various commodity reference prices. Parties can rely on these when entering into trades, making the documentation process more efficient. Other noteworthy differences with the 1993 definitions (as amended by the 2000 supplement) are as follows:

- The definition of the 'calculation period' now covers a wider range of transactions.
- The 'market disruption event' provisions are expanded. There is a new disruption event, namely 'trading disruption', which replaces the previous definitions of 'trading suspension' and 'trading limitation'. The definition of '*de minimis* trading' has been deleted in its entirety for lack of use and the default selection of market disruption event has been revised to conform to the then-current market practice.
- Two of the disruption fall-backs ('postponement – fall-back reference price' and 'average daily price disruption') from the 1993 definitions were dropped and a new disruption fall-back was included ('delayed publication or announcement'). Other disruption fall-backs were modified and the default waterfall of disruption fall-backs was updated and expanded.
- The 2005 definitions allow the parties to enter into barrier transactions by introducing knock-in and knock-out options. Those have been modelled on 2002 ISDA Equity Definitions.
- The definitions relating to currencies and business days have been amended to conform to the 2000 definitions.
- The concept of 'common pricing' was introduced. As explained later in the chapter, it applies only when the transaction refers to more than one commodity reference price.

The 2005 definitions revise and consolidate the Bullion Definitions. Some clauses of the old Bullion Definitions are included in the generic provisions relating to all types of commodity transaction, and some are included in Sub-Annex B. The main differences between the Bullion Definitions and the new 2005 definitions are as follows:

- The responsibilities of the calculation agent in the 2005 definitions are much more detailed.
- The market disruption events and disruption fall-backs have been amended significantly and standardised across different types of commodity asset.
- The 2005 definitions have no specific language relating to additional taxes.
- The 2005 definitions introduce the concept of Bermuda-style options transactions.

The definitions are divided into a table of contents, an introduction and preamble, 17 articles, four exhibits, nine sub-annexes and a user's guide. The outline structure is set out next.

2.1   2005 ISDA Definitions documents and structure

3. **Introduction and preamble to the 2005 definitions**

The 17 articles are preceded by both an introduction and a preamble. The introduction informs us that the definitions are intended for use in 'privately negotiated commodity transactions', which are governed by either the 1992 ISDA Master Agreement or the 2002 ISDA Master Agreement. That said, they can provide a useful foundation when drafting a structured product.

The introduction continues that the 2005 definitions provide the basic framework for a range of commodity derivatives financial instruments (swaps, basis swaps, options, caps, collars, floors and swaptions), as well as certain physically settled transactions. Furthermore, the introduction tells us that the 2005 definitions have fall-back provisions which apply unless the parties provide otherwise in a transaction; and that market participants may adapt or supplement them as they wish.

There is also the usual lengthy liability disclaimer, absolving ISDA from any guilt should market participants misuse the definitions, as well as a reminder that the 2005 definitions do not automatically apply to transactions which incorporated the 1993 definitions or the Bullion Definitions.

The introduction stresses that Sub-Annex B to the 2005 definitions (effectively an update of the old Bullion Definitions) has been endorsed by the London Bullion Market Association and the Financial Markets Lawyers Group – a further example that, contrary to several other ISDA definitions booklets, this one seeks to harmonise with other pre-existing regimes.

The 2005 definitions precede the 2006 ISDA Definitions (given in ISDA's general derivatives definitions booklet). In fact, they incorporate by reference various clauses from the predecessor to the 2006 definitions, the 2000 definitions. Considering that only the 2006 version is current, we recommend always specifically incorporating the 2006 definitions by reference into the documentation of all commodity transactions, and providing that all references to the 2000 definitions are deemed to be references to the 2006 definitions.

The introduction does not form part of the 2005 definitions. However, the preamble does, and it states that the definitions and provisions in the 2005 definitions may be incorporated into a document by inserting wording to the effect that the document is subject to the 2005 definitions. The preamble goes on to provide that all terms, definitions and provisions incorporated into a document will be applicable unless otherwise modified; and that is how the transaction framework, standard market definitions and logistical fall-backs are brought into the confirmation. Together with the ISDA Master Agreement, this provides the derivatives documentation infrastructure to create a commodity derivatives transaction.

4.   **Article I – Certain general definitions**

The Article I definitions cover the four distinct areas set out in the diagram below.

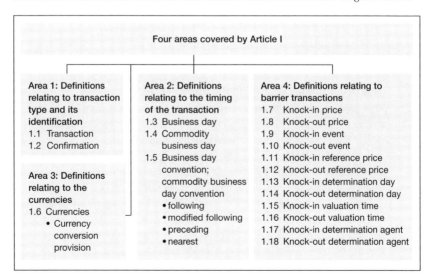

4.1 Area 1: definitions relating to the transaction type and its identification

Article I defines the scope of financial instruments that the 2005 definitions cover in the definition of a 'transaction'.

Definition of 'transaction'		
Group A • Commodity swap • Commodity basis swap • Commodity cap • Commodity floor • Commodity collar • Commodity index • Commodity forward • Commodity spot	**Group B** • Bullion transaction • Weather index derivatives transaction • NBP transaction • ZBT transaction • Gas transaction • Power transaction • Grid Trade Master Agreement transaction • EU emissions allowance transaction • Freight transaction	**Group C** • Any similar transaction to those listed in Group A and Group B • Any option with respect to any transactions in Group A and Group B • Any combination of transactions listed in Group A and Group B • Any other transaction identified as transaction in the relevant confirmation

The chart above shows how broad the definition of a 'transaction' actually is. We can divide the covered trades into three main groups.

Group A includes the main generic types of derivatives transaction (ie, commodity swap, commodity basis swap, commodity cap, commodity floor, commodity collar, commodity index, commodity forward and commodity spot).

Group B comprises the commodity-specific transactions; these are further defined in the 2005 definitions and in the relevant sub-annexes.

Group C is a fall-back category. It covers any similar transactions to those listed in Groups A and B, as well as any options and any combinations of those transactions. Group C also includes any other transaction identified as a 'transaction' in a confirmation for the purposes of the 2005 definitions.

A 'confirmation' is defined as a document or any other evidence in respect of a transaction confirming its terms.

4.2 Area 2: definitions relating to the timing of the transaction

This grouping includes the definitions relevant to the timing of the transaction. It covers the types of business day and any applicable business conventions.

Article I of the 2005 definitions provides for only two types of day: 'business day' and 'commodity business day'. However, the principal body also includes a number of references to 'bullion business days' (where this term is defined only in Sub-Annex B), as well as to 'seller business days' for option transactions.

Generally, the concept of a 'business day' is relevant only when one party needs to make a payment or a delivery to the other. A 'business day' is defined as a day on which commercial banks settle payments and are open for business in the place specified in the confirmation (eg, London and New York).

If the parties do not specify a business day in the confirmation, the business day will be determined by reference to Sections 1.5, 1.6 and 1.7 of the 2000 definitions (which are incorporated into the 2005 definitions by reference).

As the 2006 definitions have now replaced the 2000 version as the market standard, we recommend specifically incorporating that references to the 2000 definitions in the 2005 definitions will be deemed to be references to the 2006 definitions and its corresponding provisions. This is especially important if the payments are to be made in Chinese renminbi, Pakistani rupees, Vietnamese dongs, Sri Lankan rupees or Romanian lei, because these currencies are not included in the 2000 definitions but are in the 2006 definitions.

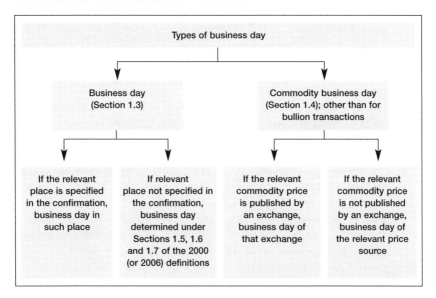

Whereas the term 'business day' is relevant for the transfer of money, the definition of 'commodity business day' is relevant whenever the commodity's reference price must be determined. Accordingly, if an exchange announces or publishes a commodity price, commodity business days will be those days on which that exchange is open for business. If, however, the relevant price is not published or announced by an exchange, commodity business days will be those days on which the relevant price source for that commodity is published.

The above 'commodity business day' definition does not apply to bullion transactions: as mentioned above, Sub-Annex B includes a separate definition of a 'bullion business day'.

Furthermore, Section 8.5 of the 2005 definitions also includes a 'seller business day' definition, which applies only to option transactions. It is defined as any day on which banks are open for business in the city where the option seller is located for the purposes of receiving notices.

A calendar day specified in a confirmation may not always fall on a business day – for example, a payment date of 7 June each year. If 7 June falls on a Sunday, as it did in 2009, an alternative date must be taken. Which date this is will be determined by the 'business day convention'. The 'business day convention' is a convention for adjusting any relevant date if that date would otherwise fall on a day that is not a business day or a commodity business day. In respect of both business days and commodity business days, there are four main conventions that the parties can elect to apply in a confirmation.

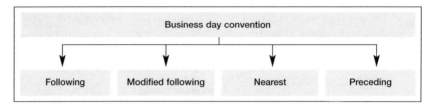

The 'following convention' means that the date will be the first following day that is a commodity business day or a business day. For example, if the confirmation for a five-year confirmation required a payment or delivery to be made on 7 June each year and the parties have elected the following convention and London business days to apply, the payment or delivery for Sunday 7 June 2009 would have to be made on Monday 8 June 2009.

The 'modified following convention' is similar to the following convention in that the relevant date will be the next following business day. However, if such day will fall in the next calendar month, the relevant day will be the first preceding day that is a business day or commodity business day. For example, if the modified following convention applied and a payment was supposed to be made on Saturday 31 July, such payment would fall on Friday 30 July.

The 'nearest convention' is slightly more complex. If the date falls on a day other than a Sunday or a Monday, the relevant date will be the first preceding day that is a business day. If, however, the date falls on a Sunday or a Monday, the relevant date will be the first following day. In essence, this means that if the relevant date falls on a Sunday or a public holiday Monday, the relevant date will be Tuesday. If it falls on a Saturday, it will be Friday. However, if there is a public holiday on a day other than Monday, the relevant day will be the first preceding business day.

Lastly, there is the 'preceding convention', which says that the relevant date will be the first preceding day which is a business day or a commodity business day.

The parties to a transaction should specify the relevant business day convention in relation to each relevant day in a confirmation. However, if the convention is not specified for a particular date, but is specified for the relevant transaction, such convention will also apply to that date.

4.3 Area 3: definitions relating to the currencies

This area covers two definitions. 'Currency' is defined as the lawful currency of any country as determined by the parties. It also incorporates by reference Section 1.7 of the 2000 definitions, which sets out the definitions of various currencies.[2]

---

2   As referred to above, this should be amended in a confirmation to incorporate the 2006 definitions.

The other defined term here is 'currency conversion provision'. This is relevant when the reference price of a given commodity is different from the currency of payment that is agreed between the parties. In that case, the parties should specify the mechanism for the currency conversion provision in the confirmation: the 2005 definitions do not provide any fall-back mechanism. The 1998 ISDA FX and Currency Option Definitions can be helpful in this regard.

4.4   Area 4: definitions relating to barrier transactions
The definitions in Sections 1.7 to 1.18 cover 'knock-in/knock-out' transactions. These are often referred to as 'barrier' transactions. They are modelled on the knock-in/knock-out provisions in the 2002 ISDA Equity Definitions and are also consistent with the 2005 Barrier Option Supplement to the 1998 FX and Currency Option Definitions.

In a 'knock-in transaction', a payment or delivery is contingent on the occurrence of a 'knock-in event' on any 'knock-in determination day' at the 'knock-in valuation time'. In turn, a 'knock-out transaction' is a right or obligation that terminates on the occurrence of the specific 'knock-out event' on any 'knock-out determination day' at the 'knock-in valuation time'. For example, a knock-out occurs when a particular level is hit (eg, the price of oil reaches US$120 a barrel) and at that point the transaction terminates. No termination payment is payable and no amounts are owed between the parties.

The parties can specify any event as the knock-in event. However, if they mark the knock-in provisions as applicable without setting out the details of the relevant event, they must provide the 'knock-in price'. In that case the obligations under a transaction are contingent on the relevant price of the transaction (the 'knock-in reference price') reaching the level of the knock-in price. The same applies in relation to the 'knock-out price'.

The job of the 'knock-in determination agent' (or the 'knock-out determination agent') is to determine whether a knock-in event (or a knock-out event) has occurred. The parties are free to name the calculation agent or a separate entity to fulfil this role.

5.   Article II – Parties
This short article contains only two definitions. A party to a commodity transaction can be either a 'fixed-price payer' or a 'floating-price payer'.

A 'fixed-price payer' makes payments of amounts calculated by reference to a fixed price, or alternatively is obligated to pay a fixed amount. In turn, a 'floating-price payer' makes payments calculated by reference to a commodity reference price, or will be obligated to pay a floating amount.

It is not always necessary to have both a fixed-price payer and a floating-price payer in every transaction. Depending on the parties' commercial intentions, there could be two fixed-price payers or indeed two floating-price payers.

The terms 'fixed-price payer' and 'floating-price payer' relate generally only to swaps and similar transactions, and may not be used at all if the payments under a trade are subject to a different payment calculation. Article II states that the terms 'fixed-rate payer' and 'floating-rate payer' do not apply to the following types of transaction: weather index derivatives transactions, National Balancing Point (NBP) transactions, Zeebruge natural gas (ZBT) transactions, gas transactions, power transactions, Grid Trade Master Agreement transactions, EU emissions allowance transactions and freight transactions. Here the parties will have other names: for instance, both weather index derivatives transactions and EU emissions allowance transactions refer to 'buyer' and 'seller'. These terms are set out in the relevant sub-annex.

6. Article III – Terms and dates

This article provides the basic definitions for transaction timings. Although it looks straightforward, it contains some traps for the unwary.

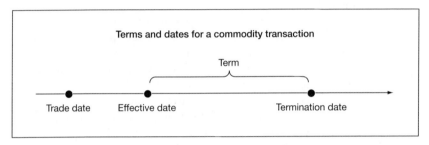

In accordance with the usual ISDA terminology, the 'trade date' is the day when the parties enter into the transaction (ie, the day when they sign the confirmation or otherwise agree terms). On the trade date, the parties will decide the first day on which the transaction's provisions will become operative (the 'effective date'), and the date when the transaction will terminate (the 'termination date'). The period of time from the effective date until the termination date is called the 'term'. Both the effective date and the termination date will be specified by the parties in the confirmation.

Article III also defines three other key dates in a transaction: the 'settlement date', the 'payment date' and the 'expiration date'. For bullion transactions only, the settlement date includes the 'bullion settlement date' and the 'bullion transaction settlement date'.

As the names suggest, the 'settlement date' and the 'payment date' are the dates when the parties settle their transaction obligations. Often, both terms are used interchangeably, but in principle the payment date is the date when an actual payment is made. The settlement date is broader and includes, for example, the date when a party exercises a swaption.

If the parties have not elected a business day convention for a settlement date or payment date, the following business day convention (or the following bullion business day convention, for bullion transactions) will apply by default. By contrast, the termination date will not be adjusted by any business day convention unless the parties have specified otherwise.

The term 'expiration date' applies to option transactions only and it is the last date or, in the case of Asian or European options, the only date when an option can be exercised. This date must be specified in the confirmation.

If the date which has been specified as the expiration date is not a commodity business day, then the first following commodity business day will be the new expiration date.

If a 'market disruption event' (as described in section 10.4 below) occurs on the originally specified expiration date, the first commodity business day on which a market disruption event ceases will be the new expiration date. However, if a market disruption event is still occurring eight commodity business days after the original disrupted commodity business day, that eighth day will be the expiration date, even if the disruption has not ceased by that time.

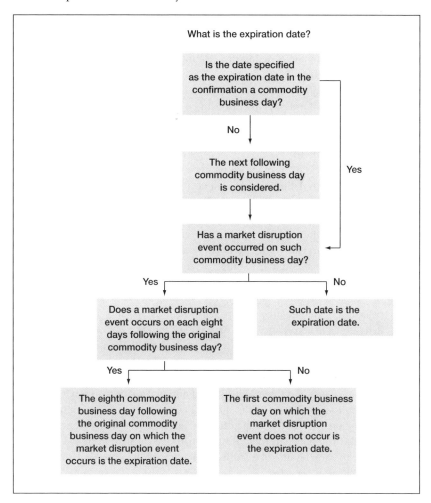

In some option transactions the option buyer can exercise the option only until the 'expiration time' on the 'expiration date'. The 2005 definitions define such time as 9:30 am on the expiration date, unless the parties specify otherwise. The 2005 definitions lack consistency here; in some sections they refer to New York time and in others to London time. Therefore, it is important always to amend the definition of 'expiration time' in accordance with the parties' needs.

Unfortunately, the 2005 definitions are also unclear as to whether this expiration time fall-back applies to all option transactions, or just the few option types specifically referred to in the relevant sub-annexes. Although the term 'expiration time' is defined in the main body of the 2005 definitions, it is not actually used there, and references to it are present only in Sub-Annex B (for bullion transactions) and Sub-Annex D (for NBP options and ZBT options). This term also appears in the 2005 definitions' exhibits. In order to avoid any confusion, we recommend always specifying the expiration time in the confirmation.

7.   Article IV – Certain definitions relating to payment

Article IV has various definitions relating to payment. We have divided these into three main areas:

- types of payment;
- types of notional quantity; and
- terms relating to calculations.

7.1   Types of payment

Sections 4.1 and 4.2 provide for two types of payment: 'fixed amounts' and 'floating amounts'. Both definitions are generic and their application is specifically excluded with respect to the following: weather index derivative transactions, NBP transactions, ZBT transactions, gas transactions, power transactions, Grid Trade Master Agreement transactions, EU emissions allowance transactions, freight transactions and any other transactions subject to a different payment calculation.

The 'fixed amount' is defined as an amount payable by the fixed-rate payer, which is specified in the confirmation or determined in accordance with Article V of the 2005 definitions. Similarly, the 'floating amount' is defined as an amount payable by the floating-rate payer, which is specified in the confirmation or determined in accordance with Article VI of the 2005 definitions. (See sections 8 and 9 below for analysis of the relevant parts of the definitions.)

7.2   Types of notional quantity

Section 4.3 provides three definitions of notional quantity – each is slightly different. The 'notional quantity' is the quantity of the relevant commodity referenced in a transaction. The 'notional quantity per calculation period' is exactly what it says it is, and it is used when there is more than one calculation period for a transaction. Lastly, the 'total notional quantity' is the sum of all notional quantities in respect of all calculation periods.

The 2005 definitions further specify that the value of each notional quantity is given in units. 'Units' is defined in Sub-Annex A as the unit of measure of the relevant commodity, as specified in the relevant commodity reference price or in the confirmation. Depending on the commodity, a unit could be, for example, a tonne, an ounce, a megawatt or a gigajoule. The intricacies of the definition of 'commodity reference price' are analysed in detail in section 10 of this chapter.

7.3 Terms relating to calculations

Article IV sets out three definitions relating to calculations: the 'calculation period', 'calculation agent' and 'calculation date'.

The 'calculation period' is a period defined by reference to two dates specified in the confirmation. The first date is the start of the calculation period and the second determines when it ends. Article IV further stresses that such dates need not be determined by reference to the effective date, termination dates or other defined terms in the 2005 definitions.

Not every transaction will have a calculation period. This term is used only when there are periodic payments made under the transaction. Each such periodic payment is made by reference to a calculation period which ends closest in time to the relevant settlement date or payment date.

For each calculation period, there is a 'calculation date' on which the calculation agent will make the relevant calculations and determinations necessary to establish the amounts that need to be paid or delivered under the transaction. There are two definitions for the calculation date: one applicable only to weather index derivatives transactions and one for all other transaction types.

In a weather index derivative transaction, the calculation date is defined by reference to a number of dates following the final date of each calculation period. The number of dates must be specified in the confirmation.

For all other transactions, the calculation date is the earliest date on which the calculation agent can give the notice of the relevant payments that must be made on the settlement date or payment date. This date can occur no later than close of business on the business day (or bullion business day) next preceding the relevant settlement date or payment date.[3] However, if the prices used to make the relevant calculations are published only on the relevant settlement date or payment date, the calculation agent must send the relevant notice at the latest time that will permit the payments due on that date to be made.

Lastly, Article IV sets out in detail the obligations of the calculation agent. Section 4.5 sets out nine specific functions of the calculation agent, which can be grouped into four main areas:

- duties relating to calculations;
- duties relating to notifications;
- duties relating to disruption events; and
- any other duties conferred on the agent by the terms of the confirmation.

---

3   The 2005 definitions suggest that the calculation date in this instance can be a 'close of business'. It confuses the date with a specific time during that date. The intention behind this definition was to create an obligation on the calculation agent to send the relevant notice by that time and this is also the market understanding of this provision. The calculation date must then be, at the latest, the first business day preceding the settlement date or the payment date. Where the relevant data is published on the related settlement date or the payment date, that day is the calculation date.

This grouping is set out in the diagram below.

Duties of the calculation agent (Section 4.5)			

Duties relating to calculations:
 • Calculating the floating price or settlement level.
 • Calculating any floating amount or cash settlement amount.
 • Calculating any fixed amount.
 • Calculating any payment amount.
	Duties relating to notifications:
	 • Giving notice on each calculation date, specifying:
	   ○ the settlement date or payment date;
	   ○ parties which need to make payments or deliveries;
	   ○ the relevant amounts; and
	   ○ calculation details.
	 • If after notice is given of any relevant details change, notifying the parties accordingly.
		Duties relating to disruption events:
		 • Determining whether a market disruption event exists and the relevant price.
		 • In relation to weather index derivative transactions, determining whether a missing date exists or data correction applies.
			Other duties:
			 • Any other duties specified in the 2005 definitions or the relevant confirmation.

Section 4.5 further specifies that if the calculation agent is required to exercise judgement in any way, it must do so in good faith and in a commercially reasonable manner after consulting the other party (or parties, if the calculation agent is a third party).

8.   Article V – Fixed amounts

This short article sets out the method for calculating fixed amounts. Generally, the parties have two options: they can specify the fixed amount quantum in the confirmation or they can provide a mechanism for determining the amount instead.

Under the default mechanism provided by the 2005 definitions, the parties need only specify a fixed price in the confirmation. This price must always be given by reference to a unit of the underlying commodity. If the parties decide to use this method, the fixed amount payable on a given settlement date or payment date will be calculated in accordance with the following formula:

Fixed amount = notional quantity (per calculation period) × fixed price

9.   Article VI – Floating amounts

This article sets out the method for calculating the floating amount. The floating amount is determined using the following formula:

Floating amount = notional quantity (per calculation period) × floating price

This is almost identical to the fixed amount formula, with the only difference being the replacement of 'fixed price' by 'floating price'. However, the definition of 'floating price' is more complex and goes to the heart of the commodity derivatives transaction's economics. The following diagram sets out definition options.

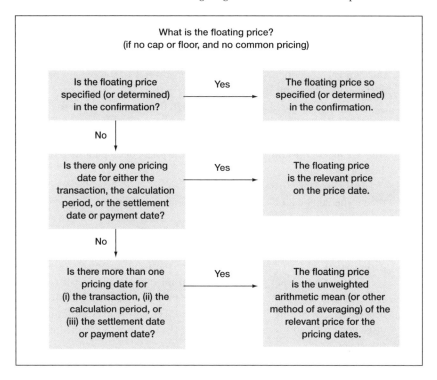

9.1 Standard determination of the floating price – no cap price or floor price, and common pricing not applicable

To determine the floating price for a transaction, we need to follow several steps and answer several questions. First, we must check whether the parties have provided a transaction-specific method for determining the floating price in the confirmation. As anywhere else in ISDA documentation, the parties are free to amend the standard wording of any set of definitions as they see fit. For now, however, we have assumed that the parties decided to follow the standard provisions of the 2005 definitions.

We must therefore check how many pricing dates there are in respect of one payment. A 'pricing date' is a date that is relevant for determining the price of a commodity and the parties can specify one or more of them in the confirmation. If there is just one floating amount payment to be made during the course of the transaction, there must be at least one pricing date specified (or determined) for the entire transaction. However, the floating amount payments often need to be made with respect to each calculation period, or on each settlement date (or payment date), and there must be at least one pricing date in respect of each payment.

For example, the parties to a commodity swap transaction referencing oil could agree that payments under the swap should be made monthly. In the confirmation, they should also specify that, say, the 15th day of each month will be the pricing date. Therefore, on the 15th of each month they will have to check what the relevant price of oil is.

If there is only one pricing date in respect of one payment, the floating price is equal to the relevant price on that pricing date. If more than one pricing date is indicated for a given transaction, calculation period or settlement (or payment) date, the floating price will be equal to an unweighted arithmetic mean of the relevant price for each pricing date. The parties are also free to specify any other method of averaging in the confirmation.

Going back to our example, even though the payments under the swap are made monthly, the parties could designate two dates in a month – say, the 15th and 16th of each month – as the pricing dates. In that case, the floating price for each payment will be equal to the arithmetic average of the prices of oil published on the 15th and 16th of each month.

In this section, we have also referred to the concept of 'relevant price' several times. The 2005 definitions define this term as a price of a given commodity on a given day, as published by the relevant price source and determined as set out in the confirmation. There are various standard price sources for different commodities; the most common are set out in the 200-plus pages of Sub-Annex A. For example, if the parties enter into a commodity derivative transaction referencing sugar, they can specify that the relevant price will be determined in accordance with the commodity reference price (White Sugar Euronext LIFFE). This is defined as a price per tonne on deliverable-grade white sugar on Euronext LIFFE on the relevant futures contract, as displayed on Reuters screen page 0#LSU. (This is further explained in section 10 of this chapter.)

9.2 Default elections for pricing date and common pricing

The parties are free to specify the pricing date in the confirmation. However, if they do not, the 2005 definitions provide some standard fall-backs.

If the transaction is a European-style option, the pricing date will, by fall-back, be the expiration date. This is logical because European options can be exercised only on the last day of their term (as explained in section 11.2 of this chapter). Therefore, the relevant price will have to be determined on that last day (ie, the expiration date).

If the parties have entered into an American-style option, the fall-back is for the pricing date to be the exercise date. An American-style option can be exercised at any time during its term, so logically the date when the option is exercised will be the pricing date.

In respect of an Asian-style option, the fall-back is for the pricing date to be "each commodity business day during the calculation period". As explained below, an Asian-style option, like a European-style option, is exercisable only on the expiration date, but its value is determined by reference to an average price throughout the term of the transaction. Therefore, each commodity business day in the relevant calculation period under an Asian-style option is a pricing date. Although in relation to other types of option the parties need not specify a calculation period, it is vital that they do so with respect to all Asian-style options. Otherwise, there will be difficulties calculating the relevant values for that transaction.

A Bermuda-style option can be exercised on each specified potential exercise day as well as on the expiration date. The pricing date fall-back for this option type is for the pricing dates to be "the potential exercise dates during the exercise period and on the expiration date". This definition is quite surprising, as it suggests that there will always be more than one pricing day in respect of a Bermudan-style option, and that the parties need to wait until the expiration date of the instrument in order to be able to determine the floating price. This is not what is normally intended, as the parties should be able to obtain the final price of a transaction on the day that the option buyer decides to exercise the option. So the default pricing date for a Bermudan-style option should have been defined as the exercise date, as it is for the American-style option. Therefore, if the parties elect to undertake a Bermudan-style option, we recommend amending the standard wording of the 2005 definitions in this respect, as required.

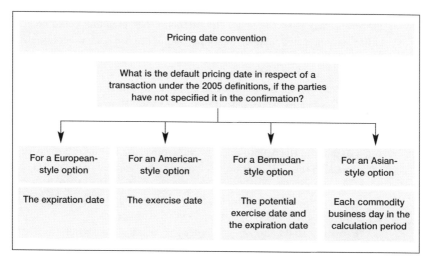

Often, a transaction references more than one commodity. For example, under a basis swap, Party A could pay to Party B a floating amount based on the value of copper and receive a floating amount based on the value of zinc. In that case, the parties may want to determine the prices of both zinc and copper on the same date. If the parties elect 'common pricing' as applicable, then a pricing date in respect of each part of the transaction will not occur until the prices of both commodities are published on the same day.

9.3   Determination of the floating price when floor price, cap price or collar applicable
Commodity derivatives are often used to hedge a party's obligations under other transactions. A party might enter into a commodity swap or option transaction to

protect itself against the adverse pricing movements in an underlying commodity. For example, an airline might want to be able to buy fuel at no more than a given price at a future date. It could enter into a commodity swap and, in return for a premium, receive a payment if fuel prices rose above the set level at the future date. The payment would reflect the difference between the agreed level and the actual level. If the agreed level were $50 a barrel of oil and actual prices rose to $80 by the future date, the airline would receive $30 a barrel of oil referenced in the transaction.

In the example above, the airline would be a fixed-price payer, whereas its counterparty would be a floating-price payer. Accordingly, the airline would be required to pay a fixed amount equal to $50 for every barrel. In turn, the floating-rate payer would have to pay the airline the actual price of oil at the relevant pricing date. If, on such date, the price was $80, then the payment obligations of each party would be offset against each other and only one of them would have to make a payment. In our scenario, the airline would receive $30 for every barrel under the swap. If, however, the actual price of oil were $45 per barrel, then the airline would have to make a payment equal to $5 per barrel ($50 – $45) to its counterparty.

Depending on the actual trading price, the market view of future prices and the agreed level (or fixed price) set at the transaction's outset, to enter into such hedge the airline may need to pay a hefty premium. The premium could be lower if the airline were prepared to accept some portion of the risk. One way of doing so would be to agree a cap price of, for example, $70 a barrel. In that case the counterparty would need to make a payment to the airline only if the price of oil rose above $70 per barrel. In our scenario, this means that at the end of the year the airline would still receive $10 a barrel referenced (instead of $30). However, if the price at the end of the year were $65, the counterparty would not have to pay anything to the airline.

The 2005 definitions allow for this by including the concepts of a 'floor price' and 'cap price' in the definition of the 'floor price'. Accordingly, if the parties specify a floor price in the confirmation, the floating price is equal to the excess of the floor price over the price determined in the usual way, as outlined above. If the parties specify a cap price instead, the floating price is equal to the excess of the price determined in the usual way, as above, over the cap price.

The parties could also agree to enter into a collar transaction. In that case one party would pay a floating amount based on the cap price, whereas the other would pay a floating amount based on the floor price. Therefore, one party would make a payment to the other if the price of the commodity rose above a certain level (the cap price), and the other party would have to make a payment to the first only if the price fell below a defined threshold (the floor price). If, however, the price of the commodity stayed within the 'collar' (ie, it did not rise above the cap price and did not fall below the floor price), no party would need to make any payment to the other.

Hypothetical example: Torre Mining Corporation

Torre Mining Corporation owns several gold mines in West Africa. It has borrowed a large amount of money from a syndicate of banks in order to develop the mines. It hopes that in a few years' time it will be able to make enough profit from the sale of gold to repay the loans. However, it is concerned that the price of gold may fall substantially from the current high level of $900 per ounce.

Vieja Jewellers International is a large corporation which owns almost 100 shops throughout Europe and the United States and sells various pieces of jewellery made of gold, silver and platinum. It has been concerned that the price of gold has recently been on the rise and it would like to hedge its exposure to this commodity. Torre and Vieja (acting through brokers) enter into a cash-settled five-year collar commodity derivatives transaction, with a floor price of $800 and a cap price of $1,000. The total notional quantity of the transaction is set at 100,000 ounces. If after five years the price of an ounce of gold is more than $1,000, Torre will make a payment to Vieja. If the price is less than $800, Vieja will make a payment to Torre. If, however, the price of an ounce of gold in five years is between $800 and $1,000, neither party makes a payment and the transaction will be terminated.

If, at the end of the term of the transaction, the price is $1,100 per ounce, Torre must pay $100 to Vieja for each ounce referenced. As the notional amount is 100,000 ounces, Torre must pay a floating amount of $10 million to Vieja.

Floating amount = floating price × total notional amount

Floating amount = ($1,100 – $1,000 per ounce) × 100,000 ounces
= $10 million

At the same time, Torre can also sell the equivalent amount of gold to third parties at the market price of $1,100. Therefore, it will still make enough profit to start repaying the interest and principal of its loan.

If, at the end of the term of the transaction, the price is $700 per ounce, Vieja must make a floating amount payment to Torre. The payment will also be equal to $10 million.

Floating amount = ($800 – $700 per ounce) × 100,000 ounces = $10 million

However, Vieja will then buy the gold more cheaply on the market at $700 per ounce. Therefore, it should still make a profit out of the drop in commodity price.

If, at the end of the term of the transaction, the price is $900 per ounce, then as the price of $900 is between the floor price of $800 and the cap price of $1,100, no party will need to make any payment to the other. The parties have hedged their exposure to the fluctuations of the price of gold, but it turned out not to be necessary. However, the more important aspect is that they obtained the hedge at zero cost and were both happy with the arrangement.

Considering that Torre actually mines gold and Vieja uses gold in its products, the parties may have decided that it would be cheaper and more cost-effective for them to enter into a physically settled transaction. This would mean that Torre would have to deliver 100,000 ounces of gold at the end of the five-year term.

The payment that Vieja must make to Torre will differ depending on the actual price of gold on the termination of the transaction. If the price stands at $1,100, Vieja will need to pay only $1,000 per ounce (ie, the cap price) for the delivery. If the price is $700, Vieja will need to pay $800 per ounce. If, however, the final price is between $800 and $1,000, Vieja will need to make the market price of gold for the delivery of the agreed 100,000 ounces. (However, in order to effect physical settlement the parties will need to use the provisions of Sub-Annex B of the Annex to the 2005 definitions, which relates to physically settled bullion transactions. The principal body of the 2005 definitions provides only for cash settlement of all transactions.)

10.   Article VII – Calculation of prices for commodity reference prices

This is the longest and probably most complex article of the 2005 definitions, and it has also undergone the most changes compared with the 1993 definitions and the 2000 supplement. It incorporates the entire Sub-Annex A of the Annex to the 2005 definitions, which forms part of Sections 7.1 and 7.2. Its six sub-sections can be divided into five different, albeit related, areas:
- incorporation of commodity reference prices of Sub-Annex A;
- Sub-Annex A of the Annex to the 2005 definitions;
- correction of the prices by the price source;
- market disruption events; and
- disruption fall-backs.

10.1   Incorporation and corrections of commodity reference prices

If the terms 'commodity reference price' or 'relevant price' appear anywhere in a transaction, the transaction incorporates by reference Sub-Annex A of the Annex to the 2005 definitions. Generally, the sub-annex should be viewed as being part of Sections 7.1 and 7.2 and forming an integral part of the main body of the 2005 definitions. The sub-annex includes hundreds of definitions as to how the price of a specified commodity is determined.

By contrast, the commodity reference prices were included in the principal body of the 1993 definitions. The 2005 version is different for two reasons:
- The inclusion of this very lengthy section in the annex made the main body of the 2005 definitions less bulky and more user-friendly; and
- The intention was that the annex would be amended from time to time to include new or updated definitions of the reference prices, and amending just the annex is easier and more transparent than changing the main body of the document.

Section 7.2 (the part still included in the main body of the 2005 definitions) specifies that when the parties use the words 'commodity reference price' or 'relevant price', they will be deemed to have incorporated Sub-Annex A as amended through the trade date of the transaction. Therefore, all amendments to the sub-annex will automatically be deemed to be included for any transaction concluded after those amendments were made.

10.2   Sub-Annex A of the Annex to the 2005 definitions

Although this sub-annex is by far the longest part of the commodity documentation, its role is quite straightforward and its application causes no major difficulties in practice. It is divided into three sub-sections:

- Section 7.1 contains 196 pages of definitions of commodity reference prices, which cover the following classes of asset: agricultural products, energy, freight, metals, paper and composite commodity indices. The main difference when compared with the 1993 definitions is the inclusion of some new definitions for agricultural products, coal, wet and dry freight, and composite commodity indices.
- Sections 7.2(a) and 7.2(b) include a few pages of definitions of the price sources (eg, Reuters and Telerate) and of the relevant exchanges (eg, the Baltic Exchange or Euronext LIFFE) which are used in Section 7.1.
- Section 7.2(c) includes the 'commodity reference price framework', which facilitates the creation of new reference prices, and it also has various other related definitions.

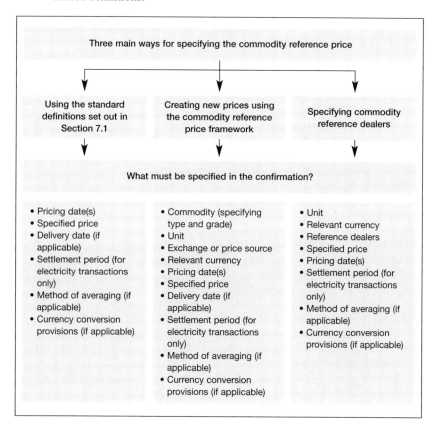

Sub-Annex A provides for three main methods for the parties to specify the commodity reference price for their transaction (see preceding diagram):

- The parties can select a commodity reference price from Section 7.1;
- The parties can create their own commodity reference price using the commodity reference price framework; or
- The parties can elect 'commodity reference dealers', in which case the price will be determined using quotations from four leading dealers.

(a)   *Determining the commodity reference price by using the definitions set out in Section 7.1*

This is the simplest method provided by the 2005 definitions for determining a price for a given pricing date. The parties need to specify one out of hundreds of commodity reference prices set out in Section 7.1, such as White Maize SAFEX for corn or Jet Fuel-Jet 55 Gulf Coast (Waterborne)-Platts US for jet fuel.

However, it is not enough just to specify one of the price codes. The definitions in Section 7.1 make reference to various terms which will be unique for each transaction. Therefore, the parties will always need to provide the details of the 'specified price' and the 'pricing dates' in each confirmation.

The term 'pricing date' has been explained in section 9.2 of this chapter. In turn, the 'specified price' is just a type of price which is published or announced on a given day and it can be one of the following:

- the high price;
- the low price;
- the average of the high price and the low price;
- the closing price;
- the opening price;
- the asked price;
- the bid price;
- the average of the bid price and the asked price;
- the settlement price;
- the official settlement price;
- the official price;
- the morning fixing;
- the afternoon fixing;
- the spot price; or
- any other type specified in the confirmation.

Therefore, the parties will need to consider what types of price of a given commodity are published or announced on a given day, and which one is used for the purposes of calculating the relevant price on the pricing dates for their transaction.

Apart from the pricing date and specified price, which will be relevant for all the commodity reference prices in Section 7.1, the parties may often need to specify the delivery date and the settlement period for some of the prices, as well as the currency conversion provisions and method of averaging. These are not always necessary, though.

As referred to above, the currency conversion provisions are necessary only if a commodity reference price is published in a currency other than the agreed currency of payment. In turn, the method of averaging is relevant only when there is more than one pricing date for a calculation period or a payment date, and the parties would like to amend the default clauses of the 2005 definitions that provide for averaging by way of unweighted arithmetic mean.

The concept of 'delivery date' needs further explanation. The exchanges and the public sources (ie, the places where the prices are published or announced other than exchanges, such as a publication or a magazine) often quote prices of the futures contract on the relevant commodities and those prices depend on the length of the relevant futures contract. The delivery date is the date or month for the delivery of the underlying commodity under that futures contract. Therefore, the delivery date helps to identify the relevant futures contract and, consequently, the price applicable to a given transaction.

The 2005 definitions provide three ways of defining the 'delivery date':
- The parties can specify either a date or a month and year in the relevant confirmation.
- The parties can specify a nearby month for the expiration of the relevant futures contract. For example, if they specify 'first nearby month', the delivery date will be the month of expiration of the first futures contract to expire following the relevant pricing date. Alternatively, the 'eighth nearby month' means that the delivery date will be the month of expiration of the eighth futures contract to expire following the relevant pricing date.
- The parties can agree any other way for determining the delivery date in the confirmation.

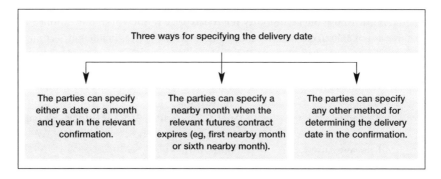

Lastly, the parties may need to specify the 'settlement period', but only if they enter into a transaction referencing electricity. As trading in electricity often takes place only on certain days and at certain times during a calculation period, the parties have to specify the applicable dates and times in the confirmation.

(b)   *Determining the commodity reference price by using the commodity reference price framework*
From the legal and documentation perspective, the commodity reference price framework is the most interesting part of this sub-annex, even though it is identical

to Section 7.1(c)(ii) of the 1993 definitions and Section 7.1(d)(ii) of the 2000 Supplement. To quote the introduction to the sub-annex, it "allows parties to specify a few key terms in order to tailor a commodity reference price for use in the relevant agreement or confirmation". It can be helpful when a reference price that the parties want to use is not set out in Section 7.1 or when the definitions set out in that section are no longer accurate.

To create a new commodity reference price under the commodity reference price framework, the parties need to specify the following details in the confirmation:

- the relevant commodity (including the type or grade of that commodity);
- the relevant unit (eg, pounds, kilograms, inches, gigajoules, megawatt hours);
- the relevant exchange (if the price of that commodity is announced or published on an exchange), or the relevant price source (if such price is not published or announced on an exchange – for example, a publication or a magazine);
- the relevant currency;
- the specified price (whether the price used in a particular transaction shall be, for example, the high price on the designated date, the opening price, the ask price, the bid price, the morning fixing); and
- if applicable, the delivery date.

Once it is understood how to create commodity reference prices, it is also much easier to understand the reference prices set out in Section 7.1 in Sub-Annex A. Any of the reference prices from Sub-Annex A can also be presented in the format provided for by the commodity reference price framework.

How to use the commodity reference price framework: As mentioned above, it is possible to convert the commodity reference prices defined in Section 7.1 into the format of the commodity reference price framework. For example, the price of corn with the reference White Maize SAFEX could be presented as:

Commodity:	Grade-WM1 yellow maize from any origin
Unit:	Metric tonne
Exchange:	SAFEX (ie, South African Futures Exchange), as displayed on Reuters Screen page 0#MAW
Relevant currency:	South African rand
Specified price:	[this will need to be decided by the parties in the confirmation – for example, the official settlement price]

The parties will also need to give the details of the specified price if they just relied on the commodity reference price as per Section 7.1.

Another example would be the commodity reference price for jet fuel under the code Jet Fuel-Jet 55 Gulf Coast (Waterborne)-Platts US, which could be translated into:

Commodity:	Jet 55 jet fuel

Unit:	Gallon
Public source:	Platts US, published under the heading "Gulf Coast 7.8 RVP Waterborne: JET 55"
Relevant currency:	US dollars
Specified price:	[this will need to be decided by the parties in the confirmation]

(c)   *Determining the commodity reference price by using the commodity reference dealer provisions*

Lastly, Sub-annex A allows the parties to specify the commodity reference price via commodity reference dealers. If the parties decide to do this, the price for a pricing date will be determined on the basis of four quotations provided by four reference dealers (or bullion reference dealers, in the case of bullion transactions). If the parties elect this method, they will also need to specify the following details in the confirmation:

- the relevant unit (eg, pounds, kilograms, inches, gigajoules, megawatt hours);
- the names of the reference dealers; and
- the relevant currency.

If the parties specify commodity reference dealers as the basis for the commodity reference price but fail to specify the reference dealers, the calculation agent will contact four leading dealers in the relevant commodity market. If the calculation agent obtains four quotations, it will discard the highest and the lowest and use the arithmetic mean of the remaining two figures to determine the relevant price. If the calculation agent obtains only three figures, then it will discard the highest and the lowest one, and the remaining value will be the relevant price for that pricing date. If there are two or fewer quotations, it will be deemed that the price cannot be determined.

10.3   Corrections of the prices by the price source

Section 7.3 covers the situation when a price used by the calculation agent to determine the relevant price is subsequently corrected by the person or body that originally published that price. If such correction has occurred within 30 days of the original publication (or 90 days in case of weather index derivatives transactions), either party may notify the other of the correction and the amount that is payable as a result. The notification must occur not later than 30 days (or 90 days for weather index derivatives transactions) after the correction has been made.

The relevant party must then make the relevant payment within three business days of the effective date of the notice. Such payment must also include any interest for the period from and including the day on which the payment was originally made, up to, but excluding, the day of payment following the correction. The interest is calculated by reference to the spot offered rate for deposits in the payments currency in the London interbank market as at 11:00 am, London time, on the relevant payment day.

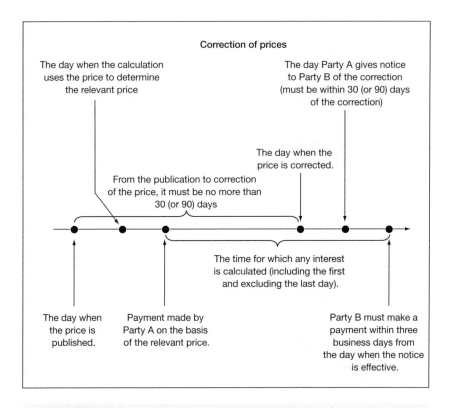

Hypothetical example: Morland Corporation

Morland Corporation is an international corporation which owns thousands of hectares of fields with orange trees. It is concerned that the price of orange juice may go down and it would like to hedge its position. For this reason, Morland enters into a commodity swap transaction on frozen concentrated orange juice with Flatland International on 5 January 2015 on the total notional amount of 1 million pounds-weight of deliverable-grade orange solids. The parties agree that Alacant Brokers will act as the calculation agent, and that the transaction will terminate on 5 January 2016.

They choose Frozen Concentrated Orange Juice No1 – NYBOT as the commodity reference price. According to Sub-Annex A, the price of the commodity is made public by the New York Board of Trade and made public on Reuters Screen Page 0#OJ.

On 5 January 2015 the price of orange juice is $1.50 per pound. The parties agreed that if the price rises above $1.50, Morland will make a payment to Flatland. However, if the price drops below this level, Flatland will make a payment to Morland.

On 5 January 2016 the price quoted on the relevant Reuters page is equal to $1.40. On the same date, Alacant calculates that Flatland needs to make a floating amount payment to Morland given by:

Floating amount = ($1.50 per pound – $1.40 per pound) × 1 million pounds
                = $100,000

Accordingly, Flatland makes this payment to Morland on 7 January 2016.

However, suppose that the price of $1.40 was published by mistake, and it is corrected on January 7 2016 to be $1.55. Flatland spots this only on 2 February 2016 and sends a notice to Morland on 3 February 2016. In the notice, Flatland specifies that the notice is effective as of 3 February. The provisions of Section 7.2 apply considering that:

- there were only two business days between publication of the wrong figure and the correct one (ie, less than 30 calendar days); and
- there were only 29 calendar days between the correction of the figure and the sending of the notice by Flatland (ie, less than 30 days).

This means that Morland must repay the $100,000 that it received from Flatland and, because the price moved against Morland, it must also make the following payment:

Floating amount = ($1.55 per pound – $1.50 per pound) × 1 million pounds
                = $50,000

Therefore, Morland must pay to Flatland the money it received originally (ie $100,000), together with the money that it should have paid at that time (ie, $50,000), plus any accrued interest. The interest is to be the spot offered rate for deposits in US dollars in the London interbank market as at approximately 11:00am, London time, calculated from, and including, 7 January 2016 (ie, the day that Flatland made the original payment to Morland) to, but excluding, the date that Morland actually makes a payment to Flatland. As Flatland specified 4 February 2016 as the effective date of the notice, Morland has until 8 February 2016 (ie, three business days later) to transfer $150,000 plus interest to Flatland.

10.4   Market disruption events

When the 2005 definitions were being drafted, the working party spent a considerable time redrafting, amending and changing the market disruption events that were set out in the 1993 definitions and the 2000 supplement. The results are contained in Section 7.4 within Article VII. This section:

- sets out the new or revised market disruption events; and
- regulates and sets out what happens if an applicable market disruption event occurs.

We have divided this sub-section of the chapter accordingly.

(a)   Description of market disruption events

The 2005 definitions provide for six standard market disruption events: 'price source disruption', 'trading disruption', 'disappearance of commodity reference price', 'material change in formula', 'material change in content' and 'tax disruption'.

Furthermore, the parties can specify and define in the confirmation any 'additional market disruption events'.

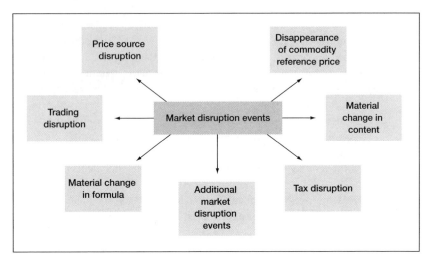

Price source disruption: The first listed market disruption event, price source disruption, can apply if the relevant price is determined by an exchange or by any other price source. It occurs when one of four events materialises:

- The price source fails to publish or announce the specified price (or the information necessary for determining the specified price) for the relevant commodity reference price;
- The price source is temporarily or permanently unavailable, or has been discontinued;
- The calculation agent could not obtain at least three quotations from reference dealers (this applies only if the parties have elected commodity reference dealers as the basis for the commodity reference price); or
- The specified price in respect of the relevant commodity reference price differs from the specified price, determined in accordance with commodity reference dealers, by a price materiality percentage. (Naturally, this applies only if the parties have specified the price materiality percentage in the confirmation.)

Trading disruption: The next market disruption event, trading disruption, is new as at 2005. It replaces two disruption events included in the previous definitions: trading suspensions and trading limitation. 'Trading disruption' is defined as "any material suspension of, or any material limitation on, trading in the futures contract or commodity on the exchange or in any additional futures contracts, options contract or commodity on any exchange specified in the confirmation".

Unlike the old definitions of 'trading suspension' and 'trading limitation', the new event clarifies what the key phrases 'material suspension' and 'material limitation' actually mean. Accordingly, a suspension can be considered 'material' in only two circumstances:

- All trading in the relevant futures contracts or the commodity has been suspended for the entire pricing date; or
- All trading on such futures contracts or the commodity is suspended subsequent to opening, provided that:
  - trading does not recommence before the scheduled closing time; and
  - the suspension is announced less than one hour before trading starts.

A limitation of trading will be considered 'material' for the purposes of trading disruption only if:
- the relevant exchange establishes limits on the range within which the price of the futures contract or the commodity can fluctuate; and
- the closing or settlement price of the futures contract or the commodity on such day is at the upper or lower limit of that range.

Disappearance of commodity reference price: This market disruption event has also been changed considerably from the previous version. It is now defined as the occurrence of one of three events:
- the permanent discontinuation of trading in the relevant futures contracts on the relevant exchange;
- the disappearance of the relevant commodity or of the trading in that commodity; or
- the disappearance or permanent discontinuance or unavailability of the specified commodity reference price.

In relation to the third item of the definition, a market disruption event will occur even if the source of the price is still available or the related futures contracts are still being traded.

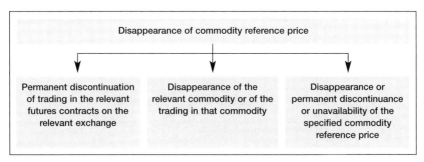

Material change in formula or content: The next two events listed above – material change in formula and material change in content – are self-explanatory and have not been changed when compared with the 1993 definitions.

A 'material change in formula' occurs when there is a material change in the formula or method of calculating the relevant commodity reference price. A 'material change in content' occurs if there is any material change in the content, composition or constitution of the commodity or the related futures contract.

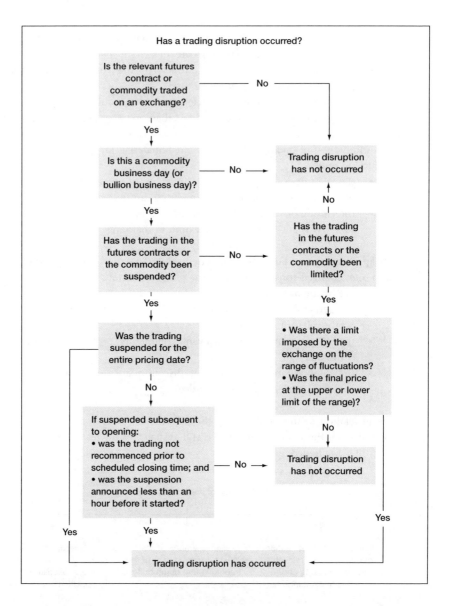

Tax disruption: The 'tax disruption' market disruption event has not changed and is defined as any imposition, change or removal of any tax on the relevant commodity which would affect the price of the transaction.

Additional market disruption events: As mentioned above, the parties are also free to define any additional market disruption events. If they decide to disapply the standard market disruption events and use their additional market disruption events instead, they need to be careful when drafting the confirmation. If they specify just 'not applicable' next to the field 'market disruption events' in the confirmation, the

2005 definitions could operate also to disapply any additional market disruption events.[4] Instead, we recommend setting out a full clause stating the intention of the parties.

Removal of *de minimis* trading event: It is also worth noting that the old market disruption event of de minimis trading has not been included in the 2005 definitions, as ISDA's working party agreed that it is no longer used and is therefore no longer relevant.

(b)   *Application and deemed application of the market disruption events provisions*
Under the 2005 definitions, the parties need not specify all market disruption events in order for them to apply. Instead, Section 7.4(d) of Article VII lists events which will be deemed to apply to any transaction other than a bullion transaction or a weather derivative transaction.[5]

Therefore, unless the parties specify otherwise, all market disruption events apart from tax disruption will apply to any transaction other than a bullion transaction or a weather index derivative transaction. However, if the parties specifically list some of the market disruption events to the exclusion of others, then only those events specifically listed in the confirmation will apply.

The definitions also make clear that if the parties elect for the standard market disruption events to apply, they can still designate in the confirmation those commodities for which a material change in formula and a material change in content will not apply.

For a bullion transaction, only the following market disruption events will be deemed to apply: price source disruption, trading disruption and disappearance of commodity reference price. As bullion transactions are standard in the market, the ISDA working party decided that there was no need for the inclusion of material change in formula and material change in content disruptions to those trades.

The 2005 definitions also clarified what happens if one event is both a market disruption event (or an additional market disruption event) and a termination event under the ISDA Master Agreement. Unless the parties decide otherwise, such event will be deemed only a 'market disruption event' (or an 'additional market disruption event'). However, this is subject to any limiting provisions in the relevant ISDA Master Agreement.

Lastly, the final paragraph of Section 7.4 stresses that if the relevant price is unavailable, the parties should first use the fall-back provisions which allow for an alternative way of determining the price. Only if this is not available can the parties terminate the transaction.

---

4   This is due to the last sentence in Section 7.4(c), which is somewhat peculiarly drafted: "The term 'not applicable' when specified in conjunction with the term 'market disruption event' means that the calculation of a relevant price will not be adjusted as a result of any market disruption event (in which case there would also be no cause to specify any additional market disruption events)".
5   Although Section 7.4(d)(i) provides that those events will apply to all transactions other than bullion transactions and does not mention any weather index derivatives transactions, the disruption events for weather index derivatives transactions are separately listed in Section 11 (Sub-annex C) of the 2005 definitions.

Deemed application of market disruption events	
Market disruption events deemed applicable to all transactions (other than bullion transactions and weather index derivatives transactions, and unless the parties specify otherwise): • price source disruption; • trading disruption; • disappearance of commodity reference price; • material change in formula; • material change in content; and • tax disruption. The parties have an option to disapply the material change in formula and material change in content to specific commodities.	Market disruption events deemed applicable to bullion transactions (unless the parties specify otherwise): • price source disruption; • trading disruption and • disappearance of commodity reference price.

(c)   ***Disruption fall-backs***

If a market disruption event occurs, the 2005 definitions provide that there will be consequences. These consequences are called 'disruption fall-backs'. The disruption fall-backs provide a basis for an alternative determination of the relevant prices for a transaction or, in certain cases, facilitate its termination once a market disruption event has occurred. Considering their importance in the transaction, the disruption fall-backs received plenty of attention from the ISDA working party which drafted the 2005 definitions.

Section 7.5 of Article VII is divided into three main areas:
- description of various disruption fall-backs available under the 2005 definitions;
- provisions regulating the deemed application of those fall-backs; and
- clauses for the general application of the disruption fall-backs.

Description of disruption fall-backs: The 2005 definitions provide for seven standard disruption fall-backs:
- fall-back reference dealers;
- fall-back reference price;
- negotiated fall-back;
- no-fault termination;
- postponement;
- calculation agent determination; and
- delayed publication or announcement.

The 2005 definitions have adopted a 'menu' approach here. The parties will specify the fall-backs that they want to apply in the order that they will apply. If the calculation agent is unable to obtain the relevant price using the first applicable disruption fall-back, the next one will apply and so on. The final disruption fall-back will provide for termination of the transaction.

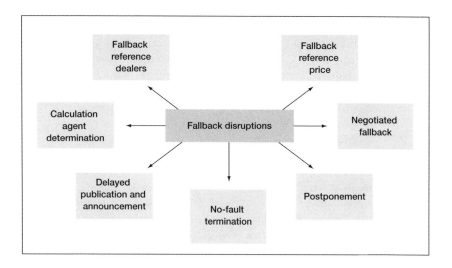

Under the 'fall-back reference dealers' disruption fall-back, the relevant price will be determined in accordance with the commodity reference price: commodity reference dealers. Obviously, it will not apply if 'commodity reference dealer' is already specified in the confirmation as the basis for the commodity reference price.

The parties can elect 'fall-back reference price' as a disruption fall-back. In that case, they will also need to specify an alternate commodity reference price. If this fall-back applies and if the calculation agent is unable to determine the relevant price using the principal commodity reference price, the alternative commodity reference price will apply.

If the 'negotiated fall-back' disruption fall-back applies, the parties will negotiate with each other with a view to agreeing on the relevant price. If they have failed to agree the price before the fifth business day (or bullion business day, for bullion transactions) following the pricing date on which the market disruption occurred, the next applicable disruption fall-back will apply.

The 'no-fault termination' disruption fall-back provides for a termination of the transaction in accordance with the provisions of the relevant ISDA Master Agreement. Accordingly, the relevant market disruption event (or additional disruption event) will constitute a termination event, and the transaction will terminate as if 'illegality' or a '*force majeure*' (as defined in the relevant ISDA Master Agreement) applied. Both parties will be deemed 'affected parties' (as defined in the relevant ISDA Master Agreement).

The 'calculation agent determination' disruption fall-back gives the calculation agent a discretionary power to determine the relevant price. However, the calculation agent must take into consideration the latest available quotation for the relevant commodity reference price and any other information that it deems relevant in good faith.

The remaining two fall-back disruptions – 'postponement' and 'delayed publication or announcement' – are the most complex in their application, not least because they appear confusingly similar.

'Postponement' was included in previous versions of the definitions, but the 2005 version sets out its application in more detail. If postponement applies, the pricing date will be deemed to be the first succeeding commodity business day (or bullion business day, for bullion transactions) on which the market disruption event (or additional market disruption event) ceases to exist. However, if the market disruption event exists for a number of days equal to the number of 'maximum days of disruption', the next fall-back disruption will apply.

Therefore, when electing postponement, the parties should also specify the maximum days of disruption in the confirmation. Considering that the result of postponement is a change in the pricing date, this may also disrupt other payment clauses in the confirmation. For example, it may be impossible to calculate the floating amount as of the original pricing date; therefore, Section 7.5 of Article VII specifies that any determination of the in-the-money amount or floating amount will also be postponed to the same extent. Furthermore, if the other party to the transaction was supposed to make a payment on the same date that the postponed floating amount would have been payable, all such other payments will also be postponed.

The 'delayed publication or announcement' disruption fall-back was introduced in the 2005 definitions and, similar to postponement, it also contemplates that a disrupted price may become available with the period of the maximum days of disruption (as specified in the confirmation). However, unlike postponement, the delayed publication or announcement disruption fall-back is retrospective and it preserves the original pricing date (the pricing announcement for which has been delayed). When it applies, the parties hope that the relevant price will eventually be published in respect of that initial pricing date.

Also similar to postponement, the delay determining the relevant price may cause disruptions to other payment dates. The determination of the in-the-money amount and the floating amount, as well as the payments of any other amounts payable on the same date, will therefore be delayed to the same extent.

Application and deemed application of disruption fall-back provisions: As with market disruption events, the parties need not specify any disruption fall-backs for certain disruption fall-backs to be deemed applicable. Selected disruption fall-backs are deemed to automatically apply in the order and manner as provided in Section 7.5(d)(i) of Article VII.

The list of deemed fall-backs was drafted by the ISDA working party on the basis of the then-current market practice (or proposed market practice) and applies to all transactions other than weather index derivatives transactions. Although the working group initially considered creating a separate fall-back 'waterfall' for bullion transactions, it decided that this could be best dealt with by the inclusion of separate bullion disruption events in Sub-Annex B (bullion transactions), which would apply only to physically settled bullion trades.

If the parties have not provided for any fall-backs in the confirmation, the following fall-back disruption will apply to the relevant transaction in this order:

- fall-back reference price;

- concurrently:
  - delayed publication or announcement;
  - postponement; and
  - negotiated fall-back;
- fall-back reference dealers; and
- negotiated fall-back.

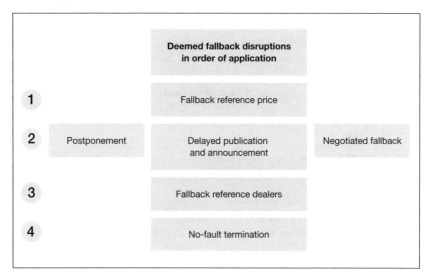

Naturally, the first provision, fall-back reference price, will apply only if the parties have specified an alternative commodity reference price. Its operation is generally straightforward and its main advantage is that the parties will know almost immediately whether this provision is capable of yielding the relevant price. If it is not, the next fall-back will apply.

The second fall-back – the concurrent operation of three disruption provisions – is complex, but it works quite well in practice. When it applies, the parties can start negotiating with a view of agreeing the relevant price under 'negotiated fall-back'. If the parties reach a settlement before a price is obtained under 'postponement' or 'delayed publication or announcement', the agreed price will apply as at the relevant pricing date. However, if postponement or delayed publication or announcement yields the relevant price before then, negotiated fall-back provisions will cease to operate.

In relation to the deemed application of the fall-back provisions under Section 7.5(d)(i) only, the 'maximum days of disruption' for both 'postponement' and 'delayed publication or announcement' is two commodity business days (or bullion business days, for bullion transactions) for both, unless otherwise specified. In the case of conflict between the two fall-back provisions, 'delayed publication or announcement' takes precedence over 'postponement'. This means that if the parties have obtained the relevant price through postponement first, they should wait until the end of the period of maximum days of disruption to see whether delayed publication or announcement could also yield the relevant price. If they have obtained a delayed price by that time, it will apply notwithstanding that a postponed price was published earlier. However, if by the end of the period of maximum days of disruption only the postponed price has been published, it will apply as the relevant price for that pricing date.

Whereas the default period for the 'maximum days of disruption' is two commodity business days (or bullion business days) under Section 7.5(d)(i), the standard of operation for negotiated fall-back, as described above, is five business days or bullion business days. Therefore, when all three fall-backs operate simultaneously, there is a potential timing mismatch.

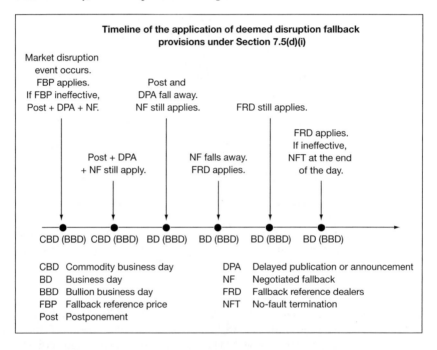

The 2005 definitions solved this by specifying that if negotiated fall-back applies simultaneously with both or either postponement and delayed publication or announcement, then negotiated fall-back will cease to operate on the first business day (or bullion business day) after the expiry of the 'maximum days of disruption' relating to postponement and delayed publication or announcement. This means that only on the second business day (or bullion business day) after the period of the maximum days of disruption will the parties be able to move on to the next disruption fall-back.

The last two deemed fall-back provisions are 'fall-back reference dealers' and 'no-fault termination'. Accordingly, the calculation agent will have three business days (or bullion business days) to obtain at least three quotations from the reference dealers. If it does not manage to get those, the transaction will terminate.

Hypothetical example: Cartagena Drinks plc

Cartagena Drinks plc is a dairy producer operating throughout the United States. It hedges itself against the price of milk rising too quickly by entering into a commodity swap agreement on Class III milk on 26 May 2016 with Lechia Corporation. Under the terms of the swap, Lechia will make a floating-amount payment to Cartagena half-yearly, starting from 1 June 2016, if Class III milk is trading above a set level at the end of the calculation period.

The parties specify the commodity reference price as Milk Class III CME. They include no provisions relating to market disruption events or disruption fall-backs in the confirmation, and specify no value for the maximum days of disruption. The selected commodity reference price is defined by reference to the Chicago Mercantile Exchange (CME), or its successor.

On 1 June 2016 trading on the CME is suspended at 2:30pm due to a serious fault in the operating system and does not recommence prior to the exchange's scheduled closing time. Thus, the criteria set out in Section 7.4(c)(ii)(A)(2) are met for the disruption to be classed as a trading disruption.

As the parties specified no market disruption events, Section 7.4(d) kicks in and various disruption events are deemed to have been specified for this trade. Trading disruption is included among those default market disruption events. As the parties specified no disruption fall-backs, the default fall-back set out in Section 7.5(d)(i) is deemed to apply.

The first fall-back is fall-back reference price. However, Cartagena and Lechia did not specify an alternative commodity reference price, so this first fall-back automatically falls away. This means that postponement, delayed publication or announcement and negotiated fall-back all begin to apply on 1 June.

The CME does not open for business on Tuesday 2 June, so it is not possible to determine the price using postponement or delayed publication or announcement. The parties negotiate to agree the relevant price, but cannot settle.

However, if the exchange had opened for business on Tuesday 2 June and had quoted the price of milk as of 9:00am on June 2 (but not with respect to 1 June), this would have meant that the parties had obtained the relevant price under the postponement disruption fall-back. At that point the parties could stop negotiating, as the negotiated fall-back would cease to apply.

Nevertheless, Cartagena and Lechia woud still need to wait until the end of Tuesday to see whether the exchange would publish the relevant price of milk as of 1 June. If the exchange did not do so, the postponed price would apply and the pricing date would be postponed from 1 June until 2 June.

Changing the scenario further, if the exchange were to publish the price of milk as of Monday 1 June at 4:00pm on Tuesday 2, that price would be the relevant price. The pricing date would still remain 1 June 2016. However, the relevant settlement date or payment date would be delayed until 2 June.

Going back to our initial scenario, the parties do not obtain a price pursuant to postponed or delayed publication or announcement on 2 June. Therefore, both of those disruption fall-backs cease to operate, but the parties can still reach an agreement pursuant to negotiated fall-back.

Further, they fail to reach an agreement as to the price by the end of 3 June. This means that negotiated fall-back falls away and the next applicable disruption fall-back (ie, fall-back reference dealers) kicks in.

The parties did not specify reference dealers in the confirmation. This means that the calculation agent has to approach four leading dealers in the market for Class III milk and obtain all least three quotations for the price of milk as of 1 June.

By the end of Friday 5, the calculation agent has obtained only two quotations for the price of milk as of 1 June.

Saturday 6 June and Sunday 7 June are not business days, so they are disregarded. Monday 8 June is the final date for the calculation agent to obtain three quotations for the price of milk. It fails to do so by the end of Monday. This means that the transaction terminates at the end of the day in accordance with the no-fault termination fall-back.

Other clauses regulating the general application of the fall-back provisions: The deemed provisions, as explained above, will apply only if the parties have not specified any disruption fall-backs in the confirmation themselves. Section 7.5 of Article VII also includes some clauses of general application regulating the operation of fall-back disruptions if the deemed provisions are not used.

Even if the deemed provisions do not apply, the parties retain the option to elect for postponement and delayed publication or announcement to apply concurrently. In such a case, delayed announcement or publication will take precedence over postponement, as explained above. Furthermore, if the parties specify both or either of the two disruption fall-backs (to operate either separately or simultaneously), negotiated fall-back will automatically apply concurrently with such fall-backs.

However, the automatic inclusion of negotiated fall-back will apply only if the parties have not referred at all to this fall-back in the confirmation. If they specifically deselected it or if they elected to use it at some other stage, such provisions will apply instead.

Lastly, the no-fault termination will apply to all transactions as the ultimate fall-back. A transaction will terminate in accordance with its provision even if the parties have not specified it in the confirmation, provided that no other fall-back manages to yield the relevant price.

11.   Article VIII – Commodity options

An option is a privately negotiated contract between two counterparties. Generally, the buyer of an option acquires a right to buy from (or sell to) the seller of the option a defined amount of assets at a specified price. However, the 2005 definitions are different from other sets of ISDA definitions in this respect, and the option buyer will never actually acquire a right to receive (or sell) any of the underlying commodity assets. Instead, on the expiry of the option, one party will only make a payment to the other.

Although the parties can provide for physical settlement if they incorporate the relevant sub-annexes to the 2005 definitions, Article VIII does not really anticipate this type of settlement in its ordinary sense (ie, the actual transfer of the underlying asset). As noted above, the same applies for swaps or any other instruments governed only by the principal body of the 2005 definitions, so this is a consistent theme throughout the document.

The eight sections of Article VIII cover the following areas:

- the description of an option and the payment of premium;
- the description of different types of option;
- terms relating to the exercise of options; and
- terms relating to the settlement of options.

11.1   Description of an option and the payment of premium

An 'option' is defined in Section 8.1 of Article VIII as a contract between the commodity option seller to the commodity option buyer, which can take one of four forms:

- a grant by the commodity option seller to the commodity option buyer of a right to receive the cash settlement amount (this term is explained later in this section) in respect of the transaction on the settlement date;
- a swaption;
- a right granted to the commodity option buyer of a right to receive any other or contingent rights as specified in the confirmation; or
- an instrument combining any of the three other forms.

A 'swaption' is an option given to the option buyer which allows it either to:

- enter into a swap identified in the confirmation (ie, the underlying transaction); or
- receive a cash settlement amount in respect of that underlying transaction on the settlement date.

The buyer of a swaption has the right to cause the underlying transaction to be effective only if the parties elect 'physical settlement' or 'contract settlement' as applicable. Otherwise, the swaption buyer will be able to receive only the cash settlement amount.

However, the principal body of the 2005 definitions does not allow for physical settlement in the sense that the parties to a transaction would actually exchange commodities. Therefore, the physical settlement of a swaption means only that the buyer will have a right to enter into the underlying swap transaction.

Considering that the 2005 definitions cover a variety of different types of asset class, option transactions relating to certain commodities have their own specific rules and definitions, set out in the annexes to the definitions. Therefore, the following transactions have been excluded from the scope of Article VIII: bullion options, bullion swaptions, weather index call options/caps, weather index put options/floors, NBP options and ZBT options. Each of these is analysed in detail in other chapters of this book.

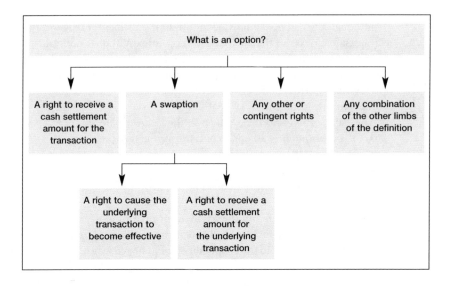

To enter into a transaction and compensate the commodity option seller for providing the option, a commodity option buyer will normally pay to the seller a specified amount of money ('total premium'). Alternatively, the parties can provide in the confirmation a value for 'premium per unit', which would then be multiplied by the relevant notional quantity to give the 'total premium'. The confirmation should also specify when such payment (or payments) should be made (the 'premium payment date(s)').

11.2 Types of option

There are two main classifications of option transaction. An option could be either a put option or a call option. It could also be either a Bermudan, American, Asian or European option.

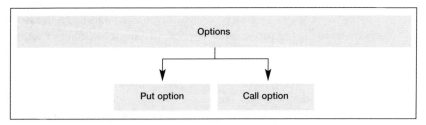

Although the main body of the 2005 definitions does not allow for the actual transfer of commodities, it is easier to understand the difference between a put and a call option if we assume, for now, that options are physically settled. In that case, a physically settled call option would give the buyer a right to purchase a specified commodity from its counterparty at the strike price or a strike price per unit (as specified by the parties in the relevant confirmation). In turn, a put option would give the buyer a right to sell that commodity at a strike price.

In a cash-settled transaction governed by the 2005 definitions, the buyer of a put option will not actually have a right to sell the specified commodity, but it gets the economic equivalent of the same. Instead of selling the commodity, the put option buyer has a right to demand a payment from its counterparty if the floating price (ie, the price of the given commodity on a given day) is lower than the strike price (as provided in the confirmation). Conversely, a call option allows its holder to demand a payment when the actual price (the floating price) is higher than the strike price. (For a fuller description of floating price, please see section 9 of this chapter.)

Another way to categorise different types of option is according to when they can be exercised. The 2005 definitions cover four of the most common types: American, Asian, Bermudan and European.

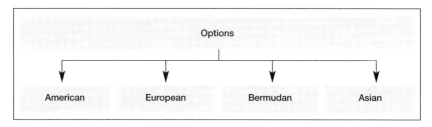

An American option can be exercised on any day during the exercise period (such period as specified in the confirmation). Such day, which can occur at any time before the option's expiry, is called the 'exercise date' if the option is actually exercised on this date (or is deemed to be exercised). However, a European and an Asian option can be exercised only on the day of their expiry (expiration date).

Whereas an American option can be exercised at any time and a European or Asian option only on the expiration date, a Bermudan option is a halfway house. It can be exercised only on specific days during the terms of a transaction as provided in the confirmation (called 'potential exercise dates'), and on the expiration date.

The 2005 definitions are quite imprecise and could suggest that the definition of the exercise date applies only to American options. However, it is a better view that a day on which any option is exercised is called an 'exercise date' in respect of that option. Therefore, the expiration day of an American or Asian option is also an exercise date if the option is actually exercised on this date (or is deemed to be exercised). Article VIII demands that an exercise date be a day which is both:

- a commodity business day; and
- a day when commercial banks are open for business in the city where the option seller is located (seller business day).

Although both European and Asian options can be exercised on the expiration date, the difference between them is quite substantial. In the case of a European (but also a Bermuda or American) option, the calculation agent uses the price of the relevant commodity on the exercise date as the floating price. However, for an Asian option, the calculation agent, when determining the floating price, uses the unweighted arithmetic mean of the relevant prices for each pricing date during the calculation period. Therefore, the value of the Asian option is effectively calculated by reference to the average price of the commodity throughout the term of the transaction.

Types of option	Day when option is exercisable	Days relevant for calculation of the relevant prices
American	Each day during the exercise period	Exercise date (the day when the option is exercised)
European	Expiration date	Expiration date
Bermudan	Each potential exercise date and the expiration date	Exercise date
Asian	Expiration date	Each pricing date in calculation period

11.3 Terms relating to the exercise of options

The main terms relating to the exercise of different types of option have already been explained and analysed in the section above. However, Article VIII also includes some key clauses from a practical perspective.

Section 8.5 provides that automatic exercise will apply to any option unless the parties specify otherwise. This means that the option will be deemed to be exercised at the close of the exercise period for that transaction (ie, the last possible moment when the option could be exercised). However, automatic exercise will not apply to a swaption to cause the underlying transaction to apply.

By comparison, automatic exercise is not deemed to apply for an option governed by the 2002 ISDA Equity Definitions. However, it is generally common practice on the market always to specify automatic exercise as applicable, which is why the working parties included this in the 2005 definitions. After all, the commercial rationale behind an option is to get the benefit of the rising (or falling) prices, without taking any economic risk if the markets are going the other way. Therefore, the default application of automatic exercise makes perfect sense from this perspective.

Unlike the 2002 ISDA Equity Definitions, the 2005 definitions do not give the option buyer a right to disapply automatic exercise during the term of the transaction.

Unless automatic exercise applies to an option, the option buyer can exercise only by giving a notice of exercise to the other party. Such notice can be given orally over the phone and, to be effective, it must be given to the option seller during the hours specified in the confirmation on a seller business day. For an American and a Bermuda option, if the notice is given after the latest time specified, it will be deemed to have been received on the next seller business day in the exercise period. Once served, the notice is irrevocable and it is effective once actually received by the seller.

Thus, the parties should be particularly careful when drafting confirmations for Bermuda options. For example, let us assume that under a Bermuda option the potential exercise dates are 15 March 2016 and 15 June 2016 and the option buyer must give notice to the option seller by 4:00 pm on the relevant day. If the option buyer serves the notice at 4.30 pm on 15 March, because of the slightly peculiar way the 2005 definitions are drafted, the seller could treat the option as exercised as of 15 June. This is particularly dangerous considering that the notice of exercise is irrevocable.

If written confirmation is specified as applicable in the confirmation or if the option seller demands it following the notice of exercise, the buyer must execute a written confirmation setting out the details of the notice. It can be delivered by fax transmission and it must be delivered within one seller business day following the date on which the notice of exercise becomes effective.

11.4   Terms relating to the settlement of options
Under Section 8.7 of Article VIII, on each settlement date for an option transaction, the seller pays to the buyer the cash settlement amount. If the parties are entering into a swaption, they must specify how this amount should be determined in the confirmation. In relation to other options, the following formula will apply, unless specifically amended:

Cash settlement amount = notional quantity × strike price differential

'Strike price differential' is, in turn, defined thus:

- for a call option, an amount which is the excess of the relevant floating price over the strike price; and
- for a put option, an amount which is the excess of the strike price over the relevant floating price.

However, the strike price differential must be a positive number. If it is negative, the option buyer will make no profit from the exercise of the option. Accordingly, the option seller need not make any payments in respect of the cash settlement amount in that case.

Hypothetical example: Javier Plantations Corp

Javier Plantations Corp owns sugar cane plantations in Latin America and it is concerned that the price of sugar may go down from the current high price of $350 per tonne. It would like to hedge against this risk, but it does not want to enter into a swap, as it would then have to give up the money that it makes if the prices continue to rise. It decides to enter into a cash-settled Asian put option with Barbastro Investments Partners, a hedge fund. They choose the commodity reference price to be White Sugar Euronext LIFFE, the notional quantity as 100,000 tonnes, and the calculation period will run from 12 March to 17 November 2015. November 17 will be the expiration date for the transaction and the strike price is agreed to be $340.

The price of sugar keeps rising to reach the level of $387 per tonne on 21 August. However, it then emerges that there is an oversupply of sugar on the markets and the price starts falling suddenly, until it reaches $284 on 17 November 2015.

The calculation agent takes the price of sugar on each commodity business day from 12 March to 17 November and calculates that the unweighted average price during the calculation period was $338.

This means that Barbastro must make the following payment to Javier:

Cash settlement amount = notional amount × strike price difference

The strike price difference is equal to the excess of the strike price over the relevant floating price. Therefore, it is equal to only $2 ($340 – $338). Thus we have:

Cash settlement amount = $100,000 × $2 = $200,000

This means that, as a result of the fall in the price of sugar, Barbastro must pay $200,000 to Javier.

12. **Article IX – Rounding**

The rounding-up provisions were introduced in the 2005 definitions for the first time. They apply to all transactions other than weather index derivatives transactions, and they provide for the rounding-up of all fixed amounts, floating amounts and cash settlement amounts to the nearest unit of the relevant currency. They also specify that each half of a unit will also be rounded up.

Both Section 9.1 of Article IX and the user's guide make it clear that those provisions are supposed to apply only to those three calculated payment amounts named above and nothing else. In particular, the rounding-up provisions do not apply to percentages or the rounding of commodity-specific prices.

13. **The exhibits and sub-annexes to the 2005 definitions**

This chapter has covered only the principal body of the 2005 definitions and Sub-Annex A of the Annex. As referred to at the beginning of the chapter, the document also includes the template confirmations to the 2005 definitions, as well as asset-specific sub-annexes. These are outside the scope of this chapter.

Emissions trading

Edmund Parker
Mayer Brown

1. Introduction

The columns and clouds of smoke, which are belched forth from the sooty throats of the city's industrial enterprises, made London in a few moments like the picture of Troy sacked by the Greeks. Its inhabitants breathe nothing but an impure and thick mist accompanied by a fulginous [sic] and filthy vapour, forcing ladies to clean their complexions with ground almonds and causing the disruption of church services by the constant coughing and spitting of the congregation.[1]

Ever since John Evelyn wrote his *Fumifugium: or the inconveniency of the aer and smoke of London* in 1661, the sooty throats of industries around the world have relentlessly devoured fossil fuels and forests, amplifying the greenhouse effect and triggering global warming: 2016 was the warmest year on record around the globe, followed closely by 2015, 2014, 2010, 2005 and 1998.[2]

This ongoing but sudden climate change is putting the world's coastal areas and nearby population centres at risk from rising sea levels, which are caused by melting glaciers and ice caps, and may potentially change existing climatic patterns. This would result in more frequent droughts and occurrences of extreme weather such as hurricanes and monsoons.

Derivatives could save the planet! That is the rationale behind emissions trading, and documentation from the 'International Swaps and Derivatives Association Inc' (ISDA) is at the forefront of this. This chapter covers the ISDA documentation platform for emissions trading. The complex nature of the underlying asset and its political ramifications make it essential for the practitioner to understand the rationale for emissions trading, together with the regulatory environment. This chapter covers these areas in detail too.

Nation states belatedly woke up to the potential dangers of global warming and began channelling their energies into the UN Framework Convention on Climate Change and the Kyoto Protocol (with the notable exception of the United States, which signed but never ratified the protocol), in a concerted effort to reduce overall greenhouse gas emissions. Among the resulting initiatives are projects to provide

---

* The publishers would like to acknowledge Avanthi Gunatilake of Mayer Brown as co-author of this chapter in the last edition.

1   John Evelyn, *Fumifugium: or The inconveniencie of the aer and smoak of London dissipated together with some remedies humbly proposed by J.E. esq. to His Sacred Majestie, and to the Parliament now assembled*, pp5–16 (London, 1661).

2   National Aeronautics and Space Administration Goddard Institute for Space Studies, GISS Surface Temperature Analysis.

economic incentives for nation states and private firms to reduce their greenhouse gas emissions by trading the right to emit such gases on an international emissions trading market. The key emissions trading schemes use a 'cap and trade' method, whereby a central authority issues emissions permits to polluting companies, subject to a cap. The polluting companies must have a sufficient number of permits to cover their emissions, failing which they must purchase emissions permits from other companies that pollute less or have otherwise obtained these permits. While maintaining an overall cap, which is lowered over time, this method provides an economic incentive for those that pollute less and imposes an economic burden on those that pollute more: fertile ground for a derivatives market.

The emissions trading derivatives market consists of financial instruments such as swaps, options and forwards, which derive their value from an underlying asset: the permits giving the right to emit a defined quantity of a greenhouse gas.

Understanding emissions trading requires a greater knowledge of the underlying asset and its regulatory framework than any other derivative. Different rules apply to different countries and greenhouse gases during different periods, all of which are driven by a regulatory infrastructure, including the framework convention, the Kyoto Protocol, and the regulatory and legislative actions of its signatories.

Without knowledge of both what global warming involves and the legislative background to emissions trading, a practitioner will not fully understand how emissions trading and its documentation platform function, both now and in the future. With this in mind, this chapter covers issues including:

- the ultimate underlying assets – greenhouse gases and their relation to climate change;
- a summary of the chain of events from the 1992 Rio Earth Summit, which produced the UN Framework Convention on Climate Change, to the resulting 1997 Kyoto Protocol, its entry into effect in 2005 and its development thereafter;
- the 'Clean Development Mechanism' (CDM) and 'joint implementation'[3] (JI) 'flexible' project mechanisms for meeting emissions targets, as well as international emissions trading, and the interaction between the three mechanisms;
- the mechanics of emissions trading;
- the 'EU Emissions Trading System' (ETS) and a brief look at developments in the United States towards a possible federal emissions trading scheme; and
- documentation for 'over-the-counter' (OTC) transactions, provided by ISDA for both Europe and the United States.

2.   Greenhouse gases and climate change

There is now an overwhelming view among the scientific community that global warming (an increase in the overall temperature of the earth's atmosphere and oceans) is occurring as, over time, the earth fails to release the sun's energy at the

---

3   Although the term 'joint implementation' was not specifically used in the protocol, it has become the market standard term for this flexible mechanism.

same rate that it absorbs it.[4] In the period between 1880 and 2012, the earth's average temperature rose by 0.85 degrees Celsius and it is predicted that by the end of this century the global temperature may increase by as much as two degrees Celsius above the 1990 level.[5] This increase in the greenhouse effect has been caused by human activities, such as fossil fuel use and deforestation, pushing up atmospheric levels of greenhouse gases, such as carbon dioxide, nitrogen dioxide and methane. The extent of the world's governments' desire to slow or halt this increase will drive the pace of the emissions trading market in future years.

The greenhouse effect works as follows:[6]

- Solar energy passes through the earth's atmosphere.
- Some of it is absorbed by greenhouse gases in the atmosphere, some is reflected by the earth's atmosphere and surface, and the rest is absorbed by, and warms, the earth's surface.
- Through absorption by the earth's surface, the solar energy is converted into heat, causing the earth to emit long-wave infrared radiation back towards space.
- Greenhouse gases, which are the atmosphere's gaseous constituents (eg, carbon dioxide, methane and water vapour) that absorb and re-emit infrared radiation, reflect some of this infrared radiation back to the earth's surface and atmosphere.
- The earth's surface gains more heat and the infrared radiation is once again emitted.
- Some of the infrared radiation passes through the atmosphere and goes into space.
- The more greenhouse gases there are in the atmosphere, the more the earth's temperature will increase.

3.   Earth Summit and UN Framework Convention on Climate Change

In 1992, the UN Conference on Environment and Development in Rio de Janeiro addressed the increasing evidence of global warming. This conference, which became known as the Earth Summit, agreed a new treaty: the UN Framework Convention on Climate Change, which entered into force in 1994. The convention acknowledged that human activities were increasing atmospheric concentrations of greenhouse gases, which in turn were exacerbating the greenhouse effect, and that this "[would] result on average in an additional warming of the earth's surface and atmosphere and may adversely affect natural ecosystems and humankind".

The convention recognised the vulnerability of certain types of geographical area to climate change, encouraged climate change scientific research and technology sharing, and agreed an ultimate objective: to stabilise greenhouse gas concentrations in the atmosphere at a level that would prevent adverse effects on the climate

---

4   Joke Waller-Hunter, executive secretary, UN Framework Convention on Climate Change, Bonn, May 2005, foreword to *Caring for Climate: A Guide to the Climate Change Convention and the Kyoto Protocol*.
5   Intergovernmental Panel on Climate Change, Fifth Assessment Report 2013.
6   *Caring for Climate: A Guide to the Climate Change Convention and the Kyoto Protocol*, UN Framework Convention on Climate Change.

system, through national policies. Its parties also agreed to record and report their greenhouse gas emissions.

The convention was a framework treaty without enforcement provisions. It committed its parties to meet annually at the 'Conference of the Parties' (COP), which monitors progress and discusses tackling climate change.

The convention was joined almost universally and signatories included all EU member states, the United States, Australia, Canada, China and India. The convention divided its signatory countries into three separate groups: Annex I parties, Annex II parties and the rest, which have become known as non-Annex I parties.

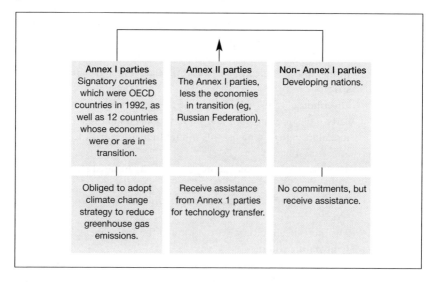

Annex I parties are those signatory countries which were OECD countries in 1992, as well as 12 countries whose economies were or are in transition (EIT parties). EIT parties include the Russian Federation, Belarus, Bulgaria, Croatia, Hungary and Ukraine. Annex II parties are the Annex I parties, excluding the EIT parties. The non-Annex I parties are for the most part the developing nations.

Each of the convention's three groups was given different obligations. Each Annex I party was obliged to adopt a climate change strategy to reduce its greenhouse gas emissions to 1990 (or, in the case of the EIT parties, a later base year) levels by 2000. This target was achieved.

The Annex I parties had to give financial assistance to the non-Annex I parties to help them reduce their greenhouse gas emissions and adapt to climate change. They also had to encourage environmentally friendly technology transfer to EIT and non-Annex I parties. The non-Annex I parties were given no additional specific commitments.

4.   Kyoto Protocol

4.1   Ratification and general content

At the third COP, which took place in Kyoto in 1997, the Kyoto Protocol was adopted. This protocol was then refined in the fourth, fifth and sixth COPs and the Marrakesh Accords in 2001, and subsequently amended by the Doha Amendment in 2012.

The protocol now focuses on seven greenhouse gases:
- carbon dioxide (CO_2);
- methane (CH_4);
- nitrous oxide (N_2O);
- hydrofluorocarbons (HFCs);
- perfluorocarbons (PFCs);
- sulphur hexafluoride (SF_6); and
- nitrogen trifluorid (NF_3).[7]

Carbon dioxide, methane and nitrous oxide account for 97% of greenhouse gas emissions, with carbon dioxide alone accounting for 76%.

The protocol's adherents must achieve legally binding greenhouse gas emissions reductions.

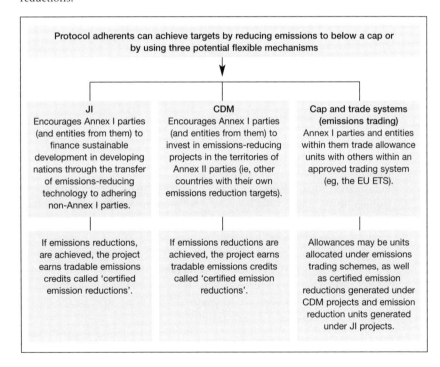

They can achieve these targets either by reducing emissions to below a cap or by using three potential flexible mechanisms: the CDM, JI, and/or emissions trading under cap and trade systems. The first two are project-based mechanisms that can generate allowances, which can then be traded along with any other allocated allowances under an emissions trading system.

Although all of the protocol's adherents are signatories to the convention, the United States is yet to ratify the protocol. Moreover, China and India are not bound by the protocol's emissions targets, as they are not Annex I parties.

4.2 Commitments to reduce emissions

Each adhering Annex I party must meet a greenhouse gas emissions reduction target. This reduction is benchmarked against 1990 emissions (or, in the case of EIT countries, a later benchmark year), and must be met on average through the protocol's compliance period (now in its third phase), which – as a result of the Doha Amendment – will now run until 31 December 2020. In addition, Annex I parties must implement climate change policies.

Overall, the Annex I parties must reduce their greenhouse gas emissions by at least 18% below 1990 levels by 2020. The European Union is treated as a single Annex I party and since 1 January 2013 has an overall emissions reduction target of 20% below 1990 levels.[8] It has allocated each EU member state's target internally. This means that some member states may increase their emissions (eg, Bulgaria by 20% and Romania by 19%), while others must reduce theirs greatly (eg, Denmark by 20% and Luxembourg by 20%). The non-Annex I parties adhering to the protocol have no emissions reductions targets.

4.3 Three flexible methods for emissions reductions

(a) CDM

While the adhering Annex I parties were able to accept greenhouse gas emissions caps, this was not feasible for developing nations, which may increase their emissions in tandem with economic growth. It is inevitable that as these nations industrialise, their emissions will increase. To help tackle this issue without hampering economic development, the protocol introduced the CDM, which encourages Annex I parties (and firms based in these countries) to finance sustainable development in developing nations through the transfer of emissions-reducing technology to adhering non-Annex I parties. If the project implementing the technology results in emissions reductions, the firm or country running the project earns tradable emissions credits (certified emission reductions). It is likely that the costs of doing so would be less than if the firm had made the corresponding reduction in emissions in its own country.

Adhering developing nations may, with the prior approval of the CDM Executive

---

8   The European Union has made a conditional offer to reduce emissions by 30% compared to 1990 levels by 2020 contingent on other developed countries signing up to comparable emission reductions and the cooperation of developing nations.

Board, carry out their own CDM projects without outside assistance and sell the resulting certified emission reductions into the open market. An example of this might be a Malaysian project to reforest 1 million hectares of sovereign territory with the certified emission reductions allocated to this 'carbon sink'[9] sold to an EU member state.

The Marrakesh Accords set out the CDM's governing rules in the Modalities and Procedures for a Clean Development Mechanism. These rules have robust procedures which require strong evidence to be shown that a CDM project has caused emissions to be lower than if the project had not taken place. The CDM Executive Board supervises all such mechanisms and a designated operational entity (ie, a private entity accredited by the board) checks each relevant project and verifies the resulting emissions reductions.[10]

CDM projects include those which can reduce emissions from production, distribution and demand for energy in manufacturing industries, in construction projects, in the chemical industry and through carbon sinks such as afforestation and reforestation projects.

CDM project cycle: a hypothetical example

Nicol International Industries, a UK corporate and major emitter of carbon dioxide, liaises with the Algerian Energy Ministry to upgrade Algeria's national grid. Algeria, a non-Annex I party, has ratified the Kyoto Protocol. The project involves a technology transfer from the United Kingdom, an Annex I party, to Algeria. The Algerian project will make Algerian energy transfer more efficient, resulting in lower carbon dioxide emissions. Nicol believes that the project will qualify as a CDM project.

Nicol is a participating installation in the EU ETS[11] and so must surrender allowances for all of its carbon dioxide emissions. Nicol has not been allocated enough allowances by the UK government to match its actual emissions. As an alternative to buying allowances on the open market, it plans to register the Algerian project as a CDM and surrender the certified emission reductions that it generates to cover the allowances that it must submit under the EU ETS.

Nicol submits the project plan to the CDM Executive Board.

Leburn Consulting Limited, a designated operational entity appointed by Nicol, and the Algerian Energy Ministry review the project plan and verify that it meets the CDM criteria.

Nicol registers the approved project with Leburn and the CDM Executive Board.

Nicol runs and monitors the Algerian project in accordance with the criteria given to it by the CDM Executive Board.

Two years later the project is complete and Freeland Partners, another

---

9   'Carbon sinks' are projects that remove carbon dioxide from the atmosphere.
10   The International Emissions Trading Association's Guidance Note through the CDM Project Approval Process (Version 1.5, May 2005) states that as of May 1 2005, 28 entities had applied for accreditation as designated operational entities, of which eight had so far been accredited.
11   For an explanation of the EU ETS, see below.

designated operational entity, verifies the reduction in carbon dioxide emissions.

The CDM Executive Board instructs the CDM Registry to credit Nicol's CDM Registry accounts with the appropriate number of certified emission reductions.[12]

The CDM Registry deducts 2% of the certified emission reductions from the total issued to Nicol as a CDM levy.[13] These 'deducted' reductions are sold into the market and the proceeds are transferred to an adaptation fund for the developing nations most susceptible to climate change risks.

The project is more successful than Nicol anticipated, leaving Nicol with more certified emission reductions than it needs to satisfy its EU ETS quota. Nicol can sell these additional reductions into the market, where they can be bought by countries or private firms.

The CDM Executive Board is made up of representatives from both adhering Annex I and non-Annex I parties. Its responsibilities include:

- formulating policies on the CDM;
- reviewing designated operational entities' decisions;
- deciding whether projects meet the CDM rules; and
- deciding on the supervisory and regulatory restrictions of CDM projects.

It also has the power to refuse the issue of certified emission reductions.

The CDM Registry is maintained by the CDM Executive Board. It records and accounts for the issue, transfer and holding of certified emission reductions. Each CDM project has its own account at the registry.

(b)   Joint implementation

The CDM relates to projects in developing nations. By contrast, JI is the protocol's mechanism for Annex I parties, or participating installations in an emissions trading scheme, to earn tradable emissions credits (emission reduction units) for investing in emissions reduction projects in the territories of other Annex I parties (ie, other countries with their own emissions reduction targets). For cost reasons, the host country for a JI project is likely to be an EIT country; this is because bigger emissions reductions can be gained from upgrading antiquated infrastructure than from improving more modern facilities.

The supervisory framework for JI is less robust than that for the CDM, as emission reduction units relate only to the transfer of the location where the emissions reduction is counted. If the host country meets all of the JI eligibility criteria, then it may apply its own procedures to the relevant JI project and issue the units directly. If it does not fulfil all of the requirements, a supervisory committee will oversee the process and decide whether the project meets the JI criteria (and if

---

12   Certified emission reductions can be issued in relation to reductions in any greenhouse gas covered by the protocol (eg, a landfill which captures methane). Importantly, certified emission reductions generated in relation to these other gases can still be surrendered by installations participating in the EU ETS to cover their carbon dioxide emissions.

13   This would not have occurred had the project taken place in a Kyoto non-Annex I party deemed to be particularly susceptible to the adverse risks of climate change.

so, how many units the host country can issue). Emissions reduction units achieved under JI projects have been eligible to be credited towards the EU ETS since 2008 (ie, during the Kyoto compliance period only).

JI project cycle: a worked example

By 2018 Austria will be facing high emissions reductions costs and is likely to be struggling to meet its Kyoto target. It decides to invest in upgrading an old Soviet-era Ukrainian power plant with carbon dioxide emissions reduction technology. Achieving similar emissions reductions in an Austrian power plant would be far more expensive.

The project is successful and achieves the anticipated carbon dioxide and sulphur dioxide reductions. Ukraine issues Austria with the corresponding emission reduction units, which Austria counts towards its emissions reduction target.

Ukraine has benefited from Austria's foreign direct investment, although to prevent double counting, the emissions reductions do not count towards Ukraine's target.

(c)   *Emissions trading*

Emissions trading is the protocol's third flexible mechanism. It allows adhering Annex I parties and the public entities and private firms within them to trade allowance units with other Annex I parties and their public entities and private firms. The allowances may be units allocated under emissions trading schemes, as well as certified emission reductions generated under CDM projects and emission reduction units generated under JI projects.

5.   Beyond Kyoto

The latest round of talks, COP 21, took place in Paris between 30 November and 11 December 2015, culminating in the Paris Agreement of 12 December 2015. Both China and the United States (the world's two biggest emitters of carbon dioxide) ratified the agreement, which entered into force on 4 November 2016.

6.   EU ETS

Currently in its third phase, the EU ETS is the European Union's compulsory 'cap and trade' project for trading carbon dioxide emission allowances. It is the most ambitious and comprehensive emissions trading system ever created and accounts for over three-quarters of international carbon trading.[14] Roughly 11,000 EU industrial installations, which are responsible for almost half of the European

---

14   From 2002 to 2006 the United Kingdom operated its own emissions trading scheme. Thirty-four organisations (including British Sugar and British Airways) voluntarily accepted emissions reduction targets (including non-carbon dioxide emissions) to reduce their greenhouse gas emissions against 1998 to 2000 levels. Participants that met their targets got an 80% reduction in their climate change levy (a business energy tax). Participants could trade allowances in the same way as under the EU ETS. The scheme ended in 2007 with participants migrating to the EU ETS thereafter. In a report appraising the four-year scheme, one lesson noted was that there is a strong case for ensuring that the number of allowances allocated promotes real emissions reductions ("Appraisal of Years 1-4 of the UK Emissions Trading Scheme", Department for Environment, Food and Rural Affairs, 2006).

Union's greenhouse gas emissions, are subject to a European-wide cap, with companies then able to purchase allowances either via free allocation or auction.

Each allowance represents the right to emit one tonne of carbon dioxide or the equivalent amount of two other significant greenhouse gases, nitrous oxide and perfluorocarbons; and each participating installation must surrender allowances equal to its actual carbon dioxide emissions (or the equivalent amount of nitrous oxide or perfluorocarbons). If its allocated allowances are insufficient to cover its actual emissions, the affected installation must go into the market and purchase additional allowances to cover the shortfall. Failure to surrender sufficient allowances to cover emissions incurs a penalty per tonne of greenhouse gas emitted; the defaulting firm will also be asked to make good the allowances in the following year. If the affected installation has an excess of allowances, perhaps through generating efficiencies, it can sell these into the market for a profit. The EU ETS aims to reduce greenhouse gas emissions by financially rewarding affected installations that reduce their emissions and penalising those that do not.

Established by the EU Emissions Trading Directive (2003/87/EC), the EU ETS began life on 1 January 2005. It became a key mechanism assisting the European Union to meet its Kyoto emissions reduction commitment. The Linking Directive (2004/101/EC) creates a link between the EU ETS and the protocol's two other flexible mechanisms: CDM and JI. All certified emission reductions and emission reduction units can be linked to the EU ETS and their allowances surrendered to meet emissions quotas, except for those relating to nuclear and sink projects.

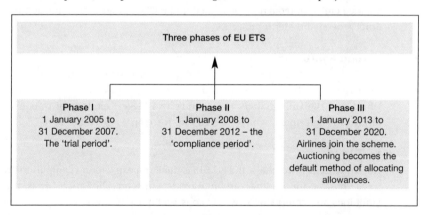

The EU ETS has been divided into three phases:

- Phase I began on 1 January 2005 and ended on 31 December 2007;
- Phase II began on 1 January 2008 and ended on 31 December 2012; and
- Phase III began on 1 January 2013 and will end on 31 December 2020, coinciding with the end of the Kyoto Protocol's second commitment period.

Participating installations are allocated allowances annually and those not used in one year can be carried over to the next. Surrendered allowances are counted towards each country's Kyoto emissions reduction target.

6.1   EU ETS: Phase I – trial period

Phase I applied to companies which emit carbon dioxide above a set threshold and are involved in:

- energy activities with a thermal capacity of at least 20 megawatts;
- the ferrous metals industry;
- the minerals industry (including cement, ceramics and glass); and
- pulp and paper production.

Phase I was intended as a trial period to establish the world's largest market for emissions trading. Several lessons were learned during Phase I which highlighted issues such as lack of accurate data to estimate allowances, over-allocation of allowances resulting in high price volatility and overall lack of progress towards Kyoto targets.

6.2   EU ETS: Phase II – compliance period

EU ETS Phase II commenced on 1 January 2008 and ended 31 December 2012.

As in Phase I, Phase II of the EU ETS covered only one greenhouse gas: carbon dioxide. However, member states had the ability to 'opt in' other greenhouse gases. In Phase II the non-compliance penalty increased to €100 per tonne of carbon dioxide, from €40 in Phase I. In addition to the EU member states, three non-members – Iceland, Norway and Liechtenstein – joined Phase II of the EU ETS.

Learning from Phase I, the European Union was careful to avoid over-allocation of allowances. The functioning of the EU ETS was based on national allocation plans designed to set out the quantum of the member state's permissible emissions to be assigned to:

- the EU ETS;
- each relevant industrial sector;[15] and
- each affected installation.

In Phase II the EU ETS took a tougher stand in reviewing the national allocation plans and the allocations sought were reduced.

Union registry: EU Regulation 389/2013 replaced national registries with a single Union registry. The online registry, which is overseen by the European Commission, records the allowances issued to participating installations, as well as each installation's annual verified emissions and compliance status, and tracks the movements of allowances between accounts (including surrender and cancellation).[16] Participating installations and individuals and organisations that wish to participate in emissions trading are among those that can open registry accounts.

---

15   As of 2013, power generators must purchase all their allowances, with certain exceptions.
16   The online registry handles accounts for stationary installations (previously dealt with by the national registries pre-2012) and aircraft operators.

European Union Transaction Log: The European Union Transaction Log, which superseded the Community Independent Transaction Log, records and checks each transaction between accounts in the Union registry.

Surrender, cancellation and trading of allowances: By 31 March each year, each affected installation must report its carbon dioxide emissions during the previous calendar year. The affected installation then has until 30 April to surrender allowances for all of its carbon dioxide emissions or face a fine. The fine is set at €100 per missing allowance. Once surrendered, the allowances are then cancelled.

Each affected installation is allocated a set number of allowances each year; if it turns out to have more allowances than it needs, it may hold these in its account to be used the following year or sell them to another party. Allowances issued under the EU ETS could not be carried over (commonly referred to as 'banking') from Phase I to Phase II, though allowances issued in Phase II could be held over for Phase III. Certified emission reductions and emission reduction units are eligible for surrender against quotas; however, as of 31 March 2015, this no longer includes credits issued during the first commitment period of the Kyoto Protocol.

EU emissions trading: a hypothetical example

Ruthven PLC is a large cement manufacturer based in Perth, Scotland. It has been allocated 300,000 emissions allowances per year (each representing an allowance to emit one tonne of carbon dioxide) under the United Kingdom's national allocation plan for Phase III of the EU ETS. At the end of the first year of Phase III, Ruthven prepared its 2013 emissions report, which was checked by an accredited verifier; the amounts are recorded at the EU registry.

The report reveals that Ruthven emitted 480,000 tonnes of carbon dioxide during 2013. Thus, the company had to surrender 480,000 allowances from its account at the EU registry by 31 March 2014 – 180,000 more allowances than Ruthven had been allocated. EU allowances are trading at €20 per tonne on the open market and Ruthven enters into three transactions to buy the missing allowances that it needs:

- It enters into a spot transaction on the 'European Climate Exchange' (ECX) with a counterparty to purchase 60,000 ECX carbon financial instruments (these are essentially cash contracts to purchase allowances).
- It enters into an 'International Emissions Trading Association' (IETA) emissions allowances single trade agreement for the EU system transaction with Strathallan PLC, a local power generating company which had more allowances than it needed, to purchase 60,000 allowances.
- It enters into an ISDA documented transaction to purchase a further 60,000 certified emission reductions from Airlie Projects, a company which has been issued certified emission reductions under a CDM project which it carried out in Tanzania.

The 180,000 allowances cost Ruthven €3.6 million: enough to make a sizeable dent in the company's bottom line. These are credited to Ruthven's registry account. Ruthven then surrenders the 480,000 allowances on 31 March 2014.

In 2014 Ruthven is again allocated 300,000 allowances into its registry account. Ruthven's board decides to upgrade the plant to reduce its carbon dioxide emissions. The upgrade costs €2 million and is completed in the first quarter.

At the end of the second year of Phase III Ruthven prepares its 2014 emissions report; once again, the report is checked by an accredited verifier and the amounts are recorded at the Union registry. The report reveals that Ruthven emitted 200,000 tonnes of carbon dioxide during 2014; the plant upgrade paid off and the company has 100,000 more allowances than it was allocated. EU allowances are now trading at €30 per tonne on the open market.

Ruthven enters into a transaction to sell 50,000 allowances to Denny PLC – a paper manufacturer which is short of allowances – and 50,000 allowances to Dunning Investments, a speculator which intends to hold the allowances on the expectation that they will rise further in value. The sale of the allowances generates €3 million for Ruthven, more than paying for the cost of the plant upgrade and leaving it with a profit of €1 million.

6.3 EU ETS: Phase III

Phase III, which commenced in 2013, introduced several bold new developments. These included:

- introducing a single EU-wide emissions cap which decreases by 1.74% annually;
- expanding the EU ETS to cover new gases and industrial sectors. Nitrous oxide and perflurocarbons from the aluminium and chemical sectors were added; and
- establishing a single Union registry, instead of national registries.

In addition, several other changes were implemented such as a move towards reducing free allocation of allowances and an increased commitment to overall reduction of emissions.

Carbon dioxide emissions from aviation have been included in the EU ETS since 2012. Airlines operating in Europe (both EU and non-EU) must verify, monitor and report their emissions and surrender allowances against these. The airlines also receive and can trade allocated allowances. The scheme is however limited to flights within the European Economic Area.

7. Emissions trading in the United States

The United States lags behind the European Union in its efforts to set up an emissions trading system. So far, these can be categorised as emissions trading at state level. The most recent attempt at introducing a federal system of emissions trading, the Clean Energy and Security Act, failed to make it to the Senate for a vote.

At state and regional level, significant progress has been made in establishing emissions trading systems.[17] In January 2009, the Regional Greenhouse Gas Initiative

---

17   David Hunter, "Market Developments at the US Federal Level: A Federal Cap-and-Trade Programme within 4 Years", *Greenhouse Gas Market Report*, 2008.

commenced. This is the first mandatory, market-based effort in the United States to reduce greenhouse gas emissions. In 2014 nine northeastern and mid-Atlantic states committed to a carbon dioxide cap of 91 million short tons.[18] This cap then reduces by 2.5% each year between 2015 and 2020.

8.   Carbon markets

The Kyoto Protocol and the EU ETS provide a framework within which a cap and trade scheme can function. However, neither the Kyoto Protocol nor the EU ETS attempted to 'design' the emissions trading market.[19] Firms may take part in trades for a number of reasons:

- to buy allowances to avoid penalties under the system;
- to trade and sell excess allowances for gain; or
- for trading purposes or to make a market.

In doing so, entities may utilise derivatives such as forwards, options and swaps to hedge against price volatility, arbitrage against pricing differences between different underlying emissions trading instruments, or secure allowances in advance. These are discussed in detail below.

Thomson Reuters Point Carbon states that overall, the year 2015 saw the equivalent of 6.2 billion tonnes of carbon dioxide being traded. This was down 19% from 7.6 billion in 2014.[20]

8.1   What factors determine the pricing of carbon credits?

A carbon credit is a right to emit carbon dioxide – that is, an allocated allowance or right acquired through JI or the CDM. The volume of carbon credits traded has continued to increase. The factors influencing the price of carbon credits and their supply and demand are complex. They may include economic factors and regulatory developments, such as changes to the EU ETS (eg, including other industries in the scheme).

Any increase in overall carbon dioxide production means that more installations will need to purchase allowances. This will inflate allowance prices. This could occur, for example, due to a cold winter driving up energy consumption and forcing power companies to emit more carbon dioxide, or because of an economic boom. Market factors such as liquidity, speculation and anticipated price movements can also affect price.

Factors which can depress carbon credit prices include:

- an economic downturn, resulting in a reduction in industrial output;
- increased carbon credit supply due to more certified emission reductions and emission reduction units arriving on the market; and
- developments in emissions reduction technology reducing demand for credits.

---

18   www.rggi.org.
19   *Ibid*, 17.
20   *Carbon Market Monitor*, Thomson Reuters.

The general ability for installations to meet their emissions quotas will also drive down prices. A switch away from coal and oil-fired power generation to renewable sources such as wind and hydroelectric power, as well as to gas and nuclear power, could also result in reduced demand for allowances.

Over-allocation or under-allocation of allowances may also affect prices. In Phase I of the EU ETS, over-allocation of allowances led to high price volatility and eventually rock-bottom prices.

Although allocated allowances, certified emission reductions and emission reduction units are all fungible for the purposes of surrendering allowances, allocated allowances currently trade at a higher price than either certified emission reductions or emission reduction units, due to uncertainty as to whether these permits will actually arrive or fears of fraud in the certification process.

8.2   Use of derivatives in the carbon markets

Trading in carbon credits proved risky in the early days due to price volatility. This risk factor, together with the increasing expansion of the market, led to the development of carbon/emissions derivatives.

Derivatives in the emissions trading arena may be used for three main reasons:

- to give the buyer protection against certain financial risks (eg, a firm in need of buying additional carbon credit may use derivatives as a way of protecting against any future increase in prices);
- as an investment class (eg, a bank may speculate that the price of carbon credits are set to come down in the future and wish to lock in this gain through a forward contract); or
- for arbitrage or trading purposes (eg, a bank may establish itself as a market maker acting as a central counterparty to buyers and sellers of emissions trading derivatives, and make a profit from the price differential).

The most commonly used types of carbon derivative in the OTC market include forwards, options and swaps.

(a)   Options

Options are bilateral contracts between an option holder and an option writer. The option writer, in consideration for a premium, grants the option holder the right, but not the obligation, to buy or sell an agreed quantity of carbon credits at a fixed price on a future date.

The most common options are put and call options. Put option holders have the right to sell or deliver carbon credits at an agreed price on a future date. Call option holders have the right to buy or receive carbon credits at an agreed price on a future date.

(b)   Forwards

In forward and futures contracts, the parties agree to buy and sell carbon credits on a future date at an agreed price. Forwards differ from options in that the buyer of a forward contract is obliged to pay the agreed purchase price even if the carbon credits are worth less than the purchase price on the settlement date, while the buyer of an option is not obliged to exercise the option and pay the purchase price.

Use of carbon derivatives: hypothetical example of a forward

Viduli Corporation operates an energy installation in Belgium and does not have sufficient allowances to cover its actual emissions during the next year. In order to avoid a penalty, it decides to purchase carbon credits from the market at the end of the year. However, it is concerned that during the remainder of the year, the price of carbon credits may escalate. Viduli needs to buy 10,000 carbon credits and is happy to pay €20 per tonne of carbon dioxide.

It enters into a forward to buy the 10,000 carbon credits at €20 per tonne of carbon dioxide at the end of the year, replacing the risk of higher carbon prices at a future date with certainty in price (ie, €200,000).

The end seller of the forward, Italian glass manufacturer Mihika, has invested in green technology and hopes to sell some of the carbon credits allocated to it which are now in excess of its needs. In order to offset some of its investment costs in green technology, Mihika looks to sell its excess allowances and lock in the current price. By selling the forwards today, Mihika removes the risk of a drop in carbon credit prices in the future.

Mihika sells the forward to Strathallan Bank, which is making a market in these forwards, for €180,000. Strathallan Bank then enters into a back-to-back transaction selling the forwards to Viduli for €200,000.

(c)   *Swaps*

As mentioned above, the trading price of EU allowances can vary from those for certified emission reductions and emission reduction units. The latter two normally trade at a discount due to the uncertainty as to whether these allowances will actually materialise, as well as fears of fraud in the verification process arising in individual projects, resulting in credits being annulled. Where an entity is involved in the production or purchase of these units, it may wish to hedge against falls of certified emission reductions or emission reduction units against EU allowances by entering into a swap protecting itself against any downward movement in the trading price.

Use of carbon derivatives: hypothetical example of a swap

Norton Folgate Industries is a glass manufacturing company. It has noticed that the price of certified emission reductions is cheaper than that of EU allowances. Norton Folgate will have sufficient allowances to meet its obligations under the EU ETS.

To realise a profit, Norton Folgate enters into a physically settled swap with a financial institution under which it delivers 30% of its EU allowances in return for a corresponding amount of certified emission reductions and a cash amount.

The financial institution has secured the certified emission reductions from a Brazilian CDM project and is pleased to have secured a good price for them. Norton Folgate can also realise a gain by submitting the certified emission reductions in place of its EU allowances.

Cash-settled EU allowances for certified emission reduction swaps are also possible. In this type of transaction the parties exchange the difference in the trading price of the two types of credit on a periodic basis. This type of transaction might be attractive to an entity participating in a CDM project which wanted to ensure that the price of certified emission reductions did not fall too far below the price of EU allowances.

(d)   **OTC trading**

When entering into a carbon trade in the OTC markets, the parties have three options as regards the documentation platforms that they use: ISDA, IETA or the European Federation of Energy Traders (EFET).[21]

(e)   **Trading through climate exchanges**

The development of exchange trading is helping the carbon credit market to reduce credit risk by providing a central counterparty, as well as liquidity, through:

- matching counterparties, trading standardised and simple contracts; and
- publishing prices.

Allowance contracts can be traded on a number of European exchanges, including the Intercontinental Exchange in the United Kingdom, Powernext in France and Nordpool in Germany.

The Intercontinental Exchange, for example, provides marketing, listing and sales of ECX carbon financial instruments: futures and cash contracts for EU ETS allowances. These are listed on ICE Futures (an electronic trading platform). Trades are then cleared through LCH.Clearnet Ltd.[22]

(f)   **Carbon pools**

Carbon pools are spot trading platforms.[23] Their members are small emitters that have been allocated allowances under the EU ETS. The pool matches their buy and sell orders together in an order book. After placing an order, the parties transfer their funds or allowances into their pool account and these are then transferred within the pool.

The advantages of carbon pools include:

- counterparty anonymity;
- the grouping of small buy and sell orders into larger orders together; and
- increased liquidity.

9.   OTC trading: documenting emissions trading under the EU ETS – ISDA

The EU ETS market has a choice of three documentation platforms for OTC transactions, each prepared by a separate trade organisation: ISDA, IETA and EFET. The key differences between the three platforms are outlined below.

---

21   See below.
22   LCH.Clearnet Ltd has a default fund of over £570 million.
23   'Spot transactions' are transactions where, once the parties have agreed a contract price, delivery and payment occur within a short time frame.

Documentation platforms		
Trade organisation	**Organisation description**	**Documentation**
ISDA	ISDA is the dominant derivatives trade association. It has over 850 member institutions based in 67 countries, which include almost all the major market players together with law firms and other interested parties.	2005 ISDA Commodity Derivatives Definitions provide in Sub-annex H a "Form of Part [7] to the Schedule to an ISDA Master Agreement for EU Emissions Allowance Transactions (incorporating options)". These emissions trading provisions are inserted into the relevant schedule to the ISDA Master Agreement. This was updated in Version 5 – Schedule to an ISDA Master Agreement for EU Emissions Allowance Transactions (incorporating options) (released in May 2012).
IETA	IETA is a non-profit organisation promoting the establishment of market-based trading systems for greenhouse gas emissions and a global greenhouse gas market using CDM, JI and emissions trading. The organisation also acts as an industry lobbying and trade body. Its members include emitters, insurers, brokers, financial institutions, law firms and management consultants.	• International Emissions Trading Master Agreement (Version 1.0 2012). • Emissions Trading Master Agreement for the EU Scheme (Version 3.0 2008). • Emissions Allowances Single Trade Agreement for the EU System (Version 5.0 2012). • CDM Emissions Reduction Purchase Agreement (Version 3.0 2006).

Continued on next page

Documentation platforms		
Trade organisation	Organisation description	Documentation
EFET	EFET is a group of over 100 European energy trading companies. It is designed to improve conditions for energy trading throughout Europe.	Allowances Appendix to the EFET General Agreement concerning the Delivery and Acceptance of Electricity (Version 4 2012).

ISDA, IETA and EFET's documentation working groups have held a number of meetings to help harmonise the three documentation platforms; each organisation's current document reflects this. However, as these three sets of documents have different origins, some differences still remain. This section of the chapter focuses in greater detail on the ISDA documents, but highlights the key areas of difference between the platforms.

9.1 The ISDA platform

As illustrated above, the ISDA platform utilises the ISDA Master Agreement and adapts its schedule by incorporating an additional section covering trading EU ETS allowances. The related confirmation is then tailored for emissions trading. As with the other platforms, the parties can trade allocated allowances under the EU ETS, certified emission reductions and emission reduction units. ISDA documentation allows the parties to select either English or New York law as the governing law. However, the parties can adapt the agreement themselves to make any other governing law applicable.

ISDA's platform is most attractive to financial institutions and other entities that are already familiar with ISDA documentation. This is particularly so when both counterparties have already entered into an ISDA master agreement and can then benefit from cross-product netting, as well as reducing basis risk through consistent documentation.

(a) Sub-annex H of 2005 ISDA Commodity Derivatives Definitions

The 2005 ISDA Commodity Derivatives Definitions provide a form of emissions trading section to insert into the schedule. This is set out in Sub-annex H as "Form of Part [7] of the Schedule to the ISDA Master Agreement for EU Emissions Allowance Transactions (incorporating options)".

This has since been updated by several revised versions, the latest of which was released in May 2012.[24] The EU ETS provisions are 36 pages long and incorporate the

---

24 Form of Part [7] to the Schedule to an ISDA Master Agreement for EU Emissions Allowance Transactions (incorporating options) (Version 5: May 2012).

2006 ISDA Definitions by reference. These areas covered by the annex are set out in the diagram below.

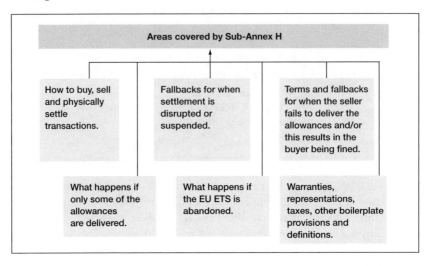

If elected, payments can be netted with respect to allowances of the same allowance type and specified compliance period and the parties can net the allowances. The documentation caters for physically settled forward and option transactions. Cash-settled transactions must be drafted on a bespoke basis.

Settlement/delivery: The provisions provide three sets of fallback where allowances cannot be delivered. This is a significant issue due to the penalties which can be imposed when an affected installation fails to deliver the require allowances into the EU ETS.

The first fallback is where neither party is at fault (the 'settlement disruption' provisions). The second, introduced in the 2008 version, refers to 'suspension events' where one party is unable to perform its obligations due to the occurrence of specific events. The third type of event is where delivery does not take place due to the fault of a party (the 'failure to deliver' provisions).

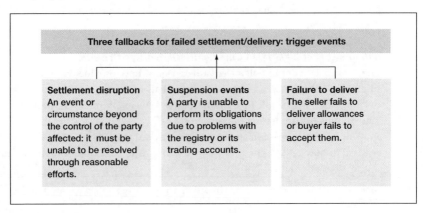

A 'settlement disruption' is an event or circumstance beyond the control of the party affected: it must not be resolvable through reasonable efforts, making it impossible for that party to perform its obligations. For the avoidance of doubt, the documentation provides that the inability of a party to deliver allowances due to low or non-allocation of allowances to it by an EU member state is not a settlement disruption event. If a settlement disruption event occurs, upon notification in writing by one party to the other, the parties' obligations under the transaction will be suspended. The parties will keep trying to settle the transaction, but if they cannot do so within a set timeframe (a 'continuing settlement disruption event'), the transaction will terminate (for more details, see the table below). Whether any payments will be made between the parties at this point will depend on what they have negotiated.

A 'suspension event' occurs when a party is unable to perform its obligations under the ISDA agreement for any of the following reasons:

- There is an 'absence of registry operation' – that is, the lack of establishment or continued functioning of the EU and international transaction logs, the relevant registry, and/or link between each of the relevant registry and transaction logs; or
- The 'occurrence of an administrator event' – where the functioning of a relevant registry or the European Union Transaction Log is suspended as a result of:
  - the relevant registry not operating in accordance with or adhering to the provisions of the registries regulation, or any other applicable law;
  - maintenance work being carried out; or
  - a suspected or actual breach of security of the registries system.

If any of these events occurs, the parties are allowed to suspend the settlement of the transaction for the duration of such event. This is subject to certain time limits and a long-stop date (for details, see the table below).

Through its own fault, a seller can fail to deliver allowances or a buyer can fail to be in a position to accept them. Both instances allow the party not at fault to trigger the 'failure to deliver' fallback provisions by delivering notice to its counterparty. These provisions do not trigger an event of default, but instead postpone settlement while the party at fault attempts to remedy the failure.

Where the seller is to blame, if it manages to deliver the missing allowances on the second delivery business day after notification of the event, it must pay the buyer default interest and, depending on the type of allowance transaction (forward or option), an amount equal to the purchase price times the number of allowances (in the case of an allowance forward transaction) or an amount equal to the strike price times the number of allowances to be delivered (in the case of an allowance option transaction). If the seller misses this deadline, the buyer can cancel the seller's obligation to deliver the allowances and demand the replacement cost of buying the missing allowances in the open market. Depending on what the parties have negotiated, this compensation may include reimbursing the buyer for any fine or excess emissions penalty and any related costs arising from the seller's failure. The selection of and interaction between three variables – excess emissions penalty, excess emissions penalty risk period and failure to deliver (alternative method) – in the confirmation will determine the amount that the seller must pay to cover these costs.

If the seller cannot deliver the allowances because the buyer has breached EU ETS requirements, the settlement date will be postponed and the seller may, by notice, request that the buyer meet EU ETS requirements. If the buyer does so, the seller will deliver the allowances and will receive default interest for the period covering the delay and either:

- an amount equal to the purchase price times the number of allowances (in the case of an allowance forward transaction); or
- an amount equal to the strike price times the number of allowances to be delivered (in the case of an allowance option transaction).

If the buyer fails to comply prior to the end of the second delivery business day after the notice, the seller may:

- discharge itself from its obligation to deliver the allowances; and
- demand that the buyer pay it the difference between the actual or estimated amount that the seller would receive under an equivalent spot transaction on the final date for surrendering allowances and the original purchase price.

Calculation of replacement cost where there is failure to deliver: If the buyer has failed to meet the settlement deadline after receiving the counterparty's notice, there are three standard elections open to the parties to determine how the seller's replacement costs are calculated.

An 'excess emissions penalty' is the fine per allowance given to an affected installation for each allowance that it fails to submit. An 'excess emissions penalty risk period' is the period of time agreed in the confirmation covering the run-up to that deadline.

The first election is where the excess emissions penalty does not apply to the particular failure to deliver. This will be either because:

- the parties have not selected 'excess emissions penalty' in the confirmation; or
- they have selected it, but have also chosen an excess emissions penalty risk period and the delivery failure occurs before the excess emissions penalty risk period begins.

If this is the case, the buyer can, by notice, cancel the seller's obligation to deliver the allowances, leaving the seller to pay it the difference between the missing allowances' original agreed purchase price and the buyer's estimated or actual cost of purchasing the missing allowances on the delivery date in a spot transaction. In addition, the seller must pay default interest on this amount from the scheduled delivery date.

Comparison of types of event that affect delivery

	Settlement disruption event	Suspension event	Failure to deliver
Delivery	Delivery is suspended until the day on which the settlement disruption event ceases.	Delivery is suspended until the earlier of 10 delivery business days following cessation of the event or three delivery business days prior to the end of phase reconciliation deadline (30 April 2021) (the 'delayed delivery date').	In most cases, the receiving party (if not at fault) may serve notice and require the delivering party to remedy the breach. The delivering party must deliver the allowances on or before the second delivery business day after such notice is given.
Long-stop date	Nine delivery business days after the original delivery date (or, where applicable, the reconciliation deadline) or three delivery business days preceding the end of phase reconciliation deadline. At this point there will be either an additional termination event or an illegality (depending on whether the 1992 or 2002 ISDA Master Agreement is used, respectively).	With regard to an obligation (delivery or acceptance) otherwise due to be performed between: • 1 January 2015 and 31 December 2016, 1 June 2018; • 1 January 2017 and 31 December 2018, 1 June 2020; and • 1 January 2019 and 25 April 2021, 25 April 2021.	The final compliance date.
Obligations of the parties	Parties have the ability to select in the confirmation whether they require all obligations to end on settlement disruption. If 'payment on termination for settlement disruption' is not selected, all obligations will cease; if not, the suspended obligations will resume on the early termination date.	It is deemed that the parties have no further delivery or payment obligations after the occurrence of the suspension event. Any payments already made will be reimbursed.	• Allowances are delivered on or before the final delivery date – the original delivery date will still apply and the delivering party must pay interest for the delay plus an amount equal to either the purchase price times the number of allowances or an amount equal to the strike price plus number of allowances to be delivered. • Allowances are not delivered on or before the final delivery date – the amount payable by the delivering party will depend on the three elections discussed below.

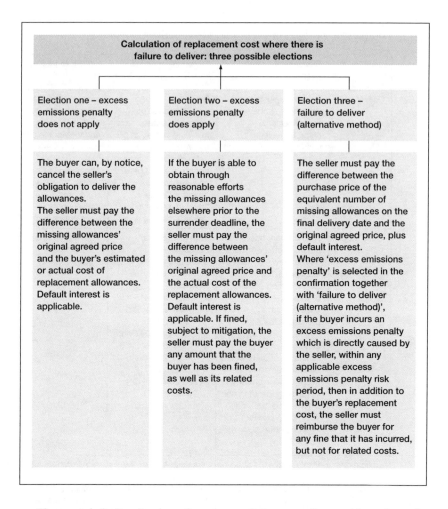

The second election is where the excess emissions penalty provisions do apply. This will be either because:

- the parties have selected 'excess emissions penalty' but not defined an excess emissions penalty risk period; or
- they have selected 'excess emissions penalty' and defined an excess emissions penalty risk period, and the delivery failure occurs within the excess emissions penalty risk period.

Following the failure to deliver and notice, the buyer must make reasonable efforts to buy the missing allowances from an alternative source before the surrender deadline. If the buyer manages to do so, the seller must then pay the difference between the missing allowances' original agreed purchase price and the actual cost of the allowances bought in. In addition, the seller must pay default interest on this amount from the scheduled delivery date.

If the buyer is unable to buy in all of the undelivered allowances before the surrender deadline, it must attempt to buy in the missing allowances as soon as possible afterwards. The seller must then pay the buyer the difference between the price of the allowances bought after the deadline and the original agreed price, as well as default interest. In addition, the seller must pay the buyer any amount that the buyer has been fined, as well as its related costs.

The buyer must also provide the seller with evidence:

- that the buyer's fine is due, either partially or entirely, to the seller's failure to deliver the allowances;
- of the extent to which the fine results from the failure to deliver; and
- that the buyer could not have used any other allowances that it held to avoid the fine.

The buyer must mitigate its losses and, to the extent possible, avoid incurring the fine. The seller must also allocate any losses that it makes due to the failure to deliver pro rata among all parties that have failed to make a delivery.

The final election involves selecting 'failure to deliver (alternative method)' in the confirmation. If this is chosen, following the buyer triggering the failure to deliver provisions, the seller must pay the difference between the purchase price of the equivalent number of missing allowances on the final delivery date and the original agreed price, plus default interest.

Where 'excess emissions penalty' is selected in the confirmation together with 'failure to deliver (alternative method)', if the buyer incurs an excess emissions penalty which is directly caused by the seller's failure to deliver within any applicable excess emissions penalty risk period, then in addition to the buyer's replacement cost described above, the seller must reimburse the buyer for any fine that it has incurred but, unlike the second election, not for related costs.

The buyer must also provide the seller with sufficient information for it to make a commercially reasonable assessment of the extent to which the buyer's allowance shortfall was directly caused by the seller's failure to deliver.

The seller's obligation to make the compensatory payment is then conditional upon the buyer demonstrating to the seller's reasonable satisfaction that it has actually incurred and paid the fine, and the extent to which the buyer's liability to pay the fine:

- is directly related to the seller's failure to deliver;
- would have existed even if the seller had delivered the allowances; and
- arose due to any third party failing to deliver it allowances.

If it transpires that the buyer's shortfall in allowances is due to a number of parties (including the buyer and seller), then the seller's compensation payment will be proportionate to its level of fault.

Other provisions: Other provisions in the document provide that if the EU ETS is abandoned, neither party will have any obligation to the other, except that the seller shall refund any amounts owed to the buyer with interest. Additionally, the parties agree that:

- on the delivery date, the seller must send the buyer an invoice;
- they will comply with the EU ETS requirements;
- the seller will deliver the allowances free and clear of encumbrances;
- all amounts are exclusive of value added tax (VAT) (although the buyer will pay the seller any VAT or taxes owed);
- they will each take responsibility for any fees and other expenses; and
- they will limit their liability in relation to certain breaches of warranty.

In the schedule's annex, the parties set out their account details, the delivery business day location and the VAT jurisdiction.

(b)   *Confirmation of OTC physically settled EU allowance forward*
The confirmation follows the standard ISDA format for a confirmation for a forward transaction. Due to the comprehensive nature of Sub-annex H, the confirmation is a relatively short document and sets out specific transaction terms and elections only. In particular, it sets out:

- the trade date;
- the buyer, seller and calculation agent's identities;
- the allowance type, price and number;
- the business, payment and delivery days;
- various failure to deliver and excess emissions penalty options; and
- whether any payment will be made if the transaction terminates following a settlement disruption event.

ISDA's published confirmations for options and forwards can also be used and adapted for spot transactions.[25]
In addition, to the extent not already set out in the schedule, the parties may insert their account details, and business day and VAT jurisdiction choices.

(c)   *Confirmation of OTC physically settled EU allowance option*
The confirmation follows the standard ISDA format for a confirmation for a forward transaction. The confirmation sets out:

- the trade date;
- the buyer, seller and calculation agent's identities;
- the allowance type, price and number;
- provisions relating to the option itself (eg, number of options, premium payment date, exercise times);
- the business, payment and delivery days;
- various failure to deliver and excess emissions penalty options; and
- whether any payment will be made if the transaction terminates following a settlement disruption event.

---

25   Under a forward transaction, the parties agree a price for the allowance upfront, but actual delivery and payment take place at a later agreed date. Under an option transaction, either the buyer or seller has the right, but not the obligation, in return for a premium, to deliver or receive the allowances at a future date.

(d)   *US Emissions Allowance Transaction Annex*

The latest edition of the US Emissions Allowance Transaction Annex was published by ISDA on 2 September 2010. It is incorporated by parties into their ISDA Master Agreement. At the same time, ISDA also released a confirmation template.

The annex covers physically settled spot, forward and option emissions trading transactions.

The annex relates to:

- nitrous oxide emissions allowances traded under the NOx SIP Call Programme;
- sulphur dioxide emissions allowances traded under the Clean Air Interstate Rule programme; and
- any emissions allowances or credits under current or future US state cap and trade programmes.

The annex differentiates between 'regulatorily continuing emissions products' and 'regulatorily non-continuing emissions products'. 'Regulatorily non-continuing emissions products' are emissions products which must comply with the rules and relevant regulations of the relevant scheme at both the trade date and the delivery date.

'Regulatorily continuing emissions products' are emissions products which must be in compliance only as of the trade date.

Due to its non-specific coverage, the annex is vague, containing none of the tailored provisions relating to excess emissions penalties or detailed fallbacks of the European annex. Such provisions may therefore have to be included in any related confirmation and tailored to the particular cap and trade scheme.

ISDA has also released a related two-page confirmation for a physically settled option transaction. Under this confirmation, the parties can elect the particular emissions product to be traded, and whether an abandonment of the particular scheme is an additional termination event for the transaction or alternative unwind mechanism.

9.2   Comparison of ISDA with IETA and EFET platforms – key differences

The ISDA and IETA standard documents are used by different types of market participant. Whereas financial institutions will be familiar with the ISDA Master Agreement and use it across a variety of derivatives products, the IETA Emissions Trading Master Agreement for the EU ETS relates only to emissions trading. The specific focus of the IETA Master Agreement means that industrial concerns without large derivatives portfolios or an ISDA Master Agreement in place are more likely to use the IETA Master Agreement. IETA documentation is governed by English law, unless otherwise agreed by the parties.

The EFET platform uses an Allowances Appendix to its General Agreement Concerning the Delivery and Acceptance of Electricity, which is drafted with various European civil law systems and English law in mind. German law is the default choice of law, although other laws may be selected. The power industry, which has several large market participants, tends to favour the EFET platform due to familiarity with the General Agreement Concerning the Delivery and Acceptance of Electricity.

The three documentation platforms are more similar than they are different. However, there are important differences due to the agreements being updated at different times, as well as the different aims of the memberships of the three organisations. Market participants need to be aware of the differences in order to be able to use the different platforms and to protect against basis risk where different documentation platforms are used in a chain of transactions.

Although there are several mechanical differences, such as the effect of oral confirmations, the key differences specific to emissions trading relate to:

- excess emissions penalties;[26]
- *force majeure*;
- settlement disruption and failure to deliver;
- differences in payment and delivery dates;
- opting out of physical settlement of delivery obligations; and
- suspension events.

Other differences relate to termination events, close-out payments and netting provisions.

Traders should note that if they buy using one set of documentation, they also enter into a sale agreement based on the same documentation. Otherwise, the differences in the terms will result in a risk for the trader.

10.   Conclusion

In 1661, when Evelyn wrote his *Fumifugium*, the pall of smoke above London had become an attraction to tourists, who climbed neighbouring church towers to see better. Evelyn and other scientists of his day argued that this situation should not continue, because it created an environment that killed people and damaged property. Evelyn therefore proposed surrounding the city with a 50-metre 'green belt' filled with "such shrubs as yield the most fragrant and odiferous flowers",[27] prohibiting burials within the city and moving the 'sooty throats' that caused pollution far from the capital. The last solution would, he assured readers, yield two principal benefits: not only would London's air regain a "universal serenity" (instead of resembling "Troy sacked by the Greeks"), but relocating noxious industries would open up prime sites within the city for the construction of prestige apartments. In the 17th as in the 21st century, environmental concerns could be turned to profit.

---

26   The excess emissions penalties in particular are more detailed in the ISDA Master Agreement and contain additional options. It is likely that subsequent versions of the corresponding IETA and EFET documentation will also incorporate these changes.

27   Perhaps the earliest reference to a carbon sink.

Weather derivatives

Paul O Oranika
Africa Business World

1. Introduction

Weather derivatives trading came into existence during the mid-1990s as a strategy used by companies to monitor and protect their businesses from adverse conditions generated by weather changes. According to the Chicago Mercantile Exchange (CME):

> One-third of businesses worldwide are directly affected by weather conditions. These products enable firms to manage weather–related risk while also offering opportunities to speculate – absorbing that risk in exchange for possible profit on weather variations. The products are based on a range of weather conditions in cities around the globe.[1]

The ultimate purpose of weather derivatives commodity trading is to help companies control their business risks associated with weather fluctuations. On the surface, the trading of weather derivative may look complex, but the process is very simple. When a company wants to reduce its weather-related risks, such company may transfer some of the risks to an investor or seller willing to assume some of these risks. More on this will be discussed through the course of this chapter.

1.1 Definition

'Weather derivatives' are traded financial assets used to hedge against losses which may result from circumstances beyond anyone's control, such as unpredictable weather. The underlying asset in weather derivatives trading (wind, frost, rain or temperature and others) have no direct value attached to them with respect to the price of the weather derivative asset. The seller of the weather derivative instrument bears the associated risk, and also stands to make money if all things remain as predicted. The buyer also assumes the risk of losing the committed asset if expectations are not met. At the same time, the buyer could benefit from hedging associated business risks against adverse weather conditions if its expectations are met. Temperature is the most commonly traded weather derivative. Because the underlying asset of a weather derivative contract is untradeable, it cannot be priced using pricing models such as the Black Scholes formula, which is often used in pricing and valuations for other derivatives assets.

1.2 Purpose of weather derivatives trading

Farmers and producers of agricultural commodities can use weather derivatives trading to hedge against poor harvests which can be caused by weather-related

---

1   CME Group, 'About Weather'. Accessed on 1 August 2015 from www.cmegroup.com/trading/weather/.

conditions beyond their control. For instance, if there is inadequate or excessive rainfall during the growing season, such condition can adversely affect the level and quality of the harvest.

Theme parks, for example, can insure themselves against rainy weekends during the summer, considered as the peak periods during which they generate most of their revenues and profits. Other companies, such as power-generating companies or gas producers, can plan ahead and use heating degree days (HDDs) or cooling degree days (CDDs) to level up their earnings.

Another illustration of how weather derivatives trading can help companies limit their losses is a sports-managing company hedging against rainfall on the day of an event which may limit ticket sales.

The most common type of weather derivatives contracts is based on the CME HDD Index. HDD Index contracts are largely traded during the months of November through March when the average daily temperatures generally fall below 65 degrees Fahrenheit (°F) or 18 degrees Celsius (°C). During this period, a cumulative temperature count (of a given location) is undertaken and weather derivatives traders can initiate positions or use call and put option or swap strategies to profit from their positions if the trade goes their way.

2.   History and evolution of weather derivatives

Several factors and drivers led to the evolution of weather derivatives markets, among which is, arguably, a convergence between the capital markets and the insurance markets. It started with the introduction of so-called 'catastrophe bonds' in the early 1990s at the Chicago Board of Trade to help insurance companies mitigate the risk of disasters such as hurricanes and earthquakes. Weather derivatives trading evolved out of this convergence of capital markets and insurance markets. It is important nonetheless to say that insurance markets and products are different from weather derivatives products. The author will discuss the differences between both markets through the course of this chapter.

Then, the United States experienced the El Niño (ie, warm) winter of 1997–98, regarded as the strongest El Niño on record. The event generated much publicity in the US news media, and many firms faced significant earnings shortfall resulting from such mild winter. Some companies consequently took a position that they needed to hedge some of their seasonal winter risks. The insurance underwriting business at that time was in a position to provide sufficient resources dedicated to hedging weather risk. Such liquidity from the insurance establishment was fundamentally responsible for the development of month-to-month seasonal swaps which took place in the weather derivatives market.[2]

The first weather derivative contract was traded in July 1996. Under this deal, an energy company called Aquila Energy undertook a dual commodity hedge on behalf of Consolidated Edison Company (ConEd).[3] Through this transaction ConEd

---

2   Geoffrey Considine, 'Introduction to Weather Derivatives', Weather Derivatives Group, Aquila Energy. Accessed on 1 August 2015 from www.cmegroup.com/trading/weather/files/WEA_intro_to_weather_der.pdf.

3   Mark Nicholls, 'Confounding the Forecasts', *Environmental Finance*, 4 July 2008.

purchased electric power provided by Aquila for the month of August. Both buyer and seller agreed on a specific price for this transaction, but a weather clause was also embedded into this deal. The weather clause stated that the seller would pay a rebate price to the buyer if the weather for the contract month (August) turned out to be cooler than what was expected.

It was also agreed that a specific measurement standard would be used, referred to as 'CDD' (see above at section 1.2), which would be measured using the temperature recorded at the weather station at the Central Park of New York City. An expected CDD temperature was established at 320°F (the standard temperature for cooling buildings during the summer). If the total CDDs ranged from 0% to 10% below 320°F, the buyer would not be entitled to a discount. However, if the CDDs ranged from 11% to 20% below the normal expected temperature, then the buyer would be paid a US$16,000 discount. This agreement also made provision for greater discounts to the buyer if the CDDs showed greater variation from the normal expected average temperature.

In 1997, weather derivatives contracts began trading over the counter at the CME, which subsequently introduced the first weather derivative-traded contract in the futures market.

By 1999, weather derivatives contracts were traded on 25 cities in the United States. In Europe, similar derivative contracts were being traded on 11 cities, with six more cities in Canada, three in Australia and three in Japan. Among some of the earlier pioneers in weather derivatives trading was Enron Corp, the Texas-based energy giant which eventually became bankrupt. Hedge funds soon discovered weather derivatives trading as a suitable investment asset class used to hedge their investment risks.

Other counterparties including farming conglomerates, utilities, individual companies, as well as insurance establishments, also began using weather derivatives trading to hedge some of their investment risks. Fund of funds investors also adopted weather derivatives trading strategies, which provide non-correlated alternative investment instruments.

3.   **Weather derivatives versus weather insurance**

Prior to the evolution of weather derivatives trading, insurance policies were the sole tools for companies to protect themselves against weather-related damages and risks. Consequently, some people wrongly equate weather derivatives to a kind of insurance policy. The truth is that they differ significantly: weather derivatives are a form of asset traded in stock exchanges or over the counter, as the case may be. They generally cover low-risk, high-probability occurrences. By contrast, weather insurance covers high-risk, low-probability events.

A company which anticipates an unusually warm or cold winter could purchase a weather derivative commodity to hedge against the effect and impact of such weather conditions on the production, or marketing of its product, services or any other aspect of its manufacturing operations. This same company may, however, buy weather insurance policy to protect itself from loss, damage or destruction of its property or equipment through a weather-related catastrophic occurrence such as a flood, hurricane, tornado, earthquake or tsunami. Weather derivatives trading offers no protection against such natural disasters.

4. US energy deregulation and impact on weather derivatives trading

Weather derivatives markets developed rapidly mainly because of the deregulation of the US energy industry. Changes and fluctuations in seasonal weather patterns often lead to volatility in energy prices. Seasonal weather patterns have always produced volatility in energy prices. The deregulation in the US energy markets provided an opportunity for various actors in the industry, such producers, marketers and other interested parties, to increase their participation in such unfolding opportunities.

In so doing, companies whose business operations have significant exposure to weather and environmental influences are able to control the weather risk exposure largely responsible for the production and delivery cost of energy. It is estimated that close to 20% of the US economy is directly influenced by changes in weather and temperature factors. These points were also echoed by government official statements relating to energy cost. In a 1998 testimony to Congress, former US Commerce Secretary William Daley stated: "Weather is not just an environmental issue; it is a major economic factor. At least $1 trillion of our economy is weather-sensitive."[4]

Many sectors in the US economy are directly influenced by weather patterns and fluctuations. Such major industries as agriculture, entertainment, energy, construction and travel are to some degree influenced by weather changes. Today many more industries, actors and participants are trading weather derivatives, including insurance and reinsurance companies, banks and hedge funds industries. Energy and weather transactions are structured in such a way as to recognise many weather-related variables including, but not limited to, temperature, rainfall, snow, wind speed and humidity. Payout for these risks may be valued from several thousand to millions of dollars.

6. Impact of the Enron bankruptcy on energy derivatives trading

Enron was among the pioneers of the conception and execution of weather derivatives transactions in 1997. These early transactions in energy derivatives trading were not as structured as one might expect. They were organised as privately negotiated, over-the-counter deals to protect against unusual weather. Those engaged in weather derivatives trading sought to hedge their energy-exposed operations and risks against unusual weather exposure.

The collapse of Enron, the biggest name in the energy sector at that time in the United States, created much panic and uncertainty regarding energy trades and particularly trades involving Enron itself. Thirty-six of Enron's 48 trading desks shut down following Enron's bankruptcy.

Enron problems may have also facilitated the rapid development of weather derivatives markets. Linda Clemons, president of Element Re – the Connecticut-

---

4   Carabello Felix, 'Introduction to Weather Derivatives'. Accessed on 18 February 2010 from www.investopedia.com/articles/optioninvestor/05/052505.asp.

based weather trading arm of reinsurance firm XL Capital – said that there are now about 30 companies looking at weather derivatives prices in the United States alone on a daily basis. Valerie Cooper, executive director of the Weather Risk Trade Association – an industry watchdog group for the international weather risk industry – said that the weather derivatives market has been experiencing significant growth over the years, and was worth more than US$8 billion at that time. Cooper expects such trend to continue.

7. Illustration of the process of buying and selling weather derivatives

7.1 Example 1 – if extreme weather occurs
When the weather derivative buyer wants to reduce the risk from extreme weather, it wants to transfer some of that risk to the seller, which in turn takes in some premium as an exchange for assuming such risk. When such extreme condition occurs, the buyer then receives some payment in line with the insured amount to cover their business losses.

7.2 Example 2 – if extreme weather does not occur
If extreme weather does not occur, the buyer does not incur any business losses; the purchased derivative does not pay off and the paid premium becomes profit to the seller.

8. Scope of energy markets and associated risks
As indicated earlier, temperature is the most widely traded weather derivative in the weather exchange markets. The following points explain the rationale for energy risks and trades:

- Energy consumers often trade temperature derivatives. Some of the factors may include the fact that there are lower energy sales during warmer winters and cooler summers. There is also a higher level of heating or cooling associated with colder winters and warmer summers.
- Beverage producers generally trade temperature derivatives because there are lower sales of beverages during cooler summers or severe winters.
- Construction companies generally trade temperature derivatives because of delays in meeting their scheduled construction activities, partly because severe winters tend to force many construction sites to shut down.
- Building materials manufacturers generally trade temperature and snowfall derivatives. This is related to depressed sales during severe winters, which may also lead to a shutdown of many construction sites.
- Ski resorts often trade snowfall derivatives because they generally experience lower sales and revenues during winters with lower levels of snowfall.
- Agricultural industries tend to trade temperature and snow fall derivatives because their industries experience significant losses from extreme temperature and rainfall.
- Municipal governments trade snowfall derivatives because of the higher costs experienced through higher snow removal charges.

- Other companies such as road salt firms trade snowfall derivatives because of the lower sales they get during low snowfall winters.
- Hydroelectric power generation companies often trade precipitation derivative because they usually experience depressed sales during droughts.

9. Weather derivatives – global implications

The weather derivatives market has now become international. Outside the United States, weather transactions have been completed in Australia, France, Germany, Japan, Mexico, Norway, Sweden and the United Kingdom. Exchange-traded weather derivatives contracts are now traded in the CME, the Inter Continental Exchange (IC), the London International Financial Futures and Options Exchange (LIFFE, now part of IC) and many others, including Asian exchanges.

10. Securities and Exchange Board of India plans to launch weather derivatives trading

As the trading of weather derivatives spreads across the world, new reports released in early 2016, indicated that the panel of the Securities and Exchange Board of India's (SEBI) was analysing the suitability of weather derivatives trading on its exchange. According to the report, SEBI "plans to allow trading in weather derivatives, a financial instrument for managing this risk in the agricultural sector". One of the reasons cited for introducing weather derivative trading is that it offers immense benefits for Indian farmers and the agricultural sectors.

According to a survey conducted by the Weather Risk Management Association, between 1 April 2001 and 31 March 2002 over 3,900 weather derivatives transactions were conducted, representing a growth rate of 43% over the previous year. Such transactions added up to a total of about US$4.3 billion in exposure. Data from the Weather Risk Management Association shows that "the weather market, recently reported a total notional value of over $10 billion for weather derivative trades in the year 2002/2003".[5] Many weather derivative analysts believe that the numbers of weather derivative transactions may have quadrupled between 2003 and 2015.

11. Elements of weather derivatives contracts

Several elements commonly feature in weather derivatives trading:

- Weather stations as a reference point – all weather contracts must use actual observations as a reference point. There must be a weather station from which readings and observations data are derived from. Sometimes a weighted combination of readings must be derived from more than one weather station for some types of contract.
- Indices – these are key components of weather derivative trading because they help to define certain measurement standards and payout conditions which may govern specific contracts. Such indices includes HDDs and CDDs (see sections 1 and 2 above) to produce a cumulative average daily

---

5   Chicago Mercantile Exchange and Weather Risk Management Association, 'Weather Contracts Achieve Record Growth'. Accessed in February 2010 from www.wrma.org/wrma/library/file468.doc.

temperature ranging from 65°F, or 18°C, depending on where such contract is traded.
- Terms – trading terms are needed by all weather derivative contracts explaining the start date and end date of each traded contract. The standard contract terms often employed are 1 November through to 31 March, referred to as 'the winter season' and 1 May through 30 September for summer contracts.
- Structure – certain standard derivative structures are used, including puts, calls, swaps, strangles, straddles and collars. Elements such as strike price are used to denote a price level where each contract may start its payout. Other elements such as the tick price are used to denote the payout amount per tick up to the maximum payout for each contract.
- Premium – all weather derivative option buyers pay a premium price generally between 10% and 20% of the notional value of the traded contract.

12. Other actors in the weather derivatives market

All transactions in the weather derivatives market involve two parties and one possible use of weather derivatives is for hedging purposes. Hedgers include industries seeking to use weather derivatives to reduce and or eliminate their weather risks. Others that participate in the weather derivatives markets are speculators such as hedge funds or individual speculators, or traders seeking opportunities to profit from market movements and fluctuations arising from market inefficiencies. Hedgers may also speculate in the derivatives markets when they see an opportunity to make money; speculators may also hedge as a risk control mechanism.

Speculators may include banks, hedge funds or insurance traders, or firms whose primary motive is either to make money or to protect their assets. The interaction between all the participants in the weather derivatives market maintains integrity and the needed liquidity in the market. Today, a brand new sector has emerged, and new companies have emerged, with the purpose of helping weather and energy-related businesses to manage their risks better. One of the pioneering firms in energy-related risk management is the New York-based Storm Exchange. David Smith, vice president of sales, who was formerly at the CME during the early formative stages of the weather derivatives market.

13. Role of the CME in weather derivatives trading

The CME has been on the forefront of weather derivatives trading, and has developed and taken weather derivatives trading to another level by trading all kinds of weather derivative-related asset on its exchange. In 1999, the CME introduced weather futures and options on futures. These products were considered the first in their class. These assets comprise monthly and seasonal average temperatures of 15 cities in the United States and another five European cities. The values of these contracts are determined by a company called Earth Satellite Corp, while the prices of the European contracts are determined by several European weather firms.

13.1 Exchange-traded weather derivatives

The CME offers trading of futures contracts on weather derivatives and options, and has also unveiled exchange-traded derivatives products similar to exchange-traded funds (ETFs). All weather derivatives contracts are based on actual weather observations as recorded in several stations.

13.2 CME measurement index for weather derivatives

The pioneers of weather derivatives trading realised that temperatures could be indexed. They also realised that this indexing could be done on a seasonal and a monthly basis. Once this was done, monetary value could be added to the developed index, making such index a tradable asset. Traders of weather derivatives receive various weather outlooks from government and independent weather forecasters. The CME launched exchange-traded weather derivatives with the creation of its HDD Index in 1999 and CDD Index in 2000.[6] HDDs and CDDs are also used in calculating weather derivatives index values. The cumulative values are used in calculations of the winter and summer monthly values. The monthly index values are the total of the cumulative values for 10 days of the month. At the CME, the weather futures contract values are calculated by multiplying either the CDD or the HDD by US$20. The result is the contract settling price for the month in question.

13.3 Options on weather derivatives

The CME also pioneered the options trading on weather derivatives. Simple options such as puts and calls, as well as advanced option strategies such as butterfly, strangles or straddles, are tradable options on weather derivatives. Options require more knowledge and experience, and are considered 'wasting assets' (ie, assets whose value depreciates) and may not be suitable for all investors.

The buyer of a weather derivative option, such as a simple call option, believes that the price of such call option may increase in value, and may be greater than the established strike price over the trading duration of such an option. The buyer pays a premium price to purchase such option. If its analysis holds true, the buyer stands to make a profit on its trades prior to the option expiration date. Option trades expire on the last day of trading for that particular option, often referred to as the 'expiration date'. The buyer could make or lose money, based on the direction of the underlying option price. The put option, by contrast, bets on declines in the price of such option. If the price of the underlying option gains value, the purchaser of a put option may lose all or part of the premium money used to purchase such option. The CME offers many option derivatives products for trading purposes.

14. Conclusion

This chapter discussed the concept of 'weather derivatives trading', which came into being in the mid-1990s. Since the introduction of weather derivatives trading, the weather markets have experienced significant growth from many industries and sectors seeking to use this tradable asset to limit their companies' exposure to

---

6   *Ibid.*

weather risk. Weather derivatives trading instruments are bought or sold in the trading exchanges or over the counter. These transactions involve two parties, a buyer and a seller. The buyer wants to reduce its company's risk exposures from extreme weather conditions by transferring some of the risk to the seller. The seller receives some money payment for assuming such risk.

The chapter also discussed the history and evolution of the weather derivatives market, from the early pioneers such as Enron to many other industry participants that sought to take advantage of Enron's collapse and the deregulation in the US energy markets to stake positions in the US energy markets.

No other exchange played a more significant role in the evolution and expansion of the weather derivatives markets than the CME. The CME took energy trading to higher levels by developing many types of weather derivative commodity trading asset, using weather and temperature variations as the basis of such trades. Today, weather derivatives trading has become international with weather trading exchanges across the world. The future growth of the global weather derivatives industry looks promising – a conclusion also drawn by knowledgeable weather derivatives industry analysts and observers.

Energy derivatives and hedging strategies

Christopher Clancy
Cyriel de Jong
KYOS Energy Consulting

1. Introduction

The next few decades are expected to see another big rise in energy consumption. Depletion of existing energy sources and the need to comply with environmental regulations will simultaneously mean a shift towards alternative energy sources. This will bring huge shifts to the energy landscape and require massive investments. Without doubt, efficient derivatives markets will be a great help in making the right investments. They help to provide the right forward-looking price signals, assess future volatility levels and provide instruments now and in the future to manage energy exposure on both the production and consumption sides.

What makes trading and hedging in energy markets special? That is the central theme of this chapter. There is a wide variety of energy commodities and products, which reduces liquidity in individual products. Differences also exist in product specifications of the traded products, price behaviour and relevant hedging schemes. This chapter devotes considerable attention to power, the purest and most ready-to-use form of energy. The difficulty of storing and transporting power makes it an ideal candidate to demonstrate various properties of energy derivatives in general. Given the large variety of energy products, it is not always evident which derivatives product and which hedging scheme will be most effective in reducing exposures. Therefore, proxy hedging is worth a reasonably detailed discussion, taking both an electricity end user and an electricity generator as examples. Finally, the chapter contains a detailed case study of using weather derivatives to hedge exposures resulting from seasonal and weather-driven demand for energy. It shows that a company's profit and loss can be directly affected by volume variations, and how weather derivatives can assist to mitigate that risk.

2. Strategic considerations for energy hedging

While many companies have quite strict policies for (almost) fully hedging foreign exchange (FX) exposures, the hedging of energy exposures is often left to the discretionary insight of individual managers. In most cases less than 50% of the exposure for the upcoming two to three years is actually hedged. In our corporate commodity advisory practice, we find that the desired level of hedging is badly defined: even the largest and most professionally managed companies may leave such decisions to local plant or business unit managers. This is surprising, given the

---

* This chapter remains unchanged since the last edition.

sometimes large share of energy costs in the total cost structure, in combination with the significant volatility in energy prices. The past few years have demonstrated that energy prices can double within a year, leading to volatility levels that are four to five times higher than those of the primary FX rates.

We believe that there are at least three important explanations for the somewhat limited (but increasing) attention paid by corporate firms to the central and active management of energy exposures. First, because of their physical nature, energy exposures are less easily recognised as a financial risk. It is often necessary to involve local managers in signing commodity and country-specific purchase contracts. Aggregation of natural exposures and contracts to financial risk figures is generally perceived as a difficult next step to apply consistently throughout the company.

A second explanation is the large diversity in energy exposures that companies may face, in terms of both products and geographical locations. This complicates consistent reporting and effective financial risk management. Furthermore, each product and market has its own product specifications and trading conventions, making it necessary to involve a range of specialists to perform the financial analysis and execute transactions. The handful of dealers dominating the market, notably Goldman Sachs and Morgan Stanley, assist companies in carrying out transactions; but at the same time they have a natural comparative advantage to arbitrage pricing differences and among their customers.

The third hurdle for consistent energy risk management among corporate firms is the difficulty of defining an appropriate benchmark. On the one hand, it may be argued that income stability is the ultimate goal for any company – avoiding the cost of financial distress, making it more attractive to work for and do business with and lowering the cost of capital, among other things. The logical consequence would be to hedge all exposures as many years into the future as possible. On the other hand, company shareholders actually prefer certain exposures so that they can choose their own level of hedging. For example, investors deliberately take an oil price exposure by investing in oil majors. For this and other reasons, companies may choose a hedging strategy that aligns well with their competitors. Still, given the huge variations in energy prices, whatever the outcome it is important for companies to define a clear benchmark. This benchmark can be communicated internally for better financial control and reduced transaction costs, and communicated to investors for transparency.

3. Energy derivatives contract structures

The bulk of derivatives trading is in products that are based on a financial concept or product, such as FX rates, interest rates or company stocks. In contrast, trading in energy derivatives, and commodity derivatives in general, means that the underlying is a physical product. This physical product or underlying must be defined very exactly and price formation must be the result of a fairly active trading activity to make a derivatives product viable. The example below provides details for European steam coal. Due to the large diversity in energy products in terms of quality and location, the standardisation and publication of generally accepted indices are not evident. In practice, only a limited number of physical indices become successful and form the basis for hedging strategies. This also means that actual exposures might differ from the hedge product, and companies face the challenge of maximising hedge effectiveness (as discussed later in this chapter).

Example: Coal API-2 – physical indices as the underlying for financial derivatives
Steam coal is the largest fuel for power generation worldwide, but is not a homogeneous product. The usual unit of measurement is based purely on weight, but weight alone is not suitable for comparing prices, due to substantial differences. Standardisation to a specific quality level offers a solution. The most typical specifications of steam coal imported into Europe are, for example, based on a calorific value of 6,000 calories per kilogram, an ash content of 8% to 15% and a size of 0 millimetres (mm) to 50 mm. Most European coal trading is for coal with exactly those specifications and delivered in one of the northwest European harbours (Amsterdam, Rotterdam or Antwerp). The most commonly used index, API-2, is published each week in the jointly owned *Argus/McCloskey's Coal Price Index Report*. It is an estimated average price for physical coal transactions following those specifications. Derivatives products, mainly swaps, are traded with this 'physical' API 2 index as an underlying. Importantly, the coal swap market can thrive only if the underlying physical market has been standardised and is liquid enough to avoid price manipulation.

The flexibility in energy assets and the embedded flexibility (optionality) in various long-term contract structures would suggest that energy market players trade options actively. Options could help to manage the risks from those more basic physical positions. However, although in oil and weather markets option structures may have gained some popularity, in the other energy markets trading activity is generally quite low. The (limited) activity is primarily over-the-counter based. Probably the main explanation is again the fragmentation of products and markets. This makes it difficult to channel enough trading activity to a specific product type.

Derivatives products that trade a linear pay-off are swaps, futures and forwards. Naming can be quite confusing, with forwards and futures being traded on the same exchange. Many exchanges for trading energy derivatives exist worldwide, ranging from the well-known New York Mercantile Exchange and Intercontinental Exchange to rather small exchanges for regional power markets. Nevertheless, various studies indicate that the abundance of trading activity is over the counter. Financially settled swaps are the most popular instruments in oil and coal markets; physically settled forwards are generally most popular in power and gas. The forward structures demonstrate most clearly the 'flow' nature of power and gas: a forward delivery means the delivery over the full maturity period (month, quarter, season, year) of a constant volume during every hour of the day.

4. From price exposure to spread exposure

Although price developments of different energy products may not be the same over shorter time periods, the overall trend over a three to five-year period (or less) is often very similar. The improved transportability helps to tighten the links between geographic locations. Larger oil tankers and bulk carriers, and especially the boom in liquefied natural gas facilities, have supported this trend. At the same time, energy commodities have natural interdependencies. For example, the power production sector is the primary end user of coal and natural gas; natural gas prices are often priced against refined oil prices (especially in Europe and Asia); and crude is naturally linked to refined oil. Also, developments in emissions trading markets, such as the EU Emissions Trading Scheme, create further linkages: the power sector is the largest emitter of carbon dioxide and nitrogen oxide, followed by the oil and gas industry.

Crack spreads, spark spreads, dark spreads, winter-summer spreads, Atlantic-continental spreads, contracts for differences – the price risk management of energy exposures often comes down to the management of spreads, as follows:

- A gas storage operator primarily manages the flexibility of the storage asset to capture time spreads. It can use the flexibility as a hedge against expected and unexpected load fluctuations from the rest of its portfolio (eg, customers, gas-fired power plants) or use it as a source of trading revenue itself.
- A shipping company or the owner of pipeline capacity manages the flexibility to exploit locational spreads. For example, the Interconnector gas pipeline between Bacton, United Kingdom and Zeebrugge, Belgium attracts a variety of trading companies. The capacity is used to exploit price differences between the UK National Balancing Point (NBP) and continental European gas prices. In addition, it is used to enjoy the flexibility of using gas of one market (typically, the more liquid NBP) as a physical hedge against positions in the other market.
- Intra-commodity spreads are the primary concern for processing companies (eg, refineries and fuel-fired power plants). For example, the spark spread of a gas-fired power plant is the gross margin of that plant for a set of power prices, gas prices and (if applicable) emission prices. A rise in the power price does not mean an increased profit margin, as it may be accompanied by an equal or even larger rise in gas prices. In practice, a power plant owner is exposed to a range of spark spreads: various maturities and various production types can be distinguished, including base load (all hours of the day), peak load (business hours only) and off-peak (non-business hours).

Later in the chapter the management of spark spreads is described in detail. However, before jumping to that rather advanced topic, there are a couple of general principles that apply to the management of energy commodities in general.

5. Optimal hedge ratio and hedge effectiveness

Important questions for a portfolio or risk manager to address include the following:

- What is my exposure?
- How can I optimally hedge it?
- What is the effectiveness of the hedge?

Various aspects come into play to address these basic questions: volatility, correlations, hedging costs, risk premiums and volume uncertainty, to name a few. We go on to explain how each of these elements plays a role, starting simply and then moving to a more advanced example. One of the most advanced examples, the hedging of a power station, is worked out in detail at the end.

When a company can make an accurate forecast of its exposure, and when that exposure is a tradable contract, the optimal hedge equals the exposure. Take, for example, a mobile phone manufacturer in Finland. Suppose that on January 1 it has a firm expectation that its electricity demand in the following year will be 1,200 megawatt-hours (MWh) per day, spread equally over the day. The exposure exactly matches with 50MW of the base-load front-year calendar contract on the Nordpool Exchange. Some statistics are as follows:

- Assuming that the year-ahead contract currently trades at €50/MWh and has an annual volatility of 20%, a movement of 20% up or down is very likely.
- Under the assumption of normally distributed returns, the 5% worst-case movement would be to a level of €70/MWh around the end of the current year.
- With about 5% probability, the (commodity) cost for the electricity demand can therefore rise from the present €21.9 million (365 x 50 x 1,200) to €30.66 million or more.
- The difference is the one-year 95% value-at-risk, which equals €30.66 million minus €21.9 million – €8.76 million. Leaving this position open may turn profits into a loss.

As a solution, the company may buy a 50MW base-load year-ahead contract on Nordpool for delivery in Finland. When the contract is for physical delivery, the electricity can be used for the plant directly. However, in most cases the contract (whether financial or physical) will serve merely as a financial hedge, giving the company time to negotiate an end-user contract with an electricity supply company. Among other things, the end-user contract will contain the necessary flexibility for some variation in offtake, in contrast to the fully constant load from a tradable contract. However, because the end-user contract will be directly priced as the Nordpool market price plus a mark-up, the Nordpool hedge of 50MW provides the full financial protection; it is the optimal hedge. At the time the company signs an end-user contract, the contract will be unwound.

In practice, the exposure might not be equal to a liquid tradable contract. The solution is to find a tradable product whose price movements closely mimic the actual exposure. This is a 'proxy' (or 'basis') hedge. There are multiple reasons for a proxy hedge:

- The commodity specifications may be different;
- The location may be different;
- The delivery period of the contract may be different; or
- The contract size may not match what is needed.

With a proxy hedge, various items start to influence the optimal hedge size and the hedge ratio. In this example, the base-load demand is replaced by a peak-load demand. On Nordpool, the peak-load contract is considerably less liquid than the base load, which is a good reason to consider using the base-load contract to hedge the peak exposure. There are four different types of hedge:

- Volume hedge – with a demand of 50MWh per hour in peak hours (8:00am to 8:00pm on business days) and 3,168 peak hours a year, the total demand equals 158.4 gigawatt-hours. It is not uncommon to hedge this with the (approximately) same volume in the proxy product. In this case, that would mean buying 18.1MW of base-load power (158.4/8.76; 8,760 hours in a year). The implicit or explicit assumption behind a volume hedge is that an increase in the underlying exposure is compensated by an equal price movement in the hedge product. For example, when the peak price moves from €60 to €80 per MWh, the base load must move from €50 to €70 per MWh in order to have a perfect hedge.
- Value hedge – there is a lot of statistical evidence that the correlation between many market prices is stronger in terms of percentage price changes than in terms of absolute price changes. For example, when the peak price moves from €60 to €80 per MWh, the comparable movement in the base-load product would be from €50 to €66.67 per MWh. If so, it is more effective to take a position in the hedge product that matches the value of the exposure instead of the volume. The company's profit and loss would be unaffected if the value of the hedge equalled €9.5 million (158,400 x 60), or a tradable base-load volume of 21.7MW.
- Optimal correlation-based hedge – both volume and value hedge ignore the possibility that the price of the hedge product may not move in tandem with the exposure. If the correlation between price returns is less than 100%, then (under certain assumptions) statistical models demonstrate that the value at risk of the combined position is minimised when the value hedge is rescaled with the correlation. For example, an 85% return correlation between base-load and peak-load year-ahead contracts implies an optimal hedge of 0.85 × 21.7 = 18.4MW base load. This number can be further scaled down if the volatility of the hedge product is actually higher than that of the exposure, and vice versa. Even though such a hedge is the best that can be achieved, it does not bring the value at risk to zero. It brings the value at risk down by 53% (the square root of 1-85%2) of the initial value at risk.
- Optimal correlation and co-integration based hedge – most risk management systems have the functionality to calculate value at risk or similar risk measures. Most of the calculation methods rely on volatilities and correlations of daily price returns. In commodity markets, many pairs of price series actually move more closely together than the correlation of daily price returns suggests. In other words, the daily return correlation underestimates the true linkage between prices. For example, while (Dutch) title transfer facility and (UK) NBP gas prices might not show returns that are the same on each day, the overall trend is rarely different over one week or one month. This implies that the spread between the markets is mean-reverting. Such a co-movement of spreads has been modelled successfully by so-called 'co-integration' or 'error-correction' models. Although a simple optimal hedge rule is not available as for correlation, a stronger co-integration generally implies that the optimal hedge ratio moves from 85% closer to 100%. The co-integration also makes the hedge more effective. At the same time, one must

be careful that the effectiveness of a hedge typically looks better on paper than it performs in real life: a hedge is often unable to provide protection against occasional market disruptions (eg, due to pipeline failures).

What to do in practice? In order to define an optimal hedge programme, it is first important to have a good view on the actual aggregate exposures. This requires the right systems and risk management tools to be in place (eg, aggregating the forecasts and exposures from various production locations). Second, the goals of the hedging programme must be crystal clear and part of a policy covering issues such as the following:

- What is the horizon being hedged?
- What percentage of price uncertainty is left 'open'?
- Who is responsible for implementation and monitoring?
- What products can be traded and with what counterparts?
- What should be done in extreme market situations?

Furthermore, the discussion of the four hedging approaches highlights that a company should define whether its goal is to minimise short-term mark-to-market variations in its exposure (eg, minimise one or 10-day value at risk), or whether longer-term cash flow at risk or profit at risk is the central aim. In the former case, the correlations and volatilities provide all statistical information to define 'optimal hedges'; in the latter case, the co-integration parameters must be incorporated. In any case, the expectations for the effectiveness of a hedge should not be set too high because markets are likely to behave differently than expected.

6. Hedging exposures with 'flexibility': the case of a power plant

Many of the peculiarities of energy hedging come together in the management of a gas-fired power station. First, the exposure is not a single commodity, but a spread (the clean spark spread). Second, the management involves the use of products with multiple maturities and granularities, ranging from spot to multiple calendar forwards. Finally, a gas-fired power station has a flexible level of generation and its exposure therefore varies with the spark spread in the market.

Let us first review the 'natural' unhedged position. Without any forward hedge and any other position (eg, a customer portfolio), the plant will sell its production in the spot market. When its spark spread (gross margin) is positive in a certain period, it will produce; otherwise it will not – or at least not at full capacity. This could mean that the plant:

- generally runs at maximum capacity (eg, 400MW) Monday to Friday from 6:00am to 11:00pm;
- is switched off over the weekend when spreads are clearly negative; and
- runs at minimum stable generation (eg, 200MW) in the night hours of Monday to Friday when spreads are negative, but a start-stop is too costly.

Any hedging scheme will leave this optimal dispatch pattern unaffected: it merely stabilises the total income. Even if this production pattern is known with certainty, there is no perfect hedge because it does not coincide with standard traded blocks. In this case, depending on the market's peak-load definition, the exposure is a combination of 100% peak load and a little off-peak (early morning and late evening full capacity, and night hours minimum capacity).

Still assuming full dispatch certainty, a market hedge would first mean selling forward 400MW peak-load power and buying corresponding volume of gas and (potentially) emission credits. Based on a risk analysis involving volatilities, correlations and co-integration, the off-peak hedge might be 100MW. The peak-load hedge will certainly mean that a positive margin is locked in, but the off-peak 'lock-in' can be negative, since in this example only a few off-peak hours are expected to be positive. This negative lock-in is often difficult to understand; the logic stems from the fact that the plant will actually produce only in a small percentage (roughly 25%) of the hours. When it comes to spot trading, about 75% of the forward sold off-peak power will be repurchased, while for the remaining 25% additional power will be sold in the market. From a profit-stabilising perspective, this is preferred above selling the full off-peak production volume in the spot market. The loss from the forward lock-in will be compensated for by a profit-in-spot market. This can be compared to the hedging of an out-of-the-money financial option.

In reality, the optimal future dispatch is not certain. When forward spark spreads rise, the expected production will rise, as will the hedge volumes. A delta sensitivity of the power plant towards a specific tradable contract (eg, power, gas, emissions) equals the sensitivity of the plant value due to changes in those market prices. An approximation to this delta sensitivity can be calculated using variations of the Margrabe spread option formula. However, ideally, this plant value is calculated on the basis of a large number of potential future price scenarios, because that is the only way to incorporate technical constraints (eg, start-stop) and the special dynamics of forward and spot power prices, as well as co-integration. With sophisticated power plant simulation and valuation models, a market player can therefore hedge more accurately and stabilise a larger proportion of its plant value.

The weather markets

It is taken for granted that weather impacts on the agricultural, commodity and energy markets. The news headlines of Summer 2010 were replete with disastrous crop failures in Russia, heatwaves in North America and calamitous rains in parts of Asia. What, if anything, can be done to mitigate the economic losses caused by the weather?

Fortunately, the answer is quite a lot. The Chicago Mercantile Exchange (CME) offers weather products related to temperatures, hurricanes, snowfall and frost. Furthermore, weather hedge funds, reinsurance companies and weather market makers offer weather cross-commodity products for agricultural and energy participants requiring idiosyncratic weather risk coverage. In this section the motivation for a weather hedge and the weather hedge's effectiveness are presented for a fictional natural gas retailer (Amigos) doing business in the northeastern United States.

Case study: weather derivatives

Retail natural gas providers are directly affected by weather. Consider Amigos, a fictional natural gas distribution company doing business in the northeastern United States. The reason that Amigos desires a weather hedge is because in a colder than average (normal) winter heating season, Amigos will sell greater volumes of natural gas to its end users. Conversely, in a warmer than average heating season, Amigos will sell smaller volumes of natural gas to its customers.

The weather risk endemic to Amigos' natural gas operations is illustrated in Table I. The second column shows the total heating degree days accumulated during the winter heating season, November 1 to March 31 for the 14 heating seasons spanning 1997 to 2010. As can be seen in the table, lower average temperatures result in higher heating degree day totals. What is striking is that New York heating degree day totals for the 1997 to 2010 winter heating seasons range from a minimum of 3,063 (in 2002) to a maximum of 4,254 (in 2003).

In the third column it is readily apparent that in cold winter heating seasons, Amigos' unhedged margins are concomitantly higher than during mild winter heating seasons because Amigos sells greater volumes of gas to its end users.[1] To obtain a sense of the weather risk, note that Amigos' expected (average) margin is $18.582 million. In the mild winter of 2002 Amigos realised unhedged margins of $16.525 million, an approximate shortfall of $2 million on the company's expectation. In contrast, in the very cold 2003 winter, Amigos realised unhedged margins of $20.785 million, an approximate windfall of $2.1 million. Put differently, Amigos' margins swung by more than $4.1 million between the 2002 and 2003 heating seasons.

Table 1

This shows the heating degree days at LaGuardia Airport and the unhedged margins at Amigos. The expected margin is $18.5 million and ranges from $15.9 million to $21.2 million.

Year	Heating degree days	Unhedged margins
1997	3753.5	$19,022,500
1998	3473.0	$17,455,000
1999	3556.5	$17,467,500
2000	3535.0	$17,980,000
2001	4132.0	$21,070,000

continued overleaf

---

1   We assume for ease of exposition that price margins are fixed and hedged.

Year	Heating degree days	Unhedged margins
2002	3063.0	$16,525,000
2003	4254.0	$20,785,000
2004	3994.5	$20,037,500
2005	4007.0	$19,645,000
2006	3475.5	$16,682,500
2007	3443.0	$15,960,000
2008	3701.5	$17,977,500
2009	3977.5	$21,212,500
2010	3658.0	$18,330,000

The senior management at Amigos decides to hedge this weather risk. The hedge envisaged is to be structured such that Amigos will receive payment when a winter heating season is warmer than normal (relatively fewer heating degree days) and Amigos will make payment when a winter heating season is colder than normal (relatively more heating degree days). This hedging strategy enables Amigos to recoup any margin shortfall associated with a warmer than normal heating by forfeiting potential windfall profits associated with a colder than normal heating season. Another way to consider the hedge is that Amigos can decrease the volatility of its winter heating season margins.

The weather hedge
In order to hedge its weather risk effectively, Amigos must:
- be confident that there is a statistically significant relationship between its unhedged margins and the weather at a particular location (LaGuardia Airport heating degree days); and
- determine the type and size of the hedge to be implemented.

With respect to the first point, CME offers a seasonal strip heating degree days index futures swap contract for 24 US cities.[2] The contract is so named because the strip specifies a (consecutive) series of futures contracts that span a specific time period. The winter heating season strip typically spans November 1 to March 31.

---

2   For a full list of CME weather products see www.cmegroup.com/trading/weather/.

Further, a heating degree day is a temperature metric. Specifically, a heating degree day = max(65 – T, 0), where max is the maximum operator and T is the daily average temperature in degrees Fahrenheit.[3] For example, if the average temperature on a day is 35 degrees, the corresponding heating degree day is calculated as max(65-35, 0) = 35. As a counter example, if the average temperature on a day is 75 degrees, the corresponding heating degree day is calculated as max(65-75, 0) = 0. Third, the CME contract specifies a location. For our example, a New York winter heating season index is equal to the sum of the daily heating degree days from November 1 to March 31 at LaGuardia airport. The contract size is $20 times the respective CME Seasonal Strip Heating Degree Days Index.

In addition to the contract specifications, it is necessary to distinguish between the buyers and sellers of the futures contract. Buyers are deemed to be long the contract and sellers are said to be short the contract. To clarify further, consider one LaGuardia contract that trades on October 25 2009. The futures swap is traded at 3,760 heating degree days for the winter heating season, November 1 2009 to March 31 2010. Suppose further that the heating degree day index settles at 3,685 heating degree days. The pay-off to the long is (3685 – 3760) x $20 = -$1,500 and the pay-off to the short is +$1,500. Another useful way to think of the pay-offs is that the index settled warmer than 3,760 heating degree days and this profited the short.

Fortunately for Amigos, as shown in Figure I, there is in fact a 92% correlation between heating degree days and Amigos' unhedged margins and this convinces Amigos that a weather hedge will be effective. The type of hedge will be a heating degree day swap so that, as discussed above, Amigos receives payment in a mild heating season and Amigos pays out in a cold heating season. Amigos is said to be short the swap. To determine the size of the swap, Amigos estimates that each New York heating degree day is equivalent to approximately $5,000 in margin.

Figure I depicts the correlation between winter heating degree days (at LaGuardia Airport in New York) and Amigos' unhedged margins.

Utilising the standardised CME weather contract requires Amigos to sell $5,000/$20 = 250 contracts to hedge its weather exposure.

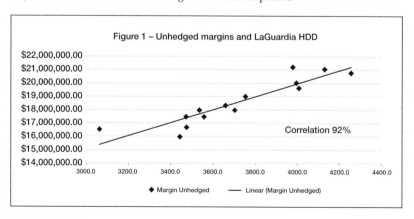

T, the average daily temperature, is the average of the daily high and daily low temperatures.

Hedge results

The impact of any one heating season's weather hedge is contained in Table 2. Amigos' unhedged margins, the swap pay-out and its hedged margins are compiled for the entire 14-year sample. For example, in the colder than normal 1997 heating season, Amigos' unhedged margin was $19.022 million and the weather swap required Amigos to pay out $0.188 million, such that the hedged margins totalled $18.835 million. In contrast, the warmer than normal 1998 heating season resulted in unhedged margins of $17.455 million, and the weather swap paid $1.215 million to Amigos, such that the hedged margins totalled $18.670 million.

The swap was agreed at 3,716 heating degree days. The standard deviation of the unhedged margins is $1.6 million and the standard deviation of the hedged margins is $0.675 million.

Table 2

Year	Heating degree days	Unhedged margins	Swap pay-out	Hedged margins
1997	3753.5	$19,022,500.00	$(187,500)	$18,835,000
1998	3473.0	$17,455,000.00	$1,215,000	$18,670,000
1999	3556.5	$17,467,500.00	$797,500	$18,265,000
2000	3535.0	$17,980,000.00	$905,000	$18,885,000
2001	4132.0	$21,070,000.00	$(2,080,000)	$18,990,000
2002	3063.0	$16,525,000.00	$3,265,000	$19,790,000
2003	4254.0	$20,785,000.00	$(2,690,000)	$18,095,000
2004	3994.5	$20,037,500.00	$(1,392,500)	$18,645,000
2005	4007.0	$19,645,000.00	$(1,455,000)	$18,190,000
2006	3475.5	$16,682,500.00	$1,202,500	$17,885,000
2007	3443.0	$15,960,000.00	$1,365,000	$17,325,000
2008	3701.5	$17,977,500.00	$72,500	$18,050,000

continued overleaf

Year	Heating degree days	Unhedged margins	Swap pay-out	Hedged margins
2009	3977.5	$21,212,500.00	$(1,307,500)	$19,905,000
2010	3658.0	$18,330,000.00	$290,000	$18,620,000

In addition to looking at any particular season's hedge, it is edifying to look at the backcast of all the hedges. In Figure II the unhedged margins are plotted side by side with the hedged margins. A quick inspection of Figure II suggests that the hedged margins are less variable than the unhedged margins. In fact, this is the case, with the unhedged margins having a standard deviation of $1.678 million and the hedged margins having a standard deviation of $0.675 million. Moreover, recalling that the expected margins are $18.582 million, the hedged margins are also $18.582 million. This is an artifact of ignoring transaction costs associated with the weather hedge. In practice, the hedged margins will be reduced by an amount proportional to brokerage commissions and the bid-ask spread in the weather market.[4]

Figure 2 illustrates the reduction in margin volatility for Amigos.

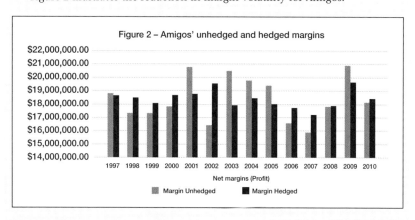

Figure 2 – Amigos' unhedged and hedged margins

Conclusion

Weather derivatives can be extremely effective hedges of volumetric risk. The weather hedge presented above is highly stylised and in our experience, our clients often seek hedging strategies that manage extreme (tail) weather risks. Weather options are particularly useful for managing extreme (non-linear) weather risks. Combining options and futures positions makes it possible to tailor

---

4   Brokerage rates are negotiable. Assuming a one-quarter of a tick brokerage rate, Amigos would pay $5,000 / 4 = $1,250 in brokerage. New York (LaGuardia) is considered a deep and liquid seasonal heating degree day weather market.

a more effective weather hedge. Moreover, utilising weather options may benefit the hedger because of increased market depth, liquidity, price discovery and lower total costs.

Weather derivatives are increasingly incorporated in cross-commodity transactions. To wit, our clients are engaged in designing, managing and transacting weather contingent power and/or gas options. For example, gas retailers reticent to buy (sell) incremental gas volumes on very cold (warm) winter days, can purchase (sell) temperature contingent gas options. The main advantage of layering weather onto gas options is that a hedger can benefit from the correlation between temperatures and gas prices.

Finally, weather derivatives and hedges range from the plain vanilla to the complex and exotic. As discussed earlier in this chapter, the fundamental co-integrated nature of the gas, power, coal and commodity markets generally extends naturally to weather markets.

Introduction to equity derivatives

Edmund Parker
Marcin Perzanowski
Mayer Brown

1. Introducing equity derivatives

This chapter provides an overview of equity derivatives, describing the common types of equity derivative instrument, their uses and the practical considerations relating to each. It also explains how equity derivatives are traded and hedged. Equity derivative instruments fall into five principal categories: options, forwards, futures, swaps and structured products – each described in this chapter.

2. Equity derivatives: form and purpose

An 'equity derivative' is a financial instrument that references and offers economic exposure to the performance of an equity asset or other equity-related variable from which the instrument's price or value is derived.

Equity derivatives may be traded on an exchange or over the counter (OTC). They may also be funded or unfunded. Equity derivatives are often used by funds and investors as speculative investments, and by end users and banks as commercial hedges. However, they also have a variety of other uses.

Equity derivatives make up a relatively small segment of the derivatives market. According to statistics published by the Bank for International Settlements, equity derivatives accounted for US$7.1 trillion (or 1.44%) out of a total of about US$493 trillion in outstanding notional derivatives transactions as at the end of 2015. The derivatives market is largely dominated by interest rate swaps, currency swaps and credit derivatives such as credit default swaps (CDS).

3. Underlying equity asset

In the case of equity derivatives, the asset referenced by the instrument is almost always an equity security or a basket of different equity securities, or a single index unit or a basket of indices.

3.1 Deriving value from underlying assets

Under an equity derivatives contract, one party pays to the other an amount linked to the change in value of one or more equity assets. This amount is based on certain elections, which are agreed by the parties in the transaction document at the outset of the transaction. The equity asset referenced in an equity derivatives instrument is said to be 'underlying' the derivative.

Value in equity derivatives is often derived from the leverage that they provide in supplying exposure to equity assets, as will be explained later in this chapter. In the context of equity markets, 'going long' means, broadly speaking, buying shares and holding them in the expectation that their value will rise (or otherwise ensuring that you profit if the price rises); 'going short' involves agreeing to sell a certain number of shares on an agreed future date at a specified price (usually the current market, or 'spot', price) in the hope that the share price falls (or otherwise ensuring that you profit if the price falls).

Though long transactions can be leveraged, short transactions are inherently leveraged because, unlike long positions, they allow a potential return without any initial investment other than the premium required to enter into the transaction. This is a fractional amount of the cost of purchasing the actual shares. A large proportion of all synthetic equity positions (ie, positions created by the use of equity derivatives) provide leverage.

3.2   Common types of underlying asset

Type of underlying equity asset	Value derived from underlying equity asset

Single equity security or index unit (securities indices such as those offered by Markit Group and others, are priced and sold in 'units', with one unit being the smallest denomination in which an interest in an index may be purchased)	• The total return on the single equity security over a specified term. (The 'return' on an index unit is the value of the aggregate return on the individual shares comprising all or part of the index.)
	• The difference in trading price of the single equity security or index unit between specific dates.
	• The difference between:
	  ◦ the trading price of the single equity security or index unit on a specific date or dates; and
	  ◦ a price specified in the transaction confirmation (which may be derived from a formula detailed in the transaction confirmation).

Basket of equity securities or index units	• The total return on the basket of equity securities or index units (aggregate return on the individual shares comprising all or part of the index) over a specified term.
	• The difference in trading price of the basket of equity securities or index units between specific dates.
	• The difference between:
	  ◦ the trading price of the basket of equity securities or index units on a specific date or dates; and
	  ◦ a price or prices specified in the transaction confirmation (which may be derived from a formula detailed in the transaction confirmation).
	• The difference in trading prices between the constituent shares or levels of the constituent indices:
	  ◦ between specific dates;
	  ◦ against a price or levels specified in the transaction confirmation on a certain date or dates (which may be derived from a formula detailed in the transaction confirmation); or
	  ◦ against each other on certain dates.

5. Equity options

An 'equity option' is a bilateral contract in which the buyer of the option acquires the right, but not the obligation, to sell to (in the case of a put option) or buy from (in the case of a call option) the option seller a defined amount of an underlying equity asset:

- at a price agreed at the contract's outset, referred to as the 'strike price'; and
- on a certain date or dates agreed at the contract's outset, referred to as the 'exercise date(s)'.

The underlying asset in an equity option is usually an equity security or index unit or basket of equity securities or index units. The 'strike price' is either a specified price or one determined by reference to a formula or set of rules set out in the transaction confirmation. Exercise dates and other elements of the option may also be based on a formula.

The option buyer pays a premium to the option seller, as set out in the transaction confirmation, in return for the seller providing the option. This premium payment includes:

- the option seller's cost of hedging its position under the option; and
- a profit element.

Equity options may be traded on an exchange or OTC, and may be funded or unfunded.

5.1 Puts and calls

(a) Put options

A put option holder has the right to sell an underlying asset (shares or index units) to its counterparty for an agreed price (the strike price) on an agreed future date (the exercise date). A put option is a contingent short position, in which the sale of an underlying equity asset is contemplated. For purposes of simplicity, these underlying equity assets are referred to in this chapter, generally, as 'shares', though it is understood that other types of equity asset may be referenced by an equity derivative.

(b) Call options

A call option holder has the right to buy an underlying asset from its counterparty at an agreed price (the strike price) on an agreed future date (the exercise date). A call option is a contingent long position, in which the purchase of shares is contemplated.

(c) Exercise of the option

Whether or not the option buyer chooses to exercise the option depends on whether the market price of the underlying share is above or below the strike price on the exercise date:

- If the investor holds a call option and the market price (or spot price) of the underlying equity security on the exercise date is above the strike price, the investor will exercise the option, which is said to be 'in-the-money'. If the option holder were to exercise this option, it would be buying the shares at a lower price through its exercise of the option and immediately selling them at a higher price in the market.

- If the investor holds a call option and the spot price of the underlying shares on the exercise date is below the strike price, the investor will not exercise the option, which is said to 'out-of-the-money'. If the option holder were to exercise this option, it would be buying the shares at a higher price than the then current market price.
- If the investor holds a put option and the spot price of the underlying shares on the exercise date is above the strike price, the investor will not exercise the option, which is out-of-the-money. If the option holder were to exercise this option, it would be selling the shares at a lower price than the then current market price.
- If the investor holds a put option and the spot price of the underlying shares on the exercise date is below the strike price, the investor will exercise the option, which is in-the-money. If the option holder were to exercise this option, it would be selling the shares at a higher price through its exercise of the option than the then current market price.

5.2   Cash settlement and physical settlement
Both put and call options can be either physically settled or cash settled.

(a)   *Physically settled options*
A physically settled call option buyer has the right to acquire certain agreed-upon shares from the seller at the strike price on the exercise date. These terms are specified in the transaction confirmation.

A physically settled put option buyer has the right to deliver certain agreed-upon shares to the option seller at the strike price on the exercise date. These terms are specified in the transaction confirmation.

(b)   *Cash-settled options*
A cash-settled call option buyer has the right to a payment from the option seller if, on the exercise date, the spot or settlement price of the agreed-upon underlying shares is higher than the strike price set out in the confirmation. The amount of the payment is equal to the difference between the settlement price and the strike price multiplied by the number of shares specified in the confirmation.

A cash-settled put option buyer has the right to a payment from the option seller if, on the exercise date, the spot or settlement price of the agreed-upon underlying shares is lower than the strike price set out in the confirmation. The amount of the payment is the difference between the settlement price and the strike price multiplied by the number of shares specified in the confirmation.

5.3   Option categories
Options are also categorised by when they can be exercised, and by the manner in

which certain terms are determined. There are a number of different kinds of equity option (which may be either put or call options), the three most common types of which are the first three listed below:

- American options – An American option can be exercised on any trading day during the option's term. This means that it can be exercised on any trading day before its expiration date.
- European options – A European option can be exercised only on its expiration date.
- Bermudan options – A Bermudan option can be exercised on specific dates throughout its term, as set out in the transaction confirmation. These dates are called 'potential exercise dates'.
- Asian options – Options can also be categorised by the method by which the strike price or exercise price is determined. An Asian option uses the average price of the underlying shares over a period of time or on particular dates specified in the transaction confirmation to determine the strike price.
- Barrier and range options (knock-in transactions) – In a knock-in transaction, a payment or physical delivery of the underlying shares (as applicable, depending on whether the option is cash settled or physically settled) is contingent on the occurrence of a 'knock-in event' on any 'knock-in determination day', which is usually a trading day or date falling within a pre-defined period or range of dates specified in the transaction confirmation. 'Knock-in events' are usually the crossing of a threshold price level by a share or index. In range knock-in transactions, payment is typically required when the share or index price falls within a certain range.
- Barrier and range options (knock-out transactions) – In a knock-out transaction, the transaction will terminate without the option being exercised if a 'knock-out event' occurs on any 'knock-out determination day' (usually a trading day or date falling within a pre-defined period or range of dates specified in the transaction confirmation). 'Knock-out events' are usually the crossing of a threshold price level by a share or index. In range knock-out transactions, payment is typically required when the share or index price falls outside of a certain range.

5.4   Equity options and leverage: an example

If an investor believes that the price of Company A shares will rise in the future, it might buy a call option on shares of Company A stock instead of purchasing the shares directly. Let us assume (for purposes of simplicity) that a physically settled call option is contemplated and:

- on day 1, the option purchase date, the market price of Company A shares is £2 per share;
- on day 1, the option premium (ie, the cost of purchasing a call option on one share of Company A stock) is £0.50; and
- the investor, looking to speculate on a potential upward price movement, has £100 to invest.

On day 1, the investor could either:

- buy 50 shares of Company A stock; or
- buy a call option for 200 shares of Company A stock with a strike price of £2 per share.

On day 30, the option exercise date, the price of Company A stock has increased to £4 per share.

If the investor had invested directly in shares of Company A stock on day 1, it would have:

- held the shares for 30 days (equivalent to the call option term); and
- sold the shares at their market price on day 30.

The investor's net profit with the direct share purchase would have been £100 (50 shares at £4 per share = £200 – £100 initial investment = £100).

If the investor had bought the (physically settled) call option on 200 Company A shares on day 1, it would have:

- exercised the option on day 30, at which time 200 Company A shares would have been delivered to it, for which it would have been required to pay £400 (200 shares at the strike price of £200 = £400); and
- sold the 200 Company A shares in the market at the then-current spot/market price of £4 per share, for a gross return of £800 (200 shares at £4 per share = £800).

The investor's net profit with the call option purchase would have been £300 (200 shares at £4 per share = £800–£400 paid for shares under the option –£100 cost of entering into the option = £300).

5.5   Mechanics of a basic in-the-money, physically settled call option

The leverage, illustrated by the example above, that the option gives the investor is one of the key benefits of trading in options.

Note that the investor does not begin to make a profit until the share price moves beyond £2.50 per share (the breakeven point), which is the per-share strike price plus the per-share cost of the option. If the share price moves to the breakeven point, the investor's option is said to be 'at-the-money'. If the strike price is below the market price of an underlying share of Company A stock, the option is in the money because the investor can:

- exercise the option and profit from taking delivery of the underlying shares for a price (the strike price) that is lower than their prevailing market price; or
- immediately sell the shares at their (higher) then-market price.

The option is considered out-of-the-money (and therefore not worth exercising) until the share price reaches the breakeven point of £2.50.

Figure 1. Mechanics of a physically settled call option

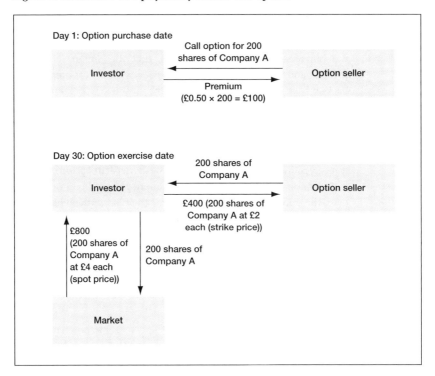

5.6 Hedging equity options

The option seller's profit is limited to the amount of the premium paid by the investor (£100), less the cost of any hedge of its position under the option that it may enter into. Absent a hedge of its position under the option, the potential loss that can be suffered by the option seller is unlimited, as the price of the underlying Company A shares could soar, dramatically raising the cost to the option seller of purchasing the shares in the market on the option exercise date to cover its short position and deliver the shares to the investor.

The option seller would therefore want to use a portion of the investor's premium payment to finance a hedge of its position under the options by entering into a so-called 'back-to-back' or 'offsetting' transaction with a third party in which it takes the opposite position to that which it holds under the Company A option that it has sold to the investor. On the day that it enters into the option with the investor, it enters into an identical option for Company A shares with a third party under which it takes the same position as the investor holds under the call option with it. The back-to-back option will reference the same shares (issuer, quantity), have the same per-share strike price and the same exercise date, only it will carry a slightly lower premium than the option seller receives from the investor under the initial call option. Since the option seller is typically a bank or broker-dealer, it pays a lower (interbank) premium to enter into its hedge than the investor pays to it.

This arrangement permits the option seller to:
- hedge its exposure fully under the Company A option with the investor; and
- include a small profit element in the premium payment that it has received from the investor for entering into the Company A option, which is equal to the difference between the premium that the option seller charges the investor and the fee that the option seller pays to its counterparty under the back-to-back option.

Under this arrangement:
- if the option is physically settled and in-the-money to the investor on the exercise date, the option seller simply delivers to the investor the shares that it receives under its back-to-back (physically settled) option; or
- if the option is cash settled and in-the-money to the investor on the exercise date, the option seller pays the investor the cash settlement amount that it receives under its back-to-back (cash-settled) option, which will equal the cash settlement amount it owes the investor.

There are also several other methods for an option seller to hedge its position under the option, including buying the underlying shares itself.

6.   Equity forwards and futures

Equity forwards and futures are different types of contract to purchase certain equity assets on a specific future date for a specified price. The principal difference is that futures are standardised and exchange traded, and forwards are entered into OTC, between two parties. Terms of forward contracts may be specially tailored to the needs of the counterparty. This cannot be done with a futures contract.

6.1   Equity forwards

'Forward contracts' are private, bilateral contracts for the sale and purchase of specified equity securities in which each party incurs:
- market risk on the shares or indices that are the subject of the forward contract; and
- a credit risk on its counterparty.

Forward contracts are traded OTC and therefore include exposure to counterparty credit risk.

There are two primary types of forward equity derivative contract: physically settled forwards and cash-settled forwards.

(a)   Physically settled forwards

Under a physically settled equity forward contract, one party agrees to sell and the other agrees to buy certain equity assets on an agreed future date for a specified price set out in the confirmation (the 'forward price'). The forward price may be agreed on in advance or determined by reference to a formula or an average price over a number of dates, similar to strike price determination in an Asian option. In a physically settled forward, the buyer takes physical delivery of the shares on the forward's maturity date.

(b)   *Cash-settled forwards*

Under a cash-settled equity forward contract, the parties exchange the difference between the forward price, as specified in the transaction confirmation, and the market price (or spot price) of the underlying shares on an agreed future date, multiplied by the number of shares specified in the transaction confirmation. Payments on index forwards are based on the difference between the price of an index unit on the agreed future date and the price set out in the confirmation.

The payment mechanics of a cash-settled equity forward work as follows:

*   If the forward price of an underlying share on the expiry date is above the spot price, Party A pays to Party B that amount multiplied by the number of shares specified in the confirmation.
*   If the forward price of an underlying share on the contract's expiry date is below the spot price, Party B pays to Party A that amount multiplied by the number of shares specified in the confirmation.

Cash-settled equity forwards can also relate to a basket of shares or basket of indices. If so, the amount paid on expiry of the swap is equal to the differences between the forward prices of the shares or index units specified in the confirmation and their spot prices, netted against one another. Payment is made by the party that is out-of-the-money on the aggregate of these price differentials.

As with certain customised, complex options and equity swaps, the forward prices of the shares or indices in a forward transaction may be determined by a formula set out in the transaction confirmation. The formula may accord the value or price movement of certain shares or indices greater weight in the determination as to whether the forward price is reached, or this may be determined based on the occurrence or non-occurrence of certain events, such as the crossing of or failure to cross certain price thresholds or levels on certain dates.

Equity forward contracts are typically documented using standard documents. This is in contrast to securities lending and securities repurchase (or 'repo') agreements that have similar mechanics to a funded equity forward, but which are documented using repurchase agreements and securities lending or stock loan agreements, such as the Global Master Securities Lending Agreement.

Equity forward positions may be hedged in a manner similar to option-seller hedging of options, as explained above.

6.2   Equity futures

In an equity futures contract, a party purchases the right to obtain certain agreed equity assets on an agreed future date. However, unlike forwards, futures contracts are standardised, exchange-traded contracts with limited counterparty credit risk. A central counterparty, or clearing house, clears the trade and assumes the credit risk of the parties that enter into futures contracts. While forwards reflect both counterparty credit risk and market risk, futures aim to eliminate credit risk to the extent possible, leaving only market risk. (The exchange itself, however, does present a small amount of credit risk.)

Exchanges (eg, the London International Financial Futures and Options Exchange (LIFFE)) offer futures packages from which parties select specific contract terms that fit their needs. For example, a party can choose to buy an equity futures contract for 1,000 shares of Company X to be delivered on 1 January 2017. Each equity futures contract is for a set amount of the underlying shares of an issuer or index. The equity futures contracts on many exchanges each represent the right to receive delivery of (or exposure to, in the case of cash-settled futures in which there is no physical delivery) 1,000 shares of an issuer or index on the contract's expiry date. If the buyer is looking for exposure to more than 1,000 shares on the same terms, it must buy two or more contracts. The buyer can gain exposure to shares only in multiples of 1,000. The inflexible nature of the terms of futures contracts is one of their principal disadvantages. If a buyer is looking for exposure to 1,200 shares, for example, it may instead need to enter into a forward contract, which is more easily customised.

In futures contracts, as noted, a clearing house acts as a central counterparty guaranteeing performance of its member banks and broker-dealers, and collecting and holding margin collateral from customers, often referred to as 'participants' (usually funds and end users). The clearing house will transact with, or clear trades involving, only institutions (banks and broker-dealers) with a seat on the affiliated exchange.

This means that a party looking to enter into a futures contract must enter into a futures-account agreement with an exchange member. These agreements contain extensive collateral and margining obligations for the non-broker counterparty and are not subject to extensive negotiation, as the counterparty has little negotiating leverage with the exchange member if it wishes to transact in futures. As a result, futures contracts are almost always funded transactions.

(a) **Settlement and pricing of equity futures**
Equity futures, like equity options and forwards, may be physically settled or cash settled.

Physical settlement: On the contract's expiry date, the buyer of the futures contract is entitled to receive delivery of the underlying shares. Most physically settled futures contracts do not reach their delivery/expiry date as they are most often traded throughout the life of the contract and the positions are then closed out before delivery in what is known as an 'offsetting' or 'closing' sale. If the original futures contract is:

- long, the offsetting contract will be for the same quantity of underlying shares, with the same issuer and other characteristics, but will be a short contract; or
- short, the offsetting contract will be for the same quantity of underlying shares, with the same issuer and other characteristics, but will be a long contract.

The offsetting contract will need to be cash settled, with the buyer responsible for any price differential resulting from any price movement in the underlying shares during the life of the contract.

Cash settlement: Cash settlement of equity futures works in the same manner as cash settlement of equity forwards. If, on the contract's expiry date, the contract price of an underlying share is:

- above the spot price, Party A pays to Party B that amount multiplied by the number of shares specified in the contract; or
- below the spot price, Party B pays to Party A that amount multiplied by the number of shares specified in the contract.

As with equity forwards, whether the price of the shares on the contract's expiry date has increased or decreased from the contract price, the price movement will be borne by the counterparty. Losses of the customer (non-dealer) counterparty are typically covered by initial margin collateral that has been posted by the customer at the transaction's inception with the exchange's clearing house.

The price of a futures contract is calculated by reference to a number of factors, including:

- the then-current cash (spot) price of the underlying shares on the date the contract is entered into;
- the expected future market movement of the underlying shares;
- current and expected supply and demand for the underlying shares;
- the fee to be paid to the seller of the futures contract (included in the premium payment paid by the customer to enter into the futures contract); and
- funding costs (included in the premium payment paid by the customer to enter into the futures contract).

(b)   *Example of an equity futures contract*

An investor believes that the price of Company Y shares is on the rise. The current price of Company Y shares is £4.55. In what is referred to as the 'opening purchase', the investor buys a three-month future on Company Y shares at £4.60 per share. The investor in this instance is speculating that the value of the shares will rise in the next three months to more than £4.60. Assuming that the investor predicts the market accurately, and the value of the shares rises to £4.80 on the contract's expiry date:

- if the contract is physically settled, the investor can:
  - take possession of the shares and sell them in the market at £4.80. The investor then realises a gain of £0.20 per share; or
  - sell the contract in the market at the then-current market price of £4.80 per share in an offsetting or closing sale and realise a gain of £0.20 per share. This can be done if the contract is a physically settled contract and the investor does not want to take physical delivery of the shares. For example, a hedge fund may be restricted from doing so for a variety of

reasons, or may wish to avoid the administrative inconvenience of selling the shares in the market; or

- if the contract is cash settled, the investor receives an amount that represents the upward movement in the value of an underlying share from the contract price (the difference between contract price and spot price; in this example, £0.20 per share) multiplied by the number of shares specified in the contract. As with all cash-settled derivatives contracts, there is no physical delivery of shares contemplated by this transaction.

If the price were to move negatively in the above example, the investor would suffer a corresponding loss – however, the mechanics would be the same.

(c) *Hedging equity futures*

Funding costs for equity futures typically include the contract seller's costs of financing its purchase of shares that are identical to those specified in the contract (at the outset of the transaction), minus any cash flows such as dividend distributions generated by the underlying shares during the interim period between share acquisition and delivery. These costs are sometimes known as 'costs of carry'. It would be expected that costs of carry would increase over time and, therefore, the price of a futures contract on the same shares would be greater the further out the contract's expiry date is.

The seller can hedge its position under the futures contract with the investor by doing one of two things. The first option is for the seller to purchase the underlying shares in the market when the futures contract is entered into (in this example, at the market price of £4.60) and holding them until the expiry date of the futures contract. Then:

- if the contract calls for physical settlement, the seller can simply deliver the shares to the investor on the contract's expiry date; or
- if the contract calls for cash settlement, the seller can hold the shares until the contract's expiry date and then sell them in the market on that same date at their market price (£4.80). This enables the seller to make the payment that it owes to the investor under the futures contract: the amount by which the per-share spot price exceeds the per-share contract price (£0.20 per share in this example) multiplied by the number of shares specified in the contract. The contract seller uses the remaining £4.60 to cover its share purchase outlay. The seller is covered on the financing costs (interest expense) of its hedge share purchase by the funding payment paid to it by the investor. The contract seller therefore breaks even on its hedge.

The contract seller profits on the amount of the premium collected from the investor that exceeds its funding costs.

If the spot price is below the contract price on the contract's expiry date, the seller will realise a loss on its holding of the shares, but will receive the difference from the investor under the futures contract.

The second option is for the seller to enter into a futures contract with a third party that is essentially identical to contract that it has sold to the investor. Under this back-to-back futures contract, the contract seller takes the opposite position to that which it holds under the futures contract that it sold to the investor. However, the seller is typically able to pay a lower fee than that which it receives from the investor because it is usually a bank or broker-dealer.

This back-to-back contract requires delivery to the seller of the same shares on the same date at the same price as it is required to deliver under the contract that it has sold to the investor. Banks and broker-dealers typically profit from the sale of futures contracts (and other derivatives contracts) in this manner, which allows them to take advantage of their lower cost of funds.

The seller's position in this example remains neutral because it has, either way, effectively hedged its risk under the futures contract that it has sold to the investor and will not profit from or suffer a loss on its delivery obligations (whether physical or cash) under the futures contract. As noted, the seller earns a fee from the investor that is included in the price of the futures contract.

6.3   Contracts for differences

A 'contract for differences' (CFD) is similar to a cash-settled forward or futures contract. CFDs are derivatives instruments that give the holder an economic exposure to the change in price of an underlying financial asset (typically, shares), without having to buy the asset itself. The amount of the cash settlement represents the difference between the underlying asset's price agreed at the outset of the contract and its market price at the date of the settlement of the contract.

CFDs can be long (where the holder gains from a rise in the price of the underlying asset) or short (where the holder gains from a fall in the price of the underlying asset). However, unlike forwards and futures, CFDs are open-ended contracts with no fixed settlement date and can be closed out by the holder on demand.

CFDs can offer exposure to a variety of financial assets, including single or multiple share indices, debt securities, commodities and currencies. When applied to shares, a CFD is an equity derivative under which the holder generally has neither voting rights nor a call option over the underlying shares.

CFDs are not permitted in the United States.

Disclosure regime for CFDs: Since 1 June 2009, the United Kingdom's regulatory framework governing disclosure of share holdings captures any instruments giving a pure economic exposure to shares without conferring voting rights (eg, CFDs). The Disclosure and Transparency Rules (Disclosure of Contracts for Differences) Instrument 2009 (FSA 2009/13) establish a general disclosure regime for long CFD positions with aggregation of CFD holdings and shareholdings with an initial disclosure threshold of 3%. The aim of these rules is to enhance transparency in share dealings by preventing parties from concealing their economic interest in a company's shares through the use of CFDs (stake-building) to bypass the normal rules of disclosure for major shareholdings. The rules are reflected in amendments to DTR 5 of the Financial Conduct Authority's Disclosure Rules and Transparency Rules (DTR) sourcebook.

7.   Equity swaps

An 'equity swap' is a bilateral contract that allows a party to acquire economic exposure to the performance of an equity asset for a specified term without actually owning that asset. The underlying equity asset can be a share or basket of shares, or an index or basket of indices. Equity swaps are inherently leveraged – that is, they allow an investor to acquire exposure to equity price movements in shares without the cash outlay required to purchase those shares, similar to equity options.

Customised, more heavily negotiated equity swaps are likely to be traded OTC, while more standardised equity swaps are often traded on a recognised exchange. Equity swaps may be funded or unfunded.

In a basic equity swap, on certain 'measurement dates' set out in the transaction confirmation, if the value of the underlying equity asset has:

- risen since the swap's execution or previous measurement date, the 'equity amount payer' pays to the 'equity amount receiver' an amount equal to the value of that increase multiplied by the number of shares specified in the transaction confirmation; or
- decreased since the swap's execution or previous measurement date, the equity amount receiver pays to the equity amount payer an amount equal to value of that decrease multiplied by the number of shares specified in the transaction confirmation.

If the swap references a basket of shares or basket of indices, the amount paid on these dates is equal to the changes in the prices of the shares or index units specified in the confirmation netted against one another on such dates. Payment is made by the party that is out-of-the-money on the aggregate of these price changes.

There are several variations on the basic equity swap, including:

- total return swaps (TRSs);
- index-linked swaps;
- share-linked swaps;
- relative value swaps;
- equity default swaps.

This section examines the most common form of equity swap: TRSs.

(a)   TRSs

TRSs simulate the economic benefits and burdens of ownership or disposal of an equity asset or basket of assets such as shares and/or index units. For purposes of simplicity, these are referred to here, generally, as 'shares', though it is understood that other types of equity asset may be referenced in a TRS. Under a TRS, the parties receive/pay the 'total return' (ie, all gains and losses that are generated) on the underlying shares, which are referenced in a TRS confirmation. The position replicated in a TRS may be either:

- a synthetic long position, in which the ownership of shares is replicated; or
- a synthetic short position, in which the disposal of shares is replicated.

(b)   Synthetic long TRSs

A synthetic long TRS replicates for the synthetic long investor, the ownership of underlying shares without the cash outlay required for the purchase of those shares. Under a synthetic long TRS, the synthetic long investor is the equity amount receiver (sometimes referred to as the 'total return receiver') and the swap provider, usually a bank or broker-dealer, is the equity amount payer (sometimes referred to as the 'total return payer'). In a synthetic long TRS, the parties exchange the cash flows outlined below, which are specified in the TRS confirmation.

Monthly exchange amounts: The following amounts are often netted against one another to arrive at a single monthly exchange amount paid on each monthly payment date specified in the TRS confirmation by one party to the other:

- Equity appreciation/depreciation payments – the parties to a synthetic long TRS often elect, in the TRS confirmation, to transfer a payment between them (often monthly) that reflects the composite movement of the underlying shares referenced in the TRS confirmation between two monthly measurement dates. If the underlying shares referenced in the TRS confirmation:
    - increase in value between monthly measurement dates, the equity amount payer pays the amount of the increase to the equity amount receiver on the following monthly payment date; or
    - decline in value between monthly measurement dates, the equity amount receiver pays the amount of the decrease to the equity amount payer on the following monthly payment date.

  As an alternative to monthly equity appreciation/depreciation payments, the parties may elect in the TRS confirmation to make a lump sum equity appreciation/depreciation payment (sometimes called a 'total return payment') as a final exchange amount at the conclusion of the transaction.

- Manufactured dividends – the equity amount payer pays to the equity amount receiver the dividend amounts that an investor would have received on the underlying shares referenced in the TRS confirmation had it actually owned the shares during the period between monthly measurements dates. These payments are often called 'manufactured dividends'. The amount of the manufactured dividends paid by the equity amount payer may vary, depending on whether it is agreed that they should be paid by reference to their gross amount or net of withholding tax. Some TRSs are structured so that the dividends are treated as if they were reinvested in additional underlying shares when paid.

  The equity amount payer is often also responsible for forwarding to the equity amount receiver any accrued interest on manufactured dividends that are not paid by the equity amount payer to the equity amount receiver until the following monthly payment date. This interest accrues from the date the actual dividend is paid by the issuer of the underlying shares to its investors, until the next monthly payment date on which the manufactured dividends are paid to the equity amount receiver.

  If the equity amount payer has hedged its position under the TRS by holding the underlying shares specified in the TRS confirmation, it receives these dividend payments from the issuer and simply passes those payments on to the equity amount receiver.

- Funding payments – the monthly exchange amount in a synthetic long TRS also includes a funding payment made by the equity amount receiver to the equity amount payer. The amount of each such payment typically equals the product of:
  - a factor that is usually expressed as a funding rate (eg, LIBOR or EURIBOR); and
  - the swap's notional amount. In a TRS, the swap's notional amount is equal to the purchase price of the underlying shares specified in the TRS confirmation on the date the swap is entered into.

  The funding payments under a synthetic long TRS are designed to cover the equity amount payer's monthly cost of borrowing the swap's notional amount. This amount will likely be used by the swap provider (the equity amount payer) to hedge its position under the synthetic long TRS by purchasing the underlying shares specified in the TRS confirmation (the hedge shares) on the date the swap is entered into.

  Regardless of whether the swap provider actually goes into the market and borrows the funds used to purchase the hedge shares or funds the purchase of the hedge shares itself, it still receives the monthly funding payments from the equity amount receiver.

  As an alternative to monthly funding payments, the funding payment may be made by the equity amount receiver to the equity amount payer in a lump sum as an initial exchange amount at the inception of the transaction.

- Premium/spread – a premium or profit element is typically paid by the equity amount receiver, as the synthetic long investor under a synthetic long TRS, to the swap provider (equity amount payer) for entering into the transaction. This monthly 'spread' is usually expressed as a specified number of basis points ('over' the relevant funding rate, such as LIBOR) multiplied by the swap's notional amount.

Initial exchange amount: As an alternative to monthly funding payments, the parties may elect that a lump sum funding payment is to be made by the equity amount receiver to the equity amount payer at the inception of the transaction. This amount essentially functions as a loan from the equity amount receiver to the equity amount payer, often used to fund the equity amount payer's purchase of the hedge shares. The initial exchange amount is therefore usually equal to the purchase price of the underlying shares specified in the TRS confirmation.

Final exchange amount: If the parties have elected not to make monthly equity appreciation/depreciation payments to one another during the life of the synthetic long TRS, then on the swap's maturity date the parties make one of the following payments to one another (often referred to as the 'total return payment'). If the underlying shares specified in the TRS confirmation have:

- appreciated in value during the life of the swap, the equity amount payer pays the amount of the net increase to the equity amount receiver on the swap's maturity date; or
- depreciated in value during the life of the swap, the equity amount receiver pays the amount of such net decrease to the equity amount payer on the swap's maturity date.

If a lump sum funding payment has been made by the equity amount receiver to the equity amount payer as the initial exchange amount under the synthetic long TRS, this amount is typically repaid by the equity amount payer to the equity amount receiver on the swap's maturity date. This amount may be netted, as appropriate, against the total return payment.

The mechanics of a cash-settled synthetic long TRS replicate for the synthetic long investor (the equity amount receiver) the gain or loss that it would realise or incur had it actually:

- purchased the underlying shares specified in the TRS confirmation on the date the swap was entered into;
- held the shares for the term of the swap; and
- sold the shares on the expiration date of the swap.

If the synthetic long TRS moves in favour of the synthetic long investor (ie, if the underlying shares referenced in the TRS confirmation have appreciated in value during the life of the swap), then the synthetic long investor has effectively 'bought low' on the underlying shares, and subsequently 'sold high'. Under these circumstances, the synthetic long investor is in the money on the maturity of the swap.

If the synthetic long TRS moves against the synthetic long investor (ie, if the underlying shares referenced in the TRS confirmation have depreciated in value during the life of the swap), the synthetic long investor is out-of-the-money on the maturity of the swap.

(c)   *Hedging a synthetic long TRS*

Because the synthetic long investor enters into the synthetic long TRS for commercial or speculative purposes, it will not look to hedge its position under the synthetic long TRS. Hedging its position would negate for the synthetic long investor the exposure to the underlying shares specified in the TRS confirmation that it seeks in entering into the synthetic long TRS.

The swap provider, by contrast, will look to hedge its position under the synthetic long TRS because it wants to nullify any commercial impact of the transaction and simply profit from the premium paid to it by the synthetic long investor.

The swap provider, as equity amount payer under a synthetic long TRS, has a synthetic short position. The swap provider's hedge under a synthetic long TRS therefore attempts to replicate the position of its counterparty: long on the underlying shares specified in the TRS confirmation.

Figure 2. Mechanics of a synthetic long TRS, including hedge

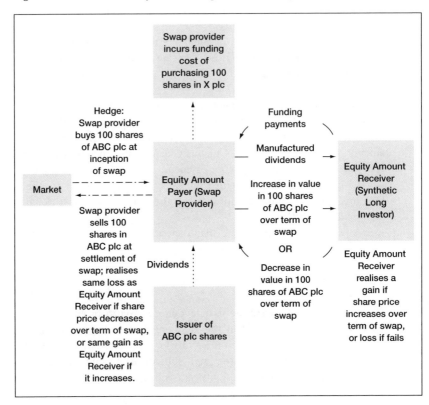

The mechanics of the swap provider's hedge, as equity amount payer, under a synthetic long TRS typically operate as follows:

- The swap provider either uses its own funds or borrows the funds to purchase shares in the market equivalent to the underlying shares (same issuer, number of shares) specified in the TRS confirmation on the date that the swap is entered into (the hedge shares). The hedge shares are therefore purchased by the swap provider at or near the price specified in the TRS confirmation.
- The swap provider holds the shares for the term of the swap.
- During the term of the swap, the swap provider uses the funding payments made by the equity amount receiver under the synthetic long TRS to make the interest payments on its loan (or to compensate it for the interest expense on the funds it has used to buy the hedge shares if it has funded the purchase of the hedge shares itself).
- On the maturity date of the swap, the swap provider sells the hedge shares into the market at their then current market price.

In this manner, the swap provider realises for itself any gain from appreciation in value of the underlying shares during the term of the swap that it would then be obligated to pass along to the equity amount receiver under the synthetic long TRS, either through the monthly equity appreciation/depreciation payments made during the life of the swap or in the final exchange amount/total return payment paid on the swap's maturity date. The swap provider is therefore hedged against any increase in the value of the underlying shares referenced in the TRS confirmation during the life of the swap.

If the underlying shares have declined in value over the term of the swap, the swap provider receives the net amount of such depreciation from the equity amount receiver under the synthetic long TRS, either through the monthly equity appreciation/depreciation payments made during the life of the swap or in the final exchange amount/total return payment paid on the swap's maturity date. The swap provider is therefore hedged against any losses it has incurred under its hedge.

(d)   *Synthetic short TRSs*

A synthetic short TRS replicates for the synthetic short investor the disposal of an underlying equity asset or basket of equity assets. Under a synthetic short TRS, the synthetic short investor is the equity amount payer and the swap provider is the equity amount receiver. In a synthetic short TRS, the parties exchange the cash flows outlined below, which are specified in the TRS confirmation.

Monthly exchange amounts: The following amounts are often netted against one another to arrive at a single monthly exchange amount paid on each monthly payment date specified in the TRS confirmation by one party to the other:

- Equity appreciation/depreciation payments – the parties to a synthetic short TRS may elect, in the TRS confirmation, to transfer a payment between them (often monthly) that reflects the composite movement of the underlying shares referenced in the TRS confirmation between two monthly measurement dates.

  Equity appreciation/depreciation payments under a synthetic short TRS operate in the same manner as under a synthetic long TRS (as explained above), only the parties are reversed.

  As under a synthetic long TRS, in the alternative to monthly equity appreciation/depreciation payments, the parties may elect in the TRS confirmation to make a lump sum equity appreciation/depreciation payment (sometimes called a 'total return payment') as a final exchange amount at the conclusion of the transaction.

- Manufactured dividends – under a synthetic short TRS, manufactured dividends are paid by the synthetic short investor as equity amount payer to the swap provider as equity amount receiver. These amounts equal the dividend amounts that an issuer would have paid on the underlying shares referenced in the TRS confirmation during the period between the monthly measurements dates. Manufactured dividends under a synthetic short TRS operate in the same manner as under a synthetic long TRS.

- Funding payments – the monthly exchange amount in a synthetic short TRS also includes a funding payment. The swap provider, as equity amount receiver under a synthetic short TRS, pays to the synthetic short investor, as equity amount payer under a synthetic short TRS, the same or similar funding payments as under a synthetic long TRS.

The funding payments under a synthetic short TRS are designed to approximate the interest return that the synthetic short investor would otherwise realise by placing in a deposit account the proceeds from the sale of the underlying shares referenced in the TRS confirmation (the swap's notional amount) on the date that the swap is entered into for a period equal to the term of the swap. As noted, however, the synthetic short investor does not typically use these payments to hedge its position under the synthetic short TRS, unlike an equity amount payer under a synthetic long TRS.

As under a synthetic long TRS, though, in the alternative to periodic funding payments, the equity amount receiver may make the funding payment to the equity amount payer in a lump sum as a final exchange amount at the inception of the transaction.

- Premium/spread – also factored into the monthly exchange amount is a premium or profit element paid by the synthetic short investor, as equity amount payer, to the swap provider, as equity amount receiver, for entering into the swap. This payment is usually expressed as a specified number of basis points multiplied by the swap's notional amount, as under a synthetic long TRS.

Note that unlike under a synthetic long TRS, under a synthetic short TRS the equity amount payer pays the premium to the equity amount receiver. This is because the synthetic short investor is the equity amount payer under a synthetic short TRS and the swap provider is the equity amount receiver.

Initial exchange amount: As under a synthetic long TRS, as an alternative to monthly funding payments, the parties to a synthetic short TRS may elect that a lump sum funding payment is to be made by the equity amount receiver to the equity amount payer at the inception of the transaction. The initial exchange amount under a synthetic short TRS works the same way as under a synthetic long TRS.

Final exchange amount: If the parties have elected not to make monthly equity appreciation/depreciation payments to one another during the life of the synthetic short TRS, then on the swap's maturity date, a payment is made based on the net appreciation or depreciation of the underlying shares referenced in the TRS confirmation over the life of the swap (the total return payment), as under a synthetic long TRS.

If the equity amount receiver makes a lump sum funding payment to the equity amount payer under the synthetic short TRS, the equity amount payer typically repays this amount to the equity amount receiver on the swap's maturity date.

The mechanics of a cash-settled synthetic short TRS replicate for the synthetic short investor (the equity amount payer) the gain or loss that it would realise or incur had it actually:

- borrowed shares, for example, under a securities lending arrangement, equivalent to the underlying shares specified in the TRS confirmation (same issuer, same number of shares) on the date that the swap was entered into and immediately sold them into the market on the same date at their then current market price; or
- bought shares equivalent to the borrowed/underlying shares specified in the TRS confirmation on the maturity date of the swap at their then-current market price and delivered them to its securities lender.

If the synthetic short TRS moves in favour of the synthetic short investor – that is, if the underlying shares referenced in the TRS confirmation have depreciated in value during the life of the swap – the synthetic short investor will have effectively sold high on the underlying shares referenced in the TRS confirmation, and subsequently bought low. In these circumstances, the synthetic short investor is in-the-money on the expiration of the swap.

If the synthetic short TRS moves against the synthetic short investor – that is, if the underlying shares referenced in the TRS confirmation have appreciated in value during the life of the swap – the synthetic short investor is out-of-the-money on the expiration of the swap.

(e)   Hedging a synthetic short TRS

As in the case of the synthetic long investor under a synthetic long TRS, the synthetic short investor under a synthetic short TRS will not want to hedge its position under the synthetic short TRS. Hedging its position would negate the exposure to the shares specified in the TRS confirmation that the synthetic short investor seeks in entering into the synthetic short TRS.

The swap provider, by contrast, will look to hedge its position under the synthetic short TRS because it wants to nullify any commercial impact of the transaction and simply profit from the premium paid to it by the synthetic short investor.

The swap provider, as equity amount receiver under a synthetic short TRS, has a synthetic long position. A swap provider's hedge under a synthetic short TRS therefore attempts to replicate the position of its counterparty: short on the underlying shares referenced in the TRS confirmation.

The mechanics of the swap provider's hedge, as equity amount receiver, under a synthetic short TRS typically operate as follows:

- The swap provider borrows shares, for example under a securities lending arrangement, which are equivalent to the underlying shares (same issuer, same number of shares) specified in the TRS confirmation on the date that the swap is entered into (the hedge shares).
- The swap provider then immediately sells the hedge shares into the market, also on the date that the swap is entered into. The hedge shares are therefore sold by the swap provider in the market at or near the price specified in the TRS confirmation.
- The swap provider holds the proceeds from the sale of the hedge shares in an account that pays a market rate of interest.

Figure 3. Mechanics of a synthetic short TRS, including hedge

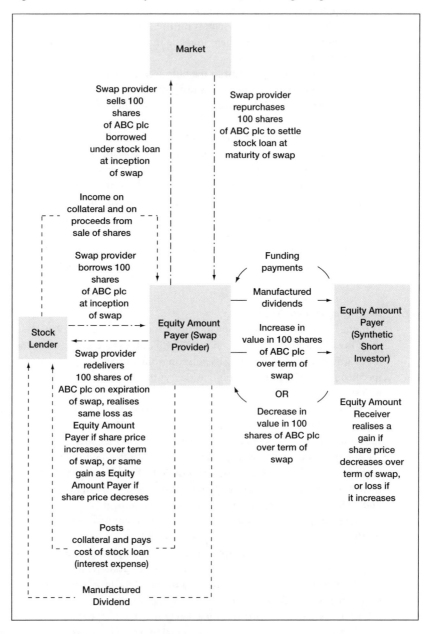

- On the expiration date of the swap, the swap provider buys shares in the market that are equivalent to the hedge shares (same issuer, same number of shares) at their then-current market price.
- The swap provider delivers the purchased shares back to its securities lender

and uses the interest accrued on the proceeds from its sale of the borrowed shares on the date that the swap was entered into to pay its securities lender the interest on the securities loan.

In this manner, the swap provider realises for itself any gain from a decline in the value of the underlying shares during the term of the swap that it would then be obligated to pass along to the equity amount payer under the synthetic short TRS, either:

- through the periodic equity appreciation/depreciation payments made during the life of the swap; or
- as the final exchange amount/total return payment made on the swap's maturity date.

The swap provider is therefore hedged against any decrease in the value of the underlying shares referenced in the TRS confirmation during the life of the swap.

If the underlying shares have appreciated in value over the term of the swap, the swap provider receives the net amount of the depreciation from the equity amount payer under the synthetic short TRS, either:

- through the periodic equity appreciation/depreciation payments made during the life of the swap; or
- as the final exchange amount/total return payment made on the swap's expiration date.

The swap provider is therefore hedged against any losses that it has incurred on its repurchase of the underlying/hedge shares. (This amount would equal any shortfall between the share repurchase price paid by the swap provider on the swap's expiration date and the swap's notional amount held in the deposit account for the life of the swap.)

7.2   FATCA: implications for equity swaps

(a)   *Introduction to FATCA*

The US Foreign Account Tax Compliance Act (FATCA), enacted in 2010, imposes a system of information reporting, requiring foreign (non-US) financial institutions (FFIs) and certain non-financial foreign entities (NFFEs) to disclose the identity of their US account holders and provide certain information on those accounts. FATCA also imposes a 30% withholding tax on 'withholdable' payments made by US persons and others to FFIs and NFFEs that do not meet the information reporting requirements.

Therefore, FATCA affects foreign payees, including foreign banks, securities dealers, investment funds (including private equity and hedge funds), securitisation vehicles and private investment vehicles that receive payments from US payers.

Withholdable payments potentially subject to the 30% FATCA withholding tax include, but are not limited to, US-source dividends and the gross proceeds from the sale of any property of a type that can produce US-source interest or dividends (including payments made under certain equity swaps over US shares).

FATCA withholding generally applies to:

- payments of US-source dividends, interest, rents, royalties and compensation made on or after 1 July 2014 to a FATCA non-compliant FFI or NFFE; and
- payments of gross proceeds from the sale or other disposition of any property of a type that can produce US-source interest or dividends (including certain equity swaps over US shares) made on or after 1 January 2019 to a FATCA non-compliant FFI or NFFE.

(b)   ***Dividend equivalent payments***

FATCA has potentially cumbersome implications for equity swaps because it also changes the US income sourcing rules for 'dividend equivalent' payments made to a foreign recipient under certain equity swaps. Before FATCA, dividend equivalent payments made to a foreign recipient under an equity swap typically were not subject to the general 30% US withholding tax, because these payments were treated as foreign-source payments. Under FATCA, dividend equivalent payments made on or after 14 September 2010 to a foreign recipient under an equity swap are treated as US-source income subject to the general 30% US withholding tax if both:

- the payment is contingent on, or determined by reference to, the payment of a dividend from US sources (eg, a dividend on US shares); and
- the equity swap is a 'specified notional principal contract'.

Therefore, dividend equivalent payments made to a foreign recipient under equity swaps are now potentially subject to the general 30% US withholding tax and the 30% FATCA withholding tax (subject to the FATCA grandfathering rule discussed below). However, any amounts withheld under FATCA can generally be credited against the general US withholding tax.

Under US statutory transition rules and final US Treasury regulations, the new US income sourcing rules for dividend equivalent payments made between 14 September 2010 and 31 December 2016 apply only if the US Treasury identifies the equity swap as a 'specified notional principal contract' or if the equity swap has one or more of the following features:

- The long party (the party entitled to receive the dividend equivalent payments) transfers the underlying shares to the short party (the party obligated to pay the dividend equivalent amounts) in connection with entering into the equity swap (referred to as 'crossing in').
- The short party transfers the underlying shares to the long party in connection with the termination of the equity swap (referred to as 'crossing out').
- The underlying shares are not readily tradable on an established securities market.
- The underlying shares are posted as collateral by the short party with the long party in connection with entering into the equity swap.

Under final US Treasury regulations (generally effective for payments made on equity swaps issued on or after 1 January 2017), any payment to a foreign recipient under an equity swap that references dividends on US shares will generally be treated as a dividend equivalent payment subject to the general 30% US withholding tax and the 30% FATCA withholding tax (subject to the grandfathering rule discussed below) if the equity swap has a delta of 0.80 or greater with respect to the underlying US shares at the time that the equity swap is issued. 'Delta' is the ratio of the change in the fair market value of the equity swap to the change in the fair market value of the underlying US shares.

(c) FATCA grandfathering

Under a special grandfathering rule, equity swaps outstanding on the date that is six months after the date on which equity swaps of that type first become subject to the US-sourcing rules for dividend equivalent payments are not subject to the 30% FATCA withholding tax on US-source dividends or gross proceeds. However, dividend equivalent payments made under these equity swaps may still be subject to the general 30% US withholding tax.

(d) Impact on ISDA master agreements

Parties negotiating new cross-border equity swaps (eg, under an ISDA (International Swaps and Derivatives Association Inc) Master Agreement) may want to:

- carve out from the definition of 'indemnifiable tax' (taxes for which the payer must gross up the payee) the US withholding tax on dividend equivalent payments;
- require any foreign long party to represent that it has not crossed into, and will not cross out of, the transaction;
- provide a termination right if payments under the equity swap become subject to a tax on dividend equivalent payments; and
- require any foreign party to represent that, as of the time any withholdable payment is made, it meets the FATCA information reporting requirements.

ISDA 2015 Section 871(m) Protocol: ISDA has published a protocol (2015 Section 871(m) Protocol) that is designed to facilitate amendment of existing ISDA master agreements, among other things, to carve out from the definition of 'indemnifiable tax' (taxes for which the payer must gross up the payee) the US withholding tax on dividend equivalent payments.

ISDA 2012 FACTA Protocol: ISDA published a similar protocol in August 2012 to address the effects of FATCA withholding tax on payments under derivatives transactions. The FATCA protocol:

- carves out the FATCA withholding tax from the payer tax representations that parties to the ISDA Master Agreement must make under Section 3(e) of the agreement; and
- places the burden of the FATCA withholding tax on the recipient of payments by carving out the FATCA withholding tax from the definition of 'indemnifiable tax' in the ISDA Master Agreement.

(e)   *US/UK Model I IGA*

A UK FFI can meet its FATCA obligations, without having to enter into an agreement with the US Internal Revenue Service (IRS), by reporting relevant information to Her Majesty's Revenue and Customs (HMRC, the UK treasury). This alternative method of compliance became possible because, on 12 September 2012, the governments of the United Kingdom and the United States signed an intergovernmental agreement (Model I IGA) to improve international tax compliance and implement FATCA. The Model I IGA sets out a framework for information exchange, which is based on the use of existing bilateral tax treaties for information exchange between tax authorities, rather than direct reporting by FFIs to the IRS. The agreement addresses current legal impediments to compliance. It ensures that compliant UK financial institutions will be treated as deemed-compliant FFIs under FATCA and will not be required to withhold tax on withholdable payments that they make or have FATCA withholding tax imposed on income that they receive.

The International Tax Compliance (United States of America) Regulations 2013 (SI 2013/1962) were issued on 6 August 2013 to implement the UK/US Model I IGA and came into force on 1 September 2013 in the United Kingdom. The 2013 regulations reflected the IRS's extension and delay to the FATCA timelines, including by treating the Model I IGA as if it had been amended. HMRC's latest guidelines were also updated to reflect the six-month postponement of the commencement of FATCA to 30 June 2013. Since the 2013 regulations were made, however, the United States has entered into FATCA agreements with other countries on more favourable terms than the Model I IGA with the United Kingdom, triggering that agreement's 'most favoured nation' provision. Accordingly, a revised set of regulations, the International Tax Compliance (United States of America) Regulations 2014 (SI 2014/1506), were issued on 9 June 2014 to replace the 2013 regulations. The 2014 regulations came into force on 30 June 2014 and are designed to reflect, from a UK perspective, the revised timelines and most favoured nation changes.

Note that UK FFIs (regardless of the UK government's signing of the Model I IGA) are still required to register with the IRS, as deemed-compliant FFIs, to avoid FATCA withholding.

8.   Structured products

Even experts often struggle to define what types of transaction are encompassed by the term 'structured products'. They are usually multi-layered products that typically consist of:

*   a debt security, such as a bond or a note; and
*   an 'embedded' equity derivative, such as an equity option.

These two products are 'wrapped' into a single instrument. Structured products are often traded on an exchange, though some are traded OTC.

The debt security that is used in structured products is called a 'wrapper'. The wrapper may be a certificate, note, bond, warrant or other debt security. The specific form that a wrapper takes will depend on investor preference, relative market liquidities, and tax and regulatory matters. However, rather than including a traditional interest coupon as part of the debt security, in a structured product the investor receives a contingent equity interest, such as a call option, on certain specified shares. The contingent equity interest replaces the interest component of the debt instrument.

8.1   Equity-linked notes

One of the most common types of structured product is an equity-linked note (ELN), such as a convertible or exchangeable bond. Convertible and exchangeable bonds allow the holder to convert the bond into shares if the price of the issuer's shares reaches a specified level (the strike price) on the option's exercise date. Convertible bonds permit the holder to exchange the bond for a newly issued security of the same issuer. Exchangeable bonds permit the holder to exchange the bond for existing securities of a third-party issuer.

A typical, standard principal-protected ELN works as follows:

- The investor purchases the ELN at its par value (which is equal to the face and redemption value of the note). However, though the purchase price of the ELN equals its par value, this price does include a discounted note purchase price plus a premium payment – the so-called 'notional discount amount' – which, together, equal the note's par value. It is assumed, as is common, that this note is principal protected – that is, the investor will at least be repaid its principal at the conclusion of the transaction, because it will receive the note's full redemption value at that time, subject to the creditworthiness of the seller.
- On maturity of the note, which is also the exercise date of the underlying option, the investor receives no interest payment, but rather receives a cash-settled call option on certain pre-agreed shares. If the market price of the underlying shares that are subject to the option exceeds the option's pre-agreed per-share strike price, the option is exercised and the investor receives a payment equal to the difference between the strike price and the market price, multiplied by the number of shares specified in the option documentation. This amount is the value of the equity call option.

The investor in a simple ELN with this structure is in the same position as if it held both:

- a zero-coupon note of the same value and maturity as that included in the ELN; and
- a cash-settled call option on the same terms and for the same shares as the embedded call option.

In the example illustrated above, the wrapper contained in the ELN has an original issue price of £930 and a redemption value of £1,000. The extra £70 paid by the investor is the notional discount amount. Most of this amount is used by the issuer to purchase the call option that is included in the ELN. The remainder of this amount is retained by the issuer as profit.

In this example, the embedded call option is for 100 shares of XYZ plc at a strike price of £10 per share. If the value of an XYZ plc share has risen above £10 on the

Figure 4. Mechanics of a two-year principal-protected ELN with embedded call option

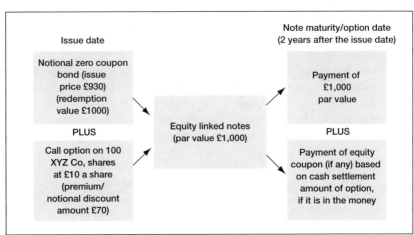

note maturity/option exercise date, the embedded call option is in-the-money. If the final value of the XYZ plc shares on the valuation date is, for example, £12 per share, the call option would be worth £200 (£12–£10 = £2 × 100 shares = £200). This is because the embedded call option is cash settled. Consequently, the holder of the ELN would receive a 20% equity coupon at maturity and, therefore, a total final repayment of £1,200, which includes the £1,000 redemption value/principal return, subject to the issuer's creditworthiness.

If the value of an XYZ share has fallen below £10 on the exercise date, the embedded call option would be out-of-the-money and would not be exercised by the investor. If the option is out-of-the-money on the exercise date, the investor would still receive back its initial investment of £1,000, representing the zero-coupon element of the transaction (assuming that the ELN is 100% principal protected). In economic terms, this would represent an opportunity cost for the investor, as it receives no return on its investment. If the original investment amount had been used to acquire a low yield but safe investment (eg, a government bond), the investor would have received at least a marginally higher return. For example, an investment of £1,000 in a debt security paying compound interest of 3% per year during the same period would have resulted in a final payment of £1,060.90.

The characteristics of the shares (issuer, number of shares) on which the option is purchased are determined by the transaction's manager or arranger, and are often based on investor preference. Many structured products are specifically tailored to offer an investor the potential (upside) exposure to the shares of a particular issuer, or to certain markets via a basket of shares, an index or basket of indices. Once this is determined, the number of shares that will be the subject of the option will be equal to the maximum number of the selected shares on which a cash-settled call option can be purchased, with that portion of the premium/notional discount amount paid by the investor that is not retained as profit by the issuer.

If a variety of shares or indices are included in the basket on which the option is held, the relative number may be determined by a formula or based on investor preference. The composition of the shares that are subject to the option may also change over time before the maturity date of the ELN, based on certain risk-weighting, algorithmic or other factors.

The potential upside of an ELN like the one described in this example is unlimited, unless a cap is built into the product. If the underlying security, index or basket performs well, it will result in a valuable coupon. Downside risk is often limited by the insertion of full (as in the above example) or partial principal protection so that the noteholder should, subject to the creditworthiness of the issuer, receive the return of all or a specified proportion of its original investment if it holds the ELN until maturity.

This is a very simple example of an ELN. Numerous variables can be built into ELNs. This might include the occurrence of exercise and payment dates throughout the life of the transaction, the final return being capped or a guaranteed rate of return being built in. A 'participation rate' can also be built in. This is the rate at which the investor participates in the appreciation of the underlying security, index or basket. Therefore, if the value of the option on the exercise date is 20% above the strike price (as in the above example) and the participation rate is 50%, the investor receives an equity-linked coupon worth 10% of the option's strike price. All of these features have an effect on the pricing of an ELN.

In practice, the issuer may hedge its contingent obligation to pay the equity coupon by entering into a back-to-back call option on exactly the same terms as the call option included in the ELN.

So-called 'CoCo' (contingent convertible) bonds are one example of an ELN. These are typically held institutionally and issued by banks for regulatory-capital compliance purposes.

8.2   Fund-linked notes

Another form of equity derivative structured product relates to fund investments. The structure of these products is similar to the ELN example discussed above. The primary difference is that with fund-linked notes (FLNs), the amount that represents the difference between the note purchase price and the initial investment/note redemption value (the notional discount amount) is invested in units of a fund (or, in certain cases, multiple funds) instead of an equity option.

The issuer typically hedges its obligations under the FLN by the direct holding of the fund shares or units into which the wrapper debt security is convertible. As an alternative to this, the issuer could also enter into call options for the fund assets, if available.

(a)   Example of an FLN

The diagram above shows a straightforward principal-protected FLN. The mechanics of a basic FLN work as follows:

- The note is sold to the purchaser on the issue date.
- The proceeds from the sale of the FLN are invested by the issuer in both:

Figure 5. Mechanics of a two-year principal-protected FLN

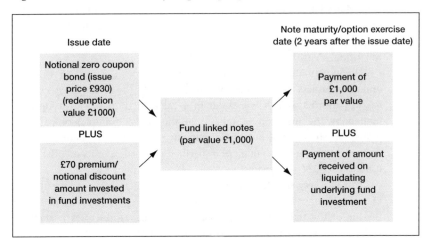

- • a zero-coupon note priced to redeem at the par value of the FLN (in this example, £1,000); and
- • a fund investment or portfolio of fund investments in the amount of the notional discount amount (in this example, £70), less any profit retained by the issuer.
- • On maturity, the investor receives:
  - • the return of its initial investment, the par value of the FLN, which will be paid from the redemption proceeds of the zero-coupon note (in this example, £1,000); and
  - • the value of the fund investments on the maturity date.

This structure enables investors to obtain the benefit of any growth in the value of the fund investment, together with its original investment, subject to the issuer's creditworthiness. However, the likelihood of the investor receiving a significant return on its original investment is limited. This is because the vast majority of the note sale proceeds will need to be invested in the zero-coupon element of the structure to fund the principal protection. With a view to seeking to enhance potential returns, structures involving a more dynamic management of the assets underlying the security have been devised. These structures include so-called 'constant proportion portfolio insurance' (CPPI) structures. CPPI structures are beyond the scope of this chapter.

(b) *Advantages of FLNs*

Fund-linked products provide a number of potential advantages for investors. An investor may face legal, regulatory, tax or practical difficulties in making a direct investment in an underlying fund. Certain investors (particularly pension funds and insurance companies) may be prohibited or restricted from investing directly in funds. Certain funds (including some hedge funds) include limitations on the type or size of eligible investor. Further, a direct investment in the fund may require a significant outlay of capital, as a high minimum investment is often required. It may, however, be permissible for these investors to obtain indirect exposure to the fund by investing in a structured product issued by another entity, particularly where full or partial principal protection is built into the product.

9.   OTC and exchange-traded equity derivatives

Some equity derivatives are entered into OTC, while others are traded on an exchange.

An OTC financial instrument is a bilateral contract usually sold to a customer by a financial institution such as a bank or broker-dealer, often referred to as the 'swap provider'. The contract is tailored to the specific requirements of the customer. The buyer and seller of an OTC derivative typically take on each other's credit risk by entering into the contract, unless the contract is fully funded. The principal advantage of an OTC derivatives contract is the degree of flexibility that the parties have in specifying terms.

Exchange-traded instruments are bought and sold directly on an organised, registered exchange. An exchange-traded derivative has a standard set of terms that apply to each type of contract, detailing the obligations of each party. Each exchange uses a standard form for each type of transaction. The principal advantage of an exchange-traded derivative is that counterparty performance (payment) is guaranteed through a related clearing house, minimising counterparty credit risk. The primary limitation of exchange-traded derivatives is the lack of flexibility of contract terms.

The principal exchange-traded equity derivative products are futures and options. In the light of global regulatory initiatives designed to attempt to minimise systemic risk in the global financial industry, many types of equity swap are increasingly becoming more standardised and traded on exchanges. Equity forwards, certain complex, non-standardised options and equity swaps are entered into OTC.

Equity forwards and futures are both contracts to purchase specified equities on a specific future date at a specific price. The principal difference is that futures are standardised and exchange traded, and forwards are generally entered into OTC between two parties so that terms may be specially tailored to the needs of the counterparty (this cannot be done with a futures contract).

Most structured products such as convertible or exchangeable notes, bonds or warrants are traded on exchanges. More complex, specially tailored structured products are entered into OTC.

Documenting OTC equity derivatives

The principal documentation of OTC derivatives is provided by ISDA.

ISDA's suite of documents for equity derivatives consists of:

- framework documents applicable to all derivatives areas covered by ISDA (including interest rate swaps, currency swaps and credit derivatives such as CDS). These documents include:

- the ISDA Master Agreement;
- the ISDA Schedule;
- the transaction confirmation (the confirmation is the document that contains the deal-specific commercial terms of a derivatives transaction); and
- the ISDA Credit Support Annex.

The ISDA Master Agreement, Schedule and Credit Support Annex are umbrella documents that contain general terms. These terms often apply to multiple derivatives transactions entered into between two parties.

- the 2002 ISDA Equity Derivatives Definitions, which are designed to be used in connection with confirmations relating primarily to option transactions, forward transactions and equity swaps governed by an ISDA Master Agreement already entered into by the parties. The 2002 definitions provide a framework of market-standard terminology and contingencies for when:
  - prices cannot be obtained;
  - trading days for exchange operation or the processing of calculations are disrupted; or
  - underlying shares are nationalised or merged.
- individual template confirmations prepared by ISDA. These are designed to work in conjunction with the ISDA Master Agreement, the ISDA Schedule and the 2002 definitions.

The 2002 definitions are analysed in depth in the next chapter of this book.

10. Collateralising equity derivatives

Most of the parties to OTC equity derivatives transactions are major dealers and funds. The swap documentation between such parties almost always consists of an ISDA Master Agreement, which will typically be supplemented by an ISDA Credit Support Annex. The credit support annex governs margin collateral matters relating to the transactions entered into under the corresponding ISDA Master Agreement.

Under the applicable credit support annex in place between the parties, each party will typically be fully collateralised against its exposure to its counterparty under the equity derivatives transactions entered into under the relevant ISDA Master Agreement. Therefore, the question of whether an equity derivative transaction is funded or unfunded is not applicable in most cases, as it is in many other types of derivative transaction.

As noted above, standardised equity derivatives transactions, such as most equity options and futures, are prepaid contracts purchased on an exchange and cleared through a clearing house. Margin collateral posting for these contracts is governed by clearing house margin rules.

11. Why use equity derivatives?

The principal purposes for which equity derivatives are used include:

- monetising shareholdings;
- enhancing corporate finance and investment strategies;
- facilitating M&A transactions;
- reducing transaction costs;
- hedging and mitigating risk; and
- providing leverage.

11.1 Monetising shareholdings

For a variety of reasons, a shareholder may need to retain ownership of certain shares, but at the same time may be looking to lock in or realise the current value of those shares. A common strategy for achieving these goals through the use of equity derivatives is to enter into a TRS for the shares, which transfers the economic exposure of that asset to a counterparty for a specified term, on a specific date in return for the cash value of those shares. This strategy allows the shareholder to:

- monetise its holdings (ie, obtain the monetary value of its shares on a specific date while retaining the actual shares);
- potentially avoid realisation of a taxable gain on the sale of the shares;
- retain voting rights under the shares (if the total return swap is so structured);
- avoid any restrictions placed on disposition of shares (eg, the shares may be held in trust); and
- dispose of large blocks of shares without distorting market prices.

11.2 Enhancing corporate finance and investment strategies

Companies sometimes use equity derivatives as part of their corporate finance strategies through the issuance of convertible or exchangeable bonds such as ELNs. These transactions allow the issuer to issue debt that pays a lower rate of interest than might otherwise accompany a comparable bond, because the holder instead looks to a greater potential return on the underlying shares.

Equity derivatives can also allow users to pursue certain investment strategies that permit them to take a view as to the relative performance of indices or individual shares or sectors within a basket. They can also provide exposure to certain markets and funds to which they otherwise may not be able to gain access.

11.3 Facilitating M&A transactions

Equity derivatives are frequently used in M&A transactions to build up a stake in the target company (so-called 'stake-building'). This is frequently done through the use of:

- call options;
- CFDs;
- forward transactions; and
- equity swaps.

Call options can give an acquiring company certainty that it will be able to secure the shares of the target company at a certain price (the strike price), if at all. The option allows an acquirer to walk away from the acquisition at a much lower cost if it decides that it does not wish to proceed because, with an option, share-purchase transaction costs and sale losses can be avoided if the deal falls through. Options typically require a relatively lower cash outlay to purchase them than would be required for a purchase of the underlying shares.

The use of options also allows the acquirer to build up a large potential stake in a company without attracting attention that would cause the share price of the target company to rise (known as 'hidden ownership').

Over the years, the cash-settled equity derivatives market has seen a rise in the concealment of economic ownership of shares through the use of hidden ownership techniques. This attracted the attention of policy makers and, in October 2011, the European Commission published proposals for a directive to amend the Transparency Directive (2004/109/EC) with a view to enhancing the disclosure requirements for cash-settled derivatives, which offer the economic equivalent of holding a long position in shares (synthetic long positions).

The concern is that the holder of a cash-settled derivative can have an economic exposure to shares underlying the derivative and will be directly affected by their performance, even without having any direct voting rights to those shares. The new measures, which were adopted by the European Parliament in June 2013, require holdings in synthetic long positions to be subject to the same disclosure requirements that apply to major shareholdings (positions equal to or greater than 5% of an issuer's total voting rights must be disclosed).

Directive 2013/50/EU amending the Transparency Directive came into force on 26 November 2013. The date of 26 November 2015 was laid down as being the deadline by which EU member states were to have transposed the new measures into national law (although similar rules have been in place in the United Kingdom since December 2009).

A synthetic long position provides the potential bidder with economic exposure to the shares of the target during the period leading up to the bid, and gives the bidder (if it elects physical settlement) the right to purchase the number of target shares specified in the confirmation at the initial price under the swap at the end of its term (or earlier, if the bidder so chooses). The bidder may want exposure to the target shares during the period leading up to the bid so it is hedged if the bid process drives up the share price. The swap is therefore a valuable instrument to the bidder, looking to acquire a sufficient number of shares in the target to complete its acquisition.

When entering into the swap, a number of key terms will be negotiated between the bidder and the swap provider. Key terms address how the price of the shares is set for the purpose of the swap at the outset (the initial price) and at conclusion of the transaction (the final price). In a stake-building transaction, it is likely that at least one if not both of these amounts will be determined on a more complex basis than simply a daily average share price.

11.4   Reducing transactions costs

There are costs involved in both purchasing and selling shares and, particularly where transactions involve only short-term holdings, these costs can be high. In most jurisdictions, stamp duty is payable on the sale of equity shares. Where a broker is used, that broker will also charge a fee. In addition, investing in foreign equity markets can create exposure to foreign exchange risks, as shares may be denominated in a foreign currency.

Equity derivatives can reduce these costs. Stamp duty is not levied on equity derivatives and foreign exchange risk is minimised because no currency exchange is necessary to enter into an equity derivative contract such as a TRS that provides exposure to foreign equities markets. Further, exposure can be provided to shares for limited periods of time, minimising purchase and sale costs.

11.5 Hedging and risk mitigation

Equity derivatives can provide protection against volatility and adverse price movement in a number of ways. One of the most common occurs when companies use equity derivatives to hedge against volatility in the price of their own shares. This is usually done using put or call options, or forwards. Equity forward contracts provide certainty regarding the future purchase or sale price of equity assets, and options provide caps or floors on the per-share price an issuer has to pay for its shares.

For example, a company may have a stock option plan as part of its executive remuneration structure. The executives are likely to exercise their options when the company's share price is at its perceived highest. A company may enter into call options that allow it to purchase its own shares at a fixed price on certain dates to hedge against having to purchase those shares at a higher price to fulfil its obligations when the options are exercised. The option in this case functions as a cap on the issuer's cost of acquiring its own shares. In the alternative, a company may enter into a forward transaction that requires it to purchase its own shares on a specific future date at an agreed price.

The company may also enter into a share buyback arrangement in which it pays a financial institution to sell it shares at an average price determined based on per-share price movement over a specified period. A company may wish to buy back its own shares for the purpose of:

- obtaining shares for delivery under an employee stock option plan;
- increasing its earnings per share (same earnings spread over fewer shares);
- adjusting its leverage ratio; and/or
- benefiting shareholders.

Equity derivatives can also be used to hedge against volatility in the securities of other entities, as well as in indices or baskets of securities or indices, which may be held by:

- banks:
  - for regulatory purposes; or
  - in the course of their securities-lending activities; or
- businesses:
  - for supply, factoring and other commercial purposes; or
  - in the course of their securities-lending activities.

11.6 Providing leverage

Equity derivatives can provide leverage that enhances returns. The derivative permits the holder to take a position on a security, index or basket that it may not own, providing the investor with the opportunity for leveraged returns. In the context of equity markets, going 'long' means buying shares and holding them in the expectation that their value will rise. Going 'short', however, involves agreeing to sell a certain number of shares on an agreed future date at a specified price (usually the current market price) in the hope that the share price falls.

Though long transactions can, of course, be leveraged, short transactions are inherently leveraged because, unlike long positions, they allow a potential return without any initial investment other than the premium required to enter into the transaction, which is a fractional amount of the cost of purchasing the actual shares.

Equity derivatives can be used to leverage a short sale of an equity security using a forward contract or put option, under which the investor agrees to sell a fixed number of shares (or a number of shares determined by a formula) to its counterparty on an agreed future date in the hope that the share price falls. This may also be done using baskets or indices.

Going short may also involve securities lending – that is, borrowing or purchasing shares from a shareholder, often a financial institution, for a premium, and agreeing to return or sell back the shares (or equivalent shares, which is permitted under most securities lending agreements) later at the same price. This strategy is based on the anticipation that the share price will fall in an amount greater than the fees paid. This purchase-and-sale arrangement is known as a 'repurchase agreement' or 'repo', and a securities repo or securities loan is often used as part of a short transaction. This strategy may provide the opportunity for returns from:

- derivative instruments that create a right to dispose of a security on a future date if certain conditions are met, making it possible to enter into the investment without the necessity of share ownership; and
- negative share performance, as well as positive.

Stock lenders and repo counterparties are able to earn a premium on the underlying shares they sell (under a repo) or lend (under a securities-lending agreement). Major financial institutions often simply borrow the securities to be loaned or sold themselves at a lower premium than they are receiving from their borrower, or they may enter into a forward contract themselves for the shares that they are lending at a lower premium than they are receiving from their borrower.

Overview of the 2002 ISDA Equity Derivatives Definitions

Edmund Parker
Marcin Perzanowski
Mayer Brown

1. The 2002 definitions: the classic

The International Swaps and Derivatives Association Inc (ISDA) released new, all singing, all dancing equity derivatives definitions in July 2011. Why then include in this book in-depth coverage of the 2002 ISDA Equity Derivatives Definitions?

The 2011 definitions were indeed intended to displace the 2002 definitions. However, due to their complexity, the 2011 definitions have not been widely adopted and the market participants continue to use the older version of the document, which therefore remains ISDA's flagship document for market standard documentation platform and framework for over-the-counter (OTC) equity derivative transactions. Even though ISDA continues to publish supporting documentation for the 2011 definitions, the actual trades are few and far between.

This is a shame. The authors are conscious of the enormous efforts put into this project back in 2010 and 2011 by the ISDA working group, which produced a truly impressive document that is over 320 pages long. The main body of the 2011 definitions is then complemented by an appendix, the fourth version of which runs into more than 140 pages. The documentation was supposed to bring a very high level of standardisation to all equity derivatives transactions, but the sheer ambition of the project planted the seeds of its potential failure.

The much more compact 2002 definitions (which are merely 71 pages long, and have no appendix) continue as the equity derivatives definitions of choice for most types of equity derivatives transaction. Does this means that the 2011 definitions will remain a rather large footnote in the history of ambitious, but ultimately unsuccessful documentation projects? We hope not, but we have not yet seen much evidence to the contrary.

This is also the reason why this book provides an in-depth analysis of the still popular 2002 definitions.

The terms defined in the 2002 ISDA Equity Derivatives Definitions are denoted by the use of single quotation marks when defined or used for the first time in this chapter. Thereafter, those terms are spelled without using any capital letters or punctuation marks, unless they appear in direct excerpts from the definitions.

1.1 History of the definitions

The 2002 definitions were the third iteration of equity derivatives definitions released by ISDA. The inaugural definitions were released as the 1994 ISDA Equity

Option Definitions, just 16 pages long, which were followed by the 1996 ISDA Equity Derivatives Definitions – an easily digestible 32 pages.

The 2002 definitions were developed to cover a range of equity derivative products and underlying equity assets, as well as to reflect the developing market practices in the global derivatives industry.

Greater in length, complexity and in the range of products covered, the 2002 definitions have a general structure that reflects market practices and substantially follows the format of their 1996 predecessor.

The 2002 definitions are designed to be used with three types of OTC equity derivative transaction: the option, the forward and the swap. No standard documentation exists for equity derivatives structured products – for example, warrants or certificates – the return on which is based on an underlying equity asset, such as a share or an index.

It is standard in these structured transactions to adapt the 2002 definitions so that the relevant fall-backs, definitions and contractual framework operate almost identically, except with the relationship of the parties adjusted to an issuer/security holder relationship, instead of a bilateral counterparty arrangement.

1.2 How do the 2002 definitions fit into the ISDA infrastructure?

ISDA has produced a documentation infrastructure for documenting OTC derivatives transactions. At the centre of this is the ISDA Master Agreement.

From time to time, ISDA has produced definitional booklets for the different asset classes of derivatives – for example:

- interest rate derivatives use the 2006 ISDA Definitions;
- currency derivatives utilise the 1998 FX and Currency Option Definitions;
- the world of credit derivatives uses the 2003 Credit Derivatives Definitions; and
- the commodity derivatives sphere utilises the 2005 ISDA Commodity Definitions.

Definitional booklets have three roles. First, they provide a contractual framework – that is, provisions for when a derivatives agreement starts, when it ends and what happens during its term. Second, they provide standardised definitions – for example, for 'business days' and 'payment periods' – to save the parties negotiating these on a bespoke basis. Third, they provide fall-backs, which essentially address the following questions:

- What happens when it all goes wrong?
- What happens if an underlying share is delisted?
- What happens if the exchange on which an underlying share is listed closes early?
- What happens if an index referenced in a transaction is no longer compiled?

Definitions are brought to life through incorporation by reference in an OTC 'confirmation'. That confirmation will also incorporate the parties' ISDA Master Agreement, as amended by a schedule and possibly a credit support annex. In addition to setting out the pricing information for the transaction, the confirmation will select various elections from the 2002 definitions to craft the transaction's terms, definitions and fall-backs, with the efficiency of the 2002 definitions providing market certainty and allowing complex OTC equity derivatives products to be documented in just a few pages.

1.3 Secondary rationale for the 2002 definitions: 'sell side' v 'buy side'
The primary rationale of the 2002 definitions is to provide a contractual framework, standardised contract terms and fall-backs. There is a secondary rationale integral to understanding the 2002 definitions: hedging.

The dominant influence in drafting the 2002 definitions was market-making banks, which are known in the market as the 'sell side'. The sell side makes its money by entering into an equity derivatives transaction with one client for an agreed price and then simultaneously entering into an opposite transaction either with another client, or by purchasing or selling an opposite position – for instance, buying a share or trading a future or an option.

The differential between these two prices represents the sell side's profit. The sell side's corresponding position is called its 'hedge', and the greatest risk to its potential profit or loss is a mismatch between the two positions. This can occur if the hedging transaction is disrupted in any way – for example, if its cost increases substantially or the bank is prevented from holding the hedging position by legal or regulatory requirements, or if valuation of the hedging trade becomes difficult or impossible.

Much of the 2002 definitions is taken up with eliminating as far as possible this hedging risk from the point of view of the sell side, and providing maximum discretion and subjective flexibility to do so.

The sell side would argue that this is justified because it is not taking a speculative risk, but rather using its position to create a market in equity derivatives, and offer this service to its clients.

Since the 2002 definitions were introduced, the 'buy side' – made up of increasingly strong hedge funds and asset managers – has become more sophisticated and has gained strong bargaining powers in an increasingly competitive field. The buy side was less content to allow all the subjective decisions regarding underlying equity assets and early termination of transactions to be made by the sell side.

After 2002, ISDA produced a series of master confirmation agreements, which are intended to allow the parties to enter into a large volume of trades on standardised terms. The master confirmation agreements, which were specific to regions and transaction types, were heavily influenced by the buy side and, on the whole, are more objective than the 2002 definitions.

1.4 Overview of the 2002 definitions
The definitions are 59 pages long and divided into a table of contents, an introduction and preamble, and 13 articles, which are each then sub-divided.

Table of contents of the 2002 definitions

Overview of the 2002 ISDA Equity Derivatives Definitions

Article 13 – Miscellaneous
13.1. Non-Reliance
13.2. Agreements and
    Acknowledgments Regarding
    Hedging Activities

13.3. Index Disclaimer
13.4. Additional Acknowledgments

2. Introduction and preamble

The 13 articles are preceded by both an introduction and a preamble. The introduction states that the definitions are intended for use in "confirmations of individual equity derivatives transactions" which are governed either by the 1992 ISDA Master Agreement or the 2002 ISDA Master Agreement. It continues that:

- the 2002 definitions can provide the basic framework for documenting privately negotiated equity derivatives transactions;
- they have fall-back provisions which will apply where the parties do not provide otherwise in a transaction; and
- market participants may adapt or supplement them as they wish.

There is also a brief overview of the new features, highlighting the major developments as compared with the 1996 version.

Apart from a lengthy liability disclaimer absolving ISDA from any guilt should market participants misuse the definitions, there is a reminder that the 2002 definitions will not automatically apply to transactions which incorporated the 1996 definitions. The introduction also sets out that the 2002 definitions are free standing and, therefore "for most equity derivatives transactions, there is no need to incorporate any other ISDA definitions booklets into the Confirmation of an equity derivative transaction".

Many equity derivatives transactions will contain a funding leg – that is, one party will pay an interest rate or funding amount to the other, perhaps in exchange for a total return payment on a share or index. The 2002 definitions, though, do not incorporate the corresponding interest rate definitional booklet. Therefore, for any equity derivatives transactions which have a funded element, the parties need to incorporate by reference into the confirmation the ISDA 2006 Definitions.

The 2006 definitions will most commonly be incorporated into:

- 'equity swap transactions', where one leg of the 'transaction' involves payments of 'floating amounts' linked to interest rates or currency exchange rates; and
- 'option transactions', in respect of the stock loan rate.

The introduction does not form part of the 2002 definitions. The preamble does. It states that the definitions and provisions in the 2002 definitions may be incorporated into a document by inserting wording that "the document is subject to the 2002 ISDA Equity Derivatives Definitions (as published by the International Swaps and Derivatives Associations, Inc.)". The preamble goes on to provide that all terms, definitions and provisions incorporated into a document will be applicable unless otherwise modified.

3.   Article 1 – "Certain general definitions"

Article 1 sub-sections

1.1 Transaction	1.27. Clearance System
1.2. Option Transaction	1.28. Index Sponsor
1.3. Forward Transaction	1.29. Exchange Business Day
1.4. Equity Swap Transaction	1.30. Scheduled Closing Time
1.5. Index Transaction	1.31. Scheduled Trading Day
1.6. Share Transaction	1.32. Currency Business Day
1.7. Index Basket Transaction	1.33. Settlement Currency
1.8. Share Basket Transaction	1.34. Euro
1.9. Basket Option Transaction	1.35. EC Treaty
1.10. Basket Forward Transaction	1.36. Clearance System Business Day
1.11. Basket Swap Transaction	1.37. Settlement Cycle
1.12. Confirmation	1.38. Cash-settled
1.13. Index	1.39. Physically-settled
1.14. Shares	1.40. Calculation Agent
1.15. Basket	1.41. ISDA Master Agreement
1.16. Issuer	1.42. Knock-in Price
1.17. Trade Date	1.43. Knock-out Price
1.18. Buyer	1.44. Knock-in Event
1.19. Seller	1.45. Knock-out Event
1.20. Number of Shares	1.46. Knock-in Reference Security
1.21. Number of Baskets	1.47. Knock-out Reference Security
1.22. Multiplier	1.48. Knock-in Determination Day
1.23. Relevant Price	1.49. Knock-out Determination Day
1.24. Equity Notional Amount	1.50. Knock-in Valuation Time
1.25. Exchange	1.51. Knock-out Valuation Time
1.26. Related Exchange	

At first sight, the 51 "certain general definitions" of Article 1 appear to be a hotchpotch of mechanical and boilerplate definitions to be utilised or adapted in all equity derivatives transactions. However, looking more closely, the Article 1 definitions cover the seven distinct areas set out in the diagram below.

Seven areas covered by Article 1		
Area 1: Definitions relating to transaction type/ financial instrument	**Area 2: Definitions relating to the underlying assets and transaction value**	**Area 3: Definitions relating to the timing of the Transaction**
1.1. Transaction	1.20. Number of Shares	1.17. Trade Date
1.2. Option Transaction	1.21. Number of Baskets	1.29. Exchange Business Day
1.3. Forward Transaction	1.22. Multiplier	1.30. Scheduled Closing Time
1.4. Equity Swap Transaction	1.23. Relevant Price	1.31. Scheduled Trading Day
1.5. Index Transaction	1.24. Equity Notional Amount	1.32. Currency Business Day
1.6. Share Transaction	1.13. Index	1.36. Clearance System Business Day
1.7. Index Basket Transaction	1.14. Shares	1.37. Settlement Cycle
1.8. Share Basket Transaction	1.15. Basket	
1.9. Basket Option Transaction	1.16. Issuer	**Area 6: Definitions relating to Settlement Type**
1.10. Basket Forward Transaction	1.25. Exchange	1.38. Cash-settled
1.11. Basket Swap Transaction	1.26. Related Exchange	1.39. Physically settled
1.12. Confirmation	1.27. Clearance System	
1.41. ISDA Master Agreement	1.28. Index Sponsor	
Area 4: Definitions relating to barrier transactions	**Area 5: Definitions relating to the identity of the parties**	
1.42. Knock-in Price	1.18. Buyer	
1.43. Knock-out Price	1.19. Seller	
1.44. Knock-in Event	1.40. Calculation Agent	
1.45. Knock-out Event		
1.46. Knock-in Reference Security	**Area 7: Curency definitions**	
1.47. Knock-out Reference Security	1.34. Euro	
1.48. Knock-in Determination Day	1.35. EC Treaty	
1.49. Knock-out Determination Day	1.33. Settlement Currency	
1.50. Knock-in Valuation Time		
1.51. Knock-out Valuation Time		

3.1 Area 1: definitions relating to the transaction type/financial instrument

Thirteen of the definitions in Article 1 relate to types of equity derivatives transaction/financial instrument. Article 1 defines the scope of financial instruments that the 2002 definitions cover in the definition of 'transaction': 'option transactions', 'forward transactions', 'equity swap transactions' or any other transaction which incorporates the 2002 definitions.

'Confirmation' is defined as document(s) in respect of a transaction confirming its terms. The definition of 'ISDA Master Agreement' provides that this means one of ISDA's standard form master agreements; it also incorporates by reference the definitions of 'event of default', 'affiliate' and 'early termination date' from the master agreement into the 2002 definitions.

Article 1 further defines 18 basic types of equity derivatives financial instrument, as listed below. ISDA has also published a separate 121-page document with sample confirmations for each of these.

List of the 18 types of basic equity derivatives transaction
1. 'Cash-settled index option transaction'
2. 'Cash-settled share option transaction'
3. 'Physically-settled share option transaction'
4. 'Cash-settled index basket option transaction'
5. 'Cash-settled share basket option transaction'
6. 'Physically-settled share basket option transaction'
7. 'Cash-settled index forward transaction'
8. 'Cash-settled share forward transaction'
9. 'Physically-settled share forward transaction'
10. 'Cash-settled index basket forward transaction'
11. 'Cash-settled share basket forward transaction'
12. 'Physically-settled share basket forward transaction'
13. 'Cash-settled index swap transaction'
14. 'Cash-settled share swap transaction'
15. 'Physically-settled share swap transaction'
16. 'Cash-settled index basket swap transaction'
17. 'Cash-settled share basket swap transaction'
18. 'Physically-settled share basket swap transaction'

These transaction types are also represented in the diagram below.

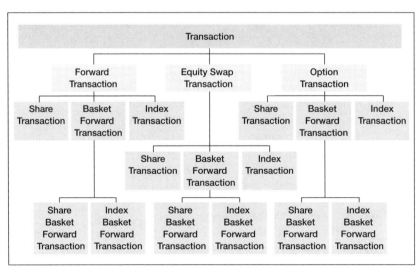

3.2   **Area 2: definitions relating to the underlying assets and the transaction value**

Article 1's definitions also relate to the type and quantity of underlying assets referenced by the equity derivatives financial instruments (defined and provided for in Area 1), where those underlying assets are traded, and the value which the financial instrument can derive from those underlying assets.

The 2002 definitions cover the following types of underlying equity asset: individual shares, baskets of shares, individual indices and baskets of indices. Article 1 provides standard definitions to cover these underlying assets with definitions for 'number of shares', 'number of baskets', 'index', 'shares', 'basket', 'issuer', 'exchange', 'clearance system', 'related exchange'and 'index sponsor', all relating to the underlying equity asset and where it is traded.

'Shares' are defined as the shares which are the underlying asset in a transaction and which are specified in the confirmation. This is a vanilla definition which does not include depository receipts, shares in exchange-traded funds and fund units. This was intentional given the sophistication of the broader equity derivatives market at the time of publication of the 2002 definitions. Later, ISDA published two Depository Receipts Supplements which can be incorporated into individual confirmations by reference for transactions that have depository receipts as their underlying asset; for transactions referencing fund units, ISDA's surprisingly rarely used 2006 ISDA Fund Definitions provide an alternative infrastructure. Significant work was also done on documentation infrastructure for exchange-traded fund assets, but this work was not completed.

We would advise parties referencing more exotic underlying equity assets to pay particular attention to changes which should be made to adapt the 2002 or 2011 definitions.

'Issuer' is defined as the company or entity which has issued those shares.

'Index' is defined as the index specified in the confirmation, as determined and announced by the index sponsor, which is referenced under a given transaction. The definition of 'index' is also simplistic. Where an index consists of component shares which are traded on multiple exchanges, such as the EURO STOXX 50, the parties should consider adding an annex to the relevant confirmation setting out the additional language suggested in the user's guide to the 2002 definitions. In summary, this language expands the scope of the disruption provisions to cover each exchange on which a component security is traded.

The parties also have an option to choose a group of shares or indices to underlie a transaction. Such 'groups' are referred to as 'baskets'. The 2002 definitions contain no provisions for adapting a transaction's pay-out according to the relative performance of the shares in the basket. For example, 'worst of' basket transactions base their return on the performance of the worst performing share in a basket, and 'best of' basket transactions base their return on the performance of the best performing share in a basket. These transactions are documented on a bespoke basis in confirmations by the parties. The 2011 definitions specifically provide for these types of transaction and much more complex structure, though.

The definition of 'number of shares' provides that in the case of a 'share option transaction' this is the number of shares obtained by multiplying the 'number of options' by the 'option entitlement' (each of which are defined in Article 2). In the case of a 'share forward transaction' or a 'share swap transaction', the definition provides that the number of shares is as specified in the relevant confirmation. The definition of 'number of baskets' also provides that this will be as specified in the individual confirmation.

The role of these simplistic, self-explanatory definitions is to provide a market-standard way of describing underlying assets in transactions.

In the case of indices, 'exchange' is defined as the exchange or quotation system provided for in the confirmation and any successor or exchange to which trading is temporarily relocated. A similar definition is provided for exchanges in relation to shares.

The definitions of 'exchange' and 'related exchange' are relevant to the several of the fall-back provisions set out elsewhere in the 2002 definitions, which relate to trading disruptions. They are particularly relevant where shares or indices trade on multiple exchanges, and/or there is a merger of stock exchanges.

The definition of 'clearance system' provides that this will be set out in the confirmation, and is relevant for facilitating settlement in physically settled transactions. If the clearance system is not so specified, it will be the principal clearance system customarily used for settling trades in the relevant shares.

Three of Article 1's definitions also relate to the value which the financial instrument can derive from the underlying assets. These are 'equity notional', 'multiplier' and 'relevant price'.

Equity notional amount is used only in relation to equity swap transactions and is the amount, as agreed by the parties and specified in the confirmation, relating to the shares which represents the parties' exposure under the transaction. This amount may be reset in certain circumstances as described further below.

'Relevant price' is a term used very often in the 2002 definitions, especially in the sections relating to settlement of transactions. This is the price of a share or level of an index, as determined by the 'calculation agent' at the relevant time on a prescribed day in accordance with the usual market practices.

'Multiplier', which is defined as the percentage amount specified in the calculation, allows the parties to add leverage to any transaction.

3.3 Area 3: timing of the transaction

The 2002 definitions provide a contractual framework for transactions. This contractual framework includes various timing definitions, in particular specifying milestone dates and business days. These days and dates then link into other definitions, to establish when a party's contractual obligations must be performed and the specifics of those obligations. Several of these are included in Article 1:

- the date when the parties agree to enter into a transaction – the 'trade date';
- the number of days within which the settlement will normally occur – the 'settlement cycle'; and
- a transaction's relevant business days – 'exchange business day', 'currency business day', 'clearance system business day' and 'scheduled trading day'.

It is crucial to bear in mind that, throughout the 2002 definitions, four definitions of business days are used to calculate the relevant time periods, which may produce different results!

(a)　　*Trade date*

The milestone 'trade date' is defined as "in respect of a Transaction, the date specified in the related Confirmation". Although not specifically mentioned, the market convention is for this to be the date when the parties agree the transaction's terms, which in common banking parlance is the date when the transaction is traded.

'Trade date' is used in several other definitions, providing assessment points for fall-back mechanics and disruption events. In the 'knock-in event' definition (see further below), trade date is integral to the fall-back position where a confirmation does not specify a particular event, but is instead determined through the price of an underlying reference security. Here, trade date is used as a basis date for two alternative triggers:

> *In the event that the related Confirmation does not specify such an event or occurrence but specifies a Knock-in Reference Security and/or a Knock-in Price, a Knock-in Event shall occur for a Transaction for which such Knock-in Reference Security is also the Index, Share or Basket specified in the related Confirmation: (i) where, on the Trade Date, the Knock-in Price is greater than the Initial Price, Strike Price, Forward Price or other initial level set for the Transaction, when the level, price or amount of the Knock-in Reference Security determined as of the Knock-in Valuation Time on any Knock-in Determination Day is greater than or equal to the Knock-in Price; and (ii) where, on the Trade Date, the Knock-in Price is less than the Initial Price, Strike Price, Forward Price or other initial level set for the Transaction, when the level, price or amount of the Knock-in Reference Security determined as of the Knock-in Valuation Time on any Knock-in Determination Day is less than or equal to the Knock-in Price.*

For American option transactions, a fall-back 'commencement date' is tagged to the trade date:

> *"Commencement Date" means, in respect of an American Option Transaction, the date specified as such in the related Confirmation or, if such date is not a Scheduled Trading Day, the next following Scheduled Trading Day. If no such date is specified, the* Commencement Date shall be the Trade Date.

The definition of 'premium payment date', which relates to option transactions, provides that *"If the Premium Payment Date is not specified in the related Confirmation, the Premium Payment Date will fall on the date that is* one Settlement Cycle following the Trade Date".

The 'trade date' definition is often integral to when observation and assessment periods begin. For example, the 'first period' definition, which relates to dividends, provides that "the initial Dividend Period will commence on, and include, the Clearance System Business Day that is one Settlement Cycle following the Trade Date".

Lastly, the 'trade date' definition is relevant to various hedging and disruption events where it is used as a base date for assessing whether circumstances have changed since the parties entered into the transaction. For example:

- the definition of 'change in law additional disruption event' begins with "Change in Law" means that, on or *after the Trade Date* of any Transaction (A) due to the adoption of or any change in any applicable law or regulation..."; and

- the definition of 'increased cost of hedging additional disruption event' begins with "Increased Cost of Hedging" means that the Hedging Party would incur a materially increased (*as compared with circumstances existing on the Trade Date*) amount of tax, duty, expense or fee (other than brokerage commissions) to..."

(b)   *Settlement cycle*

The definition of 'settlement cycle' covers the trading of shares underlying a transaction, either directly or as component parts in an underlying index, or options or futures for an exchange-traded contract used for hedging or valuing a transaction.

The settlement cycle is the customary period of clearance system business days required to clear those securities – that is, once an order to transfer a security has been made, how long it takes to appear in the clearing system account of the transferee.

The 'settlement cycle' definition links into other definitions, to establish when a party's contractual obligations must be performed and the specifics of those obligations.

The definition is relevant for settlement. It is used in the 'settlement date' definition, which specifies the settlement date for shares being delivered in physically settled transactions in option transactions as "the date that falls one Settlement Cycle following [the] Exercise Date...".

In a number of instances, the definition integrates with fall-back provisions. For example, in the definition of 'premium payment date' if the confirmation does not specify the premium payment date, it is deemed to fall "on the date that is one Settlement Cycle following the Trade Date, or if such date is not a Currency Business Day, the next following Currency Business Day".

A similar provision applies for pre-paid forwards where in the definition of 'prepayment date', if the confirmation does not specify a prepayment date, the prepayment date is deemed to fall "on the date that is one Settlement Cycle following the Trade Date".

The 'settlement cycle' definition is also relevant for some disruptions. For example, where the official settlement price of an exchange-traded contract is corrected and the correction published "within one Settlement Cycle for the related Exchange-traded Contract after the original publication", parties may notify the calculation agent who may then adjust the transaction.

The 'settlement cycle' definition is relevant to the 'failure to deliver' additional disruption event. This definition makes multiple uses of settlement cycles – for example, to determine the timing for notifying that the event has occurred. This must be done one settlement cycle prior to the settlement date for forward transactions and equity swap transactions.

(c)   Trading days and business days

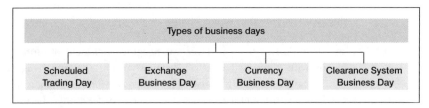

It is not only the actions of the transaction parties which control the operation of an equity derivatives transaction. Equity derivatives transaction most commonly reference liquid shares, and to be liquid a share must be listed or traded on an exchange. So whether or not that exchange is open for business or is disrupted in any way must be contemplated in the equity derivatives transaction.

Many of the fall-backs and basis for timings in the 2002 definitions reference exchanges. Four different business days are used: 'scheduled trading day', 'exchange business day', 'currency business day' and 'clearance system business day'.

'Scheduled trading day': This term is referenced as "any day on which each Exchange and each Related Exchange are scheduled to be open for trading during their respective regular trading sessions". This is a facilitative definition for 'exchange business day'; it is also relevant in certain of the fall-backs where the trading of shares and publishing of indices are disrupted.

The introduction to the 2002 definitions states:

'Scheduled' is designed to offer a clear yet flexible standard, reflecting the possibility that exchanges' schedules may change from time to time, for a variety of reasons, without market participants necessarily wanting to treat such changes as market disruptions.

Much of the 2002 definitions relate to fall-backs for where the markets for an underlying share or index are disrupted. Where there is a disruption preventing the calculation agent from following the prescribed valuation procedure, the 2002 definitions permit that the "valuation may be delayed for up to eight Scheduled Trading Days after the originally scheduled Valuation Date".

Scheduled trading days are relevant in barrier transactions where "Knock-in Determination Day" means, in respect of a Transaction for which a Knock-in Event is specified as being applicable, each Scheduled Trading Day specified...".

The definitions which apply to option transactions use the 'scheduled trading day' definition in multiple places. For example, the 'commencement date' definition provides that American option transactions will commence on "the date specified as such in the related Confirmation or, if such date is not a Scheduled Trading Day, the next following Scheduled Trading Day...".

A similar fall-back is provided for determining valuation dates for swap and forward transactions, with the 'valuation date' definition providing that this will be "each date specified as such or otherwise determined as provided in the related Confirmation (or, if such date is not a Scheduled Trading Day, the next following Scheduled Trading Day)...".

'**Exchange business day**': This term is defined as "any Scheduled Trading Day on which each Exchange and each Related Exchange are open for trading during their respective regular trading sessions".

Some actions involving underlying shares and indices can take place only when an exchange is actually open – for example, settlement cycles for exchange-traded contracts, which are described above, are referenced to "the period of Exchange Business Days following a trade in such Exchange-traded Contract on the Exchange in which settlement will customarily occur according to the rules of such Exchange".

Exchange business days can be important for determining market disruption events. The definition of 'early closure market disruption event' requires "the closure on any Exchange Business Day of the relevant Exchange...prior to its Scheduled Closing Time...".

The provisions for adjusting cancelled underlying indices, where the parties have elected a 'cancellation and payment' consequence in their transaction, provide for the transaction to be cancelled "on the later of the Exchange Business Day immediately prior to the effectiveness of the Index Cancellation and the date the Index Cancellation is announced by the Index Sponsor".

Some payments are also made referencing exchange business days too – for instance, payments following a 'merger event' affecting an option transaction must "be paid by Seller to Buyer... as agreed promptly (and in any event within five Exchange Business Days) by the parties after the Merger Date...".

'**Scheduled closing time**': This term refers, in respect of each exchange or related exchange, to the scheduled weekday closing time for such exchange or the relevant scheduled trading day, without regard to after hours or any other trading outside of the regular trading session hours. For example, the scheduled closing time of the London Stock Exchange (LSE) is 4:30 pm.

3.4   Area 4: barrier transactions

Extract from a template of an equity derivatives transaction
[Knock-in Event: [Applicable]
Knock-in Price: [ ]
Knock-in Reference Security: [ ]
Knock-in Determination Day(s): [ ]
Knock-in Valuation Time: [ ]]
[Knock-out Event: [Applicable]
Knock-out Price: [ ]
Knock-out Reference Security: [ ]
Knock-out Determination Day(s): [ ]
Knock-out Valuation Time: [ ]]

The Article 1 definitions cover the 'knock-in'/'knock-out' transactions. Knock-in/knock-out transactions are also known as 'barrier transactions'. Elsewhere in the ISDA universe of template documentation, barrier transactions are common for foreign exchange derivatives. Indeed, ISDA released a specialist publication: the 2005 Barrier Option Supplement to the 1998 FX and Currency Option Definitions. This document can also be useful for the equity derivatives practitioner documenting an equity derivative barrier transaction, as the foreign exchange template contains useful definitions, contractual terms and fall-backs which are not present in the 2002 definitions, which can be extracted and adapted.

Primer: knock-in/knock-out or barrier transactions

'Knock-in/knock-out' or 'barrier' transactions are types of contingent derivative. This means that a transaction's main operative provisions begin or cease operating only once a contingency occurs.

For knock-in transactions, payments or deliveries start only once a knock-in event or barrier event happens. The knock-in event might be that a referenced index reaches a certain level (eg, the FTSE 100 reaches 6,900 points), or it could be that the price of a referenced share achieves a certain price (eg, RBS reaches 300 pence a share).

By contrast, for knock-out transactions the payments or deliveries cease when a knock-out event or barrier event happens. The knock-out event might be that a referenced index goes below a certain level (eg, the Dow Jones goes below 17,000 points), or it could be that the price of a referenced share goes below a certain price (eg, Lloyds goes below 50 pence a share).

Knock-in and knock-out transactions can be embedded into swaps, options or forwards. For each transaction type, the parties will agree what the knock-in/knock-out event will be, how and when this will be determined, as well as how and when a referenced security or index will be valued for making any determination. The parties will also agree which of them will be responsible for making any determinations.

The terms of the related swap, option or forward transaction will then be set out separately in the confirmation, either in a separate section or sometimes in an annex.

The rationale for knock-in/knock-out transactions is to allow parties to have operative hedging or trading arrangements which apply or cease when pre-agreed market conditions occur. This can be useful for a party that wishes to purchase protection only against risks that it is unwilling to absorb, rather than against all of the risks that it is exposed to. This, in turn, can make derivatives protection more affordable.

The 2002 definitions provide that in a knock-in transaction, a payment or delivery is contingent upon a knock-in event occurring on any 'knock-in determination day'. The parties can specify any event as a knock-in event, and this does not have to be related to the underlying equity asset. Mostly, the parties will want to link the knock-in event to an equity asset, which in the 2002 definitions is called the 'knock-in reference security'. Again, this does not have to be the same share or index to which the main transaction relates. The 2002 definitions provide some further fall-backs and if the parties switch on the knock-in provisions, but do not specify the knock-in reference security, the equity asset which is the subject of the main transaction will become the knock-in reference security by default.

If the parties have decided to link the knock-in event to a knock-in reference security, then they also need to specify a knock-in price which would trigger such an event. Further, they have to specify a knock-in determination date on which the knock-in reference security should reach or exceed the knock-in price for the knock-in event to occur. If the parties do not specify a knock-in determination date, here also the 2002 definitions provide a standard fall-back, and each scheduled trading day – from the beginning until the end of the main equity derivative transaction – will be a knock-in determination date.

Lastly, the parties may specify a 'knock-in valuation time'. This is the point in time on the knock-in determination date when the calculation agent determines whether the knock-in price has been reached for the relevant knock-in reference security. If the parties have not provided for the knock-in valuation time, the ever-helpful 2002 definitions provide that the valuation time for the main equity derivative transaction shall be the knock-in valuation time. If there is no valuation time, then the knock-in valuation time will be the scheduled closing time for the exchange where the knock-in reference security is listed.

Importantly, it is only the knock-in valuation time which counts when making the determination. Where the knock-in reference price is reached earlier or later in the knock-in determination day, but not at the knock-in valuation time, this is not relevant to any determination.

For a knock-out transaction, a right or obligation is subject to the non-occurrence of the specific knock-out event on any knock-out determination day.

The parties can specify any event as the knock-out event, but if they mark it as applicable without giving the details of the relevant event, then they must fill out the section of the confirmation relating to knock-out reference security.

In that case, the obligations under a transaction are contingent upon the relevant price of the knock-out reference security reaching the level of the knock-out price. If the confirmation does not specify knock-out reference security, then it is the same as the index, share or basket under that transaction.

The provisions for knock-out valuation time apply in the same way as those for knock-in valuation time.

When documenting a knock-in/knock-out, a practitioner should bear in mind that the template confirmations available from ISDA are not comprehensive, and it is usually necessary to add operative provisions setting out further details of how the events occur, and the consequences. As mentioned, this transaction type is dealt with in greater detail both in the 2011 definitions and in the 2005 Barrier Option Supplement to the 1998 FX and Currency Option Definitions.

Hypothetical example of a knock-in transaction: Elstree Holdings and Radlett Inc

Elstree Holdings is a New York-based asset manager. It owns 100,000 shares in Hamwood Enterprises, a Bermudan insurer. Elstree believes that Hamwood's share price is unlikely to go above $20 a share, principally because it thinks that regulatory changes on the horizon will require Hamwood to hold excessive amounts of capital, hampering profit-making opportunities.

If Hamwood's share price did rise over $20, this would at least partly be due to the regulatory changes not having the impact feared. Elstree would therefore be happy to give up some of that benefit in return for premium earned in the meantime, which would protect it against the risk of adverse regulatory change.

Radlett Inc is a New York hedge fund. It believes that Bermudan insurers are currently undervalued due to the concerns about future regulatory burdens, and that once the market realises that capital requirements will not be as onerous as feared, the companies share price will soar.

Elstree and Radlett agree to enter into a knock-in transaction. They agree that the knock-in event will be the planned insurance regulations coming into force – something which may happen any time in the next two years. They agree that their transaction will have a term of three years, and that each business day during the term will be a knock-in determination day. If a knock-in event occurs, then an option transaction will crystallise between Elstree and Radlett, giving Radlett as option buyer the right to purchase the 100,000 Hamwood shares at $21 a share.

Two years later the insurance regulations come into force. Elstree has been earning premium payments during the intervening period.

Following heavy lobbying by the insurance industry, though, the capital holding requirements had been watered down, the insurance industry has also been better prepared than expected, and the regulations do not have the restrictive effect once feared. Hamwood shares are now trading at $25 a share, mainly in recognition of the light regulatory burden. Radlett chooses to exercise its option to purchase the 100,000 Hamwood shares at $21 a share.

The knock-in transaction has allowed the parties to take opposing views of the risks inherent in regulatory change. Elstree has been able to hedge itself partially against adverse change through earning premium payments in the intervening period; and Radlett has been able to make a strategic return on regulatory risk.

3.5   Area 5: identity of parties

The Article 1 definitions cover the identity and location of the parties, with definitions of 'buyer', 'seller' and 'calculation agent'.

The definitions of 'buyer' and 'seller' are relevant only to option and forward transactions. 'Buyer' and 'seller' are each defined as the "party specified as such in the related Confirmation". These definitions are facilitative, with the actual roles and duties contained in other provisions – for example, Section 2.4, which relates to the payment of premiums in option transactions, provides: "In respect of an Option Transaction, Buyer shall pay Seller the Premium on the Premium Payment Date". Also Section 4.2, which relates to payment of prepayment amounts in forward transactions, provides that "Buyer shall pay Seller the Prepayment Amount on the Prepayment Date".

For swap transactions, the transacting parties are not called 'buyer' and 'seller', but instead 'equity amount payer' and 'equity amount receiver', and these terms are defined in Sections 5.1 and 5.2. The concept of buyer and seller for swaps is only relevant for 'swaptions' (ie, an option to enter into a swap).

The 2002 definitions give flexibility to the calculation agent throughout a number of provisions. Various external events may affect the shares underlying equity derivatives transactions such as a merger, take-over, nationalisation or tender offer, underlying indices may have their methodology varied, or may not be published following a disruption. Where the parties elect in a confirmation, the calculation may be instilled with the discretion to make suitable changes or adjustments. This is discussed in detail in the sections below.

The definition of 'calculation agent' provides that "when a Calculation Agent is required to act or to exercise judgement in any way, it will do so in good faith, and in a commercially reasonable manner".

Although this general duty provides some protection to the parties, it is common for one of the parties to fulfil the role of calculation agent; and this may be perceived as a conflict, particularly where party fulfilling the calculation agent function has a broader position in the underlying security.

Either one or both of the parties is usually a market making financial institution, and it is usually the financial institution which takes the role of calculation agent, as it has the market infrastructure to carry out the role, and it will normally have the stronger bargaining position.

Where both counterparties are financial institutions, or a counterparty is more savvy, alternative provisions to ensure the impartiality of the calculation agent's function are often negotiated into the confirmation. The preparation of the 2011 definitions focused heavily on the provisions for the calculation agent, and the changes made there are substantive. Increasingly, even where parties still elect to use the 2002 definitions, they will choose to incorporate the calculation agent provisions from the 2011 definitions.

Common negotiated changes to the 2002 definitions' calculation agent provisions may include appointing both parties as calculation agent, or requiring the other party to agree any determination.

The parties may also provide that where a determination cannot be agreed that the parties will appoint an alternative calculation agent to make the determination. Sometimes the parties will provide that where they are unable to agree on an alternative calculation agent, they will each appoint a dealer, and the dealers will between them agree on an alternative calculation agent. On other occasions, this right will apply only where the original calculation agent is in default. The parties may also set out which party will pay the costs of any dispute.

The negotiated changes may be many and varied. The below clause is a hypothetical example of a calculation agent provision heavily negotiated between a fund and a market-making bank.

Example of a negotiated calculation agent provision

Calculation Agent:
The Calculation Agent is Party B. Provided, however, that if an Event of Default occurs and is continuing in respect of Party B, the Calculation Agent will be Party A or an independent dealer reasonably selected by Party A and agreed by Party B. A party (the 'Objecting Party') has the right to dispute in good faith and on commercially reasonable grounds a particular determination made by the Calculation Agent, provided that the Objecting Party notifies the other party and the Calculation Agent (if the other party is not the Calculation Agent) of such dispute promptly (but in no event later than 10 Business Days) after the Calculation Agent has provided the Objecting Party and the other party (if the other party is not the Calculation Agent) with notice of such determination. In any such instance, the parties shall, within five Business Days after such notice, jointly select three independent dealers (or, if the parties cannot jointly agree on three, each party shall select an independent dealer, which two independent dealers shall jointly select a third independent dealer). Each such independent dealer shall be requested by the Calculation Agent to make a determination as to the disputed matter within five Business Days after its appointment.

In the event that two or three independent dealers provide a determination as to the disputed matter within five Business Days after their respective appointments then (A) if a majority of the responding independent dealers provided the same determination, such determination shall be binding on the parties for the disputed matter, absent manifest error, or (B) if a majority of the independent dealers did not provide the same Determination, the responding independent dealers will jointly appoint a fourth independent dealer (the 'Resolver'). The Resolver will select, within five Business Days after its appointment, from the Determinations originally provided by the responding independent dealers, with the selected Determination being binding on the parties for the disputed matter, absent manifest error.

3.6 Area 6: definitions relating to settlement type

Article 1 provides the base definitions for 'cash-settled' (a transaction where cash settlement is applicable) and 'physically-settled' (a transaction where physical settlement is applicable). Both of these simplistic definitions are useful for providing a market standard way for any transaction's settlement method to be efficiently elected in a confirmation. Index transactions are always cash settled, whereas transactions referencing specific shares or groups of shares (or baskets) can be either cash or physically settled.

3.7 Area 7: currency

Lastly, there are two definitions relating to currency. One for the euro and one for the EC Treaty, which is relevant to the definition of the euro.

4.   Article 2 – "General terms relating to option transactions"

> Article 2 sub-sections
>
> 2.1. Certain Definitions and Provisions Relating to Option Transactions
> 2.2. Option Style
> 2.3. Option Type
> 2.4. Terms Relating to Premium

An 'option' is a privately negotiated contract between two counterparties. Generally, the buyer of an option acquires a right to buy from (or to sell to) the seller of the option a defined amount of securities at a specified price.

Article 2 is only two pages long and sets out the basic definitions applicable to option transactions. It covers the following areas:

- payment of premium;
- call and put options;
- European, American and Bermuda options; and
- number of options and option entitlement.

4.1   Premium

> Extract from a template of an option transaction
>
> Premium: [ ] [(Premium per Option [ ])]
> Premium Payment Date: [ ]

An option buyer pays an amount of money ('premium') to the option seller, as determined in the relevant confirmation, to compensate it for providing the option. The confirmation would also normally specify when such payment should be made ('premium payment date'), but if it does not, the 2002 definitions provide a fall-back (one settlement cycle following the trade date). An additional fall-back is provided if the premium payment date is not a currency business day: the premium will be payable on the next currency business day. If the buyer acquires more than one option, the parties can specify a premium per option.

4.2   Call and put options

> Extract from a template of an option transaction
>
> Option Type: [Call] [Put]
> Strike Price: [ ]

Options can be divided into 'call' and 'put' options. If physical settlement applies, a call option gives the buyer a right to purchase shares or baskets of shares from its counterparty at the 'strike price' (as specified by the parties in the relevant confirmation). A put option, however, gives the buyer a right to sell shares (or baskets of shares) at a strike price.

For a cash-settled transaction, however, a holder of a put option has a right to demand a payment from its counterparty if the settlement price (ie, the price of the underlying shares, basket of shares or the level of the relevant equities index, eg, FTSE 250, on a given day) is lower than the strike price (as provided in the confirmation). Conversely, a call option allows its holder to demand a payment when the actual price (the settlement price) is higher than the strike price. (For a fuller description of settlement price, please see section 9.2 below).

4.3 American, European and Bermuda options

> *Extract from a template of an option transaction*
>
> Option Style: [American] [Bermuda] [European]

Another way to categorise different types of option is according to when they can be exercised. The 2002 definitions cover three of the most common types: American, Bermuda and European.

An American option can be exercised on any scheduled trading day (ie, any day on which the stock exchange in respect of the relevant shares is scheduled to be open for trading). This means that it can be exercised at any time before its expiry. A European option, however, can be exercised only on the day of its expiry ('expiration date'). A Bermuda option is a halfway house that can be exercised on specific days as provided in the confirmation (called 'potential exercise dates').

4.4 Number of options and option entitlement

> *Extract from a template of an option transaction*
>
> Number of Options: [ ]
> [Option Entitlement: [ ] Share(s) per Option]

The parties also specify the number of options in the confirmation. In the case of a share-related option, if the number of options is 100, then the buyer in an option transaction has a right to buy (or sell) 100 shares. However, the parties could decide that one option should relate instead to a number of shares. For example, if in an option transaction the 'option entitlement' is 10 shares per option, then a buyer of a put option would need the number of options to be only 10 to able to sell 100 shares.

5. **Article 3 – "Exercise of options"**

> Article 3 sub-sections
>
> 3.1. General Terms Relating to Exercise
> 3.2. Procedure for Exercise
> 3.3. Multiple Exercise
> 3.4. Automatic Exercise

Like Article 2, Article 3 also relates to options and its key provisions cover:
- the period when an option can be exercised;
- the procedure for exercise;
- what happens when parties specify 'multiple exercise' as applicable; and
- what happens when the parties specify 'automatic exercise' as applicable.

> *Extract from a template of an option transaction*
>
> Procedures for Exercise:
> [Commencement Date: [ ]]
> [Potential Exercise Date(s): [ ]]
> [Latest Exercise Time: [ ][am/pm] (local time in)]
> Expiration Time: [ ] [am/pm] (local time in)
> Expiration Date: [ ]
> Multiple Exercise: [Applicable][Not Applicable]
> [Minimum Number of Options: [ ]
> Maximum Number of Options: [ ]
> Integral Multiple: [ ]]
> Automatic Exercise: [Applicable][Not Applicable]

5.1 **Time when an option is exercised**

Section 3.1 of the definitions sets out some further details as to the day and time American, European and Bermuda options can be exercised.

An American option can be exercised on all scheduled trading days from the commencement date until the expiration date between 9:00 am local time until the latest 'exercise time'. The latest exercise time is as specified in the confirmation, or if it is not, it is the same as the 'expiration time'.

A Bermuda option can be exercised on each potential exercise date and the expiration date from 9:00 am local time until the latest exercise time.

The buyer can exercise a European option only on the expiration date from 9:00am until the expiration time.

Article 3 provides that if either a potential exercise date or expiration date is a 'disrupted day' (which means that a 'market disruption event' has occurred, as explained in section 8.2 below), then the potential exercise date or expiration date will be the first succeeding scheduled trading day which is not a disrupted day.

However, if the relevant date is succeeded by eight disrupted days, then the eighth disrupted day is deemed to be the potential exercise day or the expiration date.

5.2 Procedure for exercise

Unless 'automatic expire' occurs, an option buyer must give irrevocable notice to the seller that it wants to exercise the option. Such notice can be given over the phone, but must be followed by a written confirmation. However, if the seller does not receive such written confirmation on the same day, the oral notice is valid nonetheless.

5.3 Multiples exercise

The parties can specify in the confirmation that 'multiples exercise' applies, which means that the buyer can exercise it more than once. Naturally, this is only applicable to American and Bermuda options, as the European one can be exercised only once on the day of its expiry. The parties can also specify the maximum and/or minimum amount of the underlying that such exercise will relate to. In order to do so, they must specify this in the 'minimum number of options' or 'maximum number of options' in the confirmation.

5.4 Automatic exercise

The parties can decide in the confirmation that the option shall be exercised automatically (ie, without the need for formal notification) on the date specified as the final date before the option ceases to exist (expiration date). Before that day, however, the buyer still has an option to notify the seller that it wants to disapply the automatic exercise.

If automatic exercise applies to a physically settled option, then such option will be exercised only if it is 'in-the-money'. This means that, in case of a call option, the current market price (or the 'reference price') is equal to or greater than (and, in case of a put option, such price is equal to or lower than) the price for a share at which any 'related exchange' would automatically exercise the relevant option. As the term 'related exchange' refers to any exchange on which options on the relevant shares are listed, this follows the rules of the relevant exchange to ensure that it makes commercial sense for the buyer to exercise its option. If the difference between the strike price and the reference price is too small, the costs of exercising the option may outweigh any benefits.

If parties have elected for physical settlement to apply in respect of an option, it may make sense to take a closer look at the rule of any potential related exchanges. The listed option market rules of such exchanges may have different automatic exercise thresholds for different types of customer, so parties may wish to consider amending this provision, depending on the underlying share or index.

A provision analogous to the in-the-money language is not necessary in relation to cash-settled options, because of the way such options are settled (please see section 10.1 on cash settlement).

6.   Article 4 – "General terms relating to forward transactions"

> Article 4 sub-sections
>
> 4.1. Certain Definitions Relating to Forward Transactions
> 4.2. Terms Relating to Prepayment

In a forward transaction, one of the parties agrees to sell, and the other one agrees to buy, a defined number of shares or a basket of shares at a defined point in the future for a defined price (if the transaction is physically settled). If the transaction is cash settled, the parties exchange the difference between the actual price of the underlying asset at the future date and the price set out in the confirmation. A forward can also relate to an index (in which case it will be cash settled), and the parties will instead exchange payments based upon a settlement price related to the level of the index at the future date as compared to the level set out in the confirmation.

6.1   Variable obligation

Article 4 is the shortest article in the 2002 definitions, although the concepts that it refers to are complex. The article provides that both 'forward floor price' and the 'forward cap price' are as specified in the relevant confirmation. Before explaining these concepts, we should understand the economics behind an equity forward transaction.

> *Extract from a template of an equity forward transaction*
>
> Variable Obligation: [Applicable]
> Forward Floor Price: [ ]
> Forward Cap Price: []

The buyer under a forward transaction makes a gain if at the expiration of the contract the price of the underlying asset is higher than the seller expects, whereas the opposite is true for the seller. For example, let us assume that Party A (the buyer) agrees that it will buy a share of Nokia for $10 from Party B (the seller) in three months' time. If after that time one Nokia share can be bought for $10.5 on the market, then Party A makes a profit. If the transaction is physically settled, Party A buys the share from Party B for $10 and makes an immediate profit of $0.5 if it sells the share at the current market price.

However, if after the agreed three months' time the current market price of a Nokia share is $9, then Party B makes a gain. Party A is still obliged to buy the share for $10, thus paying $1 more than it would on the market. If the price of a Nokia share after the agreed time is exactly $10, then no one makes any profit and no money is exchanged at the expiration of the contract. Such price is also often referred to as the 'breakeven point'.

The concepts of a forward floor price and forward cap price were introduced to create a collar by 'extending' the breakeven point. To continue with our example, Party A and Party B might have agreed that the forward floor price for a Nokia share should be $9.5 and they set the forward cap price at $10.5. If on the expiration of the contract the price of a Nokia share is between $9.5 and $10.5, then no money changes hands. Party A (the buyer under the transaction) makes a profit only if the price falls below $9.5, whereas Party B (the seller) will make a gain only if the price of a Nokia shares rises above $10.5. (The details of the settlement provisions under the 2002 definitions will be discussed in details in sections 9 and 10 below).

If the parties want the forward floor price and forward cap price to apply, they need to mark 'variable obligation' in the confirmation as applicable and specify the agreed floor and cap prices.

6.2 Prepayment

Article 4 also allows for 'prepayment' under which the buyer under the forward transaction shall pay a defined amount of money (or the 'prepayment amount') to the seller on the 'prepayment date'. Both the prepayment amount and the prepayment date need to be specified in the confirmation.

Extract from a template of an equity forward transaction

Prepayment: [Applicable]
Prepayment Amount:[ ]
Prepayment Date:[ ]

Normally, no money changes hands until the expiration of the contract. However, for a range of commercial reasons, the parties may decide that the buyer should pay a specified amount for the underlying that it has contracted to buy at any point during the term of the transaction. Then on the contract's expiration this amount is taken into account when the final calculations are being prepared. (See sections 10.2 on cash settlement and 11.3 on physical settlement).

Sometimes both prepayment and variable obligations are applicable at the same time. In that case, the prepayment amount is often equal to the forward floor price.

7. Article 5 – "General terms relating to equity swap transactions"

Article 5 sub-sections

5.1. Equity Amount Payer
5.2. Equity Amount Receiver
5.3. Initial Exchange Amount
5.4. Initial Exchange Date
5.5. Final Exchange Amount
5.6. Final Exchange Date
5.7. Rate of Return

5.8. Initial Price
5.9. Final Price
5.10. Equity Notional Reset

An 'equity swap' can allow a party to acquire economic exposure to an underlying equity asset without the need of actually buying that asset.

Extract from a template of an equity swap transaction

Equity Amounts payable by [Party A][Party B]

Equity Amount Payer: [Party A][Party B]
[Equity Amount Receiver: [Party A][Party B]]

In any equity swap transaction, there is an equity amount payer and an equity amount receiver. The equity amount payer assumes a short position in relation to the underlying equity asset and, as such, it believes that the value of such underlying will have fallen at the particular measurement point set out in the contract. If this turns out to be the case, it will receive a payment (called an 'equity amount') from the equity amount receiver. Conversely, if the value of the shares or of the relevant indices has risen at the measurement point, then the equity amount payer is obliged to make a payment to the equity amount receiver.

It is important to bear in mind that the equity amount payer does not always pay, and the equity amount receiver does not only receive payments. The equity amount payer pays only if the value of the equity assets has gone up, and it receives a payment if the prices gas gone down. Conversely, the equity amount receiver is obliged to make a payment if the value of the underlying has decreased, and it receives the relevant amount if the price has increased.

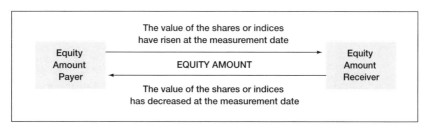

Extract from a template of an equity swap transaction

[Initial Exchange Amount payable by [Party A][Party B]:

[Party A][Party B] Initial [ ]
Exchange Amount:
[Party A][Party B] Initial [ ]]

Exchange Date:

[Final Exchange Amount payable by [Party A][Party B]:

[Party A][Party B] Final [ ]
Exchange Amount:
[Party A][Party B] Final [ ]]
Exchange Date:

The parties may also decide that one party should make a payment to the other one at the beginning or at the end of the transaction. These payments are defined as 'initial exchange amount' or 'final exchange amount' and are made on the 'initial' or 'final exchange date' as specified by the parties in the relevant confirmation. These provisions are new and have been introduced in the 2002 definitions to permit certain market access structures to be covered.

These provisions are entirely optional; they constitute a way of transferring an amount of money from one party to the other, equivalent usually to the funding cost of the equity amount payer funding or monetising the underlying equity asset. For example, if a hedge fund wants to acquire a long position in an emerging market share, its counterparty may require it to provide cash in the form of an initial exchange equal to the hedge fund's intended exposure to that share.

Although these provisions were introduced with market access products in mind, they could be used in a variety of ways. For example, one party may want to give the other a loan. Instead of the more traditional way of entering into a loan agreement, the parties may specify the initial amount exchange and the final exchange amounts. The initial exchange amount would then represent the loan from Party A to Party B, and the final exchange amount is the amount that Party B needs to return to Party B; it may include the capital together with the equity amounts payable by the equity amount payer representing the return component of the loan. If these provisions apply, the parties must also specify when the relevant transfers of money should be made – the initial exchange date and the final exchange date.

Lastly, Article 5 contains four other clauses which are used when calculating the amount owed by one party to the other: 'rate of return', 'initial price', 'final price' and 'equity notional reset'.

Extract from a template of an equity swap transaction

Equity Notional Amount: [ ]
Equity Notional Reset: [Applicable][Not Applicable]
[Multiplier: [ ]]
Initial Price: [ ]
Final Price: [ ]

As mentioned above, the amount of money which is transferred from one party to another is called the 'equity amount'. This is defined as a product of the equity notional amount and the rate of return.

Equity amount = equity notional amount × rate of return

'Equity notional amount' is the amount specified in the confirmation, whereas rate of return is calculated as follows:

Rate of return = (final price – initial price) / initial price × multiplier (if any)

The parties specify how the initial price and the final price should be calculated, but it is the job of the calculation agent to deliver the calculations to the parties as and when appropriate.

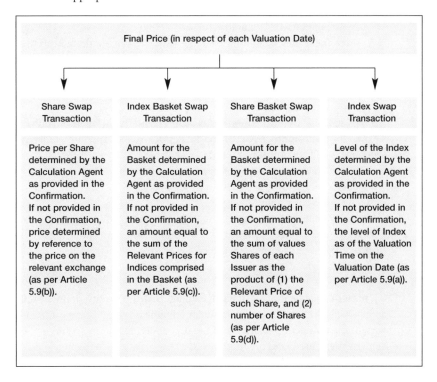

The multiplier can be used if the parties decide that they want to extend their exposure to or leverage on particular shares or share indices. If this is the case, the amount which would normally be payable is multiplied by the amount specified in the confirmation. However, the parties may decide that the multiplier shall be less than 1, and by doing this they can limit their exposure to the shares or indices (or rather limit any potential gains or losses on the movement of the share price).

Example: Sunrise Brothers plc

Regina Bank enters into a cash-settled share swap agreement with Nowak Corporation, under which Regina is the equity amount payer and Nowak is the equity amount receiver. The relevant share is issued by Sunrise Brothers plc, the initial price of which (as specified or otherwise determined in the confirmation) is €100. The parties agree that the equity notional amount is equal to €1 million. Regina and Nowak also agree that the multiplier is equal to 1 and that they will make payments to each other on a monthly basis.

After the first month

After one month, the share has risen in value and it now stands at €110 (which is the final price). This means that the rate of return is calculated as follows:

Rate of return = (€110 – €100)/€100 × 1 = 0.1

Therefore, the equity amount is as follows:

Equity amount = €1 million × 0.1 = €100,000

Since the shares have risen in value (and the value representing the equity amount), Regina (the equity amount payer) must make a payment to Nowak (the equity amount receiver) equal to €100,000.

After the second month

However, in the following month the shares of Sunrise Brothers fell down to €85. Now, the initial price is €110, the final price is €85 and the equity notional amount is still equal to €1 million.

Accordingly, the new rate of return is calculated as follows:

Rate of return = (€85 – €110)/€110 × 1 = -0.22727

The new equity amount will be:

Equity amount = €1 million × -0.22727 = -€ 227,270

As the share price has fallen and the equity amount is now negative, Nowak (the equity amount receiver) will need to make a payment to Regina (the equity amount payer).

In our example above, we have assumed that the 'equity notional reset' is not applicable and that the equity notional amount does not change throughout the term of the transaction. However, if the parties decide that the equity notional reset applies, then the equity amount in respect of each cash settlement period date is added to the equity notional amount. The purpose of this feature is for the sell side entity to avoid a punitive capital treatment by, effectively, converting any posted collateral into absolutely paid amounts. To continue with our example:

Example: Sunrise Brothers plc
Equity notional reset: applicable

After the first month
Assuming that Regina and Nowak had chosen equity notional reset to apply, the payments for the first month would remain unchanged.

After the second month
After the second month, the equity amount in respect of the previous period (ie,

€100,000) should be added to the old equity notional amount (ie, €1 million) to give €1.1 million.

This does not affect the rate of return, which is still -0.22727, but the equity amount for the second month is now as follows:

Equity amount = €1,100,000 × -0.22727 = -€249,997

This means that Nowak has to pay €22,727 more to Regina if equity notional reset applies.

After the third month

On the following payment date, the new equity notional amount would be calculated as follows:

Equity notional amount = €1,100,000 + (-€249,997) = €850,003

It is common for parties to a swap transaction to include a 'funding leg', such that the equity notional receiver would have to compensate the equity amount payer for its funding costs. Such costs would be determined by applying the agreed floating rate (eg, LIBOR or EUIRIBOR) to the agreed notional amount of the transaction. The parties would incorporate, and rely on, the 2006 ISDA Definitions here.

If equity notional reset is applicable and the parties have specified that the notional amount for funding payments will be equal to the equity notional amount, such notional amount for funding payments will be adjusted in the same way as the equity notional amount. The parties should consider carefully a scenario where the payment of any funding amounts do not fall on the same date as the payments of equity amounts, as there may be a mismatch between the notional amounts used.

8.   Article 6 – "Valuation"

Article 6 sub-sections

6.1. Valuation Time
6.2. Valuation Date
6.3. General Terms Relating to Market Disruption Events
6.4. Disrupted Day
6.5. Scheduled Valuation Date
6.6. Consequences of Disrupted Days
6.7. Averaging
6.8. Futures Price Valuation

The key provisions of Article 6 relate to:
- the basics of valuation;
- definitions of various market disruption events;
- consequences of market disruption events;
- the averaging provisions; and
- the futures price valuation.

8.1   Basics of valuation

Sections 6.1 and 6.2 of the 2002 definitions, which provide the definitions of 'valuation time' and 'valuation date', govern when a price in respect of various equity derivative transactions can be determined.

Extract from a template of an equity derivative transaction

Valuation Time: At [ ] [am/pm] (local time in [ ])]
Valuation Date[s]: [ ] [[The][Each] Exercise Date]

...

Exchange(s): [ ]

Accordingly, 'valuation date' is each date as specified or otherwise determined in the confirmation in relation to equity swap transactions and forward transactions. However, in relation to options, the valuation date will be the exercise date (or, if the option can be exercised more than once – each exercise date).

'Valuation time' is also usually specified in the relevant confirmation. However, if the parties did not specify any details, then the valuation time is the 'scheduled closing time' on the relevant exchange as provided in the confirmation.

8.2   Market disruption events

Share trading is often disrupted on world stock exchanges, either because of technical failure or to counter plunging markets. An equity derivative contract, which references an underlying equity asset which could be affected by these events, must cater for these in the contract. The 2002 definitions provide a series fall-backs to deal with all contemplated scenarios. These are called 'market disruption events' and impact on the valuation, exercise and expiration of equity derivative transactions. A market disruption event under the 2002 definitions can be one of the following:

- a 'trading disruption';
- an 'exchange disruption'; or
- an 'early closure'.

(a)   'Trading disruption'

This is defined as any suspension or limitation imposed by the relevant exchange relating to the relevant shares (or other securities) comprising 20% or more of the level of the relevant index. Examples of trading disruption could include a significant drop in the level of an index such as the Dow Jones Industrial Average which is blamed on computer failures halting trading.

(b)   'Exchange disruption'

This is defined as any event (other than early closure) that disrupts or impairs the ability of the market participants to effect transactions in, or obtain market values for, shares on the relevant exchange or exchanges comprising 20% or more of the level of the relevant index. This is a new definition, without its equivalent in the 1996 definitions, introduced as a result of the technological problems on NASDAQ when the Russell Index was being rebalanced in June 2001.

(c)   *'Early closure'*
This means a closure of the relevant exchange(s) prior to the scheduled closing time, unless such earlier closing is announced at least an hour prior to the earlier of the actual closing time for the regular trading session, or the submission deadline for orders on such business day.

In relation to trading and exchange disruption only, there is an additional requirement that the calculation agent must determine that such disruption is material "at any time during the one hour period that ends at the relevant Valuation Time, Latest Exercise Time, Knock-In Valuation Time or Knock-Out Valuation Time".

Example: Ding Corporation Pte Ltd
On 2 September 2008, Petronas Ltd sold an option to buy a specified number of shares of Ding Corporation Pte Ltd, a company listed and traded on the Stock Exchange of Singapore (SGX), to Sitiawan International plc. Petronas and Sitiawan agreed that the Sitiawan would have the right to purchase the shares only if their value falls down to S$9 (ie, they agreed that the knock-in event for this transaction occurs when the price of Ding's shares is at or below S$9).

At 1:00 pm on 21 October 2008, the share price was S$9.15; at 1:15 pm, though, the SGX computers suffered a glitch and no prices could be displayed until 2:30 pm. At the conclusion of this disruption, the share price of Ding had fallen to S$8.96. Trading then continued as normal and at 3:30 pm Ding's share price stood at S$8.88.

This meant that the knock-in event occurred only at 3:30 pm, as this is the first time that there is no market disruption event during the hour preceding the relevant valuation time. However, if the price of Ding shares had recovered and had risen to above S$9 before 3:30 pm, then the knock-in event would have been deemed not to have occurred.

8.3   'Disrupted day'
This is defined as a scheduled trading day on which either the relevant exchange fails to open for trading or a market disruption event occurs. If a market disruption event occurs on a day which would otherwise be a valuation date, averaging date, potential exercise day, knock-in determination date, knock-out determination date or expiration date, it is a duty of the calculation agent to notify the parties accordingly.

Example – Tokyo, 18 January 2006
It is often very difficult to decide whether an event should be classified as 'trading disruption', 'exchange disruption' or 'early closure'. After the suspension of trading on the Tokyo Stock Exchange on 18 October 2006, the market participants could not agree as to which event had occurred.

At around 2:30 pm on that day, an announcement was made that the exchange would be closing early. The first reaction of the market was that this was 'early closure' as defined under Section 6.3(f) of the 2002 definitions (as it appeared to be very similar to the suspension of trading at the New York Stock Exchange on 1 June 2005 at 3:56 pm without notice). The foreign press, including The Financial Times, also reported that early closure had occurred.

At about 2:40 pm the trade of shares and convertible bonds was indeed suspended as the exchange could not cope with a surge in selling orders. However, the exchange itself was opened until its usual closing time of 3:00 pm and the trading in futures and options continued until that time.

ISDA organised market conference calls and the general consensus was that a trading disruption occurred on that day, although some have also made a case for an exchange disruption. However, the question of 'materiality' was left unanswered and it was up to the calculation agent in each case to decide this and notify the parties as soon as practicable.

Consequences of disrupted days: The 2002 definitions provide three scenarios for determining a new valuation date when the original proposed valuation date happened to fall on a disruption day:

- for 'index transactions' and 'share transactions';
- for 'index basket transactions'; and
- for 'share basket transactions'.

In relation to index transactions and share transactions, the valuation date will be the first succeeding scheduled trading date that is not a disrupted day. However, if the there are nine disruption days in a row, then the ninth disruption day is deemed to be valuation date for the relevant transactions. It is worth noting that the 2002 definitions specify what happens if "eight Scheduled Trading Days immediately following the Scheduled Valuation Date" are disrupted days. However, we also need to include in this determination the original disrupted day, which means that the fall-back applies on the ninth scheduled trading day (counting from, and including, the original scheduled valuation date).

At that point, the calculation agent will:

- in respect of index transactions, determine the level of the relevant index "in accordance with the formula and method for calculating the Index last in effect prior to the occurrence of the first Disrupted Day"; or
- in respect of share transactions, determine its good-faith estimate of the value of the relevant shares.

As for index basket transactions, the valuation date for each index not affected by the relevant disruption event will still be the scheduled valuation date. In respect of each affected index, the valuation date will be the first scheduled trading date following the disrupted day. However, if there are nine consecutive disrupted days, the ninth one is deemed to be the valuation date. (Again, the 2002 definitions refer to "eight Scheduled Trading Days immediately following the Scheduled Valuation

Date", which means that the ninth day of continuous disruption is the fall-back valuation date.) On such day, the calculation agent will have to determine the level of the relevant indices – as above – "in accordance with the formula and method for calculating the Index last in effect prior to the occurrence of the first Disrupted Day".

In relation to share basket transactions, the valuation date for each share not affected by the relevant disruption event will still be the scheduled valuation date. In respect of each affected share, the valuation date will be the first scheduled trading date following the disrupted day. As above, if there are nine disrupted days in a row (from, and including, the original scheduled valuation date), the ninth one is deemed to be the valuation date. The calculation agent will then have to determine its good-faith estimate of the value of the relevant shares.

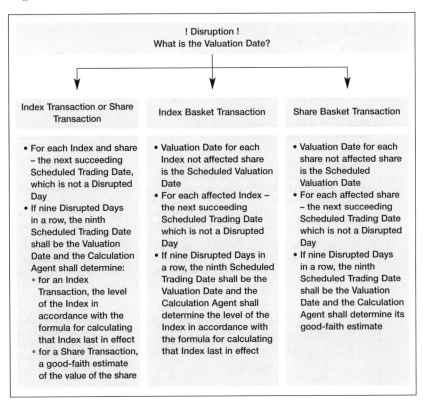

8.4   Option for averaging

Equity markets can be volatile; a price on a particular day may not reflect the then-prevailing market trend and may be a one-off spike caused by, for example, market rumours. Section 6.7 provides an option for averaging; selecting this option in the confirmation will ensure that any monies exchanged between the parties, or the value of shares to be delivered, are closer to the general market trends in respect of selected shares and indices.

> *Extract from a template of an equity derivative transaction*
>
> Valuation:
> Valuation Time: At [ ] [am/pm] (local time in)
> Valuation Date:
> [Averaging Dates: [[In relation to each Valuation Date]]
> Averaging Date Disruption: [Omission][Postponement][Modified Postponement]
> Relevant Price: [ ]]

The averaging sections provide how the relevant settlement price or final price is to be calculated. First, the parties need to decide on the 'averaging dates' (ie, the dates which will be considered for the purposes of determining the relevant prices).

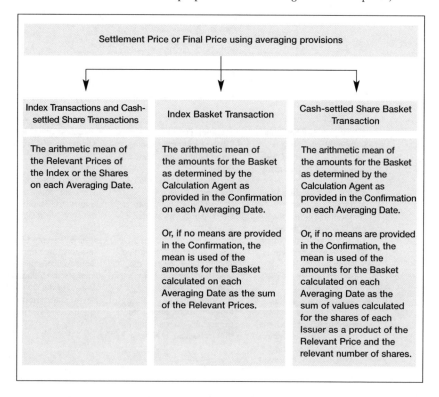

This section also uses the term 'relevant price', which was first introduced in Article 1. The 'relevant price' is the level of an index or the price of a share as determined by the calculation agent as provided in the confirmation as of the valuation time on the averaging date. (This would usually be the price of the share (or level of the index) as at the scheduled closing time of the relevant exchange on each averaging date.) The parties will also need to specify in the confirmation the averaging dates, so the dates which are taken into account when calculating the final price or the settlement price.

The standard averaging provisions are relatively simple. There are three different procedures here:

- for index or cash-settled transactions;
- for index basket transaction; and
- for cash-settled share basket transactions.

The details are set out in the diagram above. However, in principle, the final price, or the settlement price, is calculated as the arithmetic mean of the relevant prices on each averaging date.

8.5 Averaging date disruption

The parties are free to designate any scheduled trading day as an averaging date. However, any averaging date may also become a disrupted day. The 2002 definitions also provide for this with three alternative options, which may be elected in the confirmation: 'omission', 'postponement' and 'modified postponement'.

'Omission' means that if an averaging date falls on a disrupted day, it is disregarded (ie, there is one averaging date less for the purposes of the calculations). If the parties have chosen postponement as applicable, then the averaging date is postponed until the next scheduled trading date which is not a disrupted day. This means, however, that if the next scheduled trading date is already designated as an averaging date, then the price on such day would be used twice in calculating the relevant price. For this reason, the 2002 definitions also offer modified postponement as an election, under which the averaging date is the next scheduled trading day which is neither a disrupted day nor already an averaging date.

Example: Walsh Solutions PLC

Speight Enterprises Inc and Coles Capital Corporation entered into a cash-settled share transaction referencing Walsh Solutions PLC. Speight and Coles have chosen averaging to be applicable and the averaging dates are November 11, 12 and 13. Walsh is listed on the LSE. There were some glitches in the LSE communications system on 12 November and, as a result, that day was a disrupted day.

The relevant prices of Walsh Solutions in that week were as follows:

11 November: £65.80

12 November: N/A (disrupted day)

13 November: £66.60

14 November: £61.30

If Speight and Coles have chosen omission as the applicable election, then 12 November would be disregarded and the final price will be the arithmetic mean of the relevant prices on November 11 and 13:

(£65.80 + £66.60) / 2 = £66.2

If the parties have elected postponement, then the next scheduled trading day after November 12 is November 13. As it is already an averaging date, it would count double in the calculations:

(£65.80 + £66.60 + £66.60) / 3 = £66.33

If the parties have elected modified postponement to apply, the final price will be the arithmetic mean of the relevant prices on November 11, 13 and 14:

(£65.80 + £66.60 + £61.30) / 3 = £64.57

8.6   Futures price valuation

> *Extract from a template of an index transaction*
>
> Equity Amounts payable by [Party A][Party B]:
>
> [Futures Price Valuation: [Applicable][Not Applicable]
> Exchange-traded Contract: [ ]]

The 'futures price valuation' is available only for index transactions and index basket transactions. In some circumstances, the parties may decide that a final price or settlement price should be determined by reference to a particular contract, usually a futures or an options contract, listed on a particular futures or options exchange (the 'exchange-traded contract'). The parties need to specify all relevant details for such contract, such as the index to which it relates, its delivery month and exchange on which it is listed.

If futures price valuation applies, the valuation date will be a date when the official settlement price of the exchange-traded contract is published by the relevant exchange or clearing house (the 'official settlement price'). Accordingly, in respect of an index transaction, the settlement price or final price for such transaction is the official settlement price of the chosen exchange-traded contract on the relevant valuation date. For an index basket transaction, the official settlement price represents the relevant price for each index to which futures price valuation is applicable.

Lastly, if futures price valuation applies, then the settlement price and final price are determined by reference to the official settlement price irrespective of whether the relevant valuation date is a disrupted day or not.

Futures price valuation may often be very handy for the sell side institutions, which will hedge their transaction with a counterparty by entering into the relevant futures or options contract on the relevant futures or options exchange. By specifying this feature as applicable, they will ensure that the valuation of their OTC transaction documented using the 2002 definitions is the same as under the exchange-trade contract that they have separately purchased.

9.   Article 7 – "General terms relating to settlement"

> Article 7 sub-sections
> 7.1. Settlement Method Election
> 7.2. Settlement Method Election Date
> 7.3. Settlement Price

This is another short article, which applies to both cash as well as physical settlements and covers two areas – 'settlement method election' and definition of 'settlement price'.

9.1 Settlement method election

> *Extract from a template of an equity derivative transaction*
>
> Settlement Terms:
>
> [Settlement Method Election: [Applicable][Not Applicable]
> Electing Party: [Buyer][Seller]
> Settlement Method Election Date: [ ]
> Default Settlement Method: []]

Article 7.1 provides for an option to elect the settlement method (ie, whether the transaction should be cash or physically settled) during the term of the transaction. If applicable, the parties must specify:

- which party is the 'electing party' (ie, has the right decide whether the transaction is cash or physically settled);
- what is the 'settlement method election date' (ie, the date on which, or prior to which, the election must be notified by the electing party to the other party); and
- what is the 'default settlement method' (ie, what settlement applies if the electing party fails to notify the other party of its choice before the settlement method election date).

If settlement method election applies, but the parties have failed to specify the default settlement method, then:

- physical settlement will apply to 'share forward transactions' and 'share basket forward transactions'; and
- cash settlement will apply to index transactions and equity swap transactions.

However, there is no default settlement method in relation to option transactions.

9.2 Settlement price
Section 7.3 defines the settlement price for a type of transaction, as per the diagram below. The term 'settlement price' is crucial for determining the parties' payment and settlement obligations, as further explained below.

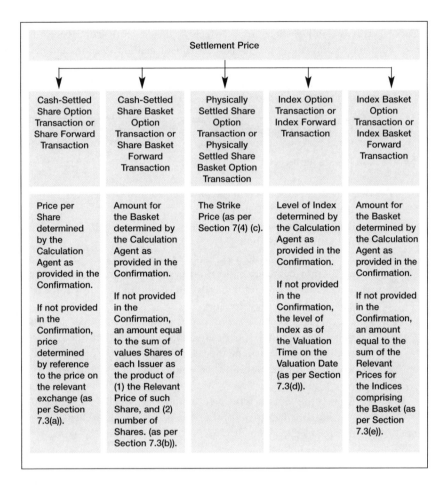

Settlement Price				
Cash-Settled Share Option Transaction or Share Forward Transaction	Cash-Settled Share Basket Option Transaction or Share Basket Forward Transaction	Physically Settled Share Option Transaction or Physically Settled Share Basket Option Transaction	Index Option Transaction or Index Forward Transaction	Index Basket Option Transaction or Index Basket Forward Transaction
Price per Share determined by the Calculation Agent as provided in the Confirmation. If not provided in the Confirmation, price determined by reference to the price on the relevant exchange (as per Section 7.3(a)).	Amount for the Basket determined by the Calculation Agent as provided in the Confirmation. If not provided in the Confirmation, an amount equal to the sum of values Shares of each Issuer as the product of (1) the Relevant Price of such Share, and (2) number of Shares. (as per Section 7.3(b)).	The Strike Price (as per Section 7(4) (c).	Level of Index determined by the Calculation Agent as provided in the Confirmation. If not provided in the Confirmation, the level of Index as of the Valuation Time on the Valuation Date (as per Section 7.3(d)).	Amount for the Basket determined by the Calculation Agent as provided in the Confirmation. If not provided in the Confirmation, an amount equal to the sum of the Relevant Prices for the Indices comprising the Basket (as per Section 7.3(e)).

10.   **Article 8 – "Cash Settlement"**

Article 8 sub-sections

8.1. Cash Settlement of Option Transactions

8.2. Option Cash Settlement Amount

8.3. Strike Price Differential

8.4. Cash Settlement of Forward Transactions

8.5. Forward Cash Settlement Amount

8.6. Cash Settlement of Equity Swap Transactions

8.7. Equity Amount

8.8. Cash Settlement Payment Date

Cash settlement is less complicated than physical settlement, which is why this article is also relatively short. Article 8 covers three areas:

- cash settlement of option transactions;
- cash settlement of forward transactions; and
- cash settlement of equity swap transactions.

The article specifies in the final Section 8.8 that any relevant payments shall be made on the 'cash settlement payment date'. Generally, this is the date as agreed by the parties in the confirmation; the 2002 definitions also however include fall-back provisions. The definition of 'cash settlement payment date' applies to all three types of transaction.

10.1 Cash settlement of option transactions

Under Section 8.1, for each exercise date for an option transaction, the seller pays to the buyer the 'option cash settlement amount'. The option cash settlement amount has different provisions applicable depending on whether the parties entered into a transaction referencing a share (or a basket of shares) or an index (or a basket of indices).

(a) Index option transactions and index basket transactions

In relation to 'index option transactions' and 'index basket option transactions', the 'option cash settlement amount' is defined as follows:

Option cash settlement amount = NO × SPD × USC × M

where 'NO' means the number of options, 'USC' means one unit of the settlement currency, 'M' means the multiplier and 'SPD' means 'strike price differential', which is, in turn, defined as:

- for a call option, an amount which is the greater of:
  - the excess of the relevant settlement price (ie, the market price of the relevant equity underlying at the relevant time) over the strike price (ie, the price specified as such in the confirmation for each transaction); and
  - zero; and
- for a put option, an amount which is the greater of:
  - the excess of the strike price (ie, the price specified as such in the confirmation for each transaction) over the relevant settlement price (ie, the market price of the relevant equity underlying at the relevant time); and
  - zero.

(b) Share option transactions and share basket option transactions

Here, the option cash settlement amount is calculated as follows:

Option cash settlement amount = NO × OE × SPD

where 'NO' means the number of options, 'OE' means 'option entitlement' (ie, the number of shares per option) and 'SPD' means strike price differential (as defined above).

Example: Vidlak International Inc

Saffron Partners sold one cash-settled call option referencing Vidlak International Inc to Konopka Enterprises on 4 February 2016. The option was a European option and could be exercised only on 16 June 2016. The parties also decided that this one option would be in relation to 1,000 shares of Vidlak (ie, the option entitlement was 1,000). The strike price (ie, the price per share for which Konopka would have a right to buy Vidlak share) was agreed at $70.

On 4 February, Vidlak's share price was $66, but it later soared and on 16 June it was at a high of $82.

This meant that Konopka had made a profit, which was determined as follows:

Cash settlement amount = NO × OE × SPD

NO is 1 (there is only one option)

OE is 1,000 (one option refers to 1,000 shares of Vidlak)

SPD is equal to the greater of the excess of the settlement price ($82) over the strike price ($66) and zero. The excess of the settlement price over the strike price is equal to $16, and $16 is greater than zero. Therefore, the SPD here is $16.

Lastly, the option cash settlement amount was:

1 × 1,000 × $16 = $16,000

This meant that as a result of the rise in the Vidlak's share value, and Konopka exercising its option, Saffron had to pay $16,000 to Konopka.

10.2 Cash settlement of forward transactions

As explained above, the parties to a forward transaction can elect prepayment as applicable in all transactions, and variable obligation as applicable in relation to the share forward transactions and share basket forward transactions. Naturally, those elections affect settlement.

As explained in more detail in section 6.2 above, 'prepayment' means that the buyer under a forward transaction has already paid (or will pay before the expiry of the transaction) a specified price in respect of the share, basket of shares, index or a basket of indices that is referenced under the transaction.

'Variable obligation' applies only to share forward transactions and share basket forward transactions (and not to any forward transactions referencing indices). If it is applicable, then parties to a transaction need not make any payments at the maturity of the transaction, as long as the price of the relevant share stays within a specified range.

Any payments are made on each cash settlement payment date and, at each such time, one party pays the 'forward cash settlement amount' to the other. If the forward cash settlement amount is a positive number, then the seller makes such payment to the buyer; if the amount is negative, then the buyer pays to the seller.

The position is slightly more nuanced if prepayment applies, as the buyer will have already made a payment for the relevant shares to the seller. In that case, on the 'cash settlement payment date', the seller pays to the buyer the sum of the forward cash settlement amount together with the 'excess divided amount' (as defined in section 12.3 below). In short, the excess dividend amount is included to give the buyer the benefit of all dividends payable by the issuer of the relevant underlying equity asset from the time that the buyer has made a payment of the prepayment amount to the seller.

These are the methods for determining the forward cash settlement amount (FCSA) for each type of transaction.

(a)   *Index forward transactions and index basket forward transactions (without prepayment)*

FCSA = (settlement price – forward price) × USC × M

For example, Party A as a seller agreed with Party B as a buyer to enter into a forward transaction for an index and they decided that:

- the forward price is €100;
- the multiplier is 1; and
- the unit of settlement currency (USC) is €1.

If the settlement price was in fact €120, then:

FCSA = (€120 – €100) × €1 × 1 = €20.

As the FCSA is a positive number, Party A (the seller) pays €20 to Party B (the buyer).

(b)   *Index forward transactions and index basket forward transactions (with prepayment)*

FCSA = settlement price × USC × M

This is a very similar formula to above. However, Party B (the buyer) has already paid the relevant amounts in respect of the index to Party A, which is why the calculations do not include the forward price. If our numbers stay the same, the FCSA will be determined as follows:

FCSA = €120 × €1 × 1 = €120

Party A pays €120 to Party B.

(c)   *Share forward transactions and share basket forward transactions (without prepayment or variable obligation)*

FCSA = NS × (settlement price – forward price)

'NS' is the number of shares or the number of baskets, as applicable.

Let us stick to our original example, but instead of referencing an index, Party A and Party B decided for their forward transaction to reference, say, five shares. Then FCSA is:

FCSA = 5 × (€120 – €100) = €100

Party A pays €100 to Party B.

(d)   *Share forward transactions and share basket forward transactions (with prepayment but without variable obligation)*

FCSA = NS × settlement price

As explained above, Party B (the buyer) has made the relevant payment in respect of the shares already, so you do not include the forward price in the calculations. To continue with our example:

FCSA = 5 × €120 = €600

Party A pays €600 to Party B.

(e) **Share forward transactions and share basket forward transactions (without prepayment but with variable obligation)**

If variable obligation is applicable, then parties need to agree both a forward floor price and forward floor cap. If the settlement price is higher than the floor, but lower than the cap, then no payments need to be made by either party.

If, however, the settlement price is less than, or equal to, the forward floor cap, then the FCSA is calculated as follows:

FCSA = NS × (settlement price – forward floor price)

If the settlement price is more than, or equal to, the forward floor cap, then the FCSA is:

FCSA = NS × (settlement price – forward cap price)

Let us now assume that Party A and Party B agreed the forward floor price to be €100 and the forward cap price to be €105. If the settlement price turns out to be €80, then:

FCSA = 5 × (€80 – €100) = -€100

As this is a negative number, Party B pays €100 to Party A.

(f) **Share forward transactions and share basket forward transactions (with prepayment and variable obligation)**

FCSA = NS × settlement price

This scenario is much less complicated, as the buyer has already made a requisite payment and there is no need to include the forward floor price or forward cap price for the calculations. In our example:

FCSA = 5 × €80 = €400

Party A pays €400 to Party B.

10.3   Cash settlement of equity swap transactions

In principle, on each cash settlement payment date, one party pays the equity amount to the other party. (The term 'equity amount' has been more fully analysed already in section 7 above). However, this can be slightly more complicated, depending on whether the parties want to include any dividends for the purposes of the calculations, as explained below.

Extract from a template of an equity derivative transaction

Equity Amounts payable by [Party A][Party B]:
Type of Return: [Price Return][Total Return]
...
Dividends:
Reinvestment of Dividends: [Applicable][Not Applicable]

If the parties have chosen 'price return', then the equity amount receiver does not get the benefit of any dividends and is exposed only to any movements in the price of the relevant shares or indices. In that case, if the equity amount is a positive number, then the equity amount payer makes such payment to the equity amount receiver. Conversely, if the equity amount is a negative number, then the equity amount receiver pays the relevant sum to the equity amount payer.

Alternatively, the parties can also choose 'total return' as applicable. Then the equity amount receiver is exposed to, and gets the benefits of, any declared dividends in relation to the referenced shares or indices. The manner in which the equity amount receiver benefits from this provision depends on whether the parties decide to specify 'reinvestment of dividends' as applicable.

If reinvestment of dividends is not applicable, then the parties calculate the equity amount in the same way as under price return. However, in addition to the equity amount, the equity amount payer will also pay to the equity amount receiver the relevant 'dividend amount' (if any) on each 'dividend payment date'.

If reinvestment of dividends applies, then the way the calculation agent determines the equity amount changes and, on each dividend payment date, the relevant dividend amount is added to the equity notional amount. This means that the equity amount receiver does not get the benefits of the dividends by way of direct payments, but instead its exposure to the relevant shares or indices increases by an appropriate amount.

11. Article 9 – "Physical settlement"

Article 9 sub-sections
9.1. Physical Settlement of Option Transactions
9.2. Physical Settlement of Forward Transactions
9.3. Physical Settlement of Equity Swap Transactions
9.4. Settlement Date
9.5. Number of Shares to be Delivered
9.6. Number of Baskets to be Delivered
9.7. Fractional Share Amount
9.8. Settlement Disruption Event
9.9. Expenses
9.10. Delivery Versus Payment
9.11. Representation and Agreement
9.12. Indemnification for Failure to Deliver

Physical settlement is a slightly more complicated process, as one party usually needs to make a payment, whereas the other one is obliged to deliver the relevant equity assets. Article 9 covers:

- provisions relating to settlement common to all types of transaction;
- the physical settlement of each of option transactions;
- the physical settlement of forward transactions;
- the physical settlement of equity swap transactions; and
- various boilerplate provisions in relation to physical settlement.

11.1 Common provisions
The article includes a few definitions which apply to settlement for each type of

transaction – namely, 'settlement day', 'number of shares to be delivered', 'number of baskets to be delivered' and 'fractional share amount'. 'Settlement day' is the day when a given transaction is settled; it is different for various practical and operational reasons for each type of transaction. The definition also covers a situation when the relevant clearance system cannot clear the transfer of the relevant share and there is a separate definition of a 'settlement disruption event'.

The definitions of 'number of shares to be delivered' and 'number of baskets to be delivered' are quite lengthy; they set out what exactly shall be delivered under each type of transaction on each settlement day. Some transactions are structured in such a way that a number of shares or baskets to be delivered is expressed as a fraction. As you cannot deliver a half of a share, then in addition to delivering defined shares and baskets a party will also need to pay an amount representing the fraction of such share or basket that you are required to deliver. such amount is defined as 'fractional share amount'.

11.2 Physical settlement of option transactions

For a call option, the buyer will pay to the seller the settlement price (expressed per share or per basket) multiplied by the number of shares (or baskets) to be delivered. In return, the seller will deliver to the buyer the number of shares (or baskets) to be delivered together with any fractional share amount.

For a put option, the buyer will deliver to the seller the number of shares (or baskets) to be delivered and will pay any fractional share amount. In return, the seller will pay to the buyer the settlement price multiplied by the number of shares (or baskets) to be delivered.

	Buyer delivers to the seller	Seller delivers to the buyer
Call option	Settlement price x number of shares (or baskets) to be delivered	Number of shares (or baskets) to be delivered + fractional share amount
Put option	Number of shares (or baskets) to be delivered + fractional share amount	Settlement price x number of shares (or baskets) to be delivered

11.3 Physical settlement of forward transactions

Physical settlement of forward transactions is slightly more complicated depending on the use of the additional elections: prepayment and variable obligations. It is summarised in the tables below.

For share forward transactions:

	Buyer delivers to the seller	Seller delivers to the buyer
P – VO –	Forward price × number of shares	Number of shares to be delivered + fractional share amount (if any)
P – VO +	Forward floor price × number of shares	Number of shares to be delivered + fractional share amount (if any)
P +	N/A	Number of shares to be delivered + excess dividend amount (if any) + fractional share amount (if any)

Above, 'P –' means that prepayment does not apply, whereas 'P +' means that it does. 'VO –' means that variable obligation does not apply and ' VO +' means that it does.

In the last scenario, in which prepayment is applicable, it is irrelevant whether variable obligation applies or not. However, this is crucial when calculating the number of shares to be delivered on the seller's side. Furthermore, as in the scenario where the buyer has made the prepayment, on the settlement day it is not required to deliver anything to the buyer.

For share basket forward transactions:

	Buyer delivers to the seller	Seller delivers to the buyer
P – VO –	Forward price × number of baskets	(Number of shares of each issuer × number of baskets to be delivered) + fractional share amount (if any)

continued on following page

	Buyer delivers to the seller	Seller delivers to the buyer
P – VO +	Forward floor price × number of baskets	(Number of shares of each issuer × number of baskets to be delivered) + fractional share amount (if any)
P +	N/A	(Number of shares of each issuer × number of baskets to be delivered) + excess dividend amount (if any) + fractional share amount (if any)

11.4 Physical settlement of equity swap transactions

This is the simplest settlement method. On the settlement day, the equity amount payer delivers to the equity amount receiver the number of shares (or baskets) to be delivered and pays the fractional shares amount (if any). In return, the equity amount receiver pays to the equity amount payer the equity notional amount (as agreed at the outset of the transaction).

11.5 Boilerplate provisions in relation to physical settlement

Article 9 also contains several sections dealing with the transfer of shares. Accordingly, all expenses relating to the transfer of shares are to be paid by the party that would pay such expenses according to the market practice for such transactions. Any transfer usually occurs on a delivery basis rather than a payment basis, and the transferor makes various representations relating to its ownership of the relevant shares. Lastly, the transferee will be indemnified in case the transferor fails to the deliver the shares.

12. Article 10 – "Dividends"

Article 10 sub-sections
10.1. Dividend Amount
10.2. Dividend Payment Date
10.3. Dividend Period
10.4. Re-investment of Dividends

> 10.5. Dividend Payment Obligations Relating to Physically-settled Option
>   Transactions
> 10.6. Extraordinary Dividend
> 10.7. Excess Dividend Amount

Shares underlying equity derivative transactions will often pay a dividend. In equity derivative transactions where any payment is related to the return on those shares, the treatment of those dividends, and the period for when dividends are taken into account in the transaction, are dealt with in Article 10.

This article covers the following areas:

- the mechanics of the determination and payment of dividend amounts relating to underlying shares and how these are treated in an equity derivatives transaction;
- special provisions in relation to equity swap transactions and option transactions; and
- provisions in relation to excess or extraordinary dividend.

> *Extract from a template of an equity derivative transaction*
>
> Dividends:
> [Dividend Period: [First Period][Second Period]
> Dividend Amount: The [Record Amount][Ex Amount][Paid Amount]
> multiplied by
> the Number of Shares
> Excess Dividend Amount: The [Record Amount][Ex Amount][Paid Amount]
> multiplied by
> the Number of Shares
> Dividend Payment Date: [ ]]
> [Extraordinary Dividend: [ ]]

12.1 Mechanics of the determination and payment of dividends

Dividend amounts are paid on the dividend payment date, which usually falls on the last day of the dividend period.

Article 9 provides that a dividend amount can consist of a 'record amount', an 'ex amount' or a 'paid amount', or any combination of them. All these sums are calculated before any applicable withholding or other deduction of taxes. Any 'extraordinary dividends' or 'excess dividend' amounts (as defined below) are excluded, though.

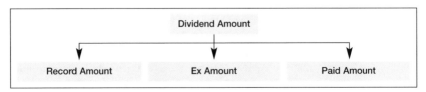

'Record amount' is any dividend declared by the relevant issuer during the relevant dividend period, whereas 'paid amount' is any dividend paid by the issuer during the relevant dividend period. 'Ex amount' represents any dividends declared by the relevant issuer if the relevant shares started trading ex-dividend during the dividend period.

When choosing the type of dividend amount, the parties should bear in mind any averaging provisions. For example, if the first averaging date falls on the last day on one dividend period and the second one on the first day of the new dividend period, then the price of the relevant share will be distorted.

As the type of dividend amount is determined by reference to the dividend period, it is crucial to be able to determine when that period starts and ends. This, in turn, depends on whether the parties choose 'first period' or 'second period' as applicable. 'First period' focuses on payment and settlement cycles and starts on the cash settlement payment date (in relation to cash settlement) or settlement date (for physical settlement) and runs up to, but excluding, the next cash settlement payment date or settlement date. 'Second period', in turn, concentrates on the valuation dates and runs from, but excluding, one valuation date, to another valuation date. This is also the default option if the parties fail to make a choice here.

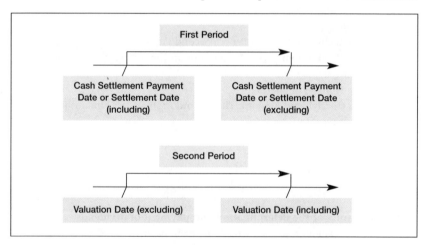

Lastly, 'dividend payment date' is a date specified in the confirmation, or, if not specified, the last day of the relevant dividend period.

12.2 Special provisions relating to equity swap transactions and option transactions

Another two important sections in Article 10 are Section 10.4 relating to re-investment of dividends and Section 10.5 relating to physically settled options.

The concept of 'reinvestment of dividends' normally applies only in relation to cash-settled equity swap transactions; it has been briefly discussed in section 10.5 above. If the concept applies, then the dividend amount is added to the equity notional amount, which means that the equity swap receiver is synthetically exposed to more of the relevant shares as the received dividends are used to acquire such additional exposure.

However, under the standard provision of the 2002 definitions, the dividend amount will not be reinvested until the next cash settlement payment date. This means that there is some delay in gaining the synthetic exposure to the additional shares between the moment when dividend is declared and the time when such amounts are added to the equity notional amount. If the parties want the newly declared dividend to be added to the equity notional amount immediately, they need to amend the 2002 definitions accordingly. The appropriate wording can be found in the user's guide.

Section 10.5 simply states that any dividends under cash-settled option transactions "will be payable to the party that would receive such dividends in accordance with the market practice for the sale of such Shares that are settled through the relevant Clearance System".

12.3   Extraordinary dividend

From time to time, companies declare a special, extraordinary dividend. These are usually paid when the relevant company has not declared any dividend for a year or longer, and represent the capital or the surplus of the relevant company. In principle, it is any other 'special' cash or non-cash dividend which is paid outside the normal operations or normal dividend procedures of the issuer.

Surprisingly, the 2002 definitions do not include a definition of the term 'extraordinary dividend' (although there are some suggestions in the user's guide), and the parties need to provide the details in the confirmation. If they do not define this term in the confirmation, however, it will be as determined by the calculation agent.

In any case, extraordinary dividend is not included under the ordinary dividend amount. The reason for is that the declaration of extraordinary dividend constitutes a potential adjustment event (as explained in the next section of this chapter).

'Excess dividend amount': This is an amount of extraordinary dividend which is calculated for each dividend period. As with ordinary dividend amount, depending when such dividend is paid or declared, it can be a record amount, ex amount or paid amount.

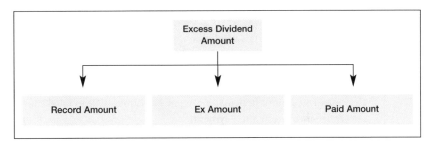

Even though extraordinary dividend is normally excluded from all obligations relating dividends (on the basis that its payment constitutes a 'potential adjustment event'), there is one exception. In forward transaction where prepayment is specified as applicable, the buyer has already paid for its exposure to the relevant equity assets, so it is only fair that it should get the benefit also of any extraordinary dividend. For this reason, the 2002 definitions specify that the seller would be required to pay any excess dividend amount to the buyer.

Parties to a forward transaction where prepayment is applicable may also want to specify that such dividend may accrue interest between the time it is paid and the cash settlement payment date (or the settlement date, for physically settled transactions).

13. Article 11 – "Adjustments and Modifications affecting Indices, Shares and Transactions"

Article 11 sub-sections

11.1. Adjustments to Indices

11.2. Adjustments to Share Transactions and Share Basket Transactions

11.3. Adjustments to Certain Share Transactions and Share Basket Transactions in European Currencies

11.4. Correction of Share Prices and Index Levels

Article 11 provides a framework to "compensate the affected party for the dilutive or concentrative effect of certain specified events on the theoretical value of the relevant Shares". This means that the parties are to be protected from an unfair result if an unusual event happens which was not foreseen at the transaction's outset. The article covers the following areas:

- adjustments to indices;
- adjustment to share transactions and share basket transactions;
- adjustment on the introduction of the euro; and
- correction of share prices and index levels.

13.1 Adjustment to indices

Extract from a template of an index transaction or index basket transaction

Index Adjustment Event:
    Index Cancellation: [Calculation Agent Adjustment][Negotiated Close Out][Cancellation and Payment]
    Index Modification: [Calculation Agent Adjustment][Negotiated Close Out][Cancellation and Payment]
    Index Disruption: [Calculation Agent Adjustment][Negotiated Close Out][Cancellation and Payment]

Section 11.1 sets out what happens if the relevant index has been replaced or if there is a successor to the index sponsor. In each case, the calculation agent needs to determine whether the new index – or the old index, but now calculated and announced by a new index sponsor – is calculated using substantially the same formula and calculations as before. If it is, then the new index (or the 'successor index') simply replaces the old one. If it is not, then there is an index cancellation or index modification event (as explained below).

Article 11 also allows the parties to decide what should happen if one of the three 'index adjustment events' occurs: 'index cancellation', 'index modification' or 'index disruption'. Accordingly, the parties can choose between three options for each event: 'calculation agent adjustment', 'negotiated close-out' and 'cancellation and payment'.

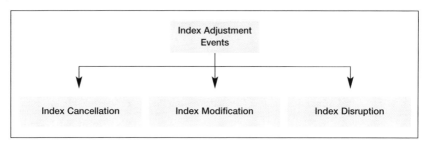

(a)   Index cancellation
As the name suggests and as explained above, this means that the relevant index was cancelled and no successor index exists.

(b)   Index modification
This means that the relevant index sponsor announces that it will make a material change in the formula or method for calculating the index.

(c)   Index disruption
This occurs when, on any valuation date, the index sponsor fails to calculate and announce the relevant index.

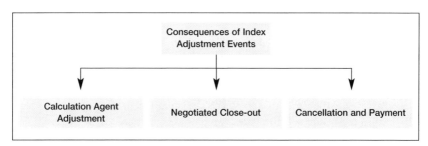

In the confirmation, the parties specify the consequence for each of the index adjustment events.

Calculation agent adjustment: If the parties elect calculation agent adjustment, then the calculation agent will calculate the level of the relevant index using the formula and method for the calculation of such index last in effect. At that point, the calculation agent will determine all the relevant prices (eg, the relevant settlement price, final price, knock-out price, forward price, etc) accordingly.

Negotiated close-out: This, in turn, means that the parties may, but they do not have to, agree to terminate the transaction on mutually acceptable terms. If they do not agree to terminate, then the transaction continues on the modified terms. This means, for example, that if index modification occurs, then transaction will continue using the materially changed formula or method for the calculation of the index.

Cancellation and payment: Under 'cancellation and payment', the transaction will be either cancelled automatically, or, in the case of index modification, at the option of either party. If a transaction is cancelled, then it will be valued using the formula for the calculation of the index immediately in effect prior to the index adjustment event.

13.2 Adjustment to share transactions and share basket transactions

Extract from a template of an share transaction or a share basket transaction

Adjustments:
Method of Adjustment: [Options Exchange Adjustment][Calculation Agent Adjustment]
[Options Exchange: [ ]]

In share transactions and share basket transactions, the parties need to decide between two choices: 'options exchange adjustment' and 'calculation agent adjustment'.

If they choose options exchange adjustment, then they must specify the relevant options exchange. Then, if there is any adjustment to the exercise, settlement, payment or other term of options on the relevant shares traded on the selected options exchange, the calculation agent will make the corresponding adjustments to the relevant terms in the transaction (eg, strike price, knock-in price, forward cap price, equity notional amount). The calculation agent will also decide the effective date of any such changes.

Naturally, this election can apply to all types of share and share basket transaction (ie, to share option transactions, share forward transactions and share swap transactions), and not only to option transactions – the rationale being that any changes to terms of options on the relevant shares listed on the relevant exchange should correctly reflect the "dilutive or concentrative effect on the theoretical value of the Shares" which has been caused by the relevant adjustment event. If the sell side party to the transaction has hedged its trade by entering into an exchange traded option, this will also ensure that there is no basis risk with its hedge position.

The calculation agent has also very wide powers to change the relevant terms of the transaction if the parties have elected calculation agent adjustment. Here, a potential adjustment event must occur and the calculation agent must determine if such an event has the required "diluting or concentrating effect". In practice, the calculation agent adjustment is the preferred election for the sell side entities, as it allows for maximum flexibility.

'Potential adjustment event' is defined in Article 11.2(e). Generally, it is any event that may have a diluting or concentrative effect on the theoretical value of the shares, in particular:

- subdivision, reclassification of the relevant shares;
- granting of any special, unusual rights to the existing shareholders;
- an extraordinary dividend;
- a call by the issuer for the relevant shares that are not fully paid;
- a repurchase of shares by the issuer; or
- some arrangements which could be classified as a 'poison pill'.

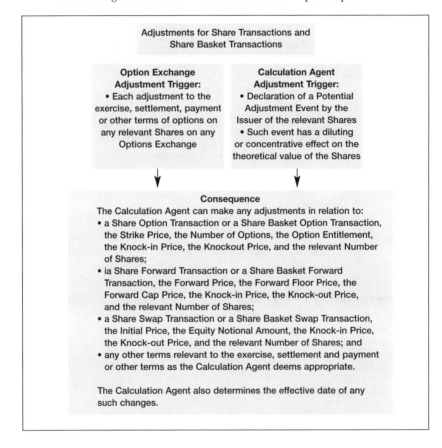

13.3 Adjustment on the introduction of the euro

Section 11.3 applies only to such share transactions and share basket transactions which relate to shares originally listed or quoted in a currency of a member state of the European Union that has not adopted the euro. If such a country adopts the single currency in the future, the calculation agent will adjust any terms of the transaction accordingly. At the time when the 2002 definitions were drafted, no one anticipated that any member state could leave the European Union or the euro, so that possibility was not specifically addressed.

13.4 Correction of share prices and index levels

Lastly, Section 11.4 covers the eventuality that any price or level published on any relevant exchange or by the index sponsor is subsequently corrected and such correction is published within one settlement cycle of the original publication. In such case, either party has a right notify the other party of the correction, and then the calculation agent will adjust the terms of the transaction accordingly.

This provision is new and was inserted as a result of the technological problems experienced by NASDAQ in June 2001 when the Russell Index was being rebalanced. In particular, the last sale price for a number of shares as published on Friday 29 June 2001 was later corrected on Monday 2 July and Tuesday 3 July 2001.

14. Article 12 – "Extraordinary Events"

> Article 12 sub-sections
> 12.1. General Provisions Relating to Extraordinary Events
> 12.2. Consequences of Merger Events
> 12.3. Consequences of Tender Offers
> 12.4. Settlement Following a Merger Event or Tender Offer
> 12.5. Composition of Combined Consideration
> 12.6. Nationalization, Insolvency and Delisting
> 12.7. Payment upon Certain Extraordinary Events
> 12.8. Cancellation Amount
> 12.9. Additional Disruption Events

Thirteen pages long, this is by far the longest article in the 2002 definitions. This article provides for the consequences of certain defined events (each, an 'extraordinary event') that may occur in relation to the underlying company under the transaction. To avoid confusion, it is important to remember that the events described here do not relate to the counterparties themselves, but only to the issuers of shares referenced in a transaction.

Altogether, there are 15 extraordinary events, which are defined in Section 12.1 as:

- 'merger event';
- 'tender offer';
- 'nationalisation';
- 'insolvency';
- 'delisting';
- any of the three 'index adjustment events' (ie, index cancellation, index modification and index disruption); and
- any of the seven 'additional disruption events' (ie, change in law, failure to deliver, insolvency filing, hedging disruption, increased cost of hedging, loss of stock borrow and increased cost of stock borrow).

Article 12 covers the following areas:
- merger events, tenders offers and their consequences;

- nationalisation, insolvency, delisting and their consequences; and
- additional disruption events and their consequences.

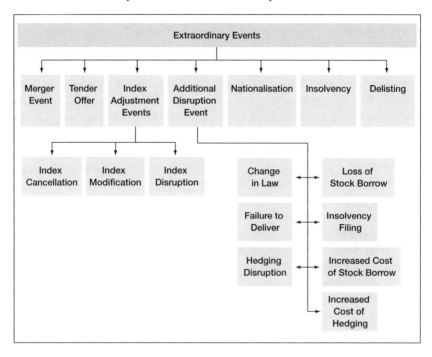

14.1 Merger events, tender offers and their consequences

Companies consolidate, amalgamate and merge with other companies or are taken over all the time. But what happens if, for example, we have an option to buy one share of, say, HBOS, but later HBOS merges with Lloyds TSB? The framework for dealing with these types of situation is covered in Article 12.

Section 12.1 defines a 'merger event' as any:

- reclassification or change of shares that results in transfer of all of such shares to another entity;
- consolidation, amalgamation, merger or a binding share exchange;
- takeover offer, tender offer, exchange offer, solicitation or proposal to acquire 100% of the shares of the relevant issuer; and
- a reverse merger (ie, when the issuer still exists, but all of its shares before the merger are less than 50% of all outstanding shares after such merger).

A 'tender offer' is very similar to the third definition above of a merger event, as it is defined as any takeover offer, tender offer, exchange offer, solicitation or proposal to purchase the relevant shares. Here, however, the potential buyer must aim to acquire more than 10%, but less than 100%, of all outstanding shares.

'Tender offer' is a new term that was not addressed in the 1996 definitions. In the meantime, however, tender offers became a more common means of acquiring control of the target, especially in the United States. This is why it was included as an additional option in the 2002 definitions. However, the parties must specify it as applicable in the confirmation for it to apply.

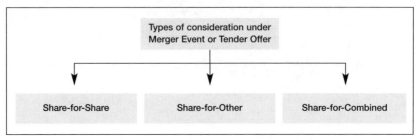

There are three ways in which a merger event or tender offer can occur. First, if you hold a share of an issuer which is being taken over, you may receive a number of shares of the new, merged company (the new shares) in consideration. For example, if you hold two shares of say, HBOS, you may receive one share of the new company resulting from the merger between HBOS and Lloyds TSB. This type of consideration is defined as 'share-for-share'.

Alternatively, instead of getting one share of the new Lloyds TSB/HBOS, you could receive just cash or other securities (which are referred to as 'other consideration'). In our example, your two shares of HBOS are exchanged for cash at the current market value. This is then called 'share-for-other'. Lastly, assuming that you still hold your two shares of HBOS, you may receive one share of Lloyds TSB/HBOS, but also, in addition to the share, you will receive some cash. This is referred to as 'share-for-combined'.

Extract from a cash-settled share basket option transaction
Consequences of Merger Events:

Share-for-Share: [Alternative Obligation] [Cancellation and Payment ([Agreed
    Model][Calculation Agent Determination])] [Options Exchange
    Adjustment] [Calculation Agent Adjustment] [Modified
    Calculation Agent Adjustment] [Partial Cancellation and Payment
    ([Agreed Model][Calculation Agent Determination])]

Share-for-Other: [Alternative Obligation] [Cancellation and Payment ([Agreed
    Model][Calculation Agent Determination])] [Options
    Exchange Adjustment] [Calculation Agent Adjustment]
    [Modified Calculation Agent Adjustment] [Partial
    Cancellation and Payment ([Agreed Model][Calculation Agent
    Determination])]

Share-for-Combined: [Alternative Obligation] [Cancellation and Payment
([Agreed Model][Calculation Agent Determination])] [Options Exchange
Adjustment] [Calculation Agent Adjustment] [Modified
Calculation Agent Adjustment] [Partial Cancellation and Payment
([Agreed Model][Calculation Agent Determination])][Component
Adjustment]

[Options Exchange: [ ]]
[Stock Loan Rate: [ ]]

[Tender Offer: [Applicable]]
Consequences of Tender Offers:

Share-for-Share: [Cancellation and Payment ([Agreed Model][Calculation Agent
Determination])] [Options Exchange Adjustment] [Calculation
Agent Adjustment] [Modified Calculation Agent Adjustment]
[Partial Cancellation and Payment ([Agreed Model][Calculation
Agent Determination])]

Share-for-Other: [Cancellation and Payment ([Agreed Model][Calculation Agent
Determination])] [Options Exchange Adjustment] [Calculation
Agent Adjustment] [Modified Calculation Agent Adjustment]
[Partial Cancellation and Payment ([Agreed Model][Calculation
Agent Determination])]

Share-for-Combined: [Cancellation and Payment ([Agreed Model][Calculation
Agent
Determination])] [Options Exchange Adjustment] [Calculation
Agent Adjustment] [Modified Calculation Agent Adjustment]
[Partial Cancellation and Payment ([Agreed Model][Calculation
Agent Determination])][Component Adjustment]

[Options Exchange: [ ]]
[Stock Loan Rate: [ ]]

The parties to a transaction are free to choose a consequence for each share-for-share, share-for-other or share-for-combined type of merger event (and tender offer, if applicable), if any of these events occur in relation to an underlying share. Generally, they can choose between seven events common to both merger events and tenders offers (ie, cancellation and payment, partial cancellation and payment, component adjustment, options exchange adjustment, calculation agent adjustment and modified calculation agent adjustment). In relation to merger events only, they can also elect alternative obligation. Furthermore, section 12.4 provides some further details on settlement following a merger event or tender offer.

14.2 Consequences of merger events and tender offers

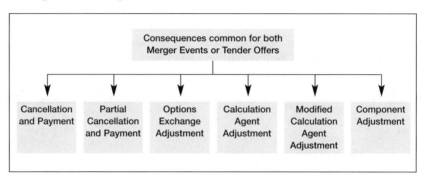

(a) Cancellation and payment

This means that the transaction will be cancelled and appropriate payments will be made in accordance with Section 12.7. In relation to option transactions only, the parties can choose how such payment shall be calculated. This will either be an 'agreed model' or 'calculation agent determination'.

Under the agreed model, the calculation agent tries to determine the value of the option transaction as it was before the extraordinary event had occurred, and then adjusts it by taking into account the change in value as a result of a change in the level of volatility of the underlying shares following such extraordinary event. If the parties elect calculation agent determination, however, the calculation agent has wide discretion and may, but is not obliged to, base its determination on the agreed model.

If cancellation and payment has been elected as a consequence of a merger event or tender offer under any swap transaction or forward transaction, the parties can decide that one or both of them shall be a 'determining party'. The determining party is responsible for calculating the 'cancellation amount', which, depending on whether it is a positive or negative number, will be paid over by one party to the other.

The definition of cancellation amount is quite lengthy and is set out in section 12.8. In principle, however, it is based on the formulation of the close-out amount in the 2002 ISDA Master Agreement. This means that the determining party will be calculating its own costs of replacing or providing the economic equivalent of the terminated transaction. It is important that the calculation agent is not chosen as a determining party, as it is not able to calculate its own costs of replacing the transactions and the provisions may not work.

(b) Partial cancellation and payment

Another consequence that the parties can elect applies only to share basket transactions. If chosen, the transaction will be terminated, but only in respect of such shares which are subject to the relevant merger event or tender offer (the 'affected shares'). Cancellation and payment, as set out above, will apply to such affect shares, whereas the transaction will continue in respect of all the other shares in the basket.

(c)   *Options exchange adjustment*

This operates in the same way as for index adjustment events, explained above. Accordingly, the calculation agent considers the impact of the relevant extraordinary event on the terms of options on the relevant underlying shares traded on the options exchange (as chosen by the parties). Then, the calculation agent makes appropriate adjustments to the relevant terms in the transaction (eg, strike price, knock-in price, forward cap price, equity notional amount). the calculation agent will also decide the effective date of any such changes.

(d)   *Calculation agent adjustment*

Another consequence of calculation agent adjustment is that it leaves a lot of discretion to the calculation agent to adjust the term of the transaction to account for the economic effect of the merger event or tender offer. However, when changing the terms, the calculation agent is not allowed to make any adjustments which account solely for changes in volatility, expected dividends, stock loan rate or liquidity relevant to the transaction.

(e)   *Modified calculation agent adjustment*

The definition of 'modified calculation agent adjustment' is almost identical, with the exception that the calculation agent can take into account any changes in volatility, expected dividends, stock loan rate or liquidity when adjusting the terms of the original transaction. Such changes may often have significant impact on the economic terms of the transaction.

In relation to calculation agent adjustment and modified calculation agent adjustment, if the calculation agent determines that no changes will produce a commercially reasonable result, cancellation and payment will be deemed to apply.

(f)   *Component adjustment*

Another election, component adjustment, can be chosen by the parties to apply in respect of a share-for-combined merger event or tender offer. This means that the consequences specifying for share-for-share will apply in relation to consideration consisting of new shares, whereas share-for-other will apply with respect to any other consideration.

Lastly, but in relation to a merger event only and provided this is not a reverse merger, the parties can choose alternative obligation. This means that the referenced shares and the referenced issuer under the transaction will change. The new underlying shares will be such as a holder of such shares would be entitled to receive in substitution for the ones it was holding before the merger event.

14.3   Composition of combined consideration

The provisions relating to merger events and tender offers are quite complex and there are various elections the parties can agree on in the transaction. Combined consideration is another special feature.

> *Extract from a template of an equity derivative transaction*
>
> Composition of Combined Consideration: [Applicable][Not Applicable]

In relation to any share-for-combined consideration merger event or tender offer, the parties can specify the composition of the combined consideration. Often, during a merger the acquirer offers the existing shareholders of the target company a choice as to what they would like to receive for their shares (ie, the shares of the acquirer, cash or anything else which the acquirer offers) and in what proportion.

If the parties to a transaction specify composition of combined consideration as applicable in the confirmation, then to the extent that the composition of the combined consideration could be determined by the shareholder, it is deemed to be new shares to the maximum value permitted.

However, if the holder could make any choice other than new shares, then the party that has long exposure to the share and will receive either such shares (if the transaction is physically settled) or a payment (if cash settled) on the transaction's maturity, can give notice to the other party and specify what it wants to receive.

The payee or deliveree must give at least two scheduled trading days' notice before the last time when an election can still be made by the holder of actual shares. In case the payee or deliveree does not specify what it would like to receive before the deadline, then the party that delivers the shares or makes a payment can in its sole discretion determine the composition of consideration.

If the parties specify composition of combined consideration as not applicable, then the first step is identical as to when this feature applies. Accordingly, to the extent that the composition of combined consideration could be determined by the shareholder, it shall be deemed to be new shares to the maximum value permitted. However, if the shareholder can choose consideration other than new shares, then the calculation agent decides in its sole discretion, what this should be.

Parties specify composition of combined consideration as applicable usually when one of them is hedging its position by buying the underlying shares. In that case, assuming that the party that needs to make a payment or deliver the shares under the relevant transaction is also holding the actual shares, than it can elect what it receives in exchange for its actual shares, as directed by the payee or deliveree.

Example: Machau Bank NA
Ottavio Global Inc has bought a call cash-settled option referencing 1,000 shares of Machau Bank from Poseidon Bank. This is a European option (ie, it can be terminated only on the expiration date), with the trade date of 22 July 2015 and the expiration date of 22 February 2016. This is a call option, so Ottavio gets a right to buy 1,000 Machau shares.

As the elected consequences of merger events, the parties have chosen alternative obligation in relation to share-for-combined. They have also specified composition of combined consideration as applicable. Poseidon Bank has hedged its position by buying 1,000 Machau shares.

Extract from the confirmation between Ottavio and Poseidon
Trade Date: 22 July 2015
Option Style: European
Option Type: Call
Seller: Poseidon Bank NA
Buyer: Ottavio Global Inc
Shares: The ordinary shares of Machau Bank NA (the Issuer)
Number of Options: 1,000
Expiration Date: 22 February 2016
Calculation Agent: Poseidon Bank
Consequences of Merger Events:

Share-for-Share: Modified Calculation Agent Adjustment
Share-for-Other: Modified Calculation Agent Adjustment
Share-for-Combined: Modified Calculation Agent Adjustment

Composition of Combined Consideration: Applicable

On 12 September, Lamping Bank and Machau announce a merger. In accordance with the merger's terms, the shareholders of Machau have some choice as to what they will receive in exchange for their shares. Accordingly, a holder of 1,000 shares, could get the following:

- 150 shares of Lamping for the first 750 shares of Machau;
- 20 shares of Lamping or cash in respect of another 100 shares of Machau. Machau shareholders have a choice until 4 November 2015 to decide whether they wanted cash or shares; and
- cash or 15 shares of Lamping Fund (a subsidiary of Lamping Bank) in respect of the final 150 shares of Machau. Machau shareholders must specify before 4 November 2015 whether they want to receive cash or shares of Lamping Fund.

As Machau does not exist as a separate entity after the merger with Lamping, the transaction between Ottavio and Poseidon needs to be adjusted. A merger event has clearly occurred and the related applicable election has been share-for-combined, as the shareholders were offered both cash and shares of Lamping.

The relevant consequence under the equity derivatives transaction is that a modified calculation agent adjustment applies, which means that Poseidon (as the calculation agent) has a right to make adjustments to any terms of the transaction as it determines appropriate to account for the economic effect on the transaction of the merger event. When making the adjustments, it can take into account any changes in volatility, expected dividends, stock loan rate or liquidity relevant to lamping shares.

Poseidon's discretion will be limited by the fact that the parties have chosen composition of combined consideration. Accordingly, when making the adjustments Poseidon will have to assume that 850 shares of Machau would be exchanged for 170 shares of Lamping.

In respect of the final 150 machau shares, Ottavio can give notice to Poseidon (in its capacity as seller) until 2 November (ie, two scheduled trading days before the holders of Machau shares can make the election) and specify what those 150 shares should represent for the purposes of the transaction. If it does not so, then Poseidon (as seller), can make the choice at its sole discretion. Lastly, Poseidon (as the calculation agent) will be able to make the necessary adjustments.

14.4   Nationalisation, insolvency, delisting and their consequences

---

Extract from a template of a cash-settled share basket option transaction

Nationalisation, Insolvency or Delisting: [Negotiated Close-Out] [Cancellation and Payment
([Agreed Model][Calculation Agent Determination])]
[Partial Cancellation and Payment ([Agreed
Model][Calculation Agent Determination])]

[Stock Loan Rate: [ ]]

This section of the 2002 definitions provides the parties with various elections to be made in the confirmation as to the consequences of nationalisation, insolvency and delisting of the issuer of the underlying shares.

The definitions of the trigger events are quite straightforward. Accordingly, 'nationalisation' means that all the shares or all substantially all the assets of the issuer have been transferred to any arm of the government.

'Insolvency' is very narrowly defined as any type of insolvency proceedings due to which either:

- all the shares of the issuer are required to be transferred to a trustee or liquidator; or
- the holders of the shares are legally prohibited from transferring them.

There is a very clear distinction between this event and 'insolvency filing', as described in the additional disruption events section below.

Lastly, 'delisting' means that the shares cease to be listed on the relevant exchange (other than for the reasons of merger event or tender offer) and are not immediately relisted.

The parties can choose one of the three consequences: negotiated close-out, cancellation and payment and partial cancellation and payment. As for a potential adjustment event, 'negotiated close-out' means that the parties may terminate the transaction on mutually agreed terms. If they do not, then the transaction continues on the terms and conditions then in effect.

'Cancellation and payment' means that the transaction will be cancelled in accordance with Section 12.7 (as explained above), whereas 'partial cancellation and payment', which applies only to share basket transactions, means that the transaction will be cancelled only to the extent that the shares in a basket are affected by nationalisation, insolvency or delisting.

14.5   Additional disruption events and their consequences

Extract from a template of an equity derivative transaction

Additional Disruption Events:
[Change in Law: [Applicable]]

[Failure to Deliver: [Applicable]]

[Insolvency Filing: [Applicable]]

[Hedging Disruption: [Applicable]
Hedging Party: [ ]]

[Increased Cost of Hedging: [Applicable]
Hedging Party: [ ]]

[Loss of Stock Borrow: [Applicable]
Maximum Stock Loan Rate: [ ]
Hedging Party: [ ]]

[Increased Cost of Stock Borrow: [Applicable]I
Initial Stock Loan Rate: [ ]
Hedging Party: [ ]]

[Determining Party: [Buyer][Seller][Buyer and Seller]]

All additional disruption events are entirely optional and must be specified to be applicable in any particular transaction. They relate to the underlying shares and allow the parties to cancel or adjust the terms of the transaction if one of those events occurs.

As with any derivative transaction, neither of the parties needs to hold any of the underlying shares under the transaction. However, the commercial reality is that often parties, and in particular market-making banks, do buy the relevant shares to hedge their position under the transaction. That is why the occurrence of an event affecting the shares can in turn affect the party holding the shares (the 'hedging party'). The 2002 definitions specifically provide for such situations.

If any of additional disruption events are specified as applicable in a confirmation, the parties must also specify one or both of them as the determining party. Similarly as under the merger event and tender offer provisions, the role of the determining party is to calculate the relevant amounts where applicable.

As mentioned above, there are seven additional disruption events:

- change in law;
- failure to deliver;
- insolvency filing;
- hedging disruption;
- increased cost of hedging;
- loss of stock borrow; and
- increased cost of hedging.

14.6   Change in law and insolvency filing

(a)   *Change in law*

This means that due to a change in the law, a party to a transaction determines in good faith that either:

- it has become illegal to buy, hold or dispose of the shares relating to the transaction; or
- it will incur a materially increased cost in performing its obligations under the transaction.

In practice, it is not uncommon to amend this definition to replace the word 'shares' with 'hedge positions', to acknowledge the fact that the hedging party may decide to hedge not by buying the actual underlying shares (but, eg, by buying an exchange traded option referencing such shares).

(b)   *Insolvency filing*

This means that a regulatory authority has initiated insolvency proceedings against the issuer of the relevant shares relating to the transaction, or that the issuer consents to any insolvency proceedings or a petition presented by its creditors.

If either change in law or insolvency filing occurs, then either party may terminate the transaction upon at least two scheduled trading days' notice to the other party specifying the date of such termination. The determining party will calculate the cancellation amount accordingly.

14.7   Failure to deliver

The parties may specify this event as applicable only in relation to a physically settled transaction. 'Failure to deliver' occurs when one party fails to deliver the relevant shares under the transaction, where such failure is caused by illiquidity in the market for such shares.

If failure to deliver applies, then such event does not constitute an event of default under the original ISDA Master Agreement. If it occurs, the party which is required to deliver the relevant shares (the 'delivering party') must give notice to the other party (the 'receiving party').

On the relevant settlement date following such notification, the delivering party must deliver to the receiving party such number of shares that it is able to deliver. The receiving party's obligation to pay for the shares is then reduced proportionately.

Depending on the type of transaction, the receiving party can then elect to elect to terminate a part or all of the remaining transaction, and it will be the determining party for the purposes of calculating the cancellation amount.

14.8 Hedging disruption

This occurs when the hedging party is unable to acquire, maintain or dispose of any transaction or assets that it deems necessary to hedge the risk of entering into and performing its obligations under the transaction, or it is unable to realise or recover the proceeds of any such hedging transaction.

If hedging disruption occurs and is continuing, the hedging party can terminate the transaction upon at least two scheduled trading days' notice to the non-hedging party. The determining party will then calculate the cancellation payment.

14.9 Increased cost of hedging

This is very similar to hedging disruption. Whereas under hedging disruption the hedging party is unable to acquire, maintain or dispose of any hedging transactions or realise the proceeds thereof, under increased cost of hedging, the hedging party would incur a materially increased amount of tax, duty, expense or fee for doing the same.

If this event occurs, the hedging party must give prompt notice to the non-hedging party that increased costs have been incurred, and that a price adjustment will be made to the transaction. At this point, the non-hedging party has two scheduled trading days to elect one of the following:

- it can agree to amend the transaction to take into account the price adjustment;
- it can pay the hedging party an amount calculated by the calculation agent that corresponds to the price adjustment; or
- it can terminate the transaction as of the second scheduled trading day.

If the non-hedging party does not make an election, then the hedging party may terminate the transaction by the end of the second scheduled trading day.

14.10 Loss of stock borrow

This event is relevant only if the non-hedging party has assumed a short position in relation to the underlying shares (eg, if it is the equity amount payer under the transaction). To acquire a hedge, the hedging party may then need to short the shares and, in order to do that, it first needs to borrow them.

The 'loss of stock borrow' event means that the hedging party is unable to borrow the number of shares it deems necessary to hedge its position under the transaction at a rate equal to or less than the maximum stock loan rate. If the parties decide that this event is applicable, they also need to specify the maximum stock loan rate in the confirmation.

If such event has occurred, then the hedging party must notify the other party accordingly. Then, the non-hedging party has to lend or procure that such shares are lent to the hedging party at a rate equal to or less than the maximum stock loan rate. Otherwise, the hedging party has a right to terminate the transaction.

14.11 Increased cost of stock borrow

This is related to loss of stock borrow and means that the hedging party would incur a rate to borrow shares in relation to the transaction that is greater than the 'initial stock loan rate'. If this event applies, the parties must specify the initial stock loan rate in the confirmation.

Similarly as under increased cost of hedging, the hedging party must give prompt notice to the non-hedging party that increased cost of stock borrow has occurred, and that a price adjustment will be made to the transaction. At this point, the non-hedging party has two scheduled trading days to elect one of the following:

- it can agree to amend the transaction to take into account the price adjustment;
- it can pay the hedging party an amount calculated by the calculation agent that corresponds to the price adjustment; or
- it can terminate the transaction as of the second scheduled trading day.

To avoid the price adjustment or the cancellation, the non-hedging party can lend (or procures that any other entity lends) the hedging party the relevant shares at a rate equal to or less than the initial stock loan rate.

Both the 'loss of stock borrow' and 'increased cost of stock borrow' aim to protect the hedging party if the costs of borrowing the underlying shares exceed the parties' initial expectations. There is a good argument that only one of those events should apply, and the hedging party should decide whether it wants to protect its position by reference to the 'initial stock loan rate' or the 'maximum stock loan rate'. In practice, however, sell side participants often insist on applying both events in their transactions.

15. Article 13 – "Miscellaneous"

Article 13 sub-sections
13.1. Non-Reliance
13.2. Agreements and Acknowledgments Regarding Hedging Activities
13.3. Index Disclaimer
13.4. Additional Acknowledgments

The final article contains four sections each setting out various representations, which are quite standard and of a boilerplate nature. They cover the following areas:

- 'non-reliance';
- 'representations' relating to hedging activities;
- 'index disclaimer'; and
- 'additional acknowledgments'.

Extract from a template of an index transaction

Non-Reliance: [Applicable][Not Applicable]

> Agreements and Acknowledgments
> Regarding Hedging Activities: [Applicable][Not Applicable]
>
> Index Disclaimer: [Applicable][Not Applicable]
>
> Additional Acknowledgments: [Applicable][Not Applicable]

15.1 Non-reliance

Section 13.1 lists various representations that parties are making to each other. Accordingly, if non-reliance applies, "each party represents to the other party that it enters into the Transaction as principal and not as agent; that neither the other party nor any of its Affiliates is acting as a fiduciary for it; that it is not relying on any representations other than those expressly set forth in the ISDA Master Agreement; that it has consulted with appropriate advisers and has made its own decisions based on its own judgement; and that it enters into the Transaction with a full understanding of the terms, conditions and risks of such Transaction".

15.2 Representations relating to hedging activities

If the parties specify this as applicable, then they represent to each other that they do not rely on the manner or method by which the other party or its affiliates enters into, maintains or disposes of its hedging arrangements in relation to the original transaction.

15.3 Index disclaimer

This provision is relevant only in relation to index transactions. If it applies, then the parties represent to each other that the transaction is not sponsored or promoted by the index or index sponsor. They also agree that the index sponsor makes no representations in relation to the index, and that neither party will have any liability for any act or omission by the index sponsor.

15.4 Additional acknowledgements

Lastly, if the parties specify additional acknowledgements are to apply, they represent to each other "that the other party and its Affiliates are not providing any specialised advice in respect of the Transaction; that it has been given the opportunity to obtain information on the terms and conditions of the Transaction that are necessary for it to evaluate the merits and risks of the Transaction; and that the other party and its Affiliates may engage in trading on the Shares of the Issuer underlying the Transaction".

Introduction to credit derivatives

Edmund Parker
Mayer Brown

1.　Introduction

A snapshot of the credit default market at the end of 2015 showed a total outstanding notional amount of US$12.3 trillion of total credit default swap contracts, with a gross market value of US$421 billion and net market value of US$113 billion. This comprised US$7.2 trillion of single name credit default swaps and US$5.1 trillion of multi-name instruments, consisting mainly of index products (US$4.7 trillion).[1]

The range of credit derivative products had developed quickly following the release by the International Swaps and Derivatives Association Inc (ISDA) of the 1999 ISDA Credit Derivatives Definitions, accelerating through the launch of the 2003 ISDA Credit Derivatives Definitions and ending with the commencement of the financial crisis in the latter half of 2007. Complexity rocketed during this era – single name credit default swaps evolved into:

- basket, constant maturity, constant proportion and portfolio credit default swaps;
- full and tranched index trades;
- 'collateralised debt obligation' (CDO) squared;
- CDO cubed;
- 'constant proportion portfolio insurance' (CPPI); and
- 'consent proportion debt obligation' (CPDO) transactions.

But just as with evolution itself, the initial species did not die. The financial crisis brought an end to CDO cubed transactions, CPDOs and much of the synthetic CDO transaction market. Will we ever see them again? The author would not rule it out, but not for a very long time.

Since 2007, the documentation focus of the credit derivatives asset class has been on building infrastructure to increase transparency and objectivity. Credit derivatives remain a strong and useful tool in the derivatives market. To understand what credit derivatives are, we must also look at the definition of 'derivatives'. The main legal definition of a 'derivative' is in Article 2(5) of the European Market Infrastructure Regulation[2] (EMIR) as a financial instrument as set out in points (4) to (10) of Section

---

1　Bank for International Settlements, Semiannual OTC Derivatives Statistics (OTC, credit default swaps, by type of position), May 2016.
2　Regulation 648/2012 4 July 2012 on over-the-counter (OTC) derivatives, central counterparties and trade repositories.

C of Annex I of the Market in Financial Instruments Directive (MiFID),[3] which applies a prescriptive list, for example:

Options, futures, swaps, forward rate agreements and any other derivative contracts relating to securities, currencies, interest rates or yields, or other derivatives instruments, financial indices or financial measures which may be settled physically or in cash;" and "Derivative instruments for the transfer of credit risk.

A more helpful and practical definition is:

a financial instrument referencing an underlying asset or other variable, from which the financial instrument's price or value is derived, entered into by the parties for a purpose.

This definition divides a derivative into four constituent parts. These are:

- a financial instrument;
- referencing an underlying asset or other variable;
- from which the financial instrument's price or value is derived; and
- entered into by the parties for a purpose.

This allows us to analyse each constituent part in turn to form a fuller picture of the nature of derivatives.

The financial instrument – the first constituent part – will fall into one of the three main categories of commodity derivative financial instrument:

- 'over-the-counter' (OTC) and 'centrally cleared' derivatives;
- structured products; and
- exchange-traded products.

In the case of OTC and centrally cleared derivatives, the financial instrument will be a swap, forward or option. In the case of a structured product it will be a note, certificate, warrant, fund unit or bespoke swap. In the case of an exchange-traded product, it will be a future, an option or one of the structured products.

The second constituent part is the underlying asset or other variable. This may be a standardised quantity of a commodity such as bullion, metals, agricultural products, freight prices, paper, gas, power, emissions allowances or a weather index. It might be an interest rate, a pair of currencies, or it may be an equity share or index. It may also be a debt instrument, such as a bond or loan, a basket of the same, or borrowed money.

The price or value of the underlying asset from which the financial instrument derives its value – the third constituent part – may be:

- the change in the price of an underlying commodity or future referencing it;
- the level of an equity index over a period of time or between specific dates; or
- the perceived likelihood of a credit event impacting on the underlying debt of a third-party reference entity.

Alternatively, it may be the relative price or level of different underlying assets over a period of time or specific dates such as currencies, or the total return on single

---

3   Directive 2004/39/EC as implemented by Article 38 and 39 of Regulation 1287/2006.

or multiple underlying assets (eg, indices or futures contracts) over a period of time. These prices or levels may be determined on specific or multiple dates and often in accordance with a formula.

The purposes for which the parties enter into a derivative transaction – which make up the fourth constituent part of a derivative – can be many and varied. Reasons might include:

- commodity producers such as mining companies looking to hedge against sale proceeds being insufficient to cover production costs;
- property developers hedging their loans against rises in the floating rate of interest;
- manufacturers hedging against rises in raw material prices which would erode sale margins;
- speculators making leveraged investments in shares; and
- funds looking to diversify their investments away from traditional asset classes such as debt and equities.

This analysis is clarified further by the diagram on the next page.

2.   The first constituent part of a credit derivative: the financial instrument

Figure 1: The constituent parts of a derivative: the financial instrument

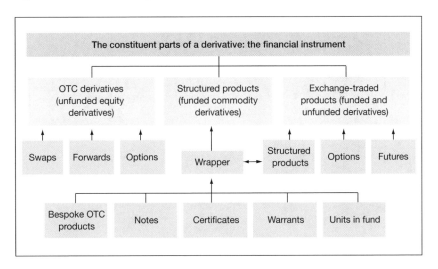

Any derivative financial instrument will be a sub-type of at least one of the three derivatives categories:

- OTC derivatives and centrally cleared derivatives;
- structured products; and
- exchange-traded products.

Figure 2: Definition of a derivative

Definition of a derivative:
• a financial instrument; • referencing an underlying asset or other variable; • from which the financial instrument's price or value is derived; • entered into by the parties for a purpose.

Price or value of the financial instrument derived from the underlying commodity asset or variable.

Leveraged return on underlying asset.

Underlying asset variable: Future price of or level of underlying asset(s) on specified date(s), perhaps by reference to strike price or formula.

Strategic return on the underlying asset:
• tax
• accounting
• selective.

• Protection against specific events.

Underlying asset or related variable referenced by the financial instrument (including categories below).

Equities; FX; inflation; commodities; interest rates; and credit.

Parties make a gain or suffer a loss on the financial instrument depending on the relevant value of the underlying commodity asset or variable at a particular time or times.

Purpose
The parties will enter into a derivative for a purpose. This purpose will direct:
• which financial instrument is used;
• the underlying commodity asset; and
• the value to be derived from the underlying asset or variable.
Purposes include those below:

Investment strategy

Monetising

Reducing financing costs

Hedging

Financial instrument (the financial instrument will be from one of the three categories below).

Exchange-trade products:
• funds
• futures
• options
• structured products.

Structure products:
• notes
• warrants
• certificates
• bespoke OTC Products.

OTC derivatives:
• options
• swaps
• forwards.

Each financial instrument is to some extent bilateral, either between counterparties (OTC), issuer and instrument-holders (structured products), or exchange and holder (exchange-traded products).

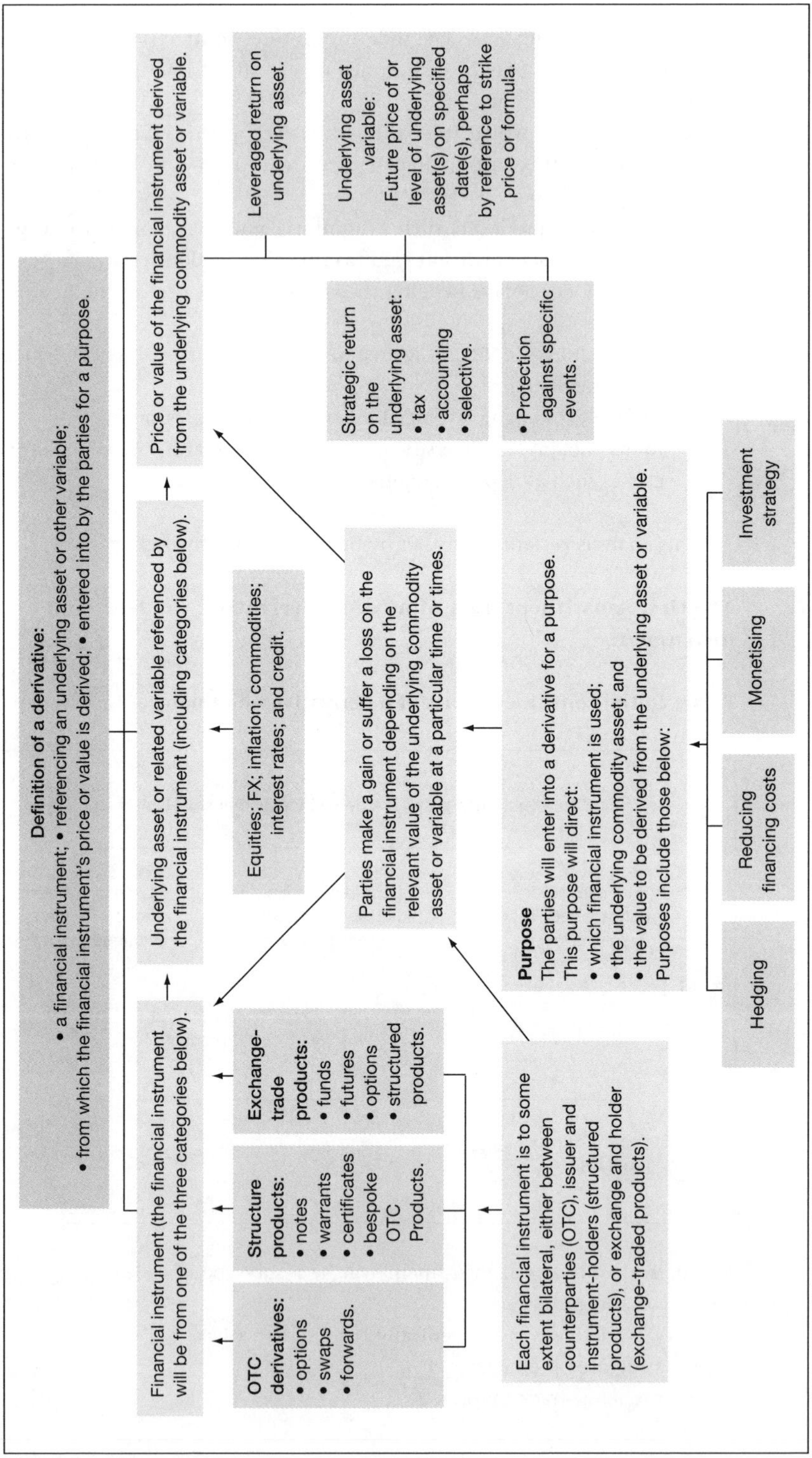

An OTC derivative financial instrument will be a swap, a forward or an option. A structured product financial instrument will be a note, a certificate, a warrant, a unit in a fund or a bespoke OTC product. An exchange-traded product financial instrument will be a future or an option or, if it is listed on an exchange, one of the four types of structured product financial instrument.

The term OTC (or 'over-the-counter') derivatives refers to these financial instruments being specifically tailored or bespoke instruments between the two parties, usually either two market makers or a market maker and an end user.

Just as with the clothing trade, many of these products have become commoditised and standardised, allowing an 'off-the-peg' alternative. The off-the-peg alternative is a 'centrally cleared' transaction. The development of this market in credit derivatives has been driven largely by regulators and law makers who, through Title VII of the Dodd-Frank Act in the United States and EMIR in the European Union, have pushed to have standardised derivatives contracts centrally cleared.

Central clearing and central counterparties (CCPs):

At a meeting in Pittsburgh in September 2009, the G20 leaders resolved that:

All standardised OTC derivative contracts should be traded on exchanges or electronic trading platforms, where appropriate, and cleared through central counterparties by the end of 2012 at the latest.

Centrally cleared derivatives involve two counterparties entering into an OTC derivative financial instrument, the parties then give up the trade to a CCP. The CCP will then face a 'clearing member' on one side of the transaction, and another clearing member on the other side of the transaction. The idea of central clearing is to reduce the systemic risk of a network of bilateral back-to-back trades.

The CCP will therefore be a 'buyer to every seller' and a 'seller to every buyer'. This means that each clearing member takes credit risk only against the CCP. To protect itself against these dual credit risks, the CCP will receive both initial and variation margins.

Now the clearing members may or may not be the original parties to the OTC transaction. Most likely, one of the parties to the original transaction will be a member or the CCP. This is because almost all OTC derivative transactions are between either a market maker and end user or customer, or between two market makers. Generally speaking, the market maker will be a clearing member of the relevant CCP. OTC derivatives contracts which are not between clearing members are not centrally cleared.

Centrally cleared derivatives therefore consist of one standardised OTC derivative being given up to a CCP to form two standardised OTC derivatives (one between the seller and the CCP, and one between the buyer and the CCP).

If a transaction is given up to central clearing, then this will not alter the overall structure of the OTC derivative, other than in relation to the parties involved.

The ambition of the G20 leaders to move all standardised OTC derivative contracts to central clearing by the end of 2012 proved too ambitious. On 1 March

2016, the European Commission introduced a mandatory clearing determination under EMIR with credit default swaps linked to iTraxx Europe Main (five-year tenor, series 17 onwards, EUR settlement) and iTraxx Europe Crossover (five-year tenor, series 17 onwards, EUR settlement) indices becoming subject to mandatory clearing with authorised or recognised CCPs. This obligation takes place on a phased basis, first affecting clearing members for these contracts from 9 February 2017, then financial counterparties and alternative investment funds, exceeding a threshold – with other users being captured in further phases until May 2019. Where the credit default swap is between counterparties in two separate categories, the clearing obligation takes effect from the later applicable date.

Under certain conditions in Europe, the clearing obligation can apply to third-country (non-EU) counterparties including when EU counterparties trade with entities established outside the European Union, or when both counterparties are established outside the European Union, but an impact on EU markets arises.

Similar requirements also exist in other jurisdictions such as the United States. There, clearing members are called 'Future Commission Merchants' (FCMs) and only they can contract directly with the CCP. A first phase of clearing of credit default swaps was introduced on 11 March 2013 in the United States, with credit default swaps linked to certain high-yield and high-grade indices becoming subject to mandatory clearing.

Other types of standees OTC credit default swap will follow, and indeed non-mandatory clearing of a number of other products, including single name credit default swap and other credit derivatives indices takes place on a voluntary basis in various jurisdictions. For example, ICE Clear Credit cleared US$100 billion of notional single name credit default swaps in the first seven months of 2016, up from US$33.3 billion in 2015. The platform with its affiliate ICE Clear Europe clear more than 500 single name and index credit default swap instruments.[4]

2.1 OTC derivatives/centrally cleared derivatives

There are three categories of derivatives OTC/centrally cleared financial instrument: options, forwards and swaps. Each type has various sub-types. Sub-types of option are European, American, Bermudan, Asian and barrier options. Among the sub-types of forward are contracts for difference, while sub-types of swap include index-linked and basket swaps. For credit derivatives, by far the most common OTC financial instrument is the swap; however, to a lesser extent options and forwards do exist in the market, and may be used in more bespoke transactions.

(a) Options

An 'option' is a bilateral contract. The buyer of the option acquires a right to buy (or sell to the seller of the option) a defined amount of an underlying asset at a price agreed at the contract's outset (the 'strike price'). This price will be either a specific

---

4   "ICE Clear Credit surpasses US$100 billion in client cleared single name credit default swaps for 2016", Institutional Asset Manager, 12 August 2016.

Figure 3: OTC derivatives/centrally cleared derivatives

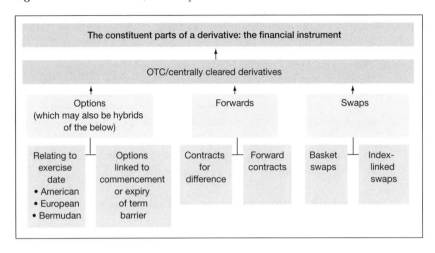

price or one determined by reference to a formula or set of rules set out in the confirmation. The underlying asset is usually a single asset such as a share or commodity or basket of shares or commodities, or an index or basket of indices.

The option buyer pays an amount of money (a 'premium') to the option seller, as determined in the relevant transaction confirmation, to compensate it for providing the option.

Options are either call options or put options, and are also either cash settled or physically settled.

In the arena of credit derivatives, a credit spread product is usually structured as a put or call option. A put option gives the buyer the right, but not the obligation, to sell the seller a reference bond at a future date. The price payable would be referenced to the credit spread. A call option gives the buyer the right, but not the obligation, to buy that credit spread at a future date.

Alternatively, swaptions (which are combinations of swaps and options) give under the option part of the agreement one party – the swaption buyer – the right, but not the obligation, to compel the swaption seller to enter into a credit default swap with it. Under this credit default swap part of the agreement, the swaption seller will either buy or sell credit protection at a price agreed at the outset of the swaption.

(b) *Forwards*
A forward transaction is a bilateral sale and purchase contract. In a physically settled transaction, one of the parties agrees to sell and the other agrees to buy a defined amount of the underlying asset at a defined point in the future for a specified price (if the transaction is physically settled). In both cases, sale prices can instead be determined by reference to a formula or an average price over a number of dates.

In a cash-settled transaction, the parties exchange the difference between the actual trading price of the underlying asset at the future date and the price set out in the confirmation.

A forward can also relate to an index (in which case it will be cash settled), and the parties will instead exchange payments based on a settlement price related to the level of the index at the future date as compared to the level set out in the confirmation.

(c)   Swaps

Swaps are by far the most common type of credit derivative financial instrument. A credit default swap or 'CDS' is a bilateral contract that allows one party to acquire economic exposure to the creditworthiness of a corporate or sovereign (the 'reference entity') without the need of investing in the debt of the reference entity. The other party, meanwhile, is hedged against the reference entity's credit risk. There are several variations including single name/reference entity swaps, basket reference entity swaps and portfolio reference entity swaps.

2.2   Documentation platform for options, forwards and swaps

(a)   ISDA

The principal provider of documentation for OTC derivatives transactions is ISDA. This is particularly so for credit derivatives, where ISDA has taken the driving seat in creating a structure for documenting derivatives transactions. The organisation is the dominant derivatives trade association. It numbers 850 member institutions spread across 67 countries among its worldwide membership of banks, corporates and other derivatives participants. All major credit derivatives market participants are ISDA members.

(b)   ISDA's suite of credit derivatives documentation

ISDA's credit derivatives suite of documentation for OTC credit derivatives consists of three inter-linking platforms: a primary platform, a secondary platform and a tertiary platform. The primary platform is the same for all ISDA's suites of derivatives documentation (eg, equity derivatives, interest rate derivatives and inflation derivatives). The other two platforms, though, are distinct.

Figure 4: The primary platform

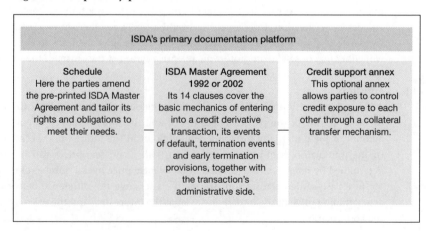

ISDA's suite of credit derivatives documentation for OTC credit derivatives utilises the primary platform of an ISDA Master Agreement (as amended by a schedule) and also an optional credit support annex to that Master Agreement.

The ISDA Master Agreement may either be the 1992 Master Agreement or the 2002 Master Agreement (the latter now being by far the most common). The 2002 Master Agreement has 14 clauses. These cover the basic mechanics of entering into the transaction, its events of default, termination events and early termination provisions, as well as the administrative side of things. This pre-printed form is amended by the parties in a pre-printed schedule, where they make certain elections and tailor the Master Agreement to their requirements.

The parties may also optionally enter into a credit support annex (or sometimes a credit support deed) which will form part of the Master Agreement and under which they will make transfers of collateral (either unilaterally or bilaterally) to control their risk exposure to each other. The primary platform will be used by the two parties for all of their derivatives transactions (eg, interest rate swaps, currency swaps, equity derivatives transactions and credit derivatives transactions).

Figure 5: The secondary platform

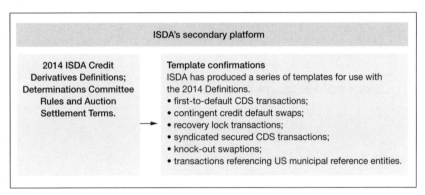

Standing on the shoulders of the primary platform is a secondary platform. This consists of the 2014 ISDA Credit Derivatives Definitions, the Determinations Committee Rules and Auction Settlement Terms, as well as a series of template confirmations and protocols.

Each template confirmation incorporates the parties' ISDA Master Agreement (as amended by the schedule) and, if applicable, a credit support annex. A confirmation also incorporates the 2014 ISDA Credit Derivatives Definitions.

The most basic form of confirmation template – one for single name credit default swaps – is provided in Exhibit A to the 2014 definitions.

Additionally, ISDA has produced templates for various specific types of credit derivatives transaction. Prior to the financial crash, each new template was produced for a new product as soon as was merited by business flow. Some of these templates are obsolete, or are likely to be used only in highly bespoke arrangements, such as 'credit default swaps on asset-backed securities' (CDS on ABS).

Others have recently been updated to take account of the 2014 definitions. These are the template confirmations for:

- first-to-default credit default swap transactions;
- contingent credit default swaps;
- recovery lock transactions;
- syndicated secured credit default swap transactions;
- knock-out swaptions; and
- transactions referencing US municipal reference entities.

The tertiary platform: Some reference entities or reference obligations may have specific features, which mean that specific amendments must be made to the 2014 definitions and template confirmations.

Because the transactions occur only sporadically, ISDA has produced various 'additional provisions' documents which can be incorporated by reference into a confirmation and which amend the terms of the template confirmation or modify the 2014 definitions. ISDA has produced additional provisions documents to cover the more widely traded variations, which include, for example, the Additional Provisions for the Republic of Hungary and the Additional Provisions for LPN (loan participation notes) Reference Entities.

A second leg includes supplements, such as the CoCo Supplement described below, which can be incorporated into a confirmation to bring specific variations to the 2014 definitions.

Figure 6: The tertiary platform

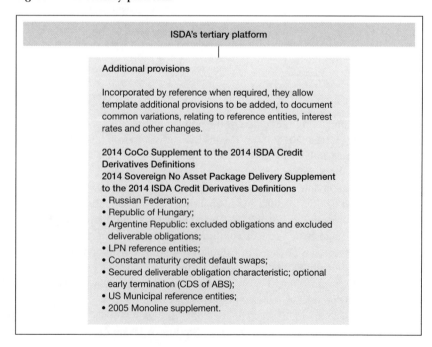

2.3 Structured products

For structured products, the financial instrument is called a 'wrapper'. The wrapper may be a certificate, note or warrant or, for more bespoke OTC derivatives, the standard ISDA documentation framework. The specific format that a wrapper takes will depend on investor preference, efficiency, liquidity, and tax and regulatory issues.

Although notes or certificates can be issued as standalone instruments by an issuer (usually a financial institution or one of its specially created subsidiaries), for reasons of documentation efficiency they are more commonly issued under a programme. The programme will establish a master documentation platform, under which future issues of instruments will be documented.

The programme will have a prospectus which, if listed on a stock exchange, will make the structured product also an exchange-traded derivative. Where this occurs, in Europe this is most commonly the Luxembourg Stock Exchange or the Irish Stock Exchange.

The prospectus will set out the conditions of any instruments issued under the programme. These conditions will usually adapt many of the provisions from the 2014 definitions to make them suitable for inclusion in a certificate, note or warrant. The prospectus will also contain risk factors and disclosure on the issuer and any other relevant parties.

The programme will also have an agency agreement which will set out the roles and responsibilities of the various other parties to the transaction – such as the calculation agent and paying agents.

Each time the issuer issues instruments to investors, it will complete a final terms document. This will make various elections contained in the conditions (set out in the prospectus) and will set out the pricing information and specific terms (eg, the identity of the underlying asset) for the particular issue.

The final terms will be attached together with the conditions to a global instrument (which will represent all of the securities for a particular issue), and will be deposited into a clearing system. In Europe, this will usually be either one or both of Euroclear and Clearstream. The instruments can then be traded.

Sometimes, but not always, the individual issue of securities will be listed on the same stock exchange as the programme. This helps to make the securities more liquid and also meets the investment requirements of many institutional investors. This means that commodity derivatives structured products can also be exchange-traded products.

2.4 Exchange-traded products

Exchange-traded credit derivatives are derivatives traded on an organised exchange. The product is popular in the form of listed structured notes or certificates as described above.

Exchange-traded derivatives may also be centrally cleared. The principal exchange-traded credit derivative products of this nature are cleared swaps. This product is currently in its infancy, but with a regulatory push coming through MiFID II, it is likely to be increasingly prominent. The additional difference here is that swaps can be entered into with brokers on the basis of bid/ask prices listed on the exchange.

3. The second constituent part of a derivative: the underlying asset

In the case of commodity derivatives, the underlying asset being referenced by the financial instrument is almost always a single commodity or a basket of commodities, or a single commodity index or a basket of commodity indices.

In equity derivatives transactions, the underlying asset is fairly simple: shares or indices related to them. The complexity lies in the regulation, the extreme volatility of the underlying asset and the sophisticated structures set up to manage these.

For credit derivatives transactions, the underlying asset is the creditworthiness of a reference entity in relation to its borrowings.

This concept can be best explained through an example. SG Warburg arranged the first eurobond: a US$15 million, 5% 10-to-15-year bond issued by Italian Autostrada on 1 July 1963. The bondholders in that issue of securities accepted the bundle of risks set out in the graph below.

Figure 7: Isolation and separate trading of credit risk

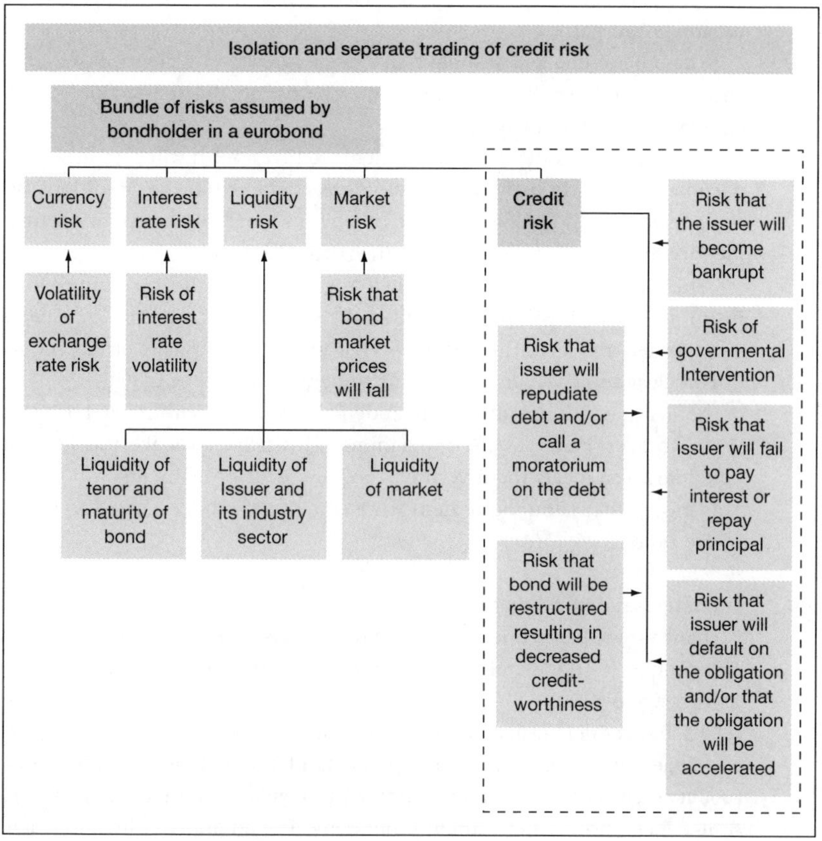

The international bondholders took on the currency risk that the exchange rate of the dollar would collapse against the domestic currencies of their own jurisdictions. The bonds were fixed-rate bonds so they also assumed interest rate risk – if floating-rate interest rates rose above the fixed-interest rate of the Autostrada bonds, then a bondholder would suffer this negative exposure (ie, the yield of the bonds would be low in comparison to other then current investments). Investors were also taking the risk that both the tenor of the securities and their term could prove to be illiquid.

Lastly, investors were taking a risk on Autostrada's creditworthiness – the risk that:

- Autostrada could become bankrupt;
- Autostrada could default on the payment of interest or repayment of principal;
- the bond could default for other reasons or be accelerated;
- Autostrada could repudiate the debt or declare a moratorium; or
- Autostrada could restructure the bond leading to a material decline in the company's creditworthiness.[5]

Those investors that wished only to assume and invest in the credit risk of Autostrada were forced to assume all of the other risks related to its obligations as well: currency risk, liquidity risk, interest rate risk, maturity risk and all other risks making up the bundle of risks inherent in any capital markets security. And this was the way it was for all bond and loan market investors until the invention of credit derivatives in the 1990s.

All derivatives derive their value from an underlying asset. In the case of credit derivatives, the underlying asset is the credit risk of an underlying reference entity, be it corporate, sovereign or a similar organisation. Credit derivatives aim to isolate the credit risk of a reference entity (eg, the issuer of a bond) from the other risks inherent in its obligations (ie, those described above). Credit risk can then be separately traded.

Let us take the Italian Autostrada example above. Imagine that credit derivatives had been invented in 1963 – 30 years earlier than they actually were. An investor entering into a credit derivative transaction referencing Autostrada could have sold credit protection to gain exposure to Autostrada's credit risk instead of buying eurobonds containing the rest of the bundle of risks. Instead of the investor assuming a portion of the eurobond's interest rate corresponding to credit risk, that investor's derivatives counterparty would be paying it a premium in return for it assuming the same credit risk.

Bilateral derivatives contracts require counterparties to take opposite views. That investor's counterparty might have chosen to purchase a corresponding amount of eurobonds to gain exposure to the other risks comprising the bundle of risks, while buying protection against Autostrada's credit risk. This investor would have assumed

---

5   In fact, none of these events happened. The bonds were repaid in full and Autostrada returned to the eurobond markets in 2006.

Figure 8: What is 'credit risk' in a debt obligation?

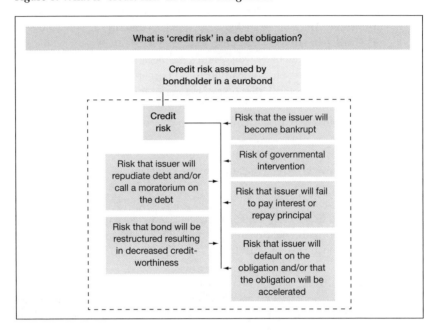

currency risk, interest rate risk, liquidity risk and market risk, but would have been protected against the credit risk in return for it paying a premium.

The Autostrada eurobond also preceded the interest rate and currency rate derivatives markets which developed in the 1960s and 1970s, but had these markets existed, an Autostrada bondholder could have hedged itself against currency movements with a currency swap or against interest rate movements with an interest rate swap.

Credit derivatives, like their sister products currency derivatives and interest rate derivatives, allow particular risks to be isolated and separately traded. As we shall see below, credit risk can never be entirely isolated from other risks, but the credit derivatives product allows other risks to be minimised.

The above example reflects the fact that a credit derivative in its simplest form could replicate the credit risk of an individual cash asset. More complex credit derivatives repackage and redistribute the credit risk of a portfolio of different assets among different investors in accordance with their appetite for risk.

How credit derivatives work: Taking credit derivatives in their simplest form, and taking as the central premise of a credit derivative the isolation, transfer and separate trading of credit risk, a party entering a credit derivative will seek to buy or sell the credit risk of a reference entity – perhaps a FTSE 100 company. This reference entity will not be a party to the credit derivatives contract; indeed, most reference entities will probably be unaware of its existence.

The credit derivatives contract will be most commonly documented as a swap.

The reference entity may be any corporate, a sovereign or any other form of legal entity which has incurred debt. For OTC derivatives contracts, a credit derivatives contract will (unless it is a structured 'funded' transaction) be made between two parties. One party, the buyer, will purchase protection against the credit risk of the relevant reference entity. To do this, it will pay a premium to the other party, the seller. Please also note the discussion above on centrally cleared derivatives.

The credit derivatives market is very standardised and, in the majority of contracts, it views the credit risk of a reference entity as having seven potential categories.

Figure 9: A reference entity's seven categories of credit risk

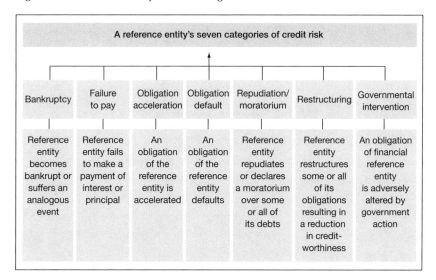

These seven categories are as follows:
- bankruptcy – where the reference entity becomes bankrupt or suffers an analogous event;
- failure to pay – where the reference entity fails to make a payment of interest or principal;
- obligation acceleration – where one of the reference entity's obligations is accelerated;
- obligation default – where the reference entity defaults on one of its obligations;
- repudiation/moratorium – where the reference entity repudiates or declares a moratorium over some or all of its debts;
- restructuring – where the reference entity arranges for some or all of its debts to be restructured causing a material change in their creditworthiness; and
- governmental intervention – where a reference entity is a financial institution, and its obligations are materially altered (eg, by amending principal or interest provisions), through government action.

These categories of credit risk are known as 'credit events' and in each contract, usually on the basis of market practice, the parties choose which credit events will apply to the transaction. As important as which credit events apply is the identity of the obligations on which credit protection is bought and sold. The parties will decide minimum threshold amounts of obligations that must be affected by a credit event in order for credit protection to apply. They must also choose which of the reference entity's obligations are subject to credit protection and, in this regard, whether credit protection should apply to:

- a single obligation only;
- a category of obligations; or
- a category of obligations fulfilling pre-determined characteristics.

Figure 10: Credit derivatives contracts

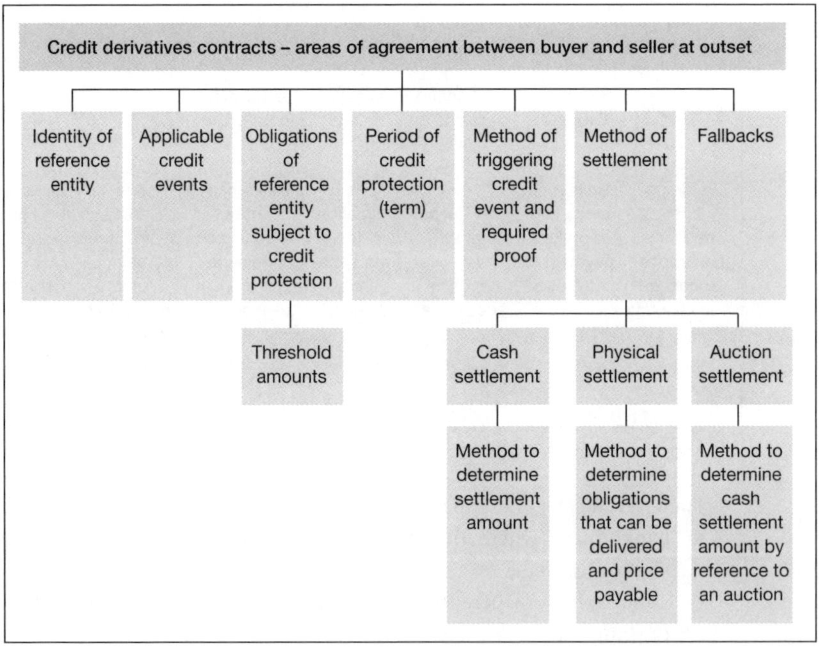

The parties agree:
- which of them may trigger a credit event;
- how this is done;
- what proof of the credit event must be shown; and
- whether a transaction will be settled by a payment of cash (and how this amount is determined, such as through an auction or formula) or the delivery of actual physical obligations in return for a full cash payment.

Lastly, the parties will agree the term of a transaction and a list of fallback positions for when 'unforeseen foreseeables' occur.

4. **The third constituent part of a derivative: the price or value of the**
financial instrument derived from the underlying asset or variable

The third constituent part of a derivative is the price or value of the financial
instrument derived from the underlying asset or variable. In the case of a credit
derivative, the price of the derivative will be based mainly upon the perceived
creditworthiness of the obligations of the reference entity or basket of reference
entities underlying the transaction.

Let us take an example: in the summer of 2006, a credit protection buyer under
a single name credit default swap which had Lehman Brothers as the reference entity
would have to pay a relatively small credit protection premium to purchase credit
protection on Lehman Brothers obligations.

However, the same credit derivative entered into in September 2008, immediately
prior to the Lehman bankruptcy, would have had a very high credit protection
premium. This would have been because the credit risk relating to Lehman Brothers,
as perceived by the market, would have grown. A seller would charge a higher amount
to take on the risk, and a buyer would be willing to pay it. The tradeable value of the
credit derivative (ie, the difference and volatility in premium) is the price or value of
the financial instrument derived from the underlying asset.

5. **The fourth constituent part of a derivative: purpose of entering into**
the derivative transaction.

5.1 Users

To understand the purposes of entering into credit derivative transactions, we must
first look at who is using these transactions.

Figure 11: Major credit derivatives market participants

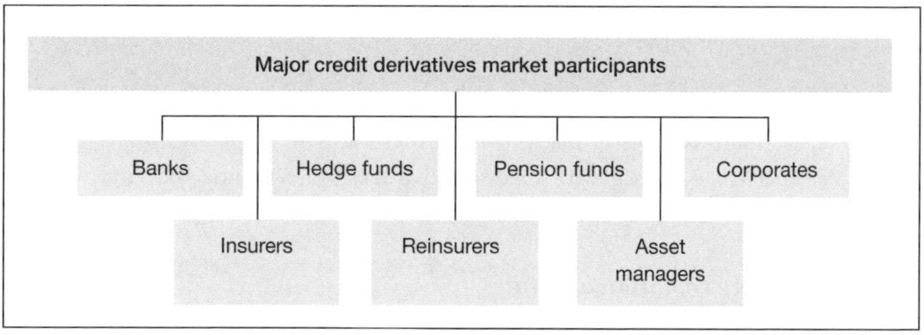

Credit derivatives market makers are financial institutions that quote a price for
buying credit protection on a reference entity at the same time that they quote a
price for selling credit protection. In doing so, they hope to make a profit on the
bid/offer spread and create a credit derivatives market by allowing end buyers and
end sellers to find each other.

Credit derivatives transactions are concentrated among relatively few
institutions. The nine largest market makers in 2016 were Bank of America NA,

Barclays Bank, BNP Paribas, Citibank NA, Credit Suisse International, Deutsche Bank AG, Goldman Sachs International, JPMorgan Bank and Mizuho Securities Co.

The end buyers and the end sellers of credit protection generally fall into the same categories of institution, although the percentage make-up of each group is quite different. The buyer and seller groups both consist of banks, hedge funds, pension funds, general corporates, insurers, reinsurers, asset managers and a limited group of other investors.

5.2 Reasons for using credit derivatives products

Different categories of market participant have different reasons for entering into credit derivatives transactions.

Figure 12: Reasons for entering into credit derivatives transactions

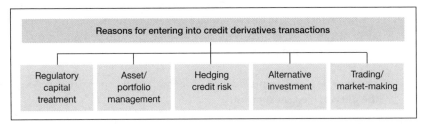

The principal reasons for entering into credit derivatives contracts usually consist of one or several of the following:
- regulatory capital treatment;
- portfolio management;
- hedging credit risk;
- alternative investments; and
- trading and market-making.

Some of these overlap and, depending on the type of institution, the importance of each motivation is likely to be different. There are also many other ancillary reasons for entering into credit derivatives transactions that may influence any decision to buy or sell credit protection.

(a) Regulatory capital treatment

Banks and insurance companies are major users of credit derivatives. Both these categories of institution are subject to regulatory capital requirements – requirements imposed by governments and regulators to protect the financial system against systemic collapse and market shocks. These requirements force a regulated institution to hold minimum levels of capital against its risk exposure. Determining the level of risk inherent in a specific amount of an obligation can be complex. Additionally, because the legally imposed requirements are minimum requirements, a financial institution will also have its own internal capital requirements to manage risk. These may oblige it to hold potentially greater amounts of capital against its credit risk.

Because credit derivatives allow financial institutions to isolate and separately trade credit risk, credit derivatives can allow regulated banks to continue to hold assets, while reducing the amount of capital they must hold against these assets for regulatory capital purposes.

(b)   *Credit risk management*

A financial institution's desire to limit and/or diversify credit risk concentrations in its debt portfolios can make credit derivatives an attractive proposition and useful tool. Let us take an example. A bank with a successful business extending loans to French car part manufacturers might find that its loan portfolio becomes overly exposed to the French auto manufacturer sector, breaching its internal risk concentration limits and stopping it from expanding an otherwise lucrative area of business.

This bank could offset credit risk concentrations by entering into credit derivatives products as a credit protection buyer referencing relevant entities from the sector. Another institution looking to diversify its own portfolio by including exposure to the French auto manufacturer sector, but without the business capability to do so through the traditional lending route, might choose to enter into similar credit derivatives products as a credit protection seller.

For credit protection sellers, credit derivatives products allow these market participants to gain exposure to particular and diverse sectors. This can be done more easily through the cash bond market where the number of available obligations may be limited.

(c)   *Hedging credit risk*

A financial institution's desire to hedge its actual credit exposure to particular obligations may be satisfied by using credit derivatives. Imagine that a UK bank has a key client, a multinational drinks distributor. That bank has entered into a debt facility with its client and, although pleased with its fee and excited at the prospect of further work, it is worried about the amount of exposure that it has. Selling the loan would cause offence to the client, but if the overall bank business were to grow, keeping the client (and the loan) would fit in well with the bank's business model. Entering into a credit default swap referencing the drinks distributor would hedge the bank's credit risk.

(d)   *Alternative investment*

A hedge fund, fund manager, insurance company or any other entity with a portfolio of investments will usually try to diversify those investments. Diversification is important not only among the assets of a particular class – for example, the manager of a portfolio will not wish to be overly exposed to a particular obligor, sector or geographical location – but also among the classes of assets themselves.

If the equity market crashes, the bond market may not; likewise, the credit derivatives market may also be protected. Credit derivatives provide an alternative class of investment. This in itself makes the product appealing.

(e) *Trading/market making*

Prior to the advent of credit derivatives, the inability to separate credit risk from the other bundle of obligations making up a security made credit risk illiquid. Trading credit risk separately attracts more participants to the market, allowing trading to take place. Financial institutions can make a market by entering into back-to-back transactions (perhaps with the assistance of a central counterparty), taking as profit the difference between buy and sell prices. Other innovations, such as tranching (allowing investors to take particular slices of credit exposure depending on their risk appetite), also help to attract new participants to the market.

6. Additional and inherent risks of credit derivatives

As stated above, a credit derivative's objective underlying asset is the isolation and separate trading of a reference entity's credit risk. If only this were the sole risk that the buyer or seller was trading in a credit derivatives transaction!

Unfortunately, although credit derivatives products go a long way towards achieving this goal, other residual risks remain. Credit protection buyers and sellers assume many other risks in addition to the credit risk of the reference entity.

Figure 13: Non-reference entity risks in credit derivatives products

Non-reference entity risks in credit derivatives products						
Basis/ mismatch risk	Market risk	Liquidity risk	Regulatory risk	Counter-party risk	Documentation and legal risk	Operational and reputational risk

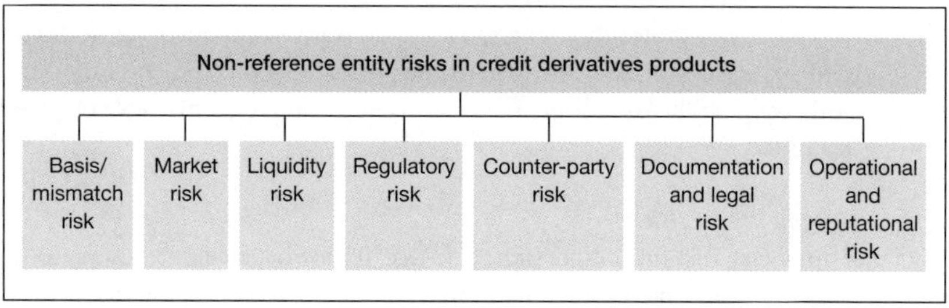

These residual risks fall into seven categories:
- basis/mis-match risk;
- market risk;
- liquidity risk;
- regulatory risk;
- counterparty risk;
- documentation and legal risk; and
- operation and reputational risk.

6.1 Basis/mis-match risk

Credit derivatives are often used to hedge against specific obligations held by the credit protection buyer. Problems may arise where:
- a reference entity, following a corporate reorganisation, is succeeded by multiple reference entities;
- standardised credit derivatives documentation does not match a bespoke transaction; or

- a corporate reorganisation or refinancing, perhaps pursuant to leveraged buy-out or private equity financing, leads to a shortage of deliverable obligations.

Examples include where a reference entity is succeeded by multiple successors and, under the rules applied by the 2014 definitions, several new credit derivatives transactions are created, forcing the buyer to purchase protection on entities that it does not want and leaving it with insufficient credit protection to hedge those assets which it actually holds.

Further examples of basis/mis-match risk can occur where the currency of a reference obligation does not match the currency of the derivatives transaction or where the maturity of an obligation does not match that of the relevant credit derivatives contract.

6.2   Market risk

Connected to liquidity risk is market risk. This can affect the price of credit protection. Spread movements and the availability of bipolar positions regarding the purchase and sale of credit protection can impact on the price of a credit derivative.

A further issue arises when a market participant tries to value its credit derivatives portfolio for accounting purposes. Some transactions, particularly those that are not market standard, may be very difficult to value on a mark-to-market basis. An alternative valuation method called 'mark to model' is reliant on the accuracy of the model used. A failure to use the correct modelling or to value a credit derivatives portfolio correctly can expose a market participant to considerable market risk – something highlighted during the credit crisis. Whether a model gives a true picture of market risk is also known as 'model risk'.

6.3   Liquidity risk

Credit derivatives markets are not as liquid as the bond and other debt markets. This may mean that if a credit derivative is not as liquid as the obligations that underlie the derivatives contract, then the price of the credit derivatives against the relevant obligations may become distorted and prone to wider fluctuations in price.

6.4   Regulatory risk

Credit derivatives regularly catch the attention of regulatory bodies. There have been many calls, particularly in the United States, to outlaw credit derivatives, or to restrict their trading severely.

6.5   Counterparty risk

In OTC credit derivatives, both the credit protection buyer and the credit protection seller are exposed to each other's credit risk. The buyer is exposed to the risk that, on settlement, the seller will not be in a position to pay the settlement amount, leaving it without the credit protection that it had purchased.

The seller will be left with the lesser risk that at any point during the transaction's term, it will not receive the fixed payments it is due. This risk is however being increasingly reduced through the introduction of enhanced margin requirements, as well as by central clearing.

To a certain extent, counterparty risk is inherent in all derivatives transactions. The parties can deal with this risk using existing ISDA documentation architecture (ie, the credit support annex and/or other collateral and credit support-related documentation).

A further risk is that a counterparty does not have the correct legal authority to enter into a credit derivatives transaction. The early landmark cases relating to derivatives and capacity occurred in the 1980s and apply to derivatives in general. Proper diligence on any counterparty is essential and will depend to a large extent on the type and jurisdiction of the relevant reference entity. Otherwise, the risk remains that any credit derivatives contract could be unenforceable and/or that any fixed payments made were recoverable.

6.6   Documentation and legal risk

Regulators remain concerned about the documentation risks existing in the credit derivatives market. The first major question is whether the credit derivatives documentation will work in any given circumstance. Does it do what is intended and is it legal, valid, binding and enforceable? The credit derivatives market is now well established and the standardisation efforts of ISDA have now reduced these risks as much as possible (eg, ISDA has obtained legal opinions in over 40 jurisdictions around the world on various enforceability issues). Indeed, the market survived major defaults such as the Lehman and Icelandic bank credit events. However, there is still a risk, particularly in the case of more bespoke products and/or where English or New York law is not used as the governing law, that documentation will not perform as intended and will not be legal, valid, binding and enforceable.

6.7   Operational/reputational risk

Market participants in the credit derivatives market are often large financial institutions. Legitimately, those institutions may try to hedge their loan or bond book through the use of credit derivatives. Problems may arise where a borrower under a loan or bond provides non-public price-sensitive information to a lender or arranger, which then hedges its position through credit derivatives. Such information may have a material impact on the pricing of credit derivatives transactions and particular care must be taken to ensure not only that the use of such information does not breach any law or regulation, but also that it causes no reputational damage to the market participant concerned.

Operational risk arises where, due to the sheer volume of transactions entered into by a market participant, either transactions are entered into without proper authorisation or diligence being carried out, or delays arise in the documenting transactions after they have been agreed.

7. Types of credit derivative product used with the 2014 ISDA Credit Derivatives Definitions

The following sections provide an overview of the products which are used in conjunction with the 2014 ISDA Credit Derivatives Definitions, as well as, for historical purposes a discussion of some of the now less frequently used products. The definitions are discussed in detail in the next chapter.

7.1 The credit derivatives product range: unfunded credit derivatives

Unfunded credit derivatives are bilateral, privately negotiated credit derivatives contracts, which are subject to varying levels of standardisation. The most common example is a simple single name credit default swap between two counterparties. These products are described as 'unfunded' because the seller makes no upfront payment to cover its potential future liabilities.[6]

The seller will make a payment in an unfunded credit derivative only if an event determination date occurs and a cash, physical or auction settlement becomes payable. An event determination date is the date on which a credit event is determined. This then kicks off the settlement process and the parties to the transaction must then perform their respective obligations in accordance with the settlement method (cash, physical or auction settlement) or fallback settlement method, as specified in the transaction confirmation.

Unfunded credit derivatives include single name credit default swaps, index trades, basket products, credit spread options, swaptions, constant maturity swaps and recovery credit default swaps. An overlap exists with funded credit derivative products, in that these products are often embedded into a note structure when creating a funded credit derivative.

A funded credit derivative involves the issue of a debt obligation either by a 'special purpose vehicle' (SPV) or a financial institution, which is purchased by the effective credit protection seller – the noteholder. The proceeds of the notes are 'collateralised' by investing their proceeds in highly rated securities, such as OECD country government bonds or in a 'guaranteed investment contract' (GIC) account.

The note proceeds are used to fund the payment of any cash, physical or auction settlement amount. This must either be paid pursuant to a credit default swap entered into by an SPV issuer, or absorbed by the issuer pursuant to the conditions of the notes.

The structure of funded credit derivatives involves embedding a credit derivative product into the structure of the transaction. The type of credit derivatives embedded may include many of the unfunded derivatives products mentioned above. Funded credit derivatives are generally credit-linked notes or synthetic securitisations.

---

6   With ever-increasing collateralisation requirements, any unfunded derivative may of course be subject to collateral arrangements to support a potential close-out amount.

(a) ***Single name credit default swaps***

Figure 14: Simple credit default swap

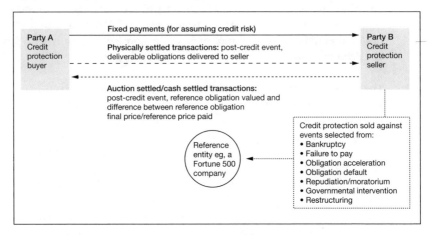

The single name credit default swap is the cornerstone credit derivatives product. Most other credit derivatives products have been adapted from it.

A solid understanding of single name credit default swaps is essential for an understanding of the more complex credit derivatives products such as index-linked credit default swaps.

In a nutshell, the product can be defined as a privately negotiated, albeit highly standardised, bilateral contract between a 'buyer' and a 'seller', referencing the third-party credit risk of a single reference entity.[7]

In a standard transaction, the parties agree that the buyer will purchase a pre-agreed notional amount of protection against the credit risk of the reference entity's obligations. The specific obligations against which the seller sells credit protection are decided at the outset. They may be specific named securities of the reference entity such as a €200 million floating-rate note, or they may be a category of obligation, such as borrowed money, displaying certain characteristics (eg, listed bonds with a maximum maturity date of less than 30 years).

The credit risk against which the seller sells credit protection covers only the risk of certain pre-agreed credit events occurring in relation to a minimum amount of the obligations (or, in the case of the bankruptcy credit event, the reference entity itself). Credit events are likely to match a significant deterioration in the reference entity's credit quality: they will be any agreed combination of bankruptcy, failure to pay, the acceleration of an obligation, an obligation default, a repudiation or moratorium of debts, a governmental intervention or a debt restructuring. In return for the seller assuming this credit risk, the buyer will periodically pay a premium. This will usually be a percentage of the credit default swap's notional amount, expressed in basis

---

7   References to bilateral private negotiated contracts are also deemed to be references to standardised centrally cleared transactions, which have been given up to clearing members.

points. The amount of the premium will reflect the credit risk of the particular reference entity, with greater risks reflected in higher premiums.

The parties document their transaction by entering into an ISDA Master Agreement and schedule, and setting out the transaction's terms in a confirmation incorporating the 2014 definitions. All of the market standard variables are set out in the 2014 definitions. The parties select the applicable credit events, business days, and other variables in accordance with market practice, which in turn may rely on the reference entity's jurisdiction of incorporation and/or its characterisation.

ISDA has produced a matrix, which accompanies a standard form single name credit default swap template. Its usage is market standard. The matrix takes the form of an Excel spreadsheet, which provides a heading column of transaction types, together with a heading column of elections from the 2014 definitions. Where the matrix is incorporated and a confirmation specifies a transaction type, the elections from the matrix are deemed to apply automatically.

A transaction will settle following an event determination date. In most cases – for instance, auction settled transactions – this will be the date on which a relevant ISDA Determinations Committee determines that a credit event is deemed to have occurred.

If auction settlement is not applicable (eg, instead there is cash or physical settlement), and in certain other limited circumstances, then there will be a right to trigger a credit event and event determinations date only and not an obligation to do so. Here, the party triggering the credit event is called the 'notifying party' and the date on which it delivers a credit event notice is the 'event determination date'.

A note on Determinations Committees and auction settlement
Credit Derivatives Determinations Committees are committees established to make determinations for credit derivative transactions incorporating the 2014 definitions. Each committee is governed by the Credit Derivatives Determinations Committees Rule. These committees analyse the facts of market events, based on publicly available information, and determine in particular:
- whether a credit event has occurred;
- the identity of any successor reference entity;
- whether an auction should be held to determine a settlement final price; and
- whether the obligations should be delivered or valued at any auction.

ISDA has also published Auction Settlement Terms which interact with the 2014 definitions and enable parties to settle some transactions based upon an auction final price determined according to an auction of selected deliverable obligations of an affected reference entity following a credit event.

Where the credit event does not occur automatically, because of a determinations committee resolution, the credit event notice is addressed to the counterparty, specifies that a credit event has occurred and gives the facts relevant to that determination. A notice of publicly available information is usually incorporated into the credit event notice. It cites publicly available information from public sources (usually two), such as Bloomberg and the *Financial Times*, confirming facts relevant to the credit event's determination.

If it is determined that a credit event has occurred, the Determinations Committee will also determine whether or not to hold an auction of the affected reference entity's obligations. A Determinations Committee is not obliged to declare whether a particular credit event has occurred. Once a credit event has been determined by a Determinations Committee, then ISDA will also usually organise an auction of defaulted bonds and loans related to the credit event, and through an observance mechanism, determine a final price.

In cash-settled transactions, the calculation agent (usually the seller) selects and values a reference entity obligation. Either the reference obligation is specified in the confirmation or the confirmation will provide a selection mechanism similar to that for establishing the reference entity's obligations, in which case the calculation agent will notify the counterparties of the reference obligation in a reference obligation notification notice.

The transaction will detail when the reference obligation will be valued. Usually, this valuation date is sufficiently far from the event determination date to allow a reference obligation's trading price to settle.

On the valuation date (which may be on one date or several dates), the calculation agent will go into the market and ask for quotations from dealers for a pre-agreed amount of the reference obligation. The calculation agent will then calculate the reference obligation's final price. The 2014 definitions provide numerous options and fallbacks for the number of valuation dates, the amount of quotations that must be sought (and from whom), and how the final price is to be calculated.

The final price is expressed as a percentage (ie, the percentage value of the current value of the reference obligation compared to its nominal amount or a reference price), and is calculated using a pre-selected valuation method. The calculation agent notifies the parties of the final price in a final price notification notice. The transaction is then settled an agreed number of days later. The cash settlement amount paid by the seller will usually be the transaction's notional amount multiplied by the reference price (usually 100%), minus the final price (eg, 50%). The transaction will then terminate. The same mechanism is used for auction-settled transactions, except that the final price is instead the price determined at the auction of obligations of the affected reference entity.

Where the parties have specified that physical settlement applies, following an event determination date, the buyer has 30 calendar days to serve a notice of physical settlement. The transaction confirmation will set out either a specific obligation or the deliverable obligation category and the deliverable obligation characteristics which a reference entity obligation must satisfy for it to be a deliverable obligation. The notice of physical settlement sets out the actual deliverable obligations that the buyer will deliver on the physical settlement date. These deliverable obligations will usually be equal in face value to the transaction's notional amount.

The physical settlement date will be either as agreed by the parties or within the longest period customary in the market. On the physical settlement date, the buyer will deliver the deliverable obligations and the seller pays an amount equal to their face value.

(b) *Basket credit default swaps*
Basket credit default swaps are a step up in complexity from credit default swaps. In basket credit derivatives products, there are a number of reference entities instead of just one. Basket products consist of two separate products: nth-to-default swaps and portfolio credit default swaps.

Figure 15: Basket credit default swap

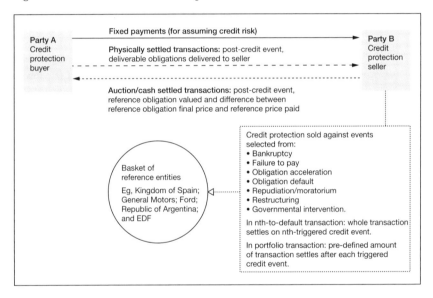

In a basket credit default swap, there are a number of reference entities (eg, Kingdom of Spain, General Motors, Ford, Republic of Argentina and EDF). In an nth-to-default transaction, the transaction is structured so that when there have been an agreed number of credit events, the transaction will cash settle, physically settle or auction settle, depending on which settlement method the parties have elected. In a portfolio credit default swap, an agreed portion of the notional amount of the credit default swap will settle after each event determination date.

Nth-to-default credit default swaps: The 'nth' in 'nth to default' refers to the number of defaults required before the transaction settles (eg, a first-to-default credit default swap or a second-to-default credit default swap). A basket credit default swap may be a first-to-default product, which, using the example in the diagram above, would mean that if any of the five named reference entities suffered a credit event and accompanying event determination date, then the transaction would settle.

If the basket credit defaults wap were a third-to-default product, then if the Kingdom of Spain and the Republic of Argentina suffered credit events (and both event determination dates had occurred), the transaction would settle if, and only if, one of General Motors, Ford or EDF suffered a credit event and event determination date. The transaction would then settle based on the transaction's full notional amount.

The seller in an nth-to-default credit default swap receives a flow of fixed payments until either the 'nth' default occurs or the termination date.

First-to-default credit default swaps allow the seller to leverage the credit risk that it is selling and so earn a higher overall yield than that which it would be able to obtain on any of the constituent reference entities forming the basket for a credit default swap with the same overall notional amount.

This leverage, though, is accompanied by greater risk for the seller. If a first-to-default credit default swap has a notional amount of US$1 million and a term of three years, and the basket is composed of five reference entities, the likelihood of a credit event affecting one of these five reference entities is much greater than the corresponding risk in a single name credit default swap for the same notional amount referencing just one of these reference entities.

One way to view a first-to-default credit default swap is as a bundle of single name credit default swaps between the buyer and seller (ie, one credit default swap for the full notional amount for each reference entity). If an event determination date occurs for any of these credit default swaps are met, then the date on which this occurs will be the termination date for all of the other credit default swaps and the parties' obligations to each other will cease.

A seller wishing to leverage its credit risk to a lesser extent, but still wanting to receive a higher yield than that available under a single name credit default swap, might choose to enter into a second or third-to-default credit default swap. This will mean that the seller is less likely to suffer a credit event, but also that because the leverage is less, the premium will also be lower.

The amount of the fixed payments received by the seller in an nth-to-default credit default swap will be determined by several factors. These include:

- the number of defaults which must occur before the transaction settles;
- the number of reference entities which are in the basket (the more reference entities in the basket, the greater the risk of a credit event occurring);
- the credit spread of each of the reference entities in the basket;
- the correlation between the reference entities (eg, if all of the reference entities are in the automobile sector and that industry encounters tough times, the likelihood of one of the reference entities defaulting increases);
- the likely recovery rate of the reference entity which defaults; and
- the term of the transaction (the longer the term, the more likely that the nth level of default will be reached).

Buyers and sellers may be attracted to nth-to-default credit default swaps because they can take a view on the likely correlation of defaults by the reference entities comprising the basket. If a seller believes that there is a high implied correlation between the reference entities, selling first-to-default credit protection may be attractive because of the likelihood that a business environment may indeed cause all of the reference entities to default. If the seller believes that there is a low implied correlation between the reference entities, selling second-to-default credit protection may be attractive because of the likelihood that different sectors would have to suffer poor business conditions for more than one reference entity to default.

Credit protection buyers are most likely to utilise nth-to-default credit default swaps to hedge portfolio credit derivative products that they hold. In these circumstances an nth-to-default credit default swap may be cheaper than entering into several single name credit default swaps.

Portfolio credit default swaps: Portfolio credit default swaps form the second category of credit derivative basket products. As with an nth-to-default credit default swap, the buyer purchases credit protection on a basket of reference entities. The number of reference entities in the basket tends to be greater than in nth-to-default credit default swaps. Instead of the relevant reference entities being referred to as a basket of reference entities, they are referred to as a portfolio of reference entities.

Portfolio credit default swaps operate very similarly to single name credit default swaps. The easiest way to conceptualise the product is to view it as consisting of a bundle of credit default swaps, with one credit default swap being in place (between the buyer and the seller) for each reference entity in the portfolio. This then provides documentation, pricing, administrative and diversification advantages benefits to the parties.

Each time a credit event and event determination date occurs in relation to a reference entity, the settlement procedure is the same as for a single name credit default swap, except that instead of the transaction terminating on the settlement date, the reference entity will be removed from the basket or portfolio and the transaction will continue.

In portfolio credit default swaps, the transaction will have an overall notional amount (eg, US$10 million) and consists of a notional amount for each reference entity. This is usually an equally weighted amount, with credit protection sold for each reference entity's reference entity notional amount only. This is called an 'untranched' portfolio credit default swap.

Where credit protection applies only for a specific slice of the portfolio, this is called a 'tranched' portfolio credit default swap. Tranched portfolio credit default swaps work by settlement amounts being paid by the credit protection seller only once losses have impacted the portfolio up to an agreed level – for instance, at an attachment point of 4% of the notional amount of the portfolio, detaching at an exhaustion point of 6% of the notional amount of the portfolio.

The attractions of entering into a portfolio credit default swap for both buyer and seller include both the diversity and/or low correlation of the reference portfolio. Portfolio credit default swaps were often used as the embedded credit derivative in the hey day of synthetic CDO transactions. The same technology is used in tranched and untranched index-linked credit default swaps.

(c)   ***Index trades***

A 'credit derivatives index' (or 'credit index') is an index comprising a managed portfolio of commonly traded reference entities.

A credit derivative index usually consists of a portfolio of equally weighted reference entities that are rebased on a periodic basis. The rebalancing takes place under pre-agreed rules using the input of credit derivatives market makers. Inclusion of a reference entity in an index is generally merited by a combination of some or all of the following:

- trading volume;
- geographical location;
- industry category; and
- creditworthiness over the previous six-month period.

Generally, a credit derivative index is a licensed product, which may have many uses. A market participant can use the index on payment of a fee to create its own product, perhaps a synthetic CDO referencing a credit index as it is periodically updated, or by entering into a bilateral OTC transaction with another market participant; or it may even create a market itself, standing as a central counterparty buying and selling credit protection on the index and taking the credit risk of each counterparty.

Credit indices increase market liquidity by increasing transaction volumes and lowering market entry barriers. Market makers create markets for trading linked credit derivative products based on standardised documentation. Participants can rely on the reference entity names and related obligations being correct and so reduce their transaction costs. This standardisation also allows automated matching and trading of products.

Credit indices can also allow funded products to have a quasi-form of management. For example, if a single tranche synthetic CDO references the most recent version of a credit index, this will mean that every six months the transaction will reference the most liquid names in a particular sector, possibly saving on management fees.

The credit derivatives index market began with several banks setting up their own credit derivatives indices. They then launched indices in partnerships with other banks. Rival ventures sprang up and this was then followed by a period of mergers which has resulted in two dominant families of indices, each administered by the same administrator and owned by substantially the same parties: iTraxx and CDX. Further consolidation between these two behemoths seems inevitable.

Index families publish rebased indices in March and September each year. The process for updating the names in each series works generally as follows. In accordance with set rules, participating market makers submit the credit default swap volumes that they have dealt with over the previous period. A provisional list of reference entities selected in accordance with these rules is then published. The reference entities are then agreed and a finalised list is published. The coupon levels for each reference entity are then agreed and trading of the new issue begins.

(d) Credit spread options

Credit spread products compare a reference entity obligation's creditworthiness with a risk-free benchmark. In North America, US Treasury bonds are used as the risk-free benchmark. In Europe and other markets, it is the general interest rate benchmark; this is known as the 'asset swap spread'.

Credit spread is calculated by subtracting the risk-free benchmark's yield or the asset swap spread from the reference entity bond's yield (to leave a percentage figure which reflects the credit risk of the reference entity). For example, in a European transaction, if the asset swap spread is 3% and the yield of a bond is 5%, then the credit spread equals 2%. Credit spread products assume that movement in the risk-free benchmark's yield or asset swap spread will be due to external market risk factors, such as interest rate fluctuations, which will equally affect the reference entity's obligation (eg, a bond). As the risk-free benchmark or asset swap spread will, by definition, be free of credit risk, any divergence between the two yields is assumed to be due to credit risk. For example, if the asset swap spread rises to 3.5% and the reference entity bond's yield stays at 5%, then the credit spread has decreased. However, if both the asset swap spread and the yield rise by half a percentage point, then the credit spread has not changed.

Credit spread products are structured mainly as put and call options. A credit spread put option gives the put option buyer the right, but not the obligation, to sell its counterparty a specified reference bond (ie, a bond issued by the reference entity) at a future date. The option may be exercised when the reference bond's credit spread over the risk-free benchmark or asset swap spread, exceeds a pre-determined level (the 'strike spread'). The price payable by the put option seller is referenced to this strike spread, and will be a price greater than the market price of the reference bond at the time when the option is exercised (ie, generally speaking, a price which excludes the decline the reference bond's creditworthiness).

Figure 16: Relationship between credit spread movements and bond prices

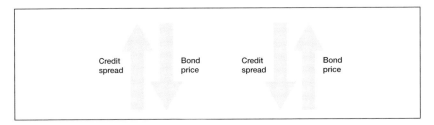

A credit spread call option gives the call option buyer the right, but not the obligation, to buy from its counterparty a reference bond specified in the confirmation at a future date at a price linked to the strike spread. The option may be exercised when the reference bond's credit spread over the risk-free benchmark or asset swap spread, goes below the strike spread. The price payable by the call option buyer is referenced to this strike spread, and will be a price lower than the market price of the reference bond at the time which the option is exercised (ie, generally speaking, a price which excludes the improvement in the reference bond's creditworthiness).

(e) Swaptions

A 'swaption' is a combination of a swap and an option. The option part of the agreement gives one party, the swaption buyer, the right, but not the obligation, to compel the swaption seller to enter into a credit default swap with it. Under this credit default swap part of the agreement, the swaption seller will either buy or sell credit protection at a price agreed at the outset of the swaption.

It is standard for credit derivatives swaptions to have a 'knock-out' option. 'Knock-out' options are option contracts where the option terminates if a specified event occurs. In credit derivatives swaptions, the knock-out event is where a credit event occurs in relation to the underlying reference entity prior to the swaption seller exercising its option to enter into the credit default swap. The knock-out event is triggered by the delivery or deemed delivery of a credit event notice and notice of publicly available information, just as in a standard credit default swap.

Credit derivatives swaptions usually use European-style options (ie, the option can be exercised only on a fixed date). The swaption buyer will pay the swaption seller a premium for assuming the risk that the underlying reference entity's credit spread will increase between the swaption's trade date and the option's exercise date. If the projected fixed rate under the credit default swap is below the market rate at the date on which the swaption buyer is to exercise its option, it will let the option expire. If the market rate is above the transaction's projected fixed rate, then the swaption seller will gain the benefit of the difference between the two prices.

Credit derivative swaptions allow market participants to take a leveraged view of the future direction of a reference entity's credit spread. The motivation to enter into a swaption also depends on the buyer and seller having divergent views on the future direction of the reference entity's credit spread. The buyer must take the view that over time the reference entity's credit spread will widen (ie, meaning the purchase price of credit protection will increase) and the seller must take the view that this credit spread will narrow (ie, meaning that the sale price of credit protections will reduce).

(f) Recovery swaps

A recovery (or recovery lock) credit default swap allows each party to express different views of what the recovery rate will be for the obligations of a reference entity if a credit event and event determination date occur are met.

Recovery swaps are usually physically settled transactions. They work as follows: following a event determination date the buyer purchases deliverable obligations from the seller in an amount equal to the credit default swap's notional amount. The price that the buyer pays to the seller for the deliverable obligations is agreed at the transaction's outset and set out in the confirmation. This is the strike price. The buyer can then sell the deliverable obligations into the market or use them itself as seller in a back-to-back credit derivative transaction.

(g)   Constant maturity credit default swaps

Constant maturity credit default swaps (also known as 'CMCDS transactions') are standard credit default swaps with one exception. Instead of the fixed payments from buyer to seller being for a fixed percentage amount of the transaction's notional amount throughout the life of the transaction, each fixed payment is reset at the outset of each fixed-rate payer calculation period.

This is done at each reset date by referring to the existing credit spread of the relevant reference entity or reference entities (ie, the percentage rate figure for buying credit protection on the reference entity).

Constant maturity credit default swaps can perhaps be viewed as a series of credit default swaps referencing the same reference entities, with each credit default swap being for the length of the fixed-rate calculation period. There are, of course, differences: a credit event which occurred during a previous calculation period could be triggered in a future one; however, the parties effectively take a new view of the reference entity's credit risk at the start of each fixed-rate calculation period.

Therefore, the idea behind constant maturity credit default swaps is that the price of credit protection should vary in accordance with the market risk at any given point in time. The fixed leg of the credit default swap effectively becomes an additional floating leg.

Mechanically, the method for setting the quantum of fixed-rate payments in any fixed-rate payer calculation period usually takes the following form.

The parties may take the relevant reference entity's credit default swap spread for a given period (eg, three years). Alternatively, where the relevant reference entity is traded in a credit index, the parties may use the corresponding published rate for that reference entity. The rate taken is called the 'reference rate'.

At each reset date the reset date is multiplied by a 'participation rate' or 'gearing factor' to provide the percentage amount of the credit protection premium. The participation rate is a percentage proportion of the reference rate.

Constant maturity credit default swaps require the buyer and seller to take divergent views of whether the cost of purchasing credit protection against a particular reference entity will increase or decrease. Sometimes constant maturity credit default swaps also have caps and floors; although reaching a cap or floor will cause a constant maturity credit default swap to behave more like a standard credit default swap.

7.2   Funded credit derivatives

So far we have discussed 'unfunded' credit derivatives: bilateral credit derivatives contracts, usually between counterparties of a strong economic standing (eg, a bank and an insurance company; or a hedge fund and pension company).

By contrast, 'funded' credit derivatives are structured transactions where the credit derivatives contract is embedded in a debt obligation. These products were hardest hit by the financial crisis, and there market size is a fraction of what it once was. The markets remain, though, even if the more complex forms are perhaps confined to history.

For funded credit derivatives, this underlying and embedded credit derivatives contract will often be based on a corresponding ISDA contract. The funded credit derivative structure will usually involve either:

- a thinly capitalised SPV issuing securities and entering into a credit derivatives contract with a financial institution; or
- a financial institution issuing securities with the credit derivatives terms set out in the conditions of the notes.

In a funded credit derivatives structure the SPV or bank issues a debt obligation which will fund (at least some of) the potential losses on the credit derivatives contract and pay an interest rate on the principal amount of the debt obligation, together with an amount corresponding to the premium for providing credit protection under the credit derivatives contract: the debt obligation 'funds' any credit protection payments which must be made under the embedded credit derivative following an event determination date relating to a reference entity.

Of course, it is more complicated that that. The proceeds of the notes must be invested to generate a return, and the debt obligations themselves will often be tranched (and rated) according to priority of payment. They may also be listed on a stock exchange. The credit derivatives contracts themselves are often more complex too: the portfolio of reference entities referenced by a credit default swap may be managed by a manager who will decide on a periodic basis which reference entities may be included in the pool; this selection may be made following the application of complex tests. The notes themselves may be subordinated to an 'unfunded', 'super senior' credit default swap, meaning that the credit derivatives contract is only partly funded.

(a)   ***Synthetic CDOs and synthetic securitisation***
Overview:

What is a synthetic CDO (full capital structure)[8]?
In a standard synthetic CDO, a thinly capitalised SPV enters into a portfolio credit default swap with a counterparty, usually the transaction's arranger. This portfolio credit default swap is usually cash settled.

Under the portfolio credit default swap, the SPV sells an amount of credit protection to the counterparty for each reference entity (eg, in a US$200 million CDO, it might sell US$2 million of credit protection for each of 100 reference entities in a portfolio).

This generates an agreed return in the form of fixed payments in relation to the notional amount of each of the reference entities in the portfolio, perhaps 0.75% per annum. The reference entities themselves will be selected from diverse industries and geographical locations to try to minimise the level of correlation between potential credit events: this will particularly be so in the case of rated transactions.

The SPV is thinly capitalised, perhaps having only US$2 capitalisation. It has no funds to make any credit protection payment should a credit event and event determination date occur on a reference entity in the portfolio: it must therefore be funded.

---

8   See further discussion below, or partial capital structure/single tranche CDOs.

To fund its potential obligations under the credit default swap, the SPV first issues debt obligations in the form of notes to investors. These notes are often tranched, with progressively deeper levels of subordination. For example, the SPV could issue three classes of note: a senior, a mezzanine and a junior tranche. Losses incurred under the credit default swap would attach first to the junior notes, then to the mezzanine and lastly, if the principal amount of that tranche were exhausted, to the senior notes.

Second, the SPV enters into an unfunded 'super senior' credit default swap on the whole of the reference portfolio with a highly rated bank or other financial institution. Under this swap the SPV will be the buyer and the financial institution the seller. The super senior credit default swap will make up most of the capitalisation of the structure; losses will impact upon it only once the principal amounts of all of the tranches of notes have been exhausted. The super senior swap is unfunded from the perspective of the financial institution, but because it is a back-to-back swap, it funds the SPV in the main credit derivatives transaction. In a rated transaction, the super senior swap is sometimes perceived to be above AAA by certain investors. The size of each tranche of notes will usually be driven (in rated transactions) by rating criteria designed to achieve an AAA rating for the senior tranche of notes and target ratings for the other tranches.

The proceeds of the debt obligations are invested, directly or indirectly (perhaps through a repurchase ('repo') agreement), in high-quality securities, or a 'guaranteed investment contract' (GIC) account or a deposit account: along with the SPV's rights under the super senior credit default swap and other transaction documents, this is the 'collateral' of the collateralised debt obligation. The noteholders receive a blended return based on the credit protection payments received from the SPV and the return on the collateral, with the quantum of return also being referenced to the amount of risk assumed by a noteholder. The super senior credit default swap counterparty will receive only its share of the credit protection payments on the credit default swap received by the SPV.

Following any credit event under the credit default swap, any credit protection payment in the form of a cash settlement amount will be funded by selling an appropriate amount of highly rated securities[9] and delivering the proceeds to the SPV's swap counterparty. The principal amount of the notes will then be reduced accordingly. If the notes are tranched with differing levels of subordination, then the most deeply subordinated notes are always reduced in principal amount first. If the principal amounts of each class of notes become exhausted, the super senior credit default swap counterparty will be required to make payments under the super senior credit default swap to fund the SPV's payments under the credit default swap.

At the transaction's maturity the proceeds of the collateral are used to repay the remaining principal amount of the notes.

---

9   The sale of any collateral may take place through the repo agreement or alternatively by a withdrawal from a GIC account or deposit account.

The objective of a synthetic CDO is for the noteholders (and the super senior swap counterparty) to take synthetic exposure to a portfolio of static or actively managed reference entities or reference obligations, through a credit derivative. The underlying credit derivatives transaction can be documented in one of two ways. Either (and less commonly) the credit derivatives terms can be set out in the conditions of the notes (adapting the 2014 definitions) and the arranger will book the transaction as a swap internally, or the SPV and the arranger will enter into a credit default swap utilising ISDA and/or index standard documentation, including the 2014 definitions.

A further type of synthetic CDO is a 'synthetic collateralised loan obligation' now more commonly called a 'synthetic securitisation'. Here, credit protection is provided by the SPV against loans which are held on the books of an originating bank. The originating bank is able to achieve regulatory capital relief on its loan assets, without transferring them (or notifying its customers). The originating bank will either structure the transaction itself or enter into a back-to-back swap with an arranging bank, which will then enter into the portfolio credit default swap with the SPV. The structuring of the transaction will be substantially similar, although credit protection will usually be limited to the particular loan assets held by the originating bank.

SPVs: why are they used in synthetic CDOs and securitisations and issues of credit-linked notes?

In a synthetic CDO or securitisation, an SPV is established with the objective of the transaction parties utilising it in a structured finance transaction to issue debt instruments, acquire underlying assets and/or enter into derivatives contracts with a view to providing a return to investors.

The transaction's arranger will establish the SPV in a low-tax or no-tax jurisdiction, such as the Cayman Islands or Jersey; or a country that has introduced a specific low-tax regime for SPVs such as Ireland, the Netherlands or Luxembourg.

The SPV will generally be an orphan company, run by directors from the relevant jurisdiction with its shares held in trust for the noteholders and/or a charity (so the SPV will not be categorised as a subsidiary of the arranger).

The assets held by the SPV will be secured so that they are available only to the holders of the related series of notes and/or any other secured parties under the transaction; in no circumstances are they available to any other creditor of the SPV.

Securities issued by the SPV will be 'limited recourse' securities. This means that the claims of the noteholders and other secured parties under a CDO will be limited only to the proceeds of the secured obligations. To the extent that secured obligations do not yield sufficient funds to satisfy the claims of the noteholders and the other secured parties, their claims will be extinguished.

Synthetic CDOs generally fall into two types: full capital structure or multi-tranche CDOs and partial capital or single-tranche CDOs. They are both described below.

(b) *Full capital structure synthetic CDOs*

Figure 17: Synthetic CDO – full capital structure

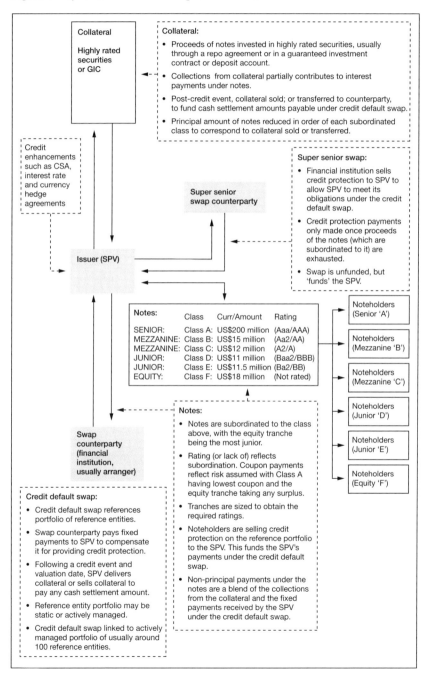

Full capital structure synthetic CDOs tend to be multi-tranched, with an SPV issuing several classes of note, each called a 'tranche'.

Tranching

Tranching allows investors to take different slices of risk exposure in accordance with their risk/return appetite. It also acts as a form of credit enhancement.

Tranches of notes in a full capital structure synthetic CDO

Figure 18: Tranches of notes in a full capital structure synthetic CDO

	Class	Curr/Amount	Rating
Senior:	Class A:	US$20 million	(Aaa/AAA)
Mezzanine:	Class B:	US$15 million	(Aa2/AA)
Mezzanine:	Class C:	US$12 million	(A2/A)
Junior:	Class D:	US$11 million	(Baa2/BBB)
Junior:	Class E:	US$11.5 million	(Ba2/BB)
Equity:	Class F:	US$18 million	(Not rated)

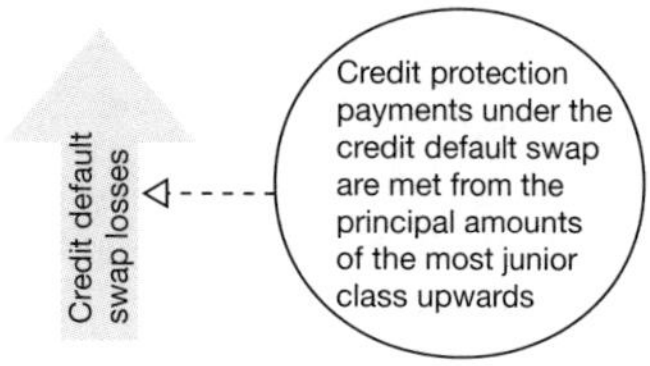

Credit default swap losses

Credit protection payments under the credit default swap are met from the principal amounts of the most junior class upwards

In a full capital structure synthetic CDO, the SPV will issue different classes (or tranches) of notes. The tranches will fall into four separate categories (in descending order of priority): senior debt, mezzanine debt, subordinated debt and equity. There may be multiple tranches within those categories.

If there is a credit event and event determination date under the credit default swap, then following the valuation date(s), the issuer will be required to pay a settlement amount.

Payment of the cash settlement amount will be funded by the issuer either delivering an amount of collateral equal to the cash settlement amount or selling a corresponding amount of collateral, the proceeds of which are then paid to the counterparty. The collateral is usually held in the form of a deposit in a guaranteed investment account or in the form of highly rated securities invested pursuant to a repo agreement.

The corresponding amount of the principal amount of the lowest available tranche of notes is then reduced. Each tranche of notes is protected by the tranche below it. This means that the more senior the tranche of notes, the less likely it is to suffer losses.

Usually, the notes are rated and the level of ratings will correspond to the seniority of any tranche of notes. Likewise, the higher level of risk attached to a tranche of notes, the higher its coupon, and the lower its rating will be. As credit events impact on the portfolio, though, the level of return will diminish.

Above the tranches of notes often sits a more senior obligation: an unfunded credit default swap with a highly rated entity. This is called a 'super senior credit default swap', and sometimes it makes up over 80% of the synthetic CDO's notional amount.

Super senior credit default swaps

The super senior credit default swap usually makes up over 80% of a synthetic CDO's capitalisation. Unlike most of the tranches of notes below it, it will not be rated.

In a super senior credit default swap the seller will usually be an insurance company or a financial institution and, due to the subordinated tranches of notes below it, will regard its investments as representing a low risk. The buyer will be the SPV. The SPV therefore enters into a back-to-back credit default swap transaction.

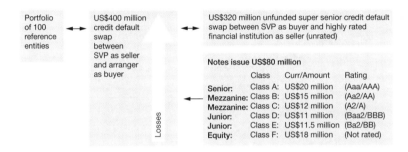

A super senior credit default swap will involve the seller selling credit protection on the entire reference portfolio, but losses will attach to the super senior credit default swap only once the principal amount of the tranches below it have been exhausted.

If the portfolio of reference entities is fixed at the issue date, this is known as 'static synthetic CDO'. Alternatively, a manager may be appointed who will switch reference entities in and out of the portfolio with a view of maximising returns in return for a fee: this is known as a 'managed synthetic CDO'.

(c)   ***Single tranche CDOs/partial capital structure CDOs***
A single tranche or partial capital structure CDO is a structured securities transaction where the transaction's arranger sells only a single tranche of a full capital structure synthetic CDO to an investor.

7.3   Credit-linked notes: an overlap with synthetic CDO structures

(a)   ***Credit-linked notes issued by an SPV***
Credit-linked notes may be issued either by an SPV or by a financial institution. Where an SPV issues a credit-linked note, it may either be as part of a CDO transaction, with issues of multiple tranches or a single tranche issue. The cost of establishing an SPV and related documentation means that most financial institutions will arrange to issue single tranche CDOs only through a repackaging programme.

Figure 19: Single tranche synthetic CDO

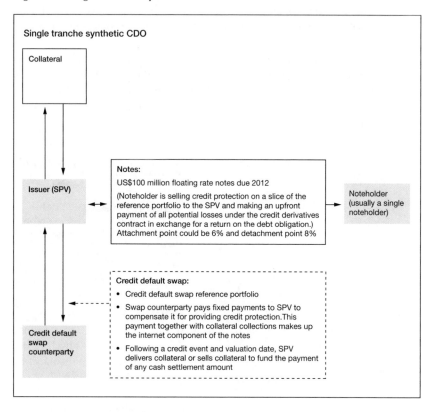

Most financial institutions that arrange large number of single tranche, credit-linked notes now establish structured note programmes utilising an SPV structure based on a modular system. Originally, financial institutions set up programmes that mirrored the structure of vanilla debt securities 'medium-term note' (MTN) programmes (see the discussion of credit-linked notes issued directly by financial institutions below). Under these MTN-style programmes, an SPV and the various other transactions parties would enter into programme documentation consisting of a principal trust deed, a programme dealer agreement, an agency agreement and a custody agreement. The conditions, disclosure and risk factors would be set out in a programme-offering document. For each issue, a separate final term, which is supplemental to the offering document, a supplemental trust deed, a purchase agreement and swap documentation would be documented.

This structure had the disadvantage that as an arranging bank's credit derivative/repackaging business expanded and it established a number of special purposes and programmes, the same documentation would have to be produced (and updated) for each issuer. In addition, each of issue of credit-linked notes produced a large amount of documentation, which tended to be identical, or virtually identical, for each issue.

Initially, the banks tackled the problem by establishing multi-issuer programmes, where a standard documentation platform was put in place and each new SPV issuer would then accede to this documentation. However, any non-standard amendments for an issue of notes greatly increased the amount of documentation required and each individual issue of notes was 'document heavy'. To avoid this, most banks began to adopt a more streamlined approach by using the modular structure.

Modules are prepared for every possible aspect of trades issued under the bank's SPV structured note programmes. These modules set out standard terms. Separate modules are also prepared which contain:

- the trust provisions and conditions of the notes (normally set out in the trust deed);
- the agency provisions (normally set out in the agency module);
- the swap provisions (normally set out in an ISDA Master Agreement) and schedule; and
- the custody provisions (normally set out in the custody agreement).

Some issues of notes may be bearer securities and other may be registered security. Some SPV issuers may be Irish incorporated or Netherlands incorporated – these are subject to different insolvency regimes. The modular system is very versatile, so separate modules can be prepared for different types of note: a module can be prepared for bearer securities, with a separate module for registered securities. A module containing conditions of notes for Irish issuers, which incorporate the vagaries of the Irish insolvency regime, can be prepared, along with another one for Dutch issuers which reflects the specific provisions of Dutch insolvency law.

These relevant modules are then incorporated by reference and amended as necessary into a trust instrument, which is prepared for each issue of notes (see further description below). This trust instrument will constitute the issue of notes and will provide that each module relevant to the particular issue of notes is incorporated by reference. The trust instrument will then set out in a separate section any relevant amendments that must be made to each module to reflect the structure of the issue of notes.

The most significant amendments must be made to the terms and conditions module to reflect the terms of the transaction (eg, denomination, principal amount, currency; maturity date, specific collateral). The trust instrument will also often incorporate some of the ancillary documentation present in a synthetic CDO transaction, such as the letter regarding completion of the global notes and the common depositary instruction letter.

In addition to the trust instrument, each transaction will have an offering document. It is standard practice for each issuer to have a base prospectus which has been approved by a listing authority (eg, the Irish Stock Exchange). The base prospectus will set out similar information to the offering document in a synthetic CDO transaction (eg, investment considerations, risk factors, the conditions of the notes themselves, disclosure regarding the issuer, the arranger bank, selling restrictions).

The programme will have a large issue size – usually around €10 billion or equivalent. When an issue of notes is made under the programme, a prospectus will be issued which will then incorporate the base prospectus into it by reference. The prospectus will set out:

- more specific investment considerations;
- risk factors and selling restrictions;
- the terms of the notes (which are set out in the trust instrument);
- summaries of the swap agreements (sometimes the credit default swap is included as an exhibit);
- disclosure information on the highly rated securities which the proceeds of the notes are invested in; and
- the reference entities relevant to the credit derivatives transaction.

Where the issue of notes is listed, this disclosure will be more detailed as it must comply with the more exacting requirements of the EU Prospectus Directive (2003/71/EC) and the particular stock exchange.

For each issue, the issuer will enter into two swap agreements with the arranging bank: an asset swap confirmation and a credit default swap confirmation. The terms of the swap agreement which are normally set out in an ISDA Master Agreement and schedule will be set out in the swap module. However, the swap confirmations will take the form of standard confirmations as used in synthetic CDO transactions.

As with a synthetic CDO transaction, there will be a transaction proposal letter and also legal opinions from the issuer and arranger's counsel.

The MTN approach in structured note programme is still applicable where an arranging bank only intends to issue a limited number of structured securities. Where an arranging bank intends to establish a number of SPVs or to issue a wide variety of transactions, the modular approach provides more streamlined and cost-effective documentation.

Additionally, credit linked notes may be structured as nth-to-default transaction, single name credit default transactions, CMCDS transactions or in many other forms, with the credit derivative element of the transaction performing as described in the unfunded credit derivatives chapter; and the funded element as described above.

(b)   *Credit-linked notes issued by a financial institution*
Where a credit-linked note structure does not utilise an SPV, a financial institution may issue the credit-linked note. Every financial institution has an active euro MTN programme. Financial institutions and large corporations used euro MTN programmes as a streamlined documentation platform for issuing bonds to meet their general funding requirements. When a financial institution issues a credit-linked note, it is issued by utilising the existing euro MTN programme.

This means that the documentation for a credit-linked note issued by a financial institution will be substantially the same as for any euro MTN issue. A base prospectus will already be in place. This is substantially similar to a base prospectus for a repackaging programme; however, the disclosure in relation to the issuer will be far greater. The conditions of the notes will have to be substantially amended for those of a vanilla programme to facilitate the issuance of credit-linked securities.

The terms of any individual issuance will beset out in a final terms document.

The remaining documentation for a financial institution issue of credit-linked notes is simpler than for an SPV issue. The issue of credit-linked notes is a direct obligation of the financial institution, so the proceeds of the notes are not invested in securities to be held as collateral. An arranger's legal opinion is not normally necessary either. This removes the need for a custody agreement and an asset swap agreement. The securities will usually be placed by the financial institution itself, removing the need for a placement agreement. It is also unusual for there to be a trustee, as much of the trustee's function is usually performed by a fiscal agent in a standard euro MTN programme. Any enforcement action would be against the assets of the bank itself rather than any collateral.

Additionally, although the issuing financial institution may itself hedge its liabilities in relation to the credit derivatives element of the transaction, it is unusual for any credit default swap to form part of the transaction documentation.

Overview of the 2014 ISDA Credit Derivatives Definitions

Edmund Parker
Mayer Brown

1.   Introduction

The International Swaps and Derivatives Association Inc (ISDA) published the first set of credit derivatives definitions in 1999. These definitions summarised the market practices of the then nascent credit derivatives market. Given how new the market was, the definitions were light on detail and subjective in tone, with the 'transaction calculation agent' regularly required to make good-faith determinations.

A series of updates by supplement followed in response to market events. One related to how to deal with a 'reference entity'[1] which split or merged; another with the treatment of convertible and exchangeable bonds; and another brought in a new set of rules for 'restructuring credit events'.

These supplements were incorporated into a revised and enhanced set of definitions which were published in April 2003 and supplemented in May of that year. The 2003 definitions, were quickly supplemented a month later by the May Supplement, which quickly dealt with some minor flaws in the new definitions. These definitions have become known as the 'Original 2003 Definitions'.

Up to this point, the updates to the definitions had tried to standardise 'transactions' to promote their growth. However, the definitions soon had to be supplemented to deal with their own success, when reference entities which filed for bankruptcy had the amount of their outstanding bonds and loans, dwarfed by the size of the position taken by the credit derivatives market on the reference entity's credit risk.

This had the effect of artificially driving up the price of defaulted 'deliverable obligations'. In some cases, it meant that where a seller had to purchase a deliverable obligation in a physically settled transaction in order to settle, the inflated price meant that its overall recovery amount was below the level that could reasonably have been expected. This increased the risk of a transaction taking market risk, as well as credit risk.

Problems arose in particular following the Delphi 'credit event',[2] where the volume and price of Delphi 'deliverable obligations' traded at a higher price after it filed for bankruptcy before then declining. These high bond prices occurred even

---

[1]   Terms in single quotation marks in this chapter refer to defined, capitalised terms in the 2014 definitions (they appear in single quote marks here only at first mention). Where the context requires, however, these terms may also refer to the corresponding capitalised terms in earlier versions of the definitions.
[2]   "Delphi, Credit Derivatives and Bond Trading Behavior After a Bankruptcy Filing", 28 November 2005, Fitch Ratings.

though rating agency recovery models showed that Delphi's bonds should have been trading at significantly lower prices than beforehand.

ISDA was proactive. It produced a cash-settlement protocol for the next series of major credit events: Dana Corporation, Delphi Corporation, Dura Corporation, Calpine Corporation, Delta and North West Airlines and CKC.

This protocol allowed parties adhering to it to amend the terms of their physically settled credit default swaps on a multi-transactional basis. The protocol amended each covered transaction in relation only to the affected credit event to allow 'cash settlement' instead of 'physical settlement', with a 'final price' for a 'reference obligation' determined through a complex auction process.

The auction process was refined with each major credit event and accompanying protocol. Once the mechanism could be tweaked for finality, the Original 2003 Definitions were updated by two supplements in 2009. These were informally known as the 'Big Bang' and the 'Small Bang' Supplements. Together they were also called the 'Auction Settlement Supplements'.

The Auction Settlement Supplements hard wired auction settlement into contracts and modified the obligations that could be delivered and valued in an auction settlement process.

The Auction Settlement Supplements also introduced the idea of objective 'Credit Derivatives Determinations Committees' (DC), composed of the significant players from the sell and buy side of the market who would objectively determine (assisted by ISDA and appointed administrators), among other things, whether credit events and 'succession events' had occurred and how auctions would be run.

For this new infrastructure, ISDA established separate Credit Derivatives Determinations Committees for different geographic regions: the Americas, EMEA (Europe, Middle East and Africa), Asia (excluding Japan), Australia, New Zealand and Japan. Each consists of 15 voting members and three non-voting (consultative) members.

These committees make decisions on questions, submitted to ISDA by market participants, that are sufficiently important to the market as a whole and do not rule on transactional disputes between parties to individual transactions.

They also determine:

- whether a credit event has occurred, and if so, the type and date of the credit event;
- whether the 'credit event notice' submitted to the Credit Derivatives Determinations Committee satisfies the requirements of 'publicly available information'; and
- the date on which the DC is deemed to have received the request. This date is relevant for various other timings in the settlement process.

If it is determined that a credit event has occurred, the DC will also determine whether or not to hold an auction of the 'reference obligations'; and for 'restructuring credit events', the 'maturity buckets' for each auction.

DCs are not obliged to declare whether a particular credit event has occurred.

If a submitted question relates to the occurrence of a succession event, the DC determines whether a succession event has occurred and the date of the occurrence of the event. If a succession event has occurred, the committee will determine, among other things, the identity of any 'successors' and the proportion of the reference obligations that each successor will succeed to.

ISDA published a consolidated version of the 2003 Credit Derivative Definitions in 2010, incorporating the changes introduced by the May Supplement and the Auction Settlement Supplements (as so supplemented, the 'Updated 2003 Definitions').

Although the Updated 2003 Definitions generally performed well in the euro sovereign debt crisis of 2011 and 2012, certain weaknesses were exposed which gave impetus to producing a fully updated set of credit derivatives definitions.

When the Updated 2003 Definitions were drafted, the euro sovereign debt crisis and potential euro break-up seemed the remotest of possibilities, with no previous G8/EU bond defaults having occurred for decades. In addition, the success of credit derivatives almost became their downfall, with the product then so mainstream that there were incentives for governments to structure defaults and restructurings so that they would not trigger credit events.

The overall complexity of these, mainly restructuring, credit events exposed various weak spots and points for improvements in the Updated 2003 Definitions. Also, the bail-in legislation introduced for financial institutions in Europe (primarily through the Bank Recovery and Resolution Directive (2014/59/EU)), which was also unforeseeable in 2003, needed to be addressed to prevent not only these types of event falling outside the credit derivatives definitions, but also to cater for the situation in which some classes (particularly subordinated classes) of debt defaulted or were restructured and others not.

Mandatory clearing and exchange trading of derivatives, as introduced by the European Market Infrastructure Regulation (648/2012) (EMIR) and the US Dodd-Frank Act, could also not have been foreseen in 2003. Accordingly, an update to the definitions was required to facilitate the standardisation of credit default swaps for these purposes. The above events, combined with market participants pushing for more objective terms for contracts, meant that the first comprehensive update of the credit derivatives definitions in over a decade was carried out with the 2014 ISDA Credit Derivatives Definitions.

The 2014 definitions are the market standard definitions for credit derivative transactions.

2.   Introduction and preamble

The introduction to the 2014 definitions provides that they are intended for use in "Confirmations of individual Credit Derivatives Transactions, which are governed either by the 1992 Master Agreement or the 2002 Master Agreement". It goes on to say that the 2014 definitions:

- can provide the basic framework for documenting privately negotiated credit derivatives transactions;
- have fallback provisions that will apply where the parties do not otherwise provide in a transaction; and
- market participants may adapt or supplement as they wish.

Apart from a lengthy liability disclaimer, the introduction also sets out that the 2014 definitions are free standing and so "for most Transactions, there is no need to incorporate any other ISDA definitions booklets (such as the ISDA 2006 Definitions) into the Confirmation of a Credit Derivatives Transaction".

It is not uncommon for bespoke credit derivatives transactions to incorporate the ISDA 2006 Definitions. However, unless there are floating rate interest payments to be made, this is usually unnecessary as the 2014 definitions set out all of the relevant interest rate and 'business day' provisions.

The introduction does not form part of the 2014 definitions. The preamble though does.

> **2014 ISDA Credit Derivatives Definitions**
> Any or all of the following definitions and provisions many be incorporated into a document by wording in the document indicating that to, or to the extent to which, the document is subject to the 2014 Definitions.

It states that the definitions and provisions in the 2014 definitions may be incorporated into a document by inserting wording that "the document is subject to the 2014 ISDA Credit Derivatives Definitions (as published by the International Swaps and Derivatives Associations, Inc. ('ISDA')) (the 'Definitions')".

It is universal in transactions to include the following wording in the first paragraph of the confirmation:

> The definitions and provisions contained in the 2014 ISDA Credit Derivatives Definitions (the 'Credit Derivatives Definitions'), as published by the International Swaps and Derivatives Association, Inc, are incorporated into this Confirmation. In the event of any inconsistency between the Credit Derivatives Definitions and this Confirmation, this Confirmation will govern.

The preamble goes on to provide that all terms, definitions and provisions incorporated into a document will be applicable unless otherwise modified. It also states that any definitions of currencies in a document incorporating the 2014 definitions will have the same meaning as the 2006 ISDA Definitions. This reinforces that it is not necessary to incorporate the 2006 ISDA Definitions into a credit derivatives transaction which incorporates the 2014 definitions.

3.   **Article I – "Certain general definitions"**

Article I's definitions cover six distinct areas. These are:
- the transaction's identity and documentary structure;
- definitions relating to the transaction's fixed time parameters;
- various Credit Derivatives Determinations Committee provisions;
- definitions and terms for determining and notifying a credit event;
- time parameters fixed once an actual or potential credit event occurs; and
- the identity and location of the parties.

3.1   Area I: transaction identity and documentary structure

Article I provides definitions for confirming the transaction's identity as a credit derivatives transaction and its documentary structure. Section 1.1 specifies that any transaction will be a credit derivatives transaction if it identifies itself as such or it incorporates the 2014 definitions. In practice, this is done in the way set out in the extract above.

Section 1.2 provides that a credit derivative transaction is confirmed or its terms evidenced by taking together "one or more documents and other confirming evidence exchanged between the parties or otherwise effective which, taken together confirm or evidence all of the terms of that Credit Derivatives Transaction".

Section 1.55 states that various terms used but not defined in the 2014 definitions – 'additional termination event', 'affected party', 'affected transaction', 'affiliate', 'close-out amount', 'stamp tax' and 'tax' – have the same meaning as in the 2002 ISDA Master Agreement. Various sections of the 2014 definitions use these defined terms: for example, Section 11.4, which uses 'additional termination event'.

3.2   Area II: definitions relating to the transaction's fixed time parameters

Article I also covers a transaction's landmark dates, for example:

- the date when the parties agree to enter into a transaction ('trade date');
- the date when the term will begin ('effective date'); and
- when the term is scheduled to end ('scheduled termination date').

Each transaction confirmation will set out as specific terms, in its general terms section, the date when the parties agree to enter into a transaction as the trade date: Section 1.13. This is usually a few days before the effective date (which is defined in Section 12.10). The effective date is the date specified in the transaction, or if not specified, the 'fixed rate payer payment date' falling at least one calendar day after the trade date.

A transaction's term runs from the effective date until the scheduled termination date, which is the agreed date for credit protection to end, unless a credit event or a potential credit event causes the transaction to terminate either before or after the scheduled termination date.

'Business day conventions' are used to ensure that events which are required to take place on 'business days', such as notice deliveries are deemed to occur on business days. When the relevant date occurs on a date that is not otherwise a business day, the 2014 definitions provide various options that the parties can select to decide whether the relevant business day selected is a preceding or following one.

Article I provides definitions for four types of business day: 'grace period business day' (Section 1.47); 'business day' (Section 1.51); 'calculation agent city business day' (Section 1.44) and 'TARGET settlement day' (Section 1.52).

3.3   Area III – Credit Derivatives Determinations Committee provisions in Article I

For the determination of credit events, Article I contains many of the provisions relating to Determinations Committees/DCs and their decision-making process. These include definitions for 'DC Rules', 'DC secretary', 'DC party', 'resolve', 'DC question', 'DC announcement coverage cut-off date', 'post dismissal additional period' and 'credit event resolution request date'.

Under the 2014 definitions, the DC is not obliged to determine whether or not any particular credit event has occurred, and even if it does, it is not compulsory for it to rule that an auction should take place. The DC will weigh up, among other things, how heavily traded the reference entity name has been (ie, whether it is worth the trouble, time and expense).

Where a DC rules that an auction is to take place, the DC secretary together with one or more 'administrators' will organise an auction.

Section 6.1 provides that if auction settlement is the applicable settlement method in the transaction confirmation and an event determination date occurs, then on or prior to the 'auction final price determination date', a seller will be obliged to pay to the buyer an 'auction settlement amount' on the 'auction settlement date'.

Article I houses several of the important provisions for DCs, as well as the decision-making process for determining credit events and whether an auction should take place.

The most important of these are set out in the table below.

Article I DC definitions	Summary
Section 1.6 ("Credit Derivatives Determinations Committee")	'Credit Derivatives Determinations Committees' are defined as being each committee established on the basis of the DC Rules for reaching DC resolutions in connection with credit derivative transactions.
Section 1.7 ("DC Rules")	'DC Rules' in turn are defined as the Credit Derivatives Determinations Committees Rules, as published by ISDA on its website at www2.isda.org (or any successor website thereto) from time to time, as amended.
Section 1.9 ("DC Secretary")	The DC secretary was ISDA from 2009 to 2016, with an independent entity then becoming responsible for this role.
Section 1.10 ("DC Party")	This is defined in the DC Rules to include the Depository Trust & Clearing Corporation, the DC secretary, various administrators, 'participating bidders' in an auction, as well as any 'external reviewer'.

continued on next page

Article I DC definitions	Summary
Section 1.11 ("Resolve")	'Resolved'/'resolve'/'resolving' is defined in the DC Rules as a DC making a specific determination through a binding vote, and – where the applicable voting threshold is not met for a binding vote – the specific determination that is deemed to be made by a DC following an external review process. These determinations are defined as DC resolutions.
Section 1.19 ("No Event Determination Date")	Where there is a 'DC no credit event announcement' for a potential credit event, then there is deemed to be 'no event determination date' for that event.
Section 1.24 ("Post Dismissal Additional Period")	This is the period from and including the date of a 'DC credit event question dismissal' to and including the date 14 calendar days later. The definition is relevant to the timings in the definitions of 'termination date', 'event determination date', 'non-standard event determination date' and 'credit event backstop date' discussed below.
Section 1.25 ("DC Credit Event Meeting Announcement")	This is a public announcement by the DC secretary that a DC is to be convened to resolve the matters described in a DC credit event question.
Section 1.26 ("DC Credit Event Question")	This is a notice to the DC secretary which requests convening of a DC to resolve whether a credit event has occurred.
Section 1.27 ("DC Credit Event Question Dismissal")	This is a public announcement by the DC secretary that a DC has resolved not to determine the matters described in a DC credit event question.
Section 1.28 ("DC Credit Event Announcement")	This is a public announcement by the DC secretary that the relevant DC has resolved that an event that constitutes a credit event. The announce will confirm that this has occurred on or after the credit event backstop date and on or prior to the 'extension date'.

continued on next page

Article I DC definitions	Summary
Section 1.29 ("DC No Credit Event Announcement")	This is a public announcement by the DC secretary that the DC has resolved that an event that is the subject of a DC credit event question was not a credit event.
Section 1.30 ("Credit Event Resolution Request Date")	For a DC credit event question, this is the date that the DC secretary publicly announces that the DC has resolved to be the date on which the DC credit event question was effective and on which the DC was in possession of applicable publicly available information.
Section 1.54 ("Final List")	Deliverability is crucial in 'auction settled transactions' as only obligations that satisfy the 'deliverable obligation category' and 'characteristics' are deliverable into an auction. Only obligations that appear on the 'final list of deliverable obligations' published by ISDA for a relevant auction may be bought and sold into that auction to determine the 'auction final price'. The actual 'final list' definition is set out in the DC Rules from time to time, with the 2014 definitions cross-referring to the DC Rules.

3.4   Area IV – definitions and terms for determining and notifying a credit event

Article I definitions provide definitions and terms for determining and notifying a credit event. These include the definitions of 'event determination date', 'credit event notice', 'publicly available information', 'public source', 'specified number', 'notice of publicly available information', 'notifying party', 'notice delivery date', 'public source', 'requirements regarding notices', 'calculation agent city' and others.

Primer on credit event notices and event determination dates

Under the Original 2003 Definitions, a credit event was triggered by a notifying party delivering a credit event notice, together usually with a notice of publicly available information. This formed the 'conditions to settlement'.

Under the 2014 definitions, the equivalent to meeting the conditions to settlement is the occurrence of an event determination date.

Once an event determination date occurs, a potential settlement process begins – be it auction, cash or physical. So what is, and what is not an effective event determination date is crucial.

The introduction of the DC in the Updated 2003 Definitions removed and reduced much of that burden from the 'transaction parties', for standard transactions, for triggering a credit event, and replaced it with increased complexity, which was further added to in the 2014 definitions.

The 2014 definitions crystallise a credit event for a reference entity by triggering an event determination date (the determination that a credit event has occurred). This is done either through the actions of the DC or through delivery of a credit event notice by a transaction party, depending on the underlying circumstances.

Event determination date following DC credit event announcement for auction settled transactions

A notifying party is one or both of the transaction parties, as specified in the 'physical settlement matrix' or 'confirmation'. The confirmation or physical settlement matrix will specify either 'buyer' or 'buyer or seller' as the notifying party.

Section 1.16(a) provides that the event determination date is the credit event resolution request date for auction settled transactions where 'buyer or seller' is specified, and there is:

- a 'DC credit event announcement' (a public announcement by the DC secretary that the relevant DC has resolved that an event that constitutes a credit event); and
- a DC has resolved that an event relating to a reference entity constitutes a credit event.

The 'credit event resolution request date' is the date on which a DC credit event question was effective and on which the DC was in possession of applicable publicly available information (see below for more on publicly available information).

A 'DC credit event question' is a notice from a market participant to the DC secretary which requests convening of a DC to resolve whether a credit event has occurred.

Event determination date for 'buyer or seller' auction settled transactions where there is no DC credit event announcement and no DC no credit event announcement

For these auction settled transactions, Section 1.16(a) provides that an event determination date will occur on the notice delivery date where, for a reference entity, there is:

- no DC credit event announcement (ie, a determination by a DC that there has been a credit event); and
- no DC no credit event announcement (ie, a determination by a DC that there has not been a credit event).

This is likely to occur only for more thinly traded reference entities.

The notice delivery date is the first date on which both an effective credit event notice and an effective notice of publicly available information have been delivered by a notifying party to the other party. If notice of publicly available information is specified as not applicable in the confirmation, then it is of course not required. There is no obligation for either party to trigger an event determination date.

Cash settlement and physical settlement transactions (and auction settled transactions where buyer is the notifying party)

Section 1.16(a) covers certain auction settled transactions only – namely, where 'buyer or seller' is specified as the notifying party. Event determination dates for cash settlement and physical settlement transactions are covered under Section 14.1. Auction settled transactions where the buyer is the specified notifying party are covered here too.

Similarly to Section 1.16(a), Section 14.1 provides that where, for a reference entity, there is neither a DC credit event announcement nor a DC no credit event announcement, then an event determination date will occur on the notice delivery date.

Also, similarly, the event determination date will automatically be the credit event resolution request date should a credit event resolution request date occur, if 'buyer or seller' is the specified notifying party. No credit event notice and notice of publicly available information is required to be delivered between the transaction parties in these circumstances.

For auction settled transactions, where 'buyer' only is specified as the notifying party, then the credit resolution request date will also be the event determination date – but only if a credit event notice is actually delivered within time limits by the buyer (no notice of publicly available information is required).

The same applies for M(M)R restructuring credit events, where 'buyer or seller' is specified as the notifying party.

Exceptions and nuances

There are some exceptions and nuances for the above. These are discussed in more detail below. For example, for non M(M)R restructuring credit events, delivery of a credit event notice is required for an event determination date to occur where there is a DC credit event announcement, which occurs prior to the transaction's trade date, and also prior to any 'DC announcement coverage cut off date' (ie, an auction final price determination date, auction cancellation date, or 14 calendar days following any no auction announcement date).

(a)   *Credit event notice*

Section 1.32 defines a 'credit event notice' as an irrevocable notice from a notifying party which describes a credit event that occurred on or after the 'credit event backstop date' and on or prior to the 'extension date'.

The credit event notice must describe the facts relevant to the credit event in reasonable detail. Importantly, the credit event need not be continuing at the time the credit event notice is delivered.

'Credit event backstop date' is defined in Section 1.39 and is the date from which credit protection runs, and following which a credit event can be declared. The definition provides that the credit event backstop date will be the date which is 60 days prior to:

- the date of a credit event resolution request date; or
- the notice delivery date, if the notice delivery date occurs during the notice delivery period.

Regardless of the trade date or the effective date, a credit derivative transaction can be triggered only by a credit event occurring no more than 60 days before the credit event resolution request date or before the notice delivery date.

This restriction/provision also applies if the applicable event occurred before the trade date or the effective date.

The 'credit event notice' definition is supported by a number of other provisions within Article I (excluding those relating to publicly available information, which are set out in the section below the table). The supporting sections are described in the table below.

Article I credit event notice supporting definitions	Summary
Section 1.21 ("Notifying Party")	This is the buyer or seller under the transaction, unless otherwise specified.
Section 1.22 ("Notice Delivery Date")	This is the first date on which both an effective credit event notice and effective notice of publicly available information have been delivered by a notifying party to the other party. If notice of publicly available information is specified as not applicable in the confirmation, then it is of course not required.
Section 1.23 ("Notice Delivery Period")	This is the period from and including the trade date to and including the date 14 calendar days after the extension date.
Section 1.38 ("Requirements Regarding Notices")	The credit event notice can be delivered in writing (including by fax or email) or by telephone.

continued on next page

Article I credit event notice supporting definitions	Summary
Section 1.40 ("Extension Date")	This is defined as the 'scheduled termination date'. However, it will instead be the 'grace period extension date' if: • 'failure to pay' and 'grace period extension' are specified in the confirmation; and • the 'potential failure to pay' with respect to the relevant failure to pay occurs on or prior to the scheduled termination date.

A form of credit event notice is set out in Exhibit A to the 2014 definitions.

(b) *Publicly available information*

Publicly available information is relevant to the process of determining a credit event and event determination date.

Section 1.22 specifies that the 'notice delivery date' is the first date on which a notifying party has delivered both an effective credit event notice and an effective notice of publicly available information to the other party. Only in rare cases will a notice of publicly available information not be specified as applicable in the confirmation (eg, in a credit default swap on a specific loan).

'Notice of publicly available information' is defined in Section 1.34, which provides that a notice of publicly available information is an irrevocable notice from the party delivering the credit event notice to the other party. This delivering party is the notifying party.

The notice must cite 'publicly available information', and this publicly available information must confirm that the credit event described in the credit event notice has actually occurred. The notice can confirm this by doing one of two things. It can attach the publicly available information (eg, the relevant news cuttings), or it can give a description in reasonable detail of the publicly available information.

Section 1.34 also states that a notice of publicly available information can be given either on its own or incorporated into a credit event notice. A form of notice of publicly available information is set out in Exhibit B to the 2014 definitions; however, it is market practice for the notice of publicly available information to be incorporated into the credit event notice.

The notice of publicly available information is used not only with credit event notices, but also with 'repudiation/moratorium extension notices'.

Section 1.35 defines what constitutes publicly available information: it is information that confirms the facts relevant to determining the credit event described in the credit event notice.

Publicly available information can come from various potential sources. First, it can be information that has been published in a 'specified number' of 'public sources'. These terms are defined in Section 1.37 and Section 1.36 respectively.

Alternatively, publicly available information may be information received from or published by the reference entity. Where the reference entity is a sovereign, the information may come from "any agency, instrumentality, ministry, department or other authority thereof acting in a governmental capacity (including, without limiting the foregoing, the central bank) of such Sovereign".

Publicly available information may also be information "from a trustee, fiscal agent, administrative agent, clearing agent, paying agent, facility agent or agent bank for an Obligation" of the reference entity.

Lastly, publicly available information may be "information contained in any order, decree, notice, petition or filing, however described, of or filed with a court, tribunal, exchange, regulatory authority or similar administrative, regulatory or judicial body".

The first option, in paragraph (a), in the definition of 'publicly available information' provides that publicly available information can be information that has been published in a specified number of public sources. The definition of a 'public source' is set out in Section 1.36. The relevant public source can be specified in the confirmation itself, for example the *Financial Times* and *Dow Jones News Wire*.

3.5   **Area V – time parameters fixed once an actual or potential credit event occurs**
Article I provides time periods sets running and key dates fixed when a potential or actual credit event occurs. These include:

- the definitions of 'event determination date' and 'grace period extension date';
- the definitions of periods in the credit event settlement process in which the parties may deliver notices ('notice delivery period', 'grace period extension date', 'grace period and potential failure to pay', 'extension date', 'exercise cut-off date');
- the date when the transaction will end before or after its scheduled termination date; and
- additional timing provisions, to provide contractual certainty.

(a)   *Event determination date and non-standard event determination date*
The event determination date is a key definition in the 2014 definitions. It is the date on which a credit event is determined. This then kicks off the settlement process in Article V. Please note the primer section above on credit event notices and event determination dates in section 3.4.

Settlement: 'cash settlement', 'physical settlement' and 'auction settlement':
Section 5.1 provides that following an event determination date, and other conditions, "the parties will perform their respective Obligations in accordance with the Settlement Method or Fallback Settlement Method, as applicable".

For auction-settled transactions, there is a further key reference: Section 6.1 provides that "if an Event Determination Date occurs on or prior to the Auction Final Price Determination Date, Seller shall, subject to Section 5.1 (Settlement), pay to Buyer the Auction Settlement Amount on the Auction Settlement Date".

For cash-settled transactions, the event determination date can be relevant for determining the cash settlement date. Here, where the 'cash settlement amount' or the 'final price' is specified in the confirmation, the 'cash settlement date' will be the number of 'business days' specified in the confirmation (failing which, three business days) following the event determination date.[3]

The 'event determination date' definition is divided into two; one for standard contracts (set out in Section 1.16), where auction settlement, combined with 'buyer or seller' specified as the notifying party, applies; and the other for non-standard contracts (set out in Section 14.1). This latter part will apply not only where either cash or physical settlement is the elected settlement method, but also where a 'fallback settlement' to cash or physical settlement has become operative. It applies also to auction settlement transactions where 'buyer' only is specified as a notifying party.

(b) Fixing the termination date

Section 1.15 provides that following a 'termination date', the parties have no further 'obligations' towards each other under their transaction. That is other than in respect of obligations that have become due on or prior to the termination date which have yet to be performed.

Section 1.15 sets out that a transaction's termination date means either:

(a) the date as determined in accordance with Section 2.12 (Reference Obligation Only Trade), 5.1 (Settlement), 6.3 (Auction Settlement Date), 7.2 (Cash Settlement Date), 8.17 (Physical Settlement Date), 9.1 (Partial Cash Settlement Due to Impossibility or Illegality), 9.6(b) (Partial Cash Settlement Terms), 9.10 (Cap on Settlement), or 11.2(c)(ii) (Additional Representations and Agreements for Physical Settlement), as applicable; or

(b) if none of such Sections is applicable, the later of the final day of (i) the Notice Delivery Period and (ii) the Post Dismissal Additional Period, if any.

In the absence of an event determination date or for a 'reference obligation only trade', where a 'non-standard reference obligation' has been redeemed in full, in practice, this means that the termination date will be the last day of the 'notice delivery period' (ie, the date 14 calendar days after the extension date).

The extension date is relevant because Section 1.22 defines the 'termination date' as the final day of the period from and including the trade date to and including the date 14 calendar days after the extension date.

Section 1.40 defines 'extension date' as the latest of:

(a) the Scheduled Termination Date, and (b) the Grace Period Extension Date if (i) 'Failure to Pay' and 'Grace Period Extension' are applicable in the Confirmation, and (ii) the Potential Failure to Pay with respect to the relevant Failure to Pay occurs on or prior to the Scheduled Termination Date.

Section 1.14 defines 'scheduled termination date' as "the date specified as such in the related Confirmation". Grace period extension date is discussed in detail in the section below.

---

3   See Section 7.2.

Section 1.24 provides that if later than the extension date, the termination date is 14 calendar days after the date of a DC credit event question dismissal.

Where an event determination date has occurred, or in a reference obligation only trade, a non-standard reference obligation has been redeemed in full, then the termination date will be as set out in the table below:

Section 2.12 ("Reference Obligation Only Trade")	If a non-standard reference obligation is redeemed in whole in a reference obligation only trade, the 'substitution event date' is the termination date.
Section 5.1 ("Settlement")	If physical settlement is the 'settlement method' or is applicable as the 'fallback settlement method', and an effective 'notice of physical settlement' is not delivered by the buyer on or prior to the 'NOPS cut-off date' (ie, the final date for delivering a notice of physical settlement), then the NOPS cut-off date is the termination date.
Section 6.3 ("Auction Settlement Date")	In an auction-settled transaction, the auction settlement date is the termination date.
Section 7.2 ("Cash Settlement Date")	In a cash-settled transaction, the cash settlement date is the termination date.
Section 8.17 ("Physical Settlement Date")	If all 'deliverable obligations' specified in the notice of physical settlement or any 'NOPS amendment notice' (ie, a notice amending a notice of physical settlement) are 'delivered' on or before the physical settlement date, the date that the buyer completes the 'delivery' is the termination date.
Section 9.1 ("Partial Cash Settlement Due to Impossibility or Illegality")	The date when deliverable obligations in the notice of physical settlement or any NOPS amendment notice which were not delivered are subsequently delivered is the termination date.
Section 9.6(b) ("Partial Cash Settlement Terms")	The cash settlement date is the termination date.

continued on next page

Section 9.10 ("Cap on Settlement")	Subject to limited exceptions, if the '60 business day cap on settlement' election is applicable and the termination date has not occurred on or prior to 60 business days following the physical settlement date, that 60th business day is the termination date.
Section 11.2(c)(ii) ("Additional Representations and Agreements for Physical Settlement")	The termination date is the latest of: • the date when the buyer completes 'delivery of deliverable obligations' in the notice of physical settlement or NOPS amendment notice; • the date when the seller completes a buy-in for all 'bonds' in the notice of physical settlement or NOPS amendment notice, where the buyer has failed to complete delivery; • the date when an alternative delivery under Section 9.8 has been completed for all 'loans' in the notice of physical settlement or NOPS amendment notice, where the buyer has failed to complete delivery; or • the date when an alternative delivery under Section 9.9 has been completed for all assets in the notice of physical settlement or NOPS amendment notice, where the buyer has failed to complete delivery.

(c)   *'Potential failure to pay', 'grace period', 'grace period business day' and 'grace period extension'*

What is a 'grace period'? As far as payments are concerned, a grace period is a provision in a company or sovereign's debt documentation giving it an additional penalty-free period to make a payment, when it is unable to do so on a scheduled payment date. A grace period provision is intended to prevent a missed payment due to administrative reasons triggering an actual default.

In international capital markets loans and bonds, grace periods are almost universal and the length of these periods is often heavily negotiated. They may vary from a few days to a month or longer, depending on the jurisdiction and the relevant market standard for the type of borrower or issuer.

How do the grace period provisions in the 2014 definitions work? The 2014 definitions have several definitions covering payment grace periods in a 'reference entity's obligations' and how to deal with them, if they become relevant in a credit derivatives transaction.

Section 1.48 defines a 'potential failure to pay' as a failure by the reference entity to make, when and where due, any payments in an aggregate amount of not less than the 'payment requirement' under at least one of its 'obligations' in accordance with the terms of such obligations. This is without having regard of any grace period or any conditions precedent to the commencement of any grace period applicable in the obligation.

'Payment requirement' is defined in Section 4.9 as the amount specified as such in the confirmation or its equivalent in the relevant obligation currency. Where the payment requirement is not specified, it is US$1 million or equivalent, determined at the date of the potential failure to pay.

Therefore, if a reference entity's potential default is for less than the payment requirement, there will be no potential failure to pay.

Whether a potential failure to pay occurs in relation to any of a reference entity's obligations is determined by applying the criteria set out in the definitions of 'potential failure to pay', 'failure to pay' (as defined in Section 4.5) and 'payment requirement'.

If these criteria are satisfied, the 2014 definitions' operative grace period provisions – 'grace period', 'grace period business day', 'grace period extension date' – are applied to determine how the potential failure to pay is treated in any credit derivatives transaction.

The grace period provisions do not apply automatically to a credit derivatives transaction.[4] The parties must state 'grace period extension: applicable' below 'failure to pay' in the credit event section of a confirmation.

If this is not done and a potential failure to pay occurs on or before the scheduled termination date, but the actual failure to pay does not occur until after the scheduled termination date, then the buyer will not have any credit protection for the later default, because the transaction's period of credit protection will not extend beyond the scheduled termination date.

If 'grace period extension: applicable' is inserted in the confirmation, either directly or through the 'physical settlement matrix', and a potential failure to pay occurs on or prior to the scheduled termination date, the period of credit protection will be extended out until the grace period extension date. A potential failure to pay covers when a reference entity fails to make "when and where due, any payments in an aggregate amount of not less than the Payment Requirement under one or more Obligations".

The definition requires this failure to be determined without taking into account any grace period in the relevant obligation's documentation or any conditions precedent to the grace period beginning.

The 'grace period extension date' will be the date which is the number of days in the grace period after the potential failure to pay.[5] 'If 'grace period' has been defined in the confirmation as being a set number of days though – for example:

---

4   Section 1.46 states: "If Grace Period Extension is not specified as applicable in the related Confirmation, Grace Period Extension shall not apply to the Credit Derivative Transaction."
5   Section 1.45(b).

Credit events: Failure to pay
                        Grace period extension: applicable
                        Grace period: 10 days

and this period is shorter than the grace period in the obligation documentation, then the number of days in the grace period set out in the confirmation will be the grace period.

Alternatively, if the relevant obligation does not have the benefit of a grace period in its documentation or if it does have a grace period but it is for less than three grace period business days, then the grace period will be three grace period business days. A 'Grace period business day' is effectively defined as being a business day in the obligation documentation, failing which a business day in the jurisdiction of the obligation currency.

3.6   Area VI – identity and location of the parties

Article I definitions cover the identity of the parties, with definitions of 'buyer', 'seller' and 'calculation agent'.

Section 1.5 provides that the calculation agent is the party to a credit derivatives transaction (or a third party) specified in the confirmation. Where no party is specified, it is deemed to be the seller.

The calculation agent is responsible for making all determinations required to be made by the calculation agent under the 2014 definitions and as also set out in the confirmation.

Section 1.5 provides that whenever the calculation agent is required to act or to exercise judgement, it has to do so in good faith and in a commercially reasonable manner.

The calculation agent is also required under Section 1.5 to "as soon as practicable after making any of the required determinations, notify the parties of such determination".

Lastly, Section 1.5 provides that "each party agrees that the calculation agent is not acting as a fiduciary for or as an advisor to such party in respect of its duties as Calculation Agent in connection with any Credit Derivative Transaction".

The buyer, who buys credit protection on a reference entity, and the seller, who sells that credit protection, are the two counterparties in any transaction. The 'buyer' is defined in Section 1.3 as 'the fixed rate payer' and the 'seller' in Section 1.4 as 'the floating rate payer'.

These terms are in turn defined in Section 12.6 and Section 12.16 respectively, where each is defined as "the party specified as such in the related Confirmation".

4.   Article II – "General terms relating to credit derivative Transactions"

Article II provides a mechanism for identifying and establishing a transaction's reference entity and reference obligation, as well as providing two separate paths for dealing with reference entities which are financial institutions and those which are not.

Article II covers three areas: 'financial reference entity terms', the reference entity and its 'successors', and provisions for determining a reference entity's reference obligations.

Reference entities are important because these are the entities in credit derivative transactions on which credit protection is sold. However, a reference entity may or may not, for example, change following a merger, demerger or spin-off.

Following a corporate event, its obligations could even be split between a number of different companies. Reference entities are of course not always corporates. They may be 'sovereigns' too; and countries can split and merge, as could have happened with the 2014 Scottish independence vote shortly before the 2014 definitions were released. Article II provides complex provisions for determining 'successor reference entities'.

Reference obligations are important, because in cash settled transactions, the reference obligation specified in a confirmation is the obligation valued to determine the final price. In physically settled transactions, the reference obligation is always a deliverable obligation (even if it does not satisfy the deliverable obligation 'category' and 'characteristics'). In all transactions the reference obligation will be deemed to be an obligation if the chosen obligation category is reference obligation only'.

Deliverability is also crucial in auction-settled transactions as only obligations that satisfy the deliverable obligation category and characteristics (and appear on the final list of deliverable obligations published by ISDA for the relevant auction) are bought and sold in auctions to determine the auction final price.

Reference obligations may also mature, cease to exist as obligations to meet criteria specified in the 2014 definitions, or be transferred to another obligor. Article II provides a detailed substitution mechanism to determine successor reference obligations.

Many of the more complex market events relate to financial institutions; for they are the subject of state interventions, bail-out, bail-ins and official and legal pressures for holder of debt obligations to accept modified rights. So Article II adds the concept of the 'financial reference entity terms'. This is an election applying where the reference entity is a financial institution, and sets in place a hierarchy of terms, which will apply differently depending on whether credit protection is being traded on senior or subordinated debt of that financial institution.

4.1 Area I: financial reference entity terms

Events during the financial crisis which staved off insolvency of financial institutions such as debt write-downs, expropriations and nationalisations provided severe tests and risks for the credit derivatives market.

These included credit derivatives transactions being triggered unexpectedly, or not, when the market thought they would be. Other challenges involved successors to senior obligations and subordinated obligations differing but determinations under the existing credit derivatives definitions resulting in a sole successor, leaving some aggrieved counterparties.

The financial reference entity terms address these challenges through parties to Transactions with financial institution reference entities electing 'financial reference entity terms' either in the confirmation directly or by incorporating the physical settlement matrix.

This election sets in place a hierarchy of terms, with differing results depending on whether credit protection is being traded on senior or subordinated debt of that financial institution.

Article II's financial reference entity terms cover three tiers of debt for financial institutions: 'senior obligations', 'subordinated obligations' and 'further subordinated obligations'. This concept recognises that financial institutions' multiple rankings of debt have different pricing and expected recoveries.

Within Article II, the financial reference entity terms apply in relation to determining relevant obligations for the successor provisions.

Under the definition of relevant obligation in (Section 2.2(f), if 'financial reference entity terms' is specified as applicable in the confirmation and the transaction is a senior transaction, the relevant obligations are deemed to include senior obligations falling within the 'bond or loan' obligation category.

Alternatively, where 'financial reference entity terms' is specified as applicable and the transaction is a subordinated transaction, relevant obligations are deemed to exclude senior obligations and any further subordinated obligations of the reference entity falling within the bond or loan obligation category. However, there is a proviso that if no such relevant obligations exist, 'relevant obligations' has the same meaning as if the transaction were a senior transaction.

'Senior transaction' is defined in Section 2.22 as a "Credit Derivative Transaction for which (a) the Reference Obligation or Prior Reference Obligation .... is a Senior Obligation; or (b) there is no Reference Obligation or Prior Reference Obligation". This links to the definition of 'senior obligation', which is defined in Section 2.23 as any obligation which is not 'subordinate' to any unsubordinated 'borrowed money obligations'.

'Subordinated transaction' is defined in Section 2.24 as a "Credit Derivative Transaction for which the Reference Obligation or Prior Reference Obligation ... is a Subordinated Obligation".

This links to the definition of subordinated obligation, which is defined in Section 2.25 as any obligation which is subordinated to any unsubordinated borrowed money obligation, or which would be so subordinated if any unsubordinated borrowed money obligation of the reference entity existed.

Where a transaction is a 'subordinated transaction', in the same circumstances, if the credit event affects a senior transaction or a subordinated transaction, it will be valid; but an event impacting on a further subordinated obligation, which is defined in Section 2.26 as an obligation subordinated to a subordinated obligation, will be excluded.

'Prior reference obligation' is defined in Section 3.2(b)(C) as in circumstances where there is no applicable reference obligation:

(I) the Reference Obligation most recently applicable thereto, if any, and otherwise, (II) the Obligation specified in the related Confirmation as the Reference Obligation, if any, if such Reference Obligation was redeemed on or prior to the Trade Date and otherwise, (III) any unsubordinated Borrowed Money Obligation of the Reference Entity.

The financial reference entity terms interact with the new 'governmental intervention credit event', which is set out in Article IV, and is the new credit event aimed at capturing government bailouts of banks.

Where the 'governmental intervention credit event' is specified in a confirmation and is accompanied by the election for 'financial reference entity terms', other provisions in the 2014 definition come into play. These include Section 3(f), which provides:

If 'Financial Reference Entity Terms' and 'Governmental Intervention' are specified as applicable in the related Confirmation, if an Obligation would otherwise satisfy a particular Obligation Characteristic or Deliverable Obligation Characteristic, the existence of any terms in the relevant Obligation in effect at the time of making the determination which permit the Reference Entity's Obligations to be altered, discharged, released or suspended in circumstances which would constitute a Governmental Intervention, shall not cause such Obligation to fail to satisfy such Obligation Characteristic or Deliverable Obligation Characteristic.

Where the 'financial reference entity terms' are specified as applicable and the transaction is a senior transaction, then any subordinated obligation will be excluded when determining whether a governmental intervention and/or restructuring credit event has occurred (see further discussion below regarding Section 3.6).

The financial reference entity terms are also relevant where 'asset package delivery' is applicable (ie, the provisions of the 2014 definitions which preserve deliverability of obligations following governmental interventions (and, in some cases, restructurings)).

4.2   Area II: the reference entity and its successors

Credit derivatives transactions have as their underlying asset the credit quality of a third party which is not party to the transaction – the reference entity. Section 2.1 provides that that these reference entities are those specified in the confirmation, together with any successor determined pursuant to the successor provisions in Section 2.2.

'Reference entity' is defined in Section 2.1 as "the entity specified as such in the related Confirmation".

The definition then goes on to provide a two-pronged fallback for determining any successor to the reference entity.

The first is any successor reference entity "identified by the Calculation Agent pursuant to Section 2.2 (Provisions for Determining a Successor) on or following the Trade Date".

The second is any successor reference entity:

identified pursuant to a DC Resolution in respect of a Successor Resolution Request Date and publicly announced by the DC Secretary on or following the Trade Date shall, in each case, with effect from the Succession Date, be the Reference Entity for the relevant Credit Derivative Transaction or a New Credit Derivative Transaction (as determined pursuant to such Section 2.2 (Provisions for Determining a Successor)).

(a)   *Provisions for determining a successor*

Credit derivatives transactions deal with the isolation and separate trading of a reference entity's credit risk. So when a corporate reference entity merges, is spun off or undergoes another corporate event, or when a sovereign reference entity partitions or is invaded, this is likely to impact on the reference entity's overall credit quality.

Section 2.2(l) of the 2014 definitions sets out the method by which eligible market participants place an applicable successor question to the DC, with a notice to the DC secretary requesting that a DC be convened to resolve one or more successors.

Section 3.5 of the DC Rules relates to successor determinations and provides at paragraph (b) that a convened DC may make a DC resolution to resolve market questions on an affected reference entity under Section 2.2.

For non-sovereigns the relevant DC may determine, using 'eligible information', the relevant obligations of an affected reference entity, the proportion of relevant obligations to which a purported successor accedes, together with any adjustments related to a 'steps plan' and the succession date (see discussion of each of these below). For sovereigns, the DC may additionally also determine if a sovereign successor event has occurred.

Following this, the DC will determine the identity of the successor and its resolution will have affect from the succession date.

Where no question is presented to a DC, or the DC declines to accept a question, then any relevant determination is made by the calculation agent instead.

Section 2.2(b) provides that the calculation agent is not permitted to make a determination if, at the time of determination, "the DC Secretary has publicly announced that the relevant Credit Derivatives Determinations Committee has Resolved that there is no Successor based on the relevant succession to Relevant Obligations".

The calculation agent or DC, as applicable, will make its calculations and determinations under Section 2.2 on the basis of eligible information.

'Eligible information' is defined in Section 2.3 as information "which is publicly available or which can be made public without violating any law, agreement, understanding or other restriction regarding the confidentiality of such information".

Stage 1 – determining whether a succession has occurred, what the relevant obligations are and whether a steps plan exists: Central to the determinations made under Section 2.2 is the definition of what 'succeeds' and 'succession' mean.

For a reference entity and its relevant obligations, Section 2.2(d) specifies that 'succeed', 'succeeded' and 'succession' are construed to mean that an entity (other than the reference entity) assumes or becomes liable for a relevant obligation by way of exchange bonds or loans, or by operation of law or otherwise.

'Relevant obligations' is defined in Section 2.2(f) as meaning obligations of the reference Eentity which fall within the bond or loan obligation category and are outstanding immediately prior to the succession date (or, where there is a steps plan, immediately prior to the legally effective date of the first succession).

'Succession date' is defined in Section 2.2(j) as the legally effective date of an event in which some or all of the relevant obligations of the reference entity are acceded to.

Section 2.2(i) provides that a 'steps plan' is a plan evidenced by eligible information showing that there will be a series of successions to some or all of a reference entity's relevant obligations. Section 2.2(b) requires an aggregation of all successions under a steps plan to form a single succession, when applying the successor tests set out in Section 2.2(a).

Under the definition of 'relevant obligation', if 'financial reference entity terms' is specified as applicable in the confirmation and the transaction is a senior transaction, then the relevant obligations are deemed to include senior obligations falling within the bond or loan obligation category.

Alternatively, where 'financial reference entity terms' is specified as applicable and the transaction is a subordinated transaction, relevant obligations are deemed to exclude senior obligations and any further subordinated obligations of the reference entity falling within the bond or loan obligation category.

Stage 2 – 'successor backstop date', 'universal successor' and being a successor under Section 2.2(c): Section 2.2(c) provides that an entity may be determined as a successor only if the succession date occurs on or after the successor backstop date; otherwise no determination can be made.

'Successor backstop date' is defined in Section 2.2(k). For purposes of any DC successor determination, this is specified as the date 90 calendar days prior to the 'successor resolution request date'.

Where there has been no successor resolution request date, the successor backstop date is deemed to be 90 calendar days prior to the date when the successor notice becomes effective.

Section 2.2(a)(vii) also provides a universal successor mechanism to combat unnoticed 'succession events'. This section provides that, notwithstanding the occurrence of a successor backstop date, a new (non-sovereign) entity will be the sole successor (the 'universal successor') if the new entity assumes all of the reference entity's obligations, including at least one relevant obligation, and the reference entity either:

- has ceased to exist; or
- is in the process of being dissolved and it has not issued any borrowed money obligations.

Section 2.2(c) fuses these elements together by providing that an entity may only be a successor if either:

- the succession date occurs on or after the successor backstop date; or
- the entity is a universal successor and the succession date occurred on or after 1 January 2014.

Stage 3 – determine successor(s) (if any) by applying Section 2.2(a) tests using eligible information: If the relevant DC accepts, following a successor resolution request date, to make a successor determination, then the next stage is carried out by the DC, as soon as reasonably practicable. If not, and as long as the DC has not already ruled that there is no successor, then the calculation agent will carry out the next stage as soon as reasonable practicable after delivery of the 'succession notice'. The determination will take effect from the succession date.

Whether it is the DC or the calculation agent making a successor determiniation, both will apply the seven tests set out in Section 2.2(a) for all affected reference entities, including the universal successor test set out in Section 2.2(a)(vii) and described above. Only one test can be satisfied.

In making the determinations under Section 2.2(a), Section 2.2(h) provides that where two or more entities, as 'joint potential successors', succeed to a relevant obligation (a 'joint relevant obligation') either directly or through guarantee, then the joint relevant obligation is treated as having been succeeded to by the joint potential successors in equal parts.

Test I – Section 2.2(a)(i): If another entity has succeeded (directly or as a provider of a 'relevant guarantee') to at least 75% of the reference entity's relevant obligations, the new entity will be the sole successor. This first test will be satisfied where the reference entity is taken over by and merged with another company.

Test II – Section 2.2(a)(ii): If one entity only has succeeded (directly or as a provider of a relevant guarantee) to over 25% (but less than 75%) of the reference entity's relevant obligations and the original reference entity retains not more than 25% of its relevant obligations, then the new entity will be the sole successor for the whole credit derivatives transaction.

Test III – Section 2.2(a)(iii): The third test is satisfied if more than one entity succeeds (directly or as a provider of a relevant guarantee) to over 25% of the reference entity's relevant obligations, but the original reference entity retains 25% or less of its relevant obligations. If this test is satisfied, each of the new succeeding entities will be successor reference entities and the original reference entity will cease to be a reference entity. If one or more of these successors has not assumed a reference obligation specified in the confirmation, then the calculation agent must determine a successor reference obligation.[6] The third test might be satisfied where the same example scenario applied as in second test, but instead the holding company spun off two subsidiaries to different purchasers.

Test IV – Section 2.2(a)(iv): The fourth test is satisfied if one or more entities each succeed (directly or as a provider of a relevant guarantee) to 25% or more of the reference entity's relevant obligations, but the original reference entity itself also retains more than 25% of its relevant obligations. If this test is satisfied then each of

---

6   Successor reference obligations are determined in accordance with Section 2.30.

the succeeding reference entities will be a successor reference entity and the original reference entity will also remain a reference entity.[7]

Test V – Section 2.2(a)(v): The fifth test is satisfied if one or more entities succeed (directly or as a provider of a relevant guarantee) to only part of the reference entity's relevant obligations, but none of them succeeds to more than 25% of them and the reference entity continues to exist. In the case there will be no successor reference entity and the original reference entity will remain the same.

Test VI – Section 2.2(a)(vi): The sixth test is satisfied if one or more entities succeed (directly or as a provider of a relevant guarantee) to part of the reference entity's relevant obligations, but no entity succeeds to more than 25% of them, and the reference entity ceases to exist.

If this test is satisfied, the entity that succeeds to the greatest percentage of the original reference entity's bonds and loans will be the only successor. However, if two new entities succeed to the same percentage of the reference entity's relevant obligations, the new entity which succeeds to the greatest percentage of obligation (ie, obligations including trade debt, letters of credit and other liabilities which would fall under the 'payment' obligation category) will be the only new reference entity and the sole successor to the original reference entity.

Test VII – Section 2.2(a)(vii): The seventh, universal successor, test is satisfied if a new entity assumes all of the reference entity's obligations, including at least one relevant obligation, and the reference entity either:
- has ceased to exist; or
- is in the process of being dissolved and it has not issued any borrowed money obligations.

Stage 4 – notify the parties of any successor, joint successors and (if applicable) create 'new credit derivatives transactions': The DC or the calculation agent will notify the determination as soon as reasonably practicable. In the case of the DC, this will be through market announcement on the ISDA website, and for the calculation agent, to the individual parties.

Additionally, where either the second or third test is satisfied (ie, there is more than one successor) under Section 2.2(a), then pursuant to Section 2.2(n) the following happens:
- With effect from the succession date, the affected transaction is divided into as many new credit derivatives transactions as there are successors. Where the original reference entity continues to be a reference entity, it is also deemed to be a successor for these purposes.
- Each successor will be a reference entity for one of the new credit derivatives transactions.
- The amounts specified in the original confirmation for the fixed rate payer

---

7   A successor obligation will be determined as in the above footnote.

calculation amount and the floating rate payer calculation amount will be deemed to be divided by the number of successors, and the resulting figures applied to the new credit derivatives transactions.

All of the terms in the original confirmation will be deemed to be replicated in each new transaction.

(b)   *Determining a sovereign successor*

Section 2.2(c) of the 2014 definitions provides that where a sovereign is the reference entity, another entity may only be a successor if the entity succeeds to the relevant obligations by means of sovereign succession event.

Section 2.2(d) provides that 'succeed', 'succeeded' and 'succession' means for a sovereign reference entity and its relevant obligations that an entity other than the sovereign assumes or becomes liable for the relevant obligations whether by operation of law or pursuant to any agreement (including any protocol, treaty, convention, accord, concord, entente, pact or other agreement).

Section 2.2(e) defines 'sovereign succession event' as an "annexation, unification, secession, partition, dissolution, consolidation, reconstitution or other similar event".

'Sovereign' is then defined in Section 2.4 as "any state, political subdivision or government, or any agency, instrumentality, ministry, department or other authority acting in a governmental capacity (including, without limiting the foregoing, the central bank) thereof".

4.3   Area III: determining the reference obligation

Article II contains multiple definitions for determining the reference obligation following a credit event, which may:

- be valued in cash-settled transactions to determine the final price;
- be a deliverable obligation (even if it does not satisfy the deliverable obligation category and characteristics) in physically settled transactions; and
- be deemed to be an obligation if the chosen obligation category is 'reference obligation only'.

(a)   *The reference obligation and related provisions*

Section 2.5 defines 'reference obligation' as the "Standard Reference Obligation, if any", before listing a series of provisos where this will not be the case.

Standard Reference Obligation is defined in Section 2.6 (*Standard Reference Obligation*) as "the Obligation of the Reference Entity with the relevant Seniority Level, which is specified from time to time on the SRO List".

The 'SRO List', defined in Section 2.18, is the list of standard reference obligations which is published by ISDA on its website. This list is a new initiative to reduce reference obligation mis-matches between back-to-back credit derivatives swap trades and also to facilitate clearing of standardised contracts.

The SRO List of Standard Reference Obligations, which consists of commonly traded obligations for a reference entity, are deemed to apply for each credit derivative transaction where 'standard reference obligation' is specified as applying in the confirmation. These trades automatically update to the current standard reference obligation if changed by ISDA.

Section 2.17 provides definitions of 'senior level' and 'subordinated level'. This states that whether an obligation of the reference entity is senior level or subordinated level will be as specified in the relevant confirmation.

Where no election is made in the confirmation, then 'senior level' is deemed to apply, unless the reference obligation is a 'non-standard reference obligation', in which case the senior level applies if the reference obligation is a senior obligation, and subordinated level applies if the reference obligation is a subordinated obligation.

Where 'standard reference obligation' is specified as 'not applicable' in the confirmation, the reference obligation will be the non-standard reference obligation (see Section 2.7).

'Non-standard reference obligation' is defined in Section 2.7 as the 'original non-standard reference obligation' or the 'substitute reference obligation'. Section 2.8 defines 'original non-standard reference obligation' as the obligation specified as the reference obligation in the related confirmation.

(b)   *'Substitute reference obligations'*

Circumstances can occur affecting a transaction's reference obligation which means that it no longer exists. For standard reference obligations, where a standard reference obligation ceases to exist the substitutions will be deemed to occur through the mechanics described in the section above (ie, there will still be other standard reference obligations in existence or a new standard reference obligation will be added to the SRO List).

However, for non-standard reference obligations, Section 2.10 and Section 2.11 provide a fallback framework for determining a substitute reference obligation.

The provisions of Section 2.10 are dependent on a 'substitution event' first having occurred.

'Substitution event' is defined in Section 2.11. It means for a non-standard reference obligation, when any of the following take place:

- the non-standard reference obligation is redeemed in whole;
- the aggregate amounts due under the non-standard reference obligation have fallen below US$10 million or equivalent; or
- for reasons other than due to a credit event, the non-standard reference obligation is no longer an obligation of the reference entity.

Notwithstanding the foregoing, the substitute reference obligation provisions do not apply for 'reference obligation only trades', and, pursuant to Section 2.12, these transactions terminate on the substitution event date.

Following the occurrence of a substitution event, the substitute reference obligation will either be chosen through a determination of the DC, or by the calculation agent.

In the case of the former, this is because Section 2.21 has introduced 'substitute reference obligation resolution request date'. This in conjunction with the DC Rules allows eligible market participants to ask the DC to determine a substitute reference obligation.

If a DC determines a substitute reference obligation (and it is not obliged to do so), then this will be the new substitute reference obligation. If the DC makes no determination, the calculation agent will make a decision pursuant to Section 2.10.

Where the decision falls to the calculation agent, it follows an objective set of criteria to determine the substitute reference obligation for trades with non-standard reference obligations.

5. Article III – "Terms Relating to Obligations and Deliverable Obligations"

Credit derivatives isolate and separately trade a reference entity's credit risk. To do this, they focus not only on a reference entity's bankruptcy risk, but also specifically on providing and quantifying compensation for events which materially impact on the credit quality of the reference entity's obligations, such as a failure to pay.

The parties to a transaction may contract that the scope of credit protection applied to a reference entity should cover only the reference entity's obligations which are unsubordinated borrowed money; or perhaps, more specifically, they may decide that only those obligations which are 'listed' bonds and loans should be covered.

It is the reference entity's obligations that are at the heart of a transaction, triggering six of the seven possible credit events.

The 2014 definitions provide a framework, which is set out in Article III, to allow the parties to determine which of a reference entity's obligations are the subject of the credit protection provided under a relevant credit derivative transaction.

Article III covers the following three principal areas:

- the reference entity's obligations which are subject to credit protection, including obligation categories and obligation characteristics;
- the reference entity's obligations which may be delivered as part of the physical settlement or auction settlement process after an event determination date. These include the 'deliverable obligation categories' and 'deliverable obligation characteristics', as well as specific variations for restructuring credit events; and
- the treatment of guarantees of obligations.

5.1 Area I: determining which obligations are 'obligations'

Section 3.1 defines 'obligation' as "(a) any obligation of the Reference Entity (either directly or as provider of a Relevant Guarantee) determined pursuant to the method described in Section 3.13 (*Method for Determining Obligations*); and (b) the Reference Obligation".

As noted above, obligation includes any obligation of the reference entity as provider of relevant guarantees. Article III provides complex provisions discussed further below, which cover what is and what is not included in these relevant guarantees.

Section 3.13 states that:

for the purposes of Section 3.1(a) the term 'Obligation' may be defined as each Obligation of each Reference Entity described by the Obligation Category specified in the related Confirmation and having each of the Obligation Characteristics (if any) specified in the related Confirmation.

The definition provides that the timing for this test is "immediately prior to the Credit Event which is the subject of either the Credit Event Notice or the DC Credit Event Question resulting in the occurrence of the Credit Event Resolution Request Date, as applicable".

So this means that if the parties decide not to limit the 'obligation' definition to specific named securities, the seller will sell credit protection to the buyer in relation to all of the reference entity's obligations which:

- fall within a selected one of the six categories listed in Section 3.13(a); and
- have any of the selected characteristics from Section 3.13(b).

In reality, and as discussed above, the parties will select the obligation category and obligation characteristics according to the market standard terms for a particular reference entity, decided by the reference entity's type and location, set out in the physical settlement matrix, rather than on a case-by-case basis.

(a)   Obligation categories

Section 3.13(a) lists six obligation categories. Only one obligation category can be selected for each reference entity. The obligation categories are:

- payment (ie, any present, future or contingent obligations to repay money (including 'borrowed money') – a broad category that includes contingent payments such as guarantees, trade debts and derivative transactions, such as swaps and repurchases (repos);
- borrowed money (ie, any obligation to pay or repay borrowed money) – a narrower category than payment because the obligation must be borrowed rather than just owed. It excludes trading debts and many derivatives transactions, such as swaps and repos, but specifically includes deposits (which would catch payments owed by a bank to its account holders) and reimbursement obligations under letters of credit;
- 'reference obligation only' (ie, any obligation that is specified as a reference obligation in the confirmation);
- bond (ie, borrowed money in the form of a bond, note (other than a note delivered under a loan) or debt security);
- loan (ie, borrowed money documented by a term loan agreement, revolving loan agreement or other similar credit agreement); and
- bond or loan (ie, any obligation that is either a bond or loan).

Some categories are wider than others, and selecting one category as opposed to another will affect the number of the reference entity's obligations that will be 'obligations'. 'Payment' is the broadest obligation category and 'reference obligations only' the narrowest. The market standard terms, set out in the physical settlement matrix, will vary between selecting borrowed money, or bond or loan, with the other elections being chosen in more bespoke transactions.

(b) *Obligation characteristics*

Section 3.13(b) sets out seven obligation characteristics:

- 'not subordinated' – an 'obligation' of the relevant reference entity which must not be 'subordinated' to "(I) the Reference Obligation or (II) the Prior Reference Obligation, if applicable";
- 'specified currency' – which limits a reference entity's obligations to those with the major currencies);
- 'not sovereign lender' – which excludes any obligation owed primarily to a sovereign or supranational organisation (including Paris Club debt);
- 'not domestic currency' – which excludes obligations payable in the reference entity's home currency (where in general the reference entity is incorporated in an emerging market jurisdiction);
- 'not domestic law' – obligations not governed by the domestic law of the reference entity's home jurisdiction, with the exception that the laws of England and the laws of the State of New York are not deemed to constitute a domestic law;
- 'listed' – the obligation must be quoted, listed or ordinarily purchased and sold on an exchange; and
- 'not domestic issuance' – this limits obligations to those issued (or reissued), or intended to be offered for sale primarily in the domestic market of the reference entity.

Provided that they are not contradictory, any number may be chosen in the confirmation to apply. Obligation characteristics are the second method by which the parties limit the amount or number of reference entity obligations that are the subject of credit protection. Obligation characteristics are not specified in all transactions and they tend to be selected to apply in transactions when it is necessary to isolate a reference entity's more liquid and internationally traded obligations from those which may be less so.

5.2 Area II: determining which of the reference entity's obligations are deliverable

The definition of 'deliverable obligation' in Section 3.2, together with the provisions for determining them in Section 3.15, are relevant to physical settlement, cash settlement and auction settlement, following an event determination date.

In physically settled transactions, the obligations of the reference entity which fall within the definition of deliverable obligation are those which may be delivered by the buyer to the seller in return for payment of the physical settlement amount.

In the case of cash-settled transactions, although the deliverable obligations provisions are meant to relate only to physically settled transactions, it has been common to adapt them in cash-settled transactions as a method for selecting a reference obligation to be valued, when none is chosen in the confirmation (in the absence of any standard reference obligation).

In auction-settled transactions, the deliverable obligations are delivered into the auction and then valued for the purposes of determining an auction settlement final price.

(a)   *Deliverable obligation*

Section 3.2 defines 'deliverable obligations' as:

- "any Obligation of the Reference Entity (either directly or as provider of a Relevant Guarantee) determined pursuant to the method described in Section 3.14 (*Method for Determining Deliverable Obligations*)";
- any reference obligation;
- any 'sovereign restructured deliverable obligation', where 'asset package delivery' (see later discussion of this area below) is not applicable, the reference entity is a sovereign and there is a restructuring credit event; and
- where 'asset package delivery' is applicable (ie, an asset package credit event has occurred) and either 'financial reference entity terms' is specified as applicable, or the reference entity is a sovereign: any 'prior deliverable obligation' (for the relevant financial reference entity) or any 'package observable bond' (for the sovereign).

An obligation will not constitute a deliverable obligation if it is an 'excluded deliverable obligation' or it has an 'outstanding principal balance' (or 'due and payable amount') of zero.

(b)   *Excluded deliverable obligation*

Any excluded deliverable obligation will be excluded from being a deliverable obligation, as set out in Section 3.2.

'Excluded deliverable obligation' is defined in Section 3.7 and is a similar provision to the definition of 'excluded obligation' in Section 3.6. As with excluded obligations, excluded deliverable obligations may be specified only on a bespoke basis.

However, the definition of 'excluded obligation' has in place of the provisions relating to 'senior' and 'subordinated' transactions, two further categories of obligation which will be excluded deliverable obligations. These will be:

- any obligation specified as such in the relevant confirmation;
- any principal-only component of a bond from which the interest components have been stripped; and
- if 'asset package delivery' is applicable, any obligation issued after the date of the asset package credit event.

(c)   *Determining which obligations are deliverable obligations*

Section 3.14 states that:

> for the purposes of Section 3.2(a) the term 'Deliverable Obligation' may be defined as each Obligation of each Reference Entity described by the Deliverable Obligation Category specified in the related Confirmation and, subject to Section 3.15 (*Interpretation of Provisions*) having each of the Deliverable Obligation Characteristics (if any) specified in the related Confirmation…

The definition provides that the timing for this test is "as of both the NOPS Effective Date (ie, the effective date of the Notice of Physical Settlement) and the Delivery Date of a Deliverable Obligation (unless otherwise specified)".

Deliverable obligation category: There are six 'deliverable obligation categories'. These replicate the obligation categories (described above). In the case of deliverable obligations, 'reference obligation only' has the effect of fixing the deliverable obligation at the transaction's outset.

Deliverable obligation characteristic: There are 14 'deliverable obligation characteristics'. Seven of these are replicated from the obligation characteristics. These are not subordinated, specified currency, not sovereign lender, not domestic law, listed and not domestic issuance. The deliverable obligation characteristics perform the same function as the obligation characteristics (ie, to isolate a reference entity's more tradable obligations).

There are also seven new characteristics. These are 'assignable loan', 'consent-required loan', 'direct loan participation', 'transferable', 'maximum maturity', 'accelerated or matured' and 'not bearer'.

These seven new characteristics are outlined below:

- Assignable loan – this is a loan that can be assigned or novated, without the consent of a reference entity or any guarantor, to at least a commercial bank or financial institution which is not already one of the loan lenders or syndicate members. This characteristic can only apply to loans and is only relevant if loans are included as a deliverable obligation category.

- Consent-required loan – this is a loan that can be assigned or novated to another party (not only a commercial bank or institution), but only with the consent of the reference entity, any relevant guarantor or a syndicate agent. If both 'assignable loan' and 'consent-required loan' are specified, then it will be necessary for an obligation to have only one of these deliverable obligation characteristics. This characteristic can apply only to loans and is relevant only if loans are included as a deliverable obligation category.

- Direct loan participation – this refers to loans where the buyer can transfer a specified share of the loan's principal and interest payments to the seller. The direct loan participation characteristic applies only to loans and is relevant only if loans are included as a deliverable obligation category.

- Transferable – this does not apply to loans. The obligation must be transferable to institutional investors "without any contractual, statutory or regulatory restriction". The definition carves out US resale restrictions under the Regulation S and Rule 144A safe harbours. All eurobonds are subject to one or other of these safe harbours.

- Maximum maturity – this means that on the physical settlement date, the deliverable obligation must not have a maturity date later than the period specified in the confirmation.

- Accelerated or matured – this refers to obligations that "the total amount owed, whether at maturity, by reason of acceleration, upon termination or otherwise (other than amounts in respect of default interest, indemnities, tax gross-ups and other similar amounts), is, or on or prior to the Delivery Date" will be fully due and payable in full in accordance the obligation's terms. This also applies where this would have been the case, but for the application of insolvency laws.

- Not bearer – by its nature, this relates only to bonds. To meet the requirements of this deliverable obligation characteristic, the bonds must be either registered bonds or, if they are bearer bonds, cleared via Euroclear, Clearstream or any other internationally recognised clearing system.

(d)   *Asset package delivery provisions*
The asset package delivery provisions in the 2014 definitions preserve deliverability of obligations following governmental interventions (and, in some cases, restructurings) of banks through concepts including 'prior deliverable obligation' and 'package observable bond', which are set out in Article III.

The governmental intervention credit event, which is set out in Article IV, is the new credit event aimed at capturing government bailouts of banks. It is accompanied by the election for 'financial reference entity terms'.

Under the definition of 'deliverable obligation' in Section 3.2, we noted that 'deliverable obligation' means any obligation of the reference entity that satisfies the deliverable obligation category and deliverable obligation characteristics, as well as the reference obligation.

In addition to these, we discussed two alternatives which broaden the scope of what may be a deliverable obligation. The second option is where 'asset package delivery' is applicable (ie, an asset package credit event has occurred) and either 'financial reference entity terms' is specified as applicable, or the reference entity is a sovereign. In these circumstances, any prior deliverable obligation (for the relevant financial reference entity) or any package observable bond (for the sovereign), as applicable, are deliverable obligations.

The asset package delivery provisions are split between Articles III and VIII.

The provisions in Article III hang off the definition of 'asset package credit event', which is set out in Section 8.9. The asset package credit event is not a new credit event, but instead is designed to enable obligations which existed immediately prior to certain governmental intervention or restructuring credit events as capable of being deliverable, notwithstanding that the intervention changed their characteristics and prevented them from being otherwise deliverable.

Pursuant to Section 8.9, the following events constitute asset package credit events:

- For financial reference entities, if 'governmental intervention' is specified as applicable in the relevant trade confirmation, then either a governmental intervention or a restructuring shall constitute an asset package credit event.
- For sovereign reference entities, if 'restructuring' is specified as applicable in the relevant trade confirmation, then restructuring shall constitute an asset package credit event.

The provisions set out in Article III which relate to asset package delivery provisions are Section 3.3, Section 3.4 and Section 3.5.

The definition of 'prior deliverable obligation' provides that, following a governmental intervention credit event, an obligation will be a prior deliverable obligation if the obligation:

- existed immediately prior to the governmental intervention;
- was the subject of the governmental intervention; and
- fell within the definition of 'deliverable obligation' immediately preceding the date on which the governmental intervention was legally effective.

In the case of a restructuring credit event, which does not also constitute a governmental intervention, then the prior deliverable obligation will be only the reference obligation.

'Package observable bond' applies only to sovereigns, and refers to a bond that is specified on a list published by ISDA on its website and which falls within the first two limbs of the definition of 'deliverable obligation (see Section 3.2) immediately prior to the legally effective date of the relevant asset package credit event.

As mentioned above, the definition of 'deliverable obligation' in Section 3.2 provides that solely for a restructuring credit event relating to a sovereign, where 'asset package delivery' is not applicable, any sovereign restructured deliverable obligation will be a deliverable obligation.

Section 3.5 provides that a sovereign restructured deliverable obligation is an obligation issued by a sovereign reference entity that has experienced a restructuring credit event and constituted deliverable obligations immediately prior to such restructuring credit event.

(e)   *Variation of the restructuring credit event*

When a corporate or sovereign finds that it is unable to pay its debts when they fall due, this can be either because it simply does not have enough money to do so and is unlikely to have in the future, or because it has had a cash flow crisis – that is, it is unable to pay its debts now, but with some adjustment of maturity dates, modification of interest rates or rolling over of loans, it will be able to meet its obligations in the future. Corporate and sovereign debt restructurings are regular occurrences in the capital markets.

The 'restructuring credit event' is defined in Section 4.8. In addition, several other provisions in the 2014 definitions relate directly to the restructuring credit event:

- Section 3.5 ('Sovereign Restructured Deliverable Obligation');
- Section 3.31 ('Mod R'), which contains definitions for 'fully transferable obligation', 'restructuring maturity limitation' and 'eligible transferee';
- Section 3.31 ('Mod R Mod R'), which contains definitions for 'conditionally transferable obligation', 'modified restructuring maturity limitation' and 'modified eligible transferee'; and
- Section 1.33 ('Credit Event Notice after M(M)R Restructuring').

Restructuring originally became problematic as a credit event for two reasons. First, if credit derivatives are intended to isolate and separately trade credit risk, with payments made from seller to buyer intended to reflect a decline in the creditworthiness of the reference entity, then a restructuring which prevents a further decline in the creditworthiness of the reference entity (eg, perhaps through lengthening the maturities of its bonds and the reference entity granting security over its assets) is arguably a contradiction, especially if in the long term the reference entity's creditworthiness improves.

Other than in the case of sovereigns, the fact that a reference entity does not file for bankruptcy demonstrates that its directors, shareholders and creditors believe in the reference entity's long-term financial health.

The second reason is what has become known as the 'moral hazard of the cheapest to deliver option'. Restructurings do not always relate to all of the reference entity's obligations. The creditors of restructured obligation are likely to seek greater protection for agreeing to any restructuring, such as the reference entity granting security over its assets. This can mean that a restructured obligation trades at a much higher price than those obligations of the reference entity which have not been restructured.

Following a credit event, the reference obligation valued in cash-settled transactions or the deliverable obligation delivered in physically settled and (into the auction) in auction-settled transactions need not be the restructured obligation.

Once again, this can lead to a contradiction: the event which has occurred to the restructured obligation which represents the decline in creditworthiness of the reference entity is measured against other obligations which may now be worth far less than the restructured obligation.

Section 4.7 provides that a restructuring credit event occurs when any one of a list of specified events binding all of the holders occurs to an aggregate amount of the reference entity's obligations at least equal the 'default requirement' (as determined by Section 4.7(a)).

These events must not be contemplated under the obligation's terms in effect at the later of the trade date or the obligation's issue date.

The specified events are:

- an interest payment or accrual reduction;
- a principal or premium reduction;
- a postponement of payment of accruals or interest, or principal or premium;
- a change of an obligation's priority of payment, causing that obligation's subordination; and
- any change in currency of interest or principal other than to a permitted currency.

Section 3.31 ('Mod R') and Section 3.33 ('General Terms Relating to Mod R and Mod Mod R'): Mod R (modified restructuring) aims to reduce the moral hazard of the 'cheapest to deliver' option for deliverable obligations in physical settlement and auction settlement, described above. It is used mainly for North American reference entities.

Paragraph (a) of Section 3.31 requires that physical settlement be the specified settlement method or the 'fallback settlement method'. Also required is that 'Mod R' must be specified in the relevant confirmation. This will usually be immediately below where 'restructuring' is specified as a credit event.

If all these criteria are satisfied, then paragraph (a) states that a deliverable obligation may be specified or deemed to be specified in the notice of physical settlement or in any later NOPS amendment notice, as applicable, only if the deliverable obligation:

- is a 'fully transferable obligation'; and
- has a final maturity date not later than the applicable 'restructuring maturity limitation date',

in each case, as of both the NOPS effective date and the delivery date.

Section 3.31(b), (c) and (d) contain the three definitions contained in paragraph (a). These are 'fully transferable obligation', 'restructuring maturity limitation date' and 'eligible transferee'.

Section 3.33 then contains definitions for 'limitation date', 'restructured bond or loan' and 'restructuring date', which are relevant to both Mod R and Mod Mod R (described below).

The Mod R criteria, set out in paragraph (a) of Section 3.31 require first that the deliverable obligation must be a fully transferable obligation.

This is defined in Section 2.32(b) as meaning that the deliverable obligation is a bond which is transferable (as defined in Section 3.14). Alternatively, it can be an obligation other than a bond which is capable of being assigned or novated without consent; this will most likely be a loan as the obligation category for each of ISDA's standard terms is 'bond or loan'.

It is also a criterion that these loans are transferable to eligible transferees. 'Eligible transferee' is defined in Section 3.31(d) and includes various finance and corporate entities or their affiliates with total assets of at least US$500 million, as well as individual and groups of investment vehicles with total assets of at least US$100 million; and also sovereigns, sovereign agencies and supranational organisations.

The definition of 'fully transferable obligation' specifically states that "any requirement that notification of novation, assignment or transfer be provided to a trustee, fiscal agent, administrative agent, clearing agent" will not be considered to be a consent for these purposes.

The deliverable obligation's maturity date must be no later than the restructuring maturity limitation date. 'Restructuring maturity limitation date' is defined in Section 3.31(c) to mean, for a deliverable obligation, the limitation date occurring on or immediately following the scheduled termination date.

An exception to this, set out within the provision, relates to where the final maturity date of the restructured bond or loan with the latest final maturity date of any restructured bond or loan occurs prior to the '2.5-year limitation date' and the scheduled termination date occurs prior to the final maturity date of that obligation.

That obligation is defined as the 'latest maturity restructured bond or loan') and the provision states that in this case, the restructuring maturity limitation date will be the final maturity date of the latest maturity restructured bond or loan.

Section 3.33 sets out definitions used in both Section 3.31 and Section 3.32.

'Limitation date' is defined to mean the first of 20 March, 20 June, 20 September or 20 December in any year to occur on or immediately following the date that is one of the following numbers of years after the restructuring date: two and a half years (the '2.5-year limitation date'), five years, seven and a half years, 10 years (the '10-year limitation date'), twelve and a half years, 15 years or 20 years, as applicable. This definition clarifies that limitation dates will not be subject to adjustment in accordance with any business day convention.

'Restructured bond or loan' is defined as an obligation that is a bond or loan and in respect of which a relevant restructuring has occurred.

'Restructuring date' is defined as meaning the date on which a restructuring is legally effective in accordance with the terms of the documentation governing the restructuring.

Section 3.33(d) provides that, for the purposes of making a determination pursuant to Sections 3.31 and 3.32, the final maturity date shall be determined on the basis of the terms of the deliverable obligation in effect at the time of making the determination. It further provides that where a deliverable obligation that is due and payable, the final maturity date will be deemed to be the date on which such determination is made.

Section 3.32: Modified restructuring has never applied to European reference entities, on the basis that it does not fully take account of European loan market practice. In particular, Mod R excludes consent-required loans from being deliverable obligations, preventing loans documented according to Loan Market Association standards from being deliverable obligations.

To deal with these concerns, the 2014 definitions include a further option for the European market known as 'modified modified restructuring' or 'Mod Mod R'.

Paragraph (a) of Section 3.32 requires that physical settlement is the specified settlement method, or the fallback settlement method. Also, 'Mod Mod R' must be specified in the relevant confirmation. This will usually be immediately below where 'restructuring' is specified as a credit event, and will be applied through the physical settlement matrix.

Restructuring also has to be the only credit event specified in a credit event notice delivered by the buyer.

If all these criteria are satisfied then paragraph (a) states that a deliverable obligation may only be specified or deemed to be specified in the notice of physical settlement or in any later NOPS amendment notice, as applicable, if the deliverable obligation:

- is a 'conditionally transferable obligation'; and
- has a final maturity date not later than the 'modified restructuring maturity limitation date'.

in each case, as of both the NOPS effective date and the delivery date.

As with the Mod R provisions, an exception to the above is where the deliverable obligation is a prior deliverable obligation and 'asset package delivery' applies due to a governmental intervention (see further discussion above), in which case it can be a deliverable obligation irrespective of the Mod Mod R provisions.

Unlike the Mod R provisions, the 'Mod Mod R' definition provides a further exception in its paragraph (a). Here, where there is a restructured bond or loan with a final maturity date on or prior to the 10-year limitation date, the final maturity date of that bond or loan shall be deemed to be the earlier of that final maturity date or the final maturity date of that bond or loan immediately prior to the relevant restructuring (ie, where the maturity date has been extended as part of the restructuring).

Section 3.32(b), (c) and (d) contain the three of the definitions contained in paragraph (a). These are 'conditionally transferable obligation', 'modified restructuring maturity limitation date' and 'eligible transferee'.

The Mod Mod R criteria, set out in paragraph (a) of Section 3.32, require first that the deliverable obligation be a conditionally transferable obligation.

This is defined in Section 3.32(b) as meaning that the deliverable obligation is a bond which is transferable (as defined in Section 3.14).

Alternatively, it can be an obligation other than a bond which is capable of being assigned or novated without consent; this will most likely be a loan as the obligation category for each of ISDA's standard terms is 'bond or loan'.

It is also a criterion that these loans can be transferred to 'modified eligible transferees' (in contrast with 'eligible transferees' in modified restructuring).

'Modified eligible transferees' are defined in Section 3.32(e) as "any bank, financial institution or other entity which is regularly engaged in or established for the purpose of making, purchasing or investing in loans, securities and other financial assets".

'Modified eligible transferees' are therefore a wider category of transferee than 'eligible transferees'. This definition is based on the broader loan market association standard form and includes any bank, financial institution or other entity regularly involved in making, purchasing or investing in loans, securities and other assets.

As with the definition of 'fully transferable obligation', the definition of 'conditionally transferable obligation' specifically states that "any requirement that notification of novation, assignment or transfer be provided to a trustee, fiscal agent, administrative agent, clearing agent" will not be considered to be consent for these purposes.

In addition, the definition of 'conditionally transferable obligation' states that a loan will not be a deliverable obligation where the reference entity, agent or any guarantor's consent is required for a novation, assignment or transfer, as long as the terms of the obligation provide that "such consent may not be unreasonably withheld or delayed".

Also, the deliverable obligation's maturity date must be no later than the modified restructuring maturity limitation date.

'Modified restructuring maturity limitation date' is defined in Section 3.32(d) as the limitation date occurring on or immediately following the scheduled termination date.

The definition does, however, provide an exception where the scheduled termination date is later than the 10-year limitation date. In this case, the modified restructuring maturity limitation date will be the scheduled termination date.

Lastly, Section 3.32(c) provides that where the conditionally transferable obligation requires consent to novate, assign or transfer and the requisite consent is refused (whether or not a reason is given for such refusal and, where a reason is given for such refusal, regardless of that reason), or is not received by the physical settlement date (in which case it is deemed to be refused), the buyer is then required promptly to notify the seller of this. Section 11.2(c)(iv) is then deemed to apply with respect to the seller as the designator.

The above, though, is provided that the designee need not be an 'affiliate' of the seller. Also, if the seller does not designate a third party that takes delivery on or prior to the 'loan alternative procedure start date', then Section 9.8 applies.

5.4   Area III: guarantees of obligations

In any credit derivatives transaction, it is of paramount importance to determine the extent of credit protection provided against the relevant reference entity. This is done (with the exception of the 'bankruptcy credit event') by determining the identity of the reference entity's obligations covered – that is, which of the reference entity's obligations are 'obligations' and, post-credit event, which of these obligations can be valued as reference obligations in cash settlement or delivered as deliverable obligations in physical settlement, or delivered into an auction in auction settlement.

Article III provides extensive provisions on guarantees to allow the parties to make these determinations, relating to the breadth of credit protection provided, as simply, comprehensively and decisively as possible.

Under the definition of 'deliverable obligation' in Section 3.2, we noted that deliverable obligation includes any obligation of the reference entity that satisfies the deliverable obligation category and deliverable obligation characteristics, as well as the reference obligation. The words "any Obligation of a Reference Entity" are followed on by "either directly or as provider of a Relevant Guarantee". 'Relevant guarantee' is also relevant in exactly the same way in Section 3.1.

Section 3.22 is also used throughout Section 2.2 on determining a successor, as well as in the definition of 'sovereign restructured deliverable obligation' in Section 3.5.

'Relevant guarantee' is defined to mean a 'qualifying affiliate guarantee' or, if 'all guarantees' is specified as applicable in the related confirmation, a 'qualifying guarantee'. It is used in the definition of 'guarantee', set out at Section 3.30, which provides that 'guarantee' means a relevant guarantee or a guarantee which is the reference obligation.

Unless the parties select 'all guarantees' as applicable in the confirmation, the fallback is for 'qualifying affiliate guarantees' to be deemed to apply instead. This selection is made either in paragraph 1 of the confirmation or through the physical settlement matrix.

Section 3.21 provides that a qualifying guarantee is a guarantee evidenced by a written instrument (which may include a statute or regulation) to pay all amounts of principal and interest due under an 'underlying obligation', for which the 'underlying obligor' is the obligor, other than amounts in excess of a fixed cap.

'Underlying obligation' is defined in Section 3.23 as meaning "with respect to a guarantee, the obligation, which is the subject of the guarantee". 'Underlying obligor' is defined in Section 3.24 as meaning, with respect to an underlying obligation, "the issuer in the case of a Bond, the borrower in the case of a Loan, or the principal obligor in the case of any other Underlying Obligation".

'Qualifying affiliate guarantee is defined in Section 3.27 as a qualifying guarantee provided by the reference entity only to one of its 'downstream affiliates'.

'Downstream affiliate' is defined in Section 3.28 as "an entity whose outstanding Voting Shares were, at the date of issuance of the Qualifying Guarantee, more than fifty per cent-owned, directly or indirectly, by the Reference Entity". 'Voting shares' are in turn defined in Section 3.29 as shares or other interests which have the board of directors or similar governing body of an entity.

'Qualifying guarantee' will be selected as an election in transactions where a reference entity is from a jurisdiction where market participants believe that upstream and cross-stream guarantees have a greater legal risk than downstream guarantees.

6.   Article IV – "Credit Events"

Article IV relates to the credit events themselves. There are seven credit events and Section 4.1 lists them. These are then defined in Sections 4.2 to 4.7:

- 'bankruptcy' (Section 4.2);
- 'obligation acceleration' (Section 4.3);
- 'obligation default' (Section 4.4);
- 'failure to pay' (Section 4.5);
- 'repudiation/moratorium' (Section 4.6);
- 'restructuring' (Section 4.7); and
- 'governmental intervention' (Section 4.8).

Section 4.1 also sets out, for clarification, various circumstances, such as a lack of authority, which will not prevent an event that otherwise meets the criteria in any of the individual credit event definitions from being a credit event.

6.1   Credit events

Section 4.1 defines 'credit event' as meaning "one or more of Bankruptcy, Failure to Pay, Obligation Acceleration, Obligation Default, Repudiation/Moratorium, Restructuring or Governmental Intervention". The credit events that the parties select are likely to depend upon relevant market standards for the reference entity's jurisdiction and characterisation, as indicated in the physical settlement matrix.

In addition to providing the definition of 'credit event', Section 4.1 carves out four sets of common law defences and circumstances that a party could potentially use to argue that a particular credit event was not valid. These are where:

- the reference entity is alleged to or actually lacks the authority to enter into an obligation or guarantee an underlying obligation;

- any obligation or underlying obligation is alleged to be or actually is unenforceable, illegal, invalid or impossible;
- the relevant circumstance or defence arises from a law, a court or administrative decision or interpretation, or similar; or
- a monetary or other authority changes or imposes exchange controls or capital restrictions.

(a)   *Bankruptcy*

Bankruptcy is the only credit event which relates to the reference entity itself rather than its obligations. Section 4.2 provides a list of eight circumstances which will be deemed to constitute a bankruptcy credit event.

There will be a bankruptcy credit event if the reference entity is dissolved other than due to a consolidation, amalgamation or merger; and likewise if the reference entity becomes insolvent or unable to pay its debts, or fails to pay them when due. If the reference entity admits in writing "in a judicial, regulatory, or administrative proceeding or filing" that it is unable generally to pay its debts when they become due, this will also be a bankruptcy credit event; similarly where the reference entity makes a "general assignment, arrangement, scheme or composition with or for the benefit of its creditors generally, or such a general assignment, arrangement, scheme or composition becomes effective"; or where the reference entity has instituted or has had instituted against it a proceeding seeking a bankruptcy or insolvency judgment or similar relief.

If a petition is presented or proceeding initiated requesting that the reference entity be wound up or liquidated, this will be a bankruptcy credit event only if:

- it results in an actual bankruptcy or insolvency judgment, or an order for relief, winding-up or liquidation; or
- the petition or proceeding is not "dismissed, discharged, stayed or retrained" within 30 calendar days of it being presented.

There is also a bankruptcy credit event if the reference entity itself passes a resolution for it to be wound up or go into an official management or liquidation, other than due to a consolidation, amalgamation or merger.

Appointments made for certain of the roles (eg, liquidators, receivers and trustees) relating to bankruptcies which apply to all, or substantially all, of the reference entity's assets are bankruptcy credit events.

If a secured party takes possession of "all or substantially all" of the reference entity's assets this will be a bankruptcy credit event. This will also be the case where a "distress, execution, attachment, sequestration, or other legal process" is applied to "all or substantially all" of the reference entity's assets and the secured party maintains possession. In each case, it will not constitute a bankruptcy credit event if the relevant process is "dismissed, discharged, stayed, or restrained" within 30 calendar days.

Lastly, Section 4.2 provides a catch-all provision stating that any event under the applicable laws of any jurisdiction which has an 'analogous effect' to any of the other circumstances listed in Section 4.2 will also be a bankruptcy credit event.

(b)   *Obligation acceleration*

When an obligation is accelerated, it means that following an event of default the noteholders, lenders or trustee declare that the obligation is immediately due and payable. Section 4.3 limits the obligation acceleration credit event to where the obligation's lenders or bondholders accelerate a greater amount of one or more obligations in aggregate totalling more than the default requirement (Section 4.8(a)). Carved out of the obligation acceleration credit event is where the event of default under the obligation is a failure to pay, which is instead covered by the provisions of the failure to pay credit event.

(c)   *Obligation default*

Obligation default, which is set out in Section 4.4, mirrors the obligation acceleration credit event, except that there is no requirement for the obligation to be accelerated following the event of default. Obligation acceleration and obligation default are alternative credit events and only one can be selected per reference entity.

(d)   *Failure to pay*

The failure to pay credit event is defined in Section 4.5. A failure to pay credit event will occur if the reference entity fails to pay any amounts equal to or greater than the payment requirement under any of its obligations. The failure to pay must take place after the expiration of an obligation's grace period (this period is set out in the obligation itself) or after the satisfaction of any conditions precedent to that grace period commencing. If an obligation does not have a grace period, or if it has a grace period of less than three business days, then the grace period is deemed to be three business days.

(e)   *Repudiation/moratorium*

Under English law, a party repudiates its debts or obligations if it states that it does not intend to honour them. A moratorium occurs if a party declares that it intends to delay honouring its obligations. Both a repudiation and a moratorium can occur prior to any actual default or failure to pay. Both are also most closely associated with the acts of sovereigns. It is market practice for the repudiation/moratorium credit event to apply only to sovereign reference entities; and this credit event is not included in any of ISDA's standard terms relating to non-sovereign reference entities, other than for sukuks.

The repudiation/moratorium credit event is defined in Section 4.6. It has two limbs which must both be satisfied in order for a repudiation/moratorium credit event to occur.

First, a reference entity's authorised officer or, alternatively, a governmental authority (eg, a minister of finance) must repudiate or declare a moratorium on any of the reference entity's obligations. This must be in an aggregate amount of at least the 'default requirement' (as defined in Section 4.9). This first test is defined in Section 4.6(c) as a 'potential Repudiation/Moratorium'.

Second, this potential repudiation/moratorium must be followed by an actual failure to pay or restructuring on or prior to the repudiation/moratorium 'evaluation date' (Section 4.6(d)). This actual failure to pay is determined without regard to the payment requirement and a restructuring will be determined without regard to the default requirement.

(f)   *Restructuring*

When a corporate or sovereign finds that it is unable to pay its debts when they fall due, this can be either because it simply does not have enough money to do so and is unlikely to have in the future, or because it has had a cash flow crisis – that is, it is unable to pay its debts now, but with some adjustment of maturity dates, modification of interest rates or per rolling over of loans, it will be able to meet its obligations in the future.

Section 4.7 provides that a restructuring credit event occurs when any one of a list of specified events binding all of the holders occurs to an aggregate amount of the reference entity's obligations at least equal to the default requirement (as determined by Section 4.9(a)). These events must not be contemplated under the obligation's terms in effect at the later of the trade date or the obligation's issue date. The specified events are:

- an interest payment or accrual reduction, including by way of redenomination;
- a principal or premium reduction, including by way of redenomination;
- a postponement of payment of accruals or interest, or principal or premium;
- a change of an obligation's priority of payment, causing that obligation's subordination; and
- any change in the currency of any payment of interest, principal or premium to any currency other than the lawful currency of Canada, Japan, Switzerland, the United Kingdom and the United States of America and the euro and any successor currency to any of these (which in the case of the euro, means the currency which succeeds to and replaces the euro in whole).[8]

Exceptions are set out in Section 4.7(b):

- where an EU member state converts its currency into the euro;
- where a member state government triggers a redenomination from euros into another currency, this will not trigger a restructuring credit event where the following two conditions are met:
  - there is a freely available market rate of conversion between euros and the new currency at the time of redenomination;
  - the redenomination does not result in a reduction of principal, interest or premium;
- where a restructuring event occurs because of an administrative, accounting, tax or technical adjustment in the ordinary course of a Reference Entity's business; and
- where the restructuring event does not directly or indirectly result in the reference entity's creditworthiness or financial condition deteriorating.

---

8   This provision makes it easier to trigger a restructuring credit event where a single EU member state leaves the euro, putting all member states on an equal footing.

The carve-out is structured so that a restructuring credit event will occur if there is a deterioration in the creditworthiness of the reference entity, combined with a redenomination from euros into another currency. The carve-out is also further restricted, in Section 4(a)(iv), so that no deterioration in the creditworthiness of the reference entity is required for the credit event to occur where both:

- a member state government triggers a redenomination from euros into another currency; and
- the value of the new currency results in a lower amount of interest, principal or premium payable, by reference to the new rate of exchange.

(g)   *Governmental intervention*

Under the governmental intervention credit event, a credit event occurs due to an action or announcement by a governmental authority pursuant to a restructuring and resolution law (or any similar regulation) which directly or indirectly applies to the reference entity in a form which is binding (irrespective of whether such event is expressly provided for under the terms of such obligation). This action or announcement must be one which affects creditors' rights by causing any of the following to happen to an obligation (including obligations for which the reference entity is acting as provider of a guarantee):

- a reduction in interest payable or accruing (including through redenomination);
- a reduction in principal or premium payable at redemption (including through redenomination);
- a postponement or deferral of either:
  - interest payments; or
  - accruals or principal payments or premiums payable; or
- a change in the reference obligation's priorities of payment, causing the 'subordination' of such obligation to any of the reference entity's other reference obligations.

A governmental intervention credit event will also occur when:

- there is an expropriation, transfer or other event which mandatorily changes the beneficial holder of the obligation;
- a mandatory cancellation, conversion or exchange takes place; or
- any event that is analogous to any of the events otherwise specified in this definition occurs.

6.2   'Multiple holder obligation'

Whereas Sections 3.31, 3.32 and 3.33 limit the deliverable obligations which can be delivered in physically settled and auction settled, transactions following a credit event, Section 4.10 limits the obligations that can actually trigger a restructuring credit event.

Section 4.10 provides that unless 'multiple holder obligation' is specified as being not applicable in the relevant confirmation, a restructuring credit event can occur only in relation to a multiple holder obligation.

'Multiple holder obligation' is defined as an obligation held at the time of the restructuring credit event:

- by at least four non-affiliated holders; and
- whose terms require that 66.2/3% of the holders consent to the restructuring (provided that any obligation that is a bond is deemed to satisfy this requirement).

The role of this provision is to prevent a creditor in a limited creditor group agreeing to a restructuring which is not advantageous, safe in the knowledge that it will not suffer the consequences of what it has agreed to because it has hedged its credit risk by entering into a credit derivatives transaction.

6.3   Redenomination

A failure to pay credit event will occur if the reference entity fails to pay any amounts equal to or greater than the payment requirement under any of its obligations.

The failure to pay credit event is modified by Section 4.11. This provides that if a government-driven redenomination would cause a failure to pay, but a freely available market rate of conversion between the original currency and the new currency existed at the time of the redenomination, then this will not constitute a failure to pay unless the redenomination itself causes a reduction of principal, interest or premium at the time of redenomination. Note that these redenomination carve-out provisions are not restricted to euros, as in the restructuring credit event amendments.

This means that if the new currency later falls in value, bringing a reduction of interest, principal or premium when compared to that which would have been received in the old currency, this will not constitute a failure to pay.

7.   Article V – "General Terms Relating to Settlement"

Article V is an enabling provision which defines 'settlement' in Section 5.1, the 'settlement method' in Section 5.2 and the 'settlement date' in Section 5.3.

Section 5.1 provides that following an event determination date "the parties will perform their respective Obligation in accordance with the Settlement Method or Fallback Settlement Method, as applicable".

So for cash-settled transactions and auction-settled transactions, the occurrence of an event determination date is enough to trigger the settlement process.

If the transaction is to be physically settled, either because 'physical settlement' is the elected settlement method in the confirmation, or is the 'fallback settlement method' under the 'auction settlement' provisions in Section 6.1, then there is a further requirement: the buyer must deliver a notice of physical settlement to the seller that is effective on or prior to the NOPS cut-off date. Following this, the settlement process begins, and "the parties will perform their respective Obligations in accordance with the Settlement Method or Fallback Settlement Method, as applicable".

Section 5.2 sets out that 'settlement method' means:

if (a) 'Auction Settlement' is specified as the Settlement Method in the related Confirmation, or if no Settlement Method is specified as applicable in the related

Confirmation, Auction Settlement, (b) 'Cash Settlement' is specified as the Settlement Method in the related Confirmation or is deemed to be applicable, Cash Settlement, or (c) 'Physical Settlement' is specified as the Settlement Method in the related Confirmation, Physical Settlement.

The 'settlement date' is defined in Section 5.3 as the auction settlement date, as defined in Section 6.3, the cash settlement date, as defined in Section 7.2 or the physical settlement date, as defined in Section 8.17.

Section 5.4 is relevant to auction settled transactions only.

It applies where, under Section 6.1, 'auction settlement' is the transaction's specified or deemed settlement method, but:

- an 'auction cancellation date' occurs;
- a 'no auction announcement date' occurs; or
- there is a DC credit event 'question dismissal'.

The fallback settlement method may also apply where the relevant credit event notice falls outside of a cut-off for delivery.

Section 5.4 provides that where 'auction settlement' is the settlement method, if 'cash settlement' is specified as the fallback settlement method in the related confirmation, then cash settlement will be the fallback settlement method, otherwise it will be physical settlement.

In cash-settled and auction-settled transactions, once the reference obligation has been determined, it must then be valued in accordance with Article VII for cash-settled transactions, and Article VI for auction-settled transactions. The amount determined as the cash settlement amount or auction settlement amount must be paid by the seller to the buyer.

In cash-settled transactions, this 'valuation methodology' uses a final price. Section 7.4 provides that this is expressed as a percentage amount. To determine the cash settlement amount, the calculation agent complies with Section 7.3. This provides that the cash settlement amount will be the greater of:

- the 'floating rate payer calculation amount' multiplied by the reference price less the final price; and
- zero.

The 'floating rate payer calculation amount' is defined in Section 12.17 as being the amount specified in the confirmation, subject to certain reductions. It is normally the same as the 'fixed rate payer calculation amount' (ie, the amount of credit protection sold).

Auction-settled transactions take the same approach as cash-settled transactions. Section 6.5 provides that this is as defined in the auction settlement terms, but will however be expressed as a percentage amount. How to determine the auction settlement amount is governed by Section 6.4, which provides that the auction settlement amount will be the greater of:

- the floating rate payer calculation amount multiplied by the reference price less the final price; and
- zero.

'Reference price' is defined in Section 2.4 as the amount specified in the confirmation or, if none is specified in the confirmation, 100%. The reference price is intended to reflect the original price of the security at the outset of a transaction, before the decline in the reference entity's creditworthiness.

8. Article VI – "Terms Relating to Auction Settlement"

Article VI provides the basic framework for auction settlement, which is then supported by the 'form of credit derivatives auction settlement terms'. The form is updated and crafted for each individual auction following an applicable event determination date. The crafted document will contain terms specific to that auction, such as the deliverable obligations, which would be valued, as well as specific terms relating to the deliverable obligations. Article VI acts as the linchpin to the 2014 definitions linking into the auction settlement terms.

Auction-settled transactions are transactions which specify 'auction settlement' as the applicable settlement method, and for which the DC resolves to hold an auction, following a determined credit event.

Article VI and the auction settlement terms allow parties to 'auction covered transactions' to settle these transactions on the basis of an auction final price determined in an auction of deliverable obligations, involving market participants.

8.1 Auction settlement and auction final price

Section 6.1 provides that if 'auction settlement' is the applicable settlement method in the transaction confirmation and an event determination date occurs, then on or prior to the auction final price determination date, a seller will be obliged to pay to the buyer an auction settlement amount on the auction settlement date.

'Auction final price' is defined in Section 6.5 together with the 'auction settlement terms' as:

> the price, if any, determined to be the Auction Final Price pursuant to Section 12 of these Credit Derivatives Auction Settlement Terms (expressed as a percentage, in increments equal to the Relevant Pricing Increment, of the Outstanding Principal Balance, rather than the face amount, of Deliverable Obligations).

This is the amount determined at the auction of deliverable obligations of the reference entity.

'Auction settlement amount' is defined in Section 6.4 and is:

the greater of:

(a) (i) the Floating Rate Payer Calculation Amount; multiplied by

(ii) an amount, expressed as a percentage, equal to the Reference Price minus the Auction Final Price; and

(b) zero.

The floating rate payer calculation amount will be specified in the relevant confirmation, and is the amount of credit protection sold. The reference price will be specified in the confirmation, and usually 100%.

'Auction settlement date' is defined in Section 6.3. It is the transaction's termination date and is either a specified number of business days, or – if not specified – three business days after the auction final price determination date.

8.2   Auction cancellations

Article VI contains provisions for where an auction is cancelled or never announced, following an event determination date by the DC.

Section 6.12 allows for cancellation of previously planned auctions where a final price is not determined and for this 'auction cancellation date' to be announced. Section 6.11 provides that where either the DC secretary announces that no auction settlement terms will be published, or – despite earlier announcements – no auction will occur, then a 'no action announcement date' will occur. This is particularly relevant for Section 6.1, as this provides that settlement will take place through the fallback settlement method instead, usually physical settlement.

8.3   Parallel auctions

'Parallel auctions' relate to M(M)R restructurings; these are transactions where 'Mod R' or 'Mod Mod R' are specified in the confirmation. Separate or 'parallel' auctions are carried out for the different maturity buckets of deliverable obligations.

'Parallel auction settlement terms' are defined in Section 6.9 as:

following the occurrence of an M(M)R Restructuring, any Credit Derivatives Auction Settlement Terms published by ISDA with respect to such M(M)R Restructuring, and for which the Deliverable Obligation Terms are the same as the Deliverable Obligation Provisions applicable to the relevant Credit Derivative Transaction and for which such Credit Derivative Transaction would not be an Auction Covered Transaction.

The parallel auction settlement terms work in the same way as the auction settlement terms described above, except instead of establishing a single auction final price, multiple final prices will be established for different maturity buckets of deliverable obligations.

Under parallel auction settlement terms, affected credit default swap transactions are grouped into maturity buckets. The aim is to reduce the deliverable obligations package combinations that are deliverable under transactions with different maturities, and combat the price distortions that can occur when restructured deliverable obligations of different maturities can have different final prices.

This works as follows: if an event determination date for a restructuring credit event occurs, then the deliverable obligations for the auction are determined by reference to the maturity bucket (eg, two years, five years or 10 years) into which the relevant transaction falls, classed by its outstanding maturity.

Section 6.13 fulfils the same purpose as Section 6.12, allowing for cancellation of a parallel auction.

9.   Article VII – "Terms Relating to Cash Settlement"

9.1   Overview

Section 7.1 provides that 'cash settlement' applies to a transaction if 'cash settlement' is specified as the settlement method in a transaction confirmation, or if:

- cash settlement is the fallback settlement method for an auction settlement transaction in accordance with Section 6.1; or

- cash settlement is deemed to apply, fully or partially, because physical settlement is the transaction's specified settlement method but:
    - is impossible or illegal;
    - a relevant consent cannot be obtained for a 'consent-required loan', which the seller wishes to deliver; or
    - an assignable loan or direct loan participation cannot be delivered before the 'latest permissible physical settlement date'.

So cash settlement can apply to a transaction if the parties specifically selected it, or it becomes applicable as a fallback.

Article VII covers five different areas of the cash settlement process. These are as follows:

- The definition of 'cash settlement' and the key dates and times in the cash settlement process – cash settlement (Section 7.1), cash settlement date (Section 7.2), 'valuation date' (Section 7.8) and 'valuation time' (Section 7.14).
- How the reference obligation is valued – 'valuation method' (Section 7.5), 'market value' (Section 7.6), 'quotation' (Section 7.7), 'quotation method' (Section 7.9), 'full quotation' (Section 7.10) and 'weighted average quotation' (Section 7.11).
- How much of the reference obligation is valued – 'quotation amount' (Section 7.12), 'minimum quotation amount' (Section 7.13) and 'representative amount' (Section 7.16).
- Who values the reference obligation – 'dealer' (Section 7.15).
- What the reference obligation's value is and, therefore, what the cash settlement amount is – final price (Section 7.4) and cash settlement amount (Section 7.3).

Section 5.1 states that upon the occurrence of an event determination date, the parties will perform their respective obligations in accordance with the settlement method or fallback settlement method.

Section 7.1 then provides that where cash settlement applies, "the Seller shall, subject to Section 5.1 (*Settlement*), pay to Buyer the Cash Settlement Amount on the Cash Settlement Date".

Section 7.3 defines 'cash settlement amount' (unless otherwise specified in the confirmation) as:

the greater of:

(a) (i) the Floating Rate Payer Calculation Amount;[9] multiplied by

    (ii) the Reference Price[10] minus the Final Price;[11] and

(b) zero.

To calculate the cash settlement amount, Article VII provides that the calculation

---

9   Defined in Section 12.17.
10   Defined in Section 5.6.
11   Defined in Section 7.4.

agent must arrange for the reference obligation applicable to the transaction to be valued to ascertain its current market value.

Article VII provides for the calculation agent to do this by contacting an agreed number of dealers on the valuation Date(s) at the valuation time and asking them to provide quotations for an amount of each reference obligation specified in the confirmation. The quotation method – for example, bid or offer – and the amount of the reference obligation for which the calculation agent asks for quotations will be set out in the confirmation.

The calculation agent will apply a valuation method to the quotations to calculate the reference obligation's final price. Whether the calculation agent will take the highest or the lowest price, or perhaps an average of prices, will be specified in the confirmation.

The final price represents the decline in the value of the reference obligation and is expressed as a percentage. The calculation agent then multiplies the floating rate payer calculation amount by the reference price (usually 100%) to give a percentage figure, and then subtracts the final price (also a percentage figure) to determine the cash settlement amount (ie, a percentage of the floating rate payer calculation amount). The seller must then pay the cash settlement amount to the buyer on the cash settlement date, which will be the transaction's termination date. Alternatively, in a fixed recovery transaction, the cash settlement amount will be set out in the confirmation, meaning that there will be no requirement to value a reference obligation. Article VII also makes provision for this.

Article VII also provides the parties to a transaction with a whole range of options and fallbacks for how cash settlement should take place: there are nine different options for valuation method, three different options for quotation method, two different options for valuation date, plus detailed fallbacks for obtaining the requisite number of quotations to calculate a Final Price.

Cash settlement, as set out in Article VII, also operates in a similar way where there is a fallback to 'partial cash settlement' in a physically settled transaction, although Section 9.6 modifies and/or replaces 10 of Article VII's definitions – in some cases significantly, in others by deeming certain elections to apply. The definitions amended or modified are 'cash settlement amount', 'cash settlement date', 'reference obligation', 'valuation date', 'valuation method', 'quotation method', 'quotation amount', 'valuation time', 'market value' and 'quotation'.

9.2 Cash settlement date

Section 7.2 sets out the provisions for determining which date should be the cash settlement date.

The seller must make its settlement payment to the buyer on the cash settlement date. The cash settlement date can be specified in the confirmation to be a number of days after the calculation agent has calculated the final price; if not, it is be deemed to be three business days after the calculation agent has calculated the final price.

9.3 Valuation date

The calculation agent must approach dealers in the reference obligation at a specified time or times to ask for quotations for the reference obligation, in order for it to determine the reference obligation's final price. The times when the calculation agent does this are crystallised by two definitions: 'valuation date' (Section 7.8) and 'valuation time' (Section 7.14).

'Dealer' is defined in Section 7.15 as dealers "in Obligations of the type of Obligation(s) for which Quotations are to be obtained"; they include any dealers specified in any individual confirmation, but exclude affiliates. If the confirmation does not specify any dealers, the calculation agent must consult with the parties and select the dealers.

Section 7.8 provides two options which can be selected in the confirmation: the calculation agent can obtain the quotations either on a 'single valuation date' or on 'multiple valuation dates'. In each case, Article VII provides the methodology for calculating the various averages.

The parties can specify in the confirmation that 'single valuation date' applies.

Valuation Date:[12] Single Valuation Date:
Five Business Days

Where this is the case, the valuation date will be the number of business days specified in the confirmation after an event determination date.

Valuation Date: Multiple Valuation Dates:
Five Business Days; and
each fifth Business Day thereafter
Number of Valuation Dates: three

Alternatively, the parties can specify in the confirmation that 'multiple valuation dates' apply. This is done by specifying 'multiple valuation dates', together with the number of valuation dates and the dates on which they fall.

9.4 Valuation time

The calculation agent is required not only to approach dealers to provide quotations for the reference obligation on each valuation date, but more specifically to do so at the same time: the valuation time. This is defined in Section 7.14 as the time specified in the confirmation or, where no time is specified, 11:00 am in the principal trading market of the reference obligation.

---

12   Extracted text boxes in this section are from Exhibit A to the 2014 definitions.

9.5   How the reference obligation is valued

Quotation Method:	[Bid][Offer][Mid-market]]
Quotation Amount:	[ ][Representative Amount]
Minimum Quotation Amount:	[ ]
Dealer(s):	[ ]
Quotations:	[Include Accrued Interest][Exclude Accrued Interest]]

On the valuation date at the valuation time, the calculation agent contacts the dealers (all as specified in the confirmation) and asks them to provide quotations. The calculation agent will use these quotations to calculate the final price.

(a)   Full quotation and weighted average quotation

Section 7.7 defines 'quotation' as each "Full Quotation and Weighted Average Quotation obtained and expressed as a percentage with respect to a Valuation Date". Section 7.7 then sets out the manner and method which the calculation agent must use to obtain these quotations, including how many quotations it must obtain, together with a series of fallbacks which can be used in establishing the final price.

A 'full quotation' is defined in Section 7.10 as a firm quotation obtained from a dealer at the valuation time for an amount of the reference obligation "with an Outstanding Principal Balance equal to the Quotation Amount". 'Quotation amount' itself is defined in Section 7.12 as the amount specified in the confirmation. This can be a defined amount, or the confirmation may state that it is to be determined by reference to a representative amount. 'Representative Amount' in turn is defined in Section 7.16 as "an amount that is representative for a single Transaction in the relevant market and at the relevant time", and is determined by the calculation agent in consultation with the parties.

A 'weighted average quotation' relates to where the calculation agent is unable to obtain a quotation from a dealer for the full quotation amount. Weighted averages are calculated by taking a number of quantities and multiplying each quantity by its weight or proportional relevance. The amounts are then added together and the resulting figure is then divided by the sum of the weights.

The concept of 'minimum quotation amounts' is relevant to weighted average quotations as defined in Section 7.11. When obtaining a weighted average quotation, the quotations must, to the extent reasonably practicable, be for as large a size as available and for as close to the minimum quotation amount as possible. All of these quotations must in aggregate be approximately equal to the quotation amount. The 'minimum quotation amount' is defined in Section 7.13 as either the amount specified in the confirmation or its equivalent, or the lower of US$1 million and the quotation amount.

(b)   Quotation method

Section 7.7 sets out the method by which the calculation agent determines the final price. The type of full quotation or weighted average quotation that the calculation agent seeks is determined through two other definitions: 'quotation method' (Section 7.9) and 'valuation 'method' (Section 7.5).

Section 7.9 provides three options for quotation method; whichever of the three is specified in the confirmation will determine whether the calculation agent approaches the dealers for 'bid q'uotations', 'offer quotations' or 'mid-market quotations' (ie, a bid and an offer quotation which is then averaged by the calculation agent).

Quotation Method: Bid

Section 7.7 provides that the calculation agent must attempt to obtain at least two full quotations on each valuation date from five or more dealers. If the calculation agent is unable to do this, then it must use the detailed fallbacks set out in Section 7.7 to meet the quotation criteria and determine a final price.

(c) **Valuation method**

Once the calculation agent has met the quotation criteria, it uses the quotations to determine a final price. The way it makes this determination depends upon what is specified in the confirmation as the valuation method. Section 7.5 provides eight different options that can be selected by the parties in a confirmation: 'market', 'highest', 'average market', 'average highest', 'blended market', 'blended highest', 'average blended market' and 'average blended highest'.

Valuation Method: Highest

Which valuation method the parties select will depend upon the number of reference obligations that the calculation agent has to value and the number of valuation dates. The table below sets out which valuation method can be applied depending on the number of reference obligations and valuation dates, as well as a summary of the valuation method's definition.

Valuation method	Number of Reference Obligations	Number of Valuation Dates	Definition
Market	One	One	The reference obligation's market value
highest	One	One or multiple	The highest quotation obtained (the ISDA fallback)
Average market	One	Multiple	The unweighted arithmetic mean of the market values

continued on next page

Valuation method	Number of Reference Obligations	Number of Valuation Dates	Definition
Average highest	One	Multiple	The unweighted arithmetic mean of the highest quotations
Blended market	Multiple	Single	The unweighted arithmetic mean of the market values of each reference obligation
Blended highest	Multiple	Single	The unweighted arithmetic mean of the highest quotations
Average blended market	Multiple	Multiple	On each valuation date, the blended market value is calculated. The arithmetic mean of those values is then calculated
Average blended highest	Multiple	Multiple	On each valuation date, the blended highest is calculated. The arithmetic mean of those values is then calculated

Whether the quotation for the reference obligation will include or exclude any accrued but unpaid interest will be specified in the confirmation[13] as either 'include accrued interest' or 'exclude accrued interest'.

Quotations: Exclude accrued interest

Each of the valuation methods is based either on the highest quotation given or on the market value. Highest, average highest, blended highest and average blended highest are based on the highest quotation given. Average market, blended market and average blended market are based on the market value of the reference obligation.

The concept of choosing the highest quotation given is straightforward. 'Market value', though, is more complex and is defined in Section 7.6. 'Market values' are based on the number of full quotations and weighted average quotations received. How the calculation agent determines market values for the average market blended market and average blended market valuation methods is set out in the table below.

---

13   Section 7.7(c).

Quotations received	Calculation Agent action to determine market value
More than three full quotations	Disregard the highest and lowest full quotations and calculate the arithmetic mean. If two full quotations have the same highest or lowest value, only one is discarded
Exactly three full quotations	Disregard the highest and lowest full quotations and calculate the arithmetic mean. If two full quotations have the same highest or lowest value, only one is discarded
Exactly two full quotations	Calculate the arithmetic mean of the full quotations
One full quotation and/or a weighted average quotation	Weighted average quotation used
One full quotation only or no full quotations	Five business-day period commences, operating until two or more full quotations or a weighted average quotation is obtained. If two full quotations or a weighted average quotation is not obtained by the end of the period, market value is calculated as per further fallbacks

9.6 Value of the reference obligation and value of the cash settlement amount

The concept of the reference obligation's 'final price' is defined in Section 7.4.

The final price represents the decline in value of the reference entity's obligations, and is central to calculating the payment that the seller must make to the buyer covering the difference in value of the reference entity's obligations at the transaction's outset and their current value post-credit event.

The calculation agent calculates the reference obligation's final price in accordance with the applicable valuation method. The final price is expressed as a percentage, and is a percentage of the 'outstanding principal balance' or 'due and payable amount' of the reference obligation.

As soon as practicable after obtaining all of the quotations for the reference obligation, the calculation agent must notify each of the parties in writing of each quotation that it receives and provide a written computation showing its calculation of the final price. In practice, this is known as the final price notification.

The cash settlement amount is the amount paid by the buyer to the seller on the cash settlement date. The payment represents the compensation payment from buyer to seller, which isolates the buyer from the credit risk of the reference entity. 'Cash settlement amount' is defined in Section 7.3 as either, in the case of a fixed recovery swap, the amount specified in the confirmation, or otherwise the floating rate payer calculation amount multiplied by the percentage figure of the reference price (usually 100%), less the final price. The cash settlement amount is subject to a minimum of zero. It is payable on the cash settlement date, which will then be the transaction's termination date.

10.   Article VIII – "Terms relating to Physical Settlement"
Physical settlement is relevant as a fallback mechanism when the DC elects not to have an auction, for less liquid credit default swap reference entities and in more bespoke transactions.

It is also relevant for the settlement transactions which underlie the auction settlement process. A 'representative auction-settled transaction' or 'RAST' is a physically settled credit derivatives transaction deemed to be entered during an auction. It facilitates getting an auction settlement price, and brings together buyers and sellers of deliverable obligations (the 'participating didders'), allowing physical settlement in the auction and the transfer of deliverable obligations at the prices struck at the auction.

Article VIII relates solely to physically settled transactions and provides the documentary infrastructure for physically settling credit derivatives transactions. Its provisions come into play in transactions specifying the physical settlement method once the buyer has delivered a notice of physical settlement following an event determination date.

Article VIII covers the mechanics of how physical settlement takes place, including determining the deliverable obligations that the buyer must deliver and defining what constitutes a delivery. Article VIII also covers when a delivery takes place, the amount of deliverable obligations which must be delivered by the Buyer, and the period when delivery must take place.

Article VIII is supplemented by provisions from Article IX, with detailed fallbacks for when the buyer is unable to deliver deliverable obligations to the seller or where the seller is unable to accept a delivery of deliverable obligations from the buyer. Article VIII is also supplemented by provisions from Article III, with the new 'asset package delivery' provisions, covering assets delivered as substitutes to the original deliverable obligations, following a restructuring or governmental intervention credit event. Article III also provides several important definitions for the obligations themselves, such as 'obligation' (Section 3.1) and 'deliverable obligation' (Section 3.2).

Article VIII also covers much of the asset package delivery provisions which are split between Articles III and VIII. In particular, the asset package delivery provisions in Article III hang off the definition of 'asset package credit event', which is set out in Section 8.9. The asset package delivery provisions deal with the regular concern of ensuring that a deliverable obligation exists or is available, following a credit event on a financial reference entity, to be used to settle such transaction.

10.1   How physical settlement works
Section 5.1 provides that if the transaction is to be physically settled, either because 'physical settlement' is the elected settlement method in the confirmation, or

because it is the fallback settlement method under the auction settlement provisions in Section 6.1, then there is a further requirement: the buyer must deliver a notice of physical settlement to the seller that is effective on or prior to the NOPS cut-off date (see further discussion below), following an event determination date.

Following this, the settlement process begins, and "the parties will perform their respective Obligations in accordance with the Settlement Method or Fallback Settlement Method, as applicable".

Section 8.1 then provides that the seller is obliged to accept delivery of the deliverable obligations detailed in the notice of physical settlement[14] on or before the physical settlement date. In return, the seller must pay the physical settlement amount to the buyer on the physical settlement date.

Section 8.2 sets out that a notice of physical settlement must state that the buyer will physically settle the transaction and contains a detailed description of the deliverable obligations that it intends to deliver. This detailed description includes the outstanding principal balance or due and payable amount (see further discussion below as to how these are assessed) of each deliverable obligation that it intends to deliver, as well as any available CUSIP or ISIN numbers (or, if not available, the rate and tenor of the deliverable obligation). A form of notice of physical settlement is set out in Exhibit C to the 2014 definitions.

The buyer can change its mind about the deliverable obligations that it intends to deliver to the seller as many times as it likes, and Section 8.2 provides a mechanism to do this through a 'NOPS amendment notice'.

If 'asset package delivery' is applicable (see further discussion below), the buyer is required on the NOPS effective date, or as soon as reasonably practicable thereafter (but, in any case, prior to the delivery date), to notify the seller of the detailed description of the asset package, if any, that it intends to deliver to the seller in lieu of the prior deliverable obligation or package observable bond, if any, specified in the notice of physical settlement or NOPS amendment notice.

NOPS effective date is defined in Section 8.3 as the date on which an effective notice of physical settlement or NOPS amendment notice is delivered by the buyer to the seller.

10.2 Physical settlement amount

The physical settlement amount (ie, the seller's payment to the buyer) is defined in Section 8.18 as the floating rate payer calculation amount (ie, the notional amount of the transaction) multiplied by its reference price (usually 100%, unless the reference entity's obligations are trading at a discount on the transaction's effective date).

The essence of physical settlement (ie, how the buyer isolates itself from the reference entity's credit risk) is that, post-event determination date, the seller is obliged to purchase deliverable obligations from the seller at their original price (ie,

---

14   Unless otherwise stated in this chapter, or the context requires, references to the notice of physical settlement also include a NOPS amendment notice (ie, a notice which amends a notice of physical settlement).

their price at the transaction's outset), leaving the seller to suffer the decline in value. How much of a loss the seller suffers will depend on the severity of the credit event.

Physical settlement must take place within an agreed period: the 'physical settlement period'. This is defined in Section 8.19 as either the number of business days specified in the confirmation or the longest number of business days for settling the deliverable obligation according to market practice. Market practice is determined by the calculation agent in consultation with the parties. The ISDA standard terms contained in the physical settlement matrix for each type of reference entity specify that the physical settlement period is 30 business days. This would most likely mean that if a physical settlement period is not specified in the confirmation, a calculation agent would normally determine that the market practice for settling a deliverable obligation is 30 Business days.

Subject to the various fallbacks set out in Article IX, the last day when physical settlement can take place is the physical settlement date. This is defined in Section 8.17 as the last day of the longest physical settlement period following the NOPS cut-off date. The physical settlement date is also the transaction's termination date.

Section 8.10 provides a definition for 'NOPS cut-off date' as the later of:

- the 30th calendar day after the event determination date; or
- the 10th calendar day after the DC credit event announcement or DC credit event question dismissal (or, if following an M(M)R restructuring, the 10th calendar day after the 'non-standard exercise cut-off date').

NOPS cut-off date is used in the definition of 'settlement' in Section 5.1, which requires delivery of the notice of physical settlement that is effective on or prior the NOPS cut-off date. Where a notice of physical settlement is not delivered on or prior to the NOPS cut-off date, then the NOPS cut-off date becomes the transaction's termination date.

The date when the buyer delivers (or is deemed to deliver) the deliverable obligation or an asset package to the seller is the 'delivery date'. This is defined in Section 8.16.

Section 8 also contains complex interpretation provisions for determining the amount of deliverable obligations that must the buyer must deliver on the delivery date. These are discussed below.

10.3 Asset package delivery provisions

The asset package delivery provisions in the 2014 definitions are split between Articles III and VIII, with the asset package delivery provisions in Article III hanging off the definition of 'asset package credit event' set out in Section 8.9 in particular. The asset package delivery provisions help ensure that a deliverable obligation exists, or is available – following a credit event – to be used to settle a transaction.

Section 8.5 defines an 'asset package' as all of the assets received by a 'relevant holder' in respect of an 'asset package credit event' (see Section 8.9).

Further, if the relevant holder is offered a choice of assets, the asset package will be the largest asset package (see Section 8.6).

Asset package becomes relevant where the 'prior deliverable obligation' (ie, deliverable obligations that existed prior to the governmental intervention or restructuring) no longer exists or is unavailable for delivery (eg, due to an expropriation).

When this happens, the buyer can instead deliver the related asset package. The same mechanism applies where the reference entity is a sovereign and the deliverable obligation is a 'package observable bond'.

There is, of course, a contradiction in delivering an asset package that does not exist or is otherwise unavailable. However, Section 8.12 provides that:

> if the Asset Package is zero (that is, it does not exist, or is unavailable), the Outstanding Amount of the Prior Deliverable Obligation or Package Observable Bond shall be deemed to have been Delivered in full three Business Days following the date on which the Buyer has notified the Seller of the detailed description of the Asset Package that it intends to Deliver.

'Largest asset package' is defined in Section 8.6 as the "package of Assets for which the greatest amount of principal has been or will be exchanged or converted … as determined by the Calculation Agent".

Section 8.7 provides a definition for 'asset'. This is a broad catch-all definition that includes as assets "each Obligation, equity, amount of cash, security, fee … right or other assets …" and goes on to widen these categories to include "whether tangible or otherwise, and whether issued, incurred, paid or provided, by the Reference Entity or a third party". It is difficult to imagine what would not be captured by this definition, although future market events occasionally expose cracks in the best thought-out provisions.

Section 8.8 is the definition that triggers the asset package delivery provisions. This section provides that 'asset package delivery' will apply if an asset package credit event occurs unless either:

- such asset package credit event occurred prior to the credit event backstop date (ie, before the 90 day look-back period); or
- the reference entity is a sovereign and no package observable bond exists.

Section 8.9 defines 'asset package credit event' as follows:

> (a) if 'Financial Reference Entity Terms' and 'Governmental Intervention' are specified as applicable in the related Confirmation:
>   (i) a Governmental Intervention; or
>   (ii) a Restructuring in respect of the Reference Obligation, if 'Restructuring' is specified as applicable in the related Confirmation and such Restructuring does not constitute a Governmental Intervention; and
> (b) if the Reference Entity is a Sovereign and 'Restructuring' is specified as applicable in the related Confirmation, a Restructuring, in each case, whether or not such event is specified as the applicable Credit Event in the Credit Event Notice or the DC Credit Event Announcement.

Although confusingly called a 'credit event', asset package credit event is not a new credit event, but instead is designed to enable obligations which existed immediately prior to certain governmental intervention or restructuring credit events as capable of being deliverable, notwithstanding that the intervention changed their characteristics and prevented them from being otherwise deliverable.

Section 8.12(b) provides that delivery of prior deliverable obligation or package observable bond may be satisfied by delivery of the related asset package.

Section 8.12(b) further provides that when calculating the settlement amount, the asset package is treated as having "the same currency, Outstanding Principal Balance, or Due and Payable Amount, as applicable, as the Prior Deliverable Obligation ... to which it corresponds, had immediately prior to the Asset Package Credit Event".

Without this important clarification, the settlement mechanics would not operate properly.

If the asset package is zero (eg, the relevant prior deliverable obligation or package observable bond was expropriated and the holders were given nothing in return), then the full amount of the outstanding principal balance or due and payable amount, as applicable, of the relevant prior deliverable obligation or package observable bond is deemed delivered in full three business days following the date that the buyer notified the seller of the asset package to be delivered.

11. Article IX – "Fallback Provisions Applicable to Physical Settlement"

Article IX covers the various fallbacks if problems are encountered when physically settling a transaction.

11.1 Alternative delivery procedures

The provision offers alternative procedures for when the buyer is unable to deliver the securities detailed in the notice of physical settlement. The primary fallback is for either party to designate an affiliate to deliver or take delivery of the deliverable obligations. There are different fallback provisions for bonds and for loans, each of which begins when a seller is unable to deliver the deliverable obligation within five business days of the physical settlement date.

Section 9.1 provides that if, due to an event beyond the parties' control, it is impossible or illegal for the buyer to deliver or for the seller to accept any of the deliverable obligations specified in the notice of physical settlement, then on or before the physical settlement date the buyer must deliver any deliverable obligations for which it is possible to accept or make delivery. The seller must then pay the portion of the physical settlement amount corresponding to the amount of deliverable obligations that are delivered in accordance with the current market practice for that deliverable obligation. The relevant party must give the reasons for the impossibility or illegality to the other in writing.

If, following the occurrence of any impossibility or illegality, the amount of deliverable obligations specified in the notice of physical settlement cannot be delivered before the latest permissible physical settlement date (as defined in Section 9.5), then the 'partial cash settlement terms' (as set out in Section 9.6) will apply to these 'undeliverable obligations'.

Sections 9.2, 9.3 and 9.4 each provide additional provisions to facilitate (as applicable) partial cash settlement of undeliverable loan obligations, 'unassignable obligations' or undeliverable obligations, where specified in the confirmation.

These provisions will apply only where consent required loans, 'assignable loans' and 'direct loan participations', as the case may be, are specified as deliverable obligations characteristics in the confirmation and as deliverable obligations in the notice of physical settlement, or NOPS amendment notice.

11.2   Partial cash settlement terms

The partial cash settlement terms set out in Section 9.6 will be deemed to apply if transfer of deliverable obligations is not possible due to a lack of consent in the case of consent-required loans (Section 9.2) and assignable loans (Section 9.3); and, in the case of a participation, if a participation is not effected (in each case, prior to the latest permissible physical settlement date) (Section 9.4).

Section 9.6 provides that if the partial cash settlement terms apply, physical settlement will not apply to the affected obligations; instead, the affected part of the credit derivatives transaction will be cash settled in accordance with Section 9.6, instead of by the physical settlement method. The seller will be obliged to pay the buyer a cash settlement amount on the cash settlement date, which will be the greater of:

- zero; and
- the outstanding principal balance or the due and payable amount or the currency amount (as applicable) of each relevant obligation multiplied by its reference price, less the final price.

The cash settlement date will occur three business days after the calculation of the final price on the relevant valuation date (which is two business days after the latest permissible physical settlement date). The cash settlement date is also deemed to be the transaction's termination date.

For the purposes of partial cash settlement, when calculating the final price, the following are deemed to apply:

- The reference obligation is deemed to be each undeliverable obligation, undeliverable loan obligation, unassignable Obligation, or undeliverable participation.
- The valuation method is deemed to be the highest valuation method, unless fewer than two full quotations are obtained or a weighted average quotation applies, in which case it is deemed to be the market valuation method.
- The quotation method is deemed to be the bid quotation method.
- The quotation amount is deemed to be a quotation amount equal to the outstanding principal balance or due and payable amount or currency amount (as applicable), with no minimum quotation amount.
- The valuation date is deemed to be two business days after the latest permissible physical settlement date, with the valuation time being that specified in the confirmation or, if none is specified, 11:00 am in the obligation or participation's principal trading market.

The partial cash settlement terms work by the calculation agent going out into the market and attempting to obtain full quotations on the valuation date (ie, two business days after the latest permissible physical settlement date).

11.3 Buy-in of bonds not delivered

Section 9.7 provides that where a buyer cannot deliver all of the bonds in the notice of physical settlement, then unless this is due to impossibility or illegality, the seller has the right to buy them in.

Where Section 9.7 applies, the seller must first give the buyer at least two business days' notice, in the form of a buy-in notice, of which bonds it intends to buy in.

On the buy-in date, the seller will conduct a dealer poll asking for firm quotations for the bonds (the buy-in offers). If the seller can obtain only one buy-in offer, then that will be the buy-in price; otherwise, the lowest buy-in offer will be the buy-in price.

If the seller cannot obtain a buy-in offer for the bond's full outstanding principal balance on the buy-in date, it will attempt to obtain buy-in offers for all or a portion of the bonds on each business day following the buy-in date until the fourth business day after the buy-in date or the date the buy-in price is determined, whichever is earlier.

On the date that the buy-in price is determined or as soon as practicable thereafter, the seller must deliver a buy-in price notice to the buyer of the outstanding principal balance of the bonds for which it obtained buy-in prices.

On the third business day following this notice, the buyer will be deemed to have delivered the bought-in bonds. The seller then pays the buyer. The amount paid will be equal to the portion of the physical settlement amount corresponding to the bought-in bonds reduced (but not below zero) by the relevant bonds' buy-in price (which is expressed as a percentage), and multiplied by the outstanding principal balance of the relevant bonds for which a buy-in price was determined. Any reasonable brokerage costs in relation to purchasing the relevant bonds are subtracted from this amount.

11.4 Alternative procedures relating to loans not delivered

Section 9.8 sets out alternative procedures for where the buyer is unable to deliver a loan which it has specified as a deliverable obligation in the notice of physical settlement to the seller.

Under Section 9.8, if by the fifth business day after the physical settlement date the buyer has been unable to deliver the specified loans to the seller, then the 'alternative procedures' set out in Section 9.8 apply. This fifth business day after the physical settlement date is defined as the 'loan alternative procedures start date' and the alternative procedures detailed in Section 9.8 apply unless one of the following has been specified in the confirmation:

- 'reference obligation only';
- in the case of a consent-required loan, 'partial cash settlement of consent-required loan applicable';
- in the case of an assignable loan, 'partial cash settlement of assignable loans applicable'; or
- in the case of participations, 'partial cash settlement of participations applicable'.

In these cases, instead of Section 9.8, Section 9.2 will apply to consent-required loans, Section 9.3 will apply to assignable loans and Section 9.4 will apply to participations.

So, assuming that Section 9.8 is applicable, then where the buyer cannot obtain the necessary consents to deliver a loan specified in the notice of physical settlement, it can provide a certificate, at any time after the 'alternative procedure start date', signed by one of its officers of managing director or equivalent rank certifying that it used reasonable efforts to attempt to obtain the consents. This certificate can be delivered in relation to all or part of the deliverable obligations, as applicable.

Once this has been done, the buyer is then entitled to deliver a bond (instead of a loan) that has transferable and not bearer-deliverable obligation characteristics. The buyer may also deliver an assignable loan instead. In both cases, the new deliverable obligation must meet the other deliverable obligation category and characteristics (other than consent-required loan and direct loan participation). If the relevant credit event is restructuring and either modified restructuring or modified modified restructuring applies, then the buyer must also comply with these deliverable obligation restrictions.

At any time after the 15th business day following the alternative procedure start date, if any of the loans referred to in the buyer's certificate are still undelivered and the buyer has not delivered bonds meeting the criteria set out above, then it is the seller's turn to direct proceedings.

At this point, the seller can instruct that the buyer deliver a bond to it that has transferable and not bearer-deliverable obligation characteristics; or instead, an assignable loan. In each case, the new deliverable obligation must meet the other deliverable obligation category and characteristics (other than consent-required loan and direct loan participation) on both the physical settlement date and the delivery date. If the relevant credit event is restructuring and either modified restructuring or modified modified restructuring applies, then the buyer must also comply with these deliverable obligation restrictions.

The bond or loan will then be deemed to have been specified in the notice of physical settlement. This is subject to the seller identifying a holder (other than the seller itself or one of its affiliates) of the bond or loan willing and able to deliver the bond or loan to the buyer, free of any consents, at a price less than the reference price. The relevant instrument must also be able to be delivered by the buyer to the seller, without any other person's consent.

11.5 Alternative procedures relating to assets not delivered

Section 9.9 sets out the fallback settlement procedures to be followed if the buyer does not deliver to the seller a prior deliverable obligation or package observable bond that is has previously said it would deliver.

Essentially, subject to certain conditions, Section 9.9 provides that the seller is able to compel the buyer to deliver to the seller another deliverable obligation selected by seller.

Section 9.9 applies where the buyer has notified the seller that it intends to deliver an asset package in lieu of the prior deliverable obligation or package observable bond specified in the notice of physical settlement or any NOPS amendment notice, and it is unable to make that delivery in the correct proportion, on or prior to the date that is five business days after the physical settlement date.

In these circumstances, Section 9.9 allows the seller to require the buyer to deliver instead any other deliverable obligation that the seller selects which has on both the physical settlement date and the delivery date which satisfies the requirements of a deliverable obligation under the transaction.

This is subject to:

- the seller identifying a holder of, or dealer in, the security (other than the seller or one of its affiliates) that is able to deliver the deliverable obligation to the buyer at a price less than the reference price; and
- the buyer being able to deliver the deliverable obligation to the seller without further consent.

11.6 Cap on settlement

Some market participants may be concerned that the physical settlement fallbacks may lead to a situation where settlement does not occur. The parties can therefore agree at the outset to vary these physical settlement fallbacks by specifying '60 business-day cap on settlement' as applicable in the confirmation. This is also the set election in the physical settlement matrix.

The effect of this election, which is covered in Section 9.10, is to provide that if the transaction's termination date has not occurred by the 60th business day following the physical settlement date, then that date shall be the transaction's termination date. There are two exceptions. First, if a buy-in price notice, effective at least three business days before the 60th business day, has been delivered in relation to a portion of the transaction, then the termination date for that portion of the transaction shall be the third business day after the notice becomes effective. The second exception relates to the alternative procedures relating to loans not delivered. Where, on the 60th business day, the buyer still has not delivered the deliverable obligations which the seller has specified, then the relevant portion's termination date will be the 10th business day after the seller has informed the buyer of the identity of the deliverable obligations.

12. Article X – "Effect of DC Resolutions"

Article X contains only two definitions: Section 10.1 on settlement suspension and Section 10.2 on the effect of a DC resolution. These relate to the DCs.

Section 10.1 refers to where there is a DC credit event meeting announcement following the occurrence of an event determination date, but prior to the physical settlement date or, to the extent applicable, a valuation date, there is a settlement suspension of any ongoing cash settlement or physical settlement procedures – for instance, because a notifying party had already delivered a credit event notice, commencing the settlement process.

Section 10.1 provides that the timing requirements of any section of the definitions relating to settlement will toll, and then remain suspended until either the date of a relevant DC credit event announcement or DC credit event question dismissal.

During this suspension period, the parties are neither obliged nor entitled to take any settlement action for an applicable transaction.

Once the DC credit event announcement or DC credit event question dismissal occurs, the timing requirements of the relevant settlement section (eg, Section 7.2, Section 7.8 or Section 8.1) that have previously tolled or been suspended resume on the business day after the DC secretary's announcement. Section 10.1 gives the parties the benefit of the full day, ignoring when the tolling or suspension actually began.

Section 10.2 provides that generally any DC resolution applicable to a transaction is binding on both the buyer and seller. DC resolutions are specified as binding on the parties notwithstanding:

- that the definitions or any confirmation may require the calculation agent to make the same determination; or
- an overlying master agreement or confirmation provides an alternative dispute resolution or determination mechanism.

This latter point still has the benefit, however, that the parties may specifically carve out Section 10(a)(ii) in a transaction, allowing the conflicting confirmation or master agreement provisions to apply.

13. **Article XI – "Additional representations and agreements of the parties"**
Article XI covers the various additional representations and agreements that the parties make to and with each other, as well as various fallbacks if problems are encountered when physically settling, and auction settling, a transaction.

Section 11.2(a), for example, provides that the buyer agrees that when the buyer makes a delivery, it is deemed to represent that, except in the case of direct loan participations, it is transferring full title (including counterclaims or defences).

Section 11.2(b) provides that unless the buyer provides an indemnity to the seller, the buyer is deemed to represent, when it makes a delivery, that (except for some minor exclusions) accepting the deliverable obligations will not lead to any commitment to lend additional funds (including outstanding commitments).

Section 11.3 provides that in the absence of other reasons, a transaction will not be considered frustrated or voidable, solely because the reference entity does not exist or ceases to exist on or following the trade date; or obligations, deliverable obligations or the reference obligation do not exist, or cease to exist, on or following the trade date.

Section 11.4 provides that if the reference entity in a credit derivatives transaction merges, amalgamates or transfers all or substantially all of its assets to the seller (or if the reference entity and the seller become affiliates), an additional termination event under the 2002 ISDA Master Agreement is deemed to have occurred with the seller as the sole affected party. Each credit derivative transaction that involves the relevant reference entity will be an affected transaction. The 2002 Master Agreement 'close-out amount' provision will apply, irrespective of whether the parties have a 1992 Master Agreement or 2002 Master Agreement in place. Each affected transaction will then terminate in accordance with the relevant master agreement.

14. Article XII – "Initial Payment Amount, Fixed Amounts and Floating Rate Payer Calculation Amount"

Article XII covers upfront payments the parties may make to each other: the initial payment amount. It covers the premium payment the buyer makes to the seller for assuming the credit risk inherent in the reference entity: the fixed amounts. It also covers the base amount on which these fixed amounts may be calculated: the floating rate payer calculation amount. Lastly, it covers the marker date for when credit protection begins: the effective date.

14.1 Initial payments

> Initial Payments:
> Initial Payment Payer: Seller
> Initial Payment Amount: US$1 million
> Initial Payment Date: 15 March 2016

Initial payments are the payments that one party makes to the other at the outset of the transaction. This is an election, and is only applicable if specifically included by the parties.

Any initial payment will usually be from the buyer to the seller to cover the period from the effective date to the first fixed rate payer payment date, where the first fixed rate payer calculation period is shorter than the other calculation periods in the transaction (eg, a one-week calculation period as opposed to a three-month calculation period).

In the standardised credit default swap market, if the 'transaction type' is 'standard European corporate', 'European financial corporate', 'European CoCo financial corporate', 'subordinated European insurance corporate' or 'Western European sovereign', the market standard is for the fixed rate to be one of 0.25%, 1%, 3%, 5%, 7.5% or 10%.

If the transaction type is 'standard Japan corporate', 'Japan financial corporate' or 'Japan sovereign', the market standard is for the fixed rate to be one of 0.25%, 1% or 5%. If the transaction type is a 'standard transaction type' other than those listed above, the fixed rate, to be market standard, must be either 1% or 5%.

Section 12.1 provides the framework for initial payments in credit derivative transactions, providing:

> *If an Initial Payment Payer and an Initial Payment Amount are specified in the related Confirmation, the Initial Payment Payer will pay to the other party an amount equal to the Initial Payment Amount on the Initial Payment Date.*

This allows the upfront adjustment of credit protection amounts, to allow payments of upfront amounts to make the adjustment between the actual credit protection price for the reference entity and the standarised coupon, or fixed amount.

This works by providing for an 'initial payment payer' and an 'initial payment amount' are in the related confirmation, the initial payment payer will be obliged to pay to the other party the amount specified as the initial payment amount on the date specified as an initial payment date.

So, in summary an upfront payment is made at the transaction's outset, following which the fixed rate payer pays the fixed amounts.

Section 12.2 provides that the initial payment payer is the party specified as such in the confirmation, with Section 12.3 adding that the initial payment amount is the amount specified in the confirmation. Lastly, Section 12.4 gives the final element of the system, stating that 'initial payment date' means " the date specified as such in the related Confirmation, or, if no such date is specified, the date that is three Business Days immediately following the Trade Date".

14.2   Fixed payments

1. Fixed Payments:
Fixed Rate Payer Calculation Amount: US$10 million

Fixed Rate Payer Payment Dates: 31 March, 30 June, 30 September and
31 December each year

Fixed Rate: 1%

Fixed Rate Day Count Fraction: Actual/360

Article XII has 10 definitions that cover the payments of the credit protection premium that the buyer must make to the seller during the transaction's term. These are:

- Section 12.5 ('fixed amount');
- Section 12.6 ('fixed rate payer');
- Section 12.7 ('fixed rate payer calculation amount');
- Section 12.8 ('fixed rate payer period end date');
- Section 12.9 ('fixed rate payer calculation period');
- Section 12.11 ('fixed rate payer payment date');
- Section 12.12 ('calculation of fixed amount');
- Section 12.13 ('fixed rate');
- Section 12.14 ('fixed rate day count fraction'); and
- Section 12.15 ('relating fixed rate payer payments to fixed rate payer calculation period').

2. Fixed payments:
Fixed Rate Payer
Calculation Amount: €30 million

Fixed Rate Payer Period End
Date: Each Fixed Rate Payer Payment Date

Fixed Rate Payer Payment
Date: 31 March, 30 June, 30 September and 31 December in each year

'Fixed rate payments' are the payments made by the buyer to the seller to compensate it for providing credit protection on the reference entity. The payments are made periodically during the transaction's term, with Article XII providing the necessary terms and definitions. 'Fixed rate payer' is defined in Section 12.6 "as the party obligated to make one or more payments of a Fixed Amount", which is of course, the buyer.

Section 12.12 provides the methodology for determining what the fixed amount payable by a fixed rate payer on a fixed payer payment date will be. 'Fixed rate payer payment date' is defined in Section 12.11. This will be defined (usually quarterly dates), with a fallback for where an event determination date occurs. Here the fixed rate payer payment date will usually be the earlier to occur of the termination date and the first settlement date.

'Fixed amount' either can be a numerical figure stated in the confirmation or, if a figure is not stated, determined using the formula set out in Section 12.12(b). If this formula is used, then the fixed amount will be calculated by multiplying the fixed rate payer calculation amount by the fixed rate and the 'fixed rate day count fraction' (see further discussion below).

If an actual amount is specified in the confirmation as a fixed amount, the buyer will pay that amount to the seller on each fixed rate payer payment date. Usually, though, a specific amount is not specified and the actual amount payable is calculated according to a formula set out in Section 12.1(b).

The fixed rate payer calculation amount will then be multiplied by the fixed rate. 'Fixed rate' is defined in Section 12.13 as "a rate, expressed as a decimal, equal to the per annum rate specified in the related Confirmation". This rate will be multiplied by the fixed rate day count fraction. A 'day count fraction' is a method, used generally in capital markets transactions when there is more than one interest payment in any year, to calculate the fraction of a year falling between two set dates, for determining the amount of interest payable on any interest payment date.

Each fixed amount payable is calculated on the basis of the fixed rate payer calculation period. The 'fixed rate payer calculation period' is defined in Section 12.9 as being each period from and including a fixed rate payer period end date to (but excluding) the next one. The first fixed rate payer calculation period commences on the transaction's effective date and the last finishes on the earlier of the event determination date, should one occur, or if not, the scheduled termination date. This means that credit protection payments are not payable once an event determination date has occurred or if the transaction's termination date falls after the scheduled termination date, due to the grace period provisions or repudiation/moratorium extension provisions.

'Effective date' is defined in Section 12.10; it is the marker for when the period of credit protection commences, and is usually specified in the confirmation. Where it is not, Section 12.10 provides a fallback for it to be, "the Fixed Rate Payer Payment Date falling on or immediately prior to the calendar day immediately following the Trade Date". The effective date shall not be subject to adjustment by any business day convention.

The actual 'fixed rate payer period end date' (defined in Section 12.8) is normally specified in the confirmation; if it is not, the fallback is for the fixed rate payer period end date to be the fixed rate payer payment date.

14.3 Fixed rate day count fraction

> 2. Fixed Payments:
> Fixed Rate Day Count Fraction: Actual/360

In interest rate transactions, fixed rates of interest are expressed as percentage amounts payable on a principal or notional amount (eg, 5% of a notional amount of €100 million per annum). This is also the case for payments of fixed amounts in credit derivatives transactions.

These payments, though, are often made more frequently than once a year, and in the credit default swap market the market convention is for fixed amounts to be paid quarterly, with the fixed rate payer payment dates being on 31 March, 30 June, 30 September and 31 December in each year. To work out how much is due on each fixed rate payer payment date, the parties apply day count fractions to determine how much of the annual fixed amount is payable on a fixed rate payer payment date. Day count fractions are used not only in credit derivatives, but also in fixed income securities and derivatives generally whenever there are payments of part of an annual amount more than once a year.

Section 12.3 provides five different day count fractions; the parties may select any one of them to apply to a transaction. These are:

- actual/365 or 'actual/actual';
- actual/365 (fixed);
- actual/360, act/360, A/360;
- '30/360' or 'bond basis'; and
- '30E/360'or 'Eurobond basis'.

The fixed rate day count fraction selected to apply to the transaction is set out in the fixed payments section of the confirmation. If the parties do not specify a fixed rate day count fraction, the fallback is for 'actual/360' to apply. Actual/360 is also the market standard fixed rate day count fraction.

14.4 Relating fixed rate payer payments to fixed rate payer calculation periods

Section 12.4 covers how fixed rate payer payment dates interact with fixed rate payer calculation periods (ie, whether they are they included within a fixed rate payer calculation period). Section 12.4 appears to replicate the definition of 'fixed rate payer calculation period' in Section 12.9.

Section 12.4 provides that unless otherwise specified in the confirmation, where the fixed amount is calculated according to the formula set out in Section 12.1(b), the fixed rate payer calculation period will exclude the relevant fixer rate payer period end date (which is normally the fixed rate payer payment date). This section also provides that for the final fixed rate payer calculation period, which will end on the earlier to occur of an event determination date or the scheduled termination date, the event determination date or scheduled termination date is included in the fixed rate payer calculation period.

14.5 Floating rate payer and floating rate payer calculation amount

Article XII has two definitions that cover the identity of the party making the credit protection payments to the buyer following a credit event and the quantum of credit protection that it sells to the buyer. These are:

- 'floating rate payer' (Section 12.16); and
- 'floating rate payer calculation amount' (Section 12.17).

The credit protection payments made by the buyer to the seller make up the fixed rate leg of the swap. The floating rate payments under the floating rate leg to the credit default swap will be made only if an event determination date occurs. If this happens, the seller will be required to pay a cash settlement amount, an auction settlement amount or a physical settlement amount to the buyer. This payment is called the 'floating payment'.

General terms
Fixed Rate Payer: Loretto plc (the 'Buyer')
Floating Rate Payer: Glenalmond Corporation (the 'Seller')

Floating payment

Floating Rate Payer Calculation Amount: €30 million

'Floating rate payer' is defined in Section 12.16 as "the party specified as such in the related Confirmation". This will invariably be the seller. 'Floating rate calculation amount' is defined in Section 12.17 as "the amount specified as such in the related Confirmation". This amount will be the amount of credit protection that the seller sells to the buyer. The floating payment itself will, in a cash-settled transaction, be the cash settlement amount, in an auction-settled transaction, the auction settlement amount, and in a physically settled transaction, the physical settlement amount.

15. Article XIII – "Credit Derivatives Physical Settlement Matrix"

ISDA has through its credit derivatives physical settlement matrix and accompanying confirmation adopted a strategy for standardising transactions. Each version of the matrix is released on ISDA's website, in the bookstore section, under the "ISDA Definitional, Booklets and Confirmations by Product Type", credit derivatives sub-category.

The matrix takes the form of an excel spreadsheet, which provides a heading column of "transaction types", together with a heading column of elections from the definitions.

Where the matrix is incorporated through Article XIII, and a confirmation specifies a transaction type, the elections from the matrix are deemed to apply automatically.

Here is an extract from the matrix:

Transaction Type	Standard North American corporate	Standard European corporate or Standard European financial corporate or Standard European CoCo financial corporate	Standard subordinated European insurance corporate
Business days:	If the floating rate payer calculation amount is denominated in: • USD: London and New York • EUR: London, New York and TARGET • GBP: London • JPY: London and Tokyo • CHF: London and Zurich • CAD: London, New York and Toronto	If the floating rate payer calculation amount is denominated in: • EUR: London and TARGET • USD: London and New York • GBP: London • JPY: London and Tokyo • CHF: London and Zurich • CAD: London and Toronto	If the floating rate payer calculation amount is denominated in: • USD: London and New York • EUR: London and TARGET • GBP: London • JPY: London and Tokyo • CHF: London and Zurich • CAD: London and Toronto
Calculation agent city:	New York	London	London
All guarantees:	Not applicable	Applicable	Applicable

The columns and rows of elections which are deemed to apply to a transaction depend on the nature and jurisdiction of the reference entity. For example, one set of elections applies for standard North American corporate and another for standard subordinated European insurance corporate.

These elections reflect the standard trading terms in the credit derivatives market for those types of reference entity.

The confirmation which accompanies the matrix is substantially the same as the standard ISDA single name credit default swap confirmation. The principal substantive differences comprise that paragraph 1 (general terms) includes, as its first line item, an election for transaction type and, as its third line item, a definition for 'matrix publication date'.

Through Article XIII, the matrix is automatically incorporated into the confirmation, by specifying that the 2014 definitions and a transaction type apply.

16. **Article XIV – "Non-Standard Event Determination Date and Non-Standard Exercise Cut-off Date"**

Article XIV is a short article of two sections covering 'non-standard event determination dates' (Section 14.1) and 'non-standard exercise cut-off dates' (Section 14.2) only.

'Event determination date' is defined in Section 1.16. Section 1.16(b) provides that for non-auction-settled transactions and auction-settled transactions where the notifying party is the buyer that the event determination date will instead be the non-standard event determination date, pursuant to Section 14.1, for transactions which do not fall within Section 1.16(a). See detailed discussion in paragraph 3.4 above and discussion of Section 14.1 below.

The exercise cut-off date is relevant to the cut-off point for when a valid credit event notice can be delivered, which in turn is relevant to part of the 'event determination date' definition. Exercise cut-off date is also relevant to the definition of 'movement option cut-off date' in Section 6.17.

'Exercise cut-off date' is defined in Section 1.41. As with the definition of 'event determination date', the definition is split into two.

Section 1.41(a) relates to auction-settled transactions, to which Section 1.16(a) of the 'event determination date' definitions applies, where the relevant credit event is an M(M)R restructuring credit event.

Section 1.41(b) applies to all other transactions, whether auction-settled, cash-settled or physically settled, and provides that "the Non-Standard Exercise Cut-off Date determined in accordance with Section 14.2 (Non-Standard Exercise Cut-off Date)" applies instead.

Section 14.1(a) provides that the non-standard event determination date will be as follows. If a DC credit event announcement has occurred, and a credit event resolution request date has occurred on or before the last day of the notice delivery period, then the event determination date will be either (a) the credit event resolution request date, or (b) the first date on which the credit event notice is delivered and effective.

For the event determination date to be the credit event resolution request date, Section 14.1(b)(i)(B) provides further alternative criteria:

- the buyer or seller must be the notifying party;
- cash settlement or physical settlement (and not auction settlement) must be the applicable settlement method;

- the applicable credit event cannot be M(M)R restructuring; and
- the DC credit event announcement must be before the transaction's trade date.

Alternatively, the event determination date will be the first date that the notifying party delivers the credit event notice prior to the non-standard exercise cut-off date if auction settlement applies and the buyer is the only notifying party, or 'buyer or seller' is specified as the notifying party and the applicable credit event is 'M(M)R restructuring'.

Where none of these criteria are met, the non-standard event determination date is then determined by the provisions in Section 14.1(b)(ii), and "will be the first date on which a Credit Event Notice is delivered by a Notifying Party to the other party and is effective".

The date on which the credit event notice must be effective is either during the notice delivery period or the period from and including the date of the DC credit event announcement to and including 14 calendar days later.

For Section 14.1(b)(ii) to apply, though, other alternate sets of criteria must be met. Section 14.1(b)(ii)(B) provides the first set of criteria:

- The buyer or seller must be the notifying party;
- Cash settlement or physical settlement (but not auction settlement) must be the applicable settlement method;
- The applicable credit event cannot be M(M)R restructuring; and
- The DC credit event announcement must be before the transaction's trade date, and on or prior to the DC announcement coverage cut-off date.

Section 14.1(b)(ii)(B) provides the alternative set of criteria which can be met:

(I) 'Buyer' is the only Notifying Party and the Trade Date occurs on or prior to a DC Announcement Coverage Cut-off Date; and

(II) either:

(x) 'Auction Settlement' is not the applicable Settlement Method; or

(y) 'Auction Settlement' is the applicable Settlement Method and a Credit Event Notice is delivered by a Notifying Party to the other party and is effective on a date that is later than the relevant Non-Standard Exercise Cut-off Date ...

Both of these alternative criteria are subject to the further requirements, for Section 14.1(b)(ii) to apply:

- no physical settlement date or termination date can have occurred on or prior to the date of the DC credit event meeting announcement;
- if any valuation date or delivery date has occurred on or prior to the DC credit event meeting announcement date, a non-standard event determination date is deemed to have occurred only for the portion of the floating rate payer calculation amount, if any, with respect to which no valuation date or delivery date has occurred; and
- no credit event notice specifying an M(M)R restructuring as the only credit event has previously been delivered to the seller by the buyer. This is:
  - unless the M(M)R restructuring specified in the credit event notice is also

the subject of the DC credit event question which results in the credit event resolution request date;

- unless, and to the extent that, the exercise amount specified in the credit event notice was less than the floating rate payer calculation amount; or
- unless the credit derivatives transaction is an auction-covered transaction and the deliverable obligations set out on the final list are identical to the permissible deliverable obligations for such credit derivative transactions.

Section 14.2 provides two alternatives for the non-standard exercise cut-off date, depending on whether the relevant credit event is an M(M)R restructuring or not.

Section 14.2(a) states that where the relevant credit event is not an M(M)R restructuring, the non-standard exercise cut-off date is either:

(i) *the Relevant City Business Day prior to the Auction Final Price Determination Date, if any;*

(ii) *the Relevant City Business Day prior to the Auction Cancellation Date, if any; or*

(iii) *the date that is fourteen calendar days following the No Auction Announcement Date, if any, as applicable …*

Section 14.2(b) provides that where the relevant credit event is an M(M)R restructuring, the non-standard exercise cut-off date will, if the DC secretary publishes a final list applicable to the transaction auction settlement terms and/or parallel auction settlement terms, be the date that is:

(A) two Relevant City Business Days, if the Credit Event Notice is delivered by Seller, or

(B) five Relevant City Business Days, if the Credit Event Notice is delivered by Buyer, in each case following the date on which such Final List is published[.]

Where the DC secretary does not publish a final list applicable to the transaction auction settlement terms and/or parallel auction settlement terms, or Section 14.2(b)(i) is not otherwise met, then Section 14.2(b)(ii) provides that the non-standard exercise cut-off date will be the date 14 calendar days after the relevant no auction announcement date.

Interest rate derivatives

Natalie Ashford
Vincent KP Sum
Mayer Brown

---

1. Introduction

Interest rate derivatives are complex financial instruments based on an underlying asset which, for each party, is the right to pay or receive an amount of money by reference to a given interest rate, based on a notional amount. Interest rate derivatives are usually traded over the counter (OTC) by individual investors that have either bespoke cash flow requirements or specific views on interest rate movements.

Interest rate derivatives form the largest derivatives market in the world. Businesses commonly use interest rate derivatives to control cash flows, but there are other reasons for market participants to enter into interest rate derivatives, as described below. The Bank for International Settlements reported that, as of mid-2015, the notional amount of outstanding interest rate derivatives contracts totalled US$435 trillion, representing 79% of the global OTC derivatives market.

Increasingly, interest rate derivatives are being used as tools to achieve complex regulatory, tax, capital, accounting and financing goals in highly structured transactions.

2. Why use interest rate derivatives?

Derivatives present a means of transferring and mitigating risk, which opens the door for some investors to markets that would otherwise have been inaccessible due to an unacceptable level of risk. Irrespective of market conditions, interest rate derivatives provide an opportunity to achieve a positive return and lower cost of funding. Different types of investor tend to enter into interest rate derivatives for different reasons: hedging, speculation or arbitrage.

2.1 Hedging

Banks most commonly use interest rate derivatives to hedge their risks and to promote liquidity by equalising their revenue streams and liabilities, while reducing the risk of any significant loss arising from an unfavourable movement in interest rates. The primary aim of hedging is thus not necessarily to make a gain, but rather to prevent loss.

Borrowing entities also use interest rate derivatives in a wide range of financing arrangements, typically either potentially to reduce expenditure on interest by swapping a higher fixed rate for a lower floating rate, or to hedge existing interest rate risk where there is a possibility that rates will increase in the future.

2.2 Speculation

Where an investor has an opinion as to how interest rates are going to move over the short term, interest rate derivatives provide an opportunity to speculate based on such opinion. Hedge funds typically speculate on the market in an attempt to yield large returns from high-volume, high-rate swaps.

2.3 Arbitrage

Where parties have different levels of creditworthiness, they will be able to obtain different rates in the market. Sometimes a company may be able to receive a preferential floating rate, although it actually wants a fixed rate, or *vice versa*. By entering a swap with another company in an equal and opposite position, both companies may be able to benefit.

For example, if one borrower is able to secure a loan at a fixed rate of 12% or a floating rate of LIBOR +2%, while another borrower can secure a loan only at a fixed rate of 10% or a floating rate of LIBOR +1%, then there a difference of two percentage points between the fixed rates at which they can each borrow, but only one percentage point difference in the offered floating rates. The quality spread differential (ie, the difference between the fixed-rate difference and the floating-rate difference) is therefore one percentage point. In this situation, both borrowers may be able to benefit from a swap.

The first borrower could borrow at the offered floating rate (LIBOR +2%) and pay the second borrower a fixed rate of 9.5%. The second borrower could borrow at its offered fixed rate (10%) and pay the first borrower a floating LIBOR rate. The net total owed by the first borrower would therefore be lower than if it had relied on the loan in isolation (11.5% instead of 12%), as it would for the second borrower (LIBOR +0.5% instead of LIBOR +1%). In this way, both borrowers are able to benefit from the swap equally and effectively pay the fixed or floating rate, as applicable, at a preferential rate.

3. Types of interest rate derivatives

Interest rate derivatives vary widely in their level of complexity and can be tailored to each investor's specific needs in light of current market conditions. Interest rate derivatives may be categorised into three main groups: vanilla, quasi-vanilla and exotic.

3.1 Vanilla interest rate derivatives

A 'vanilla' product is the most basic type of interest rate derivative and is also usually the most liquid. Examples include interest rate swaps (fixed for floating), interest rate caps or floors, bond options, forward rate agreements or options, cross-currency swaps, money market instruments and interest rate swaptions.

In the simplest form of an interest rate swap, one party receives interest rate payments based on a fixed rate (while making payments based on a floating rate) and another party receives interest rate payments based on a floating rate (while making payments based on a fixed rate). The two parties enter into an interest rate swap in order to exchange and net off their cash flows, and the risks associated with such cash flows, in the hope of reducing uncertainty and the risk of loss from changes in market interest rates. The value of the swap at any given time would be determined by the difference between the fixed and floating rates. At inception, the value of the swap to each of the parties would therefore be zero.

Where an investor is concerned that interest rates may rise, or may continue to rise, an interest rate cap may be entered into to place a maximum level of exposure on upward interest rate movements. The investor would pay for the cap upfront and then receive periodic payments based on the difference between the cap and floating rate over time, realising the benefit over the life of the contract. However, a payment would be made to the investor only if the prevailing floating rate exceeded the cap rate on a specified date. Similarly, if an investor is concerned about falling interest rates, an interest rate floor may be an attractive instrument in which to invest.

Options and swaptions provide the investor with a right (but not an obligation) to trigger a swap at a certain point in time. These products may be classified as European, Bermudan or American. A European-type option, the most common, can be settled for cash only on a specified expiry date. Occasionally, parties may agree to a Bermudan-type option, where the option can be utilised on a number of pre-determined occasions during the lifetime of the option, but not at any time of the investor's choosing. The most rare is an American-type option, which can be utilised at any time during the option's lifetime.

Where a company wishes to hedge its future loan exposure against rising market rates or where interbank participants believe the market may be about to turn, forward rate options are often used. Collateral is frequently required to be posted under a forward or futures contract, in an amount correlating with the change in price of the underlying asset.

An interest rate swaption may be an effective tool for providing a greater degree of certainty and minimising risk where cash flow of an underlying asset or liability is uncertain due to an exposure to default risk.

3.2   Quasi-vanilla interest rate derivatives

Still fairly liquid, although slightly more complex than the plain vanilla products described above, 'quasi-vanilla' interest rate derivatives include, for example, interest rate swaps based on two floating rates (as opposed to one fixed and one floating), in-arrears swaps, range accrual swaps or notes and constant maturity or treasury swaps.

While a vanilla swap sets the interest rate at the outset of the contract, to be paid at the end of each interest period, an in-arrears swap sets the floating rate only at the end of the relevant interest period, to be applied retrospectively and paid immediately. Where market rates rise, an investor pays the predetermined fixed rate (based upon the market position when entering into the swap) and receives the higher, floating rate that is set at the end of the interest period, when the interest rates have risen, resulting in a profit.

Under a range accrual note or swap, interest is paid out only if the floating-rate interest, which is linked to the performance of a reference rate such as LIBOR, stays within a predetermined range. Each day that the market rate falls within the pre-determined range, interest is accrued at an above-market rate. However, no interest, or a reduced rate of interest, is accrued on days when the market rate fixes outside of that range.

By making the note callable at the option of the investor (but exposing itself to reinvestment risk), the investor may benefit from even greater returns. A call option can also be valuable to the issuer, since it provides it with the right to call the note and return the principal to the investor in the event that the investor begins obtaining a high return.

Investors that heavily speculate on the market and make predictions on the yield curve may reap substantial returns from an in-arrears swap, while those confident that interest rates will not rise as far, or as fast, as the market predicts may obtain an enhanced return from a range accrual note through exposure to increased interest rate risk.

3.3 Exotic interest rate derivatives

The most complex and least liquid products are known as 'exotic' interest rate derivatives and include cross-currency swaptions, Bermudan swaptions, snowballs, targeted accrual redemption notes (known as 'TARNs'), inverse floaters and power reverse dual-currency notes.

A cross-currency swaption is a hybrid product that exchanges fixed-rate payments in one currency for receipt of floating-rate payments in another currency. On certain dates, the seller would also have the option to terminate the swap or cancel it by entering into an opposite swap (ie, to pay the floating rate and receive the fixed rate). Fixed-for-fixed and floating-for-floating cross-currency swaptions are also popular.

As discussed in relation to Bermudan-type swaps, inclusion of a Bermudan swaption would afford the payer the right, but not the obligation, to enter into an interest rate swap on any one of a number of predetermined dates.

Exotic products are highly leveraged such that, while they expose investors to greater risks, they also provide an opportunity for greater return.

A snowball, for example, adds the previous interest rate to the current interest rate on each payment date, creating the potential for a high level of return. Rates are typically floored at 0% and can also be set in arrears. Snowballs are often 'callable inverse snowballs', whereby the interest rate is priced based upon the previous interest rate, plus spread, minus a scaled floating rate, which the issuer may call on any payment date. A 'snowball' is a highly leveraged bet on the market's movements as any trend in the floating rate, whether positive or negative, causes the interest rate payments to increase or decrease, accordingly, faster than in a vanilla swap. However, in some cases, where LIBOR is above a certain threshold, the interest rate may actually be calculated as zero and therefore the accumulation will start from zero, effectively eliminating all of the investor's future returns.

There is no limit on the number of features that may be combined to create products tailored to each investor's investment requirements and risk appetite. Some products become so complex that it is questionable whether either counterparty fully understands the risks that may be involved. This concern was echoed around the world following the recent global financial crisis, which has led to regulatory reforms aimed at controlling the risks involved in derivatives trading (see section 7 below).

4. Valuation and pricing

At the start of the contract, derivative instruments have zero value: it is only as interest rates change over time that the value begins to change. Interest rate swaps used to be valued based upon one unique yield curve for each currency, which was formed by plotting yield against different maturity lengths. Some banks identified inconsistencies in this approach many years ago and begun to utilise different pricing techniques instead, although it was not until after the global financial crisis that the market widely acknowledged that this was not an appropriate method of valuation. Since then, a multi-curves formula has been used, which takes into account different interest rates (eg, one curve for three-month EURIBOR and another for six-month EURIBOR).

While a breakdown of the complex mathematical formulae is outside the scope of this chapter, the underlying methodology in a vanilla interest rate swap may illustrate some of the complexities involved. To calculate the value of the swap, the present value of the fixed leg and the floating leg must be calculated. The fixed-leg valuation is relatively straightforward as it is calculated by reference to the fixed rate agreed at the outset of the swap. Since the floating rate changes over time, this leg is more difficult to value. The floating leg is valued as the present value of the floating-rate payments as determined on the agreed dates of payment by reference to a forward yield curve, which predicts interest rates as a function of maturity.

5. Risks

Since pricing of derivatives, particularly exotic derivatives, can be complicated and each counterparty must rely on complex risk analysis models to understand fully the potential exposure to the markets, all parties face risks when entering into an interest rate derivative. Fundamentally, the value of the derivative will change as interest rates rise or fall and, even with the best-designed risk model, investors can never be fully certain how the markets will unfold. Where the derivative is not supported by collateral, these risks are amplified further, but even with collateralised trades, the value of the posted collateral may change as a result of extraneous market movements. The following paragraphs set out some of the general risks involved in interest rate derivatives.

5.1 Leverage

Derivatives provide a means for investors to earn large returns on relatively small movements in interest rates due to leverage (eg, see the discussion on snowballs at paragraph 2.3. above). While this makes the product extremely attractive, it also means that investors may experience significant losses if interest rates were to move in the opposite direction. Some reports estimate that, in the past decade, over US$39 billion have been lost by investors in the derivatives market.

5.2 Hidden tail risk

Market returns are often assumed to follow a normal distribution, a mathematical model whereby the probability of returns falling within three standard deviations of the mean (either positive or negative) is 99.97%. However, this does not always accurately reflect the market; there are times when certain unexpected and uncontrollable events may push rates outside of the normal distribution. Although rare, such events (eg, the credit crisis) can happen overnight, turning what would otherwise be a well-protected portfolio into one with significant losses.

5.3. Counterparty risk

Interest rate derivatives may be exposed to counterparty risk (ie, a risk that the counterparty will be unable to perform its obligations). The level of loss that one party may experience is often calculated based upon the perceived cost of replacement of the contract.

Counterparty risk may be managed by inclusion of a termination event relating to credit ratings. For example, a unilateral protection may be added stating that if one party's credit rating falls below a certain level, then the other party would have a right to terminate the agreement. However, this mechanism has limited effect where significant market events happen quickly, as the counterparty may not be able to act fast enough before the credit rating plummets.

While well-designed risk models may help to mitigate certain types of risk, it would be difficult – if not impossible – to eliminate risks entirely.

6. Documentation

For bilateral OTC agreements, the majority of derivatives terms remain unchanged from transaction to transaction, so the ISDA Master Agreement – a set of standard terms prepared by the International Swaps and Derivatives Association Inc (ISDA) – is usually used as a starting point for all OTC derivatives transactions. The forms of the agreement published in 1992 and 2002 are the most common in the market, depending upon which is most appropriate for the individual counterparties. A 'supplement' is also executed by the parties, in the form of a schedule, which documents any amendments to the terms provided in the standard form ISDA Master Agreement along with any additional commercial terms.

If collateral is to be provided in connection with a trade, then a credit support document (whether in the form of a deed or an annex to the ISDA Master Agreement) will be executed by the parties to document its specific terms and conditions. ISDA has published several forms of credit support documentation, allowing parties to select the one most appropriate for their transaction.

Each individual trade entered into under the ISDA Master Agreement (including the supplement) is documented by way of a 'confirmation', which sets out the specific commercial and economic terms. In order to streamline the confirmation, ISDA has published a number of definitions booklets, each relating to a different type of transaction, which may be incorporated by way of cross-reference to avoid the need for detailed and complex definitions to be set out in the confirmation itself.

The 2006 ISDA Definitions provide a basic framework for privately negotiated interest rate and currency derivative transactions; they are the market standard set of terms for governing interest rate derivatives. These definitions include specific provisions relating to the swaption straddle – an exotic derivative which includes two swaptions, each relating to a different underlying swap, and an updated form of confirmation that parties can use to document a swaption or swaption straddle.

Note that the terms defined in the 2006 ISDA Definitions are denoted by the use of single quotation marks when used for the first time in the body of this chapter. Thereafter, those terms are spelled without using any capital letters or punctuation marks (unless they are being defined, for instance).

New definitions and provisions relating to mark-to-market currency swap transactions have also been added, along with an accompanying confirmation. A mark-to-market swap eliminates exchange rate exposure arising from the beginning of one calculation period to the beginning of the next as the currency for one party (the variable currency amount) is subject to adjustment at the start of each calculation period, while the currency amount for the other party (the constant currency amount) is fixed. The variable currency amount is adjusted by reference to the constant currency amount and the then-prevailing applicable currency exchange rates.

Matrices have also been included in the 2006 ISDA Definitions to provide, for certain types of transaction, a range of standard selections of terms and provisions that would otherwise usually be negotiated and referenced in the confirmation. Where a matrix applies, the parties do not need to define all of the relevant terms in the confirmation, unless they wish to make any deviations from the relevant matrix. The 'settlement matrix' applies to swaptions and transactions that include optional or mandatory early termination features in a currency provided for by the matrix. The 'MTM matrix' (mark-to-market matrix) is deemed to apply to mark-to-market currency swaps in specified currencies. If parties do not wish for either matrix to apply, they may simply exclude it in the confirmation.

Definitions relating to rate options have also been updated in the 2006 ISDA Definitions to take account of Thomson Reuters' acquisition of the Telerate service, while day count fractions have been amended to clarify the way in which they operate in practice.

As and when appropriate in order to keep up with any changes in the market, ISDA continues to publish amendments and supplements to the 2006 ISDA Definitions on its website. These amendments are generally deemed to apply to any transactions entered into before the date of the amendment (eg, if the MTM matrix is not excluded, then any amendments to the MTM matrix would apply to the transaction as and when they become effective). However, parties may state in the confirmation if they do not wish for any future amendments to become applicable and effective in relation to that transaction.

ISDA continues to monitor the market and any new product developments so that, if appropriate, standardised documents may be created and/or updated to reflect these changes.

7.   Regulatory environment
Following the global financial crisis, governments and regulatory bodies around the world became increasingly concerned about certain types of financial instrument, including derivatives. Since many believe OTC derivatives were (at least partly) to blame for aggravating the crisis, regulators felt it important to address the perceived flaws in the market in order to create a more stable environment. A global reform

followed in an attempt to restructure the regulatory system, prevent another financial crisis and increase public confidence.

7.1 European Union

The European Union has, in response to the commitments made by the G20 leaders in Pittsburgh in 2009, taken a close look at the regulation of derivatives and subsequently introduced the European Market Infrastructure Regulation (648/2012) (EMIR). EMIR imposes a number of requirements on counterparties to derivatives transactions, including the obligation to clear standardised trades centrally, report all transactions to trade repositories and adopt certain other measures aimed at reducing the risk arising from trades that cannot be cleared. Even though EMIR came into force on 16 August 2012, some of its implementing measures (in particular, relating to margining of uncleared derivatives) are still being finalised by the EU regulators. The requirement to clear standardised trades is being phased in from early 2016, and it has already significantly changed the market in the European Union for interest rate products.

The regulation of derivatives products in the European Union is going to be further tightened when the Markets in Financial Instruments Regulation (600/2014) (MiFIR) and the new Markets in Financial Instruments Directive (2014/65/EU) (MiFID), commonly together referred to as 'MiFID 2'', come into force. The intention of MiFID 2 is to close loopholes in the existing legislation, increase transparency and ensure that trading takes place only on closely regulated markets, thereby protecting investors. Member states are required to implement the new rules by 3 January 2018.

MiFID 2 will tighten the regulation of activities relating to regulated instruments from the pricing and advising, to the trading and the reporting stages. In particular, where currently more sophisticated clients are not due certain protections, MiFID 2 will require that some of these protections are extended. In an attempt to reduce bilateral risk, OTC products will be encouraged to move to one of several approved trading venues: a regulated market, a multilateral trading facility or an organised trading facility. Indeed, one of the main purposes of creating a new category of venue – the organised trading facility – is to reduce the scope of trading that can be seen as OTC, as it reclassifies previously bilateral trades in venues such as broker crossing networks into transactions on a regulated venue.

EMIR and MiFID 2 have many cross-border implications; therefore, they will not apply only to those physically located within the European Union. The implications will be far reaching and apply to all financial services businesses undertaking business in financial instruments anywhere in the European Economic Area and to anyone participating in the European Union's financial markets, whether domestic or foreign based. Therefore, all parties must carefully consider whether the provisions of EMIR and, in the future, MiFID 2 may be triggered and, if appropriate, to ensure compliance accordingly.

7.2 United States

The Dodd-Frank Wall Street Reform and Consumer Protection Act (the Dodd-Frank Act) provides a comprehensive framework for the regulation of OTC swaps, including interest rate derivatives, overseen by the Commodity Futures Trading Commission (CFTC). The Dodd-Frank Act provides for the CFTC to implement appropriate rules in order to increase transparency and reduce systemic risks in the interest rate markets.

Most interest rate derivatives are now subject to central clearing, and those that are not must both adhere to certain threshold amounts of collateral and meet new margin requirements that are based upon an international standard developed by the Basel Committee on Banking Supervision and the International Organization of Securities Commissions. Similarly to EMIR, the CFTC has also introduced swap data reporting, imposing greater obligations upon swap participants.

Perhaps one of the best-known rules under the Dodd-Frank Act is the 'Volcker Rule', which prohibits certain banking entities (including, largely, those based, or doing business, in the United States and their affiliates) from engaging in proprietary trading.

Although the Dodd-Frank Act is directly applicable to banks and other persons in the United States, many rules have a broad extraterritorial application to banks and other financial institutions located outside the United States and, for example, may be applicable if the trade has a direct and significant connection with activities in, or effect on, commerce in the United States. Therefore, all parties to interest rate derivatives must carefully consider whether any of the restrictions under the Dodd-Frank Act are applicable in the specific circumstances of each trade.

7.3   Asia Pacific

Discussion of the large number of jurisdictions within the Asia Pacific region is outside the scope of this chapter, but a brief review of arguably the four major jurisdictions in the Asia Pacific region – Australia, Hong Kong, Japan and Singapore – follows. Each of these jurisdictions began implementing derivatives reforms in 2013, in line with their commitments to the G20 and the Financial Stability Board.

Australia's reform of OTC derivatives covers rules relating to mandatory reporting to a trade repository, mandatory clearing by a central counterparty and mandatory execution on a trading platform. The reform involved several stages, each coming into effect in turn over the course of a few years.

Similarly, Singapore introduced multiple phases of regulatory reform, with a new regulatory regime for trade repositories, an extended regime for clearing facilities and mandatory reporting and clearing of certain derivative transactions. Several phases are still ongoing and are expected to be phased in over the next couple of years.

Japan also introduced mandatory reporting for a broad range of OTC derivatives and a central clearing obligation for different types of interest rate swap, with a mandatory use of exchanges or other electronic trading platforms. The proposed margin requirements were delayed due to bilateral discussions with EU and US regulators, but are being phased in from September 2016.

The first phase of Hong Kong's Securities and Futures (Amendment) Ordinance 2014 came into effect in mid-2015, introducing mandatory reporting and record keeping obligations in relation to interest rate swaps (and non-deliverable forwards) conducted by certain entities. The second phase was introduced on 1 September

2016 and involves mandatory clearing of vanilla swaps between certain regulated persons, under certain conditions and above specified thresholds, within one business day of the trade. This phase also requires a record of all relevant transactions to be kept for at least five years after the termination or maturity of relevant trades. There are no transitional arrangements, but the first date on which applicable trades are required to clear is 1 July 2017. Rules on margining for uncleared swaps have been delayed and it is believed this may not be enforced until the European Union implements its margin requirements.

7.4   A reformed market

Firms continue to implement appropriate changes not only to ensure compliance with EMIR, the Dodd-Frank Act and any other local laws as necessary, but also to identify any commercial opportunities that may arise as a result of the changes being made to their internal processes and procedures. Regulators and governments will no doubt continue to keep a close eye on the OTC derivatives market in the coming years. Only time will tell whether the regulatory overhaul will prove effective in creating a more transparent, risk-averse environment as intended.

FX derivatives

David Johnson
First Abu Dhabi Bank PJSC

1.   Introduction

Foreign exchange (FX) transactions encompass everything from tourists buying money for their holidays abroad to multi-million US dollar payments made by governments and companies for goods and services purchased overseas. Globalisation has led to a substantial increase in the number of FX transactions. The global FX market is by far the largest financial market in the world, with average daily transaction volumes in the trillions of US dollars. Transactions involving the exchange of euros and US dollars make up the biggest proportion of this market.

FX rates are constantly changing and are affected by all kinds of economic and political factor. Positive economic data regarding a country can cause the value of its currency to soar just as easily as uncertainty from looming elections can cause it to fall. Sometimes rates change for, seemingly, no reason at all.

Famous events shaping the world's foreign currency market include the creation of the euro on 1 January 1999 when 14 EU nations each gave up their domestic currency to form the largest currency union in the world. Other well-known events include the Russian ruble crisis of the late 1990s; in 2015 the Russian ruble plummeted again following a dramatic fall in the value of oil and gas (as energy exports are the cornerstone of the Russian economy).

This volatility represents the FX risk that individuals and corporations may be exposed to. As discussed in this chapter, FX derivatives can help reduce this risk. FX derivatives can also be used to speculate upon currency fluctuations, thereby enabling market participants to profit from the rise or fall of one currency relative to the value of another.

This chapter covers:

- what FX derivatives are and their main uses;
- a description of the main kinds of over-the-counter (OTC) FX derivative;
- a discussion of the 1998 FX and Currency Option Definitions; and
- some practical points to consider when using OTC FX derivatives.

2.   What are FX derivatives?

2.1   Definition

A 'foreign exchange derivative' or 'FX derivative' is a transaction in which the payoff depends on the FX rate of two (or more) currencies. FX derivatives allow the isolation and separate trading of the change in FX rates.

A typical FX derivatives transaction is a contract entered into between two parties:

- providing for the purchase of an agreed amount of one currency by one party from another in exchange for the sale by it of an agreed amount of another currency to that other party; or
- entitling one party with a right (but not the obligation) to purchase from, or sell to, the other party a specified quantity of a specified currency at a pre-agreed price.

FX derivatives can be in the form of bilateral OTC contracts or they can be traded on exchanges. Exchange-traded products are standardised derivatives instruments that are traded on an organised exchange. 'Standardisation' means, among other things, that the parties cannot amend the price, maturity and quantity of a product traded on an exchange. OTC products, by contrast, offer participants the ability to customise their transactions to suit their particular needs.

As discussed in the chapter on the Derivatives Regulation, following the global financial crisis of the past decade, new regulations – in particular, the European Market Infrastructure Regulations and the US Dodd-Frank Wall Street Reform and Consumer Protection Act – legislate that certain kinds of derivative must be traded on exchanges. However, FX derivatives have, thus far, been exempted from much of this regulation and most of the world's FX derivatives market is traded OTC. Accordingly, this chapter focuses on OTC FX derivatives.

2.2 The 1998 FX and Currency Option Definitions

In 1997 various industry bodies, including the International Swaps and Derivatives Association Inc (ISDA), the EMTA Inc (formerly, the Emerging Markets Traders Association) and the Foreign Exchange Committee, formed a working group to develop standard documentation for FX and currency option derivatives transactions. The 1998 FX and Currency Option Definitions (the FX Definitions) were the output of this working group and are now the market standard definitions used for documenting FX and currency options derivatives transactions. Accordingly, the explanations and terminology used in this chapter are based upon the FX Definitions, and the terms used in this chapter, but not otherwise defined herein, have the meaning given to them in the FX Definitions. These terms are denoted by the use of single quotation marks when used for the first time in this chapter and/or where defined. Thereafter, those terms are spelled without using any capital letters or punctuation marks. These definitions are discussed in detail in section 4 below.

3. Types of FX derivative

There are four main types of OTC FX derivative:

- 'spot';[1]

---

[1] Some practitioners and, indeed, certain regulations do not classify FX spot transactions as derivatives. However, since most FX transactions are documented using the FX Definitions, they are discussed in this chapter.

- 'forwards';
- 'swaps'; and
- 'options'.

3.1   FX spot

(a)   Description of FX spot transactions

FX spot transactions are the simplest form of FX derivatives transactions. An 'FX spot transaction' is a contract providing for the purchase of an agreed amount of one currency by one party in exchange for the sale by that party of an agreed amount of another currency to the other party to the transaction, where the 'settlement date' (ie, the date that the two currencies are exchanged) for the transaction occurs on the market standard day for settlement, usually, two 'business days' after the date that the parties enter into the transaction (known as the 'trade date').

Market convention for expressing a two-business day settlement period is 'T+2' (ie, settlement two business days after the trade date). A notable exception to this T+2 settlement rule for FX spot transactions is those where US dollars are exchanged for Canadian dollars, for which the settlement date is one business day after the parties enter into the transaction (or, to express it another way, this pair of currencies settles T+1).

(b)   Motivations for using FX spot transactions

FX spot transactions are entered into between two parties when one wants to buy an agreed amount of one currency and another wants to sell it, in exchange for an agreed amount of another currency on the market standard settlement date, usually T+2. Unlike some other FX transactions discussed below, FX spot transactions are always 'deliverable' (ie, the underlying currencies are exchanged between the parties).

One party may be an 'end user' of the currency (ie, it needs the currency for a particular purpose, for example, to purchase something in a currency that it does not have) and the other may be a broker which is entering into the transaction in order to earn a 'spread' (ie, the difference between the rate at which it exchanges the currency with the end user and the rate at which it purchased the currency from a third party). This spread represents the profit earned by a broker from entering into FX spot transactions.

(c)   Example FX spot transaction

Tournelles SA is a company incorporated in France that manufactures widgets. Tournelles sells most of its widgets in the United States and, accordingly, receives most of its revenue in US dollars. Tournelles needs euros to pay its employees at the widget factory. Accordingly, Tournelles enters into an FX spot transaction with Greatorex Bank in order to exchange $10 million for €8 million on a T+2 basis.

Below is a diagrammatic representation of this FX spot transaction.

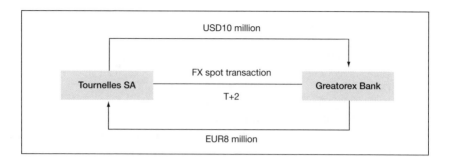

USD10 million

FX spot transaction

Tournelles SA ——————————————— Greatorex Bank

T+2

EUR8 million

3.2   FX forward

(a)   *Description of FX forward transaction*

An 'FX forward transaction' is a contract providing for the purchase of an agreed amount of one currency by one party in exchange for the sale by that party of an agreed amount of another currency to the other party to the transaction where the settlement date for the transaction occurs on a day different from the market standard day for settlement. The rate at which the two currencies will be exchanged is fixed on the trade date, even though settlement will occur in the future.

As noted above, market convention for FX spot transactions is normally T+2, whereas FX forwards can have settlement periods of any number of days, weeks, months or years (or, to express it another way, a FX forward may, for example, have a T+7 settlement date).

Deliverable and non-deliverable forwards: There are two broad categories of FX forward transaction, depending on how they settle (ie, how each party to the transaction discharges their obligations).

A 'deliverable' FX forward transaction is settled by the parties actually exchanging the agreed amount of one currency for another on the settlement date. This is the same settlement method as for FX spot transactions discussed above.

A 'non-deliverable' FX forward transaction, by contrast, does not involve the physical exchange of two currencies on the settlement date. Rather, a formula is used to determine the difference between the exchange rates for two currencies at two points in time. An FX rate is agreed by the parties on the trade date (known as the 'forward rate') and then, on the 'valuation date' (normally, two business days before the end of the transaction), the then current exchange rate is determined (known as the 'settlement rate') usually based upon the then prevailing spot rate.

Depending upon how the exchange rate has moved between the trade date and the valuation date, one party will pay the other an agreed amount of money. The amount of money that is paid is known as the 'settlement currency amount' and represents the profit by one party (which receives the payment) and loss by another (which pays it). This payment of the settlement currency amount mirrors the position that the parties would have been in had there been an actual physical exchange of the two underlying currencies (like in a deliverable FX forward transaction).

The settlement currency amount is paid in the 'settlement currency' (regardless of the two currencies referenced in the transaction), which is usually US dollars or another 'hard' currency (ie, a currency that is unlikely to depreciate suddenly or to fluctuate greatly in value over a short period of time).

The exchange rate movement is determined by comparing the value of one currency (known as the 'reference currency') to another currency (the settlement currency). It is the relative value of the reference currency to the settlement currency that determines the settlement currency amount. The settlement rate represents the values of the currencies that would be received had there been an actual exchange.

One of the parties is designated as the 'reference currency seller' (ie, the one that would have paid the reference currency on the settlement date were it to be a physically settled transaction) and the other as the 'reference currency buyer' (ie, the one that would be paid the reference currency on the settlement date were it to be a physically settled transaction). If the settlement rate exceeds the forward rate, this means that the reference currency buyer has agreed a worse exchange rate than would have been available had it simply waited until the valuation date to purchase the reference currency in a FX spot transaction. By contrast, if the settlement rate is less than the forward rate, the difference represents an entitlement to a larger amount of the reference currency than the reference currency buyer would have received had it waited until the valuation date to purchase the reference currency. To reflect these two scenarios, a payment, known as the 'settlement currency amount', is due from one party to the other.

The settlement currency amount is calculated by reference to the below formula:
Settlement currency amount = notional amount × (1 – forward rate/settlement rate)

For the purposes of the above formula, the 'notional amount' is the amount of settlement currency agreed by the parties on the trade date (ie, the size or face value of the contract) and the forward rate and settlement rate are both quoted in terms of the amount of reference currency per one unit of settlement currency.

If the settlement currency amount is a positive number (ie, the settlement rate is greater than the forward rate), then the reference currency buyer must pay that amount, in the settlement currency, to the reference currency seller. Conversely, if the settlement currency amount is a negative number (ie, the settlement rate is less than the forward rate), the reference currency seller must pay an amount equal to the absolute value thereof, in the settlement currency, to the reference currency buyer.

(b)   *Motivations for using FX forward transactions*

For deliverable FX forward transactions: Deliverable FX forward transactions are entered into between two parties when one wants to buy an agreed amount of one currency and another wants to sell it, in exchange for an agreed amount of another currency at a predetermined date in the future that is not the market standard settlement date. Accordingly, the motivation is substantially similar to FX spot transactions, but the parties agree to a settlement date that is further into the future than two business days after trading.

Example deliverable FX transaction: Leliaert SA is a Belgian commodities broker that has sold 10,000 barrels of oil to Whitehall Inc, the payment for which will be in US dollars and received in one month's time. Entering into an FX forward transaction with a bank, Pendle Bank PLC, would enable Leliaert to lock in the euro/dollar exchange rate, thereby insulating it from the effects of currency movements during this one-month period. In fact, if Leliaert entered into the FX forward at the same time as the oil sale transaction, it would be able to determine its profit margin on the oil sale, thus helping it determine whether or not to enter into the transaction in the first place. Accordingly, Leliaert enters into an FX forward transaction with Pendle pursuant to which it agrees to sell the consideration that it will receive for selling its oil (USD500,000) in exchange for EUR400,000 with a T+30 settlement date.

Below is a diagrammatic representation of this FX forward transaction (and the oil sale transaction):

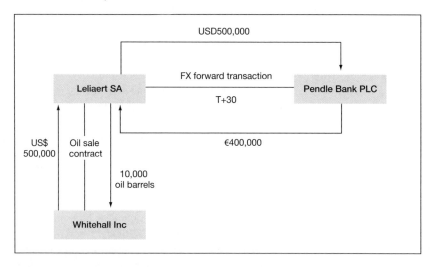

For non-deliverable FX forward transactions: Non-deliverable FX forward transactions always settle in the settlement currency regardless of the currencies traded by the parties. Therefore, the rationale for a party entering into such a transaction is, usually, different to that of a deliverable FX forward.

Non-deliverable FX forward transactions are used to hedge FX risks, or to speculate, in currencies for which there is no market in ordinary FX forward contracts, due to either illiquidity or exchange controls. This is the case, for instance, with respect to a number of Asian currencies where the governments do not allow currencies to be traded, including the Chinese renminbi, the Indian rupee, the Korean won, the Philippine peso and the Taiwanese dollar. Non-deliverable FX forward transactions enable parties to gain exposure to these currencies where a deliverable forward would not work (due to the need to deliver the underlying currencies at maturity of such deliverable transaction).

Example non-deliverable FX transaction: Galveston Limited is an investment firm in London. Galveston believes that the Chinese renminbi is going to appreciate in value versus the US dollar. Due to exchange controls, there is no deliverable FX forward market and so it decides to buy a non-deliverable FX forward contract from Saint Regis Bank PLC to benefit from any appreciation in the value of the Chinese renminbi. The key terms of the contract are as follows:

Reference currency buyer:	Galveston Limited
Reference currency seller:	Saint Regis Bank PLC
Notional amount:	USD10 million
Forward rate:	CNY6.2[2] to USD1
Settlement rate:	The spot rate on the valuation date
Settlement currency:	USD

Scenario A: The renminbi appreciates versus the dollar during the term of the transaction

Settlement rate:	CNY5.2 to USD1
Settlement currency amount:	= USD10 million x (1 – 6.2/5.2)
	= USD10 million x (1 – 1.1923)
	= USD10 million x – 0.1923
	= USD1.923 million (absolute value)

Accordingly, USD1.923 million is to be paid by Saint Regis Bank PLC, as reference currency seller, to Galveston Limited, as reference currency buyer.

Scenario B: The renminbi depreciates versus the dollar during the term of the transaction

Settlement rate:	CNY7.2 to USD1
Settlement currency amount:	= USD10 million x (1 – 6.2/7.2)
	= USD10 million x (1 – 0.8611)
	= USD10 million x 0.1389
	= USD1.389 million

Accordingly, USD1.389 million is to be paid by Galveston Limited, as reference currency buyer, to Saint Regis Bank PLC, as reference currency seller.

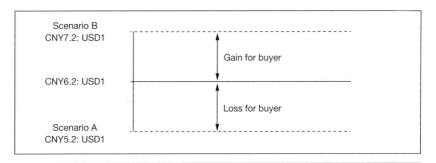

---

2   Like the United Kingdom, where 'sterling' and 'pound' both refer to the nation's currency, there are two names for China's currency: 'renminbi' is the official name of China's currency, but 'yuan' is the unit of account.

3.3 FX swaps

(a) *Description of FX swap transactions*

An 'FX swap transaction' is a contract providing for the simultaneous purchase and sale of identical amounts of one currency for another currency with two different valuation and settlement dates. Or to express it another way, an FX swap involves two parties exchanging two different currencies at the start of a transaction and then, at maturity, each party redelivers the currency that it had received from the other at the start. Also, during the term of the transaction, periodic cash flows are exchanged. Essentially, an FX swap transaction is an agreement between two parties to make a loan to each other in different currencies. The cash exchanged by the parties at the outset represents the collateral for the loans extended to each other.

In order to understand an FX swap transaction, it is helpful to deconstruct it into its component parts.

'Initial exchange' (or 'near leg'): The first part of an FX swap transaction is simply an FX spot transaction entailing the purchase of an agreed amount of one currency by one party in exchange for the sale by that party of an agreed amount of another currency to the other party to such transaction, where settlement occurs on the standard settlement date (ie, T+2). This FX swap transaction embodies the initial exchange by the parties of the principal of two different currencies at the outset of the transaction (so that each party has the use of the different currency during the term of the transaction).

'Running payments': The second part of an FX swap transaction is that the parties make interest payments to each other (in the same currency as they each borrowed) during the term of the contract. Normally, one of the parties pays a floating-interest rate and the other pays a fixed-interest rate, but both could pay floating or fixed-interest rates.[3]

'Final exchange' (or 'far leg'): The third part of an FX swap transaction is simply an FX forward transaction whereby the parties re-exchange the currencies that they bought in the first part of the transaction, but the settlement date occurs further into the future (ie, T+30) at the settlement rate pre-agreed at the outset. This part of the transaction represents the parties re-exchanging the principal amount of the swap that they initially exchanged at the start (ie, repaying the loan that they borrowed).

(b) *Motivations for using FX swap transactions*

As discussed above, an FX swap is, essentially, two collateralised loans exchanged between the parties. Each party is both a lender and a borrower, just in opposite currencies. FX swap maturities can be any length of time and market convention is that the duration can extend up to 10 years, making them a flexible method of FX borrowing.

---

3   These running payments are, effectively, an interest rate swap transaction. For further details regarding interest rate swaps, please refer to the chapter on interest rate derivatives.

FX swaps are commonly used to circumvent exchange controls or to give each party access to foreign currency to make purchases in foreign markets. By way of example, some companies may be able to borrow cheaply from banks in their own country provided that the loan is in their domestic currency. The same companies may not, however, be able to borrow at competitive interest rates in a foreign currency. If there are two companies that can borrow cheaply domestically and each would like to obtain the other's currency, then an FX swap efficiently facilitates this since under such a transaction each party receives the foreign currency that it wants at a cheaper rate than it could otherwise obtain on its own.

Parties may also enter into FX swaps as a way to enter new capital markets or to provide predictable revenue streams in another currency – typically, as a hedge against FX risk.

(c)   *Example FX swap transaction*

Kempson PLC is a British manufacturing company that would like to invest in Australian resource extraction. All of Kempson's assets and money are located in the United Kingdom and are denominated in British pounds. Kempson has an established track record with various British banks that are thus willing to lend to it at competitive interest rates, provided that the loan is collateralised and is denominated in British pounds. Kempson does not have a relationship with any Australian banks, nor does it have any assets located in Australia that it can offer as collateral for a loan from an Australian bank; accordingly, the interest rate that an Australian bank would charge for an Australian dollar-denominated loan would be higher than that charged by Kempson's British bankers for a loan in sterling.

Lambert Limited is an Australian company which would like to invest in sterling-denominated gilts. All of Lambert's assets and money are denominated in Australian dollars. Just like Kempson, Lambert can borrow cheaply from its local banks, but not from foreign banks in a foreign currency. Entering into an FX swap transaction would be mutually beneficial to both Kempson and Lambert since it would enable them to use their respective competitive advantages of borrowing cheaply domestically, while obtaining the international currencies that they seek.

Accordingly, Kempson and Lambert each take out loans from their own local banks and agree to enter into a GBP100 million/AUD200 million floating-to-fixed FX swap transaction with a term of five years as follows:

Initial exchange (constituting an FX spot transaction): Two business days after entering into the transaction, Kempson pays Lambert GBP100 million and Lambert pays Kempson AUD200 million (on the basis that the spot exchange rate on the trade date is GBP1 to AUD2).

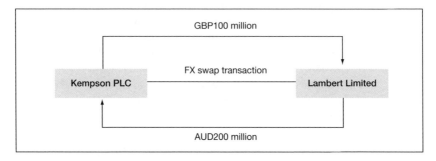

Running payment throughout the terms of the transaction (constituting interest payments on the loan): On pre-agreed dates (usually quarterly), each party pays to the other an amount of interest. Kempson pays Lambert in Australian dollars on the basis of a 4% fixed rate of interest (since it borrowed Australian dollars). Conversely, Lambert pays Kempson a floating amount by reference to the three-month British pound LIBOR rate (since it borrowed in British pounds).

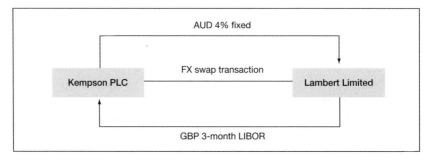

Final exchange (constituting an FX forward transaction): In five years' time, Lambert pays Kempson £100 million and Kempson pays Lambert A$200 million in repayment of their loans to each other.

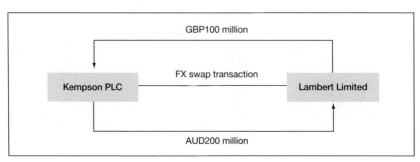

For simplicity, the above example has shown two companies entering into an FX swap directly with each other. Usually, however, a bank or other intermediary would act as a broker in between the two companies. The bank would facilitate the currency swap transaction in return for charging a fee (or spread) that would be included in the cost of the transaction. Typically, spreads on foreign exchange swaps are relatively low. Therefore, the actual borrowing rates for the companies in this example would increase slightly, but they would still be better than those offered by international banks in a foreign currency without the FX swap.

3.4   FX options

(a)   Description of FX options

'FX options' are contracts between two parties, one of which grants the option (the 'seller') and the other that buys it (the 'buyer'). The option seller, in consideration for a premium, grants the option buyer the right (but not the obligation) to buy or sell an agreed quantity of a currency at a specified price on a future date. FX options differ from FX forwards in that the buyer of a forward contract is obliged to pay the currency on the settlement date, even if the interest rate has moved out of its favour. The buyer of an FX option, by contrast, is not obliged to exercise the option and pay the settlement amount. Consequently, if exercising the FX option would cause the buyer to suffer a loss (ie, the option is 'out-of-the-money' from the buyer's perspective) due to the currency movements, then the buyer would not exercise it, and the option would simply expire.

FX options may be either a 'call' or a 'put'. A call FX option transaction gives the buyer the right, but not the obligation, to buy from the seller a specified amount of a specified currency at a specified price. The specified price is known as the 'strike price' or 'exercise price'.

A put FX option transaction gives the buyer the right, but not the obligation, to sell to the seller a specified amount of a specified currency at the strike price.

(b)   Deliverable and non-deliverable FX option transactions

There are two broad categories of FX option transaction, depending on how they settle (ie, how each party to the transaction discharges their obligations) if the option is exercised.

Deliverable FX option transactions: If exercised, a deliverable FX option transaction is settled by the parties actually exchanging the agreed amount of one currency for another on the settlement date. This is the same settlement method as for FX spot and deliverable FX forward transactions discussed above. But, unlike FX spot and deliverable FX forward transactions, an FX option is settled only if exercised by the buyer.

Non-deliverable FX option transactions: A non-deliverable FX option transaction, by contrast, does not involve the physical exchange of two currencies on the settlement date. Rather, if the option is exercised, a formula is used to determine the difference between the exchange rate for two currencies at two points in time and the resulting payment required by one party to the other. Two formulae for calculating such payment are set out in the FX Definitions and the more common one is discussed further below.

(c)   *Motivation for using FX options*

FX options give the buyer the right, but not the obligation, to buy or sell a specified amount of a particular currency at the strike price during a specified time period. FX options are used extensively for hedging because FX options allow buyers to protect their position for a relatively small cost (ie, the premium paid to purchase the option). Option sellers, however, like writing options to obtain the premium paid by the buyer. Investors utilise FX options because, as a proportion to the amount of capital invested, their potential profit is much greater than through buying the underlying currencies outright. Each of these concepts is discussed further below.

From a hedging perspective, an FX option allows a company to protect itself from decreases in value of one currency against another (ie, downside risk) while, simultaneously, still affording the company the chance of benefiting from favourable currency movements (ie, upside potential). A German company may, for example, earn a sizable proportion of its revenue in New Zealand dollars. This company is exposed to the risk that, if the New Zealand dollar depreciates against the euro, then this will negatively impact its earnings, reported in euros. At the same time, this company would like to benefit from any increase in the value of the New Zealand dollar versus the euro, since this will increase its earnings. Buying a call option on the euro (ie, the right to buy the euro using New Zealand dollars at a particular price) would enable the German company to reduce its potential downside risk, while still affording it with the upside potential described above. If the value of the New Zealand dollar fell, then the German company would exercise the option to buy euros. Conversely, if the value of the New Zealand dollar rose, then the German company would not exercise the option and the contract would simply expire.

The seller of the euro call option described above would be paid a premium by the German company. If the option is not exercised, then this premium is kept as profit by the seller. This can be an attractive revenue stream for investment banks and other FX option dealers.

From an investor's perspective, a fundamental advantage of FX options is leverage (ie, they afford the buyer with much more exposure to a currency than would be obtainable by buying the currency outright). By way of explanation, a small investment in FX options can benefit from the price movements of currencies that would either cost much more to own outright, or would require much greater risk. Continuing with the above German company example, another way to mitigate the New Zealand dollar/euro exchange rate risk would be for the company simply to buy euros with its New Zealand dollars using an FX spot transaction. However, that would consume a lot of capital; buying a euro call option would cost only a fraction of that amount. Because of leverage, FX options are useful financial instruments for hedging, or for pure speculation.

Of course, options have a downside. Although the risk is limited to the premium paid to purchase an FX option, the disadvantage of buying FX options is that they can (and often do) expire completely worthless. If the relevant FX rate does not move sufficiently in the right direction before the expiration date (ie, in-the-money to the buyer), then the buyer loses their entire investment.

(d)   *Example FX option transaction*

Let us assume that the German company mentioned above, Waldemar GMBH, bought a euro call option from Maidstone Limited, an investment firm in London. The key terms of the transaction are set out below:

Option type:	EUR call option
Option buyer:	Waldemar GmbH
Option seller:	Maidstone Limited
Option style:	European
Call currency amount:	EUR10 million
Strike price:	NZD1.10 to €1
Premium:	EUR10,000
Settlement currency:	EUR

The below diagram illustrates the profit that could be earned by Waldemar through buying this option, assuming that the value of the New Zealand dollar fell against the euro.

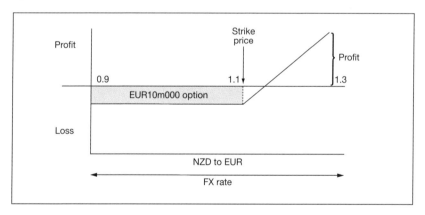

4.   The 1998 FX and Currency Option Definitions

4.1   Background

As mentioned above in section 2.2, in 1997 various industry bodies formed a working group to develop standard documentation for FX and currency option derivatives transactions. The 1998 FX and Currency Option Definitions were the output of this working group and are now the market standard definitions used for documenting FX and currency options derivatives transactions. The purpose of the FX Definitions is to provide the basic framework for documenting foreign exchange and currency options derivatives transactions.

The FX Definitions were published in two parts; the first is the main definitional booklet and the second is an annex to that booklet known as 'Annex A'. Annex A contains the terms that are expected to change from time to time, such as the 'principal financial centers' for each currency. The FX Definitions are available for purchase from ISDA and Annex A (and its various updates) can be downloaded for free from ISDA's website (www2.isda.org).

The FX Definitions are designed for use with various industry standard master agreements, including the ISDA Master Agreement. For further information regarding the ISDA documentation architecture, please see the chapter on industry standard documentation.

Although a relatively detailed overview of the FX Definitions is provided below, ISDA, EMTA and the Foreign Exchange Committee also published a *User's Guide to the 1998 FX and Currency Option Definitions*. This user's guide provides a detailed discussion of each section of the FX Definitions and is also available for purchase from ISDA.

4.2   The FX Definitions
The FX Definitions may be summarised as follows:
- Article 1 sets out general definitions for FX transactions;
- Article 2 provides general terms and settlement provisions for FX transactions;
- Article 3 sets forth general terms regarding currency option transactions, including their settlement and exercise;
- Article 4 contains definitions of currencies and their 'principal financial centers' (though most of this is actually contained in Annex A); and
- Article 5 sets out the terms relating to 'disruption events' and their respective 'fallbacks'.

Certain key provisions of each of these articles are discussed in more detail below.

(a)   Article 1
Article 1 ("Certain General Definitions") contains general definitions applicable to FX transactions and currency option transactions.

'Business day' and 'business day convention' (Sections 1.1 and 1.2): Since FX transactions and currency option transactions entail making payments, deliveries, valuations and other determinations, and they require the support of various banks and settlement systems which are open only on certain days, the FX Definitions contain provisions for determining what constitutes a business day and a process for moving events that would otherwise fall on a day that is not a business day to a day that is (known as the 'business day convention').

What constitutes a business day for the purposes of the FX Definitions is set out in Section 1.1. A day may be considered a business day for one purpose but not for another. For example, for the purposes of making payments, a business day is a day on which commercial banks effect delivery (or would have effected delivery but for the occurrence of a disruption event)[4] of the currency to be delivered on the settlement date or 'premium payment date' (as applicable) in the place specified for payment in the 'confirmation'. If a place is not so specified, there is a series of fallbacks, the first of which is that a business day is a day on which commercial banks effect delivery (or would have effected delivery but for the occurrence of a disruption event) of the currency to be delivered on the settlement date or premium payment date (as applicable) in accordance with the market practice of the FX market in the principal financial centre of such currency.[5]

If an event was to fall on a non-business day, it will be moved to a business day pursuant to the business day convention set out in Section 1.2. An event will be moved pursuant to the following business day convention rules:

- 'Following' – the event will be moved to the first following day that is a business day;
- 'Modified following' – the event will be moved to the first following day that is a business day unless it would fall in the next calendar month, in which case it will be moved to the immediately preceding day that is a business day;
- 'Nearest' – the event will be moved to the first preceding day that is a business day if the event falls on a day other than a Sunday or Monday, or it will be moved to the first following day that is a business day if it falls on a Sunday or Monday; and
- 'Preceding' – the event will be moved to the first preceding day that is a business day.

Which business day convention applies depends on what the parties have selected in their confirmation or, failing that, depends on the event in question. For example, with respect to a settlement date or premium payment date, 'following' is the default business day convention, but with respect to a valuation date, 'preceding' is the default business day convention.[6]

'Calculation agent' (Section 1.3): The 'calculation agent' is the party responsible for making various calculations and determinations required in relation to FX transactions and currency option transactions. Usually, the calculation agent is one of the parties and, if a bank is one of the parties, that bank will normally be the calculation agent since it will be adept at making the relevant calculations and have access to the required information sources. The calculation agent is required to act in good faith and in a commercially reasonable manner, and its determinations are binding upon the parties in the absence of manifest error.

'Deliverable FX transactions' and 'non-deliverable FX transactions' (Sections 1.7 and 1.13): As discussed above, a 'deliverable FX transaction' is one where the parties

---

4   As discussed further below, a date for payment will be moved if it is scheduled to fall on a non-business day. However, if a disruption event is the reason that commercial banks are not effecting delivery of the relevant currency, then moving the event to a business day undermines the purpose of disruption events. Accordingly, this caveat addresses this by providing that the day will not be so adjusted if commercial banks would have effected delivery had the disruption event not occurred. However, if the closure of commercial banks is due to a scheduled holiday, then the business day will be adjusted.
5   Section 1.1(a)(ii).
6   Sections 1.24, 3.4(b) and 1.16(f).

settle the transaction by actually delivering the underlying currencies to each other.[7] A 'non-deliverable FX transaction', by contrast, is one where an amount in the settlement currency is paid from one party to the other depending upon the difference between the forward rate and the settlement rate.[8] Pursuant to Section 1.7, unless the parties otherwise specify, a transaction will be deemed to be deliverable.

'Settlement currency', 'settlement rate', 'settlement rate option', 'spot rate' and 'valuation date' (Section 1.16): Section 1.16 sets out various provisions relating to non-deliverable FX transactions. Most of these provisions have already been discussed above, but, for ease of reference, they are summarised below:

- 'Settlement currency' – this is the currency in which payments will be made between the parties upon settlement of a non-deliverable FX transaction.[9] As discussed above, the settlement currency is usually US dollars or another 'hard currency';
- 'Settlement rate' – this is usually the prevailing spot rate on the valuation date;[10]
- 'Settlement rate option' – this is usually specified in the confirmation as the source of the spot rate and is, generally, a Reuters screen where FX rates are quoted.[11] If the parties do not specify a settlement rate option, then it will be the one set out in Annex A for the relevant 'currency pair';
- 'Spot rate' – this is the currency exchange rate determined using the settlement rate option;[12] and
- 'Valuation date' – this is the date on which the settlement rate is determined and is, usually, two business days prior to the settlement date.[13] As noted above, the valuation date will be adjusted if it falls on a non-business day and, unless otherwise specified, the business day convention for this purpose is 'preceding'.

'Reference currency' and 'reference currency notional amount' (Sections 1.19 and 1.21): As discussed above, the 'reference currency' is the currency whose relative value determines the amount to be paid when settling a non-deliverable FX transaction. It is not, however, the currency that is actually exchanged (that is the settlement currency, as noted above).

The 'reference currency notional amount' is the quantity of reference currency specified in the confirmation.[14] The FX Definitions provide that, if an amount is not so specified, then the reference currency amount will be:

- in respect of a non-deliverable FX transaction, the notional amount multiplied by the forward rate; and

7   Section 1.7(a).
8   Section 1.13.
9   Section 1.16(b).
10   Section 1.16(c).
11   Section 1.16(d).
12   Section 1.16(e).
13   Section 1.16(f).
14   Section 1.21.

- in respect of a non-deliverable currency option transaction, the 'put currency amount' or the 'call currency amount', whichever is denominated in the reference currency.

'Trade date' and 'settlement date' (Sections 1.24 and 1.25): The 'trade date' is the date on which the parties enter into their transaction and the 'settlement date' is the date on which the parties have agreed to settle their transaction pursuant to the agreed settlement method.[15] The settlement date (but not the trade date) will be adjusted if it falls on a non-business day and, unless otherwise specified, the business day convention for this purpose is 'following'.[16]

(b)   *Article 2*
Article 2 ("General Terms Relating to FX Transactions") consists of only two sections. Section 2.1 sets out the definition of 'forward rate' and Section 2.2 stipulates how deliverable and non-deliverable FX transactions are settled.

'Forward rate' (Section 2.1(a)): The 'forward rate' is the currency exchange rate agreed by the parties at the outset of a transaction and specified in the confirmation. As discussed above, for non-deliverable FX transactions, the relative value change between the forward rate agreed on the trade date and the settlement rate determined on the valuation date determines the settlement currency amount. If a forward rate is not so specified, it will be the currency exchange rate obtained by dividing the reference currency notional amount by the notional amount.

'Deliverable FX transactions' and 'non-deliverable FX transactions' (Sections 2.2(a) and (b)): Section 2.2(a) applies to deliverable FX transactions and provides that, on the settlement date, each party will pay the amount specified to be payable by it in the confirmation (subject to any applicable provisions of Article 5).[17] This is the operative provision pursuant to which the actual exchange of the agreed amount of underlying currencies between the parties is effected.

Section 2.2(b) applies to non-deliverable FX transactions. This section provides that if the settlement currency amount is a positive number, then the 'reference currency buyer' will pay that amount in the settlement currency to the 'reference currency seller', and if the reference currency amount is a negative number, the reference currency seller will pay the absolute value of thereof in the settlement currency to the reference currency buyer (subject to any applicable provisions of Article 5).

Section 2.2(b) also sets out how the settlement currency amount is determined. As discussed above, it is determined pursuant to the below formula:

Settlement currency amount = notional amount × (1 – forward rate / settlement rate)

---

15   Section 2.2.
16   Section 1.24.
17   Article 5 is discussed further below.

(c) Article 3

Article 3 ('General Terms Relating to Currency Option Transactions') sets out various provisions that are integral to currency option transactions. Selected key definitions are discussed below.

'Buyer' and 'seller' (Article 3.1(a) and (f)): The 'buyer' is the party specified as such in the confirmation; it is the party that pays the premium to the seller on the 'premium payment date'[18] in return for having the right, but not the obligation, to exercise the relevant currency option transaction during the 'exercise period'.[19]

The 'seller' is the party specified as such in the confirmation; it is the party that pays to the buyer, if the buyer exercises the option:
- in the case of a deliverable currency option transaction, the call currency amount; and
- in the case of a non-deliverable currency option transaction, the 'in-the-money amount'.[20]

Option style (Section 3.2) – 'American', 'Bermuda', 'European': The date(s) on which an option can be exercised are selected by the parties in the confirmation. An 'American option' affords the most flexibility as it can be exercised by the buyer at any time during the transactions term. A 'Bermuda option' offers limited flexibility as it can be exercised by the buyer only on certain dates during a transactions term. A 'European option' is the least flexible since it can be exercised by the buyer only on the 'expiration date'.

Option type (Section 3.3) – 'puts' and 'calls': Options come in two types – calls and puts – with the former being the right to buy a currency at a pre-agreed price (the strike price)[21] and the latter being the right to sell a currency at the strike price.[22]

More specifically, a call option entitles the buyer to a right:
- in the case of a deliverable currency option transaction, to purchase from the seller the call currency amount at the strike price; and
- in the case of a non-deliverable currency option transaction, to receive from the seller the in-the-money amount, if positive.[23]

A put option, by contrast, entitles the buyer to a right:
- in the case of a deliverable currency option transaction, to sell to the seller the put currency amount at the strike price; and
- in the case of a non-deliverable currency option transaction, to receive from the seller the in-the-money amount, if positive.[24]

---

18   Section 3.4(a).
19   Section 3.6.
20   Section 3.7(c).
21   Section 3.3(a).
22   Section 3.3(b).
23   Section 3.3(a).
24   Section 3.3(b).

'Premium' and 'premium payment date' (Section 3.4): The 'premium' is the amount specified in the confirmation (or determined pursuant to the formula specified in the confirmation); it is the price paid by the buyer to the seller for the currency option transaction.[25] The premium is payable on the premium payment date (or, in some case, the parties will agree to spread payment over multiple premium payment dates).

'Commencement date', 'exercise date', 'exercise period' and 'expiration date' (Section 3.5): Section 3.5 sets out how and when currency option transactions may be exercised by the buyer.

A currency option transaction may be exercised by the buyer during the exercise period. The exercise period depends upon the option style as follows:

- 'American 'means that the currency option transaction can be exercised during business hours of any business day between the 'commencement date' (normally, the trade date) and the expiration date (the end of the contract);[26]
- 'Bermuda' means that the currency option transaction can be exercised during business hours of 'specified exercise dates' (which are certain dates agreed by the parties throughout the term of the transaction);[27] and
- 'European' means that the currency option transaction can only be exercised during business hours on the expiration date.[28]

If a currency option transaction is exercised outside of the exercise period (eg, otherwise than during business hours), then in the case of an American option it is deemed exercised on the following business day within the exercise period (if any), and in the case of Bermuda and European options, the notice is ineffective.[29]

'Exercise' and 'automatic exercise' (Section 3.6): Section 3.6 provides details about how a currency option transaction is exercised and the circumstances in which a currency option transaction will be automatically deemed exercised by the buyer. A currency option transaction can be exercised only in whole, and not in part.[30]

A currency option transaction is exercised by the buyer delivering a 'notice of exercise' to the seller during the exercise period.[31] A notice of exercise may be delivered by various means including by fax, email and orally. If a notice of exercise is not received prior to the expiration time on the expiration date, then the currency option transaction will expire and become worthless.

To reduce the chances of the buyer of a currency option transaction failing to exercise its transaction and it expiring worthless, the FX Definitions contain provisions stipulating that if it were to be profitable for the buyer to exercise its option (ie, the option is in-the-money from the buyer's perspective), then it will be

---

25   Section 3.4(a).
26   Section 3.4(c)(i).
27   Section 3.4(c)(iii).
28   Section 3.4(c)(ii).
29   Section 3.6(a).
30   Section 3.6(a).
31   Section 3.6(a).

deemed to have exercised it.[32] Specifically, if the in-the-money amount exceeds the product of both 1% of the strike price and the call currency amount or put currency amount, as applicable, then such currency option transaction will be deemed to be exercised by the buyer at the expiration time (for major currencies, this is usually 10:00am New York time) on the expiration date.

'In-the-money amount' (Section 3.7): Section 3.7 sets forth how deliverable and non-deliverable currency option transactions are settled.

In the case of deliverable currency option transactions, the buyer must pay the put currency amount to the seller in return for receiving the call currency amount from the seller (subject to any applicable provisions of Article 5).[33]

In the case of non-deliverable currency option transactions, the seller must pay the in-the-money amount to the buyer (subject to any applicable provisions of Article 5). The 'in-the-money amount' is, effectively, the amount by which a particular currency (the reference currency) has increased or decreased in value relative to the value of the settlement currency as determined on the valuation date, when compared to the strike price agreed on the trade date.

Section 3.7(c) sets forth two ways in which the in-the-money amount is calculated. The simpler (and more popular) of the two methods is discussed below for both calls and puts. This method entails comparing the cost of buying (in the case of a call option) an agreed amount of a particular currency (the 'call currency amount') or selling (in the case of a put option) an agreed amount of a particular currency (the 'put currency amount') at two points in time.

Call option in-the-money amount calculation: The settlement rate is the cost, expressed in the 'put currency', of buying one unit of 'call currency'. If the settlement rate is greater than the strike price agreed on the trade date, then the option will be in-the-money from the buyer's perspective. This means that the buyer secured a better exchange rate by entering into the option than it would have done had it simply bought the relevant currency on the exercise date pursuant to an FX spot transaction.

Therefore, the 'in-the-money amount' is the excess of the settlement rate over the strike price multiplied by the call currency amount.[34]

Put option in-the-money amount calculation: The settlement rate is the amount that would be received, expressed in the call currency, in return for selling one unit of put currency. If the settlement rate is less than the strike price agreed on the trade date, then the option will be in-the-money from the buyer's perspective. This means that the buyer secured a better exchange rate by entering into the option than it would have done had it simply sold the relevant currency on the exercise date in an FX spot transaction.

---

32   Section 3.6(c).
33   Article 5 (*Disruption Events*) is discussed further below.
34   Section 3.7(c)(ii)(A).

Therefore, the in-the-money amount is the excess of the strike price over the settlement rate multiplied by the put currency amount.[35]

(d) *Article 4*

Article 4 ('Calculation of Rates for Certain Settlement Rate Options') sets forth the provisions for determining the settlement rate for FX transactions and currency option transactions. The vast majority of the provisions are not actually set out in the FX Definitions main definitional booklet; instead, most provisions are set out in Annex A since they are subject to change. Unless the parties otherwise agree, Section 4.2 ('Annex A') provides that the parties will be deemed to have incorporated the latest version of Annex A published as at the trade date.

Annex A contains the following definitions:

- Section 4.3 provides definitions of the currencies of certain countries;
- Section 4.4 comprises a table of the principal financial centres for certain currencies;
- Section 4.5 provides the sources for determining the settlement rate for certain currencies, which is usually a Reuters screen upon which FX rates are quoted; and
- Section 4.6 contains supporting definitions for determining the settlement rate.

Below is a table setting out the full name of selected major currencies, along with their industry standard short forms and their respective principal financial centres:

Currency	Standard abbreviation	Principal financial centre(s)
Argentine peso	ARS	Buenos Aires
Australian dollar	AUD	Sydney and Melbourne
Brazilian real	BRL	Brasilia, Rio de Janeiro or Sao Paulo
British pound sterling	GBP	London
Canadian dollar	CAD	Toronto
Chinese renminbi	CNY	Beijing
Danish krone	DKK	Copenhagen

continued overleaf

---

35   Section 3.7(c)(ii)(B).

Currency	Standard abbreviation	Principal financial centre(s)
Euro	EUR	N/A[36]
Indian rupee	INR	Mumbai
Indonesian rupiah	IDR	Jakarta
Japanese yen	JPY	Tokyo
Mexican peso	MXN	Mexico City
New Zealand dollar	NZD	Wellington and Auckland
Russian ruble	RUR	Moscow
Saudi Arabian riyal	SAR	Riyadh
Swiss franc	CHF	Zurich
South African rand	ZAR	Johannesburg
South Korean won	KRW	Seoul
United States dollar	USD	New York

(e)   *Article 5*

Article 5 ('Disruption Events') is the final article in the FX Definitions. It sets out provisions that enable parties to a transaction to allocate certain event risks (eg, the unavailability of an information source) by providing an alternative method for determining a currency exchange rate or settling such affected transactions. These event risks are known as 'disruption events' and the alternative means of determining a particular rate or settling an affected transaction are known as 'disruption fallbacks'. Disruption events can be grouped into four categories:

- price source risks (ie, unavailability or unreliability of a pricing source);
- convertibility and transferability risks (ie, the inability to transfer or convert a currency);
- sovereign risks (ie, the risk of nationalisation or government default); and
- other risks.

---

36   Since many EU countries use euros, there is no principal financial centre for euros. Rather, whether or a day constitutes a business day for euro transactions depends on whether TARGET2 (the Trans-European Automated Real-time Gross Settlement Express Transfer System – an interbank payment system for processing cross-border transfers throughout Europe) is open.

By way of example, civil unrest in Indonesia caused the unscheduled closure of the country's central bank and many of its commercial banks over two days in early 1998. Consequently, many FX transactions involving the Indonesian rupiah could not be settled on their respective settlement dates. Later that same year, the Russian government announced a moratorium on Russian residents making payments on foreign currency contracts to non-Russian counterparties. Consequently, the Russian ruble to US dollar exchange rate was severely disrupted. Through the introduction of disruption events and disruption fallbacks, the parties are now able to allocate the risk of these kinds of event.

'Disruption events': Section 5.1 defines the 13 events that constitute disruption events. Each of these events is discussed in detail in the *User's Guide to the FX Definitions* and, accordingly, rather than repeating the same information here, below is a table summarising each disruption event:

Disruption event	Summary explanation
'Benchmark obligation default' (Section 5.1(d)(i))	A default occurs with respect to a 'benchmark obligation' (which is an obligation specified in a confirmation). This is similar to a credit event occurring under a credit default swap[37]
'Dual exchange rate' (Section 5.1(d)(ii))	A currency exchange rate specified in a settlement rate option splits into two or more exchange rates
'General inconvertibility' (Section 5.1(d)(iii))	An event occurs in a particular jurisdiction making it generally impossible to convert from one currency into another within that jurisdiction
'General non-transferability' (Section 5.1(d)(iv))	An event occurs in a particular jurisdiction making it generally impossible to transfer money either from accounts in that jurisdiction to accounts outside of it, or between accounts within that jurisdiction
'Governmental authority default' (Section 5.1(d)(v))	A sovereign defaults on its obligations
'Illiquidity' (Section 5.1(d)(vi))	It is impossible to obtain a firm quote for the settlement rate on the valuation date

continued overleaf

---

37   For further information regarding credit default swaps, see the chapter on credit derivatives.

Disruption event	Summary explanation
'Inconvertibility/non-transferability' (Section 5.1(d)(vii))	An event that constitutes all of the following: • general inconvertibility; • general non-transferability; • specific inconvertibility; and • specific non-transferability.
'Material change in circumstances' (Section 5.1(d)(viii))	Due to a change in circumstances beyond a party's control, it becomes impossible for it to fulfil its obligations under the transaction
'Nationalization' (Section 5.1(d)(ix))	The expropriation, confiscation or other government action depriving a party of all, or substantially all, of its assets
'Price materiality' (Section 5.1(d)(x))	The official currency exchange rate differs from the open market currency exchange rate by a specified amount
'Price source disruption' (Section 5.1(d)(xi))	It becomes impossible to obtain the settlement rate on the valuation date
'Specific inconvertibility' (Section 5.1(d)(xii))	An event occurs in a particular jurisdiction making it impossible for a party to the transaction to convert one currency into another within that jurisdiction
'Specific non-transferability' (Section 5.1(d)(xiii))	An event occurs in a particular jurisdiction making it impossible for a party to the transaction to transfer money either from accounts in that jurisdiction to accounts outside of it, or between accounts within that jurisdiction

'Disruption fallbacks': Section 5.2 defines the 11 alternative means for determining the settlement rate or an alternative basis for settling a transaction. Each of these alternatives is discussed in detail in the *User's Guide to the FX Definitions* and, accordingly, rather than repeating the same information here, below is a table summarising each disruption fallback:

Disruption fallback	Summary explanation
'Assignment of claims' (Section 5.2(c)(i))	In respect of a nationalization, the party subject to the nationalization will assign its official claim against the relevant governmental authority to the other party to the transaction
'Calculation agent determination of settlement rate' (Section 5.2(c)(ii))	The calculation agent will determine the settlement rate
'Deliverable substitute' (Section 5.2(c)(iii))	A non-deliverable FX transaction will be converted into a deliverable FX transaction and settled accordingly
'Escrow arrangement' (Section 5.2(c)(iv))	Each party pays its obligations into an escrow account pending resolution of the disruption event
'Fallback reference price' (Section 5.2(c)(v))	The settlement rate will be determined by the calculation agent pursuant to an alternative settlement rate option specified in Annex A
'Local asset substitute-gross' (Section 5.2(c)(vi))	Delivery of a benchmark obligation in the amount equal to the notional amount of the affected currency
'Local asset substitute-net' (Section 5.2(c)(vii))	Delivery of a benchmark obligation in the amount equal to the net settlement amount
'Local currency substitute' (Section 5.2(c)(viii))	Rather than settling the transaction using the settlement currency, it will be settled using the currency affected by the disruption event and paid into a local account within the affected jurisdiction
'No fault termination' (Section 5.2(c)(ix))	The transaction will be settled as though an additional termination event under the relevant ISDA Master Agreement had occurred and both parties were 'affected parties'[38]

continued overleaf

[38] For further information regarding ISDA master agreements, see the chapter on industry standard documentation.

Disruption fallback	Summary explanation
'Non-deliverable substitute' (Section 5.2(c)(x))	A deliverable FX transaction will be converted into a non-deliverable FX transaction and settled accordingly
'Settlement postponement' (Section 5.2(c)(xi))	Settlement of the transaction will be postponed until the earlier of the disruption event ceasing to occur or the expiry of a specified waiting period

Which disruption events apply: The parties to a transaction are free to specify which disruption events apply (Sections 5.1(e)(i)). When both currencies in a transaction are hard currencies, often the parties will not specify any disruption events in their confirmation because the risk of them occurring is considered low. Where one currency is considered prone to risks, however, the parties may specify it as the 'event currency' (ie, the currency in relation to which disruption events are applicable).[39]

If the parties do not make any elections in their confirmation regarding which disruption events apply, then the position is as follows:

- Deliverable FX transactions: no disruption events apply;
- Non-deliverable FX transactions: price source disruption will be deemed to have been specified.[40]

Which disruption fallbacks apply: The parties to a transaction are free to specify which disruption fallbacks apply (and in which order) following the occurrence of particular disruption events (Section 5.2(e)(i)). If the parties do not, however, specify which disruption fallbacks apply, then the FX Definitions set out a hierarchy of which events apply and in which order.[41] Details of the order and a discussion of the same (including a flow chart) are contained in the *User's Guide to the FX Definitions*.

5.   Additional practical considerations

The final section of this chapter briefly discusses various practical considerations that are relevant to FX transactions and currency option transactions. In particular, this section discusses:

- the different market conventions for documenting FX transactions;
- the 'barrier option supplement'; and
- settlement risk and how it can be mitigated.

---

39   Section 5.4(c).
40   Section 5.1(e)(i).
41   Section 5.2(e).

5.1 Market convention for documenting FX transactions

(a) *FX Spot*

As discussed in the chapter on industry standard documentation, normally OTC derivatives transactions are evidenced by the parties signing a document which sets out the economic terms of the transaction (a confirmation). However, since FX spot transactions settle two business days after being entered into (save for the US dollar/Canadian dollar currency pair where transactions settle one business day after being entered into), most transactions complete before the documentation can be signed by both parties. Consequently, it is common for FX spot trade confirmations to not be signed by either party. Rather, the confirmation will, instead, be styled like a receipt that is issued by one party to the other (and, often, both parties will exchange receipts).

Moreover, it is quite common for FX spot trade confirmations not to refer to the relevant ISDA Master Agreement entered into between the parties. In order to ensure, however, that such transactions supplement, form a part of and are subject to the relevant ISDA Master Agreement, it is common for parties to add specific wording to this effect to their ISDA Master Agreement Schedule. An example of such wording is set out below:

Unless the parties otherwise agree in writing, this Agreement will govern all transactions (whether entered into before or after the date of this Agreement) that are FX Transactions or Currency Option Transactions, in each case, as defined in the 1998 FX and Currency Option Definitions published by the International Derivatives Association Inc., the EMTA Inc. and the Foreign Exchange Committee (the 'FX Definitions').

The definitions and provisions contained in the FX Definitions will be incorporated by reference into each Confirmation for an FX Transaction or Currency Option Transaction to the extent consistent with the terms of that Confirmation.

(b) *Non-deliverable forwards*

Non-deliverable forwards trade confirmations are always signed by the parties. Moreover, with a view to encouraging standardisation and, therefore, liquidity, EMTA has published on its website (www.emta.org/ndftt.aspx) non-deliverable forward confirmation templates for various currency pairs. Most non-deliverable forwards traded in the market use these templates.

5.2 The 2005 Barrier Option Supplement

ISDA, EMTA and the Foreign Exchange Committee published a supplement to the FX Definitions, known as the 2005 Barrier Option Supplement, which can be incorporated by parties to currency option transactions. If a currency option transaction is a 'barrier' option, then settlement will occur only if certain conditions are satisfied – for example, an exchange rate exceeding a certain level at any time within a specified time period.

ISDA, EMTA and the Foreign Exchange Committee also published a user's guide to this supplement. Both the 2005 Barrier Option Supplement and the user's guide are available for free from ISDA's website (www2.isda.org).

5.3   Settlement risk (Herstatt risk)

FX transactions and currency option transactions often entail the delivery of currencies whose principal financial centres are in different time zones, meaning that the settlement times vary. For example, British pound and euro transactions normally settle earlier in the day than US dollar transactions (since New York is five hours behind London and six hours behind most of the rest of Europe). Moreover, the FX Definitions do not operate on a payment-versus-payment mechanism whereby parties deliver different currencies at the same time. Therefore, the party that pays first is exposed to the risk that the other may not honour its obligations.

This occurred in 1974 when a German bank, Bankhaus Herstatt, had its licence withdrawn by its regulators because it was on the verge of insolvency. Some of Herstatt's counterparties had already paid Deutsche Marks to it on the presumption that they would receive US dollars later the same day. But when Herstatt's licence was withdrawn at 3:30pm in Germany (which was 10:30am in New York) Herstatt withheld its US dollar payments, leaving its counterparties short.

Settlement risk can be mitigated by various means. The three most common methods are as follows:

- Escrow arrangements – some parties to FX transactions put in place payment-versus-payment systems whereby both parties pay their respective payments to a third party, normally a bank or other highly rated financial institution, and this third party releases the first payment only once it has received the second. The third party performing this escrow agency role will usually charge a fee for this service.

- Non-deliverable FX transactions – one of the advantages that non-deliverable FX transactions have over their deliverable counterparts is that the parties are not exposed to settlement risk since only a single payment is effected to settle the transaction.

- Continuous Linked Settlement (CLS) – CLS is a payment-versus-payment system for major currencies operated by a special purpose bank, CLS Bank International, dedicated to settling foreign exchange trades. Additionally, CLS facilitates multiple transaction payment netting across currencies, thereby reducing the numbers of actual payments effected by participating institutions. This payment netting vastly reduces the actual movement of cash. Only major international banks are direct members of CLS, but they can make it available to other institutions and submit instructions on behalf of those other institutions. More information regarding CLS is available from its website (www.cls-group.com/Pages/default.aspx).

Property derivatives

Edmund Parker
Mayer Brown
Emmett Peters
Addleshaw Goddard LLP

1. Introduction

How often have you overheard young colleagues discussing their desire to purchase a property, get a foot on the first rung of the property ladder and take advantage of rising house prices (or perhaps, more accurately, apartment prices)? Likewise, institutional and private investors have been able to invest in the property market only by purchasing, holding (while occupying or renting) and later selling a property, all the while suffering large transaction costs. These transaction costs have also left those expecting a market downturn unable to short the property market as equity and bond investors[1] can with shares and bonds. They have had to wait for a downturn in the market before buying a property and then wait again for the market to take an upwards turn.

The advent of property derivatives (ie, derivatives deriving their value from the real estate market) opened up a new method of property investment, allowing investors to trade in the property market without having to buy or sell a physical property. The amount of property derivatives outstanding in the United Kingdom was estimated at around £148.9 billion in September 2016, against an estimated outstanding notional amount of US$493 trillion[2] of derivatives transactions in the world market. The property derivatives market was kick-started in the United Kingdom in the wake of favourable tax and regulatory developments and the development of benchmark property indices.

Given that real estate is the world's largest asset class, property derivatives have long been touted as the 'next big thing', ready to join interest rates, foreign exchange, commodities, equity and credit as a mainstream class of derivatives. This chapter covers:

- the problems and drawbacks associated with traditional property investment and the costs involved;
- a definition and description of 'property derivatives', with a description of the main underlying property reference indices;

---

1   The stock lending and repurchasing (repo) markets are well established in the equity and bond markets, whereby the holder of an equity security can lend or sell the security to another party with the intention of returning an equivalent security at an agreed later date. The party borrowing or purchasing the security can then sell it into the market with the expectation that the price will fall; if it does, the party which has borrowed or been transferred the security will, at the agreed future date, return an equivalent security at the agreed future date, having repurchased the security in the open market, locking in the reduction in value as profit.
2   Bank of International Settlements, Global OTC Derivatives Market Statistics Tracker.

- a description of the main types of property derivative, their documentation platform and examples of types of transaction; and
- the status and future direction of the market.

2. Problems with traditional property investment

2.1 Problems with holding a physical asset

(a) Commercial property purchase and sale

When acquiring a property, any would-be buyer faces various obstacles. First, it can take time to find a suitable investment property. Typically, it can be several months before a suitable property is identified and the negotiation of the commercial terms concluded. Second, the most desirable properties are often acquired or disposed of 'off market', and this can impact on available assets in terms of both liquidity and available quality. Third, there is a risk that a vendor may withdraw the property, attempt to procure more favourable terms or simply sell to a third party. Fourth, property acquisition costs are significant. The procuring/acquiring agent often charges the purchaser a fee of typically 1% of the purchase price. In normal circumstances, bank funding/arrangement fees can range anywhere from 0.5% to 1% of the loan amount.

The bank's legal fees must also be met – and again, these are typically up to 0.25% of the loan amount (and sometimes more). A purchaser's own legal fees are usually around 0.5% to 0.75% of the asset price, and valuation fees are around 0.5% of the property's value. Fifth, there is 'stamp duty land tax' (SDLT) to be paid at typically 5% of the gross consideration (where the consideration is above £250,000) and otherwise in accordance with the table and worked example set out below. The SDLT is invariably payable given that stamp duty savings schemes are becoming more limited. The contribution of real estate into a unit trust (eg, a Jersey property unit trust) in consideration of the issue of units in the trust being exempt from SDLT in 2006. This effectively brought an end to the establishment of Jersey property trusts and property trusts established in other jurisdictions for the purposes of saving the SDLT. Other SDLT saving schemes have also largely been closed off.

Property or lease premium or transfer value	SDLT rate
Up to £150,000¶	Zero
The next £100,000 (the portion from £150,001 to £250,000)	2%
The remaining amount (the portion above £250,000)	5%

Example

If you buy a freehold commercial property for £3 million, the SDLT that you owe is calculated as follows:

- 0% on the first £150,000 = £0
- 2% on the next £100,000 = £2,000
- 5% on the final £2,750,000 = £137,500
- Total SDLT = £139,500

Further, transactions involving the corporate acquisition of property-owning companies with the onward transfer of the property to a special purpose vehicle group company are being scrutinised by Her Majesty's Revenue and Customs to ensure that they are effected for good-faith commercial reasons and do not form part of an arrangement for which the main purpose (or one of the main purposes) is the avoidance of the SDLT. Accordingly, acquisition costs for a buyer acquiring commercial property can often be around 8% of the purchase price. For the existing property investor, the cost of disposing of a property is typically around 2% (leaving aside any broken funding costs and the acquisition costs of a new property). In any market, but in particular the current market (which is experiencing sub-5% yields on high-quality commercial investment properties in the United Kingdom), such expenditure is significant and any method of reducing or avoiding these costs will be attractive.

(b)   *Commercial property rental*
A normal commercial market/rack rent institutional lease for a term of 25 years will have a rent review every five years. Nobody knows what the rental market will be like in five years' time. Although most leases provide that rent reviews can move only upwards, it is not uncommon to see no rent increase at the first review, leaving the rent fixed at the same rate for 10 years and the landlord left with uncertainty as to both its future returns and how it will cover its funding costs. This has certainly been the situation since the economic downturn of 2008–2009. In many instances, landlords did not even bother to instigate the rent review process.

From a tenant's perspective, the risk of sizeable future increases in rent at the end of each five-year period can hinder adequate business planning. The common practice of linking rental increases to the Rental Price Index has gone some way towards addressing landlords' and tenants' concerns, but even this approach still leaves the parties in an unhedged position at the mercy of the market. Likewise, a lease that sees rent being linked to a tenant's turnover (a situation not uncommon in the hotel and retail sectors) often sees a landlord's yield being calculated on a basis over which it has little or no control. Additionally, there is the risk that a tenant cannot be found following the exercise of any break clause, leaving the landlord with a period of non-occupation (and no income) and the costs associated with procuring a new tenant.

(c)   *Residential property*
The residential property buyer may wish to buy a residential property for sole use, or may be a company or individual looking to buy one or more properties for letting purposes. Either way, it will face similar costs to the commercial buyer. These costs will be similar in quantum to commercial property costs, except for the SDLT, which

has been increased dramatically on residencies sold in excess of £925,000.

The table below sets out the bands and provides a worked example. Unlike under the previous regime, a purchaser now pays at the stepped rate and not the flat rate – that is, for each £1 over £1.5 million, the purchaser will pay SDLT at 12%.

Property or lease premium or transfer value	SDLT rate
Up to £125,000	Zero
The next £125,000 (the portion from £125,001 to £250,000)	2%
The next £675,000 (the portion from £250,001 to £925,000)	5%
The next £575,000 (the portion from £925,001 to £1.5 million)	10%
The remaining amount (the portion above £1.5 million)	12%

Example
If you buy a house for £800,000, the SDLT you owe is calculated as follows:
- 0% on the first £125,000 = £0
- 2% on the next £125,000 = £2,500
- 5% on the final £550,000 = £27,500
- Total SDLT = £30,000

Furthermore, generally where a purchaser has an existing property that he intends to retain, the additional acquisitions will see a further three percentage points added to each SDLT band. So the highest band will increase from 12% to 15%.

There has been no relief for corporate buyers of residential real estate. Unless the company in question intends to trade, redevelop or rent the property, the SDLT will be calculated at 15% where the price exceeds £500,000. An additional three percentage points will be added, unless the property being bought is subject to a lease that has an unexpired term of more than 21 years or its value is less than £40,000. There may also be an annual property tax which, in the event that the total consideration is less than £500,000, will be between 0% and 3% (as opposed to 4%, which applies to property transactions of £500,000 or more). Additionally, when letting a property, there will be agency costs and the risk of not finding a tenant.

3. What are property derivatives?
Property derivatives recognise that acquiring a physical property involves acquiring a bundle of risks:
- funding risk (that interest rates will go up,[3] minimising any potential returns);

- rental value risk (that rent will go up or down);
- letting risk (that a property cannot be let); and
- capital value risk (that capital value will increase or decrease).

In addition to the bundle of risks, there are the costs accompanying acquisition and disposal.[4] Property derivatives allow the isolation and separate trading of these risks, while reducing the cost burden. To date, property derivatives markets have developed only in capital and rental value risk, but we may see markets developing in the other risk attributes.

The typical property derivatives transaction is a bilateral contract taking the form of either an 'over-the-counter' (OTC) derivative or an embedded derivative in a bond or warrant. Presently, property derivatives are mainly structured as index-linked derivatives, with the amount payable by one party to the other depending on the value of the reference index. This chapter concentrates primarily on index-linked property derivatives, due to the overwhelming focus of the market on these products.

The property index derivatives market has remained disappointingly small compared to the size and performance of the traditional property market. Two principal reasons are the lack of standardised documentation and the lack of a homogenous product.

Property is not homogenous. It is not like a tonne of cocoa or a barrel of oil: a prime office block in the City of London is a different asset from one in the West End. Derivatives are financial instruments that derive their value from an underlying asset. So, to create a homogenous product, the mainstream property derivatives market has selected the value of an index of property values as the underlying asset from which it derives its value.

All OTC property index derivatives transactions involve the parties taking contrary views on the future levels of an index. Each index has a numerical value based on the values of its underlying component properties, just as the FTSE 100 is based on the values of its chosen 100 equity shares. The recent development of a wide range of high-quality property indices (Standard & Poor's and the Office of Federal Housing Enterprise Oversight in the United States, and 'International Property Databank Limited' (IPD) for commercial property and Halifax for residential property in the United Kingdom) has helped to form a homogenous product, leaving a lack of standardised documentation as the market's principal deficiency.

4. The underlying indices

The driving force of the property derivatives market has been transactions where payments are linked to the performance of a reference property index. In the case of commercial property, the benchmark indices are provided by IPD,[5] and for residential property the indices are provided by Halifax. Importantly, neither IPD nor Halifax owns any of the properties in the indices that it compiles, and the parties entering

3   Interest rate risk can also be dealt with through the use of derivatives by entering into an interest rate cap agreement.
4   See above.
5   The IPD was established in 1985 and is an independent organisation.

into a property index-linked swap need not own any of the properties making up the reference index.

4.1 IPD indices

The IPD produces two key indices for the United Kingdom – the UK Annual Property Index and the UK Monthly Property Index – as well as a number of indices for other European countries.[6]

(a) UK Annual Property Index

The UK Annual Property Index was established in the 1980s and has been used for many years by real estate practitioners as a benchmark for a variety of property industry-related matters.[7] Its use as a reference index for property derivatives transactions is a relatively new application.

Every year, the IPD publishes the UK Annual Property Index level for the previous year on or around 1 March. The index took 1980 as its base year[8] and awarded it 100 points. For each year since then, the IPD has published the increase or decrease on the previous year. At the end of 2015, the 23,639 properties covered by the index were valued at £198 billion.[9] Each property is value-weighted to reflect the proportion that its capital value makes up in the index. The index measures the change in valuation[10] (rather than sale price) during a one-year period of its covered assets.

The index has three categories:

- capital growth;
- income return; and
- total return.

'Capital growth' measures the average increase in capital value of each property making up the index, net of all capital investment. 'Income return' measures receivable and accrued rent: an amount gross of portfolio management costs, but net of non-recoverable costs involved in generating the income stream. 'Capital growth' and 'income return' are then added together to give the figure for 'total return'.

The performance of each category is measured against the 'all properties' index. This consists of principal sub-sectors for:

- 'retail', which measures against only the retail properties in the index;
- 'office', which measures against only the office properties in the index;
- 'industrial', which measures against only the industrial properties in the index; and
- 'residential', which measures against only the properties in the index.

---

6   The IPD also produces two other indices which relate to property funds such as the UK Quarterly Property Index.
7   For example, the indices are used by property fund managers as a benchmark to show average investment performance and as market indices as an indicator of overall market performance.
8   Although the index actually tracks price movements back to 1971.
9   IPD UK Annual Property Index Results: Year to 2 December 2015.
10   Valuations are carried out in accordance with the Royal Institute of Chartered Surveyors open market valuation industry standards.

In the results for the year to December 2015, 'retail' had 4,072 properties consisting of standard retail properties in southeast England, standard retail properties in the rest of the United Kingdom, shopping centres and retail warehouses. 'Office' had 2,519 properties, consisting of offices in the City of London, offices in the West End and mid-town London, offices in the rest of southeast England and offices in the rest of the United Kingdom. 'Industrial' had 2,895 properties, consisting of industrial properties in southeast England and industrial properties in the rest of the United Kingdom. 'Residential' had 11,579 properties and 2,574 other general commercial properties.

The IPD also produces an estimated value for the index soon after the year-end, which may be adjusted when the final figures are reported.

When derivatives users use the UK Annual Index as a reference index in their transactions, they may reference the performance of any category (eg, 'income return') and any related sector (eg, 'industrial').

(b) **IPD Monthly Index**

The IPD UK Monthly Index is also value-weighted to reflect the proportion of capital employed by each property, but covers a smaller selection of properties than the UK Annual Index. The index has a 100-point base level set in December 1986.[11] The IPD publishes the index results for the previous month on the 10th working day after the end of that month. The index is divided into the same categories and sub-sectors as the UK Annual Index. The UK Monthly Index is compiled using the same methodology as the UK Annual Index, the only differences being the frequency of compilation and the number of properties referenced.

In September 2016, the index covered 3,258 properties, with a value of over £45 billion. There were 1,345 properties in the retail sector, 750 properties in the office sector and 893 properties in the industrial sector.

Derivatives counterparties reference the UK Monthly Index when they need more frequent market figures than the UK Annual Index allows.

(c) **International indices**

The IPD has produced property indices for Canada, South Africa, Denmark, France, Germany, Italy, Ireland, the Netherlands, Norway, Portugal, Spain and Sweden, as well as a pan-European index.[12] Each country index follows a methodology broadly similar to the UK Annual Index. For example, as at December 2015 the IPD Spanish Databank covered properties in Spain with a total value of €17.6 billion, and reported on capital growth, investment return and total return for the all property, retail, office, industrial and residential sectors.

4.2 Halifax indices

The key residential property index is the Halifax House Price Index, which covers the UK housing market from 1983 onwards. The index captures its data from Halifax

---

11   The July 2010 level for the UK Monthly Index Capital Growth: 'All Properties' was 0.2%.
12   The IPD's non-UK indices are compiled in conjunction with partner organisations.

mortgages and uses this information to assess the UK residential housing market as a whole. The index consists of five main individual indices.[13] These cover both houses (existing, new and all houses) and buyers (first-time buyers and home movers). The indices are seasonally adjusted.[14] For derivatives purposes, the most common index is the seasonally adjusted index for all houses and all buyers. Each index represents the price of a typically transacted house: this is standardised (eg, location, number of rooms, type of property, age of property, tenure) to represent the inherent differences between properties. The index excludes certain types of property which may not reflect market prices, such as sales with sitting tenants or council house sales. Halifax produces both monthly and quarterly figures.

5. Advantages and disadvantages of property derivatives

5.1 Advantages
The advantages are as follows:
- Derivatives can allow a property investor to gain exposure to the property market, while avoiding the high transaction costs and long deal times associated with property acquisition and disposal.
- Investors can enter the property market without a funding obligation and so can participate in the property market without having to acquire any property.
- The national (and in future, potentially international) nature of property derivatives can allow investors to diversify their portfolio to other regions and types of property, which can help to reduce portfolio risk (eg, the underperformance of the retail market against the office market).
- An investor or institution that provides funding and finds itself over-exposed to a particular property sector (eg, a successful developer of office space in the City of London) can hedge itself against a downturn by entering into a contract for difference or property total return sector swap based on the value of retail property. In the future, this may become a requirement of financial institutions providing funding, as they seek to protect their revenue stream.
- An investor can hedge itself against its asset decreasing in value (or rental values declining) and can do so for a specific period of time.
- Investors can short the market, taking advantage of any decrease in capital or rental values, or take a position of taking gains above or below a strike price.
- Investors can view property derivatives as a separate asset class in themselves.

5.2 Disadvantages
The disadvantages are as follows:
- Although the transaction costs involved in using property derivatives are lower than those involved in the traditional property markets,[15] new users

---

13   Halifax also produces 12 regional indices which are published quarterly.
14   This is because prices in the summer tend to be lower than those in the spring.
15   In property derivatives transactions, agents' fees and bid/offer spreads can total 0.75% of a transaction. In addition, legal and other costs may arise.

may need legal advice and training in the use of derivatives. Setting up a derivatives trading platform can be expensive. In particular, for OTC transactions, where the 'International Swaps and Derivatives Association Inc' (ISDA) documentation platform is used, an ISDA Master Agreement will need to be negotiated for each counterparty.

- If not used properly, instead of limiting risk, derivatives can cause excess risk and losses, particularly where investors have failed to put sufficient controls in place. As far as property derivatives transactions are concerned, there is a lack of knowledge in the market generally, both by derivatives practitioners about property and by property practitioners about derivatives.

- There is a lack of liquidity in the market, which periodically means that property derivatives are failing to attract enough investment to create liquidity: the market needs to move from this vicious circle into a virtuous one. In December 2005, the UK Financial Services Authority agreed to allow life insurance companies to include IPD index-linked property forwards and swaps as admissible assets in their calculation of solvency ratios.[16] This may act as a spur to liquidity.[17]

- In addition to market risk in OTC transactions (and, to a more limited extent, in 'property index certificate' (PIC) and warrant transactions), an investor will be taking credit risk in its counterparty.

- A truly successful market must have differing views on its direction. In recent years the development of a property derivatives market has been hampered by a lack of counterparties willing to take a position that the market will decline.

- Property derivatives have reference indices as their underlying asset. Where a derivatives transaction is being entered into to hedge against a specific risk, the performance of the index may not match that of the physical asset being hedged.

6.   Types of property derivative

There are six main types of property derivative:

- 'contracts for differences' (CFDs);
- property total return swaps;
- PICs;
- property-linked warrants;
- property forwards; and
- property futures.

Overwhelmingly, these derivatives use one or more of the aforementioned property reference indices as their underlying asset. Although it is possible to have one or more properties as an underlying asset, no market has developed to date.[18]

---

16   This is particularly significant given that life companies own around 40% of UK commercial properties.
17   Additionally, UK tax law was amended in September 2004 to allow property derivatives to be treated the same as other derivatives.
18   This is partly due to the diligence transaction costs and credit risk which would accompany any such transaction. However, such markets may develop in the future. Other derivatives are widely used in real estate transactions (eg, interest rate cap agreements).

6.1   Property CFDs/total return swaps

(a)   Description

A 'CFD' is a cash-settled bilateral agreement which derives its value from the assessment and settlement of the difference in price of an underlying asset[19] at two points in time.[20] For example, in an equity CFD, the parties could agree to settle each month the difference in a share's price between the current and the previous month. Neither party would be obliged physically to own the underlying share.

One party would take the view that the share's overall price direction was downwards (the short position) and the other that it was upwards (the long position). If the equity CFD had 10,000 Vodafone shares as its underlying asset and the price per share was £0.10 more this month than last month, the party taking the short position would be 'out of the money' and would pay £1,000 (ie, 10,000 × £0.10) to its counterparty. If the following month, Vodafone's share price had declined by £0.05, the party taking the short position would be 'in the money' and would instead receive £500 from its long position counterparty.

In property CFDs, the underlying asset is an index level instead of a share price. The parties settle the contract at periodic intervals on the basis of a formula capturing the difference between current and previous levels of a property reference index.[21] As with equity CFDs, there is no obligation actually to purchase or invest in the underlying asset. A property CFD allows the counterparties to trade the price movement in the property market without tying up capital in physical properties.

Whereas in the equity markets, it is common to find parties willing to take opposing views on overall market direction, property market investors have tended to have a herd mentality, all believing that the market is either on the up or going down. This is now changing, with investors starting to take opposing views,[22] both as to whether the future of the market is up or down and as to the extent of any market movement. This uncertainty means that property owners and financiers are more likely to enter into property CFDs to hedge against either a declining market or minimum market growth. They are likely to find counterparties in property investors wanting to take a long position on the property market.

Where both parties take the view that the general direction of the property market is upwards, but differ in their view of the extent of the increase, they can enter into a property CFD in which the parties settle price movements above or below a strike price (eg, the movement in one year's time above or below a 5% increase on current reference index levels). CFDs are also referred to as 'total return swaps' when documented using ISDA documentation.

---

19   Such as shares, bonds, futures or index levels.
20   The Financial Services and Markets Act 2000 defines a 'contract for difference' more broadly as "a contract, the purpose, or pretended purpose, of which is to secure a profit or avoid a loss". It is market practice to regard only instruments in the narrower definition described above as being CFDs.
21   Investors can select any of the indices or sub-indices described above to gain exposure to particular property markets.
22   In the Investment Property Forum's "Consensus Forecasts Survey of Independent Forecasts UK Property Investment", February 2006, nine forecasters (25% of those sampled) expected property capital values to fall in 2008, whereas a further 12 expected a rise of under 1%.

(b)   OTC documentation platform

In the OTC derivatives market, property CFDs (as well as property total return swaps and property forwards, which are covered below)[23] are documented using the ISDA documentation platform.[24] They use the ISDA Master Agreement and Schedule, together with an individual confirmation for each transaction (which incorporates the 2006 ISDA Definitions).

On 4 May 2007, the ISDA released the ISDA 2007 Property Index Derivatives Definitions, together with two standard templates: a total return swap template and a forward transaction template. The definitions are supplemented by Annex A, which sets out definitions relating to the different index providers.

Each template was provided in two different forms: Form X and Form Y. Form X is meant for use with US property indices and Form Y for use with European property indices.

In each of the two forms of template for total return swaps (which cover synthetic sale and purchases of properties), one party (the total return payer) pays the positive difference in the level of the relevant property index between two dates, with the other party (the total return receiver) paying the amount of any decrease in the value of the index. For example, if the index value has increased from 80 to 85, the total return payer will make a payment based on multiplying this by the transaction's notional amount; if the index value has decreased from 80 to 75, the total return receiver will make a payment based on multiplying this by the transaction's agreed notional amount. This is analogous to the total return receiver having borrowed this sum to invest in the property market, taking the hit on any fall in property values and the benefit of an upward market. The total return payer, by contrast, takes the role of a synthetic lender.

In each of the two template forward contracts, the derivatives transaction is linked to the performance of a specified property index (perhaps the easiest analogy is to think of a share index such as the FTSE 100 going up and down in value over time), with the difference between the present and future value of the index being settled by the 'long party' and the 'short party' on an agreed future date. This template involves the on-selling of future property market risk and is also based on the transaction's agreed notional amount.

The main differences between Form X and Form Y for each transaction type are as follows:

- Form X provides that republication (a reassessment of the index value by the index sponsor) applies, whereas Form Y does not.
- Form X provides that index prices are linked to index publication dates and not agreed index measurement periods, and Form Y the reverse.
- Form X provides that floating rate interest amounts accrue between the relevant index's scheduled publication dates and are payable with the amount linked to the return on the index; however, Form Y provides that

---

23   PICs and property-linked warrants contain similar provisions relating to index disruption and adjustment.
24   Property CFDs traded on a trading platform will use bespoke documentation.

amounts accrue during index measurement periods and are payable on the dates specified by the parties.

The 2007 ISDA Property Index Derivatives Definitions fit into ISDA's standard documentation infrastructure. Under this infrastructure, the parties enter into an ISDA Master Agreement (the set of standard terms for derivatives transactions), amended by a schedule (a document setting out the specified variations). They can enter into one of the two categories and forms of template property index derivative confirmation described above (although they may of course create their own template confirmation). This confirmation will incorporate the agreed Master Agreement and the 2007 Property Index Derivatives Definitions. The parties may also choose to provide collateral to control their exposure to each other in the event of a default or termination, under a credit support annex to the Master Agreement.

The value of the ISDA standard terms definitions booklets and template confirmations is that they provide boilerplate market-standard language and definitions, saving parties the cost of developing and negotiating their own templates, and providing market liquidity.

The 2007 Property Index Derivatives Definitions consist of two articles and an annex:

- Article I, which covers general definitions and interpretations;
- Article II, which covers adjustments and disruptions to the index; and
- Annex A, which provides descriptions of the most commonly used indices and index providers.

Article I provides general definitions for defining and determining:

- the price of the index;
- when it is published;
- what events may constitute an 'index disruption event';
- the identity and the role of the index sponsor;
- the amounts payable by each party; and
- when those payments must be made.

Article II provides a series of fallbacks for adjustments and disruptions. These cover how to deal with a rebasing of the index, what happens if there is a delay in publication and what happens when an index disruption event occurs.

Annex A sets out descriptions of the most commonly traded indices. The annex is updated from time to time and parties incorporating the definitions into a transaction will be deemed to be incorporating the most up-to-date annex. The current version sets out shorthand index names for 23 Standard & Poor's Case-Schiller indices, 11 Office of Federal Housing Enterprise and Oversight indices and the Halifax Price Index, as well as setting out names and disclaimers for the IPD and the National Council of Real Estate Investment Fiduciaries.

(c)   *Fallback provisions: adjustment and disruption events*
Property index derivatives transactions provide two fallback categories, depending

on the reasons why the reference index cannot be calculated. The first fallback category ('adjustment events') involves the property index sponsor adjusting the index to take account of:
- rebasing;
- a manifest error in publication; or
- a publication delay.

The second fallback category ('disruption events') involves the index being permanently disrupted and ceasing to exist.

Index adjustment events: Index adjustment events generally relate to three categories:
- Rebasing of the reference index – if the underlying index is rebased, the calculation agent will make adjustments to the transaction so that the rebased index reflects the reference index's historical performance pre-rebasing.
- Manifest error in publication – if the index sponsor makes a calculation error, the calculation agent[25] will make corresponding adjustments to the transaction. Usually, the calculation agent will be required to notify the parties of the error and adjust the terms of the transaction accordingly, and the party that has received any excess payment will be required to repay the excess, plus interest.
- Delay in publication – if the index sponsor does not publish a price for the index on the valuation date, various fallbacks will be triggered. Normally, the parties will select a timeline so that if publication is delayed but the index is published within x days, the payment dates shall be deferred until after the publication date.

If the index sponsor does not publish a final price for the index within the agreed number of days and the index sponsor has published a provisional price within this period, that price shall apply.

If the index sponsor publishes no price within this period (ie, neither a final nor provisional price), it is deemed that the index is disrupted, a 'delayed publication event' has occurred and the index disruption events apply.

Index disruption events: An index disruption event can occur:
- due to a delayed publication event;
- if the index sponsor stops calculating or publishing the index; or
- if the calculation agent decides that the index sponsor has materially changed the index or the methodology for calculating it.

If a disruption event occurs, the parties will try to agree on a substitute index.

---

25   The calculation agent will usually be one of the parties to the transaction. In the case of property index certificates and property-linked warrants, this will be the financial institution issuing the security (or one of its affiliates).

Once a new index is in place, the calculation agent will make any necessary adjustments to the transaction. If the parties cannot agree on a substitute index, the transaction will terminate.[26]

Example: property CFD transaction

Cardiff Richard is a UK pension fund wanting property market exposure. It already has a physical property portfolio and is now looking to invest in property derivatives linked to retail properties, instead of making a traditional retail real estate investment. Its aim is to acquire a distinct asset class and try to reduce its property investment cost base. Cardiff Richard's analysts believe that over the next year, returns on retail property will average between 4% and 7%.

The company's broker introduces it to Ardargie, one of the United Kingdom's largest construction companies. Ardargie is engaged in three large shopping centre construction projects and expects to agree their sale in a year's time. To make an investment return, Ardargie cannot support a decrease in retail market capital values, and to ensure this it is prepared to enter into a hedging transaction and forgo any market increases above 4%. Ardargie and Cardiff Richard agree to enter into a one-year CFD using the IPD UK Annual Index's 'all retail' category and 'capital value' sector as a reference index.

The transaction has a notional amount of £200 million, roughly equal to the project costs of Ardargie's three shopping centres. The parties agree that at maturity, if the reference index has risen by more than 4%, Ardargie will pay the amount of any gains over this level to Cardiff Richard, and if the reference index has not increased by 4% (or has declined in value), Cardiff Richard will pay the percentage amount below a 4% increase to Ardargie. On the first day of the agreement, the index level stands at 1,600. By the maturity date, the reference index has risen to 1,700 – a 6.25% rise.

The difference between the strike price of 4% and the final price of the reference index is 2.25 percentage points. This is multiplied by the notional amount of £200 million to give the amount which Arargie pays to Cardiff Richard: £4.5 million. Ardargie agrees the sale of its three shopping centres at the same time as the maturity date of the CFD. The shopping centres have risen in value in line with the reference index[27] and, although Ardargie has had to make a large payment to Cardiff Richard, it was able to hedge its position. As to Cardiff Richard, it was able to invest in the retail property market without tying up capital.

6.2   Property total return swaps

Property total return swaps fall into two categories:

- synthetic sale and purchases, which swap a property amount with an interest rate amount; and

---

26   The termination will take place as if there had been an additional termination event under the ISDA Master Agreement, with both parties as the affected parties and the transaction as the sole affected transaction. Market quotation will be used as the applicable payment measure to calculate the close-out amount.

27   In reality, one of the weaknesses of using property index derivatives as a hedging tool is that individual properties may not correlate in value to the reference index.

- sector swaps, which exchange the returns on different property indices[28] (eg, the IPD UK Annual Index for 'total return' and 'all retail', and the IPD UK Annual Index for 'total return' and 'all industrial').

(a)   *Synthetic sale and purchase property total return swaps*

In a synthetic sale and purchase property total return swap, one party (the total return payer) will hold an amount of physical property and wish to hedge itself against movements in the property market.[29] The other party (the total return receiver)[30] will wish to make a synthetic investment in the property market, but also to avoid the transaction costs and complications involved in purchasing a physical asset.

The property amount leg is structured as a CFD, referenced to an underlying property reference index (not any actual physical asset). This leg of the swap will perform as per a CFD. There will be no strike price and, on a periodic basis, the total return payer will pay the receiver the amount of any increase in the reference index. In turn, the total return receiver will pay the payer the amount of any decrease in the index.[31] In the interest rate leg of the swap, the total return receiver will pay the payer a fixed or floating rate of interest on the notional amount of the swap. In this way, a synthetic sale and purchase has been made. The total return payer has made a synthetic sale of the notional amount of the swap. It will be compensated for any decrease in the overall value of the property market, and although it must pay amounts equal to the positive increase[32] in the property market, the property that it is hedging should also increase in value.[33]

The total return receiver makes its synthetic purchase by paying interest on the notional amount of the swap to the payer. This is analogous to the total return receiver having borrowed the sum to invest in the property market. Like a traditional investment, it will enjoy the gains in the property market and suffer the losses.

Example: property total return swap

Lobos Limited, a life insurance company, has £400 million of exposure to the UK

---

28   This second category does not fall within the standard definition of 'total return swap', but market usage has meant that it is increasingly classified as being a total return swap rather than an index swap.
29   It is unlikely to be a condition of any transaction that the property return party making the synthetic sale actually holds any physical assets (and, indeed, no physical asset will be referenced in the confirmation), as the property leg of the swap will be referenced to a property reference index. However, the main motivation for the total return payer entering into a synthetic sale and purchase property total return swap will be to isolate itself from property market movements.
30   Standard documentation will not usually refer to the parties as 'total return payer' and 'total return receiver'. However, for the purposes of this chapter, these definitions are used to show the respective positions that the parties are taking and draw an analogy with total return payers and receivers in bond and loan total return swaps.
31   The amount of any increase or decrease will be captured through a formula set out in the confirmation.
32   As with all index-linked property derivatives, the transaction will be an imperfect hedge, because the actual movements in value of any physical properties being hedged may not correlate with movements in the reference index.
33   This is a crucial difference from a bond or loan total return swap, and occurs because the total return is on the reference index rather than a physical property. The transaction assumes, though, that the total return payer is compensated by a corresponding increase in the value of the property being hedged (however, see footnote 37).

property market. It wants to reduce this by £200 million as soon as possible, but at the same time wants to choose the right moment to sell such a significant part of its property portfolio. Freeland Corporation is looking to gain £200 million of exposure to the UK property market, but does not want to be exposed to the high transaction costs and liquidity issues involved in traditional property transactions. Lobos and Freeland enter into a synthetic purchase and sale property total return swap.

The swap has a notional amount of £200 million (the same amount by which Lobos is seeking to reduce its exposure to the UK property market). There will be no exchange of principal and Freeland will pay Lobos three months of GBP-LIBOR-BBA plus 1% on the £200 million notional amount each quarter. This is the same amount as if Freeland Bank had actually borrowed £200 million or Lobos had placed this amount on deposit following a sale. Lobos, for its part, will then pay Freeland Bank, on a periodic basis, the total positive return of the IPD UK Annual All Properties Index multiplied by £200 million, calculated in accordance with a formula.

Freeland, in turn, must pay the amount of any decrease in the reference index to Lobos. The effect of the transaction is to create a synthetic sale of £200 million of Lobos's property portfolio to Freeland Bank. When the transaction terminates, Lobos will still have its property portfolio, but will have been insulated against market movements in the meantime.[34]

(b) Property total return sector swaps

In a property total return sector swap, the parties exchange the total return on two different property reference indices. For example, total returns on the IPD sector indices in the United Kingdom for industrial, office and retail property can vary widely. A property total return sector swap can act as a valuable tool for diversifying risk by allowing a party that wants to reduce its exposure to one particular sector (eg, perhaps it has a particularly successful industrial property portfolio) to do so by synthetically increasing its exposure to another (eg, the retail property sector). A transaction will be structured with two legs, one representing each sector (eg, a total return on the industrial property sector leg and a total return on the retail sector leg). Each leg will be structured as a property CFD, with the difference in value being netted on any payment date.

Example: property total return sector swap

Thornbank Properties has been a success story in the office development market. Its winning team has created a string of successful flagship office developments in the last five years. Unfortunately, it has been a victim of its own success. Some 95% of its £1 billion portfolio consists of office space. Although, like all property companies, it is vulnerable to a downturn in the property market, it is particularly vulnerable to a downturn in the office market.

Bridge of Earn Investments has been similarly successful in the retail property

---

34   If Lobos decides not to sell its portfolio, the transaction will have allowed Lobos to 'sit out' of the property market during the transaction's term and later re-enter the market without incurring acquisition and disposal costs.

field. It has a property portfolio of £600 million, £500 million of which is in retail property. The companies are introduced to each other by their brokers and agree to enter into a total return swap whereby each party will offset £100 million of risk from its most dominant portfolio. Each leg of the swap is structured as a CFD.

In the first leg, Thornbank will pay Bridge of Earn the total return on the IPD UK All Office Total Return Index. Thornbank will pay Bridge of Earn any increase in the index and Bridge of Earn will pay Thornbank any decrease.

In the second leg, Bridge of Earn will pay Thornbank the total return on the IPD UK All Retail Total Return Index. Bridge of Earn will pay Thornbank the value of any decrease. All payments will be netted on each payment date. The parties have successfully used a property total return sector swap to diversify their property portfolio risk.

6.3   PICs

A 'PIC' is a bond with an embedded property derivative. It is usually issued by financial institutions and listed on a stock exchange.[35] A PIC is a direct unsecured obligation of its issuer and gains its derivatives element through linkage to an underlying property index (usually one of the sectors of the IPD UK Annual Index).[36]

On the issue date, the bondholder will pay the issuer the bond's principal amount. In return, the bondholder will receive both an income return, in the form of a coupon, and a capital return on the bond's maturity through the issuer returning an amount of principal greater or lesser than the original amount.[37] Both income and capital returns are linked to the performance of the reference index, in each case less various administrative expenses. PICs contain similar index and adjustment events to those in property index-linked OTC transactions.

(a)   Income return

A bondholder receives an income return through a coupon. This may be payable quarterly, semi-annually or annually. The coupon is based on the return from the annual index[38] (subject to a minimum of zero), multiplied by the bond's outstanding principal amount.

(b)   Capital return

The outstanding principal amount of the bonds is adjusted periodically to reflect the return on the index. Depending on whether the index has gone up or down, the bondholder will receive a greater or lesser amount of its principal amount at maturity. Future coupon payments are also calculated on the basis of the adjusted principal amount.

---

35   Barclays PICs are listed on the London Stock Exchange and are issued pursuant to the bank's structured note programme.
36   For example, Barclays Bank PLC's issue of Series 3649 £200 million property index certificates due 31 March 2008 is linked to the IPD All Property Total Return Index.
37   Coupon payments may have to be adjusted where payments are made on the basis of an estimated index level. Where a final coupon payment would otherwise be based on an estimated index amount, instead a LIBOR-based amount will be paid.
38   Pursuant to the requirements of the EU Prospectus Directive (2003/71/EC).

Example: PIC

Strath Bank issues £50 million PICs, due 14 April 2009. The PICs are documented under Strath Bank's structured note programme and the issuing document takes the form of final terms.[39] The PICs are linked to the performance of the IPD UK Annual All Properties Index and are listed on the London Stock Exchange. The PICs are issued on 14 April 2006. The entire issue is subscribed by Imen Investments, a life insurance company. Imen Investments is attracted to the PICs because:

- its internal rules permit it to purchase only listed financial instruments issued by a rated company (Strath Bank has an AA rating);
- the bonds will form a separate asset class from its other investments;
- Strath Bank is making a secondary market in the PICs; and
- it sees cost benefits in accessing the property market through PICs rather than a traditional property investment.

The PICs pay a quarterly coupon based on the value of the reference index multiplied by the PICs' outstanding principal amount. From this amount, Strath Bank subtracts its administration costs. Each year the PICs' outstanding principal amount is adjusted upwards or downwards in line with the level of the reference index and future coupon payments are calculated accordingly. At maturity, the reference index has declined in value by 10% and Imen Investments receives less than its original investment back.

(c) **Advantages and disadvantages**

A PIC gives its holder some of the benefits of actually holding a physical property: a cash sum is invested and the holder takes the benefit of an overall rise or the burden of a decline in the property market, but without the downside of actual property ownership. Other advantages include:

- the issuer's credit quality;[40]
- low transaction costs;
- a secondary market;[41]
- price transparency; and
- the holding of listed securities issued by a rated issuer.[42]

The main downside of PICs is that the investor must tie up capital while investing in the property market.

6.4 Property-linked index warrants

A warrant is a tradable, listed security issued by a financial institution. In return for

---

39 Including that the securities have been issued by a rated issuer.
40 Press release by Protego Real Estate Investors, 10 October 2005, "Protego Transacts the First Significant Secondary Market Trade in Property Derivatives", disclosing a secondary market transaction for £8 million PICs.
41 This is an important criterion for many institutions.
42 For example, Goldman Sachs introduced a series of warrants linked to the value of the Halifax 'All Houses', 'All Buyers', Standardised Average House Price (Seasonally Adjusted) Index for the United Kingdom in June 2006 (Goldman Sachs Warrants & Certificates: Property Linked Warrants & Certificates, August 2004).

a premium, it gives its holder the right, but not the obligation, to buy (in the case of a call warrant) or sell (in the case of a put warrant) a specified quantity of an underlying asset on a future date or dates, at an agreed exercise price (the strike price). With put warrants, if the actual price at the exercise date is below the strike price, the holder will be out of the money and the warrant will be worthless. This is because the holder will have the right to sell the underlying asset only at the strike price and this will be below the market price, so only sale at a loss will be possible.

Conversely, with call warrants, if the actual price at the exercise date is above the strike price, the warrant will be worthless because the holder will have the right to buy the underlying asset only at above the market price. Warrants are leveraged securities because movements in the price of the underlying asset cause greater increases or decreases in the relative value of the warrant. The downside for the warrant investor is limited only to the price of the warrant. London Stock Exchange rules require that the issuing bank make a market in the warrants. All trades are executed through a broker. Property-linked warrants are cash-settled instruments that are linked to and attempt to replicate the performance of an underlying property reference index.[43]

Examples to date have used the Halifax house price indices. A typical issue of warrants will take the average house price today according to a reference index and adjust it to take account of a strike price. To create an underlying asset, the warrant will divide the average house price (according to the reference index) plus any strike price by 1,000. This would mean, for example, that if the average house price according to the reference index were £100,000 and a warrant's strike price were 110%, in a warrant issue £110,000 would be divided by 1,000, so that each warrant would give the right to buy or sell (depending on whether it was a put or call warrant) one-thousandth of an 'average house' for £1.10 on the warrant's expiry date. The initial price of the warrant will depend on how attractive buying one-thousandth of an average house for £1.10 on the expiry date is likely to be.[44] During the term of the warrant, its tradable price will go up or down depending on the level; if the price of the average house went up to £150,000, the warrant would give the right to purchase one-thousandth of an average house for £1.10, even though one-thousandth of an average house would now be worth £1.50. This would make a put warrant worth £0.40 per warrant[45] and a call warrant worthless. Had the initial price of the warrant issue been £0.20 per warrant, the warrants would now be trading at least £0.20 higher than the issue price[46] – a 100% rise in value, even though the price of the underlying asset had risen by only 36.3%.[47]

(a) Advantages

Call and put warrants allow investors to take either short or long positions on future

---

43   Warrants are cash settled so no physical amount is ever transferred.
44   Subject to any transaction costs.
45   The actual trading price would also take account of the market view, at that point in time, of future price movements.
46   This demonstrates the leverage of property-linked warrants.
47   The reference index represents the property market as a whole. Other local factors may mean that properties do not stimulate movements in the reference index.

property market movements. They benefit from the tax benefits and low transaction costs of other derivatives products, as well as the reduced credit risk involved in purchasing instruments from a rated financial institution. The London Stock Exchange rules requiring the warrant issuer to provide continuous two-way warrant prices provide market liquidity. Warrant holders can benefit from low and flexible transaction sizes – for example, a single warrant can cost as little as a few pence. As a leverage investment, if an investor has a strong view on future market direction, it can maximise profits to a far greater extent with warrants than through a traditional property investment.

(b)   *Disadvantages*

The main disadvantage of a warrant is also one of its key advantages: leverage. Investors are 'betting the house' because if a strike price is not reached, the investor will lose 100% of its investment. Additionally, because warrants track the average UK house price, like any index-linked property derivatives any actual risk being hedged in relation to specific properties may not be covered where the performance of the asset being hedged does not match that of the reference index due to local factors.

> **Example: put warrant**
>
> John owns a residential property in Manchester, which he bought for £100,000 in February 2011. According to the Halifax index, an average house in the Greater Manchester region valued at £100,000 in the first quarter of 2011 would be worth just over £160,000 in the first quarter of 2016. John is planning to emigrate to Germany in two years' time and is worried that the local residential property market may be overheated. He does not want to be caught between a potentially future booming German market and a slumped UK market, and although he is prepared to risk some decline in property values, he is concerned that a large decline will not leave him with enough money to buy a suitable property in Germany.
>
> To protect himself, John purchases put warrants linked to a Halifax property reference index from Rothesay Bank. At the purchase date, John's house is worth the same as the UK average house price according to the reference index: £160,000. The warrants are trading at £0.25 per warrant and each warrant effectively gives John the right to sell one-thousandth of a notional average house for £1.65 in two years' time. John buys 100,000 warrants for £25,000.
>
> Following John's purchase, his fears prove correct and the UK housing market suffers a large decline in value; by the warrant's exercise date, the reference index has declined by 30%, leaving the average price of a UK residential property at £112,000. John's 100,000 warrants are now worth £37,000 – that is, the strike price less the final price, so £0.37 per warrant. When John sells his property for £112,000 prior to emigrating, he has been partially hedged against the decline in property values by the warrants, so that his losses have been limited to a maximum of £25,000.

Example: call warrant

Eduardo, a trainee solicitor, wishes to take advantage of the rising property market, but although confident that after he qualifies he will earn enough money to buy a suitable property, his current salary will not generate a suitable multiple to obtain a mortgage. Worried that property prices may rise significantly in the meantime and that he will be unable to get onto the property ladder, he decides to purchase warrants that give him the right to buy a notional property for £160,000. As with a put warrant, 100,000 warrants must be exercised to equal the value of the reference index.

Through his broker, Eduardo arranges to buy call warrants issued by Rothesay Bank. The warrants have a strike price of £1.65, are trading at £0.15 per warrant and are exercisable in two years' time in 2008. Eduardo is therefore paying £15,000 (ie, 1,000 warrants at £0.15 each) for the right to buy a notional house at £160,000. If Eduardo buys a house in 2008 and the average house price is above £175,000 (ie, £160,000 plus the £15,000 cost of the warrants), the warrants will have been a good investment. When the warrants are exercised, the average UK house price has in fact risen to £200,000 and Eduardo (who has now qualified as a solicitor) is in a position to purchase a property. Through the warrants, he has the right to purchase the notional house for £160,000, meaning that the call warrants are worth £40,000. This amount is divided by 1,000, giving the warrants a value of £0.40 each. The gearing effect of the warrants means that they have risen in value by 266%, even though average house prices have increased by only 25%. If house prices had decreased, however, the warrants would have been worthless.

6.5 Forward transactions

Property derivatives forwards are the newest additions to the property derivatives product portfolio, with the first transactions having been carried out in the second half of 2005. A property derivatives forward transaction involves two counterparties entering into a derivatives transaction linked to the performance of a property index, but with differences being settled or exchange occurring only from a future date onwards.[48] To a certain extent, all property derivatives transactions are forward transactions, in that each settlement date occurs in the future on the basis of either an agreed price or a formula that agrees a future price. However, the market usage of this term in relation to property derivatives involves the on-selling of property market risk from an existing transaction.

Example: forward transaction

Mina Estates, a property developer, enters into a property derivatives forward transaction with Woodlands Trustees, a pension fund. Mina had previously entered

---

48   Other attempts to establish a market were made around the same period, in particular with property income certificates (which included single asset property companies and single property ownership trusts). However, these initiatives were more similar to property securitisations and cannot really be considered to be property derivatives.

into a three-year synthetic sale and purchase total return swap with Lexington Bank with a notional amount of £50 million. Mina enters into a back-to-back transaction with Woodlands Trustees for the second and third years of the swap, whereby Woodlands receives each payment that Mina receives under its transaction with Lexington and Woodlands pays the equivalent of each payment that Mina must make to Lexington. The effect of the transaction is that Mina has forward sold the second and third years of its property total return swap with Lexington.

6.6 Futures transaction

A future is an exchange-traded forward contract. A futures contract will, however, contain a standardised package of terms and have a set settlement date.

Property futures can be transacted in varying sizes, with a common minimum size of £50,000. They are also more liquid that other instruments, allowing an easier transaction exit. The asset class is though much less liquid than other asset classes.

7. Status of the property derivatives market

7.1 Early attempts to establish a market

The first attempt to establish a property derivatives market was made in 1991,[49] when the London Futures and Options Exchange introduced exchange-traded property futures. In all, there were four tradable contracts: two were linked to residential property prices and based on the value of the Nationwide Anglia Building Society House Price Index; the other two were linked to mortgage rates and based on the value of the exchange's mortgage interest rate index. Five months after their introduction, having failed to gain sufficient trading volumes, the contracts were suspended. The project failed mainly because of the time lags relating to the underlying indices, combined with high transaction costs. The market began in earnest again in 2005.

7.2 Current market drivers: the Property Derivatives Interest Group

The Property Derivatives Interest Group (formerly known as the Property Derivatives Users Association) is a non-profit organisation promoting the use and market development of property derivatives, as well as providing support to market participants. It is a sub-group of the Investment Property Forum, an independent membership organisation which aims to improve property investments awareness, understanding and efficiency.

7.3 Future development of property derivatives

The property derivatives market remains at a nascent stage, and has disappointed in

---

49   Quintain Estates and Development plc was reported to have entered into a transaction which forward sold a property derivatives contract to a pension fund ("Property Derivatives: the first forward sales", PLC, November 2005 Edition). Quintain entered into a three-year property index-linked swap with Barclays Bank with a notional amount of £15 million. It then forward sold the second and third years of the swap to the pension company. Quintain was able to take advantage of more competitive pricing than would have been available for a one-year swap.

its development in the past 10 years. Whether it goes on to become a mainstream derivatives market will primarily depend on liquidity, market understanding, the diversification of indices and their regularity of calculation. It is likely that the property derivatives market will continue to focus on index-based derivatives. However, as reporting and sophistication increase, those indices will become increasingly specialised (eg, perhaps a tradable index related to Bristol city centre retail property could be traded against Newcastle city centre industrial property in a property total return sector swap); if sufficient liquidity is gained, a successful exchange-traded futures market may even develop.[50]

Other index developments could include a developments index, which takes account of development costs in an index. This would enable developers to hedge against the rising costs of developments so that they could adequately assess the profitability of a proposed development. Within such an index there could be sub-indices dealing with the types of building being constructed and their locations, to take into account variables that are geographically specific. For those landlords that base their rent on turnover (eg, in hotels or retail), again, specific indices dealing with these types of property could develop. Banks and other institutions providing the finance in property transactions may also become increasingly interested in exploring property derivatives, and may incorporate property derivatives as a hedging strategy in much the same way that interest rate and credit derivatives are used today. In terms of the existing indices, we are also likely to see improvements in the timing of publication, such that there is an IPD UK Quarterly Index in place of the IPD UK Annual Index.

---

50   Other attempts to establish a market were made around the same period, in particular with property income certificates (which included single asset property companies and single property ownership trusts). However, these initiatives were more similar to property securitisations and cannot really be considered to be property derivatives.

About the authors

Paul Ali

Associate professor, Melbourne Law School,
University of Melbourne
p.ali@unimelb.edu.au

Paul Ali is an associate professor in Melbourne Law School, University of Melbourne, and a member of Melbourne Law School's Centre for Corporate Law and Securities Regulation.

Dr Ali has published widely on banking and finance law. He has worked in the banking and finance and corporate groups of two leading Australian law firms. He has also worked in the securitisation team of a major US bank, and has been a principal of a private capital firm and a consultant with a corporate governance advisory firm.

Natalie Ashford

Registered foreign lawyer, Mayer Brown
natalie.ashford@mayerbrownjsm.com

Natalie Ashford is a registered foreign lawyer (England and Wales) in the Hong Kong office of Mayer Brown JSM's finance practice.

Prior to joining Mayer Brown in Hong Kong, Ms Ashford worked in the firm's London finance practice. She also spent six months on secondment to Mayer Brown's New York finance practice and a further six months on secondment to a global bank in Hong Kong.

Ms Ashford focuses on all areas of banking and finance law and has gained experience in a range of complex, cross-border transactions including real estate and project financings, and securitisations. She has acted for major banks and financial institutions, as well as private equity funds and private companies.

Christopher Clancy

Managing director, KYOS Energy Consulting
North America
clancy@kyos.com

Christopher Clancy is managing director of KYOS Energy Consulting North America. He has worked as a senior quantitative analyst at NextEra Energy in Houston, Texas and Juno Beach, Florida. Previous to that, he worked in London as a quantitative analyst with Entergy-Koch Trading Europe. Mr Clancy has over 10 years of applied experience in the European and North American gas, power and weather markets. In addition, he was co-awarded a wind energy risk management patent in the United Kingdom, the United States and Australia.

Mr Clancy has a graduate degree in economics from Emory University in Atlanta, Georgia.
This biography remains unchanged since the last edition.

Cyriel de Jong

Director, KYOS Energy Consulting
dejong@kyos.com

Cyriel de Jong is founder and director at KYOS Energy Consulting, located in Haarlem, the Netherlands. He has been working as an adviser for the energy industry since 2001. Until 2006, he combined this with a position at Erasmus University Rotterdam.

He completed his MSc in Econometrics at Maastricht University, and finished his PhD at Erasmus University Rotterdam in 2003. His research focused on derivatives pricing and market volatility, with publications in the *Journal of Business* and the *Journal of Derivatives*.

KYOS provides quality pricing and risk management software to the energy sector as well as to companies active in other commodity markets. For the major utility companies in Europe, Cyriel de Jong has led a great number of projects related to energy market valuation, risk management, trading strategies and investment analysis. KYOS's financial models to value energy assets and contracts are based on solid stochastic optimisation methods and Monte Carlo simulation techniques. The applications are widely used by utility companies, investment banks, commodity trading houses, industrial companies, regulators and policy makers.

John D Finnerty
Managing director, AlixPartners LLP
jfinnerty@alixpartners.com

John D Finnerty is a managing director at AlixPartners specialising in valuation and hedging. He has developed innovative derivatives models for calculating a lack of marketability discount and valuing employee stock options, convertible debt and venture capital preferred stock.

Mr Finnerty is also professor of finance at Fordham University's Gabelli School of Business and was founding director of the master of science in quantitative finance programme. He has written 15 books and over 100 articles. He is a former editor of *Financial Management* and *FMA Online*.

Mr Finnerty received a PhD in operations research from Naval Postgraduate School, an MA in economics from Cambridge University and a BA in mathematics from Williams College. He was inducted into the Fixed Income Analysts Society Hall of Fame in 2011.

Ruth Frederick
Senior legal counsel

Ruth Frederick is a senior lawyer based, over the past five years, in the London office of a global asset management firm. Ruth supports the UK Fixed Income and Equity Divisions advising on a broad range of matters including European and cross-border regulation, derivatives, trading and investment compliance.

Prior to working in asset management, Ruth worked at Sidley Austin LLP in London where she acted for banks and financial institutions on a range of cross-border structured finance transactions with a particular emphasis on credit derivatives.

Ruth also has extensive experience in debt capital markets, cash and synthetic securitisations, general banking, insolvency and restructurings and cross-border asset backed financings. Ruth was seconded to Credit Suisse, London where she advised on restructurings, vendor financing transactions and emerging market credit linked trades. Ruth has lived and worked in Germany and Singapore and holds a BSc in Computer Science.

David Johnson
Associate general counsel – treasury and global markets, First Abu Dhabi Bank PJSC
David.Johnson@fgb.ae

David Johnson is a derivatives and structured finance lawyer and is currently the senior legal counsel responsible for supporting the treasury and global markets business at First Abu Dhabi Bank PJSC.

Mr Johnson's diverse experience developed while working on a range of structured finance transactions. He specialises in derivatives, securitisation and secured lending transactions.

He is a frequent contributor to legal publications and has written on a variety of derivatives topics, including articles discussing repurchasing transactions, closing-out

International Swaps and Derivatives Association Inc (ISDA) Master Agreements, the 2014 ISDA Credit Derivatives Definitions and repackaging transactions.

Paul O Oranika
Chief executive officer, Africa Business World
oranika@aol.com

Paul Oranika is the founder and chief executive officer of Africa Business World, an online business database and news services company based in Atlanta, Georgia. For over eight years, Mr Oranika taught political science at Grand Canyon University in Phoenix, Arizona and public administration at Central Michigan University in Mt Pleasant, Michigan.

He is the author of five books, including *Nigeria: One Nation, Two Systems*; *Hedge Funds: Investment Vehicles for the Global Economy*; and *Stock Market Trading: Beginner's Guide for Profitable Trading*.

Rachael W Park
Director, AlixPartners LLP
wpark@alixpartners.com

Rachael W Park is a director in AlixPartners' financial advisory services practice based in New York. She holds an MBA in finance and information systems and a Master of Science in quantitative finance. She has over 15 years of business experience, including eight years of economic valuation and litigation support experience.

Rachael has been involved in a wide variety of finance and economic projects, such as business valuation, securities valuation, solvency analysis, credit analysis and quantitative analysis. She specialises in valuing securities, including equity derivatives, fixed-income derivatives, structured finance products, restricted stocks, hybrid securities and other complex derivative instruments.

Rachael has been engaged in a number of litigation matters, such as securities valuation disputes, fair market value disputes, 10b-5 and Section 11 securities fraud litigation and tax fraud litigation.

Edmund Parker
Global head, Derivatives and Structured Products Practice, Mayer Brown
eparker@mayerbrown.com

Edmund ("Ed") Parker is global head of Mayer Brown's Derivatives and Structured Products practice, head of the firm's Banking and Finance practice in London, and serves on Mayer Brown's Partnership Board. Consistently ranked as a key individual and receiving strong market praise from the legal directories, the most recent sources say that Ed "enjoys a reputation as one of the City's leading lawyers". Clients appreciate his "unrivalled breadth and depth of knowledge across all asset classes" and regard him as "one of the lawyers who knows the most about derivatives – he wrote the book on them" (Chambers UK 2015). Ed is also described as "very user-friendly and very easy to deal with", with the same source adding that "he really knows his stuff" and is "a leader in his field". Ed was nominated for Derivatives Lawyer of the Year at the 2014 Global Capital Derivatives Awards.

Ed is the industry's most widely published lawyer on derivatives matters, with his views regularly sought by the press and on television. In addition to this book, his written works include four derivatives books, consisting of: as sole author, *Credit Derivatives: Understanding and Working with the 2014 ISDA Credit Derivatives Definitions* and *Credit Derivatives: Documenting and Understanding Credit Derivative Products*; as sole editor, *Equity Derivatives: Documenting and Understanding Equity Derivative Products*; and as co-editor, *Commodity Derivatives: Documenting and Understanding Commodity Derivative Products*.

Marcin Perzanowski
Of counsel, Mayer Brown
mperzanowski@mayerbrown.com

Marcin Perzanowski is an of counsel in the Derivatives and Structured Products Group in the London office of Mayer Brown. He has extensive experience in advising on a broad range of derivatives and structured finance transactions for banks, corporates, funds, pension schemes and insurance companies. Marcin regularly advises his clients in relation to financings structured as total return swaps, repos, securities loans and margin loans, with underlying in the form of shares, bonds and loans, and with various types of custody and collateralisation structures. He often works on investment products, such as credit linked notes or instruments referencing proprietary indices, and has advised on a number of complex derivatives transactions across several asset classes (including equity derivatives, credit derivatives, commodities, as well as FX and interest rates derivatives).

Marcin has been described by his clients as "a star in the making", "phenomenally able" and "clearly on the partnership trail", with another source adding that they were "pleased with [his] intellect and responsiveness". In addition to this book, his written works include: several chapters in *Equity Derivatives: Documenting and Understanding Equity Derivative Products*, two chapters in *Sovereign Debt and Debt Restructuring*, and he also co-edited *Commodity Derivatives: Documenting and Understanding Commodity Derivative Products*.

Emmett Peters
Partner, Addleshaw Goddard LLP
Emmett.Peters@addleshawgoddard.com

Emmett Peters has been a partner in Addleshaw Goddard's real estate division since 2005 and since 2014 has led the firm's London real estate team. Emmett has experience in acquisitions, disposals, debt funding and asset management as well as advising on property holding structures both on and offshore.

Emmett acts for investors, including institutions and private companies, and developers on a wide variety of matters. Emmett also acts for a number of banks lending both development and acquisition finance and has considerable experience in funding ground rent portfolios.

Addleshaw Goddard is an international law firm committed to delivering outstanding value and providing innovative commercial solutions to its clients' most demanding and complex legal issues. As one of the firm's key areas of expertise, real estate is at the heart of its operations.

Patrick Scholl
Partner, Mayer Brown
pscholl@mayerbrown.com

Patrick Scholl is a partner in the Frankfurt office of Mayer Brown. He has over 10 years of experience in banking and finance practice.

Dr Scholl advises on all aspects of debt capital markets products, over-the-counter (OTC) derivatives, all kinds of credit derivative and synthetic risk transfer, as well as repackaging. Dr Scholl's recent work also focuses on a number of significant issues currently affecting the OTC derivatives markets, the testing of key derivatives principles and the clearing of financial products through central counterparties, as well as on the implementation of the EU derivatives regulation (known as EMIR).

Vincent KP Sum
Partner, Mayer Brown
vincent.sum@mayerbrownjsm.com

Vincent KP Sum is a partner of Mayer Brown JSM. His practice focuses on complex capital markets matters, including structured products, securitisations, derivatives, retail and non-retail funds, secured lending and financing, and debt capital markets matters. He advises underwriters, arrangers, portfolio managers, issuers, trustees and institutional investors. He is qualified to practise in Hong Kong, New York, and England and Wales.

Mr Sum has been ranked as a leading individual in "Capital Markets: Derivatives & Structured Products and Securitisation" in both *Chambers Asia Pacific* and *Chambers Global* (2013–2016). He was accredited as a recommended lawyer in "Structured Finance and Securitisation (Hong Kong)" in *The Legal 500 Asia Pacific* (2013–2016) and a leading lawyer in both "Capital Markets: Derivatives" and "Capital Markets: Structured Finance and Securitisation (Hong Kong)" in *IFLR1000* (2013–2016).

Kunel Tanna

Associate, Mayer Brown
ktanna@mayerbrown.com

Kunel Tanna is an associate in the Derivatives and Structured Products group of Mayer Brown's London office, having qualified in March 2014.

Kunel acts for some of the world's leading financial institutions as well as multilateral organisations, hedge funds, pension schemes and corporates. He advises on a wide range of capital markets and structured finance transactions, with a particular focus on complex, cross-border derivatives, repurchase transactions, risk hedging transactions, prime brokerage, secured custody arrangements and structured lending transactions. Kunel also advises on the regulatory aspects of derivatives transactions, in particular under the European Markets Infrastructure Regulation.

Kunel has studied and worked in the law, focusing on banking and finance law, in London, Paris and Hong Kong. He has also been seconded to the legal team of one of the world's largest investment banks to advise on and manage their structured notes programmes.

Guy Usher

Head of derivatives and structured finance, Fieldfisher
Guy.Usher@fieldfisher.com

Guy Usher heads up the derivatives and structured finance group at Fieldfisher, where he became a partner in 1997. He has specialised in derivatives for over 25 years and advises global investment banks, broker-dealers, asset managers, hedge funds and corporate and other end users. He advises on putting derivatives into structured financings, as well as on specific products such as credit, equity, commodity and property derivatives. He also provides project advice on reorganisations, netting and collateral.

Mr Usher frequently writes and speaks on derivatives and co-authors the highly regarded Fieldfisher publication *Summary of ISDA Close-out Netting Opinions*. He is also an author and consulting editor of *Repo and Stock Lending: A Practitioner's Guide* (Globe Law and Business).

Related titles in derivatives

Globe Law
and Business

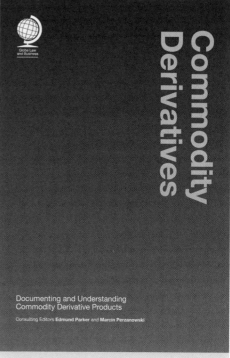

"

Mr Parker ably achieves this goal
[of creating a better understanding
of credit derivatives products]
through a combination of lucid
prose, well organized charts and
helpful examples.

Kurt Leeper
Bank Lawyers Blog

"

Move over *The Wealth of Nations*,
Das Kapital and *Capitalism and
Freedom* on your bookshelf;
Commodity Derivatives is a
worthy addition to these
economic treatises.

Michael Sackheim
Futures & Derivatives Law Report

Go to **www.globelawandbusiness.com** for full details
including free sample chapters and reviews.